NEW PERSPECTIVES ON

Microsoft® Windows® 8

COMPREHENSIVE

NEW PERSPECTIVES ON
Microsoft® Windows® 8

COMPREHENSIVE

June Jamrich Parsons
Dan Oja
Lisa Ruffolo

COURSE TECHNOLOGY
CENGAGE Learning·

Australia • Brazil • Japan • Korea • Mexico • Singapore • Spain • United Kingdom • United States

COURSE TECHNOLOGY
CENGAGE Learning·

New Perspectives on Microsoft Windows 8, Comprehensive

Editor-in-Chief: Marie L. Lee

Director of Development: Marah Bellegarde

Executive Editor: Donna Gridley

Associate Acquisitions Editor: Amanda Lyons

Product Development Manager: Leigh Hefferon

Senior Product Manager: Kathy Finnegan

Product Manager: Julia Leroux-Lindsey

Developmental Editor: Jane Pedicini

Associate Product Manager: Angela Lang

Editorial Assistant: Melissa Stehler

Brand Manager: Elinor Gregory

Market Development Managers: Gretchen Swann, Kristie Clark

Senior Content Project Manager: Jennifer Goguen McGrail

Composition: GEX Publishing Services

Art Director: GEX Publishing Services

Text Designer: Althea Chen

Cover Art: ©Philip Meyer/Shutterstock

Copyeditor: Suzanne Huizenga

Proofreader: Kathy Orrino

Indexer: Alexandra Nickerson

For product information and technology assistance, contact us at
Cengage Learning Customer & Sales Support, 1-800-354-9706
For permission to use material from this text or product, submit all requests online at **www.cengage.com/permissions**
Further permissions questions can be emailed to
permissionrequest@cengage.com

Some of the product names and company names used in this book have been used for identification purposes only and may be trademarks or registered trademarks of their respective manufacturers and sellers.

Windows® is a registered trademark of Microsoft Corporation. © 2012 Microsoft. Microsoft and the Office logo are either registered trademarks or trademarks of Microsoft Corporation in the United States and/or other countries. Course Technology, Cengage Learning is an independent entity from the Microsoft Corporation, and not affiliated with Microsoft in any manner.

Disclaimer: Any fictional data related to persons or companies or URLs used throughout this book is intended for instructional purposes only. At the time this book was printed, any such data was fictional and not belonging to any real persons or companies.

Library of Congress Control Number: 2012923172

ISBN-13: 978-1-285-08087-1

ISBN-10: 1-285-08087-4

Course Technology
20 Channel Center Street
Boston, MA 02210
USA

Cengage Learning is a leading provider of customized learning solutions with office locations around the globe, including Singapore, the United Kingdom, Australia, Mexico, Brazil, and Japan. Locate your local office at:
international.cengage.com/global

Cengage Learning products are represented in Canada by Nelson Education, Ltd.

To learn more about Course Technology, visit **www.cengage.com/course technology**

To learn more about Cengage Learning, visit **www.cengage.com.**

Purchase any of our products at your local college store or at our preferred online store **www.cengagebrain.com**

ProSkills Icons © 2014 Cengage Learning.

Printed in the United States of America
1 2 3 4 5 6 7 8 9 17 16 15 14 13

Preface

The New Perspectives Series' critical-thinking, problem-solving approach is the ideal way to prepare students to transcend point-and-click skills and take advantage of all that Microsoft Windows 8 has to offer.

In developing the New Perspectives Series, our goal was to create books that give students the software concepts and practical skills they need to succeed beyond the classroom. We've updated our proven case-based pedagogy with more practical content to make learning skills more meaningful to students.

With the New Perspectives Series, students understand *why* they are learning *what* they are learning, and are fully prepared to apply their skills to real-life situations.

About This Book

This book provides coverage of the essential topics for the new Microsoft Windows 8 operating system, and includes the following features:

- Introduction to the basics of Microsoft Windows 8, offering hands-on instruction so that students can use the operating system with confidence and ease
- Guided tours of the innovative Windows 8 Start screen for people using a traditional mouse and keyboard and for people with a touchscreen computer
- Overview of the Windows 8 desktop, apps, and file system, teaching students how to start and turn off Windows, run applications, and organize files
- Exploration of the exciting advances in Windows 8, including Start screen tiles, the new Charms bar and Apps screen, and the updated File Explorer

New for this edition!

- Each tutorial has been updated with new case scenarios throughout, which provide a rich and realistic context for students to apply the concepts and skills presented.
- Some tutorials include a new Troubleshoot type of Case Problem, in which certain steps of the exercise require students to identify and correct errors—which are intentionally placed in the files students work with—to promote problem solving and critical thinking.

System Requirements

This book assumes a typical installation of Microsoft Windows 8 Pro. (Note that most tasks in this text can also be completed using the Windows 8 edition, the basic edition of the operating system.) The browser used for any steps that require a browser is Internet Explorer 10.

The New Perspectives Approach

Context

Each tutorial begins with a problem presented in a "real-world" case that is meaningful to students. The case sets the scene to help students understand what they will do in the tutorial.

Hands-on Approach

Each tutorial is divided into manageable sessions that combine reading and hands-on, step-by-step work. Colorful screenshots help guide students through the steps. **Trouble?** tips anticipate common mistakes or problems to help students stay on track and continue with the tutorial.

VISUAL OVERVIEW

Visual Overviews

Each session begins with a Visual Overview, a two-page spread that includes colorful, enlarged screenshots with numerous callouts and key term definitions, giving students a comprehensive preview of the topics covered in the session, as well as a handy study guide.

PROSKILLS

ProSkills Boxes and Exercises

ProSkills boxes provide guidance for how to use the software in real-world, professional situations, and related ProSkills exercises integrate the technology skills students learn with one or more of the following soft skills: decision-making, problem-solving, teamwork, verbal communication, and written communication.

KEY STEP

Key Steps

Important steps are highlighted in yellow with attached margin notes to help students pay close attention to completing the steps correctly and avoiding time-consuming rework.

INSIGHT

InSight Boxes

InSight boxes offer expert advice and best practices to help students achieve a deeper understanding of the concepts behind the software features and skills.

TIP

Margin Tips

Margin Tips provide helpful hints and shortcuts for more efficient use of the software. The Tips appear in the margin at key points throughout each tutorial, giving students extra information when and where they need it.

REVIEW

APPLY

Assessment

Retention is a key component to learning. At the end of each session, a series of Quick Check questions helps students test their understanding of the material before moving on. Engaging end-of-tutorial Review Assignments and Case Problems have always been a hallmark feature of the New Perspectives Series. Colorful bars and headings identify the type of exercise, making it easy to understand both the goal and level of challenge a particular assignment holds.

REFERENCE

TASK REFERENCE

GLOSSARY/INDEX

Reference

Within each tutorial, Reference boxes appear before a set of steps to provide a succinct summary and preview of how to perform a task. In addition, a complete Task Reference at the back of the book provides quick access to information on how to carry out common tasks. Finally, each book includes a combination Glossary/Index to promote easy reference of material.

Our Complete System of Instruction

Coverage To Meet Your Needs

Whether you're looking for just a small amount of coverage or enough to fill a semester-long class, we can provide you with a textbook that meets your needs.

- Brief books typically cover the essential skills in just 2 to 4 tutorials.
- Introductory books build and expand on those skills and contain an average of 5 to 8 tutorials.
- Comprehensive books are great for a full-semester class, and contain 9 to 12+ tutorials.

So if the book you're holding does not provide the right amount of coverage for you, there's probably another offering available. Visit our Web site or contact your Cengage Learning sales representative to find out what else we offer.

CourseCasts – Learning on the Go. Always available…always relevant.

Want to keep up with the latest technology trends relevant to you? Visit http://coursecasts. course.com to find a library of weekly updated podcasts, CourseCasts, and download them to your mp3 player.

Ken Baldauf, host of CourseCasts, is a faculty member of the Florida State University Computer Science Department where he is responsible for teaching technology classes to thousands of FSU students each year. Ken is an expert in the latest technology trends; he gathers and sorts through the most pertinent news and information for CourseCasts so your students can spend their time enjoying technology, rather than trying to figure it out. Open or close your lecture with a discussion based on the latest CourseCast.

Visit us at http://coursecasts.course.com to learn on the go!

Instructor Resources

We offer more than just a book. We have all the tools you need to enhance your lectures, check students' work, and generate exams in a new, easier-to-use and completely revised package. This book's Instructor's Manual, ExamView testbank, PowerPoint presentations, data files, solution files, figure files, and a sample syllabus are all available on a single CD-ROM or for downloading at www.cengage.com.

SAM: Skills Assessment Manager

Get your students workplace-ready with SAM, the premier proficiency-based assessment and training solution for Microsoft Office! SAM's active, hands-on environment helps students master computer skills and concepts that are essential to academic and career success.

Skill-based assessments, interactive trainings, business-centric projects, and comprehensive remediation engage students in mastering the latest Microsoft Office programs on their own, allowing instructors to spend class time teaching. SAM's efficient course setup and robust grading features provide faculty with consistency across sections. Fully interactive MindTap Readers integrate market-leading Cengage Learning content with SAM, creating a comprehensive online student learning environment.

Acknowledgments

I would like to thank the following reviewers for their contributions in the development of this text: Debi Griggs, Bellevue College; Clara Groeper, Illinois Central College; and Stacy Hollins, St. Louis Community College - Florissant Valley. Their valuable insights and excellent feedback helped to shape this text, ensuring it will meet the needs of instructors and students both in the classroom and beyond.

Many thanks also to everyone on the New Perspectives team for their guidance, insight, encouragement, and good humor, including Donna Gridley and Jennifer Goguen McGrail. Special thanks go to Julia Leroux-Lindsey, whose attention to detail and thoughtful solutions make this book more accessible, appealing, and instructive. Jane Pedicini deserves special mention for her wit and spirit, which made this project fun, and for her pursuit of clarity, which elevates this book into a superior teaching tool. I also appreciate the careful work of Susan Pedicini and Serge Palladino, Manuscript Quality Assurance testers. Additional thanks go to June Parsons and Dan Oja, on whose previous work this book is based.

– Lisa Ruffolo

BRIEF CONTENTS

WINDOWS

TABLE OF CONTENTS

Appendix A Using Windows 8 with a Touchscreen Device
Mastering Touch Features in Microsoft Windows 8 . . **WIN A1**

Appendix B Exploring Additional Windows 8 Tools
Using Windows 8 Apps and Tools . . . . **WIN B1**

WINDOWS

OBJECTIVES

Session 1.1
- Start Windows 8
- Explore the Start screen
- Start and close Windows 8 apps
- Run desktop applications, switch between them, and close them
- Identify and use the controls in windows and dialog boxes

Session 1.2
- Navigate your computer using File Explorer
- Change the view of the items in your computer
- Get help when you need it
- Turn off Windows 8

Exploring the Basics of Microsoft Windows 8

Investigating the Windows 8 Operating System

Case | *Behind the Scenes*

Behind the Scenes is a small but growing temporary employment agency in St. Louis, Missouri. The agency specializes in training and providing virtual assistants, high-quality support staff that work from home to perform office tasks and projects for clients. As the training manager at Behind the Scenes, Emma Garcia coordinates staff training sessions on a wide range of professional and computer skills.

Emma recently hired you as her assistant. She has asked you to lead the upcoming training sessions on the fundamentals of the Microsoft Windows 8 operating system. As you prepare for the sessions, she offers to help you identify the topics you should cover and the skills you should demonstrate while focusing on the new features in Windows 8.

In this tutorial, you will start Windows 8 and practice some fundamental computer skills. You'll tour the Start screen and the desktop, start applications, and then navigate a computer using File Explorer. Finally, you'll use the Windows 8 Help and Support system and turn off Windows 8.

STARTING DATA FILES

There are no starting Data Files needed for this tutorial.

Session 1.1 Visual Overview:

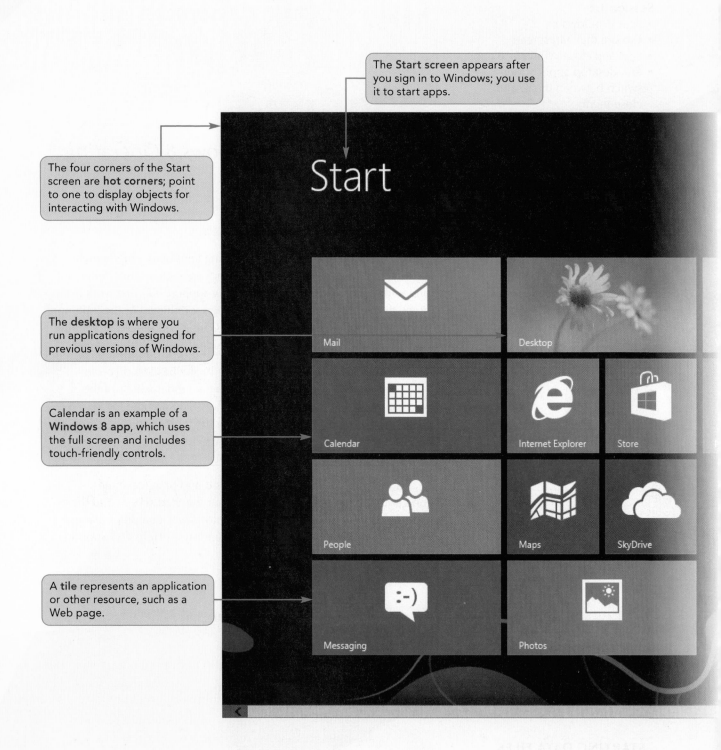

The **Start screen** appears after you sign in to Windows; you use it to start apps.

The four corners of the Start screen are **hot corners**; point to one to display objects for interacting with Windows.

The **desktop** is where you run applications designed for previous versions of Windows.

Calendar is an example of a **Windows 8 app**, which uses the full screen and includes touch-friendly controls.

A **tile** represents an application or other resource, such as a Web page.

Start

Mail

Desktop

Calendar

Internet Explorer

Store

People

Maps

SkyDrive

Messaging

Photos

Windows 8 Start Screen

The name you use to sign in to Windows appears next to the user icon.

The **user icon** identifies the current user and provides access to your account settings; you can personalize the Start screen by using a photo instead.

Scroll the Start screen to the right to display additional apps.

A **live tile** displays content that changes frequently.

An **app**, short for application, is a small program created for a specific purpose.

Click the Zoom button to reduce the size of the tiles and display more apps on the Start screen.

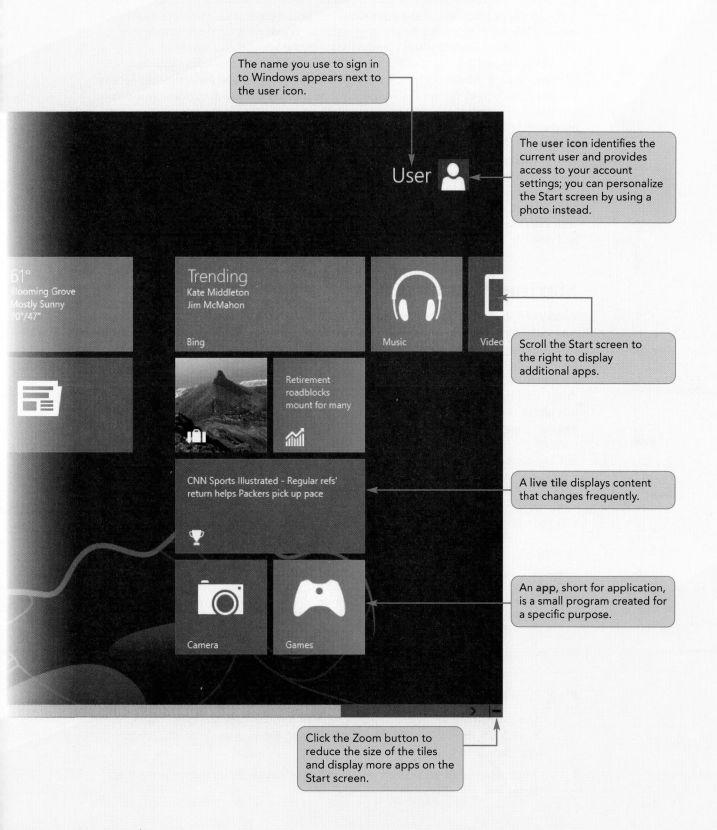

Introducing Windows 8

The **operating system** is software that manages and coordinates activities on the computer and helps the computer perform essential tasks, such as displaying information on the computer screen and saving data on disks. (The term *software* refers to the applications, or programs, that a computer uses to complete tasks.) Your computer uses the **Microsoft Windows 8** operating system—**Windows 8** for short. Windows is the name of the operating system, and 8 indicates the version you are using.

The most popular features of Windows 8 include its speed, flexibility, and design. Windows 8 runs software created specifically for Windows 8 and for earlier versions of Windows, such as Windows 7. In either case, you can use more than one application at a time and switch seamlessly from one application to another to perform your work effectively.

Windows 8 is designed to run on computers that use a touchscreen, such as tablets, and those that use a keyboard and mouse, such as a laptop or desktop computer. A **touchscreen** is a display that lets you touch areas of the screen to interact with software. To select an application button, for example, you touch the button on the tablet screen with your fingertip. However, you are not required to use a touchscreen with Windows 8. This book assumes that you are using a computer with a keyboard and pointing device, such as a mouse.

Starting Windows 8

TIP

If you have a Microsoft account, you can use the user name and password for that account to sign in to Windows 8.

Windows 8 starts automatically when you turn on your computer. After completing some necessary start-up tasks, Windows 8 displays a **lock screen**, which includes a picture, the date, and the time. You clear the lock screen to display the Welcome screen. Depending on how your computer is set up, the Welcome screen might list only your user name or it might list all the users for the computer. Before you start working with Windows 8, you might need to click your user name and type a password. A **user name** is a unique name that identifies you to Windows 8, and a **password** is a confidential series of characters that you must enter before you can work with Windows 8. If you installed Windows 8 yourself, you probably created a user name and password as you set up your computer. If not, the person who created your account assigned you at least a user name and possibly a password. After selecting your user name or entering a password, the Windows 8 Start screen appears (as shown in the Session 1.1 Visual Overview).

To begin preparing for your training session on Windows 8, Emma asks you to start Windows 8.

To start Windows 8:

▶ **1.** Turn on your computer. After a moment, Windows 8 starts and the lock screen appears.

   Trouble? If you are asked to select an operating system, do not take action. Windows 8 should start automatically after a designated number of seconds. If it does not, ask your instructor or technical support person for help.

▶ **2.** Press any key to clear the lock screen and display the Welcome screen.

   Trouble? If the Welcome screen does not appear, click the lock screen, hold down the mouse button, and then drag the picture up to display the Welcome screen.

▶ **3.** If necessary, click your user name, type your password, and then press the **Enter** key.

The Windows 8 Start screen appears, as shown in the Session 1.1 Visual Overview. Your screen might look different.

Trouble? If your user name does not appear on the Welcome screen, try pressing the Ctrl+Alt+Del keys to enter your name. If necessary, ask your instructor or technical support person for further assistance.

Trouble? If a blank screen or an animated design replaces the Start screen, your computer might be set to use a **screen saver**, a program that causes a monitor to go blank or to display an animated design after a specified amount of idle time. Press any key or move your mouse to restore the Start screen.

Trouble? If your computer is using a screen resolution other than 1366 x 768, the figures shown in this book might not match exactly what you see in Windows 8 as you work through the steps. Take the screen resolution difference into account as you compare your screen with the figures.

The screen that appears after you sign into Windows 8 is called the Start screen because you start working on your computer from this screen. The Start screen includes multicolored rectangles called tiles, which represent applications. Some tiles display an **icon**, a small picture that represents a resource available on your computer, such as an application or file. See Figure 1-1.

| Figure 1-1 | Tiles on the Start screen |

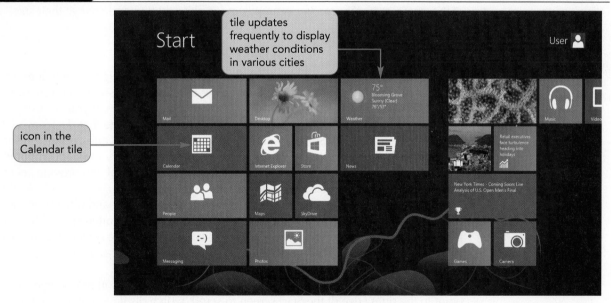

While some tiles display icons, others display pictures that preview the contents of the tile. For example, the Weather tile might display current weather conditions in cities around the world. A tile that displays updated content is called a live tile. The Weather tile is an example of a Windows 8 app. You can use this app to check the current and forecasted weather in various locations.

The Windows 8 User Interface

The part of the operating system you use when you work with a computer is called the **user interface (UI)**. The UI includes everything that lets you interact with the computer, including the layout of the screen and the controls, such as icons and buttons, that the operating system provides so you can make selections and change settings. On the Start screen, the Windows 8 UI uses a design that emphasizes large, clear text rather than graphical icons to identify screen objects. When you use a Windows 8 app, such as Calendar, the focus is on the content, so the screen is not cluttered with tools and windows. The Windows 8 UI also uses animation and fluid motions to respond to your actions and selections, which make the system seem livelier than a collection of static objects. To take advantage of wide screens, multiple monitors, and touch devices, the Windows 8 UI is more horizontally oriented than previous versions of Windows. For example, you scroll right and left to access content currently out of view.

Touring the Start Screen

The first time you start a computer after installing Windows 8, the computer uses **default settings**, those preset by the operating system. The default Start screen you see after you first install Windows 8, for example, displays a number of tiles, including those for Internet Explorer (a program you use to access the Internet), Weather, and Photos. However, Microsoft designed Windows 8 so that you can easily change the appearance of the Start screen. You can, for example, move and add tiles and change their size.

Interacting with the Start Screen

If you are using a laptop or desktop computer, you use a **pointing device** to interact with the objects on the screen. Pointing devices come in many shapes and sizes. The most common one is called a **mouse**, so this book uses that term. If you are using a different pointing device, such as a trackball or touchpad, substitute that device whenever you see the term *mouse*. Some pointing devices are designed to ensure that your hand won't suffer fatigue while using them. Some are attached directly to your computer by a cable, whereas others work wirelessly like a TV remote control and provide access to your computer without being plugged into it.

You use a pointing device to move the pointer over locations and objects on the screen, or to **point** to them. The **pointer** is an on-screen object, often shaped like an arrow, though it changes shape depending on its location on the screen and the tasks you are performing. As you move the mouse on a surface, such as a table top, the pointer on the screen moves in a corresponding direction.

If your Start screen contains more tiles than Windows can fit on one screen, you can point to the right edge of the Start screen to scroll, which displays any tiles out of view. Emma suggests that during your class, you introduce Behind the Scenes employees to the Start screen by showing them how to use the pointer to scroll.

To use the pointer to scroll:

1. Use the mouse to point to the **right edge** of the Start screen. The screen scrolls to display additional tiles not shown on the main Start screen. See Figure 1-2.

Trouble? If a bar of buttons appears on the right side of the screen, you pointed to the upper-right or lower-right corner. Point to the right edge of the screen to scroll.

Trouble? If the screen does not scroll, your Start screen might not contain additional tiles. If there are more tiles, click the right arrow button ❯ on the scroll bar at the bottom of the screen to scroll to the right.

Figure 1-2	Scrolling the Start screen

▶ **2.** Point to the **left edge** of the Start screen to scroll back to the main Start screen (or click the left scroll arrow button ❮ on the scroll bar).

When you move the pointer, a scroll bar appears at the bottom of the screen indicating that the screen includes content currently out of view. (Some screens display both vertical and horizontal scroll bars.) You can drag the scroll bar or click the arrow buttons to scroll.

Clicking refers to pressing a mouse button and immediately releasing it. Clicking sends a signal to your computer that you want to perform an action with the object you click. In Windows 8, you perform most actions with the left mouse button. If you are told to click an on-screen object, position the pointer on that object and click the left mouse button, unless instructed otherwise.

Besides scrolling the Start screen to display additional tiles, you can zoom the Start screen to make the tiles smaller (to display more tiles) or larger (to display fewer tiles). You do so by clicking the Zoom button, which appears in the lower-right corner of the Start screen when you move the pointer.

To zoom the Start screen:

▶ **1.** Move the pointer until the Zoom button ▬ appears in the lower-right corner of the Start screen. See Figure 1-3.

Figure 1-3	Displaying the Zoom button

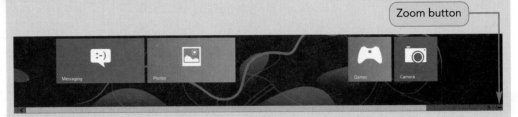

2. Click the **Zoom** button ▬ to reduce the size of the tiles. See Figure 1-4.

Figure 1-4	Zooming the Start screen

tiles are smaller to display more of them on the Start screen

3. Click a blank spot on the Start screen to return the tiles to their original size.

When you moved the pointer to the Zoom button to click it, a bar appeared on the right edge of the Start screen. This is called the **Charms bar**, and it contains buttons, also called **charms**, for interacting with Windows 8. The Charms bar appears when you point to the upper-right or lower-right corner of the screen. These locations are two of the four hot corners Windows 8 provides for mouse users. When you point to the Charms bar, it appears with a black background, indicating it is the **active object**. You can interact with active objects by clicking them, for example. When you click the Search charm on the Charms bar, a menu opens. A **menu** is a list, or group, of com-mands, and a **menu command** is text that you can click to perform a task. The **Search menu** provides access to applications, documents, settings, and much more. Emma suggests you use the Search charm on the Charms bar to open the Search menu.

To open the Search menu:

1. Point to the upper-right corner of the screen to display the Charms bar.

2. Point to the **Charms bar** to display it with a black background, which means it is active. See Figure 1-5.

TIP

You can also press and hold down the Windows key and then press C to display the Charms bar.

Figure 1-5   **Active Charms bar**

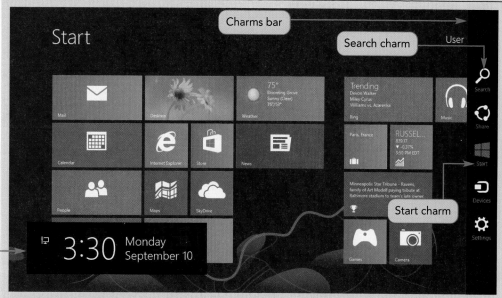

3. Click the **Search** charm on the Charms bar to display the Search menu, shown in Figure 1-6.

Figure 1-6   **Search menu**

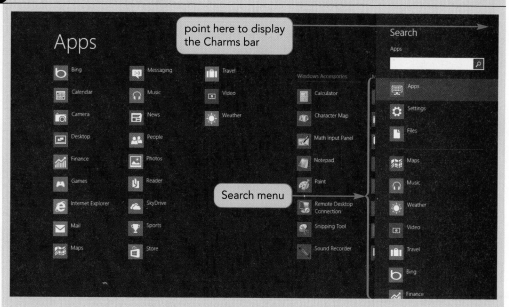

4. Point to the lower-right corner of the Start screen to display the Charms bar again, and then click the **Start** charm to return to the Start screen.

When you activate the Charms bar, a status box appears on the screen displaying the date and time. It might also display other status information, such as the strength of your network connection or battery level.

Although you can use the Search menu to find applications, settings, and files, the Start screen is designed to provide quick access to all the information, applications, and locations on your computer. For example, you can use the Start screen to display the desktop, which is your work area for using applications designed to run in previous versions of Windows.

Exploring the Desktop

In addition to the Start screen, Windows 8 includes the desktop where you can access tools for managing Windows and other programs. You also use the desktop to work with files and folders. A **file** is a collection of related information; typical types of files include text documents, spreadsheets, photos, and songs. A **folder** is a container that helps you organize the contents of your computer.

The Start screen includes a Desktop tile (shown in the Session 1.1 Visual Overview), which you click to display the Windows 8 desktop.

To display the desktop:

▶ **1.** Click the **Desktop** tile on the Start screen to display the desktop, shown in Figure 1-7. Your desktop might contain additional or different items.

| Figure 1-7 | Windows 8 desktop |

Most of the features you use on the Start screen are available on the desktop. For example, you can point to the upper-right hot corner to display the Charms bar. In addition, the desktop includes the features described in Figure 1-8.

Figure 1-8   **Features of the Windows 8 desktop**

Feature	Description
Date/time control	Control that shows the current date and time, and lets you set the clock
Desktop graphic	Part of a Windows 8 theme, which is a set of desktop backgrounds, window colors, sounds, and screen savers
Notification area	Area containing icons that correspond to services running in the background, such as an Internet connection
Pinned programs	Programs you can start by clicking their button on the taskbar
Recycle Bin	Icon for a folder that holds items deleted from the hard drive until you remove them permanently
Taskbar	Strip that contains buttons to give you quick access to common tools and running programs

© 2014 Cengage Learning

On the Start screen or the desktop, you need to select an object before you can work with it. To **select** an object on the Start screen, you point to the object, such as a tile. To select an object on the desktop, you point to and then click the object. Windows 8 often indicates that the object is selected by highlighting it, typically by changing the object's color, putting a box around it, or making the object appear to be pushed in.

Clicking an object on the desktop usually selects it. To open a folder or start the application associated with an object, you double-click the object on the desktop. For example, you can double-click a folder icon to open the folder and see its contents. **Double-clicking** means clicking the left mouse button twice in quick succession.

Emma suggests that you have students practice double-clicking by opening the Recycle Bin. The Recycle Bin holds items deleted from the hard drive until you remove them permanently.

To view the contents of the Recycle Bin:

▶ **1.** Point to the **Recycle Bin** icon, and then click the left mouse button twice quickly to double-click the icon. The Recycle Bin window opens, as shown in Figure 1-9.

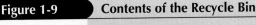

Figure 1-9   Contents of the Recycle Bin

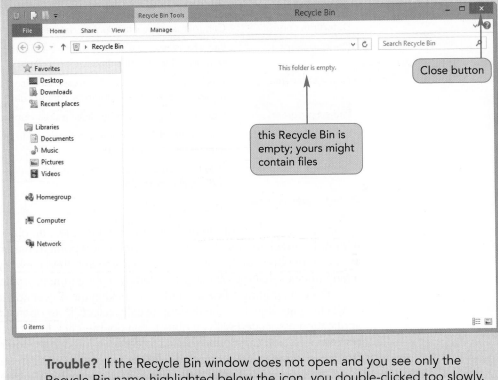

Trouble? If the Recycle Bin window does not open and you see only the Recycle Bin name highlighted below the icon, you double-clicked too slowly. Double-click the icon again more quickly.

Now you can close the Recycle Bin window.

2. Click the **Close** button [×] in the upper-right corner of the Recycle Bin window.

You'll learn more about opening and closing windows later in this session.

Displaying Shortcut Menus

Your mouse most likely has more than one button. In addition to the left button, the mouse has a right button that you can use to perform certain actions in Windows 8. However, the term *clicking* refers to the left button; clicking an object with the right button is called **right-clicking**. (If your mouse has only one button, you right-click by pressing the right side of the button.)

In Windows 8, right-clicking usually selects an object and opens its **shortcut menu**, which lists actions you can take with that object. You can right-click practically any object—a tile on the Start screen, a desktop icon, the taskbar, and even the desktop itself—to view commands associated with that object. Emma suggests that when you're not sure what to do with an object in Windows 8, you should right-click it and examine its shortcut menu. Now you can right-click the Recycle Bin icon to open its shortcut menu.

To right-click an object on the desktop:

▶ **1.** Point to the **Recycle Bin** icon on your desktop, and then right-click the icon to open its shortcut menu. This menu offers a list of actions you can take with the Recycle Bin icon. See Figure 1-10.

Figure 1-10	Recycle Bin shortcut menu

Recycle Bin icon

shortcut menu

Trouble? If the shortcut menu does not open and you are using a trackball or a mouse with a wheel, make sure you click the button on the far right, not the one in the middle.

▶ **2.** Click **Open** on the shortcut menu to open the Recycle Bin window again.

▶ **3.** Click the **Close** button [×] in the upper-right corner of the Recycle Bin window.

Now that you've explored the desktop, you can return to the Start screen and use it to start applications.

Returning to the Start Screen

You can use a few techniques to return to the Start screen. The easiest way is to use a **keyboard shortcut**, which means you press one or more keys on the keyboard to perform an action. Another way is to point to the lower-left hot corner to display a miniature image, or **thumbnail**, of the Start screen and then click. Recall that you can also click the Start charm on the Charms bar to display the Start screen.

Windows 8 provides many keyboard shortcuts for streamlining your work. The keyboard shortcut for displaying the Start screen is to press the Windows key. If you press the Windows key when the Start screen is displayed, you return to your previous location.

To return to the Start screen:

▶ **1.** Press the **Windows** key to display the Start screen.

▶ **2.** Press the **Windows** key again to display the desktop.

▶ **3.** Point to the lower-left corner of the screen until a thumbnail of the Start screen appears, as in Figure 1-11.

Figure 1-11	Start screen thumbnail

thumbnail of the Start screen

▶ **4.** Click the **thumbnail** to display the Start screen.

Trouble? If the Start screen does not appear, point to the lower-left corner of the screen again, and without moving the pointer, click to display the Start screen.

Starting Applications

Computers can run two types of software: system software and applications. **System software** is the software that runs a computer, including the operating system. An **application** is the software you use most directly to perform tasks such as writing a screenplay or viewing a Web page. In general, a computer runs system software to perform computer tasks, and you run applications to carry out your work or personal tasks.

REFERENCE

Starting an Application

- Click the application's tile on the Start screen.

or

- On the Start screen or the Search menu, type the name of the application until the application appears in the search results on the Apps screen.
- Click the application in the search results.

Windows 8 runs two types of applications. Windows 8 apps are designed to use the Windows 8 interface and work with touchscreen devices. Windows 8 apps appear only on the Start screen. For example, the Calendar tile is for the Calendar Windows 8 app, which displays a full-screen calendar where you can schedule appointments and other events. You can also use Windows 8 to run **desktop applications**, which are programs developed for previous versions of Windows. For example, WordPad is a desktop application you use to create basic word-processing documents.

To start a Windows 8 app, you click its tile on the Start screen. Emma suggests that you demonstrate how to start the Calendar app.

To start the Calendar app:

1. Click the **Calendar** tile on the Start screen to start the Calendar app. See Figure 1-12.

   Trouble? If a Sign in with a Microsoft account screen appears and you have a Microsoft account, enter your email address and password, and then click the Sign In button.

Figure 1-12   **Calendar app**

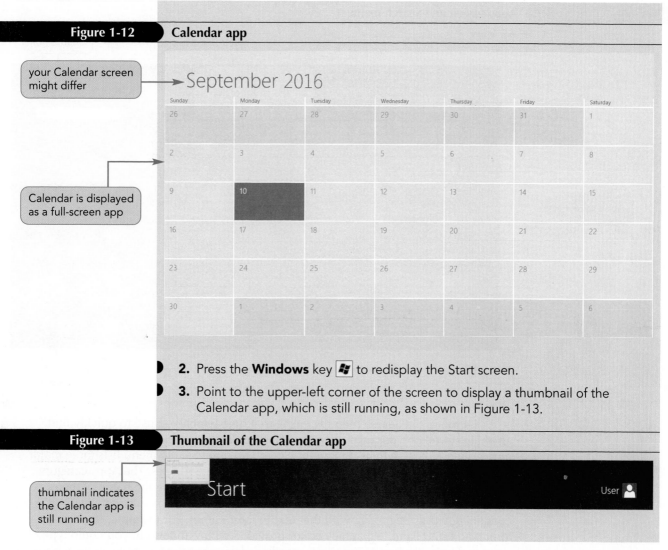

your Calendar screen might differ

Calendar is displayed as a full-screen app

> **2.** Press the **Windows** key ⊞ to redisplay the Start screen.
>
> **3.** Point to the upper-left corner of the screen to display a thumbnail of the Calendar app, which is still running, as shown in Figure 1-13.

Figure 1-13   **Thumbnail of the Calendar app**

thumbnail indicates the Calendar app is still running

Start   User

You use the upper-left hot corner to display a thumbnail for each running app, even if it doesn't appear on the screen. The list of running apps is called the **Switch List** because you can click a thumbnail in the list to switch to that app. You can display the Switch List from the Start screen, while working with a Windows 8 app, or from the desktop.

Another way to start a desktop application or a Windows 8 app is to use the Search menu, which you displayed earlier, and the Apps screen. You use the Search menu to search for or select items, including applications. When you open the Search menu, it appears on top of the Apps screen, which lists all the applications installed on your computer. See Figure 1-14.

TIP

To display the Apps screen without the Search menu, right-click the Start screen and then click the All apps button in the lower-right corner of the screen.

Figure 1-14   Apps screen and Search menu

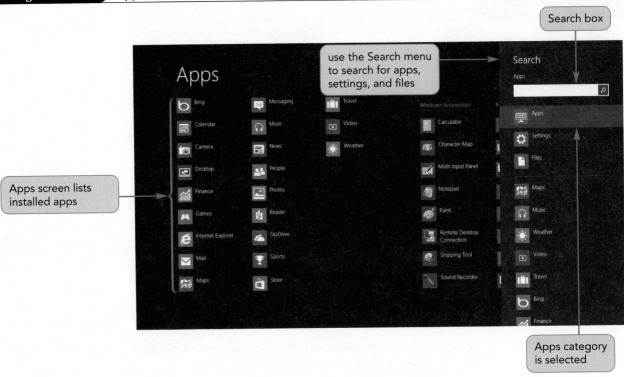

At the top of the Search menu is the **Search box**, which you use to quickly find anything stored on your computer including applications, documents, pictures, music, videos, and settings. Below the Search box, the Search menu lists three major categories of items you can search for: Apps, Settings, and Files. The Apps category is selected by default. To search for an application, start typing the name of the application. As you type, the Apps screen displays the search results: applications containing words beginning with that text in their names. For example, if you want to find and start Paint, a graphics editor provided with Windows 8, you could type *paint* in the Search box. Windows 8 searches your computer for applications whose names start with "paint" and displays them on the Apps screen, where you can click the Paint application to start it.

If you want to search for settings related to the text you entered, click Settings in the category list. For example, with "paint" displayed in the Search box, you could click Settings to display the Settings screen with system settings related to "paint," including one that lets you turn Windows features such as Paint on or off.

Searching for files works the same way: type the text related to the file you are looking for (for example, "paint") in the Search box and then click Files in the category list. The Files screen opens and displays files that contain "paint" in their filenames, contents, or file details, including files created in applications with "paint" in their names, such as a drawing created in Paint.

Below the category list in the Search menu are Windows 8 apps installed on your computer. These apps are also displayed on the Start screen.

Now that you've explored the Search menu, you're ready to use it to start an application. If you start typing on the Start screen, the Search menu opens and the text you typed appears in the Search box. Emma suggests you use this method to start WordPad, which Behind the Scenes employees can use to write and open text documents.

To start WordPad:

1. Type **wordp** to display the Search menu with "wordp" inserted in the Search box. The search results include the WordPad application. See Figure 1-15.

Figure 1-15   WordPad in the search results

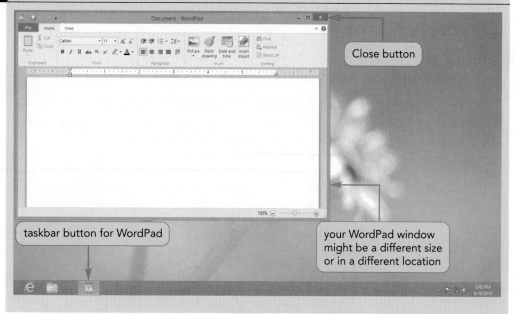

WordPad is listed in the search results

search text entered

number of apps found

no settings or files are associated with WordPad

Trouble? If settings or files appear in the search results, click Apps in the category list, and then repeat Step 1 if necessary, making sure the search term is displayed in the Search box.

2. Click **WordPad** in the search results. The WordPad window opens on the desktop, as shown in Figure 1-16.

Figure 1-16   WordPad window

Close button

taskbar button for WordPad

your WordPad window might be a different size or in a different location

Unlike Windows 8 apps, which open as full-screen programs, a desktop application opens in a **window**, which is a rectangular work area that contains tools for performing tasks. When a window is open on the desktop, a button appears on the taskbar for that window. (Recall that the **taskbar** is a strip at the bottom of the desktop that gives you quick access to common tools and running desktop applications.) **Taskbar buttons** are buttons on the taskbar that you use to work with open programs easily. These buttons are especially useful if you have many windows open on the desktop. To quickly display a particular window, you can click its button on the taskbar.

Running Multiple Applications

One of the most useful features of Windows 8 is its ability to run multiple programs at the same time. This feature, known as **multitasking**, allows you to work on more than one task at a time and to switch quickly between projects.

Two applications are now running at the same time: WordPad and Calendar. If more than one application is open on the desktop, you can click a button on the taskbar to switch between the open applications. If one of the applications is a Windows 8 app, however, you use a hot corner to switch from one application to another. You can also use the Alt+Tab keyboard shortcut to switch between applications. To do so, you hold down the Alt key and then press the Tab key to display thumbnails of all running applications (both Windows 8 and desktop), press the Tab key again to select a thumbnail, and then release the Alt key to make that application active.

To demonstrate multitasking and switching between applications, Emma suggests that you start Paint, another desktop application. You use Paint to draw, color, and edit digital pictures. You start Paint from the Start screen.

To run WordPad and Paint on the desktop:

1. Press the **Windows** key ⊞ to display the Start screen, and then type **paint**. The Search menu appears with "paint" in the Search box, and Paint appears in the search results.

2. Click **Paint** in the search results to start it. Now two applications are open on the desktop at the same time.

3. If the Paint window fills the entire screen, click the **Restore Down** button 🗗 in the upper-right corner of the window to reduce the size of the window. See Figure 1-17.

| Figure 1-17 | Two applications open on the desktop |

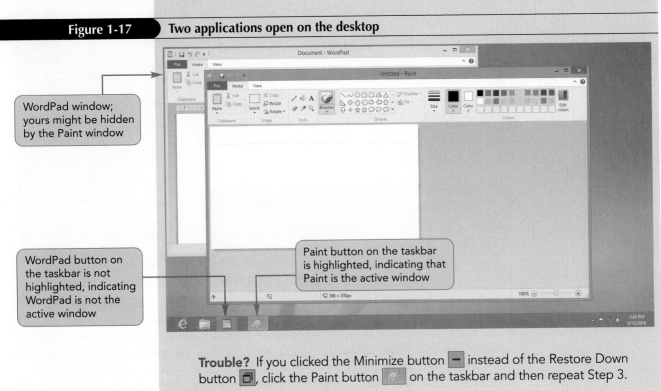

WordPad window; yours might be hidden by the Paint window

WordPad button on the taskbar is not highlighted, indicating WordPad is not the active window

Paint button on the taskbar is highlighted, indicating that Paint is the active window

Trouble? If you clicked the Minimize button ▬ instead of the Restore Down button 🗗, click the Paint button 🖌 on the taskbar and then repeat Step 3.

On the desktop, the **active window** is the one you are currently working with—Windows 8 applies your next keystroke or command to the active window. Paint is the active window because it is the one you are currently using. If two or more windows overlap, the active window appears in front of the other windows. The button for the active window is highlighted on the taskbar. The WordPad button is still on the taskbar, indicating that WordPad is running even if you can't see its program window. The taskbar organizes all the open windows so you can quickly make one active by clicking its taskbar button.

Switching Between Applications

Because only one application is active at a time, you need to switch between applications if you want to work in one or the other. On the desktop, the easiest way to switch between applications is to use the taskbar buttons.

TIP

You can also click an inactive window to make it the active window.

To switch between WordPad and Paint:

1. Click the **WordPad** button 🖼 on the taskbar. The WordPad window moves to the front, and the WordPad button appears highlighted on the taskbar, indicating that WordPad is the active window.

2. Click the **Paint** button 🖌 on the taskbar to switch to the Paint program. The Paint window is again the active window.

Besides WordPad and Paint, the Calendar app is also open and running. Because Calendar is a Windows 8 app and not a desktop application, no Calendar button appears on the taskbar. When an app is open but not visible on the screen, it is said to be running in the **background**. To access a desktop application running in the background, you click its button on the taskbar. To access a Windows 8 app running in the background, you use the Switch List to display thumbnails of open apps.

To switch to the Calendar app:

1. Point to the upper-left hot corner of the desktop to display a thumbnail of the Calendar app in the Switch List.

2. Click the **Calendar** thumbnail to display the Calendar app.

The Switch List includes thumbnails for Windows 8 apps only, not desktop applications. Because Windows 8 treats the desktop as an app, the Switch List displays one thumbnail for the desktop. WordPad and Paint are now open and running on the desktop.

If two or more Windows 8 apps are running in the background, the Switch List appears as a bar with a black background on the left of the screen. In Figure 1-18, the Weather and Calendar apps are running in addition to the desktop, so the two apps appear in the Switch List.

TIP

To display the Switch List as a bar, point to the upper-left hot corner and then move the pointer down along the left edge of the screen.

Figure 1-18   Switch List displayed on the desktop

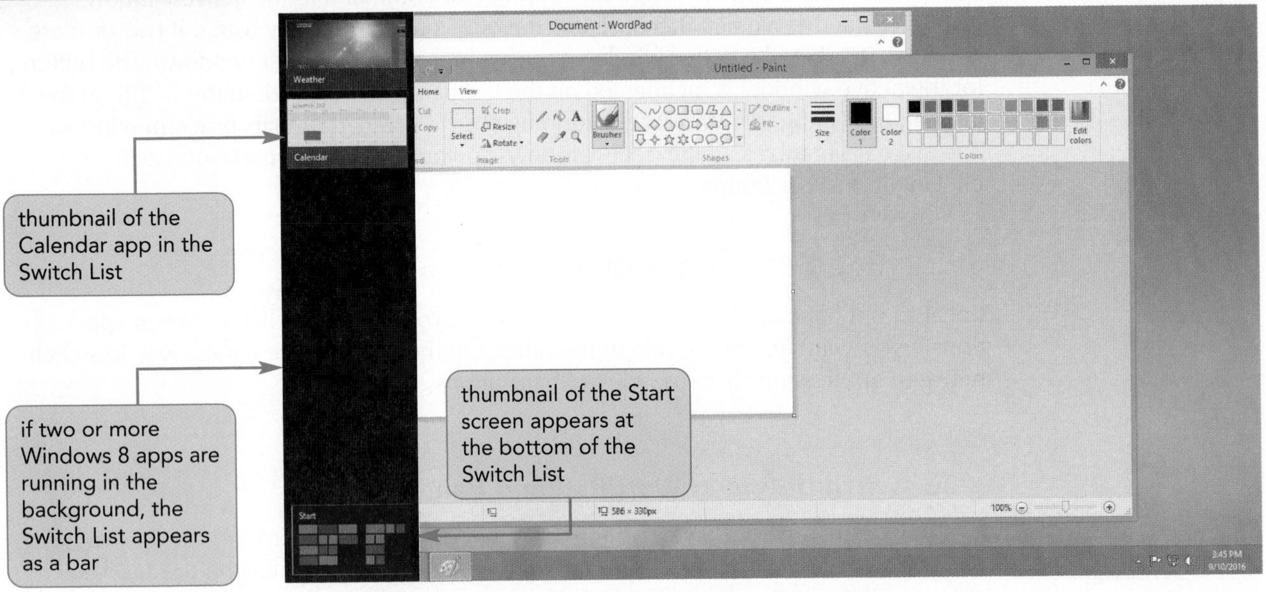

thumbnail of the Calendar app in the Switch List

if two or more Windows 8 apps are running in the background, the Switch List appears as a bar

thumbnail of the Start screen appears at the bottom of the Switch List

Manipulating Apps and Windows

Windows 8 apps start and run as full-screen programs so you can focus on your task and the content of the app. Occasionally, you need to refer to information in one app while you are working in another app. For example, if you are creating your schedule for the week in Calendar, you might want to display the Maps app to find and record directions to an appointment. If you are using a high screen resolution (at least 1366 × 768), you can **snap** an app, which means you display an app on the left or right side of the screen and leave it open as you work in other apps.

To start the Maps app and snap the Calendar app:

1. Press the **Windows** key ⊞ to display the Start screen.

2. Click the **Maps** tile to start the Maps app.

3. Point to the upper-left hot corner, and then drag the pointer down along the left edge of the screen to display the Switch List. *Insert*

4. Right-click the **Calendar** thumbnail, and then click **Snap left** on the shortcut menu to snap the Calendar app to the left side of the screen while the Maps app is open on the right. See Figure 1-19.

Figure 1-19   **Calendar app snapped on the left**

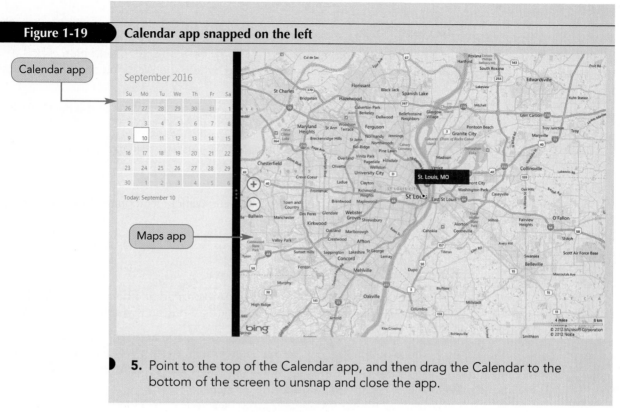

5. Point to the top of the Calendar app, and then drag the Calendar to the bottom of the screen to unsnap and close the app.

You can snap only Windows 8 apps. Because these apps usually appear in full-screen view, snapping lets you display more than one app at a time. In contrast, a desktop application appears in a window. Recall that a window is a rectangular area of the screen that contains an application, text, graphics, or data. You can open more than one window on the desktop and then manipulate the windows to display as much or as little information as you need. In most windows, three buttons appear on the right side of the title bar. See Figure 1-20. The first button is the Minimize button, which hides a window so that only its button is visible on the taskbar. Depending on the status of the window, the middle button either maximizes the window or restores it to a predefined size. The last button is the Close button, which closes the window.

Figure 1-20   **Window buttons**

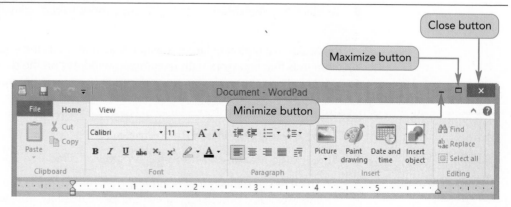

WordPad and Paint are open on the desktop, so Emma encourages you to show employees how to use their window controls. First, you will return to the desktop and then close a window so you can focus on manipulating a single window.

To close Paint:

▶ **1.** Press the **Windows** key ⊞ to display the Start screen, and then click the **Desktop** tile to display the desktop, where the WordPad and Paint windows are open.

▶ **2.** Click the **Close** button ⊠ in the upper-right corner of the Paint window. Paint closes while the WordPad window remains open.

> **Trouble?** If a dialog box opens with a message asking if you want to save changes, click the Don't Save button.

You can use the Minimize button when you want to temporarily hide a window but keep the program running.

To minimize the WordPad window:

▶ **1.** Click the **Minimize** button ▬ on the WordPad title bar. The WordPad window shrinks so that only the WordPad button is visible.

> **Trouble?** If the WordPad window closed, you accidentally clicked the Close button ⊠. Use the Search menu to start WordPad again, and then repeat Step 1. If you accidentally clicked the Maximize button ☐ or the Restore Down button ⊡, repeat Step 1.

You can redisplay a minimized window by clicking the window's button on the taskbar. When you redisplay a window, it becomes the active window.

To redisplay the WordPad window:

▶ **1.** Click the **WordPad** button 🖼 on the taskbar to redisplay the WordPad window.

> The taskbar button provides another way to switch between a window's minimized and active states.

▶ **2.** Click the **WordPad** button 🖼 on the taskbar again to minimize the window.

▶ **3.** Click the **WordPad** button 🖼 once more to redisplay the window.

The Maximize button enlarges a window so that it fills the entire screen. Emma recommends that you work with maximized windows on the desktop when you want to concentrate on the work you are performing in a single program.

To maximize the WordPad window:

▶ **1.** Click the **Maximize** button ☐ on the WordPad title bar.

> **Trouble?** If the window is already maximized, it fills the entire screen, and the Maximize button ☐ doesn't appear. Instead, you see the Restore Down button ⊡. Skip this step.

TIP

You can also double-click a window's title bar to maximize the window. Double-click the title bar again to restore the window to its previous size.

The Restore Down button reduces the window so that it is smaller than the entire screen. This feature is useful if you want to see more than one window at a time. Also, because the window is smaller, you can move it to another location on the screen or change its dimensions.

To restore a window:

▶ **1.** Click the **Restore Down** button ▣ on the WordPad title bar. After a window is restored, the Restore Down button ▣ changes to the Maximize button ▢.

You can use the mouse to move a window to a new position on the screen. When you click an object and then press and hold down the mouse button while moving the mouse, you are **dragging** the object. You can move objects on the screen by dragging them to a new location. If you want to move a window, you drag the window by its title bar. You cannot move a maximized window.

To drag the restored WordPad window to a new location:

▶ **1.** Position the mouse pointer on the WordPad title bar.

▶ **2.** Press and hold down the left mouse button, and then move the mouse up or down a little to drag the window. The window moves as you move the mouse.

▶ **3.** Position the window anywhere on the desktop, and then release the left mouse button. The WordPad window stays in the new location.

▶ **4.** Drag the WordPad window near the upper-left corner of the desktop.

   Trouble? If the WordPad window becomes maximized when you drag it near the upper part of the desktop, click the Restore Down button ▣ before performing the next set of steps.

You can also use the mouse to change the size of a window. When you point to an edge or a corner of a window, the pointer changes to the resize pointer, which is a double-headed arrow, similar to ⬃. You can use the resize pointer to drag an edge or a corner of the window and change the size of the window.

To change the size of the WordPad window:

▶ **1.** Position the pointer over the lower-right corner of the WordPad window. The pointer changes to ⬃. See Figure 1-21.

Figure 1-21   **Preparing to resize a window**

resize pointer

▶ **2.** Press and hold down the mouse button, and then drag the corner down and to the right.

▶ **3.** Release the mouse button. Now the window is larger.

▶ **4.** Practice using the resize pointer to make the WordPad window larger or smaller.

You can also use the resize pointer to drag any of the other three corners of the window to change its size. To change a window's size in any one direction only, drag the left, right, top, or bottom window borders left, right, up, or down.

Using Tools in Desktop Applications

Desktop application windows contain **controls**, which are graphical or textual objects used for manipulating the window and for using the application. Many desktop applications organize controls in two places: ribbons and dialog boxes.

Emma mentions that the WordPad program displays the controls you are likely to see in most windows, including the ribbon, which might be unfamiliar to Behind the Scenes employees. She suggests that you identify the controls on the WordPad ribbon and in WordPad dialog boxes during your first training session.

Using the Ribbon

TIP

By default, the ribbon displays the Home tab when you start WordPad. To display the contents of the View tab, you click the View tab on the ribbon.

Many desktop applications use a **ribbon** to consolidate the application's features and commands. The ribbon is located at the top of a desktop application window, immediately below the title bar, and is organized into tabs. Each **tab** contains commands that perform a variety of related tasks. For example, the Home tab has commands for tasks you perform frequently, such as changing the appearance of a document. You use the commands on the View tab to change your view of the WordPad window.

To select a command and perform an action, you use a button or other type of control on the ribbon. Controls for related actions are organized on a tab in **groups**. For example, to enter bold text in a WordPad document, you click the Bold button in the Font group on the Home tab. If a button displays only an icon and not the button name, you can point to the button to display a **ScreenTip**, which is text that identifies the name or purpose of the button. Figure 1-22 shows examples of the types of controls on the ribbon.

Figure 1-22   Examples of ribbon controls

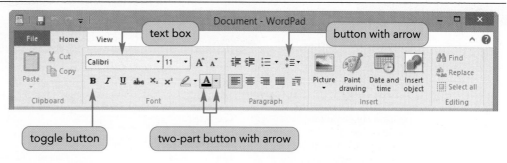

Figure 1-23 describes the types of ribbon controls.

Figure 1-23   Types of controls on the ribbon

Control	How to Use	Example
Button with arrow	Click the button to display a menu of related commands.	
Text box	Click the text box and type an entry, or click the arrow button to select an item from the list.	Calibri
Toggle button	Click the button to turn on or apply a setting, and then click the button again to turn off the setting. When a toggle button is turned on, it is highlighted.	**B**
Two-part button with arrow	If an arrow is displayed on a separate part of the button, click the arrow to display a menu of commands. Click the button itself to apply the current selection.	**A**

© 2014 Cengage Learning

Using Dialog Boxes

When you click some buttons on the ribbon, you open a **dialog box**, a special kind of window in which you enter or choose settings for how you want to perform a task. For example, you use the Print dialog box to enter or select settings for printing a document.

Besides using buttons on ribbon tabs, you can also open dialog boxes by selecting a command on the File tab. You click the File tab to display a list of commands such as Open, Save, and Print. To open a dialog box, such as the Print dialog box, you click the appropriate command, such as Print.

Dialog box controls include command buttons, tabs, option buttons, check boxes, and text boxes to collect information about how you want to perform a task. Emma says a good way to learn how dialog box controls work is to open a typical WordPad dialog box, such as the Print dialog box.

To work with a typical Windows 8 dialog box:

1. Click the **File** tab on the ribbon, and then click **Print** to open the Print dialog box. See Figure 1-24.

Figure 1-24   **Print dialog box**

tab organizes related controls; some dialog boxes have more than one tab

click a check box to turn an option off (not checked) or on (checked); you can select more than one check box in a group

option buttons appear in groups; you click one option button in a group, and a dot indicates your selection

click the text box and then type an entry

click an up or down arrow to change the entry

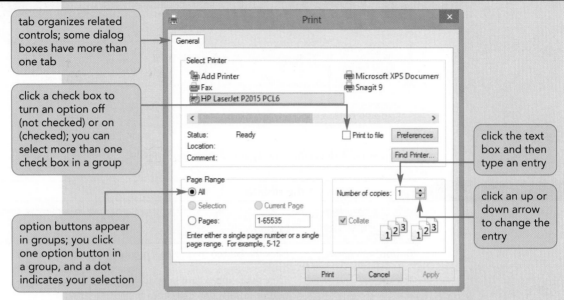

2. Click the **Pages** option button. You use this control to print only specified pages, not the entire document.

3. Double-click the **Number of copies** text box and then type **2**. You use this control to indicate how many copies of the document you want to print.

4. Click the **Cancel** button to close the Print dialog box.

TIP

You can also click an arrow button in the Number of copies text box to change the number of copies you want to print.

If you were ready to print a document with the settings you specified, you would click the Print button instead of the Cancel button. To retain your selections while you perform other tasks in a dialog box, such as setting preferences or finding a printer, you can click the Apply button, complete the other tasks, and then click the Print button.

You're finished working with applications for now, so you should close all open windows.

Closing Applications

You should close an application when you are finished using it. Each application uses computer resources, such as memory, so Windows 8 works more efficiently when only the applications you need are open.

REFERENCE

Closing an Application

- To close a Windows 8 app, display the Switch List, right-click the app's thumbnail, and then click Close on the shortcut menu; or click the top edge of the app and then drag the app to the bottom edge of the screen.
- To close a desktop application, click its Close button on the title bar, or right-click its taskbar button and then click Close window on the shortcut menu.

Emma reminds you that you've already closed an open desktop application using its Close button. You can also close an application, whether active or inactive, by using the shortcut menu associated with the application button on the taskbar.

To close WordPad using the taskbar button shortcut menu:

▶ **1.** Right-click the **WordPad** button [icon] on the taskbar. The shortcut menu for the WordPad taskbar button opens.

▶ **2.** Click **Close window** on the shortcut menu. The WordPad window closes and its button no longer appears on the taskbar.

   Trouble? If a message appears asking if you want to save changes, click the Don't Save button.

You've closed all the desktop applications, but the Maps app is still running. You can use the Switch List to close a Windows 8 app such as Maps from the desktop or the Start screen.

To close the Maps app:

▶ **1.** Point to the upper-left hot corner to display the Switch List.

▶ **2.** Right-click the **Maps** thumbnail, and then click **Close** on the shortcut menu. The Calendar app closes.

▶ **3.** Press the **Windows** key [icon] to return to the Start screen.

PROSKILLS

Problem Solving: Working with Apps Efficiently

As you work on your computer throughout the day, you may end up with quite a few Windows 8 apps and desktop applications open and running at the same time. This can lead to two common problems that affect your productivity: Finding the information you need becomes more difficult as you switch between applications, and the performance of your computer can slow significantly.

To address both these issues, decide which applications need to be running, and then close what you don't need. Closing unnecessary applications allows you to focus on the information you need for the tasks at hand, and it frees up system resources, which makes your computer faster and more responsive and can solve performance problems.

REVIEW

Session 1.1 Quick Check

1. What does the operating system do for your computer? *4 tiles*
2. The Start screen includes multicolored rectangles called _____ *tiles* , which represent _____.
3. What is a live tile?
4. When you're not sure what to do with an object in Windows 8, you can right-click the object and examine its _____ *shortcut menu*
5. Name two ways to display out-of-view tiles on the Start screen. *scroll; zoom*
6. How can you display the Charms bar? *point to the ~~left bottom right~~ upper*
7. Explain the difference between the Start screen and the desktop.
8. To access a Windows 8 app running in the background, you use the _____ *Switch List* , which displays thumbnails of open apps.

Session 1.2 Visual Overview:

The **Home tab** provides access to commands you perform frequently.

The **Address bar** shows the location of the current window in the Windows hierarchy.

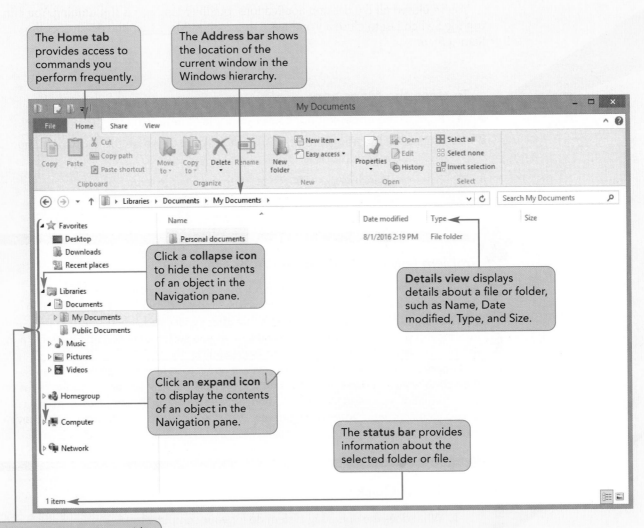

Click a **collapse icon** to hide the contents of an object in the Navigation pane.

Details view displays details about a file or folder, such as Name, Date modified, Type, and Size.

Click an **expand icon** to display the contents of an object in the Navigation pane.

The **status bar** provides information about the selected folder or file.

The **Navigation pane** provides access to resources and locations on your computer.

Working in File Explorer

The **View tab** provides controls for changing the view of the folder window and its contents.

The **ribbon** provides access to commands you can perform in a window and organizes them by task into tabs and groups.

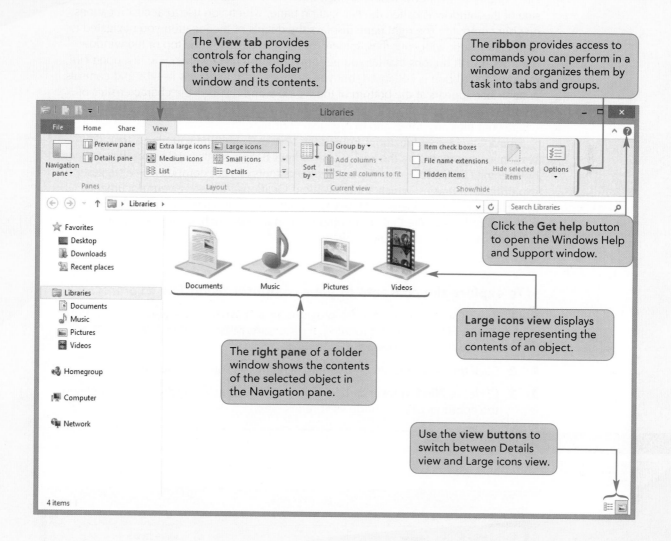

Click the **Get help** button to open the Windows Help and Support window.

The **right pane** of a folder window shows the contents of the selected object in the Navigation pane.

Large icons view displays an image representing the contents of an object.

Use the **view buttons** to switch between Details view and Large icons view.

Exploring Your Computer

To discover the contents and resources on your computer, you explore, or navigate, it. **Navigating** means moving from one location to another on your computer, such as from one file or folder to another, or from one drive to another. In Windows 8, you use **File Explorer** (as shown in the Session 1.2 Visual Overview) to navigate, view, and work with the contents and resources on your computer.

Navigating with File Explorer

File Explorer is a window that is divided into two separate areas, called **panes**. The left side of the window is called the Navigation pane, which you use to access locations on your computer. The right pane displays the details of the location you navigated to, so you can work with your files, folders, or devices easily. At the top of the window is a ribbon with buttons that let you perform common tasks. When you first open File Explorer, the ribbon is collapsed, but you can expand it to access its tabs and controls. A status bar appears at the bottom of the window and displays the characteristics of an object you select in the File Explorer window. You use File Explorer to keep track of where your files are stored and to organize your files.

Emma Garcia, the director of Behind the Scenes, is helping you plan a training session for employees on the basics of Windows 8. She wants you to start this session by opening File Explorer and exploring the contents of your computer. She suggests exploring the libraries, which are convenient locations for storing your documents, music, pictures, and videos. A **library** is a central place to view and organize files and folders stored anywhere that your computer can access, such as those on your hard disk, removable drives, and network.

To explore the contents of your computer using File Explorer:

1. If you took a break after the previous session, make sure that your computer is on and Windows 8 is running. If necessary, press the **Windows** key ⊞ to display the Start screen.

2. Click the **Desktop** tile on the Start screen to display the desktop.

3. Click the **File Explorer** button 📁 on the taskbar. A window opens showing the contents of the Windows libraries. See Figure 1-25.

| Figure 1-25 | Windows libraries |

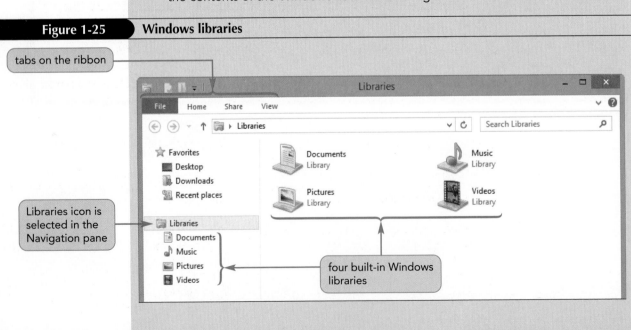

tabs on the ribbon

Libraries icon is selected in the Navigation pane

four built-in Windows libraries

> **4.** In the Navigation pane, click the **Pictures** library. The right pane of the window shows the contents of the Pictures library, which is designed for storing your photos and other picture files. See Figure 1-26. Your Pictures library might contain files and folders.

Figure 1-26   **Pictures library in File Explorer**

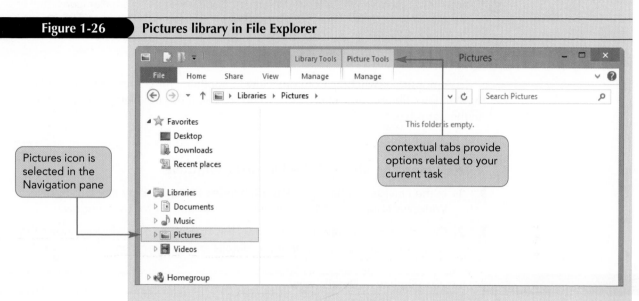

As you open folders and navigate with File Explorer, tabs might appear at the top of the window just above the standard ribbon tabs. For example, the Picture Tools Manage tab appears when you navigate to the Pictures library. This type of tab is called a **contextual tab**, and it contains options related to your current task. For example, the Picture Tools Manage tab contains options for working with pictures.

Emma mentions that you can change the appearance of most windows to suit your preferences. You'll change the view of the File Explorer window next so you can see more details about folders and files.

Changing the View

Windows 8 provides eight ways to view the contents of a folder: Extra large icons, Large icons, Medium icons, Small icons, List, Details, Tiles, and Content. The default view for any folder in the Pictures library is Large icons view, which provides a thumbnail image of the file contents. The default view for other types of folders is Details view, which displays a small icon instead of a thumbnail and lists details about each file. Although only Details view lists all file details, such as the date a photo was taken and its rating, you can see these details in any other view by pointing to a file to display a ScreenTip.

Changing the Icon View

- In File Explorer, click a view button on the status bar.

or

- Click the View tab on the ribbon.
- In the Layout group, click the view option, or click the More button, if necessary, and then click a view option.

INSIGHT

Selecting a View

When you display files in Medium icons view or larger, the icon displays a preview of the file's content. The preview images are big and easy to see; however, the window shows fewer files with large icons. When you display files using smaller icons, the window can show more files, but the preview images are not as easy to see. The view you select depends on your preferences and needs.

To demonstrate switching from one view to another, Emma says you can display the Windows libraries in Details view. To do so, you'll use the Details view button on the status bar.

To change the view of the Libraries window:

1. In the Navigation pane, click the **Libraries** link to display the four built-in Windows libraries in Tiles view, which is the default for this window.

2. Click the **Details view** button 🔲 on the status bar. The window shows the same four libraries, but with more details and smaller icons. See Figure 1-27.

Figure 1-27   Libraries window in Details view

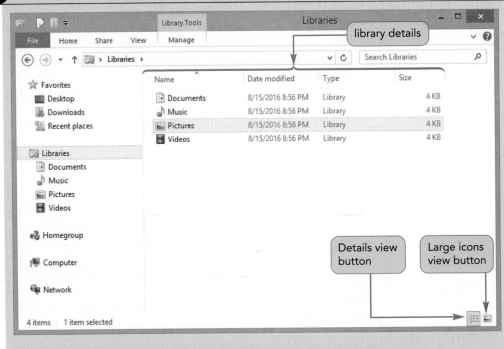

3. Click the **Large icons view** button 🔲 on the status bar. The window shows the files with large icons and no file details.

Emma suggests that you now use File Explorer to navigate your computer.

Using the Navigation Pane

To navigate your computer, you use the Navigation pane on the left side of the File Explorer window. The Navigation pane organizes computer resources into five categories: Favorites (for locations you access frequently), Libraries (for the Windows default libraries), Homegroup (for your shared home network, if any), Computer (for the drives and devices on your computer), and Network (for network locations your computer can access).

When you move the pointer into the Navigation pane, triangles appear next to some icons. An open triangle, or expand icon, indicates that a folder contains other folders that are not currently displayed in the Navigation pane. Click the triangle to expand the folder and display its subfolders. (A **subfolder** is a folder contained in another folder.) A filled triangle, or collapse icon, indicates the folder is expanded, and its subfolders are listed below the folder name. You can click a folder in the Navigation pane to navigate directly to that folder and display its contents in the right pane.

Using the Navigation pane to explore your computer usually involves clicking expand icons to expand objects and find the folder you want, and then clicking that folder to display its contents in the right pane. To display a list of all the folders on a drive, expand the Computer icon in the Navigation pane, and then expand the icon for the drive, such as Local Disk (C:). The Navigation pane shows the hierarchy of folders on the drive, so you can use it to find and manage your files and folders.

Identifying Storage Devices

Each storage device you can access on your computer is associated with a letter. The first hard drive is drive C. (If you add other hard drives, they are usually drives D, E, and so on.) If you have a CD or DVD drive or a USB flash drive plugged in to a USB port, it usually has the next available letter in the alphabetic sequence. If you can access hard drives located on other computers in a network, those drives sometimes (although not always) have letters associated with them as well. Naming conventions for network drives vary. For example, the network drive on a typical computer might have the drive letter Z.

Now you're ready to use the Navigation pane to find and open a folder people use often—the My Documents folder, which is a convenient place to store your documents and other work. The My Documents folder is stored in the Documents library by default.

To open the My Documents folder:

▶ 1. If necessary, click the **expand** icon ▷ next to Libraries in the Navigation pane to display the four built-in library folders for Documents, Music, Pictures, and Videos. (Your computer might include additional library folders.) Note that the expand icon ▷ changes to a collapse icon ◢.

   Trouble? If the expand icon ▷ does not appear next to Libraries in the Navigation pane, the Libraries folder is already expanded. Skip Step 1.

▶ 2. Click the **expand** icon ▷ next to Documents to display the folders in the Documents library. See Figure 1-28.

Figure 1-28   Folders in the Documents library

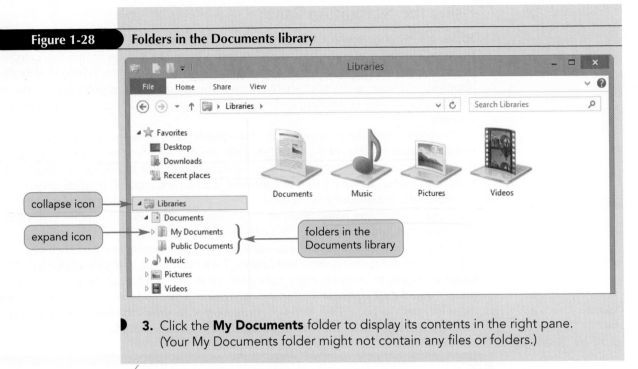

3. Click the **My Documents** folder to display its contents in the right pane. (Your My Documents folder might not contain any files or folders.)

The Address bar in File Explorer provides handy shortcuts for navigating to locations on your computer. For example, you can use the Back button to return to the last location you visited. You can use it now to return to the Sample Pictures folder.

To return to the Libraries window:

1. Click the **Back** button ⊖ on the Address bar to return to your last location: the Libraries window.

2. Click the **Close** button ✕ to close File Explorer.

3. Press the **Windows** key ⊞ to display the Start screen.

Getting Help

Windows 8 **Help and Support** provides on-screen information about the program you are using. Help for the Windows 8 operating system is available by displaying the Start screen, typing *help*, and then clicking Help and Support in the search results.

When you start Help for Windows 8, the Windows Help and Support window opens, which gives you access to Help files stored on your computer as well as Help information stored on the Microsoft Web site. If you are not connected to the Web, you have access to only the Help files stored on your computer.

Emma suggests that you start Windows 8 Help and Support, and then explore the information provided in the Windows Help and Support window.

To start Windows 8 Help and Support:

1. On the Start screen, type **help** to open the Search menu with "help" already entered in the Search box.

TIP

You can also start Windows 8 Help and Support from File Explorer by clicking the Get help button on the ribbon.

2. Click **Help and Support** in the search results on the Apps screen. The home page of Windows Help and Support opens on the desktop.

3. Click the **Maximize** button ⬜ to maximize the Windows Help and Support window. See Figure 1-29. The contents of the home page differ depending on whether you are connected to the Internet.

   Trouble? If the Help and Support window does not display the page in the figure, click the Help home link near the top of the window to view the Help home page.

Figure 1-29 Windows Help and Support window

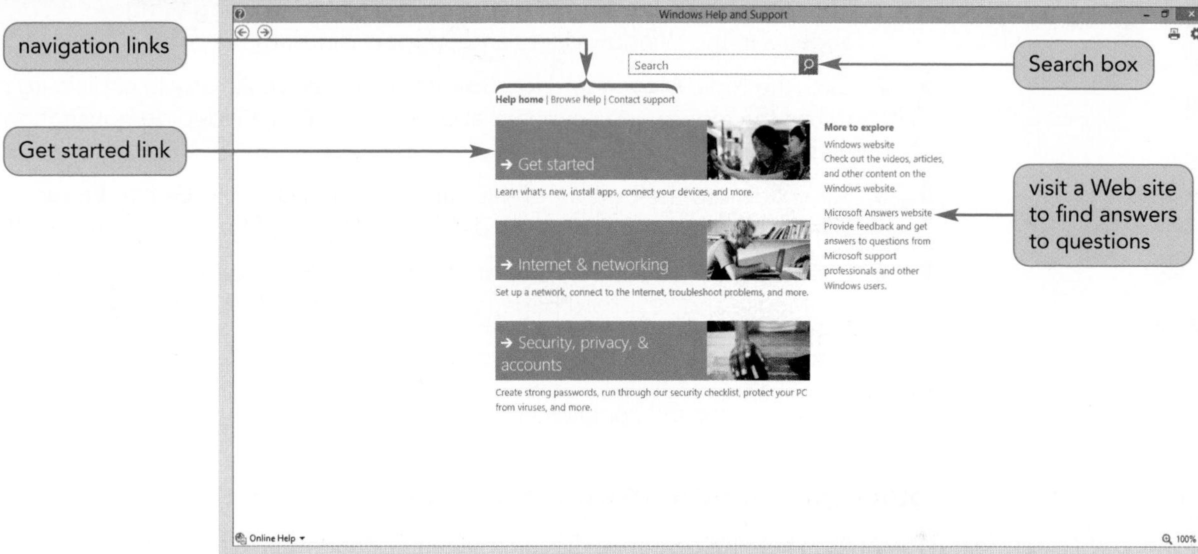

The Help home page in Windows Help and Support provides tools for finding answers and other information about Windows 8. For information about setting up your computer after installing Windows 8, click the Get started link. If you have an Internet connection, you can click the Internet & networking link to find information on setting up a network and connecting to the Internet. For help with maintaining security, privacy, and user accounts, click the Security, privacy, & accounts link. You can also connect to the Microsoft Web sites to get help. Click the Windows website link to visit the Windows pages on the Microsoft Web site. Click the Microsoft Answers website link to visit an interactive site where you can search for answers to specific questions about using Windows 8.

You can also use the other navigation links in the Windows Help and Support window to access Help topics. Click the Browse help link to display the most commonly explored Help topics, such as using files and folders. To list your options for contacting Microsoft support, click the Contact support link. These three navigation links are available on all pages in the Windows Help and Support window.

In addition to links providing access to pages in Windows Help and Support, the window contains two navigation buttons—the Back button and the Forward button. You use these buttons to navigate the pages you've already opened. Use the Back button to return to the previous page you viewed. By doing so, you activate the Forward button, which you can click to go to the next page of those you've opened. At the top of almost every Help page is the Search box, which you can use to quickly find Help content. Type any word or phrase in the Search box and press the Enter key, and Windows 8 lists all the Help pages that contain that word or phrase.

Viewing the Get Started Topics

Windows Help and Support includes instructions on the basics of using Windows 8. You can learn more about these basic topics by using the Get started link on the Windows Help and Support home page.

To view Get started topics:

1. Click the **Get started** link. A list of topics related to using Windows 8 appears in the Windows Help and Support window.

2. Click the topic **Mouse and keyboard: What's new**. An article explaining how to use the mouse and keyboard appears, including a video demonstrating these skills.

3. Scroll down to the bottom of the page and then click the **Get to know Windows 8** link. A page opens describing the new features in Windows 8.

4. Click the **Back** button ⊝ to return to the previous page you visited, which is the Mouse and keyboard page, and then click the **Back** button ⊝ to return to the Get started page.

You can access the full complement of Help pages by using the Browse help list.

Selecting a Topic from the Browse Help List

The Browse help list organizes the information in Windows Help and Support into topics and categories. You can click a link to display the titles of related categories. You can click a topic under a specific category to get help about a particular task or feature. For example, you can use the Browse help list to learn more about files, folders, and searching logically.

To find a Help topic using the Browse help list:

1. Click the **Browse help** link. A list of Windows Help topics appears in the Windows Help and Support window.

2. Click the topic **Files, folders, and search** to display a list of topics divided by categories all related to files, folders, and searching.

3. Under the Work with your files category, click the topic **How to work with files and folders**. The Windows Help and Support window displays information about that topic.

4. Scroll down to review the information on this page.

5. Click the **Top of page** link to return to the top of the page.

Another Help tool is the Search box, a popular way to find answers to your Windows 8 questions.

Searching the Help Pages

If you can't find the topic you need by clicking a link or browsing topics, or if you want to quickly find Help pages related to a particular topic, you can use the Search box. Emma provides a typical example. Suppose you want to know how to exit Windows 8, but you don't know if Windows refers to this as exiting, quitting, closing, or shutting down. You can search the Help pages to find just the right topic.

To search the Help pages for information on exiting Windows 8:

▶ **1.** Click the **Help home** link to return to the home page.

▶ **2.** Click the **Search** box. A blinking insertion point appears.

▶ **3.** Type **shut down** and then press the **Enter** key. A list of Help pages containing the words "shut down" appears in the Windows Help and Support window. See Figure 1-30. (Your results might differ.)

Figure 1-30 **Search Help results**

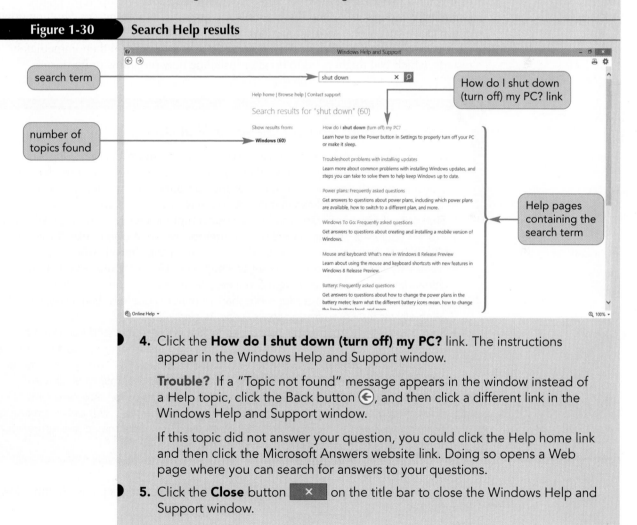

▶ **4.** Click the **How do I shut down (turn off) my PC?** link. The instructions appear in the Windows Help and Support window.

> **Trouble?** If a "Topic not found" message appears in the window instead of a Help topic, click the Back button ⊖, and then click a different link in the Windows Help and Support window.

> If this topic did not answer your question, you could click the Help home link and then click the Microsoft Answers website link. Doing so opens a Web page where you can search for answers to your questions.

▶ **5.** Click the **Close** button ☒ on the title bar to close the Windows Help and Support window.

Now that you know how Windows 8 Help works, Emma reminds you to use it when you need to perform a new task or want a reminder about how to complete a procedure.

Turning Off Windows 8

TIP

Shutting down does not automatically save your work, so be sure to save your files before selecting the Shut down or Restart option.

When you're finished working in Windows 8, you should always turn it off properly. Doing so saves energy, preserves your data and settings, and makes sure your computer starts quickly the next time you use it.

You can turn off Windows 8 using the Power button on the Settings menu. (Use the Charms bar to display the Settings menu.) When you click the Power button, you can choose the Sleep, Shut down, or Restart option. If you choose the Sleep option, Windows saves your work and then turns down the power to your monitor and computer, a condition called **sleep**. A light on the outside of your computer case blinks or changes color to indicate that the computer is sleeping. Because Windows saves your work, you do not need to close your programs or files before your computer goes to sleep. To wake a computer, you typically press the hardware power button on your computer case. Some computer manufacturers might set the computer to wake when you press a key or move the mouse. After you wake a computer, the screen looks exactly as it did when you put your computer to sleep.

If you choose the Shut down option, your computer closes all open programs, including Windows itself, and then completely turns off your computer. Shutting down doesn't save your work, so you must save your files first.

If you select the Restart option, your computer shuts down and then immediately restarts, which you might need to do after installing new programs or hardware.

PROSKILLS

Decision Making: Sign out, Sleep, or Shut Down?

If you are using a computer on the job, your organization probably has a policy about what to do when you're finished working on the computer. If it does not, deciding on the best approach depends on who uses the computer and how long it will be idle. Keep the following guidelines in mind as you make your decision:

- Sign out—If another person might use your computer shortly, sign out of Windows to protect your data and prepare the computer for someone else to use. To sign out of Windows 8, click your user icon on the Start screen and then click Sign out.
- Sleep—By default, Windows 8 is set to sleep after 15–30 minutes of idle time, depending on whether you are using a mobile or desktop computer. If you will be away from the computer for more than 15 minutes but less than a day, you can generally let the computer go to sleep on its own.
- Shut down—If your computer is plugged in to a power outlet and you don't plan to use the computer for more than a day, such as over the weekend, you save wear and tear on your electronic components and conserve energy by turning the computer off. You should also turn off the computer when it is susceptible to electrical damage, such as during a lightning storm, and when you need to install new hardware or disconnect the computer from a power source. If your mobile computer is running on battery power only and you don't plan to use it for more than a few hours, you should also turn it off to save your battery charge.

Emma suggests that you compare putting your computer to sleep and shutting down Windows 8.

To turn off Windows 8:

▶ **1.** Press the **Windows** key ⊞ to display the Start screen.

▶ **2.** Point to the upper-right hot corner on the Start screen to display the Charms bar.

3. Click the **Settings** charm on the Charms bar to display the Settings menu, shown in Figure 1-31.

Figure 1-31   **Settings menu**

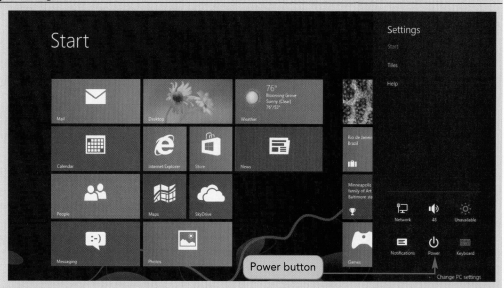

4. Click the **Power** button to display the power options.

5. Click **Sleep**. Windows 8 saves your work and then puts the computer to sleep. The light in the hardware power button changes color or blinks to indicate the computer is in a sleep state.

   Trouble? If a Sleep option does not appear when you click the Power button, your computer might be set to go to sleep only automatically. Click Shut down on the Power menu, and skip the remaining steps.

6. If the light in the hardware power button changes color or is now blinking, press the hardware power button to wake up the computer. If necessary, clear the lock screen and enter your password. Otherwise, move the mouse or press a key to wake the computer.

7. Display the Charms bar, and then click the **Settings** charm to display the Settings menu.

   Trouble? If you are instructed to sign out instead of shut down, click twice anywhere on the Start screen to close the Settings menu and Charms bar, click your user icon on the Start screen, and then click Sign out. Skip Step 8.

8. Click the **Power** button, and then click **Shut down**. Windows 8 turns off the computer.

   Trouble? If the Power button displays the Update and shut down option instead of Shut down, click Update and shut down.

In this session, you learned how to use File Explorer to navigate your computer. You also learned how to change the view of the contents of the File Explorer window. Finally, you learned how to get help when you need it and how to turn off Windows 8. With Emma's help, you should feel comfortable with the basics of Windows 8 and well prepared to demonstrate the fundamentals of using this operating system.

REVIEW

Session 1.2 Quick Check

1. _Navigating_ means moving from one location to another on your computer, such as from one file or folder to another. *30*
2. The left pane in File Explorer is called the _Navigation pane_, which provides access to resources and locations on your computer.
3. What is the purpose of the Pictures library? *31*
4. Describe the difference between Details view and Large icons view. *32*
5. In the File Explorer window, what appears in the right pane when you click a folder icon in the Navigation pane?
6. Explain how to expand a folder or other objects in the Navigation pane.
7. How do you access Windows Help and Support in Windows 8?
8. What option(s) save(s) your work before turning off your computer?

Review Assignments

PRACTICE

There are no Data Files needed for the Review Assignments.

The day before your first Windows 8 training session for Behind the Scenes employees, Emma Garcia offers to observe your tour of the operating system and help you fine-tune your lesson. You'll start working on the Start screen, with no applications open. Complete the following steps, recording your answers to any questions according to your instructor's preferences:

1. Start Windows 8 and sign in, if necessary.
2. Use the mouse to scroll the Start screen. How many full tiles appear on the screen when you scroll?
3. Zoom the Start screen to reduce the size of the tiles. How many tiles appear on the screen now?
4. Start the Calendar app.
5. Display the desktop. List the major parts of the desktop, including any icons.
6. Start WordPad. Identify each object on the taskbar (not including the notification area).
7. Start Paint and maximize the Paint window. How many buttons appear on the taskbar?
8. Switch to WordPad. How do you know that WordPad is the active program?
9. Close WordPad, and then restore the Paint window to its original size.
10. Open the Recycle Bin window. Record the number of items it contains, and then drag and resize the Recycle Bin window so that you can see both it and the Paint window.
11. Close the Paint window from the taskbar. What command did you use?
12. Display the Switch List. Which thumbnails are displayed in the Switch List?
13. Maximize the Recycle Bin window and then click the Home tab. Which buttons are active (not gray)? Use any button on the Home tab to open a dialog box. What dialog box did you open? What do you think this dialog box is used for? Click the Cancel button to close the dialog box, and then close the Recycle Bin window.
14. Change the view of the items displayed in the right pane of the File Explorer window. What view did you select and how did your selection change the appearance of the items? Close File Explorer.
15. Open Windows Help and Support. Use the Get started link to learn something new about Windows 8. What did you learn? How did you find this topic?
16. Browse Help topics to find information about customizing your computer. How many topics are listed in the Customize your PC category?
17. Use the Search box to find information about customizing your computer. How many topics are listed?
18. Close Help, and then return to the Start screen.
19. Turn off Windows 8 by using the Sleep command, shutting down, or signing out.
20. Submit your answers to the preceding questions to your instructor, either in printed or electronic form, as requested.

Case Problem 1

APPLY

There are no Data Files needed for this Case Problem.

Up and Running Up and Running is an independent firm located in major electronics stores throughout the Midwest. The firm installs software, repairs hardware, and provides training to customers of the electronics stores. Ken Mathias is the manager of a store in Red Wing, Minnesota. Ken hired you to work with customers in their homes or businesses. You are preparing for a visit to a customer who is new to Windows 8 and wants to determine the contents of his computer, including media apps and sample media files. Complete the following steps:

1. Start Windows 8 and sign in, if necessary.
2. Examine the tiles on the Start screen and use one to start an app that plays music or videos or displays photos. Which app did you start?
3. Start another media app. Which app did you start?
4. Search for apps installed on your computer related to media. What apps did you find?
5. Start one of the apps you found in Step 4. Which app did you start? Is it a Windows 8 app or a desktop application? How can you tell?
6. Start an app you could use to take photos. Which app did you start? Is it a Windows 8 app or a desktop application?
7. Use the Search menu to find settings related to media. How many settings did you find?
8. Close all open applications.
9. Start File Explorer, and then navigate to a folder that contains files. Which folder did you open? View the files in Details view, and then sort them by Size. Which file is the largest? (*Hint*: If there are no folders with files on your computer, display the contents of the Desktop.)
10. Change to Large icons view, and then point to a file to display a ScreenTip. What type of file did you select? What details are provided in the ScreenTip? Close File Explorer.
11. Open Windows Help and Support, and then find and read topics that describe two Windows features that make your PC more secure.
12. Close all open windows.
13. Submit your answers to the preceding questions to your instructor, either in printed or electronic form, as requested.

Case Problem 2

CHALLENGE

There are no Data Files needed for this Case Problem.

Austin Framing After earning a degree in fine arts and working as a conservator of prints and paintings, Danielle Reid opened a store called Austin Framing in Austin, Texas. She specializes in archival framing to preserve manuscripts and fine prints. So that she can concentrate on building her business, Danielle hired you to help her perform office tasks. She asks you to start by teaching her the basics of using her computer, which runs Windows 8. She especially wants to know which applications are installed on her computer and what they do. Complete the following steps:

1. Write down the apps listed on the Start screen.
2. Start one of the apps and then describe what it does. Close the app.
⊕ **Explore** 3. Open the Search menu, display the items in the Apps category, if necessary, and then click the Apps screen to display all the applications installed on the computer. Examine the applications in the Windows Accessories list.
4. Use Windows Help and Support to research one of the applications you examined in the previous step, such as Calculator or Notepad. Describe the purpose of the application.

5. Use the Search box in Windows Help and Support to list all the Help topics related to the application you researched in the previous step. How many topics are displayed in the results? Select a topic and review the Help information.

✛ **Explore** 6. Start the application you researched. If the application opened on the desktop, press the F1 key to display Help for the application. Click each link in the Help window to explore the Help topics. Compare these topics to the ones included in the Windows Help and Support window. Are they the same topics or different?

✛ **Explore** 7. Use Windows Help and Support to search for Help topics about WordPad. If you are connected to the Internet, also find Help information about WordPad on the Microsoft Answers Web site. Compare the two search results.

8. Close all open windows.

9. Submit the results of the preceding steps to your instructor, either in printed or electronic form, as requested.

Case Problem 3

There are no Data Files needed for this Case Problem.

Thorpe Consulting   Kara Thorpe recently started her own consulting firm in Santa Rosa, California, to help nonprofit organizations raise funds. Thorpe Consulting recommends fundraising strategies and helps clients earn grants for specific projects. Kara uses her Windows 8 laptop to create proposals, reports, and other documents and to communicate with clients. She uses File Explorer to work with files, but suspects she is not taking full advantage of its features. As Kara's new assistant, one of your responsibilities is to show her around the File Explorer window and demonstrate how to customize its appearance. Complete the following steps:

1. Start File Explorer. Click each tab on the ribbon to find out the kind of commands that are provided. Write down any commands that seem related to changing the appearance of the folder window.

2. In the Libraries window, switch to Large icons view, if necessary.

✛ **Explore** 3. Change the view to Content view. (*Hint*: Click the View tab, and then click the More button in the Layout group.) Describe the differences between Large icons view and Content view.

4. Click the Pictures library, and then describe any changes in the ribbon.

5. Click the Music library, and then describe any changes in the ribbon.

✛ **Explore** 6. Select a command on the View tab that displays a pane showing the details of the selected library. What command did you select?

✛ **Explore** 7. Select a command on the View tab that closes the Navigation pane. What command did you select?

✛ **Explore** 8. Click the Up one level button next to the Address bar. (*Hint*: Point to a button to display its name in a ScreenTip.) What happens when you click the Up one level button twice? How can you return to the Libraries window?

✛ **Explore** 9. Close the pane showing the details of the selected library, and then redisplay the Navigation pane. (*Hint*: Perform Steps 6 and 7 again.)

10. Close File Explorer, and then open the Windows Help and Support window and search for information about changing folder options. Find instructions explaining how to show hidden files. Explain how to do so. (*Hint*: A hidden file is not listed in a window, though it is actually stored in that folder.)

11. Close all open windows.

12. Submit the results of the preceding steps to your instructor, either in printed or electronic form, as requested.

CHALLENGE

Session 2.1 Visual Overview:

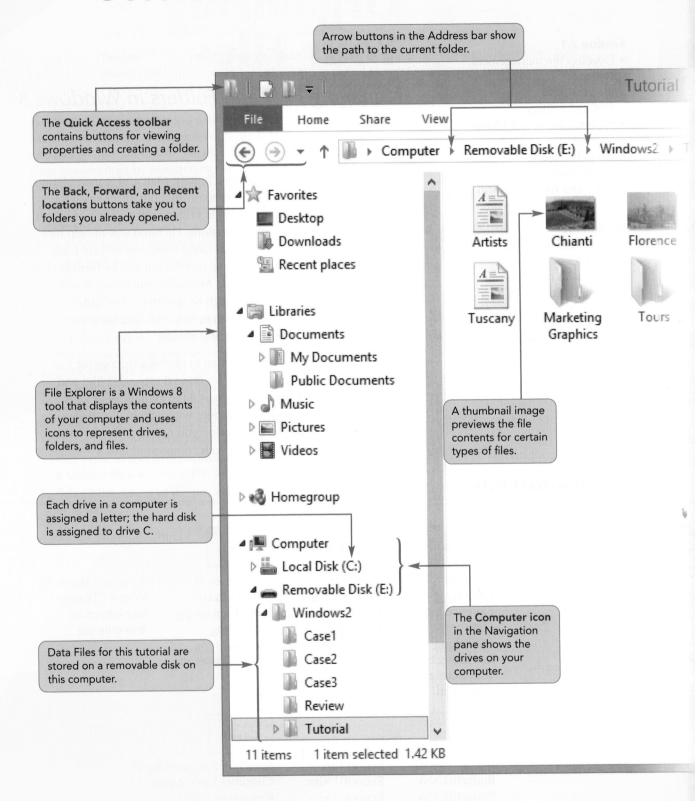

Arrow buttons in the Address bar show the path to the current folder.

The **Quick Access toolbar** contains buttons for viewing properties and creating a folder.

The **Back**, **Forward**, and **Recent locations** buttons take you to folders you already opened.

File Explorer is a Windows 8 tool that displays the contents of your computer and uses icons to represent drives, folders, and files.

Each drive in a computer is assigned a letter; the hard disk is assigned to drive C.

Data Files for this tutorial are stored on a removable disk on this computer.

A thumbnail image previews the file contents for certain types of files.

The **Computer icon** in the Navigation pane shows the drives on your computer.

Files in a Folder Window

The **file path** is a notation that indicates a file's location on your computer.

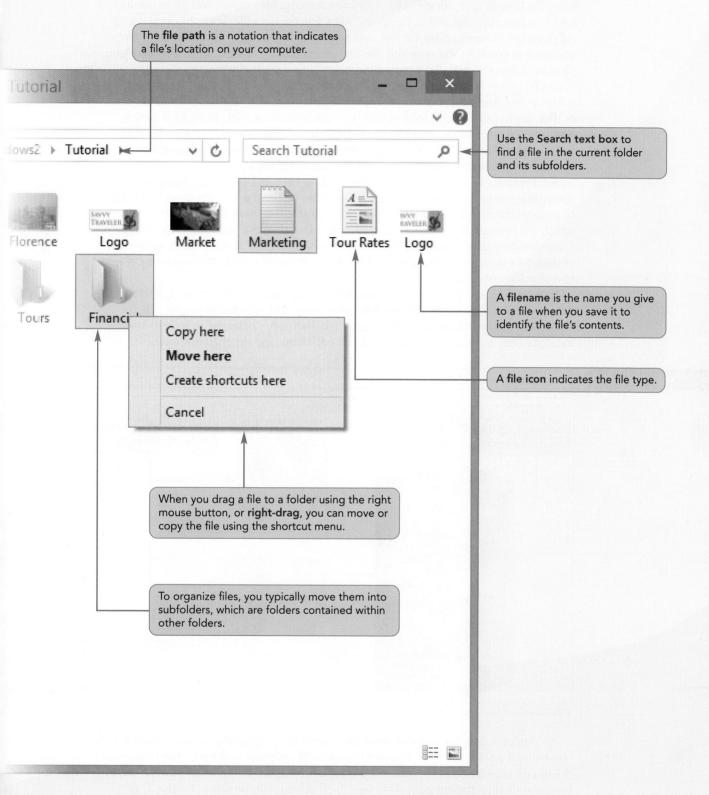

Use the **Search text box** to find a file in the current folder and its subfolders.

A **filename** is the name you give to a file when you save it to identify the file's contents.

A **file icon** indicates the file type.

When you drag a file to a folder using the right mouse button, or **right-drag**, you can move or copy the file using the shortcut menu.

To organize files, you typically move them into subfolders, which are folders contained within other folders.

Preparing to Manage Your Files

Knowing how to save, locate, and organize computer files makes you more productive when you are working with a computer. After you create a file, you can open it and edit the file's contents, print the file, and save it again—usually using the same program you used to create it. You organize files by storing them in folders. You need to organize files and folders so that you can find them easily and work efficiently.

A file cabinet is a common metaphor for computer file organization. A computer is like a file cabinet that has two or more drawers—each drawer is a storage device, or **disk**. Each disk contains folders that hold documents, or files. To make it easy to retrieve files, you arrange them logically into folders. For example, one folder might contain financial data, another might contain your creative work, and another could contain information you're gathering for an upcoming vacation.

A computer can store folders and files on different types of disks, ranging from removable media—such as **USB flash drives** (also called flash drives, thumbnail drives, or simply USB drives) and digital video discs (DVDs)—to **hard disks**, or fixed disks, which are permanently stored on a computer. Hard disks are the most popular type of computer storage because they provide an economical way to store many gigabytes of data. (A **gigabyte**, or **GB**, is about 1 billion bytes, with each byte roughly equivalent to a character of data.)

To have your computer access a removable disk, you must insert the disk into a **drive**, which is a computer device that can retrieve and sometimes record data on a disk. See Figure 2-1. A computer's hard disk is already contained in a drive inside the computer, so you don't need to insert it each time you use the computer.

| Figure 2-1 | Computer drives and disks |

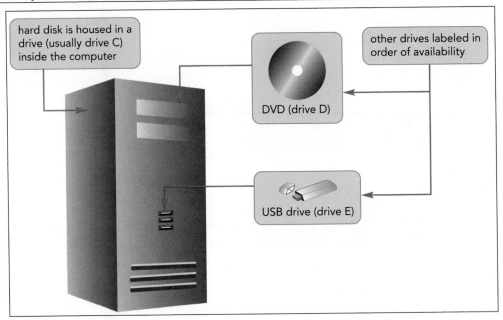

© 2014 Cengage Learning

A computer distinguishes one drive from another by assigning each a drive letter. As you learned earlier, the hard disk in a computer is assigned to drive C. The remaining drives can have any other letters, but are usually assigned in the order that the drives were installed on the computer—so your USB drive might be drive D, drive E, or drive F.

Understanding the Need for Organizing Files and Folders

Windows 8 stores thousands of files in many folders on the hard disk of your computer. These are system files that Windows 8 needs to display the Start screen and desktop, use drives, and perform other operating system tasks. To keep the system stable and to find files quickly, Windows organizes the folders and files in a hierarchy, or **file system**. At the top of the hierarchy, Windows stores folders and important files that it needs when you turn on the computer. This location is called the **root directory** and is usually drive C (the hard disk). The term *root* refers to another popular metaphor for visualizing a file system—an upside-down tree, which reflects the file hierarchy that Windows uses. In Figure 2-2, the tree trunk corresponds to the root directory, the branches to the folders, and the leaves to the files.

Figure 2-2 **Windows file hierarchy**

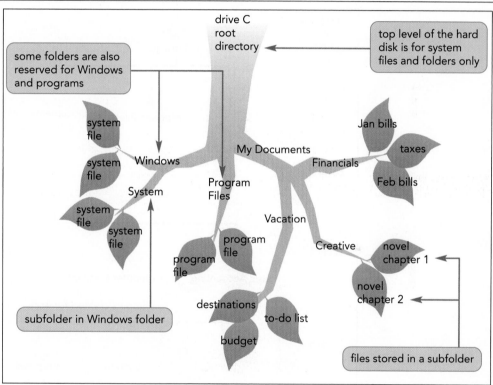

© 2014 Cengage Learning

Note that some folders contain other folders. An effectively organized computer contains a few folders in the root directory, and those folders contain other folders, also called subfolders.

The root directory, or top level, of the hard disk is for system files and folders only. You should not store your own work in the root directory because your files could interfere with Windows or a program. (If you are working in a computer lab, you might not be allowed to access the root directory.)

Do not delete or move any files or folders from the root directory of the hard disk; doing so could disrupt the system so that you can't run or start the computer. In fact, you should not reorganize or change any folder that contains installed software because Windows 8 expects to find the files for specific programs within certain folders. If you reorganize or change these folders, Windows 8 can't locate and start the programs stored in those folders. Likewise, you should not make changes to the folder (usually named Windows) that contains the Windows 8 operating system.

Developing Strategies for Organizing Files and Folders

The type of disk you use to store files determines how you organize those files. Figure 2-3 shows how you could organize your files on a hard disk if you were taking a full semester of business classes. To duplicate this organization, you would open the main folder for your documents, create four folders—one each for the Basic Accounting, Computer Concepts, Management Skills, and Professional Writing courses—and then store the writing assignments you complete in the Professional Writing folder.

| Figure 2-3 | Organizing folders and files on a hard disk |

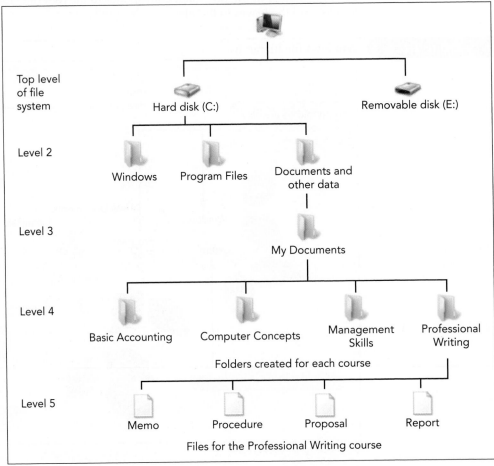

© 2014 Cengage Learning

If you store your files on removable media, such as a USB drive, you can use a simpler organization because you do not have to account for system files. In general, the larger the medium, the more levels of folders you should use because large media can store more files and, therefore, need better organization. For example, if you were organizing your files on a 12 GB USB drive, you could create folders in the top level of the USB drive for each general category of documents you store—one each for Courses, Creative, Financials, and Vacation. The Courses folder could then include one folder for each course (Basic Accounting, Computer Concepts, Management Skills, and Professional Writing), and each of those folders could contain the appropriate files.

If you have USB drives with a lower storage capacity, you might use one USB drive for your courses, another for creative work, and so on. If you need to create large documents for your courses, you can use one USB drive for each course.

PROSKILLS

Decision Making: Determining Where to Store Files

When you create and save files on your computer's hard disk, you should store them in subfolders. The top level of the hard disk is off-limits for your files because they could interfere with system files. If you are working on your own computer, store your files within the My Documents folder in the Documents library, which is where many programs save your files by default. When you use a computer on the job, your employer might assign a main folder to you for storing your work. In either case, if you simply store all your files in one folder, you will soon have trouble finding the files you want. Instead, you should create subfolders within a main folder to separate files in a way that makes sense for you.

Even if you store most of your files on removable media, such as USB drives, you still need to organize those files into folders and subfolders. Before you start creating folders, whether on a hard disk or removable disk, you need to plan the organization you will use. Following your plan increases your efficiency because you don't have to pause and decide which folder to use when you save your files. A file organization plan also makes you more productive in your computer work—the next time you need a particular file, you'll know where to find it.

Exploring Files and Folders

windows

To explore the files and folders on your computer in Windows 8, you use File Explorer. This tool displays the contents of your computer, using icons to represent drives, folders, and files. When you start File Explorer, it opens to show the contents of the Windows default libraries, making it easy to find the files you work with often, such as documents and pictures. To display only the drives on your computer, you can use another Windows tool: the Computer window. You typically open this window to perform system tasks, such as viewing system information. Like File Explorer, the Computer window is a folder window that displays locations on your computer.

A **folder window** refers to any window that displays the contents of a folder. It is divided into two sections, called panes. The left pane is the Navigation pane, which contains icons and links to locations you use often. The right pane displays the contents of your folders and other locations. If you select a folder in the Navigation pane, the contents of that folder appear in the right pane. To display the hierarchy of the folders and other locations on your computer, you select the Computer icon in the Navigation pane, and then select the icon for a drive, such as Local Disk (C:) or Removable Disk (E:). You can then open and explore folders on that drive.

If the Navigation pane showed all the folders on your computer at once, it could be a very long list. Instead, you open drives and folders only when you want to see what they contain. If a folder contains undisplayed subfolders, an expand icon appears to the left of the folder icon. (The same is true for drives.) To view the folders contained in an object, you click the expand icon. A collapse icon then appears next to the folder icon; click the collapse icon to hide the folder's subfolders. To view the files contained in a folder, you click the folder icon, and the files appear in the right pane. See Figure 2-4.

Figure 2-4 Viewing files in a folder window

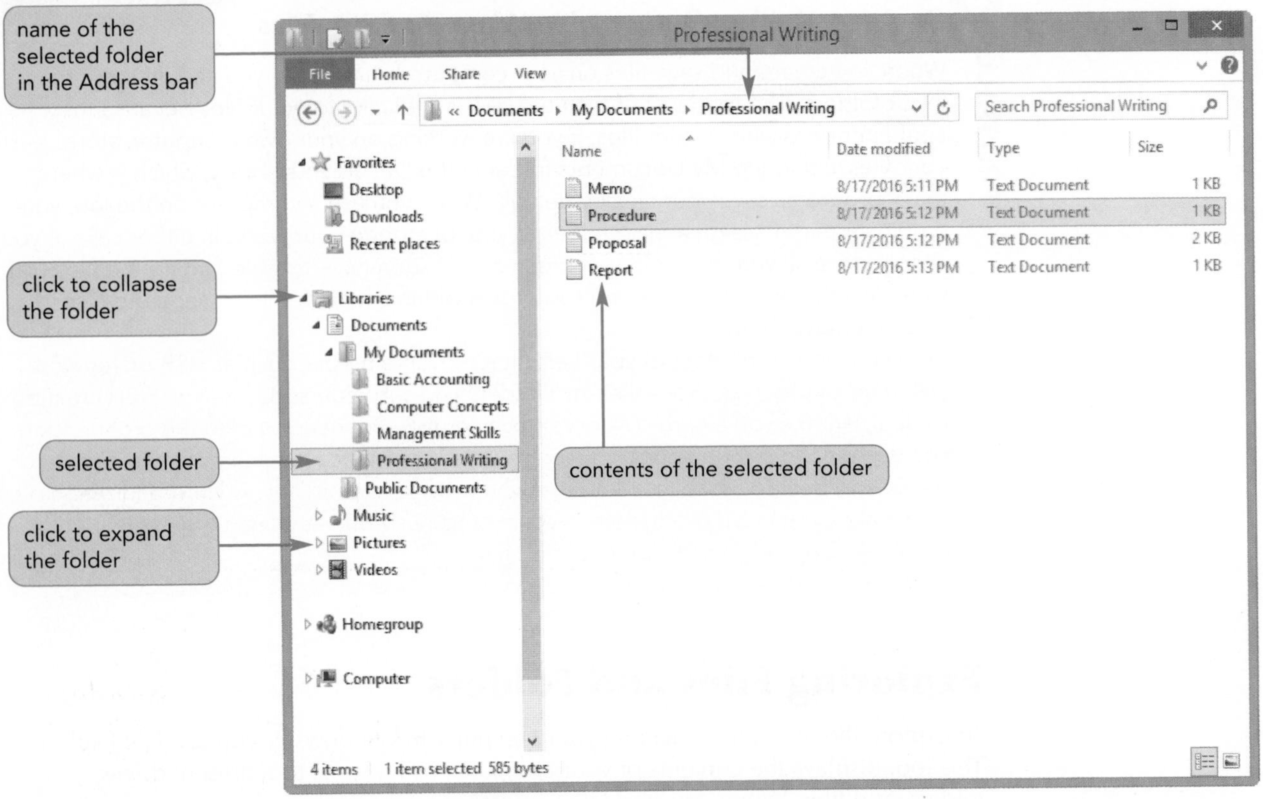

name of the selected folder in the Address bar

click to collapse the folder

selected folder

click to expand the folder

contents of the selected folder

Using the Navigation pane helps you explore your computer and orients you to your current location. As you move, copy, delete, and perform other tasks with the folders in the right pane of a folder window, you can refer to the Navigation pane to see how your changes affect the overall organization.

In addition to using the Navigation pane, you can explore your computer from a folder window in other ways. Use the following navigation techniques in any folder window and many dialog boxes:

- Opening drives and folders in the right pane—To view the contents of a drive or folder, double-click the drive or folder icon in the right pane of the folder window. For example, to view the contents of the Professional Writing folder shown in Figure 2-5, you can double-click the Professional Writing folder in the right pane.

Figure 2-5   Viewing the contents of a folder

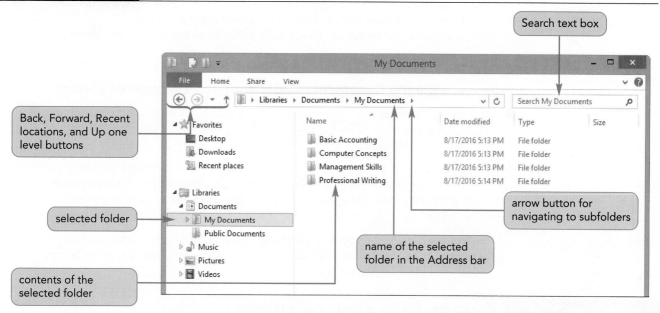

- Using the Address bar—You can use the Address bar to navigate to a different folder. The Address bar displays your current folder as a series of locations separated by arrow buttons. Click a folder name such as My Documents or an arrow button to navigate to a different location. You'll explore these controls later in the tutorial.
- Clicking the Back, Forward, Recent locations, and Up one level buttons—Use the Back, Forward, and Recent locations buttons to navigate to other folders you have already opened. After you use the Address bar to change folders, for example, you can use the Back button to return to the original folder. You can click the Recent locations button to navigate to a location you've visited recently. Use the Up one level button to navigate up to the folder containing the current folder. The ScreenTip for this button changes to reflect the folder to which you can navigate. For example, when you are working in the My Documents folder, the ScreenTip is Up to "Documents".
- Using the Search text box—To find a file or folder stored in the current folder or its subfolders, type a word or phrase in the Search text box. The search begins as soon as you start typing. Windows finds files based on text in the filename, text within the file, and other characteristics of the file, such as **tags** (descriptive words or phrases you add to your files) or the author. For example, if you're looking for a document named September Income, you can type *Sept* in the Search text box. Windows searches the current folder and its subfolders, and then displays any file whose filename contains a word starting with "Sept," including the September Income document.

Using Libraries and Folders

When you open File Explorer, it shows the contents of the Windows built-in libraries by default. A library displays similar types of files together, no matter where they are stored. In contrast, a folder stores files in a specific location, such as in the Professional Writing subfolder of the My Documents folder on the Local Disk (C:) drive. When you want to open the Report file stored in the Professional Writing folder, you must navigate to the Local Disk (C:) drive, then the My Documents folder, and finally the Professional Writing folder. A library makes it easier to access similar types of files. For example, you might store some music files in the My Music folder and others in a folder named Albums on your hard disk. You might also store music files in a Songs folder on a

USB drive. If the USB drive is connected to your computer, the Music library can display all the music files in the My Music, Albums, and Songs folders. You can then arrange the files to quickly find the ones you want to open and play.

Next, you'll navigate to the My Documents folder from the Documents library.

To open the My Documents folder from the Documents library:

▶ 1. Display the desktop, if necessary, and then click the **File Explorer** button 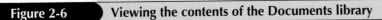 on the taskbar. The File Explorer window opens, displaying the contents of the default libraries.

▶ 2. In the Libraries section of the Navigation pane, click the **expand** icon ▷ next to the Documents icon. The folders in the Documents library appear in the Navigation pane; see Figure 2-6. The contents of your computer will differ.

Trouble? If your window displays icons in a view different from the one shown in the figure, you can still explore files and folders. The same is true for all figures in this session.

| Figure 2-6 | Viewing the contents of the Documents library |

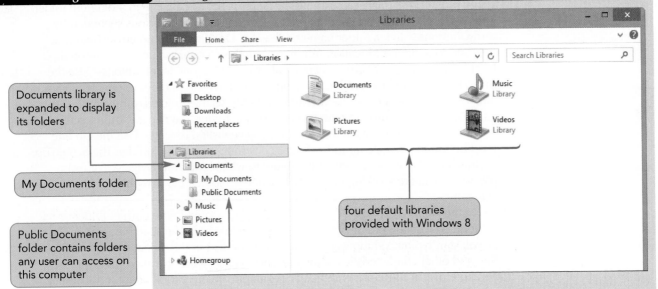

Documents library is expanded to display its folders

My Documents folder

Public Documents folder contains folders any user can access on this computer

four default libraries provided with Windows 8

▶ 3. Click the **My Documents** folder in the Navigation pane to display its contents in the right pane.

You can think of the Documents library as containing links to folders and files that are physically stored in other locations. The My Documents folder is not stored in the Documents library—it is actually located in your personal folder, which is labeled with the name you use to sign in to the computer, such as Matt. The My Documents folder is designed to store your files—the memos, reports, spreadsheets, presentations, and other files that you create, edit, and manipulate in a program. Your personal folder contains other folders that most users open frequently, such as My Pictures found in the Pictures library and My Music found in the Music library. Although the My Pictures folder is designed to store graphics and the My Music folder is designed to store music files, you can store graphics, music, or any other type of file in the My Documents folder, especially if doing so makes it easier to find these files when you need them.

Now that you've shown Matt how to display the contents of the My Documents folder from the Documents library, you can show him how to navigate to the actual location of the My Documents folder using the hierarchy of folders on your computer.

To open the My Documents folder using the hierarchy of folders on your computer:

1. In the Navigation pane of the open folder window, click the **Desktop** icon. This icon represents resources you can access from the desktop. See Figure 2-7. Your desktop might have other icons.

Figure 2-7   **Resources accessed from the desktop**

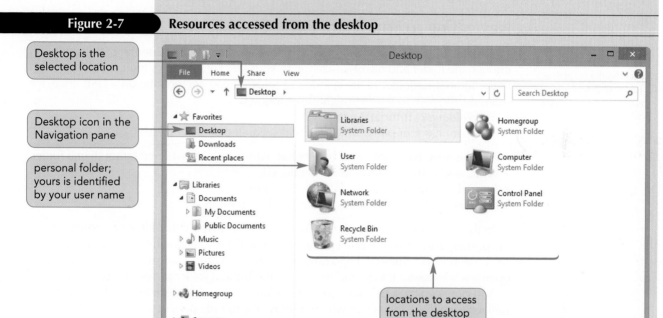

Desktop is the selected location

Desktop icon in the Navigation pane

personal folder; yours is identified by your user name

locations to access from the desktop

2. In the right pane, double-click your personal folder (the one with your user name). The personal folder shown in Figure 2-8 is named User. A list of folders stored in your personal folder appears in the right pane. Yours might appear in a different view.

Figure 2-8   **Contents of your personal folder**

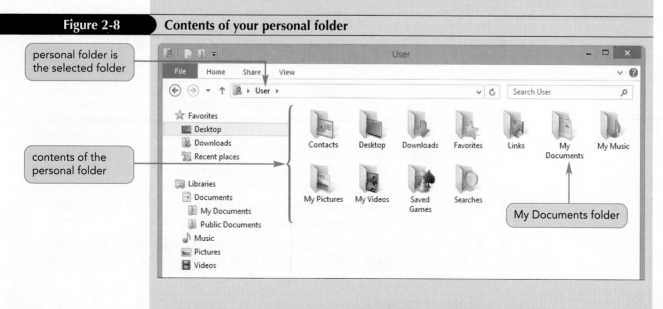

personal folder is the selected folder

contents of the personal folder

My Documents folder

TIP

When you are working in the Navigation pane, you only need to click a folder to open it, not double-click it.

3. In the right pane, double-click the **My Documents** folder. The Address bar shows the actual location of the My Documents folder on your computer—in your personal folder.

You've already mastered the basics of using a folder window to navigate your computer. If necessary, you click expand icons in the Navigation pane until you find the folder that you want. Then, you click the folder icon in the Navigation pane to view the folders and files it contains, which are displayed in the right pane. You can also double-click folders in the right pane to display their contents.

Navigating to Your Data Files

TIP

To display the file path in a folder window, click to the right of the text in the Address bar.

To navigate to the files you want, it helps to know the file path. The file path leads you through the folder and file organization to your file. For example, the Logo file is stored in the Tutorial subfolder of the Windows2 folder. If you are working on a USB drive, for example, the path to this file might be as follows:

E:\Windows2\Tutorial\Logo.png

This path has four parts, with each part separated by a backslash (\ ):

- E:—The drive name followed by a colon, which indicates a drive rather than a folder
- Windows2—The top-level folder on drive E
- Tutorial—A subfolder in the Windows2 folder
- Logo.png—The full filename, including file extension

In this example, drive E is the name for the USB drive. (If this file were stored on the primary hard disk, the drive name would be C.) If someone tells you to find the file E:\Windows2\Tutorial\Logo.png, you know you must navigate to your USB drive, open the Windows2 folder, and then open the Tutorial folder to find the Logo file.

You can keep track of your current location as you navigate between drives and folders using the Address bar, which displays the full file path in a folder window. You can use the open folder window to navigate to the Data Files you need for the rest of this tutorial. Before you perform the following steps, you need to know where you stored your Data Files, such as a USB drive. The following steps assume that drive is Removable Disk (E:), a USB drive. If necessary, substitute the appropriate drive on your system when you perform the steps.

To navigate to your Data Files:

1. Make sure your computer can access your Data Files for this tutorial. For example, if you are using a USB drive, insert the drive into the USB port.

Trouble? If you don't have the starting Data Files, you need to get them before you can proceed. Your instructor will either give you the Data Files or ask you to obtain them from a specified location (such as a network drive). In either case, make a backup copy of your Data Files before you start using them so you will have the original files available in case you need to start over. If you have any questions about the Data Files, see your instructor or technical support person for assistance.

2. In the open folder window, click the **expand** icon ▷ next to the Computer icon to display the drives on your computer, if necessary.

3. Click the **expand** icon ▷ next to the drive containing your Data Files, such as Removable Disk (E:). A list appears below the drive name showing the folders on that drive.

4. If the list of folders does not include the Windows2 folder, continue clicking the **expand** icon ▷ to navigate to the folder that contains the Windows2 folder.

5. Click the **expand** icon ▷ next to the Windows2 folder to expand the folder, and then click the **Windows2** folder so that its contents appear in the Navigation pane and in the right pane of the folder window. The Windows2 folder contains the Case1, Case2, Case3, Review, and Tutorial folders, as shown in Figure 2-9. (Because Case Problem 4 does not require any files, the Windows2 folder does not include a Case4 folder.) The other folders on your system might vary.

Figure 2-9	Navigating to the Windows2 folder

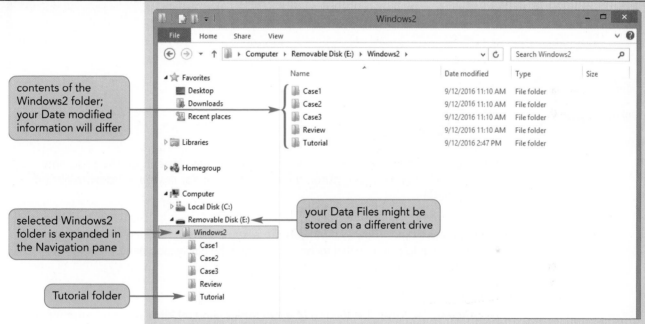

contents of the Windows2 folder; your Date modified information will differ

selected Windows2 folder is expanded in the Navigation pane

Tutorial folder

your Data Files might be stored on a different drive

6. In the Navigation pane, click the **Tutorial** folder. The files it contains appear in the right pane. To preview the contents of the graphics, you can display the files as medium icons or larger.

TIP

If you change the view of one folder, other folders continue to display files in their specified view.

7. Click the **View** tab on the ribbon, and then click **Medium icons** in the Layout group. The files appear in Medium icons view in the folder window. See Figure 2-10.

| Figure 2-10 | Files in the Tutorial folder in Medium icons view |

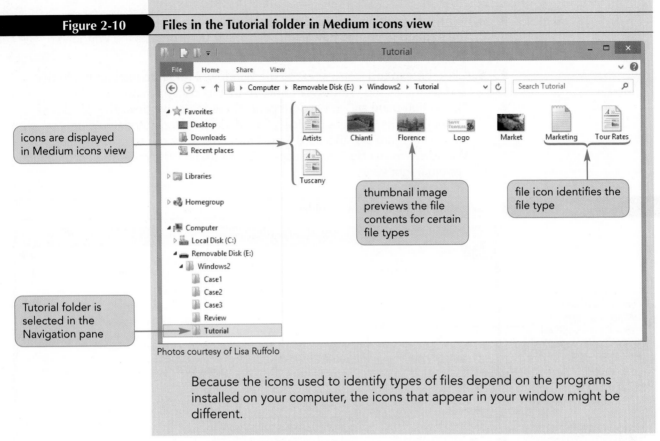

icons are displayed in Medium icons view

thumbnail image previews the file contents for certain file types

file icon identifies the file type

Tutorial folder is selected in the Navigation pane

Photos courtesy of Lisa Ruffolo

Because the icons used to identify types of files depend on the programs installed on your computer, the icons that appear in your window might be different.

Matt wants to know how to use the Address bar effectively, so you offer to navigate with the Address bar to compare that technique to using the Navigation pane.

Navigating with the Address Bar

The Address bar, located at the top of every folder window, displays your current folder as a series of locations separated by arrow buttons. For example, in Figure 2-11, the Address bar shows the Windows2 and Tutorial folders separated by an arrow button, indicating that Tutorial is the current folder and it's stored in the Windows2 folder. Click the arrow button after the Windows2 folder to display a list of subfolders in the Windows2 folder. If a chevron button ≪ appears, you can click it to list the folders and drives containing the locations displayed in the Address bar. The first item in the Address bar is Computer, which contains Removable Disk (E:). Windows2 is contained in Removable Disk (E:), and the Tutorial folder is contained in the Windows2 folder.

| Figure 2-11 | Navigating with the Address bar |

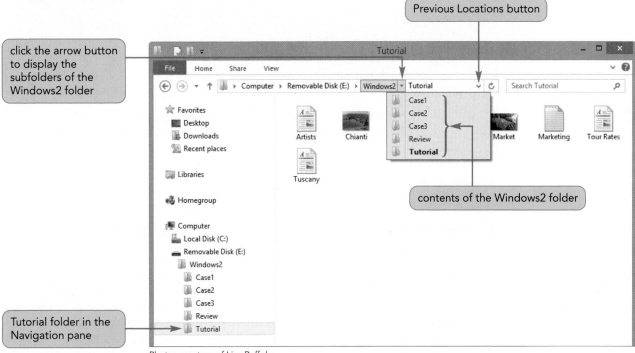

Photos courtesy of Lisa Ruffolo

To change your location, you can click or type a folder name in the Address bar. For example, you can click Windows2 to navigate to that folder. You can also type the path to the folder you want, or type the name of a standard, built-in Windows folder or library, such as the My Documents or Favorites folders or the Music or Pictures libraries.

TIP

To navigate to any location you visited in a folder window, click the Previous Locations button in the Address bar, and then click the location you want to visit.

After you navigate to a location by any method, you can click the Back, Forward, and Recent locations buttons to revisit folders you've already opened. For example, if you navigate first to drive E:, then to the Windows2 folder, and then to the Tutorial folder, you can click the Back button to open your previous location, the Windows2 folder. When you do, the Forward button becomes active. You can then click the Forward button to open the next location in your sequence, the Tutorial folder. To navigate to any recent location, click the Recent locations button, and then click a location in the list.

To navigate the hierarchy of folders and drives on your computer, recall that you can use another navigation button: the Up one level button. For example, if you are working in the Tutorial folder, you can click the Up one level button to navigate to the Windows2 folder. If you click the Up one level button again, you navigate to the root directory of your removable disk, such as Removable Disk (E:).

To navigate using the Address bar and navigation buttons:

1. In the folder window displaying the contents of your Tutorial folder, click the drive containing your Data Files, such as Removable Disk (E:), in the Address bar. The window displays the contents of the drive containing your Data Files.

Trouble? If the drive containing your Data Files is not listed in the Address bar, click the chevron button « in the Address bar, and then click Removable Disk (E:).

Trouble? If the drive letter of your removable disk is different, substitute the correct drive letter for drive E for the remaining steps.

2. Click the **arrow** button ▶ to the right of Computer on the Address bar, and then click the name of a hard disk, such as **Local Disk (C:)**.

   Trouble? If the hard disk on your computer has a different name, click that name instead of Local Disk (C:).

3. Click the **Back** button ⊖ on the Address bar two times to return to the Tutorial folder.

4. Click the **Recent locations** button ▼ to display a list of locations you visited, and then click **Windows2**. The subfolders in your Windows2 folder appear in the right pane.

Leave the folder window open so that you can work with other file and folder tools.

Using the Search Text Box to Find Files

After you use a computer awhile, you're likely to have hundreds of files stored in various folders. If you know where you stored a file, it's easy to find it—you can use any navigation technique you like to navigate to that location and then scan the file list to find the file. Often, however, finding a file is more time consuming than that. You know that you stored a file somewhere in a standard folder such as My Documents or My Music, but finding the file might mean opening dozens of folders and scanning many long file lists. To save time, you can use the Search text box to quickly find your file.

The Search text box appears next to the Address bar in any folder window. To find a file in the current folder or any of its subfolders, you start typing text associated with the file. This search text can be part of the filename, text within the file, tags (keywords you associate with a file), or other file properties. By default, Windows searches for files by examining the names of the files displayed in the folder window and files in any subfolders. If it finds a file whose filename contains a word starting with the search text you specify, it displays that file in the folder window. For example, you can use the search text *travel* to find files named Savvy Traveler and Travel Agencies. If you are searching a hard drive, Windows also looks for files that contain a word starting with your search text. If it finds one, it displays that file in the folder window. For example, using *travel* as the search text also finds files containing words such as "traveled" and "travelogue." If you are searching a removable drive, Windows searches filenames only by default. However, you can change settings to specify that you want to search other properties, including the contents. The following steps assume you are searching a removable drive.

Matt asks you to find a digital photo of an Italian market on his computer. He knows he has at least one photo of a market. You can find this file by starting to type *market* in the Search text box.

To use the Search text box to find a file:

1. In the folder window displaying the contents of your Windows2 folder, click the Search text box.

2. Type **m** and then pause. Windows 8 examines the files in the Windows2 folder and its subfolders, searching for a filename that includes a word starting with *m*. The files in the Windows2 folder that meet this criterion are displayed in the search results. You can continue typing to narrow the selection.

3. Type **ar** after the **m** so that the search text is now *mar*. Only two files have filenames that include a word beginning with *mar*. See Figure 2-12. The first three letters in each filename are highlighted. Your files might appear in a different view.

Trouble? If you are searching a hard drive, you will see additional files that contain words beginning with *mar*.

Figure 2-12	Searching for a file

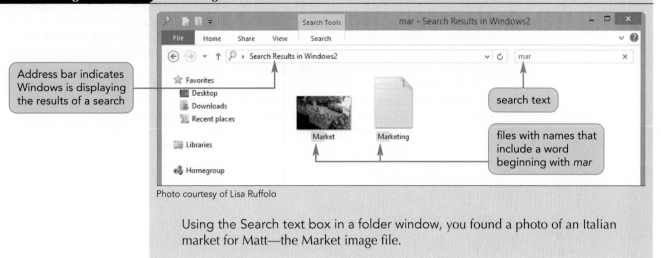

Address bar indicates Windows is displaying the results of a search

search text

files with names that include a word beginning with *mar*

Photo courtesy of Lisa Ruffolo

Using the Search text box in a folder window, you found a photo of an Italian market for Matt—the Market image file.

Now that Matt is comfortable navigating a computer to find files, you're ready to show him how to manage his files and folders.

Managing Files and Folders

After you devise a plan for storing your files, you are ready to get organized by creating folders that will hold your files. You can do so using any folder window. In this tutorial, you create folders in the Tutorial folder, which is probably stored on a USB drive, not a hard drive. When you are working on your own computer, you usually create folders within the My Documents folder and other standard folders, such as My Music and My Pictures. However, Chianti, Florence, Logo, and Market are all graphics files that Matt uses for marketing and sales. The Artists and Tuscany files were created for Italian tour descriptions. The Marketing and Tour Rates files relate to business finances.

One way to organize these files is to create three folders—one for graphics, one for tours, and another for the financial files. When you create a folder, you give it a name, preferably one that describes its contents. A folder name can have up to 255 characters. Any character is allowed, except / \ : * ? " < > and |. Considering these conventions, you could create three folders as follows:

- Marketing Graphics folder—Chianti, Florence, Logo, and Market files
- Tours folder—Artists and Tuscany files
- Financial folder—Marketing and Tour Rates files

Before creating the folders, you show your plan to Matt. You point out that instead of creating a folder for the graphics files, he could store them in the Pictures library that Windows 8 provides for photos, clip art, drawings, and other graphics. However, Matt wants to keep these marketing graphics files separate from any other files. He also thinks storing them in a folder along with the Tours and Financial folders will make it easier to find his business files later.

Guidelines for Creating Folders

Keep the following guidelines in mind as you create folders:
- Keep folder names short and familiar. Long folder names can be more difficult to display in their entirety in folder windows, so use names that are short but clear. Choose names that will be meaningful later, such as project names or course numbers.
- Develop standards for naming folders. Use a consistent naming scheme that is clear to you, such as one that uses a project name as the name of the main folder, and includes step numbers in each subfolder name (for example, 01 Plan, 02 Approvals, 03 First Draft, and so on).
- Create subfolders to organize files. If a file list in a folder window is so long that you must scroll the window, consider organizing those files into subfolders.

Matt asks you to create the three new folders. After that, you'll move his files to the appropriate folders.

Creating Folders

You've already seen folder icons in the windows you've examined. Now, you'll create folders within the Tutorial folder using the ribbon that appears in all folder windows.

Creating a Folder in a Folder Window

- In the Navigation pane, click the drive, folder, or library in which you want to create a folder.
- Click the Home tab and then click the New folder button in the New group, or click the New folder button on the Quick Access toolbar.
- Type a name for the folder, and then press the Enter key.

or

- Right-click a drive, folder, or library in the Navigation pane or right-click a blank area in the folder window, point to New, and then click Folder.
- Type a name for the folder, and then press the Enter key.

Now you can create three folders in your Tutorial folder as you planned—the Marketing Graphics, Tours, and Financial folders. You create these folders in three ways: using the Home tab, shortcut menu, and Quick Access toolbar. (The Quick Access toolbar is a row of buttons on a program's title bar that gives you one-click access to frequently used commands, including creating a folder.)

To create folders:

1. Navigate to the **Tutorial** folder included with your Data Files.

2. Click the **Home** tab, and then click the **New folder** button in the New group. A folder icon with the label "New folder" appears in the right pane. See Figure 2-13.

Figure 2-13   Creating a subfolder in the Tutorial folder

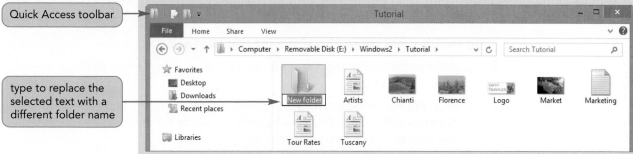

Quick Access toolbar

type to replace the selected text with a different folder name

Photos courtesy of Lisa Ruffolo

Trouble? If the "New folder" name is not selected, right-click the new folder, click Rename, and then continue with Step 3.

Windows uses *New folder* as a placeholder, and selects the text so that you can replace it immediately by typing a new name. You do not need to press the Backspace or Delete key to delete the text.

▶ **3.** Type **Marketing Graphics** as the folder name, and then press the **Enter** key. The new folder is now named Marketing Graphics and is the selected item in the right pane. To create a second folder, you can use a shortcut menu.

▶ **4.** Right-click a blank area in the right pane, point to **New** on the shortcut menu, and then click **Folder**. A folder icon appears in the right pane with the New folder text selected.

▶ **5.** Type **Tours** as the name of the new folder, and then press the **Enter** key.

▶ **6.** Click the **New folder** button 🗋 on the Quick Access toolbar, type **Financial**, and then press the **Enter** key to create and name the folder. The Tutorial folder now contains three new subfolders.

After creating three folders, you're ready to organize your files by moving them into the appropriate folders.

Moving and Copying Files and Folders

If you want to place a file into a folder from another location, you can either move the file or copy it. **Moving** a file removes it from its current location and places it in a new location that you specify. **Copying** also places the file in a new location that you specify, but does not remove it from its current location. Windows 8 provides several techniques for moving and copying files. The same principles apply to folders: You can move and copy folders using a variety of methods.

Moving a File or Folder in a Folder Window

- Right-drag the file or folder you want to move to the destination folder.
- Release the mouse button, and then click Move here on the shortcut menu.

or

- Right-click the file or folder you want to move to the destination folder, and then click Cut on the shortcut menu. (You can also click the file or folder and then press the Ctrl+X keys.)
- Navigate to and right-click the destination folder, and then click Paste on the shortcut menu. (You can also click the destination folder and then press the Ctrl+V keys.)

Matt suggests that you move some files from the Tutorial folder to the appropriate subfolders. You'll start by moving the Marketing file to the Financial folder using the right-drag technique, which you will learn next.

To move a file using the right mouse button:

▶ **1.** Point to the **Marketing** file in the right pane, and then press and hold the right mouse button.

▶ **2.** With the right mouse button still pressed down, drag the **Marketing** file to the **Financial** folder. When the Move to Financial ScreenTip appears, release the button. A shortcut menu opens.

▶ **3.** With the left mouse button, click **Move here** on the shortcut menu. The Marketing file is removed from the main Tutorial folder and stored in the Financial subfolder.

   Trouble? If you released the mouse button before you dragged the Marketing file all the way to the Financial folder and before seeing the Move to Financial ScreenTip, press the Esc key to close the shortcut menu, and then repeat Steps 1–3.

   Trouble? If you moved the Market file instead of the Marketing file, press the Ctrl+Z keys to undo the move, and then repeat Steps 1–3.

▶ **4.** In the right pane, double-click the **Financial** folder. The Marketing file is in the Financial folder.

   Trouble? If the Marketing file does not appear in the Financial folder, you probably moved it to a different folder. Press the Ctrl+Z keys to undo the move, and then repeat Steps 1–4.

▶ **5.** Click the **Back** button ⦸ on the Address bar to return to the Tutorial folder.

The advantage of moving a file or folder by dragging with the right mouse button is that you can efficiently complete your work with one action. However, this right-drag technique requires polished mouse skills so that you can drag the file comfortably. When you drag to move files, be sure to verify the destination by waiting for the Move to ScreenTip. Otherwise, you might move the file to an unintended folder and have trouble finding the file later.

Another way to move files and folders is to use the **Clipboard**, a temporary storage area for files and information that you copy or move from one place and plan to use somewhere else. Although the Clipboard does not appear in a folder window, you can use it when working with files and folders. Select a file and use the Cut or Copy command to temporarily store the file on the Clipboard, and then use the Paste command to insert the file elsewhere. Although using the Clipboard takes more steps, some users find it easier than dragging with the right mouse button.

You'll move the Artists file to the Tours folder next by using the Clipboard.

To move files using the Clipboard:

▶ **1.** Right-click the **Artists** file, and then click **Cut** on the shortcut menu. Although the file icon is still displayed in the folder window, Windows 8 removes the Artists file from the Tutorial folder and stores it on the Clipboard.

▶ **2.** In the right pane, right-click the **Tours** folder, and then click **Paste** on the shortcut menu. Windows 8 pastes the Artists file from the Clipboard to the Tours folder. The Artists file icon no longer appears in the folder window.

▶ **3.** In the Navigation pane, click the **expand** icon ▷ next to the Tutorial folder, if necessary, to display its contents, and then click the **Tours** folder to view its contents in the right pane. The Tours folder now contains the Artists file. See Figure 2-14.

Figure 2-14	Moving a file

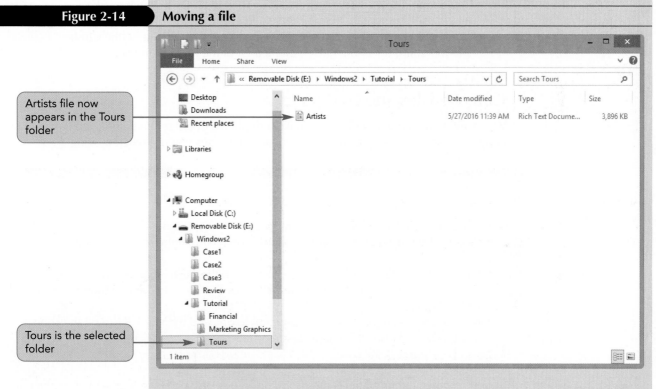

Artists file now appears in the Tours folder

Tours is the selected folder

Next, you'll move the Tuscany file from the Tutorial folder to the Tours folder.

▶ **4.** Click the **Back** button ⬅ on the Address bar to return to the Tutorial folder, right-click the **Tuscany** file in the folder window, and then click **Cut** on the shortcut menu.

▶ **5.** In the Navigation pane, right-click the **Tours** folder, and then click **Paste** on the shortcut menu. The files are moved into the Tours folder.

▶ **6.** Click the **Forward** button ➡ on the Address bar to return to the Tours folder. The Tours folder now contains the Artists and Tuscany files.

One way to save steps when moving or copying multiple files or folders is to select all the files and folders you want to move or copy, and then work with them as a group. You'll show Matt how to do that next.

Selecting Files and Folders

You can select multiple files or folders using several techniques, so you can choose the most convenient method for your current task. First, you open the folder that contains the files or folders you want to select. Next, select the files or folders using any one of the following methods:

- To select files or folders that are listed together in a folder window, click the first item, hold down the Shift key, click the last item, and then release the Shift key.
- To select files or folders that are listed together in a folder window without using the keyboard, drag the pointer to create a selection box around all the items you want to include.
- To select files or folders that are not listed together, hold down the Ctrl key, click each item you want to select, and then release the Ctrl key.
- To select all of the files or folders, click the Select all button in the Select group on the Home tab.
- To clear the selection of an item in a selected group, hold down the Ctrl key, click each item you want to remove from the selection, and then release the Ctrl key.
- To clear the entire selection, click a blank area of the folder window.

Copying Files and Folders

When you copy a file or folder, you make a duplicate of the original item. You can copy files or folders using techniques similar to the ones you use when moving them.

REFERENCE

Copying a File or Folder in a Folder Window

- Right-drag the file or folder you want to copy to the destination folder.
- Release the mouse button, and then click Copy here on the shortcut menu.

or

- Right-click the file or folder you want to copy to the destination folder, and then click Copy on the shortcut menu. (You can also click the file or folder and then press the Ctrl+C keys.)
- Navigate to and right-click the destination folder, and then click Paste on the shortcut menu. (You can also click the destination folder and then press the Ctrl+V keys.)

You'll copy the four graphics files from the Tutorial folder to the Marketing Graphics folder now.

To copy files using the Clipboard:

1. Using any navigation technique you've learned, return to the Tutorial folder window.

2. Click the **Chianti** file, hold down the **Shift** key, click the **Market** file, and then release the **Shift** key. Four files are selected in the Tutorial folder window.

3. Right-click the selected files, and then click **Copy** on the shortcut menu. Windows copies the files to the Clipboard.

4. Right-click the **Marketing Graphics** folder, and then click **Paste** on the shortcut menu.

5. Double-click the **Marketing Graphics** folder to verify it contains the four files you copied, and then return to the Tutorial folder.

Now that you have copied files using the Copy and Paste commands, you can use the right-drag technique to copy the Tour Rates file to the Financial folder. As with moving files, you point to the file, hold down the right mouse button, and then drag the file to a new location. However, when you release the mouse button, you click Copy here (instead of Move here) on the shortcut menu to copy the file.

To copy a file:

▶ **1.** Right-drag the **Tour Rates** file from the Tutorial folder to the Financial folder.

▶ **2.** Release the mouse button, and then click **Copy here** on the shortcut menu.

▶ **3.** Double-click the **Financial** folder to verify it contains the Marketing and Tour Rates files, and then return to the Tutorial folder.

When you move or copy a folder, you move or copy all the files contained in the folder.

You can use a third technique to copy or move a file or folder. You can drag the file or folder (using the left mouse button) to another location. Whether the file or folder is copied or moved depends on where you drag it. A ScreenTip appears when you drag a file to a new location—the ScreenTip indicates what happens when you release the mouse button. Figure 2-15 summarizes how to copy and move files and folders by dragging.

Figure 2-15	Dragging to move and copy files

Drag a File or Folder:	To:
Into a folder on the same drive	Move the file or folder to the destination folder
Into a folder on a different drive	Copy the file or folder to the destination folder

© 2014 Cengage Learning

Although the copy and move techniques listed are common ways to copy and move files and folders, be sure you can anticipate what happens when you drag a file or folder.

REVIEW

Session 2.1 Quick Check

1. You organize files by storing them in ___*folder*___ .
2. What is the purpose of the Address bar in a folder window? *58*
3. A(n) ___*folder file*___ can have up to 255 characters of any kind, except / \ : * ? " < > and |.
4. Explain how to use a folder window to navigate to a file in the following *56* location: E:\Courses\Computer Basics\Operating Systems.txt.
5. Describe how to find files using the Search text box.
6. One way to move files and folders is to use the ___*clipboard*___, a temporary storage area for information that you cut or copied.
7. Explain one advantage and one disadvantage of moving a folder using the right-dragging method.
8. What happens if you click the first file in a folder window, hold down the Shift key, click the last file, and then release the Shift key? *will selected*

Session 2.2 Visual Overview:

The View tab on the ribbon contains options for specifying the view of the current folder window.

Use the options in the Panes group to display or hide a pane in the folder window.

The contents of this folder are grouped by file type; a **group** displays a sequential list of all the files in a folder, grouped according to file detail, such as file type or size.

A **backup** is a duplicate copy of a file.

The zipped folder icon indicates a **compressed folder**, which stores files so they take up less disk space.

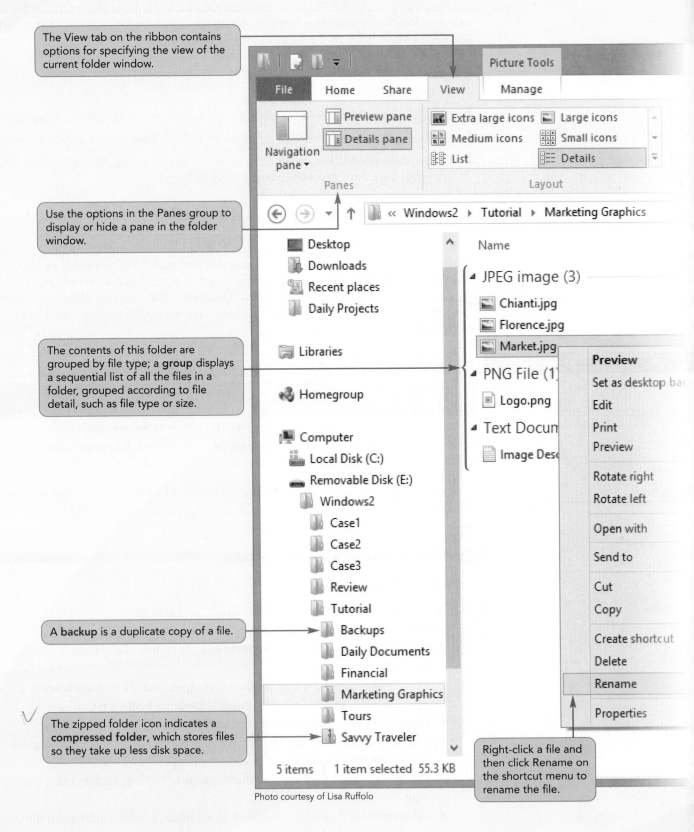

Right-click a file and then click Rename on the shortcut menu to rename the file.

Photo courtesy of Lisa Ruffolo

Customized Folder Window

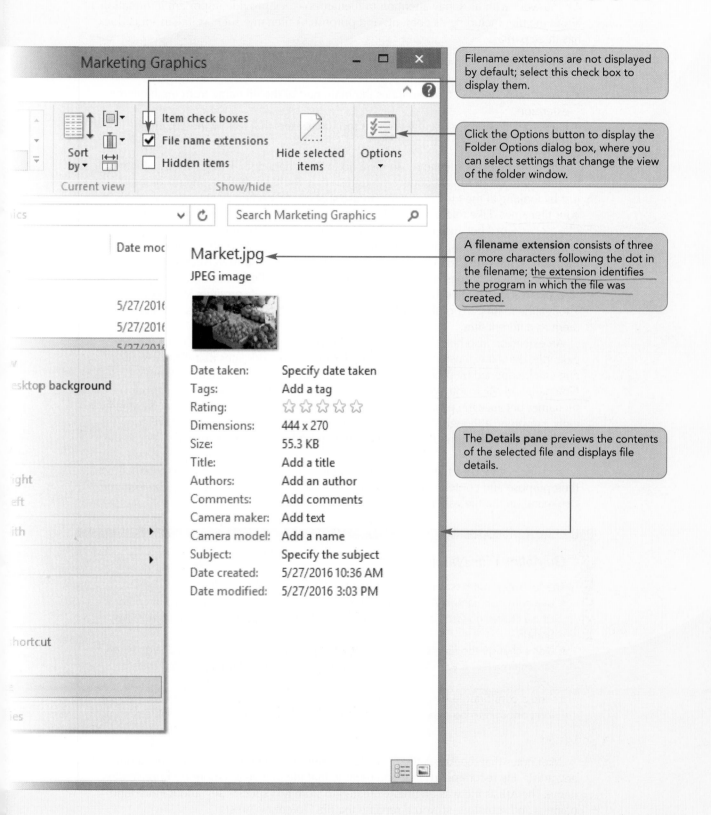

Filename extensions are not displayed by default; select this check box to display them.

Click the Options button to display the Folder Options dialog box, where you can select settings that change the view of the folder window.

A **filename extension** consists of three or more characters following the dot in the filename; the extension identifies the program in which the file was created.

The **Details pane** previews the contents of the selected file and displays file details.

Naming and Renaming Files

As you work with files, pay attention to filenames—they provide important information about the file, including its contents and purpose. A filename such as Italian Tours.docx — *extension* has three parts: *main part*

- Main part of the filename—The name you provide when you create a file, and the name you associate with a file
- Dot—The period (.) that separates the main part of the filename from the filename extension
- Filename extension—Usually three or four characters that follow the dot in the filename

The main part of a filename can have up to 255 characters. This gives you plenty of room to name your file accurately enough so that you'll know the contents of the file just by looking at the filename. You can use spaces and certain punctuation symbols in your filenames. Like folder names, however, filenames cannot contain the symbols / \ : * ? " < > or | because these characters have special meanings in Windows 8.

A filename might display its filename extension. For example, in the filename Italian Tours.docx, the extension *docx* identifies the file as one created in Microsoft Word, a word-processing program. You might also have a file called Italian Tours.png—the .png extension identifies the file as one created in a graphics program such as Paint. Though the main parts of these filenames are identical, their extensions distinguish them as different files.

An extension also helps Windows identify what program should open the file. For example, the .txt extension in a file named Brochure.txt indicates that it is a text file and can be opened by programs associated with that extension, such as WordPad, Notepad, and Microsoft Word. You usually do not need to add extensions to your filenames because the program you use to create the file adds the extension automatically. However, although Windows 8 keeps track of extensions, by default, Windows 8 is not set to display them. (You will learn how to show filename extensions later in the tutorial.)

Be sure to give your files and folders meaningful names that will help you remember their purpose and contents. You can easily rename a file or folder by using the Rename command on the file's shortcut menu.

INSIGHT

Guidelines for Naming Files

The following are best practices for naming (or renaming) your files:

- Use common names. Avoid cryptic names that might make sense now but could cause confusion later, such as nonstandard abbreviations or imprecise names like Stuff08.
- Don't change the filename extension. Do not change the filename extension when renaming a file. If you do, Windows might not be able to find a program that can open it.
- Find a comfortable balance between too short and too long. Use filenames that are long enough to be meaningful, but short enough to be read easily on the screen.

Matt notes that the Artists file in the Tours folder could contain information about any artists. He recommends that you rename that file to give it a more descriptive filename. The Artists file was originally created to store text specifically about Florentine painters and sculptors, so you'll rename the file Florentine Artists.

To rename the Artists file:

1. If you took a break after the previous session, make sure that a folder window is open, and then navigate to the **Windows2** folder included with your Data Files. Click the **Tutorial** folder in the left pane and change to **Medium icons** view, if necessary.

2. Open the **Tours** folder to display its contents.

3. Right-click the **Artists** file, and then click **Rename** on the shortcut menu. The filename is highlighted and a box appears around it.

4. Type **Florentine Artists**, and then press the **Enter** key. The file now appears with the new name.

   Trouble? If you make a mistake while typing and you haven't pressed the Enter key yet, press the Backspace key until you delete the mistake and then complete Step 4. If you've already pressed the Enter key, repeat Steps 3 and 4 to rename the file again.

   Trouble? If your computer is set to display filename extensions, a message might appear asking if you are sure you want to change the filename extension. Click the No button, and then repeat Steps 3 and 4.

> **TIP**
>
> To rename a file, you can also click the file, pause, click it again to select the filename, and then type to enter a new filename.

All the files that originally appeared in the Tutorial folder are now stored in appropriate subfolders. You can streamline the organization of the Tutorial folder by deleting the duplicate files you no longer need.

Deleting Files and Folders

> **TIP**
>
> In most cases, a file deleted from a USB drive does not go into the Recycle Bin. Instead, it is deleted when Windows 8 removes its icon, and the file cannot be recovered.

You should periodically delete files and folders you no longer need so that your main folders and disks don't get cluttered. In a folder window, you delete a file or folder by deleting its icon. When you delete a file from a hard disk, Windows 8 removes the file from the folder but stores the file contents in the Recycle Bin. The Recycle Bin is an area on your hard disk that holds deleted files until you remove them permanently. When you delete a folder from the hard disk, the folder and all of its files are stored in the Recycle Bin. If you change your mind and want to retrieve a deleted file or folder, you can double-click the Recycle Bin, right-click the file or folder you want to retrieve, and then click Restore. However, after you empty the Recycle Bin, you can no longer recover the files it contained.

REFERENCE

Deleting a File or Folder

- Click the file or folder you want to delete. (If you want to delete more than one file or folder, select them first.)
- Press the Delete key, and then click the Yes button.

or

- Right-click the file or folder you want to delete. (If you want to delete more than one file or folder, select them first.)
- Click Delete on the shortcut menu, and then click the Yes button.

Because you copied the Chianti, Florence, Logo, Market, and Tour Rates files to the subfolders in the Tutorial folder, you can safely delete the original files. As is true for moving, copying, and renaming files and folders, you can delete a file or folder in many ways, including using a shortcut menu or selecting one or more files and then pressing the Delete key.

To delete files in the Tutorial folder:

▶ **1.** Use any technique you've learned to navigate to and display the **Tutorial** folder.

▶ **2.** Click **Chianti**, hold down the **Shift** key, click **Tour Rates**, and then release the **Shift** key. All files in the Tutorial folder are now selected. None of the sub-folders should be selected.

▶ **3.** Right-click the selected files, and then click **Delete** on the shortcut menu. Windows 8 might ask if you're sure you want to permanently delete these files.

▶ **4.** If necessary, click the **Yes** button.

Make sure you have copied the selected files to the Marketing Graphics and Financial folders before completing this step.

So far, you've worked with files in folder windows, but you haven't viewed any file contents. To view a file's contents, you open the file. When you double-click a file in a folder window, Windows 8 starts the associated program and opens the file. You'll have a chance to try these techniques in the next section.

Working with New Files

The most common way to add files to a drive or folder is to create new files when you use a program. For example, you can create a text document in a word-processing program, a drawing in a graphics program, or a movie file in a video-editing program. When you are finished with a file, you must save it if you want to use the file again. To work with the file, you open it in an appropriate program; you can usually tell which programs can open a file by examining the filename extension or file icon.

Before you continue working with Matt's files, you decide to create a task list to summarize your remaining tasks. You'll create the task list file, save it, close it, and then reopen it to add some items to the list.

Creating a File

You create a file by starting a program and then saving the file in a folder on your computer. Some programs create a file when you open the program. When you open WordPad, for example, it starts with a blank page. This represents an empty (and unsaved) file. You type and format the document to create it. When you are finished, you save your work using the Save As dialog box, where you can select a location for the file and enter a filename that identifies the contents. By default, most programs save files in a library such as Documents, Pictures, or Music, which makes it easy to find the files again later.

The task list you want to create is a simple text document, so you can create this file using Notepad, the basic text-editing program that Windows 8 provides.

To create a Notepad file:

▶ **1.** Press the **Windows** key 🪟 to display the Start screen.

▶ **2.** Type **notep** to display the Search menu with "notep" inserted in the Search text box. The search results include the Notepad application.

▶ **3.** Click **Notepad** in the search results. The Notepad program window opens on the desktop. See Figure 2-16.

Figure 2-16 **Creating a file**

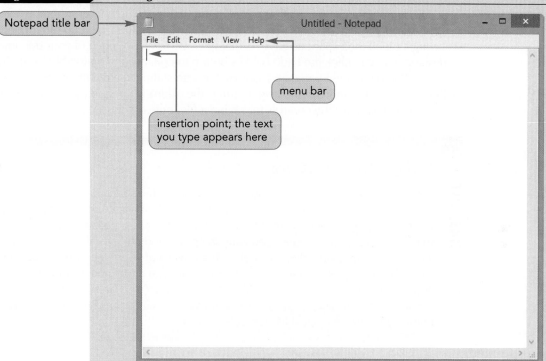

Notepad title bar

Untitled - Notepad

File Edit Format View Help

menu bar

insertion point; the text you type appears here

▶ **4.** Type the following text in the Notepad window, pressing the **Enter** key at the end of each line, including the last line:

To Do for Matt's Files

1. Organize files in a folder window.

2. Customize a folder window.

3. Show and hide filename extensions.

4. Compress and extract files.

The Notepad title bar indicates that the name of this file is "Untitled." To give it a more descriptive name, preserve the contents, and store the file where you can find it later, you must save the file.

Saving a File

TIP

After you create a file, avoid cluttering the desktop by saving the file in a subfolder on your computer, not on the desktop.

As you are creating a file, you should save it frequently so you don't lose your work. When you save a new file, you use the Save As dialog box to specify a filename and a location for the file. When you open a file you've already created, you can use the application's Save command to save the file with the same name and location. If you want to save the file with a different name or in a different location, however, you use the Save As dialog box again to specify the new name or location. You can create a folder for the new file at the same time you save the file.

The Save As dialog box can contain the same navigation tools found in a folder window, such as an Address bar, Search text box, Navigation pane, and right pane displaying folders and files. You might need to click the Browse Folders button to expand the Save As dialog box. (When the dialog box is expanded, this button changes to the Hide Folders button.) Then, you can specify the file location, for example, using the same navigation techniques and tools that are available in all folder windows.

In addition, the Save As dialog box always includes a File name text box where you specify a filename, a Save as type list where you select a file type, and other controls for saving a file. If the expanded Save As dialog box covers too much of your document or desktop, you can click the Hide Folders button to collapse the dialog box so it hides the Navigation pane, right pane, and toolbar. You can still navigate with the Back, Forward, Recent locations, and Up one level buttons; the Address bar; and the Search text box, and you can still use the controls for saving a file, but you conserve screen space.

INSIGHT

Saving Files on SkyDrive

Some Windows 8 applications, such as Microsoft Office, include SkyDrive as a location for saving and opening files. SkyDrive is a Microsoft service that provides up to 7 GB of online storage space for your files by default. Because these files are stored online, they take up no storage space on your computer and are available from any computer with an Internet connection. To protect the privacy of your files, you can designate which SkyDrive users can access them: only you, you and some other users, or anyone. To use SkyDrive, you need a free Microsoft account. (You can sign up for a Microsoft account at https://signup.live.com. If you use Hotmail, Xbox LIVE, or have a Windows Phone, you already have a Microsoft account.)

Now that you've created a task list, you need to save it. A good name for this document is Task List. However, none of the folders you've already created for Matt seems appropriate for this file. It belongs in a separate folder with a name such as Daily Documents. You can create the Daily Documents folder at the same time you save the Task List file.

To save the Notepad file:

1. In the Notepad window, click **File** on the menu bar, and then click **Save As**. The Save As dialog box opens.

2. If the Navigation pane does not appear in the Save As dialog box, click the **Browse Folders** button. The Browse Folders button toggles to become the Hide Folders button, as shown in Figure 2-17.

| Figure 2-17 | Saving a new file |

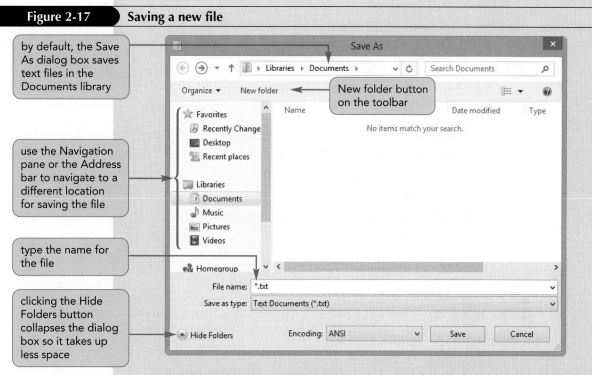

by default, the Save As dialog box saves text files in the Documents library

use the Navigation pane or the Address bar to navigate to a different location for saving the file

type the name for the file

clicking the Hide Folders button collapses the dialog box so it takes up less space

New folder button on the toolbar

By default, Notepad saves files in the Documents library on your hard drive. You want to create a subfolder in the Tutorial folder for this document.

3. In the Save As dialog box, use any technique you've learned to navigate to the **Windows2\Tutorial** folder provided with your Data Files.

4. Click the **New folder** button on the toolbar in the Save As dialog box. A new folder appears in the Tutorial folder, with the *New folder* name highlighted and ready for you to replace.

5. Type **Daily Documents** as the name of the new folder, and then press the **Enter** key.

6. Double-click the **Daily Documents** folder to open it. Now you are ready to specify a filename and save the task list file in the Daily Documents folder.

7. Click the **File name** text box to select the *.txt text, and then type **Task List**. Notepad will automatically provide a .txt extension to this filename, so you don't have to type it.

8. Click the **Save** button. Notepad saves the Task List file in the Daily Documents folder. The new filename now appears in the Notepad title bar.

9. Click the **Close** button ![X] to close Notepad.

Next, you can open the file to add another item to the task list.

Opening a File

If you want to open a file in a running application, you use the Open dialog box, which is a folder window with additional controls for opening a file, similar to the Save As dialog box. You use the application's Open command to access the Open dialog box, which you use to navigate to the file you want, select the file, and then open it. If the application you want to use is not running, you can open a file by double-clicking it

TIP

To open a file using the default program, right-click the file, point to Open with, click Choose default program, click a program, and then click the OK button.

in a folder window. The file usually opens in the application that you used to create or edit it. If it's a text file with a .txt extension, for example, it opens in a text editor, such as Notepad. If it's a text file with a .docx extension, it opens in Microsoft Word.

Not all documents work this way. Double-clicking a digital picture file usually opens a picture viewer app, which displays the picture. To edit the picture, you need to use a graphics editing application. When you need to specify an application to open a file, you can right-click the file, point to Open with on the shortcut menu, and then click the name of the app that you want to use.

To open and edit the Task List file:

1. In the right pane of the Tutorial folder window, double-click the **Daily Documents** folder.

2. Double-click the **Task List** file. Notepad starts and opens the Task List file.

    Trouble? If an application other than Notepad starts, such as WordPad, click the Close button to close the program, right-click the Task List file, point to Open with, and then click Notepad.

3. Press the **Ctrl+End** keys to move the insertion point to the end of the document, press the **Enter** key if necessary to start a new line, and then type **5. Review how to customize the Navigation pane.**

    Because you want to save this file using the same name and location, you can use the Save command on the File menu to save your work this time.

4. Click **File** on the menu bar, and then click **Save**. Notepad saves the Task List file without opening the Save As dialog box because you are using the same name and location as the last time you saved the file.

As long as Notepad is still open, you can create another simple text file that describes the graphics in the Marketing Graphics folder.

To create and save another file:

1. Click **File** on the menu bar, and then click **New** to open a new, blank document.

2. Type the following text in the Notepad window, pressing the **Enter** key at the end of each line:

    Marketing Graphics files:

    Chianti: Photo of the Chianti valley

    Florence: Photo of Florence

    Logo: Copy of the company logo for Web pages and ads

    Market: Photo of an Italian market

3. Click **File** on the menu bar, and then click **Save**. The Save As dialog box opens because this is the first time you are saving the file.

4. Navigate to the **Marketing Graphics** folder in the Tutorial folder.

5. Click in the **File name** text box, and then type **Image Descriptions**.

6. Click the **Save** button. Notepad saves the Image Descriptions file in the Marketing Graphics folder.

> **7.** Click the **Close** button ❌ to close Notepad. (Because Notepad only allows one file to be opened at a time, the program closed the first file for you when you created the new file.)

Now that you've organized Matt's files and then created and saved new folders and files, you're ready to refine the organization of the files.

Refining the Organization of Files   / улучшить

To refine the organization of your files, you can fine-tune the arrangement of your files and folders in a folder window. Changing the order of files in a list can often help you find files and identify those that share common features, such as two versions of the same file. One way to change the view is to sort your files. **Sorting** files and folders means listing them in a particular order, such as alphabetically by name or type, or chronologically by their modification date. You can also **filter** the contents of a folder to display only files and folders with certain characteristics, such as all those you modified yesterday. In short, sorting reorganizes all of the files and folders in a list, while filtering displays only those files and folders that share a characteristic you specify. Both actions change your view of the files and folders, not the items themselves.

Windows 8 provides another way to change the view of your files and folders—grouping. When you group your files by type, for example, Windows separates the files into several groups, such as Microsoft Word documents in one group and photo files (or JPEG files) in another group.

PROSKILLS

Problem Solving: Preventing Lost File Problems

Many computer users, even very experienced ones, fall into the trap of saving or moving a file to a folder and then forgetting where it's stored. You can prevent these types of lost file problems by managing your files systematically. To manage files so you know where to find them later, start by formulating a logical plan for organizing your files. Some people sketch a simple diagram of the file structure to help them visualize where to store files. Next, create the folders you need to store the files, and then move and copy your existing files into those folders. As you create files using programs, save them in an appropriate folder and use folder names and filenames that help you identify their contents. If possible, use a similar organization scheme in all of your folders. For example, if you organized the files for one project into subfolders such as Phase 1, Phase 2, Phase 3, and Follow Up, use the same organization for each project. To make it easier to find files, especially in a long file list, you can sort, filter, and group the files in a way that seems logical to you. Performing these basic management tasks helps you keep track of your files so you can easily find information when you need it.

You want to show Matt how to change the view of his files by sorting, filtering, and grouping so he can choose one view that makes the most sense for him or his current task.

Sorting and Filtering Files

When you are working with a folder window in Details view, you can sort or filter the files using the column headings in the right pane of the window. To sort files by type, for example, click the Type column heading. You can sort files in ascending order

(A to Z, 0 to 9, or earliest to latest date) or descending order (Z to A, 9 to 0, or latest to earliest date). To switch the order, click the column heading again.

Sorting is often an effective way to find a file or folder in a relatively short file list. By default, Windows 8 sorts the contents of a folder in ascending alphabetic order by filename, with any subfolders listed before the files. A file named April Marketing appears at the top of the list, and a file named Winter Expenses appears at the end. You can change the sort criterion to list files according to any other file characteristic.

If you are working with a longer file list, filtering the list might help you find the file you want. To filter the contents of a folder, you click the arrow button to the right of a column heading, and then click one or more file properties such as a specific filename, created or modified date, author, or file type. Windows displays only files and folders with those properties. For example, if you want to list only music files by a particular artist, you can filter by that artist's name.

Details view always includes column headings corresponding to file details. To sort files in other views that do not display column headings, you can right-click a blank area of the folder window, point to Sort by on the shortcut menu, and then click a file detail such as Type. (You cannot filter files in views without column headings.)

TIP

To sort by a file detail that does not appear as a column heading, right-click any column heading and then select a file detail.

To sort and filter the files in the Marketing Graphics folder:

1. Navigate to the **Marketing Graphics** folder in the Tutorial folder.

2. If necessary, click the **View** tab, and then click **Details** in the Layout group to switch to Details view.

3. Click the **Type** column heading to sort the files in ascending order according to file type. A sort arrow ▲ appears at the top of the Type column heading. The sort arrow points up to indicate the column is sorted in ascending order.

   Trouble? If the Type column does not appear in your folder window, right-click any column heading and then click Type. Then complete Step 3.

4. Click the **Type** column heading again to reverse the sort order. The sort arrow now points down, indicating the column is sorted in descending order.

5. Right-click any column heading to display a list of file details. Details with a check mark are displayed in the folder window. If the Date modified column heading does not appear in your folder window, click **Date modified** to display this column. Otherwise, click a blank area of the window. Your folder window should now display only the Name, Date modified, Type, and Size columns.

   Trouble? If your folder window contains columns other than Name, Date modified, Type, and Size, right-click any column heading, and then click the name of the column you want to remove from the folder window. The content of the column is not erased; it is just no longer visible on-screen.

TIP

When you sort files by Date modified with the most recent files on top, you can quickly find the files you created or modified recently.

6. Click the **Date modified** column heading to sort the files in descending chronological order by the date they were modified. See Figure 2-18.

Figure 2-18	Sorting files by date modified

sort arrow points down, indicating the column is sorted in descending order

files are sorted so that the most recently modified files appear first

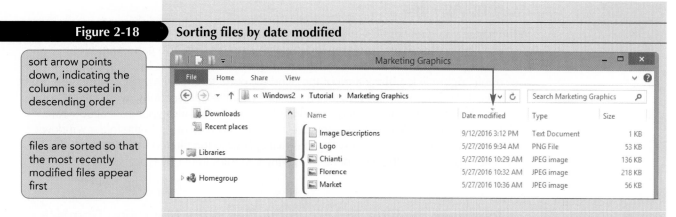

To compare sorting and filtering, you can filter the files by their modified date to display only the files you modified today.

▶ **7.** Point to the **Date modified** column heading, and then click its **arrow** button ▾ to display a list of filtering options.

▶ **8.** Click the **Today** check box to select today's date. The folder window displays only the Image Descriptions file. See Figure 2-19.

Trouble? If you modified the Image Descriptions file on a different date, click that date on the calendar.

Trouble? If you clicked Today rather than the check box, skip Step 9.

Figure 2-19	Filtering to display files modified today

only files modified today appear in the filtered list

menu of filtering options

Today check box

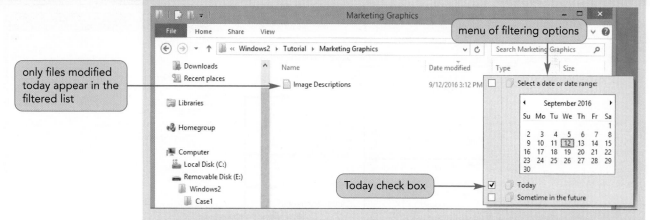

Note that you can filter by two or more properties by selecting the corresponding check boxes.

▶ **9.** Click a blank area of the window to close the list. A check mark appears next to the Date modified column heading to indicate the file list is filtered by a Date modified detail.

Next, you can group the files in the Marketing Graphics folder and compare this view to the views displayed when you sorted and filtered the files.

Grouping Files

To change your view of files and folders, you can group them—a technique that is especially effective when you are working with long file lists. You can group files according to any file detail such as Type or Authors. To group files by author, for example, right-click a blank area of the window, point to Group by, click More, and then click Authors. Windows divides the folder window into sections, with one section listing files you wrote, for example, and another section for files your colleague wrote.

Before grouping files, you must remove any filters you are using in the folder window. If you don't, you'll rearrange only the files that appear in the filtered list. After removing the filter, you'll group the files in the Marketing Graphics folder by type.

To remove the filter and group the files in the Marketing Graphics folder:

1. In the Marketing Graphics folder window, click the **check mark** on the Date modified column heading, and then click the **Today** check box (or the **Select a date or date range** check box if you selected a date on the calendar earlier) to clear the check box. Click a blank area of the folder window. The complete list of Marketing Graphics files appears in the window.

TIP

You can click the triangle next to a group name to show or hide a group of files.

2. Click the **View** tab on the ribbon, click the **Group by** button ▢ in the Current view group, and then click **Type**. Windows arranges all the files in the Marketing Graphics folder into three groups, one for each file type. See Figure 2-20.

| Figure 2-20 | Grouping files |

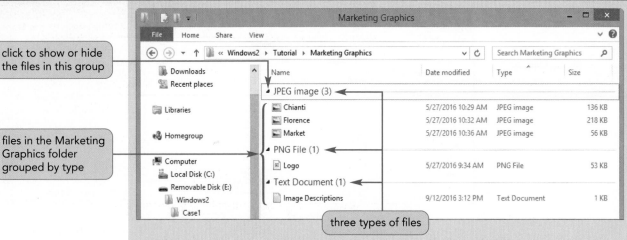

click to show or hide the files in this group

files in the Marketing Graphics folder grouped by type

three types of files

3. Click the **View** tab, click the **Group by** button ▢ in the Current view group, and then click **(None)** to ungroup the files.

4. If necessary, click the **Type** column heading to sort the files in ascending order again by type.

Now that Matt knows how to sort, filter, and group files in a folder window, he mentions that he might want to hide or show elements of the folder window itself, such as the Navigation pane. You'll show him how to customize the folder window elements next.

настройка

Customizing a Folder Window

As you learned earlier, you can change how you view your files and folders in a folder window, such as changing from large icons to a detailed list. You can make other changes to the layout of your folder windows. For example, you can hide the Navigation pane to devote more space to file lists. The View tab includes options you can use to fine-tune the layout of a folder window. You have already used some options in the Current view and Layout groups. Figure 2-21 summarizes all the options on the View tab.

Figure 2-21	View tab options

Group	Option	Description
Panes	Navigation pane	Show or hide the Navigation pane in this window only, and specify whether to expand the Navigation pane to the open folder, show all folders, or show favorites.
	Preview pane	Show or hide the Preview pane. When you select this option, you can preview the contents of a file without having to open a program.
	Details pane	Show or hide the Details pane. When you select this option, you display the most common properties associated with a selected file, such as the author of the file or its type.
Layout	View options	Select one of eight views for displaying the contents of the current folder: Extra large icons, Large icons, Medium icons, Small icons, List, Details, Tiles, Content.
Current View	Sort by	Select a file property to use for sorting, select ascending or descending sort order, and choose one or more columns to display in the current folder window.
	Group by	Group files by a file detail displayed in the current folder window.
	Add columns	Select a file detail to display as a column in the current folder window or choose a file detail not included in the list.
	Size all columns to fit	Change the width of all columns to fit the contents.
Show/Hide	Item check boxes	Show or hide check boxes next to files and folders; use the check boxes to select items.
	File name extensions	Show or hide the extensions for all files in the current folder window.
	Hidden items	Show or hide the files and folders marked as hidden.
	Hide selected items	Hide the selected files or folders.
	Options	Use the Folder Options dialog box to change settings for opening items, file and folder views, and searching.

© 2014 Cengage Learning

You'll show Matt how to change the layout of a folder window, and then how to customize the appearance of the folder contents. Finally, you'll demonstrate how to add items to the Navigation pane to suit the way he works.

приспособить
в соответ-ии

Changing the Layout of a Folder Window

You can change the layout of a folder window by showing or hiding the Navigation pane and either the Preview pane or the Details pane. The Preview pane appears on the right side of a folder window and displays the contents of a picture file and some other types of files. The Details pane also appears on the right and provides information about a selected file, such as the author and file type. Only one of these panes can be open in a folder window. Neither pane appears by default. Figure 2-22 shows a folder window with the Navigation and Preview panes open.

Figure 2-22   **Folder window displaying the Navigation and Preview panes**

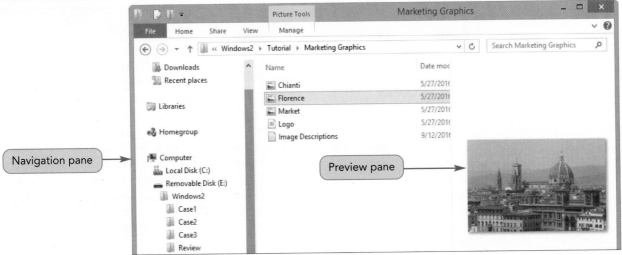

Photo courtesy of Lisa Ruffolo

Matt wants to see if he likes having the Details pane in the folder window, so he asks you to display that pane. He is also curious about the Preview pane, so you'll open that for him first. The Marketing Graphics folder window should currently be open in Details view, with files sorted according to type.

To change the layout of a folder window:

1. Click the **Chianti** file to select it, click the **View** tab on the ribbon, and then click the **Preview pane** button in the Panes group to display the Preview pane.

2. Click the **View** tab, and then click the **Details pane** button in the Panes group to close the Preview pane and display the Details pane. See Figure 2-23. Your file details might vary.

| Figure 2-23 | Folder window displaying the Navigation and Details panes |

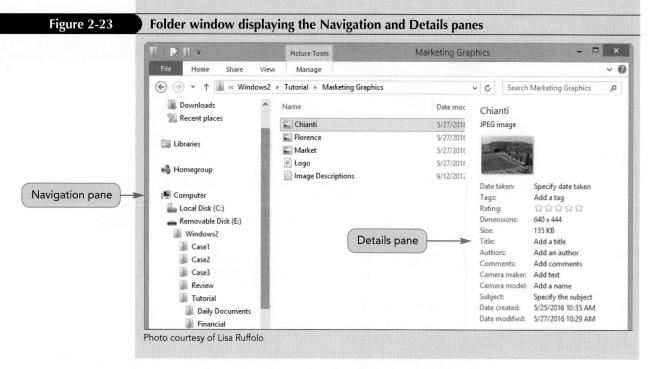

Photo courtesy of Lisa Ruffolo

You can also use options in the Show/hide group on the View tab to customize the file list.

Customizing the File List

Although Windows 8 refers to a filename extension to identify a file's type, filename extensions are not displayed by default in a folder window. Windows hides the extensions to make filenames easier to read, especially for long filenames. If you prefer to display filename extensions, you can show them in all the folder windows (as you do in the following steps).

Another type of file not displayed by default in a folder window is a **hidden file**. Windows hides many types of files, including temporary files it creates before you save a document. It hides these files so that you do not become confused by temporary filenames, which are similar to the names of the files you store on your computer. By default, Windows 8 also hides system files, which are files the operating system needs to work properly. You should keep these files hidden unless a reliable expert, such as a technical support professional, instructs you to display them. Keep in mind that hidden files still take up space on your disk.

You use the options in the Show/hide group on the View tab to show and hide filename extensions in all windows. To show and hide hidden files, you use the Folder Options dialog box.

To show filename extensions:

1. Click the **Expand the Ribbon** button 🔽 to expand the ribbon.

2. On the View tab, click the **File name extensions** check box in the Show/hide group to insert a check mark so filename extensions appear in all windows. See Figure 2-24.

| Figure 2-24 | Folder window showing filename extensions |

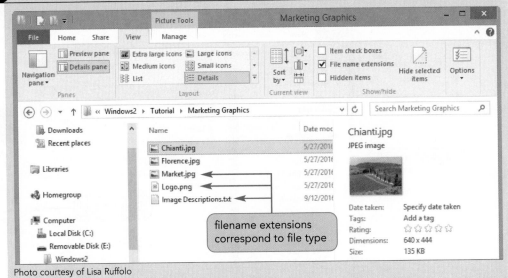

Photo courtesy of Lisa Ruffolo

▶ **3.** Click the **Options** button to open the Folder Options dialog box.

▶ **4.** Click the **View** tab in the Folder Options dialog box. See Figure 2-25. The settings selected on the View tab of your Folder Options dialog box might differ.

| Figure 2-25 | Folder Options dialog box |

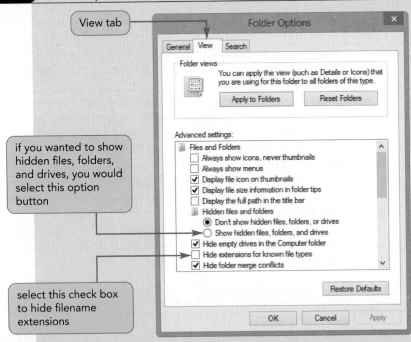

▶ **5.** Click the **Hide extensions for known file types** check box to insert a check mark, and then click the **OK** button to hide the filename extensions again.

Trouble? If the Hide extensions for known file types check box already contains a check mark, just close the dialog box.

Next, you can customize the Navigation pane by changing its appearance and adding a folder to the Favorites list.

настроить
Customizing the Navigation Pane

You can customize the Navigation pane by adding, renaming, and removing items in the Favorites list. For example, if you use the Navigation pane to open a particular folder, you can drag that folder to the Favorites list to make it one of your favorite locations.

To customize your Navigation pane, first, you'll add the Daily Documents folder as a link in the Favorites list so you can access the folder quickly. Then, you'll rename this link to distinguish it from the Documents library, which is also listed in the Navigation pane. When you rename an item in the Favorites list, you rename the link only—not the actual file or folder. Later, when you restore the settings on your computer, you'll delete this link.

To customize the Navigation pane:

1. Use any navigation method you've learned to display the folders in the Tutorial folder. Scroll to the top of the Navigation pane, if necessary.

2. Drag the **Daily Documents** folder from the Tutorial folder to the end of the Favorites list in the Navigation pane. When the Create link in Favorites ScreenTip appears, release the mouse button to insert a new link named Daily Documents in the Favorites list. See Figure 2-26.

Figure 2-26 **Daily Documents folder as a link in the Favorites list**

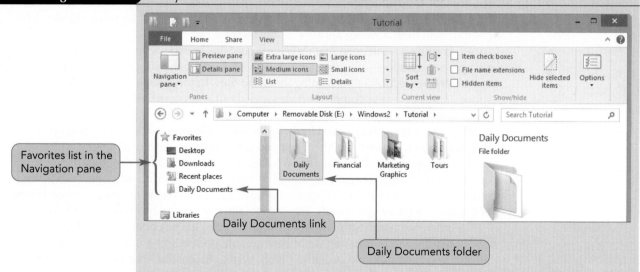

Favorites list in the Navigation pane

Daily Documents link

Daily Documents folder

---

3. Right-click the **Daily Documents** link in the Favorites list, and then click **Rename** on the shortcut menu. The current name is selected.

4. Type **Daily Projects** as the new name of this link, and then press the **Enter** key. The link is renamed, but the Daily Documents folder in the Tutorial folder still has its original name. See Figure 2-27.

Figure 2-27 **Daily Documents link renamed as Daily Projects**

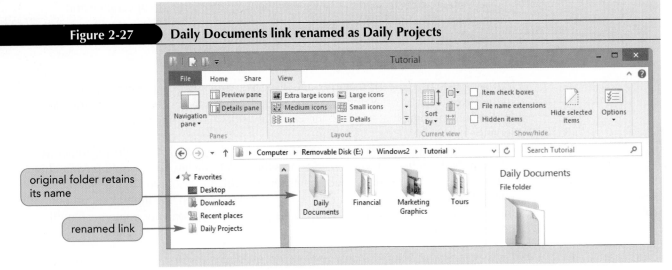

Now that you've refined your file organization and customized the folder window, you are ready to show Matt two final tasks—compressing and extracting files.

Working with Compressed Files

If you transfer files from one location to another, such as from your hard disk to a removable disk or vice versa, or from one computer to another via email, you can store the files in a compressed (zipped) folder so that they take up less disk space. You can then transfer the files more quickly. If you or your email contacts can send and receive files only up to a certain size, compressing large files might make them small enough to send and receive. When you create a compressed folder using Windows 8's compression tool, a zipper appears on the folder icon.

You compress a folder so that the files it contains use less space on the disk. Compare two folders—a folder named Photos that contains about 8.6 MB of files, and a compressed folder containing the same files, but requiring only 6.5 MB of disk space. In this case, the compressed files use about 25 percent less disk space than the uncompressed files.

You can create a compressed folder using the Zip button in the Send group on the Share tab of a folder window. Then you can compress additional files or folders by dragging them into the compressed folder. You can open a file directly from a compressed folder, although you cannot modify the file. To edit and save a compressed file, you must extract it first. When you **extract** a file, you create an uncompressed copy of the file in a folder you specify. The original file remains in the compressed folder.

If a different compression program, such as WinZip, has been installed on your computer, the Zip button might not be available on the Share tab. In this case, refer to your compression program's Help system for instructions on working with compressed files.

Matt suggests that you compress the files and folders in the Tutorial folder so that you can more quickly transfer them to another location.

TIP

Another way to compress files is to select the files, right-click the selection, point to Send to on the shortcut menu, and then click Compressed (zipped) folder.

To compress the folders and files in the Tutorial folder:

 1. Select all the folders in the Tutorial folder, click the **Share** tab on the ribbon, and then click the **Zip** button in the Send group. After a few moments, a new compressed folder with a zipper icon appears in the Tutorial window with the filename selected.

Trouble? If the Zip button is not available on the Share tab, this means that a different compression program is probably installed on your computer. Read but do not perform the remaining steps.

2. Type **Savvy Traveler** and then press the **Enter** key to rename the compressed folder. See Figure 2-28.

Figure 2-28	Creating a compressed folder

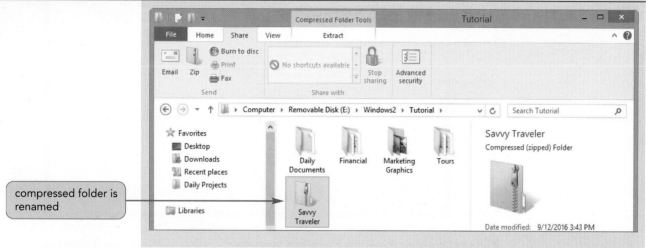

compressed folder is renamed

You open a compressed folder by double-clicking it. You can then move and copy files and folders from the opened compressed folder to other locations, although you cannot rename the files. More often, you extract all of the files in the compressed folder. Windows 8 then uncompresses and copies them to a location that you specify, preserving the files in their original folders as appropriate.

Understanding Compressed File Types

INSIGHT

Some types of files, such as JPEG picture files (those with a .jpg or .jpeg filename extension), are already highly compressed. If you compress JPEG pictures into a folder, the total size of the compressed folder is about the same as the collection of uncompressed pictures. However, if you are transferring the files from one computer to another, such as by email, it's still a good idea to store the compressed files in a zipped folder to keep them together.

To extract the compressed files:

1. Click the **Compressed Folder Tools Extract** tab on the ribbon, and then click the **Extract all** button. The Extract Compressed (Zipped) Folders Wizard starts and opens the Select a Destination and Extract Files dialog box.

2. Press the **End** key to deselect the path in the text box and move the insertion point to the end of the path, press the **Backspace** key as many times as necessary to delete the Savvy Traveler text, and then type **Backups**. The final three parts of the path in the text box should be \Windows2\Tutorial\ Backups. See Figure 2-29.

Figure 2-29　Extracting files from a compressed folder

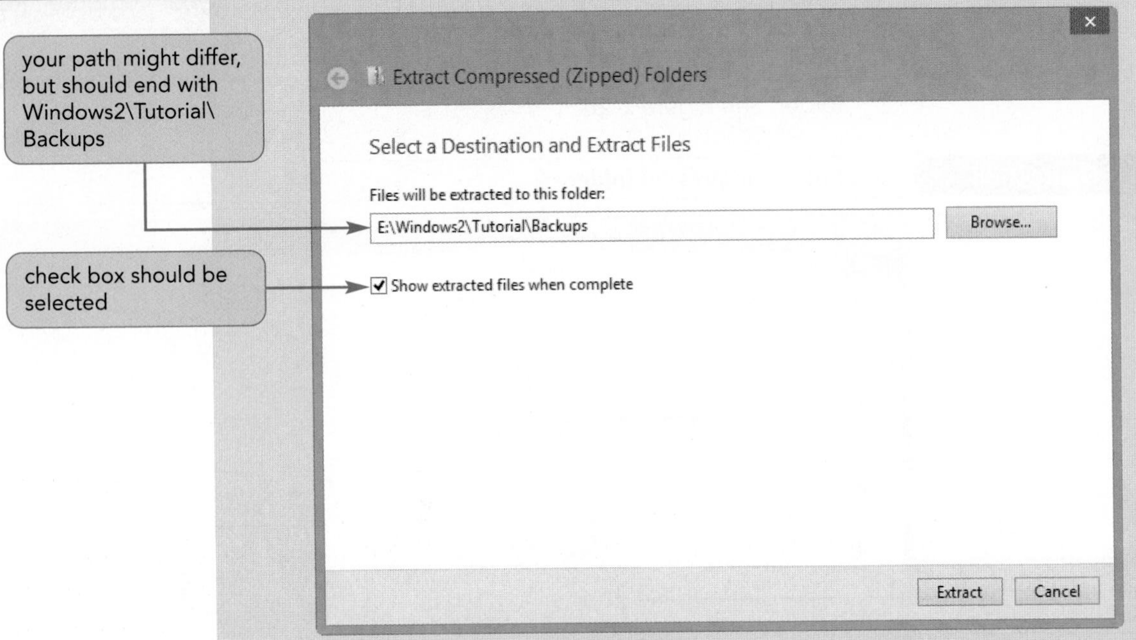

your path might differ, but should end with Windows2\Tutorial\Backups

check box should be selected

3. Make sure the Show extracted files when complete check box is checked, and then click the **Extract** button. Windows extracts the files and then opens the Backups folder, showing the Daily Documents, Financial, Marketing Graphics, and Tours folders.

4. Open each folder to make sure it contains the files you worked with in this tutorial.

5. Close the Backups folder window, and then click a blank area of the Tutorial folder window.

In this session, you renamed and deleted files according to your organization plan, and then created a file, saved it in a new folder, and opened and edited the file. Then you refined the organization of the files and folders, customized a folder window, and worked with compressed files. Before you end your Windows 8 session, you should restore your computer to its original settings.

Restoring Your Settings

If you are working in a computer lab or on a computer other than your own, complete the steps in this section to restore the original settings on the computer.

To restore your settings:

1. In the Tutorial folder window, click the **View** tab, and then click the **Details pane** button in the Panes group to hide the Details pane in the folder window.

2. Click the **Minimize the Ribbon** button to show only tab names on the ribbon.

3. Right-click the **Daily Projects** link in the Favorites list in the Navigation pane, and then click **Remove**.

4. Close all open windows.

REVIEW

Session 2.2 Quick Check

1. A filename _extension_ identifies the file's type and indicates the program that created the file.

2. When you delete a file from a hard disk, Windows removes the file from the folder but stores the file contents in the _Recycle bin_.

3. Explain one way to create a file.

4. Explain the difference between sorting and filtering files. _78 - 77_

5. If you _group_ files by author, Windows divides the folder window into sections, with each section listing files written by a different author.

6. To display the contents of pictures and some other types of files, you can customize folder windows to display the _Preview_ or the Details pane.

7. When you _extract_ a file, you create an uncompressed copy of the file in a folder you specify.

8. Describe how to create a compressed folder.

Review Assignments

Data Files needed for the Review Assignments: Banner.png, Colosseum.jpg, Lectures.xlsx, Rome.jpg, Schedule.rtf, Tours.rtf

Matt has saved a few files from his old computer to a removable disk. He gives you these files in a single, unorganized folder, and asks you to organize them logically into subfolders. Before you do, devise a plan for managing the files, and then create the subfolders you need. Next, rename, copy, move, and delete files, and perform other management tasks to make it easy for Matt to work with these files and folders. Complete the following steps:

1. Use a folder window to navigate to and open the Windows2\Review folder provided with your Data Files. Examine the six files in this folder and consider the best way to organize the files.
2. In the Review folder, create three folders: **Business**, **Destinations**, and **Supplements**.
3. To organize the files into the correct folders:
   - Move the Banner and Schedule files from the Review folder to the Business folder.
   - Move the Colosseum, Rome, and Tours files to the Destinations folder.
   - Move the Lectures file to the Supplements folder.
4. Copy the Tours file in the Destinations folder to the Business folder.
5. Rename the Schedule file in the Business folder as **2016 Schedule**. Rename the Lectures file in the Supplements folder as **On-site Lectures**.
6. Return to the Review folder and use the Search text box to find a file whose filename begins with the text *ban*. Rename this file **Company Banner**.
7. Create a Notepad file that includes the following text:
   Traveler's Tips
   Make sure your passport is up to date.
   Store photocopies of important documents.
   Arrange all forms of transportation.
8. Save the Notepad file as **Tips** in the Supplements folder. Close the Notepad window.
9. Navigate to the Supplements folder, open the Tips file, and then add the following tip to the end of the document: **Prepare electronic tools for the trip.**
10. Save the Tips file with the same name and in the same location. Open a new document in Notepad, and then type the following text:
    Eating in Rome
    Avoid main tourist area restaurants.
    Pick up sandwiches and pizza by the slice.
11. Save the file as **Eating in Rome** in the Destinations folder. Close Notepad.
12. Navigate to the Destinations folder and then perform the following tasks:
    - Sort the files by Date modified. How many files appear in the folder window?
    - Filter the files by today's date (or the date you created the two text files). How many files appear in the folder window?
13. Remove the filter, and then group the files by type. How many types are displayed? How many files are displayed of each type?
14. Navigate to the Supplements folder, and then display filename extensions in the folder window. Group the files by size.
15. Change the layout of the folder window by displaying the Details pane, and then change the grouping to (None).
16. In the Review folder, add the Business folder to the Favorites list in the Navigation pane. Rename the link **Savvy Traveler**.

17. Click the Savvy Traveler link, click the Company Banner.png file, and then press the Print Screen key to capture an image of the folder window. (*Hint*: Depending on the type of computer you are using, the Print Screen key might be labeled differently, for example, PrtScn.) Start Paint, and then press the Ctrl+V keys to paste this image in a file. Save this file as **Review** in the Windows2\Review folder provided with your Data Files. Close Paint.

18. Restore your computer's settings by hiding the Details pane, hiding filename extensions in the folder window, and removing the Savvy Traveler link from the Favorites list in the Navigation pane.

19. Create a compressed (zipped) folder in the Review folder named **Rome** that contains all the files and folders in the Review folder.

20. Extract the contents of the Rome compressed folder to a new folder named **Rome Backups** in the Review folder. (*Hint*: The file path will end with *Windows2\Review\Rome Backups*.)

21. Close all open windows.

22. Submit the results of the preceding steps to your instructor, either in printed or electronic form, as requested.

Case Problem 1

APPLY

See the Starting Data Files section at the beginning of this tutorial for the list of Data Files needed for this Case Problem.

Bay Shore Arts Center   Casey Sullivan started the Bay Shore Arts Center in Monterey, California, to provide workshops and courses on art and photography. Attracting students from the San Francisco and San José areas, Casey's business has grown and she now holds classes five days a week. She recently started a course on fine art landscape photography, which has quickly become her most popular offering. Knowing you are multitalented, Casey hired you to help her design new classes and manage other parts of her growing business, including maintaining electronic business files and communications. Your first task is to organize the files on her new Windows 8 computer. Complete the following steps:

1. In the Windows2\Case1 folder provided with your Data Files, create three folders: **Classes**, **Landscapes**, and **Management**.

2. Move the Fall Classes, Spring Classes, Summer Classes, and Winter Classes files from the Case1 folder to the Classes folder.

3. Rename the four files in the Classes folder by deleting the word *Classes* from each name.

4. Move the four JPEG files from the Case1 folder to the Landscapes folder.

5. Copy the remaining two files to the Management folder. Also, copy the Workshops file to the Classes folder.

6. Delete the Instructors and Workshops files from the Case1 folder.

7. Open the Recycle Bin folder by double-clicking the Recycle Bin icon on the desktop, and then display the window in Details view. Sort the contents of the Recycle Bin by filename in descending order.

8. Filter the files by their deletion date to display only the files you deleted today. (*Hint*: If you deleted files from the Case1 folder on a different date, click that date on the calendar.) Do the Instructors and Workshops files appear in the Recycle Bin folder? Explain why or why not. Remove the filter, and then close the Recycle Bin window.

9. Make a copy of the Landscapes folder in the Case1 folder. The name of the duplicate folder appears as Landscapes—Copy. Rename the Landscapes—Copy folder as **California Photos**.

10. Search for the Workshops file and then copy it to the California Photos folder. Rename this file **California Workshops**.

11. Compress the graphics files in the California Photos folder in a new compressed folder named **Photos**, and then move the zipped Photos folder to the Case1 folder.

12. Close all open windows.

13. Submit the results of the preceding steps to your instructor, either in printed or electronic form, as requested.

CHALLENGE

Case Problem 2

See the Starting Data Files section at the beginning of this tutorial for the list of Data Files needed for this Case Problem.

Charlotte Area Business Incubator   Antoine Jackson is the director of the Charlotte Area Business Incubator, a service run by the University of North Carolina in Charlotte to consult with new and struggling small businesses. You work as an intern at the business incubator and spend part of your time organizing client files. Antoine recently upgraded to Windows 8 and asks you to examine the folder structure and file system on his computer, and then begin organizing the files logically. Complete the following steps:

⊕ **Explore** 1. Open a folder window, click the Desktop icon in the Navigation pane, and then open and identify each folder that appears in the Desktop folder window.

2. Examine the files in the Windows2\Case2 folder provided with your Data Files. Display the Details pane in the folder window and then select each file to display its details. Based on the file-names and the descriptions displayed in the Details pane, create an organization plan for the files.

3. In the Windows2\Case2 folder, create the folders you need according to your plan.

4. Move the files from the Case2 folder to the subfolders you created. When you finish, the Case2 folder should contain at least two subfolders.

5. Rename the spreadsheet files in each subfolder as follows. (*Hint*: If Microsoft Excel is not installed on your computer, Windows displays the .xlsx filename extension as you rename the files.)

   - Budget01: **Web Site**
   - Budget02: **Marketing**
   - Budget03: **Event**
   - Report01: **Travel Expenses**
   - Report02: **Project**
   - Report03: **Balance Sheet**

6. Search for a file in the Case2 folder that contains *budget* in its filename.

7. Open the text document you found, and then add the following tip at the end of the file: **Revise the budget as the business changes throughout the year**. Save and close the file.

8. Open the folder window for one of the subfolders you created. Expand the ribbon in the folder window.

9. Change the view of the folder window to Content. Press the Print Screen key to capture an image of the folder window. (*Hint*: Depending on the type of computer you are using, the Print Screen key might be labeled differently, for example, PrtScn.) Start Paint, and then press the Ctrl+V keys to paste this image in a file. Save the image as **Content View** in the Windows2\Case2 folder provided with your Data Files. Close Paint.

⊕ **Explore** 10. In one of the Case2 subfolders, compress all Excel workbooks (that is, all XLSX files) in a new compressed folder named **Workbooks** in the Case2 folder. (*Hint*: After you create the compressed folder in a Case2 subfolder, move it to the Case2 folder.)

11. Restore your computer by hiding the Details pane and minimizing the ribbon in the folder window.

12. Close all open windows.

13. Submit the results of the preceding steps to your instructor, either in printed or electronic form, as requested.

Case Problem 3

Data Files needed for this Case Problem: Customer Satisfaction.pdf, Customer Service.pptx, Customers.accdb, Guidelines.docx, New Employees.pptx

Upcycle Products   Wally Ping founded Upcycle Products to convert discarded products such as plastic containers and cardboard packaging into useful materials and consumer products. The company's most successful products include tote bags made from discarded soda bottles. Wally recently installed Windows 8 on the company's computers, and now finds that he cannot open some files with any installed program. You offer to help him identify the file types and organize the files. Complete the following:

1. Examine the files in the Windows2\Case3 folder provided with your Data Files. In the Case3 folder, create the subfolders you need to organize the files.

2. Use the View tab on the ribbon to display the filename extensions for all of these files. List the filename extensions not already discussed in this tutorial.

⊕ **Explore**   3. Use your favorite search engine to find information about each file type you listed in Step 2. For example, search for PDF files to learn what type of program can open files with a .pdf extension.

4. Move the files from the Case3 folder to the subfolders you created.

5. Open the Guidelines file in WordPad, read the contents, and then close WordPad. Based on the contents of the Guidelines file, move it to a different folder, if necessary.

⊕ **Explore**   6. Open the Guidelines file in its new location. Type your name at the beginning of the file, and then use the Save As dialog box to save the file as a different type, such as .rtf or .txt, but using the same location. (*Hint*: Click the Save as type arrow and then click a file type.) Close the application.

7. Double-click any other file in a Case3 subfolder and describe what happens.

⊕ **Explore**   8. If an application did not start when you double-clicked the file in Step 8, right-click the file, and then click Open with. If you are connected to the Internet, look for an app in the Windows Store that might open this file. Go to the Windows Store and scroll through apps, looking for one that might open the file. Return to the desktop. Describe what you found.

9. Close all open windows.

10. Submit the results of the preceding steps to your instructor, either in printed or electronic form, as requested.

TROUBLESHOOT

Case Problem 4

There are no Data Files needed for this Case Problem.

Fort Worth Professional Employment   Doris Salazar owns Fort Worth Professional Employment, an employment agency in Fort Worth, Texas. The company works with employers and potential employees to fill positions and develop careers. Doris and her staff use Windows 8 laptop and tablet computers when they meet with employers and employees to record the details of positions and qualifications. You are working as a part-time trainer to teach the staff about using their computers efficiently. One common problem is losing files they have saved in a library subfolder. Doris asks you to prepare a lesson on troubleshooting this problem so the staff can avoid losing files in Windows 8. Complete the following:

⚙ **Troubleshoot** 1. Windows 8 provides a new feature called File History, which will be very helpful to the company employees. Use Windows Help and Support to find information on File History. What is the purpose of this feature?

⚙ **Troubleshoot** 2. Use Windows Help and Support to learn how to turn on File History. Explain how to do so.

⚙ **Troubleshoot** 3. Use Windows Help and Support to find topics about restoring (or recovering) files. Which Windows 8 tools let you restore (or recover) files?

⚙ **Troubleshoot** 4. Use Windows Help and Support to learn how to change File History settings. Explain the steps.

5. Submit the results of the preceding steps to your instructor, either in printed or electronic form, as requested.

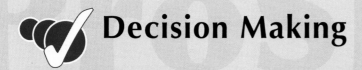 **Decision Making**

Choosing the Most Efficient Organization for Your Computer Files

Decision making is choosing the best alternative from many possible alternatives. The alternative you select is your decision. When making a decision, you typically complete the following steps:

1. Gather information
2. Make predictions
3. Select the best alternative
4. Prepare an action plan
5. Perform tasks and monitor results
6. Verify the accuracy of the decision

If you are involved in making a complex decision that affects many people, you perform all six steps in the process. If you are making a simpler decision that does not affect many people, such as how to organize your computer files, you can condense the steps or perform only those that relate to your decision.

Gather Information and Select the Best Alternative

Start by gathering information to identify your alternatives. For example, when organizing your files, you could store most of your work on your computer hard disk or on removable media, such as a USB drive or an external hard drive. Ask questions that quantify information, or use numbers to compare the alternatives. For example, how much space do you need for your files? How often do you work with your files?

Also, ask questions that compare the qualities of the alternatives. For example, is one alternative easier to perform or maintain than another? Does each alternative make sense for the long term?

After testing each alternative by asking both types of questions, one alternative should emerge as the best choice for you. If one option does not seem like the best alternative, continue comparing alternatives by listing the pros and cons of each.

Prepare an Action Plan

After you make a decision, prepare an action plan by identifying the steps you need to perform to put the decision into practice. One way to do this is to work backward from your final goal. If you are determining how best to manage your computer files, your final goal might be a set of folders and files organized so that you can find any file quickly. Start by listing the tasks you need to perform to meet your goal. Be as specific as possible to avoid confusion later. For example, instead of listing "Create folders" as a task, identify each folder and subfolder by name and indicate which files or types of files each should contain.

Next, estimate how long each task will take, and assign the task to someone. For simple decisions, you assign most tasks to yourself. If you need to use outside resources, include those in the action plan. For example, if you decide to store your files on USB drives, include a step to purchase the drives you need. If someone else needs to approve your plan or any of its tasks, be sure to include that step in the action plan.

If appropriate, the action plan can also track your budget. For example, you could track expenses for a new hard disk or backup media.

Complete the Tasks and Monitor the Results

After you prepare an action plan and receive any necessary approvals, perform the tasks outlined in the plan. For example, create or rename the folders you identified in your action plan, and then move existing files into each folder. As you perform each step, mark its status as complete or pending, for example.

When you complete all the tasks in the action plan, monitor the results. For example, after reorganizing your files, did you meet your goal of being able to quickly find any file when you needed it? If so, continue to follow your plan as you add files and folders to your computer. If not, return to your plan and determine where you could improve it.

PROSKILLS

Organize Your Files

Even if you are familiar with some features of Windows 8 or regularly use your computer for certain tasks, such as accessing Web sites or exchanging email, take time to explore the basics of Windows 8 on your computer. Decide how you want to organize the files and folders you use for course work or for job-related projects on your own computer. Be sure to follow the guidelines you learned for developing an organization strategy, creating folders, naming files, and moving, copying, deleting, and compressing files. As you begin to work through this ProSkills exercise, you will record settings on your computer. To do so, you can capture and save images of the desktop and windows you open by pressing the Print Screen key to capture an image of the screen, and then saving the image in a WordPad or Paint file. You can print these images to use as references if you experience problems with your computer later or want to restore these settings. Complete the following tasks:

1. Start Windows 8 and sign in, if necessary.

2. To solve system problems that might appear later, capture an image or two of the Start screen. (*Hint*: Zoom in on the Start screen so most, if not all, tiles appear on one screen). Start WordPad or Paint, and copy the images into a file and save it in the My Pictures folder, so you can refer to it later. Then, capture and save images of the your current desktop and the File Explorer window with the Favorites, Libraries, and Computer expanded.

3. Use a program, such as WordPad or Notepad, to create a plan for organizing your files. List the types of files you work with on a regular basis, and then determine whether you want to store them on your hard disk or on removable media. Describe the folders and subfolders you will use to manage these files. (*Hint*: Remember where you save the file.)

4. In File Explorer, create one of your main folders and then create its subfolders. Locate the file you created and move it to one of the new folders. Navigate to that folder and then use the Address bar to display the contents of this folder. Capture and save an image of this window.

5. Change the view of a folder window using two different view options. Capture and save images of the folder window in each view.

6. Start a Windows 8 app, and then capture and save an image of the app. Start a second Windows 8 app, and then display the Switch List on the desktop. Capture and save the image of the screen with the Windows 8 apps running.

7. Use Windows Help and Support to find information about a feature or technique covered in this tutorial. Choose a topic that you want to know more about. Capture and save an image of the Windows Help and Support window displaying information about this topic.

8. Use a folder window to navigate to your files. Note which tools you prefer to use for navigating your computer.

9. Create any additional folders and subfolders you want to use for your files.

10. Move and copy files to the appropriate folders according to your plan, and rename and delete files as necessary.

11. Create a backup copy of your work files by creating a compressed file and then copying the compressed file to a removable medium, such as a USB flash drive.

12. Submit your finished plan to your instructor, either in printed or electronic form, as requested.

OBJECTIVES

Session 3.1
- Personalize the Start screen
- Pin apps to the Start screen
- Create shortcuts on the Start screen
- Customize Start screen tiles
- Change the appearance of the Start screen

Session 3.2
- Personalize the desktop
- Create shortcuts on the desktop
- Customize the desktop using the Control Panel
- Change display settings
- Modify the taskbar

Personalizing Your Windows Environment

Changing Desktop Settings

Case | *Preserve Africa*

Preserve Africa is a charitable organization in Washington, DC, that raises funds for wildlife preserves in African countries. Jodi Berman started the organization with Amanda Jameson about two years ago. Amanda now travels throughout the United States and Africa to meet with donors and representatives of wildlife preserves, and Jodi runs the operations in Washington, DC.

You have been working as the office manager for Preserve Africa for a few months, providing general assistance to Jodi, Amanda, and the staff. Jodi recently upgraded the office computers to Windows 8, and now she asks you to customize the organization's computers so that everyone can access frequently used applications, important files, and computer resources. She also wants the desktop to reflect the image of Preserve Africa. You will start by personalizing Jodi's computer so she can approve the changes. Later, she will apply the changes to the other office computers.

WINDOWS

STARTING DATA FILES

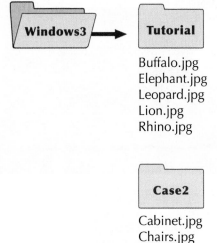

Windows3 → **Tutorial**
Buffalo.jpg
Elephant.jpg
Leopard.jpg
Lion.jpg
Rhino.jpg

Review
Giraffe.jpg
Gorilla.jpg
Impala.jpg
Lemur.jpg
Zebra.jpg

Case1
America.jpg
France.jpg
Puerto Rico.jpg
Sea Cliff.jpg
Tokyo.jpg

Case2
Cabinet.jpg
Chairs.jpg
Chest.jpg
Drawer.jpg
Table.jpg

Case3
Aqua Green.jpg
Checkers.jpg
Festival.jpg
Lime Green.jpg
Red Stripe.jpg

Case4
(none)

Session 3.1 Visual Overview:

Change the appearance of the Start screen by changing the background design and selecting a different **color scheme**, a set of colors including a background color and coordinated accent color.

Many tiles have a live tile feature that you can turn on and off.

A pinned item remains on the Start screen until you unpin it.

Use the Larger button on the Apps bar to make the selected tile larger; you can also make large tiles smaller.

Use the Turn live tile on button on the Apps bar to make the selected tile a live tile.

Photo courtesy of Oliver Wright

Personalized Start Screen

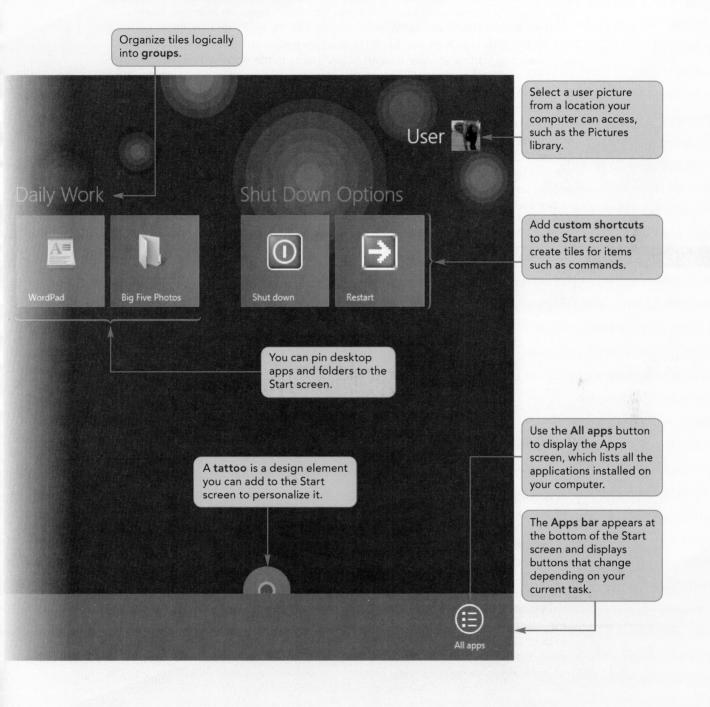

Organize tiles logically into **groups**.

Select a user picture from a location your computer can access, such as the Pictures library.

Daily Work

Shut Down Options

User

WordPad   Big Five Photos   Shut down   Restart

Add **custom shortcuts** to the Start screen to create tiles for items such as commands.

You can pin desktop apps and folders to the Start screen.

A **tattoo** is a design element you can add to the Start screen to personalize it.

Use the **All apps** button to display the Apps screen, which lists all the applications installed on your computer.

The **Apps bar** appears at the bottom of the Start screen and displays buttons that change depending on your current task.

All apps

Personalizing the Start Screen

As you know, after you start Windows 8 and sign in, the Start screen appears, displaying tiles for the apps installed on your computer. When you first install Windows 8, the Start screen displays a collection of standard apps, including Calendar, Mail, Photos, and Weather. Because the Start screen is the gateway to your computer, it should display the apps you use most often, organized in a way that makes sense for how you work.

To personalize the Start screen, you can add tiles for apps you use often and remove tiles for the apps you don't use. Each tile is a **shortcut**, a quick way to perform an action such as starting an app. Instead of navigating to the Apps screen, which lists all of the apps and system tools on your computer, and then clicking an app, you can click a tile on the Start screen to start an app. Besides shortcuts for apps, you can add shortcuts for folders such as the My Documents folder and commands such as the Shut down command. When you add a shortcut to the Start screen, you are adding, or **pinning**, a tile to the Start screen. You can arrange the tiles on the Start screen into groups. For example, you might want to keep folders in one group, entertainment apps such as Music and Games in another group, and apps for keeping in touch with people, such as Mail, Messaging, and People, in a different group.

You can also change the appearance of the Start screen to make it more appealing and useful to you. Figure 3-1 summarizes the Start screen features you can personalize.

Figure 3-1	Customizable Start screen features

Feature	Description
Background	Change the color and design of the Start screen background.
Tile	Add tiles for apps (including desktop programs), folders, and commands, and then arrange them into groups. You can also remove tiles you don't use, change the size of a tile, and turn the live tile feature on or off.
User picture	Change the picture displayed next to your user name.

© 2014 Cengage Learning

PROSKILLS

Problem Solving: Adding Apps to Work Productively

In addition to the default apps that come with Windows 8, you can purchase and install apps using the Windows Store, a Microsoft Web site accessible from the Start screen. The Windows Store provides apps created by Microsoft and other developers. It organizes apps by categories, such as Social, Productivity, Tools, and Security. If you're looking for a specific app, you can use the Search menu to search for the app by name. Most of the default apps are designed for entertainment and connecting with your contacts. The Windows Store includes Windows 8 and desktop apps to help you work productively, such as dictionaries, eBook readers, antivirus software, and even the latest version of Microsoft Office. When you sign in to Windows 8, you are eligible to purchase, download, and install apps from the Windows Store. Microsoft and other developers frequently post new apps in the Windows Store, so you should visit the site occasionally to see whether new productivity apps are available. When you visit the site, look for an App updates link on the home page. You can click this link to update apps you've already installed.

Amanda is in Kenya this week visiting a wildlife organization. This gives Jodi time to work with you to customize her computer, starting with the tiles on her Start screen. You'll also show her how to change the Start screen background and change the user picture.

Pinning Apps to the Start Screen

The Start screen displays a tile for each app that Microsoft provides by default. If you download and install an app from the Windows Store, a tile automatically appears on the Start screen. You can also add a tile for any Windows 8 or desktop app installed on your computer. When you do, you are adding a pinned item, which is a shortcut you click to open the app. Tiles are called pinned items because they remain on the Start screen until you unpin them. When you unpin an item, Windows removes the tile from the Start screen, but it doesn't remove the app from your computer.

REFERENCE

Pinning an App to the Start Screen

- Right-click the Start screen, and then click the All apps button on the Apps bar.
- Right-click an app on the Apps screen, and then click the Pin to Start button on the Apps bar.

To pin an app to the Start screen, you must first display the app on the Apps screen. In previous tutorials, you accessed the Apps screen using the Charms bar; however, the Start screen provides a quicker way to display installed apps: the Apps bar. The buttons on the Apps bar change depending on your current task. When you display the Apps bar on the Start screen, it includes one button, the All apps button, for opening the Apps screen, where you can access all of the apps and system tools installed on your computer. When you right-click an app on the Apps screen, the Apps bar opens again, this time with buttons for performing tasks with the selected app, such as pinning the app to the Start screen and uninstalling the app from your computer.

Jodi mentions that she often receives reports and other documents as **PDF files**, which are files in the Portable Document Format. Reader is a Windows 8 app that lets you read and navigate PDF documents. Because Jodi thinks she will use Reader often, she wants to add a tile for the app to the Start screen. She also uses WordPad to create and edit text documents. In addition, she wants to open File Explorer directly from the Start screen so she can access files and folders quickly.

You'll show Jodi how to pin Reader, WordPad, and File Explorer to the Start screen so they appear as tiles. You are already familiar with WordPad and File Explorer, which are desktop apps, so you will pin Reader to the Start screen first. You'll start by using the Apps bar to display all of the apps installed on Jodi's computer, including Reader. Make sure your computer is turned on and displaying the Start screen before you perform the following steps.

To display the Apps screen and pin Reader to the Start screen:

1. Right-click a blank area of the Start screen to display the Apps bar. See Figure 3-2. The apps on your Start screen might differ.

Figure 3-2   Apps bar on the Start screen

2. Click the **All apps** button to display the Apps screen, which organizes apps and system tools into categories, with Windows 8 apps listed on the left. See Figure 3-3. Your Apps screen might contain different apps.

Figure 3-3   Apps screen

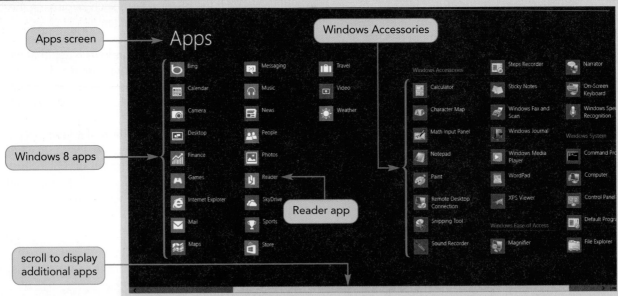

3. Right-click the **Reader** tile. The Apps bar opens again, and Reader tile appears highlighted with a check mark, indicating it is selected.

4. Click the **Pin to Start** button on the Apps bar to pin Reader to the Start screen.

5. Press the **Windows** key to display the Start screen, move your mouse to display the scroll bar, and then scroll to the right to display the Reader tile. See Figure 3-4.

Trouble? If the Reader tile appears in the main section of the Start screen, you do not need to scroll.

Figure 3-4 **Reader tile on the Start screen**

Next, you can add tiles for WordPad and File Explorer to the Start screen. Although both of these are desktop apps, you use the same technique to pin them to the Start screen as you do for Windows 8 apps. You can pin desktop apps to the Start screen and to the taskbar on the desktop. Where you pin a desktop app (the Start screen, taskbar, or both) depends on your personal preferences and where you do most of your computer work. If you routinely start and work with apps on the Start screen, and only occasionally work with a few desktop apps, pin those desktop apps to the Start screen. If you spend most of your time on the desktop working with desktop apps, include only the Desktop tile on the Start screen (where it appears by default) and pin the desktop apps you use often to the taskbar.

To pin any type of app to the Start screen, you open the Apps screen, which organizes apps and system tools into at least four categories: Windows 8 apps, Windows Accessories, Windows Ease of Access, and Windows System. Categories for other installed desktop apps appear after the Windows 8 apps in alphabetical order. Figure 3-5 describes these categories of apps.

Figure 3-5   **Categories of apps**

Category	Description
Windows 8 apps	Apps developed for the Windows 8 user interface, including the standard apps installed when you set up Windows and any apps downloaded and installed from the Windows Store
Windows Accessories	Desktop apps provided with Windows for performing basic tasks, including Paint, WordPad, Windows Media Player, and Calculator
Windows Ease of Access	Desktop apps that make the computer easier to use for people with vision, hearing, and mobility impairments
Windows System	Desktop tools for working with the operating system, files, and folders, including the Control Panel and File Explorer
Other desktop apps	Desktop apps installed on your computer, such as Microsoft Office

Jodi thinks she will often use WordPad and File Explorer as soon as she signs in to Windows, so you'll pin these desktop apps to the Start screen.

To pin WordPad and File Explorer to the Start screen:

▶ **1.** Right-click a blank area of the Start screen to display the Apps bar, and then click the **All apps** button to display the Apps screen.

▶ **2.** Scroll the Apps screen to the right to display the Windows Accessories, Windows Ease of Access, and Windows System categories. See Figure 3-6. Your screen might include additional categories of apps.

| Figure 3-6 | Scrolled Apps screen |

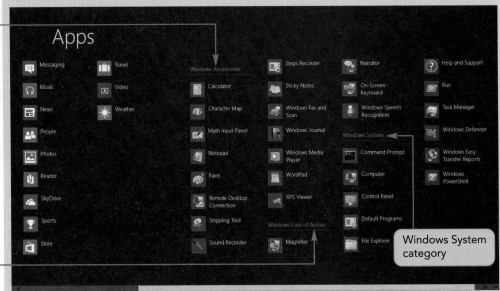

Windows Accessories category

Windows Ease of Access category

Windows System category

▶ **3.** In the Windows Accessories category, right-click the **WordPad** app to high-light it with a check mark and to display the Apps bar, which contains buttons for working with desktop apps. See Figure 3-7.

Figure 3-7 Apps bar for desktop app

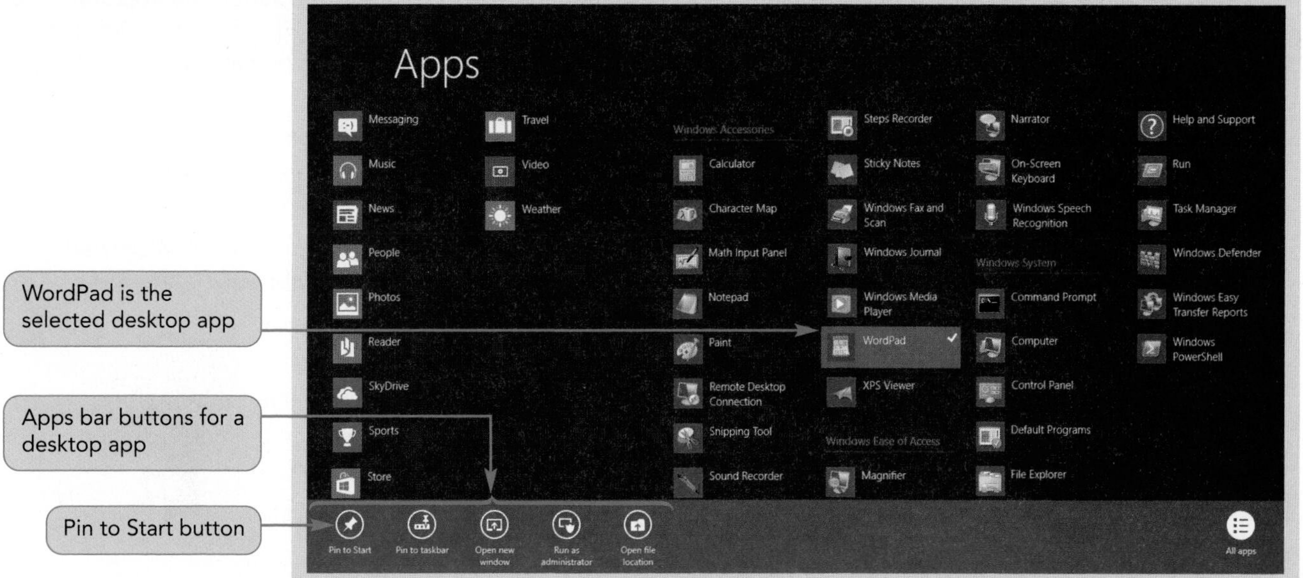

WordPad is the selected desktop app

Apps bar buttons for a desktop app

Pin to Start button

4. Click the **Pin to Start** button on the Apps bar to pin WordPad to the Start screen.

5. In the Windows System category, right-click the **File Explorer** app, and then click the **Pin to Start** button on the Apps bar.

6. Press the **Windows** key ⊞ to display the Start screen, and then scroll the Start screen to the right to display the WordPad and File Explorer tiles. See Figure 3-8.

Figure 3-8 WordPad and File Explorer tiles on the Start screen

File Explorer pinned to the Start screen

WordPad pinned to the Start screen

You can test the three new tiles on the Start screen to make sure each opens the appropriate app.

To test the Reader, WordPad, and File Explorer tiles:

1. Click the **Reader** tile on the Start screen to start Reader. When the app starts, it might display a document explaining how to convert PDF files into Word documents or it might display a Browse button, which you can click to find a PDF file to open.

2. Drag the top of the Reader app screen down until it shrinks to a thumbnail, and then continue dragging it to the very bottom of the screen to close the app.

3. Scroll the Start screen to the right, if necessary, and then click the **WordPad** tile on the Start screen. The WordPad program window opens on the desktop.

4. Click the **Close** button ❌ to close WordPad.

5. Press the **Windows** key ⊞ to display the Start screen, scroll to the right, if necessary, and then click the **File Explorer** tile to open the File Explorer window on the desktop.

6. Click the **Close** button ❌ to close File Explorer, and then press the **Windows** key ⊞ to return to the Start screen.

TIP

You can also press the Alt+F4 keys to close a Windows 8 app.

Now that you've pinned apps to the Start screen, you can add tiles for other items, including folders and commands.

Pinning Folders to the Start Screen

If you often use a folder soon after you sign in to Windows, you can pin the folder to the Start screen, where it appears as a tile. Because pinned items remain on the Start screen until you unpin them, you should unpin them when you no longer need them so the Start screen doesn't become cluttered. You can pin folders located on the hard disk to the Start screen, but not folders on removable media such as a USB flash drive.

Jodi frequently uses photos of the so-called big five African animals: the buffalo, elephant, leopard, lion, and rhinoceros. She has image files of these animals stored on a removable disk. To provide Jodi with easy access to the photos, you will create a new folder for the photos on the hard disk, copy the image files to the new folder, and then pin the folder to the Start screen. You can create the new folder in the Public Pictures folder on the hard disk. Public Pictures is one of four public folders that are available to anyone using the computer. (Public Documents, Public Music, and Public Videos are the other public folders.) People often use the public folders to share files with other users. To locate the photos so you can copy them, you can use the new File Explorer tile on the Start screen to navigate to the folder containing the African animal photos on a removable disk.

To pin a folder to the Start screen:

1. Scroll the Start screen to the right, if necessary, and then click the **File Explorer** tile on the Start screen to open File Explorer on the desktop.

2. Use any technique you've learned to navigate to the **Tutorial** folder in the Windows3 folder provided with your Data Files.

3. Select the five image files (**Buffalo**, **Elephant**, **Leopard**, **Lion**, and **Rhino**) and then press the **Ctrl+C** keys to copy the files to the Clipboard.

▶ **4.** In the Navigation pane, click the **expand** icon ▷ next to the Pictures link to display the folders in the Pictures library, and then click the **Public Pictures** folder to open the folder.

▶ **5.** If necessary, click the **Expand the Ribbon** button ⌄ on the ribbon, and then click the **New folder** button in the New group on the Home tab to create a folder.

▶ **6.** Type **Big Five Photos** and then press the **Enter** key to name the folder.

▶ **7.** Right-click the **Big Five Photos** folder and then click **Paste** on the shortcut menu to paste the five image files into the Big Five Photos folder.

▶ **8.** Right-click the **Big Five Photos** folder and then click **Pin to Start** on the shortcut menu.

▶ **9.** Press the **Windows** key 🪟 to return to the Start screen, and then scroll to the right, if necessary, to display the tile for the Big Five Photos folder. See Figure 3-9.

Figure 3-9 ▶ **Start screen with pinned folder**

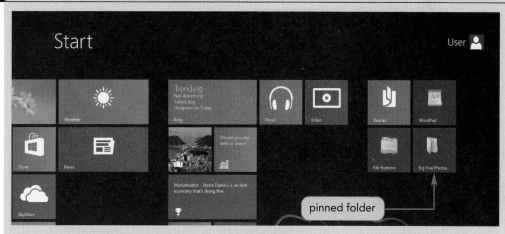

▶ **10.** To test the new pinned item, click the **Big Five Photos** tile on the Start screen. The folder opens in File Explorer on the desktop.

▶ **11.** Close all open windows, and then press the **Windows** key 🪟 to return to the Start screen.

Jodi mentions that she would like a quicker way to shut down and restart the computer without having to display the Settings menu. To accommodate this request, you will add custom shortcuts to the Start screen to shut down or restart the computer in one step.

Adding Custom Shortcuts to the Start Screen

TIP

Windows uses the term *shortcut* to refer to items you click to open a related app, file, or folder, and to refer to the menu that appears when you right-click an item.

Recall that when you pin an app or folder to the Start screen, you are creating a shortcut to the item that Windows displays as a tile on the Start screen. So far, you have pinned three apps by working directly with each one: You located the app on the Apps screen, right-clicked it, and then selected an option for pinning the item to the Start screen. In some cases, however, you can't work directly with the item you want to pin. For example, although you can click the Power button on the Settings menu to display the Shut down, Sleep, and Restart commands, right-clicking one of these commands does not display a shortcut menu or the Apps bar with the Pin to Start option. Instead, you must use the Create Shortcut wizard to create a custom shortcut on the desktop, and then pin that shortcut to the Start screen. A **wizard** is a series of dialog boxes that guides you through the steps of performing a task. The **Create Shortcut wizard** guides you through the steps of creating a shortcut.

When you start the Create Shortcut wizard, the first dialog box displays a text box for entering the location of the item. Instead of entering the path to a file or folder, you can enter the name of a Windows command, such as shutdown. The shutdown command turns off the computer or restarts it. To specify which action you want the shutdown command to take, you include a switch after the command name, such as /s. A switch starts with a slash (/) followed by a letter or number. Use the /s switch for a complete shutdown and the /r switch to restart the computer.

After entering the command, you use the Create Shortcut wizard to provide a name for the shortcut, such as Shut down or Restart. The shortcut icon appears on the desktop or in the window where you created the shortcut. Shortcut icons on the desktop include a small arrow so you can distinguish them from regular icons. The small arrow is a reminder that the icon points to an item stored elsewhere on the computer. Although custom shortcuts each use the same generic icon, you can customize the shortcut by selecting a different icon with a more meaningful image. Finally, you can right-click the shortcut icon to display a menu that includes the Pin to Start command.

You'll start by creating two custom shortcuts on the desktop—one to shut down the computer and another to restart it. You will also customize the shortcut icons so they are easy to recognize. After that, you will pin the shortcuts to the Start screen.

To create custom shortcuts:

TIP

You can also press the Windows+D keys to display the desktop.

1. Click the **Desktop** tile on the Start screen to display the desktop.

2. Right-click a blank area of the desktop, point to **New** on the shortcut menu, and then click **Shortcut** to start the Create Shortcut wizard and open its first dialog box. See Figure 3-10.

| Figure 3-10 | First dialog box in the Create Shortcut wizard |

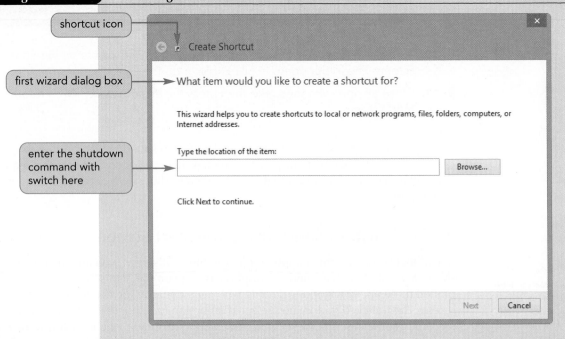

▶ **3.** Type **shutdown /s** to enter the command for performing a complete shutdown, and then click the **Next** button to open the second dialog box in the wizard, where you name the shortcut.

▶ **4.** Type **Shut down** to replace the command text with a more meaningful name for the shortcut, and then click the **Finish** button to display the Shut down shortcut icon on the desktop. Next, you can create another custom shortcut for the Restart command.

▶ **5.** Right-click a blank area of the desktop, point to **New** on the shortcut menu, and then click **Shortcut** to start the Create Shortcut wizard again.

▶ **6.** Type **shutdown /r** to enter the command for restarting the computer, and then click the **Next** button to open the second dialog box in the wizard.

▶ **7.** Type **Restart** to enter a name for the shortcut, and then click the **Finish** button to display the Restart shortcut icon on the desktop. See Figure 3-11.

| Figure 3-11 | Shut down and Restart shortcut icons on the desktop |

generic icons for both shortcuts

shortcut arrow

Both shortcuts use the same icon, which would be confusing to anyone using the shortcuts. You can customize the icon for each shortcut to make them easier to distinguish. You do so by opening the Properties dialog box for each icon. A **property** is a characteristic of an object such as a file or shortcut.

To change the icons for the shortcuts:

▶ **1.** Right-click the **Shut down** shortcut icon on the desktop, and then click **Properties** on the shortcut menu to open the Shut down Properties dialog box.

2. If necessary, click the **Shortcut** tab to display settings and options for working with shortcuts.

3. Click the **Change Icon** button to open a Change Icon dialog box with a message explaining that the shutdown command does not include any icons.

4. Click the **OK** button to acknowledge the message and to open the Change Icon dialog box containing images you can apply to the icon. See Figure 3-12.

| Figure 3-12 | Change Icon dialog box |

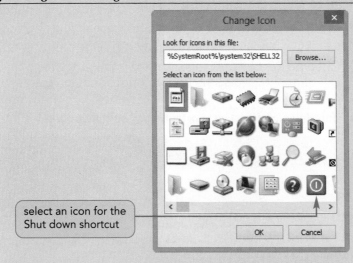

select an icon for the Shut down shortcut

5. Click the image of a red power button in the fourth row, seventh column, and then click the **OK** button to close the Change Icon dialog box.

6. Click the **OK** button to close the Shut down Properties dialog box and display the Shut down shortcut with a new icon.

You'll use the same technique to customize the icon for the Restart shortcut.

7. Right-click the **Restart** shortcut icon on the desktop, and then click **Properties** on the shortcut menu.

8. On the Shortcut tab, click the **Change Icon** button, and then click the **OK** button to close the message dialog box and open the Change Icon dialog box containing images you can apply to the icon.

9. Scroll to the right, click the image of a green arrow ➡ in the top row and then click the **OK** button.

Trouble? If an image of a green arrow does not appear in your Change Icon dialog box, click any other suitable image.

10. Click the **OK** button to close the Restart Properties dialog box and display the Restart shortcut with a new icon. See Figure 3-13.

Figure 3-13 | **Custom shortcut icons**

Now that you've created custom icons for the Shut down and Restart shortcuts, you can pin these items to the Start screen.

To pin the custom shortcuts to the Start screen:

▶ **1.** Right-click the **Shut down** shortcut icon on the desktop, and then click **Pin to Start** on the shortcut menu.

▶ **2.** Right-click the **Restart** shortcut icon on the desktop, and then click **Pin to Start** on the shortcut menu.

▶ **3.** Press the **Windows** key ▣ to display the Start screen, and then scroll to the right to display the tiles for shutting down and restarting the computer. See Figure 3-14.

Figure 3-14 | **Start screen with custom shortcuts**

Now that the custom Shut down and Restart shortcuts are pinned to the Start screen, you can return to the desktop and delete the original shortcut icons. When you pinned the custom shortcuts to the Start screen, you created a copy of each shortcut, so deleting a custom shortcut on the desktop does not affect the pinned item. Likewise, unpinning a shortcut does not affect the shortcut icon on the desktop. In this case, Jodi is in the habit of returning to the Start screen when she finishes working on the desktop, so she only needs the Shut down and Restart shortcuts on the Start screen. You'll delete the shortcut icons on the desktop.

> **To delete the custom shortcuts on the desktop:**
>
> ▸ **1.** Scroll to the left, if necessary, and then click the **Desktop** tile to display the desktop.
>
> ▸ **2.** Right-click the **Shut down** shortcut icon, and then click **Delete** on the shortcut menu.
>
> ▸ **3.** Right-click the **Restart** shortcut icon, and then click **Delete** on the shortcut menu.

No shortcut icons remain on the desktop.

Customizing Start Screen Tiles

If you continue to pin items to the Start screen, you will eventually have an unmanageable number of tiles on the Start screen. One way to keep the tiles organized is to group them so that similar tiles appear together. When you group tiles, you can assign a name to the group, which helps you quickly find the tile you want. Another way to organize the tiles is to modify their appearance. For example, you can reduce the size of tiles to fit more on the Start screen and turn live tiles on or off. If you're not using a tile, you can remove it from the Start screen, which helps to keep the Start screen uncluttered. Removing a tile from the Start screen does not remove the app from your computer. You can still use the Apps screen to start and use the app.

Grouping Tiles

In addition to the standard tiles Windows displays on the Start screen, you added six other tiles for Windows Reader, File Explorer, WordPad, the Big Five Photos folder, the Shut down command, and the Restart command. All of these new tiles appear together in their own group. You can start organizing the tiles by moving the Reader tile into the main group of tiles for Windows 8 apps. Next, you can create a group for the File Explorer, WordPad, and Big Five Photos folder tiles. Jodi will use these tiles in her daily work. Finally, you can create a group for the Shut down and Restart tiles. They should remain separate from other tiles so Jodi does not click one and turn off the computer accidentally.

REFERENCE

Grouping Tiles on the Start Screen

- To create a group, drag a tile to the left or right until a vertical bar appears. Release the tile to add it to the new group.
- To move a tile into an existing group, drag the tile to the group.
- To change the position of a tile within a group, drag the tile to a new position.

Jodi asks you to organize the tiles on the Start screen into three groups: the Reader tile in the group of Windows 8 apps; the File Explorer, WordPad, and Big Five Photos tiles in a new group; and the Shut down and Restart tiles in another new group. The new tiles were added to a new group when you pinned them to the Start screen, so you only need to move the Reader tile and create a group for the Shut down and Restart tiles.

To group the tiles on the Start screen:

1. Press the **Windows** key ⊞ to display the Start screen, and then scroll to the right to display the Reader tile.

2. Drag the **Reader** tile to the left to add it to the second group of tiles for Windows 8 apps. See Figure 3-15.

Figure 3-15   **Moving the Reader tile**

Reader tile moved to main group of Windows 8 tiles; your tile might appear in a different position

Trouble? If the Reader tile appears in a location different from the one shown in the figure, continue with the steps. Windows positions the tile in the most convenient spot in a Windows 8 apps group.

Next, you'll create a group for the Shut down and Restart files.

3. Drag the **Shut down** tile to the right until a vertical bar appears, as shown in Figure 3-16.

Figure 3-16   **Creating a group on the Start screen**

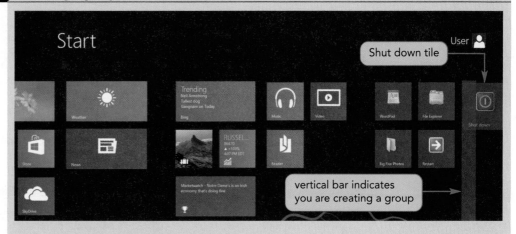

Shut down tile

vertical bar indicates you are creating a group

4. Release the Shut down tile to add it to the new group.

5. Drag the **Restart** tile just to the right of the Shut down tile to add it to the same group. Now the Start screen includes an additional group of tiles. See Figure 3-17.

Figure 3-17   Start screen with three groups of tiles

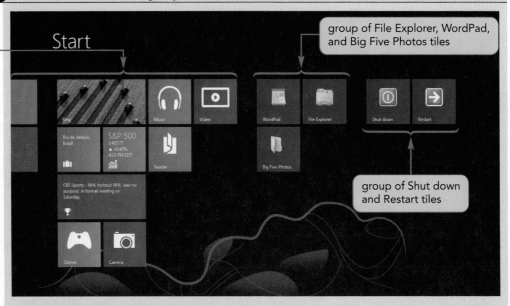

Windows 8 tiles are in two groups

group of File Explorer, WordPad, and Big Five Photos tiles

group of Shut down and Restart tiles

Trouble? If you drag the Restart tile too far to the right and accidentally create another group, drag the tile to the left of the Shut down tile.

After organizing tiles into groups, you can work with each group directly to name the group or move it to a different location on the Start screen. To do so, you must zoom the Start screen to display all of the tiles at once. Right-clicking a tile on the zoomed Start screen selects the group of tiles and displays the Apps bar.

To identify the new groups of tiles on Jodi's Start screen, you'll display a label above each new group. The group of Windows 8 apps doesn't need a label because those tiles obviously belong together.

To name the new groups of tiles:

TIP

You can also press the Ctrl+Plus (+) keys to zoom in and the Ctrl+Minus (-) keys to zoom out.

1. Point to the lower-right corner of the Start screen until the Zoom button appears, and then click the **Zoom** button ▬ to zoom in and display all of the tiles.

2. Right-click the group containing the File Explorer tile to select the group.

3. Click the **Name group** button on the Apps bar to display a text box where you can enter a group name. See Figure 3-18.

Figure 3-18 Naming a group of tiles

selected group

zoomed Start screen

enter a name for the selected group here

Name group button

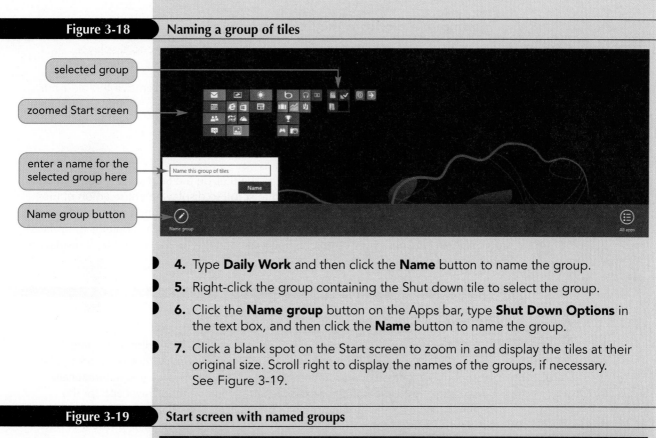

4. Type **Daily Work** and then click the **Name** button to name the group.

5. Right-click the group containing the Shut down tile to select the group.

6. Click the **Name group** button on the Apps bar, type **Shut Down Options** in the text box, and then click the **Name** button to name the group.

7. Click a blank spot on the Start screen to zoom in and display the tiles at their original size. Scroll right to display the names of the groups, if necessary. See Figure 3-19.

Figure 3-19 Start screen with named groups

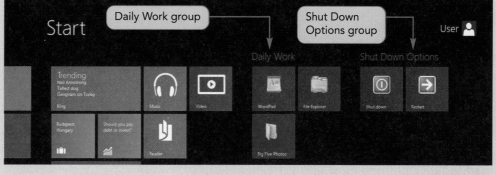

Arranging the tiles into groups organizes the Start screen so it's easier to find the tile you want.

Removing Tiles

To keep your Start screen clean and uncluttered, you can remove tiles to display only those you use often. If you discover that you want to add a tile to the Start screen again, you can use the Apps screen or desktop to pin the item to the Start screen. Keep in mind that when you remove a tile, you are only unpinning the item, not deleting an app or a folder.

Now that the Daily Work group contains tiles for File Explorer, WordPad, and the Big Five Photos folder, Jodi is reconsidering whether she needs a tile for File Explorer. She can easily open a File Explorer window by clicking the Desktop tile and then clicking the File Explorer button on the taskbar, or by clicking the Big Five Photos tile in the Daily Work group.

To remove a tile from the Start screen:

▶ 1. Right-click the **File Explorer** tile in the Daily Work group to display a check mark on the tile, indicating it is selected.

▶ 2. Click the **Unpin from Start** button on the Apps bar to remove the tile from the Start screen.

Modifying Tiles

Besides rearranging, grouping, and removing the tiles on the Start screen, you can also change their size. For example, if you need to scroll to display an entire group of tiles, you can reduce the size of large tiles to display more tiles on a single screen. You can modify tiles by making them live tiles, which change to display the contents or updated information for an app. For example, if you make the Photos tile a live tile, it displays a slide show of photos and other images.

INSIGHT

Turning on Live Tiles

As you know, many tiles on the Start screen are live tiles—they display the latest information from apps including Bing, Mail, Calendar, People, Photos, Weather, News, and Sports. When you open some apps such as News or Travel, you automatically turn on their live tile feature. For example, after you open the Travel app for the first time, its tile displays a slide show of popular travel destinations. To turn on live tiles for other apps, such as Mail and People, you need to set up an account or add information to the app. For example, after you use Mail to set up an email account, the Mail tile becomes a live tile and displays recent email messages. For the Weather app, you need to specify your location or let Windows use the location you entered during setup to have the Weather tile display up-to-date weather information for your location.

To display images in the live Photos tile, first make sure you have stored photos in a location the Photos app can access, such as the Pictures library, your SkyDrive, Facebook, or Flickr account, or a device containing photos, such as a camera, phone, or mobile computer. (*SkyDrive* is a location on a Microsoft server computer where you can store files and access them using a Web browser or other apps. Facebook is a social networking Web site you can join to share information with other members. Flickr is a photo-sharing Web site where you can post your own photos and view photos from other people.) If you store image files in a location the Photos app can access, you can make the Photos tile a live tile by right-clicking the tile and then clicking the Turn live tile on button on the Apps bar.

Jodi asks you to reduce the size of some tiles for Windows 8 apps so she can see how to display more tiles on the main part of the Start screen. She also wants to display the images in the Big Five Photos folder on the Photos tile.

To change the size of the Start screen tiles:

▶ **1.** Scroll to the left to display the **People** tile on the Start screen, and then right-click it to select the tile and display the Apps bar.

▶ **2.** Click the **Smaller** button on the Apps bar to reduce the size of the People tile. See Figure 3-20.

Figure 3-20	Reducing the size of a tile

People tile is now smaller

▶ **3.** Right-click the **Messaging** tile and then click the **Smaller** button on the Apps bar.

▶ **4.** If necessary, drag the **Messaging** tile up to fill the space created by the smaller tiles.

Because you have already stored the five animal photos in a subfolder in the Pictures library, you can make the Photos tile a live tile by starting the app. First, you'll start the Photos app to make sure it detected the files in the Big Five Photos folder. Then, you'll turn on the live tile feature.

To make the Photos tile a live tile:

▶ **1.** Click the **Photos** tile to start the Photos app, which displays five locations for storing photos. See Figure 3-21.

Trouble? If you or someone else has already added photos to a Photos location, your screen will look different from Figure 3-21.

Figure 3-21   Photos app

photos in the Big Five Photos folder in the Pictures library

Pictures library   SkyDrive photos   Devices   Facebook photos   Flickr pho

Photo courtesy of Oliver Wright

2. Close the Photos app to return to the Start screen.

3. Right-click the **Photos** tile and then click the **Turn live tile on** button on the Apps bar. The Photos tile now displays the images in the Big Five Photos folder. See Figure 3-22.

   Trouble? If the Turn live tile off button appears on the Apps bar instead of the Turn live tile on button, the Photos tile is already a live tile. Skip Step 3.

Figure 3-22   Live Photos tile

live Photos tile displays photos in the Pictures library

Photo courtesy Gary M. Stolz, U.S. Fish and Wildlife Service

Now the live Photos tile reflects the mission of the Preserve Africa organization.

Changing the Appearance of the Start Screen

Besides personalizing the Start screen to make it more useful and informative, you can change its appearance to suit your preferences. For example, you can change the background design or select a different color scheme, which is a set of colors including a background color and a coordinated accent color.

Windows displays a generic icon as the default user account picture, but you can change this picture to display a photo of yourself or anything else that identifies you. If your computer includes a built-in camera, you can use the camera to take a photo and display it as your user account picture. Otherwise, you can use any image file stored in a location your computer can access.

Changing the Start Screen Background

Windows provides a number of background patterns you can display on the Start screen—all of them designed in the Windows 8 style. You can select a background design different from the default to add your personal stamp to the Start screen. Many background designs include tattoos, which are colorful designs that can make the Start screen background distinctive and lively. In addition, you can select a color scheme for the background design.

REFERENCE

Changing the Start Screen Background

- Point to the upper-right corner of the screen to display the Charms bar.
- Click the Settings charm to open the Settings menu.
- Click the Change PC settings command to display the PC settings screen.
- Click the Personalize category in the left pane, if necessary.
- Click the Start screen link to display options for personalizing the Start screen.
- Click a background design to apply the design to the background of the Start screen.
- Drag the slider to select a color scheme for the background design.

Jodi asks you to show her the Start screen using a different background design and a brighter color scheme. You can make these changes using the PC settings screen, which you open from the Settings menu. You have used the Settings menu before to shut down the computer or put it to sleep.

To change the design and color of the Start screen background:

1. Display the Charms bar.

2. Click the **Settings** charm to display the Settings menu.

3. Click the **Change PC settings** command at the bottom of the menu to display the PC settings screen. See Figure 3-23.

   Trouble? If the Personalize category is not selected on your PC settings screen, as shown in the figure, click Personalize in the left pane to select the category.

TIP

Click the Lock screen link in the Personalize category to change the image displayed on the lock screen.

Figure 3-23   PC settings screen

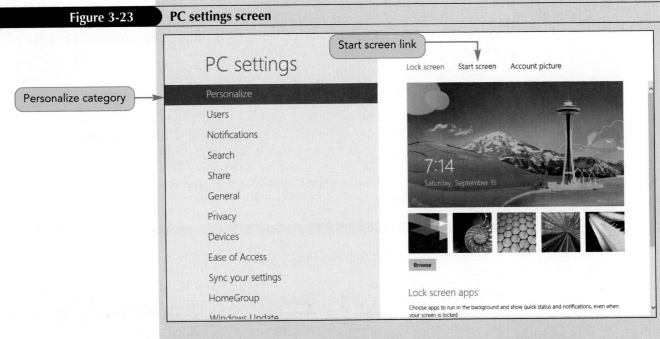

4. Click the **Start screen** link to display options for personalizing the Start screen. See Figure 3-24.

Figure 3-24   Start screen settings

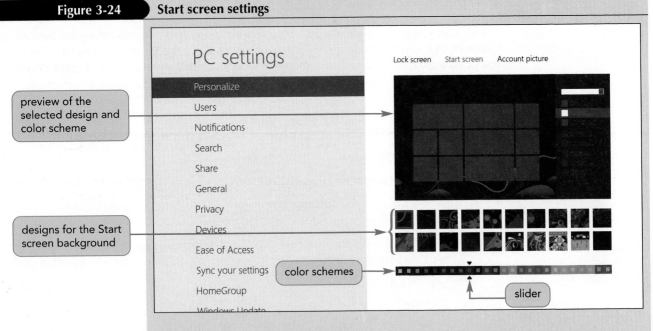

5. Click the fifth design from the left to select a new design.

6. Drag the slider two squares to the right to select a color scheme using shades of teal green.

7. Press the **Windows** key ⊞ to display the Start screen, which now appears with a new design and different color scheme. See Figure 3-25.

Figure 3-25   **Start screen with new background**

selected background design

teal green color scheme

Start screen tattoo

Photo courtesy Gary M. Stolz , U.S. Fish and Wildlife Service

Jodi likes the new Start screen background and decides to use it for a while.

Changing the User Picture

Previous versions of Windows provided a collection of images from which you selected a user picture. Windows 8 lets you select any image file stored in a location your computer can access, such as the Pictures library. You can select a photo of yourself or another identifying place or object, an illustration you or someone else created using a graphics app, or any other image stored in a file. You can also use your computer's camera to take a photo and use it as your user picture. Your user picture represents your **user account**, which is a collection of information specifying how you can use the computer and its apps and includes appearance settings such as your Start screen background and color.

Jodi wants to use the photo of an elephant stored in the Big Five Photos folder as her user picture. You'll show her how to replace the generic user icon on the Start screen with a more meaningful photo.

To change the user account picture:

1. Right-click the **user icon** on the Start screen, and then click **Change account picture** on the shortcut menu to display the PC settings screen again with the Account picture link selected. See Figure 3-26.

Figure 3-26   Changing the account picture

Account picture link

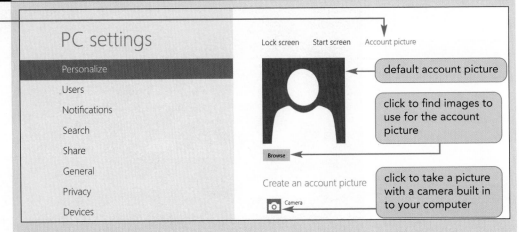

2. Click the **Browse** button to display the files and folders in the Pictures library.

3. If necessary, click the **Big Five Photos** folder to open it, and then click the **Elephant** file to select it.

4. Click the **Choose image** button to select the Elephant image as the account picture.

5. Press the **Windows** key 🏁 to display the Start screen, which now includes the new account picture.

To create an image of the Start screen that displays many of the changes you made, you can take a screen shot of the Start screen. Jodi can use that image for reference as she customizes the other Preserve Africa computers.

To create a screen shot of the Start screen:

TIP

You can also press the Windows+Print Screen keys to create a screen shot named Screenshot (1), for example, which Windows stores in a folder named Screenshots in the Pictures library.

1. Press the **Print Screen** key to capture an image of the Start screen and save the image on the Clipboard. Depending on the type of computer you are using, the Print Screen key might be labeled differently (for example, PrtScn).

2. Click the **WordPad** tile on the Start screen to start WordPad on the desktop and open a new, blank document.

3. Type **Customized Start screen** and then press the **Enter** key.

4. Press the **Ctrl+V** keys to paste the Start screen image into the new WordPad document.

5. Click the **Save** button 💾 on the Quick Access toolbar, navigate to the **Public Documents** folder in the Documents library, type **Start screen** as the name of the file, and then click the **Save** button to save the file in the Public Documents folder.

   Trouble? If necessary, click the default name in the File name text box to select it before typing a new file name. WordPad will automatically add the file extension .rtf.

6. Close WordPad.

Jodi is satisfied with the changes you made and doesn't want to further personalize the Start screen.

In this session, you learned how to pin apps, folders, and custom shortcuts to the Start screen so they appear as tiles. You also learned how to customize Start screen tiles by grouping, removing, and modifying tiles. Finally, you personalized the appearance of the Start screen by changing the design and color of the background and selecting a new user picture.

REVIEW

Session 3.1 Quick Check

1. On the Start screen, a(n) _____ appears as a tile and is a shortcut you click to open a folder or an app.
2. Explain how to use the Apps screen to add a tile to the Start screen.
3. When you use the Create Shortcut wizard to create a custom shortcut, what command do you enter to perform a complete shutdown of your computer?
4. One way to organize the tiles on the Start screen is to _____ them so that similar tiles appear together.
5. Explain how to remove a tile from the Start screen.
6. Name two ways you can change the appearance of a tile on the Start screen.
7. What are properties?
8. Which screen do you use to change the Start screen background?

Session 3.2 Visual Overview:

The background image is part of the desktop **theme**, a collection of settings that determines the appearance of the desktop.

You can change the appearance of desktop icons.

Besides the Recycle Bin, you can display additional desktop icons.

The **Peek** feature displays previews of the open windows grouped on a taskbar button.

You can change the position of the buttons on the taskbar.

Customized Desktop

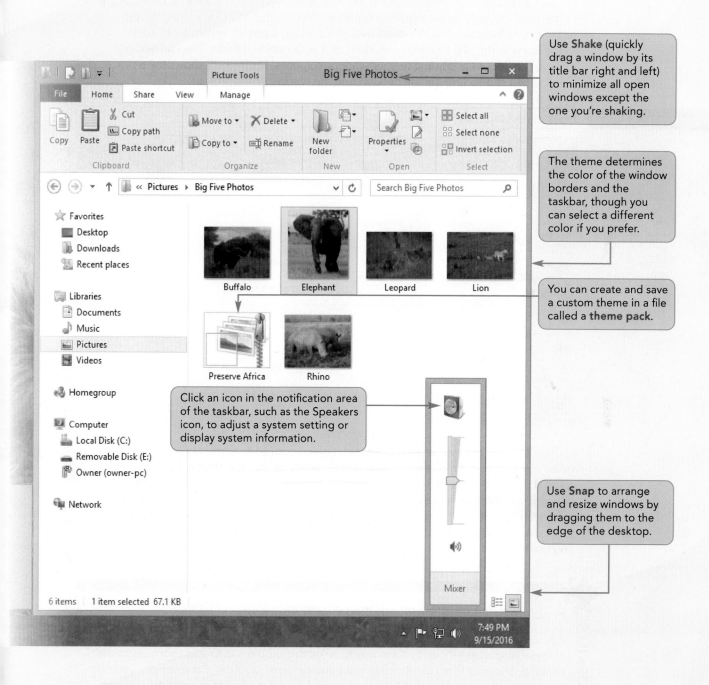

Use **Shake** (quickly drag a window by its title bar right and left) to minimize all open windows except the one you're shaking.

The theme determines the color of the window borders and the taskbar, though you can select a different color if you prefer.

You can create and save a custom theme in a file called a **theme pack**.

Click an icon in the notification area of the taskbar, such as the Speakers icon, to adjust a system setting or display system information.

Use **Snap** to arrange and resize windows by dragging them to the edge of the desktop.

Personalizing the Desktop

When you click the Desktop tile on the Start screen, Windows displays the desktop, also called the classic desktop because of its similarity to the desktop in earlier versions of Windows. The desktop displays a background image, the Recycle Bin icon, and the taskbar by default.

You can place icons on the desktop that represent objects you want to access quickly or frequently when you are working on the desktop, such as Windows tools, drives, programs, and documents. Windows provides desktop icons for system tools, such as the Recycle Bin, the Computer window, and your personal folder. You can add or remove these icons according to your work preferences. Figure 3-27 shows the types of icons you can include on the desktop and the objects they represent.

Figure 3-27 Types of desktop icons

Icon	Description
	Computer icon
	Control Panel icon
	Document shortcut icon
	Drive shortcut icon
	Folder shortcut icon
	Network icon
	Program shortcut icon (such as Paint)
	Recycle Bin icon (full and empty)
	User's folder icon

© 2014 Cengage Learning

Besides these built-in desktop icons, you can use shortcuts to start a desktop program or access an object. Similar to clicking pinned items on the Start screen, double-clicking a shortcut on the desktop opens its associated file, folder, device, or program. When you delete a shortcut or desktop icon, you delete only the icon—the file or resource it represents remains in its original location. You typically create shortcuts on the desktop (or elsewhere, such as in a folder or on the taskbar) to locations, files, and devices that you use often.

PROSKILLS

Problem Solving: Simplifying Tasks with Shortcuts

If you work with many devices, programs, or folders, it might be difficult to access all of these resources efficiently. One way to solve this problem is to add shortcuts to the desktop. Shortcut icons can simplify tasks you perform regularly. For example, you can create a shortcut icon for a USB flash drive, and then drag files to the shortcut icon to copy them to the removable disk. You also can create a shortcut icon for a desktop program you use often, such as Calculator, and then double-click the icon to start the program. Some programs add a shortcut icon to the desktop when you install the program. If you work with a particular folder often, you can add a desktop shortcut to the folder. That way, you can double-click the folder shortcut to open the folder without navigating many folder windows.

While Amanda is in Kenya, you'll continue to work with Jodi to customize her computer, starting with adding icons to the desktop for system tools she uses often. Then you'll show her how to create a shortcut icon on the desktop to a USB flash drive.

Adding Icons to the Desktop

Windows provides five standard icons that you can display on the desktop. Besides the Recycle Bin, which appears on the desktop by default, you can display the Computer icon on the desktop to provide easy access to the Computer window and therefore the drives and devices connected to your computer. If you display the desktop icon for your personal folder (that is, the folder containing the current user's files), you can quickly find and open the folders containing your documents. Having the Network icon on the desktop gives you access to a window that lists the shared computers and other devices on your network. You can also add the Control Panel icon to the desktop. The Control Panel contains specialized tools you use to change the way Windows looks and behaves.

REFERENCE

Displaying Standard Desktop Icons

- Right-click an empty area of the desktop, and then click Personalize on the shortcut menu.
- In the left pane of the Personalization window, click Change desktop icons.
- In the Desktop Icon Settings dialog box, click to select a check box for each icon you want to add to the desktop.
- Click the OK button.

Jodi mentions that the Windows tools she uses most frequently are her personal folder, the Computer window, and the Control Panel. You'll add these icons to Jodi's desktop.

To display standard desktop icons:

1. If you took a break after the previous session, make sure the desktop is displayed. Close any open windows.

   Trouble? If the Start screen is displayed instead of the desktop, click the Desktop tile on the Start screen.

2. Right-click a blank area of the **desktop**, and then click **Personalize** on the shortcut menu. The Personalization window opens.

TIP

Note that the Recycle Bin icon has two appearances: one when it is empty, and another when it contains deleted items.

3. In the left pane, click **Change desktop icons**. The Desktop Icon Settings dialog box opens. See Figure 3-28. The Recycle Bin check box is already selected, indicating that Windows is displaying the Recycle Bin icon on the desktop.

   Trouble? If you are working in a computer lab, the Change desktop icons command might not appear in the left pane. In that case, read but do not perform the remaining steps in this section and the next section.

Figure 3-28   **Desktop Icon Settings dialog box**

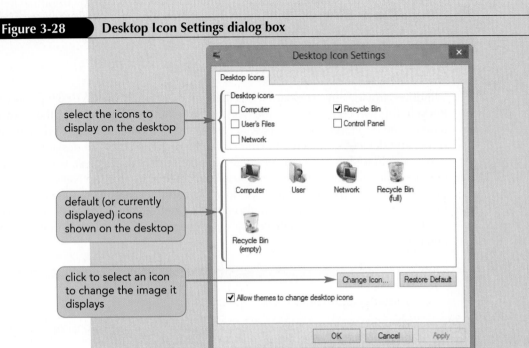

select the icons to
display on the desktop

default (or currently
displayed) icons
shown on the desktop

click to select an icon
to change the image it
displays

Trouble? If the settings in your Desktop Icon Settings dialog box differ from those in the figure, note the current options so you can restore them later, and then change the options so only the Recycle Bin check box is selected.

4. Click the **Computer**, **User's Files**, and **Control Panel** check boxes. If necessary, click the **Allow themes to change desktop icons** check box to remove the check mark. You are going to make other changes to the desktop and you do not want these icons to reflect those changes.

5. Click the **OK** button. The icons for your personal folder, the Computer window, and the Control Panel appear on the desktop after Windows applies the new settings.

Now that you've added desktop icons for Jodi, you can customize their appearance according to her preferences.

Changing the Appearance of Desktop Icons

You can change the images displayed on the desktop icons using the same Change Icon dialog box you used earlier to customize the Shut down and Restart icons. Change the image to suit your preferences or to display a more accurate image. For example, the Computer icon shows an image of a desktop computer. If you work on a notebook or tablet computer, you might want to change this image to match your computer type.

Because she works on an all-in-one computer, with the computer and monitor built in to the same case, Jodi wants to change the image for the Computer icon on the desktop. To do so, you use the Personalization window again.

To change the image of the Computer icon:

▶ **1.** In the left pane of the Personalization window, click **Change desktop icons**. The Desktop Icon Settings dialog box opens.

▶ **2.** In the box displaying desktop icons, click the **Computer** icon, and then click the **Change Icon** button. The Change Icon dialog box opens and highlights the current image. Note the image currently used for the Computer icon so you can restore it later.

▶ **3.** Click the icon of a computer monitor displaying a moon image (two icons to the left of the current icon), as shown in Figure 3-29.

Figure 3-29	Changing the default Computer icon

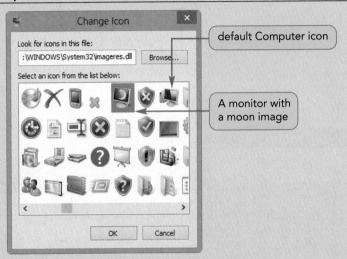

Trouble? If the computer monitor image shown in the figure does not appear in your Change Icon dialog box, click any other suitable image.

▶ **4.** Click the **OK** button to close the Change Icon dialog box.

▶ **5.** Click the **OK** button to close the Desktop Icon Settings dialog box, and then close the Personalization window. The Computer icon on the desktop now appears as a monitor displaying a moon image.

The standard Windows desktop icons provide quick access to common Windows tools. These are standard tools that Windows provides to simplify or enhance your computer work. However, other items you access often (such as documents, folders, and drives) might be different from the items other users access often. In addition, the folders you use frequently one week might differ from those you'll use frequently the next week. To personalize your desktop to provide quick access to these items, you can create and use shortcuts.

Creating Desktop Shortcuts

Many people use shortcuts on the Start screen and shortcuts on the desktop for different types of objects. They pin apps to the Start screen so they can quickly access and start an app. They create shortcuts on the desktop for other types of objects, typically folders and drives.

On the desktop, you can create shortcuts to access drives, documents, files, Web pages, programs, or other computer resources, such as a network folder. For example, you can easily open a document from the desktop by creating a shortcut icon for the document. A shortcut icon for a document works much the same way as a document icon does in a folder window—you can double-click the shortcut icon to open the document in the appropriate program. However, a shortcut icon is only a link to the actual document. If you move the icon, you move only the shortcut, not the document itself. One advantage of using shortcut icons is that if your desktop becomes cluttered, you can delete the shortcut icons without affecting the original documents.

You can also create shortcut icons for the folders, drives, and devices on your computer. This way, you can access your local hard disk, for example, directly from the desktop, instead of having to open a folder window and then navigate to the hard disk.

Windows provides several ways of creating shortcuts on the desktop. Figure 3-30 summarizes the techniques you can use to create shortcuts. The one you choose is a matter of personal preference.

| Figure 3-30 | Methods for creating shortcuts |

Method	Description
Drag (for drives and devices only)	To create a drive shortcut on the desktop, use a folder window to locate the drive icon, and then drag the icon to the desktop.
Right-drag	Use a folder window to locate and select an icon, hold down the right mouse button, and then drag the icon to a new location. Release the mouse button and click Create shortcuts here on the shortcut menu.
Right-click, Create shortcut	Use a folder window to locate an icon, right-click the icon, click Create shortcut on the shortcut menu, and then drag the shortcut icon to a new location.
Right-click, Send to	To create a shortcut on the desktop, use a folder window to locate an icon, right-click the icon, point to Send to, and then click Desktop (create shortcut).

© 2014 Cengage Learning

Next, you'll create a shortcut to a USB flash drive on the desktop. You could use any technique for creating shortcuts, but you'll use the drag method because it involves the fewest steps.

Creating a Shortcut to a Drive

To create a shortcut to a drive, you can open the Computer window, and then drag the drive icon from the window to the desktop. Windows creates a shortcut icon that looks like a drive icon with a shortcut arrow and includes an appropriate label, such as Removable (E) – Shortcut. If you drag a document icon from a folder window to the desktop, you move the actual document from its original location to the desktop. However, you cannot move a drive, a program, or another computer resource—its location is fixed during installation. Therefore, when you drag a drive icon to the desktop, you automatically create a shortcut.

TIP

You can rename a shortcut icon the same way you rename a folder.

When you create a shortcut to a USB flash drive, you can insert the drive in a USB port and then double-click the shortcut to view your Data Files. You can move or copy documents to the drive without having to open a separate folder window.

Jodi regularly copies files from her computer to a USB flash drive and wants to use a shortcut to simplify the task. You'll show her how to create a shortcut to a USB flash drive on her desktop.

To create a shortcut to a USB flash drive:

▶ 1. If necessary, insert the USB flash drive containing your Data Files into a USB port on your computer.

▶ 2. Double-click the **Computer** icon on the desktop. If necessary, move or resize the Computer window so you can see the icons along the left side of the desktop. You need to see both the desktop icons and the Computer window to drag effectively.

▶ 3. Point to the **Removable Disk (E:)** icon in the Computer window, press and hold the left mouse button, and then drag the **Removable Disk (E:)** icon from the Computer window into an empty area of the desktop.

Trouble? If your USB drive has a name other than Removable Disk (E:), substitute the appropriate name and drive on your system as you perform the steps. The steps in this tutorial assume that your Data Files are stored on Removable Disk (E:), a USB flash drive.

▶ 4. Release the mouse button. A shortcut labeled Removable Disk (E) – Shortcut now appears on the desktop. Click the desktop to deselect the shortcut icon. See Figure 3-31.

| Figure 3-31 | Shortcut to a removable disk |

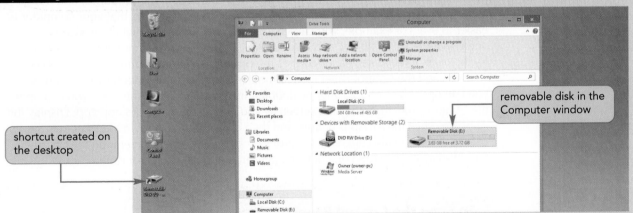

shortcut created on the desktop

removable disk in the Computer window

Trouble? If you dragged with the right mouse button instead of the left, a shortcut menu appears when you release the mouse button. Click Create shortcuts here to add the Removable Disk (E) – Shortcut to the desktop.

▶ 5. Point to the **Removable Disk (E) – Shortcut** icon to view its ScreenTip, which indicates the permanent location of the drive on your computer.

Jodi wants to copy the Start screen document from the Public Documents folder to a folder on the USB flash drive so she can refer to the document while working on different computers. Use the shortcut on the desktop to copy the file to the Windows3\Tutorial folder on the USB flash drive.

To use the removable disk shortcut:

▶ **1.** In the Navigation pane of the Computer window, click the **Documents** link to display the contents of the Documents library, which includes the Start screen document in the Public Documents folder.

▶ **2.** Double-click the **Removable Disk (E) – Shortcut** icon on the desktop. A new window opens showing the contents of the USB flash drive.

▶ **3.** Open the **Windows3** folder, and then open the **Tutorial** folder.

▶ **4.** Drag the **Start screen** file from the Public Documents folder in the Navigation Pane to the Tutorial folder window. Because you are dragging a file on a hard drive to a removable disk, Windows copies the Start screen file rather than moving it to the Tutorial folder.

▶ **5.** Close both open windows.

Using a shortcut to a drive saves a few steps when you want to make backup copies of files or transfer files from one computer to another.

Customizing the Desktop with the Control Panel

You've worked with the Start screen and with standard desktop and shortcut icons to personalize your desktop. You can also personalize Windows using the Control Panel, a window that contains specialized tools you use to change the way Windows looks and behaves. Some tools help you adjust settings that make your computer more fun to use. For example, use the Personalize tool to change the theme, which, as shown in the Session 3.2 Visual Overview, is a background plus a set of colors, sounds, and other elements. Other Control Panel tools help you set up Windows so that your computer is easier to use. For example, you can change display settings so that the desktop, icons, and windows are sharp and clear. All of the Control Panel tools provide access to dialog boxes that let you select or change the properties, or characteristics, of an object.

If you add the Control Panel icon to the desktop, as you did in a previous set of steps, you can open the Control Panel by double-clicking that icon. Otherwise, you can open the Control Panel from the Start screen as you would any other desktop app: Display the Apps bar, click the All Apps button, and then click Control Panel in the Windows System category. You can also open the Control Panel from the Settings menu on the Charms bar: Display the Charms bar, click Settings, and then click Control Panel.

To open the Control Panel:

▶ **1.** Double-click the **Control Panel** icon on your desktop. The Control Panel window opens. See Figure 3-32.

TIP

You can click the View by button arrow and then click Large icons or Small icons to list each tool in alphabetical order.

Figure 3-32   **Control Panel**

Control Panel Home page displayed in Category view

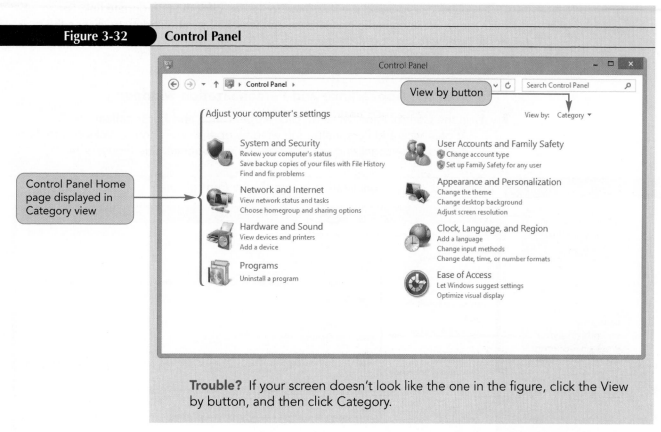

Trouble? If your screen doesn't look like the one in the figure, click the View by button, and then click Category.

The main window of the Control Panel is called the Control Panel Home page. By default, this page displays tools in Category view, which groups similar tools into categories. See Figure 3-33.

Figure 3-33   **Control Panel categories**

Control Panel Category	Typical Tasks
System and Security	Schedule maintenance checks, increase the space on your hard disk, maintain Windows security settings, and keep Windows up to date.
Network and Internet	Set Internet options, view network status, and set up a home-group to share files and perform other network tasks.
Hardware and Sound	Change the sounds on your computer, and change the settings for your printer, keyboard, mouse, camera, and other hardware.
Programs	Install and uninstall programs and Windows features, set options for default settings and programs, and work with desktop gadgets.
Mobile PC	If you are using a mobile computer such as a laptop, use this category to change battery settings and adjust other common mobility settings.
User Accounts and Family Safety	Change user account settings, passwords, and associated pictures.
Appearance and Personalization	Change the appearance of desktop items, apply a theme or screen saver, and customize the Start screen and taskbar.
Clock, Language, and Region	Change the date, time, and time zone; the language you use on your computer; and the format for numbers, currencies, dates, and times.
Ease of Access	Change computer settings for vision, hearing, and mobility.

© 2014 Cengage Learning

To open a category and see its related tools, you click the appropriate link. For example, you can open the Appearance and Personalization window to change the desktop background or to set a theme.

To open the Appearance and Personalization window:

  1. In the Control Panel window, click **Appearance and Personalization**. The Appearance and Personalization window opens, showing the tasks and tools related to personalizing your computer's appearance. See Figure 3-34.

| Figure 3-34 | Appearance and personalization options in the Control Panel |

Appearance and Personalization window

options for customizing your work environment

The Appearance and Personalization window, like the other Control Panel category windows, lists tasks and tools in the right pane and links to the Control Panel Home page and other categories in the left pane. To change the desktop background, for example, you click the Change desktop background task in the right pane. The Desktop Background window opens so you can select a new desktop background and set other background options.

Jodi wants her office computers to reflect the image of Preserve Africa, and she'd like the desktop itself to be more appealing to her and her employees. You will work with the Control Panel to personalize Jodi's desktop.

Selecting Themes

The easiest way to personalize the desktop in Windows 8 is to select a theme. When you select a theme, you select one or more desktop background images; a color for window borders and the taskbar; a collection of sounds to play to signal system tasks, such as shutting down Windows; and a screen saver. Windows themes include collections of high-resolution images. You can select one of the images in a theme to display as the desktop background, or you can play a slide show of the images and switch from one image to another after a specified amount of time. Windows also provides a few high-contrast themes, which make the items on your screen easier to see.

Selecting a Theme

- Open the Control Panel window and switch to Category view, if necessary.
- Click Appearance and Personalization.
- Click Personalization.
- Click a theme.

Jodi asks you to show her a few desktop themes to see if one would be suitable for Preserve Africa.

To change the theme:

1. In the Appearance and Personalization window, click **Change the theme** to open the Personalization window, which lists many types of themes. See Figure 3-35. Your Personalization window might differ. Note your current theme so you can restore it later.

Figure 3-35   **Personalization window**

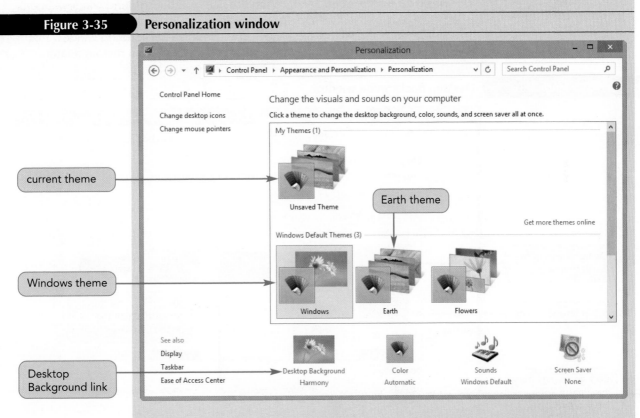

2. If necessary, scroll the themes, and then click **Earth**. The desktop background changes to an image of a glacier and its reflection, the taskbar and window borders change color, and a sound plays (if your speakers are turned on).

   Trouble? If the Earth theme does not appear in your Personalization window, select any other theme that displays photos.

3. Minimize the Personalization window.

Jodi thinks the Earth theme might work for her, but she wants to display a different image in the Earth theme collection. You'll show her how to do so by changing the desktop background.

Changing the Desktop Background

You can change the desktop background, or its **wallpaper**, to display one of the images that Windows provides, or you can select your own graphic to use as wallpaper. When you change the background, you are not placing a new object on the desktop; you are only changing its appearance. You can also determine how you want to position the picture—resized to fill the screen, resized to fit the screen, stretched across the screen (which might distort the image), tiled (repeated across the screen), or centered. If you center the wallpaper on the screen, you can select a color to frame the background image.

You and Jodi decide to examine the desktop backgrounds that Windows provides to find a suitable image.

To change the desktop background:

▶ 1. Click the **Control Panel** button ▣ on the taskbar to restore the Personalization window, and then, near the bottom of the window, click the **Desktop Background** link to open the Desktop Background window. See Figure 3-36. All six Earth images are selected because Windows uses all of the images for the desktop slide show. Your Desktop Background window might differ. Note your current desktop background so you can restore it later.

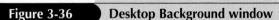

Figure 3-36 **Desktop Background window**

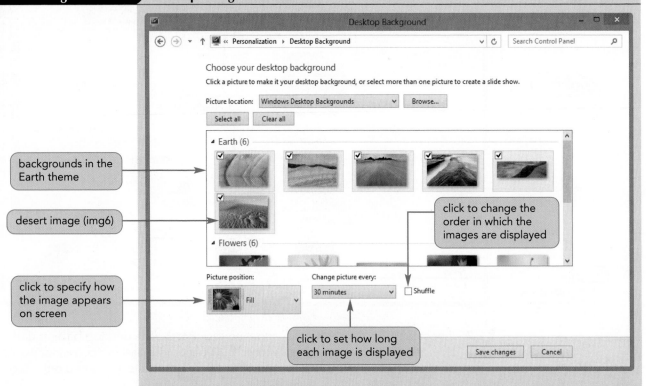

backgrounds in the Earth theme

desert image (img6)

click to change the order in which the images are displayed

click to specify how the image appears on screen

click to set how long each image is displayed

▶ 2. Click the **desert** image in the Nature category. (The ScreenTip indicates this image is named img6.) Windows displays the image you selected on the desktop. Now only the desert image is selected in the Earth category of themes.

▶ 3. Minimize the Desktop Background window to see the new background image.

After examining the desktop, Jodi doesn't think the desert image is right for her organization after all. However, she didn't notice other images in the Desktop Background window that would be more appropriate. You offer to show her how to find more desktop themes online.

To find a desktop theme online:

▶ **1.** Click the **Control Panel** button ▨ on the taskbar to restore the Desktop Background window.

▶ **2.** Click the **Back** button ⊜ to display the Personalization window and the glacier image on the desktop.

▶ **3.** Click the **Get more themes online** link to start the Internet Explorer Web browser and display a Web page on the Microsoft Web site where you can select and download desktop themes. Scroll down to display available themes. See Figure 3-37. Content on the Web changes frequently, so the themes displayed on your Web page might differ.

Trouble? If your computer is not connected to the Internet, you cannot access the Web page with additional themes. Read but do not perform the remaining steps.

Figure 3-37	Online desktop themes

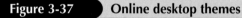

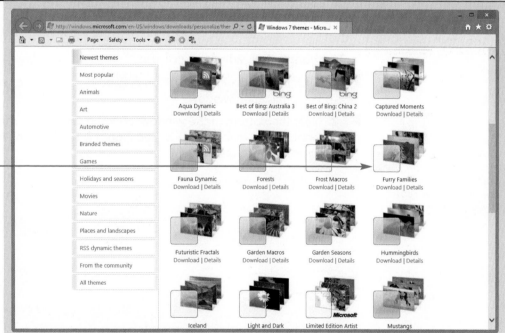

▶ **4.** Locate the Furry Families theme, and then click its **Download** link to download the Furry Families theme to your computer.

Trouble? If the Furry Families theme does not appear on the Web page, download any other theme.

▶ **5.** When an information bar appears at the bottom of the window, asking if you want to open or save the theme, click the **Open** button. Windows displays the Furry Families theme in the Personalization window.

▶ **6.** Click the **Desktop Background** link to select the images to display.

▶ **7.** Click the **check boxes** for the two polar bear images and the penguin image to deselect them because these animals are not native to Africa.

▶ **8.** Click the **Change picture every** button, and then click **15 minutes** to change the amount of time each picture is displayed in the theme slide show.

▶ **9.** Click the **Save changes** button.

▶ **10.** Minimize the Personalization window, and then close Internet Explorer to display the Furry Families theme on the desktop. Instead of displaying only one theme image, your desktop will play a slide show of the images in the Furry Families theme.

Jodi likes the new theme but comments that she would prefer a different color for the taskbar. You'll show her how to change the colors of the window borders and taskbar.

Changing Desktop Colors

Besides changing the desktop background, you can use the Color and Appearance window to set the color of windows and the taskbar. Each theme uses a particular color for window borders and the taskbar. For example, the Windows theme uses light blue by default for the window borders and taskbar, though you can change this to another color, such as orange.

To change the window colors:

▶ **1.** Click the **Control Panel** button [icon] on the taskbar to restore the Personalization window.

▶ **2.** Near the bottom of the window, click the **Color** link. The Color and Appearance window opens. See Figure 3-38. Note the current window color so you can restore it later.

Figure 3-38 **Color and Appearance window**

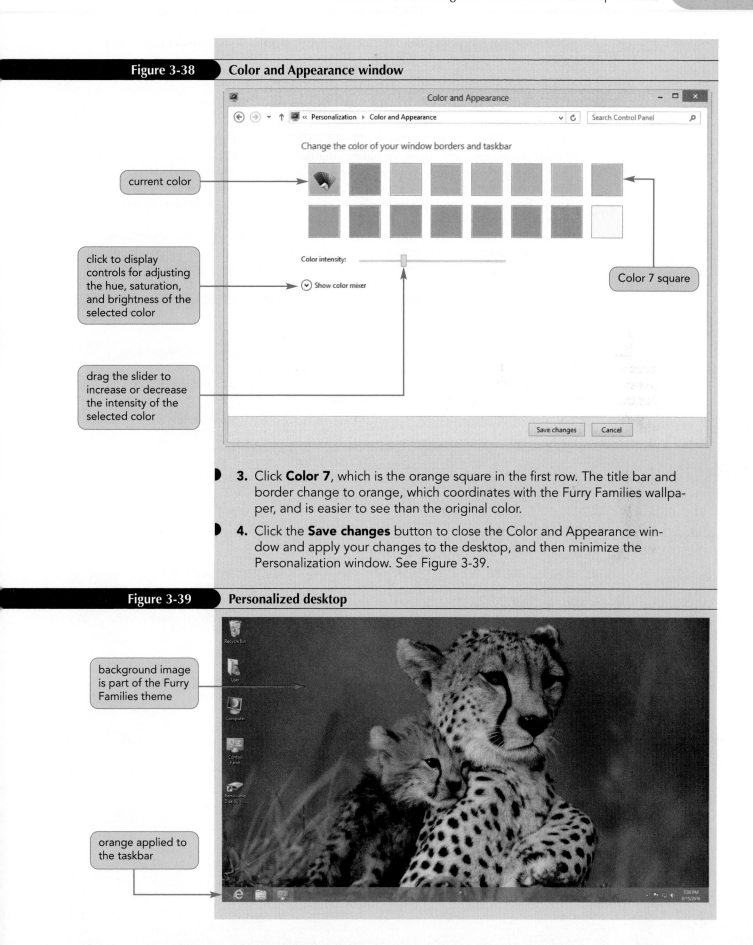

current color

click to display
controls for adjusting
the hue, saturation,
and brightness of the
selected color

drag the slider to
increase or decrease
the intensity of the
selected color

Color 7 square

3. Click **Color 7**, which is the orange square in the first row. The title bar and border change to orange, which coordinates with the Furry Families wallpaper, and is easier to see than the original color.

4. Click the **Save changes** button to close the Color and Appearance window and apply your changes to the desktop, and then minimize the Personalization window. See Figure 3-39.

Figure 3-39 **Personalized desktop**

background image
is part of the Furry
Families theme

orange applied to
the taskbar

The desktop is now personalized for Jodi. It displays the Furry Families theme and taupe window elements.

Activating a Screen Saver

A **screen saver** is a program that blanks your computer screen or displays a moving design after the computer has been idle for a specified period of time. Screen savers can be entertaining and handy for hiding your data from the eyes of others if you step away from your computer. When a screen saver is on, you restore your desktop by moving your mouse or pressing a key. Windows 8 comes with several screen savers. Some show an animated design, while others play a slide show of pictures stored on your computer.

You can select how long you want the computer to sit idle before the screen saver starts. Most users find settings between 3 and 10 minutes to be the most convenient. You can change this setting using the options on the Screen Saver Settings dialog box.

INSIGHT

Using a Screen Saver for Security

To enhance the security of your computer and prevent unauthorized people from accessing your files, take advantage of a security setting available in the Screen Saver Settings dialog box. To have the screen saver request your user name and password before displaying your desktop, select the check box in this dialog box labeled On resume, display logon screen. This means that only you and other people who know your user name and password can work with your desktop and files.

Jodi wants to examine the screen savers that Windows provides and then choose the most appropriate one for her organization.

To activate a screen saver:

1. Click the **Control Panel** button [icon] on the taskbar to restore the Personalization window, and then, near the bottom of the Personalization window, click the **Screen Saver** link. The Screen Saver Settings dialog box opens. See Figure 3-40. Note the name of the current screen saver so you can restore it later.

Figure 3-40	Screen Saver Settings dialog box

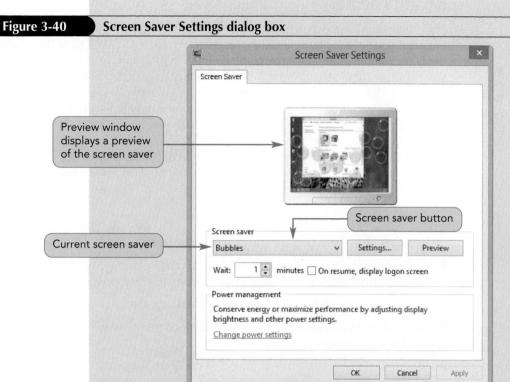

Preview window displays a preview of the screen saver

Screen saver button

Current screen saver

▶ **2.** Click the **Screen saver** button to display the screen savers installed on your computer.

▶ **3.** Click **Ribbons**. The animated screen saver plays in the Preview window. Jodi likes that screen saver, but it's not appropriate for her desktop theme. You suggest the Photos screen saver, which plays a slide show of the pictures and videos stored in the Pictures library by default.

▶ **4.** Click the **Screen saver** button, and then click **Photos**. The preview window plays a slide show of the graphics files stored in the Pictures library, including those in the Big Five Photos folder.

▶ **5.** To restrict the screen saver to display photos in the Big Five Photos folder only, click the **Settings** button to open the Photos Screen Saver Settings dialog box. You use this dialog box to specify which files to include in the slide show and other settings, such as the slide show speed.

▶ **6.** Click the **Browse** button. The Browse For Folder dialog box opens.

▶ **7.** Expand the **Pictures** library and the **Public Pictures** folder, if necessary, and then click the **Big Five Photos** folder. Click the **OK** button to indicate you want to include all the pictures in the Big Five Photos folder in the screen saver slide show.

▶ **8.** Click the **Save** button to close the Photos Screen Saver Settings dialog box. Now only the pictures in the Big Five Photos folder appear in the Preview window.

▶ **9.** Click the **OK** button to close the Screen Saver Settings dialog box.

▶ **10.** Minimize the Personalization window.

After your computer is idle for a minute or so, the screen saver will start, playing a slide show of the photos.

Saving Themes

Now that you have made changes to the desktop, you can save these settings as a theme. If you save the current settings as a theme, you can apply all of the changes—the Furry Families wallpaper, the taupe window colors, and the screen saver—at the same time, without selecting the individual settings again. By default, Windows stores the theme files in a system folder. You can create your own theme file—called a theme pack—that you can store in a folder of your choice, and then share that theme with people on other Windows 8 computers. Although you cannot move or copy a theme from a system folder, you can move or copy a theme pack. You will save the desktop settings you created for Jodi as a theme and a theme pack, both called Preserve Africa. Jodi will use the theme pack and the photos in the Big Five Photos folder to apply the Preserve Africa theme to other office computers.

To save the desktop settings as a theme:

▶ **1.** Restore the Personalization window, and then, in the My Themes section, click **Save theme**. The Save Theme As dialog box opens.

▶ **2.** Type **Preserve Africa** as the name of this theme.

▶ **3.** Click the **Save** button. The Preserve Africa theme now appears in the My Themes section.

▶ **4.** To save the theme so that others at Preserve Africa can use it, right-click the **Preserve Africa** theme in the Personalization window, and then click **Save theme for sharing** on the shortcut menu.

▶ **5.** In the Save Theme Pack As dialog box, open the **Big Five Photos** folder in the Public Pictures folder.

▶ **6.** Click the **File name** text box, if necessary, and then type **Preserve Africa**. Note that the Save as type is Desktop Theme Pack (*.deskthemepack).

▶ **7.** Click the **Save** button. Windows saves the Preserve Africa theme pack file in the Big Five Photos folder.

▶ **8.** Close the Personalization window.

Managing the Desktop with Taskbar Tools

Windows 8 includes three taskbar tools you can use to manage the windows on your desktop: Snap, Peek, and Shake. With Snap you can drag the title bar of an open window to the top of the desktop to maximize the window. To restore the window to its original size, drag the title bar away from the top of the desktop. You can also use Snap to arrange windows side by side and expand windows vertically on the desktop.

Peek also helps you manage open windows. To quickly minimize all open windows, you click the Show desktop button on the far right side of the taskbar. To preview open windows without leaving your current window, you point to a taskbar button to display thumbnails of open files, and then point to a thumbnail. Any open windows fade to reveal the selected window, and then reappear when you move the pointer away from the thumbnail. To open the window you're previewing, you click the thumbnail.

Shake is another handy tool for managing windows. Use Shake to quickly minimize all open windows on the desktop except the one you want to focus on—you don't have to minimize the windows one by one. Click and hold the title bar of the window you want to keep open, and then shake it by quickly dragging the window to the right and left. When you do, you minimize all of the other open windows. To restore the minimized windows, shake the open window again.

Jodi sometimes needs to work with two windows open as she examines images and manages her files and folders. You offer to show her how to quickly arrange windows side by side using Snap.

To arrange windows side by side with Snap:

▸ **1.** Click the **File Explorer** button 📁 on the taskbar to open File Explorer, open the **Pictures** library, and then open the **Big Five Photos** folder.

▸ **2.** Right-click the **Lion** photo, point to **Open with** on the shortcut menu, and then click **Paint** to display the photo in Paint.

   Trouble? If the Paint window opens as maximized, click the Restore Down button 🗗 to resize the window. If the window is still too large, use the resizing pointer ⤡ to make it the same size as the Big Five Photos folder window.

▸ **3.** Arrange the windows so that you can see parts of both windows.

▸ **4.** Click the **title bar** of the Paint window to make it the active window, and then drag the **title bar** to the left of the desktop until an outline of the expanded window appears. See Figure 3-41.

   Trouble? If the outline does not appear, make sure most of the Paint window appears to the left of the screen. The window will snap to the desktop when you release the mouse button.

Figure 3-41	Arranging windows with Snap

Paint will be snapped to the left side of the desktop to fill the outline

outline of the Paint window

Photos courtesy of Garibgazi; Oliver Wright; Gary M. Stolz, U.S. Fish and Wildlife Service; Ken Stansell, U.S. Fish and Wildlife Service; Komencanto

▸ **5.** Release the mouse button to expand the Paint window to cover the left side of the desktop.

▸ **6.** Drag the **title bar** of the File Explorer window to the right of the desktop until an outline of the expanded window appears.

   Trouble? If the File Explorer window is not visible on your screen, minimize the Paint window and then repeat Step 6.

▸ **7.** Release the mouse button to expand the File Explorer window to cover the right side of the desktop.

Trouble? If you minimized the Paint window, click the Paint button  on the taskbar to restore it.

Now each window covers half of the desktop, with Paint on the left and File Explorer on the right.

Jodi can use Snap when she needs to work with two windows side by side. However, she typically has many windows open, and often has to stop working with a document or an image to manage those windows. For example, she might open a few more image files and then decide to copy other files to a USB flash drive. She'd like to quickly view the desktop to verify that it contains a shortcut to the removable disk so she can copy the files using the shortcut icon. She also wants to know how to briefly display a particular window to view its contents. You'll show her how to use Peek to perform both tasks.

To use Peek:

1. Click the far right side of the taskbar (to the right of the date and time) to minimize all of the open windows. See Figure 3-42.

Figure 3-42 **Displaying the desktop with Peek**

far right side of the taskbar

2. Click the **File Explorer** button on the taskbar to display the Big Five Photos folder.

3. Right-click the **Buffalo** file, point to **Open with** on the shortcut menu, and then click **Paint** to open the Buffalo image file in Paint.

4. Minimize the new Paint window.

5. Right-click the **Elephant** file, point to **Open with** on the shortcut menu, and then click **Paint** to open the Elephant image file in Paint.

6. Minimize the new Paint window.

7. Point to the **Paint** button on the taskbar to display thumbnail previews of the three pictures open in Paint. See Figure 3-43.

Figure 3-43   **Previewing windows with Peek**

preview of Paint windows

Photos courtesy of Garibgazi; Oliver Wright; Gary M. Stolz, U.S. Fish and Wildlife Service;
Ken Stansell, U.S. Fish and Wildlife Service; Komencanto

Trouble? If a list of filenames appears instead of thumbnails when you point to the Paint taskbar button, the thumbnails feature is probably disabled on your computer. Read but do not perform Steps 8 and 9.

TIP

To restore the desktop when you're previewing a window, move the pointer away from the thumbnail.

8. To preview the Elephant image, point to the **Elephant** thumbnail. The File Explorer window fades so that the Elephant window is the only one open on the desktop.

9. Click the **Elephant** thumbnail to display the Elephant image in Paint and make it the active window. The File Explorer window is also redisplayed, but it is not the active window.

Jodi mentions that when she needs to focus on the contents of a window, she likes to minimize all of the other open windows. You suggest she use Shake to do so.

To use Shake:

1. Point to the **Paint** button ▨ on the taskbar, and then click the **Buffalo** thumbnail to open the Buffalo image in Paint.

2. Point to the **Paint** button ▨ on the taskbar again, and then click the **Lion** thumbnail to open the Lion image in Paint.

3. Point to the **title bar** of the Lion window, hold down the mouse button, and then quickly drag the window about an inch to the right and left to shake it. The Lion window remains open while all of the other open windows are minimized.

4. To restore the minimized windows, shake the **Lion** window again.

5. Click the far right side of the taskbar to minimize all open windows.

Next, you can explore the display properties that affect the sharpness of the images on your desktop.

Changing Display Settings

After working with the properties for the desktop background, theme, and screen saver, you're ready to explore the display properties that affect the computer monitor itself. The Screen Resolution window lets you control the display settings for your monitor, such as the size of the desktop and whether to use more than one monitor. Windows chooses the best display settings, including screen resolution and orientation, based on your monitor. **Screen resolution** refers to the clarity of the text and images on your screen. At higher resolutions, items appear sharper and smaller, so more items fit on the screen. At lower resolutions, fewer items fit on the screen, but they are larger and easier to see. At very low resolutions, however, images might have jagged edges. Selecting the best display settings for your monitor enhances your Windows experience.

INSIGHT

Selecting the Best Display Settings for Your Monitor

Notebook and desktop computers have either a standard or widescreen liquid crystal display (LCD) monitor. Display settings for standard LCD monitors typically differ from those for widescreen monitors. However, all LCD monitors display the sharpest images and clearest text at a particular resolution, which is called their **native resolution**. Screen resolution is measured horizontally and vertically in **pixels**, short for "picture elements," which are the tiny dots that make up a computer image. For example, most 19-inch standard LCD monitors have a native resolution of 1280 × 1024. A 22-inch widescreen LCD monitor usually has a native resolution of 1680 × 1050. You can change the resolution to a lower setting, such as 1024 × 768, to make the on-screen objects larger, though the text might not be as clear as text displayed at the native resolution. If you are using a standard monitor, be sure to select a resolution with an aspect ratio of 4:3, such as 1024 × 768. (An **aspect ratio** is the ratio of the width to the height.) If you are using a widescreen monitor, select a resolution with an aspect ratio of 16:9 or 16:10, such as 1366 × 768.

Changing the Screen Resolution

You use the Screen Resolution window to change the display settings. You click the Resolution button to display a list of available resolutions on your monitor and a slider bar. You can drag the slider bar to increase or decrease the resolution, or sharpness, of the image. You will change the screen resolution from its current setting to 1366 × 768, if that setting is not already selected.

To change the screen resolution:

▶ 1. Right-click the **desktop**, and then click **Screen resolution** on the shortcut menu to open the Screen Resolution window. Note the original setting on the Resolution button so you can restore it later.

▶ 2. Click the **Resolution** button to display the options available on your computer, and then drag the slider to 1366 × 768, if necessary. The settings appear in the Resolution box as you drag the slider. The preview area shows the relative size of the new resolution. See Figure 3-44.

| Figure 3-44 | **Changing the screen resolution** |

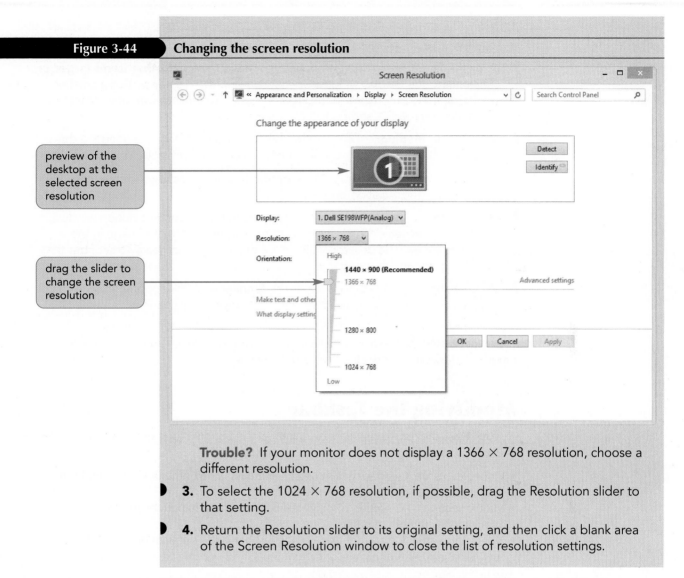

preview of the desktop at the selected screen resolution

drag the slider to change the screen resolution

Trouble? If your monitor does not display a 1366 × 768 resolution, choose a different resolution.

▶ **3.** To select the 1024 × 768 resolution, if possible, drag the Resolution slider to that setting.

▶ **4.** Return the Resolution slider to its original setting, and then click a blank area of the Screen Resolution window to close the list of resolution settings.

If you select a screen resolution recommended for your monitor, but find the text and objects are now too large or small, you can adjust the size of the text and objects.

Changing the Size of Text and Objects

Without adjusting your screen resolution, you can change the size of the text and objects such as icons on your screen. This means you can increase or decrease the size of text and objects while maintaining the native resolution of your monitor. For example, if you use a low screen resolution, such as 1024 × 768, you can make text and objects smaller to display more information on the screen. Conversely, if you use a high resolution, you can make text and objects easier to see by making them larger while retaining the sharpness of the high resolution.

Jodi's computer uses the Smaller – 100% setting, which is the default for her monitor. You'll view the other settings to see if they would improve her desktop.

To view the display settings:

▶ **1.** In the Screen Resolution window, click **Make text and other items larger or smaller**. The Display window opens, showing the display settings: Smaller – 100%, Medium – 125%, and Larger – 150%. (Your window might not include the Larger – 150% setting.)

▶ **2.** Click the **Medium – 125%** option button, and then note the image in the Preview area. This setting would not noticeably improve Jodi's desktop.

  Trouble? If the Medium – 125% option button is already selected, click the Smaller – 100% option button.

▶ **3.** If a Larger – 150% option button appears in the Screen Resolution window, click the **Larger – 150%** option button, and then note the image in the Preview area. The desktop objects are much larger and easy to see, but they take up too much space.

▶ **4.** Click the original setting, such as the **Smaller – 100%** option button, and then close the Display window without applying any changes.

You have used the taskbar to manage open windows. Next, you'll learn how to modify the taskbar to work effectively on the desktop.

Modifying the Taskbar

As you know, the bar that appears by default at the bottom of the desktop is the taskbar. The taskbar is divided into the following three sections:

- Pinned items: This section, which begins at the left side of the taskbar, contains the Internet Explorer and File Explorer icons by default.
- Middle section: This section displays taskbar (or program) buttons for desktop applications currently running.
- Notification area: On the right side of the taskbar is the notification area, which shows the current time, icons for system tools, and system status information.

In the middle section of the taskbar, Windows displays buttons for each desktop application that is running. By default, each button is identified by an icon, not a text label, to conserve space. If you open another file in one of these applications, Windows groups the buttons for that app into a single button. A few windows might be grouped on the Paint button, for example. The Paint icon would appear on top, and the outlines of the open windows would be stacked behind it.

As you saw when working with Peek, when you point to a taskbar button, Windows displays a thumbnail preview of the corresponding window. The preview is designed to help you identify a window by more than the title alone. If a window is playing a video or an animation, the video or animation also plays in the preview. When you point to a grouped taskbar button, Windows arranges the thumbnail previews in a row above the taskbar. You can click a thumbnail to open a window. To close a window, you point to a thumbnail until a Close button appears in the upper-right corner of the thumbnail, and then you click the Close button.

You can personalize the taskbar to suit your preferences. For example, you can reorder the taskbar buttons by dragging them to a new location. You can also change the appearance of taskbar buttons by displaying button labels and specifying when buttons should be grouped together. To further customize the taskbar, you can change the size and position of the taskbar or hide it altogether.

PROSKILLS

Decision Making: Monitoring the Notification Area

The icons in the notification area of the taskbar let you access certain computer settings, such as the system time. The icons also communicate the status of programs running in the background. Background programs are those programs that Windows runs to provide a service, such as an Internet connection. By default, the notification area displays only a few icons, which are usually determined by your computer manufacturer and the programs installed on your computer. One of these icons (the flag) is for the Action Center, a window that displays notification messages about security and maintenance settings. Read these messages when they appear so you can make decisions about your computer. You can also point to the Action Center icon to display a summary of Action Center issues, and then click the flag icon to open the Action Center, which categorizes messages by color. Items highlighted by a red bar are important and need your immediate attention. For example, a message reminding you to update an antivirus program is flagged as important. Items highlighted by a yellow bar are suggestions you can address later, such as recommended maintenance tasks. To respond to Action Center messages, click the Action Center icon again.

In addition, you might receive notifications from other programs running in the background about a change in status, such as the addition of a new hardware device. Read the notification to find out whether you need to respond to or correct a problem. You can also point to any icon in the notification area to display its status or name. (You might need to click the Show hidden icons button (an arrow) on the taskbar to display all of the icons in the notification area.) For example, if you're having trouble hearing sounds on your computer, point to the Speakers icon to determine whether you need to turn up the volume.

Now you can personalize the taskbar on Jodi's computer. You'll start by showing her how to pin items to the taskbar.

Pinning Desktop Apps to the Taskbar

Internet Explorer and File Explorer are pinned to the left section of the taskbar by default. If you use another desktop app often, you can also pin that app to the taskbar. Pinning an app to the taskbar increases your efficiency because the pinned app is always visible as you work on the desktop, and you can start the app with a single click. (You need to double-click desktop shortcut icons for programs.) You can rearrange the buttons for pinned and running apps on the taskbar to suit your preferences.

REFERENCE

Pinning Desktop Apps to the Taskbar

- If the desktop app is already running, right-click the program button on the taskbar, and then click Pin this program to taskbar.

or

- If the desktop app is not running, display and then right-click the Start screen, click the All apps button on the Apps bar, locate and right-click the app on the Apps screen, and then click Pin to taskbar on the Apps bar.

Because Jodi frequently uses Paint, you suggest that she pin Paint to the taskbar. This task is particularly easy because Paint is already running and its button appears on the taskbar.

To pin Paint to the taskbar:

▶ **1.** Right-click the **Paint** button on the taskbar, and then click **Pin this program to taskbar**.

▶ **2.** To confirm that Paint is pinned to the taskbar, right-click the **Paint** button on the taskbar again, and then click **Close all windows**. All of the Paint windows close, but the Paint program button remains on the taskbar.

   Trouble? If a dialog box appears asking if you want to save changes to an image, click the Don't Save button.

TIP

To unpin a file, open the Jump List, point to the filename, and then click the Unpin from this list icon.

In addition to starting a desktop app from the taskbar, you can use a pinned item to open favorite and recent files from that program. To do so, you use a **Jump List**, a list of recently or frequently opened files, folders, or Web sites. When you right-clicked the Paint button in the previous steps, you displayed the Paint Jump List, which included the image files you opened for Jodi, such as Buffalo, Elephant, and Lion. If you want to make sure you can always access one of those files, you can pin it to the Jump List. To open a pinned file, you right-click the Paint button on the taskbar to display the Jump List, and then click the recent or favorite file you want to open in Paint.

Jodi plans to use the Lion image file often, so you'll show her how to pin the file to the Paint Jump List and then open the file from the taskbar.

To pin a file to the Paint Jump List:

▶ **1.** Right-click the **Paint** button on the taskbar to display the Jump List.

▶ **2.** Point to **Lion**, and then click the **Pin to this list** icon to pin Lion to the Jump List. See Figure 3-45. The items in your Paint Jump List might be different.

Figure 3-45	**File pinned to the Paint Jump List**

Paint Jump List

Lion file is pinned to the Paint Jump List

   Trouble? If your Jump List does not include the Lion file, pin a different image file to the list.

▶ **3.** To open the Lion file in Paint, click **Lion** on the Jump List. Paint starts and opens the Lion image file.

▶ **4.** Close the Paint window.

Jodi says that the changes you made to the taskbar will help her work more efficiently. She'd also like to adjust the position of the taskbar buttons. She uses the File Explorer button more frequently than the Internet Explorer button, and she asks you to move the File Explorer button to the far left side of the taskbar for easy access.

Review Assignments

PRACTICE

See the Starting Data Files section at the beginning of this tutorial for a list of Data Files needed for the Review Assignments.

Preserve Africa keeps a computer in its conference area for any staff member to use when needed. Jodi asks you to customize that computer so it is appropriate for the organization. Jodi recently received photographs of wildlife in Kenyan game preserves and wants to make the photos available to staff members to use in promotional materials. As you perform the following steps, note the original settings of the desktop and other items so you can restore them later. Complete the following steps:

1. Insert the USB flash drive or other removable media containing your Data Files in the appropriate drive, and then create a shortcut to this drive on the desktop. Use **Review Removable Disk Shortcut** as the name of the shortcut.

2. Use the Review Removable Disk Shortcut on the desktop to copy the five image files in the Windows3\Review folder provided with your Data Files to a new folder in the Public Pictures folder. Use **Wildlife** as the name of the new folder.

3. Pin the Windows Reader app to the Start screen.

4. Pin the WordPad and Paint desktop apps to the Start screen.

5. Pin the Wildlife folder (which you created in Step 2) to the Start screen.

6. Complete the following tasks to create and pin a custom shortcut to the Start screen:
   - On the desktop, create a custom shortcut to the Restart command.
   - Name the shortcut **Restart**.
   - Change the icon to display an appropriate image.
   - Pin the Restart shortcut to the Start screen.
   - Delete the Restart shortcut icon from the desktop.

7. Add the Reader tile to a larger group of Windows 8 apps. Create an unnamed group for the Restart tile. Use **Promos** as the name of the group containing only the WordPad, Paint, and Wildlife tiles.

8. Apply a different design to the Start screen background. Change the color scheme to one that uses at least one shade of blue.

9. Change the user picture to display one of the images stored in the Wildlife folder.

10. Complete the following tasks to create a screen shot of your Start screen:
    - Display the Start screen, scroll to the right, and then press the Print Screen key to capture an image of the Start screen.
    - Start Paint, and then press the Ctrl+V keys to paste the image in the Paint file.
    - Save the file as **Review Start XY**, where *XY* are your initials, in the Windows3\Review folder provided with your Data Files.

11. Change the desktop icon settings on your computer to display the Computer and Control Panel icons in addition to the default Recycle Bin icon. Change the image for the Computer icon so that it displays any other appropriate image.

12. Change the desktop theme to any other theme that displays photographs.

13. Change the screen saver to play a slide show of the images in the Wildlife folder. Close all open windows.

14. Complete the following steps to open and work with Paint:
    - Use Paint to open the Impala image in the Wildlife folder, and then pin Paint to the taskbar.
    - Pin the Impala image file to the Paint Jump List.

15. Use Snap to align the Paint window on the right side of the desktop.

16. Press the Print Screen key to capture an image of the desktop. In Paint, press the Ctrl+V keys to paste the image in the Paint file. Save the file as **Review Desktop XY**, where *XY* are your initials, in the Windows3\Review folder provided with your Data Files.

17. Complete the following tasks to restore the settings on your computer:
   - Unpin the Windows Reader app from the Start screen.
   - Unpin the WordPad, Paint, Wildlife, and Restart tiles from the Start screen.
   - Apply the original design and color scheme to the Start screen background.
   - Restore the default image for the user picture.
   - On the desktop, restore the image of the Computer icon, and then display the original set of icons on the desktop.
   - Change the desktop theme to Windows and restore the original setting for the screen saver.
   - Unpin the Impala image file from the Paint Jump List, and then unpin Paint from the taskbar.
   - Delete the Wildlife folder in the Public Pictures folder.
   - Delete the Review Removable Disk Shortcut icon from the desktop.
18. Close any open windows.
19. Submit the results of the preceding steps to your instructor, either in printed or electronic form, as requested.

Case Problem 1

APPLY

See the Starting Data Files section at the beginning of this tutorial for a list of Data Files needed for this Case Problem.

Santa Fe Productions   Roddy Hampton started Santa Fe Productions to provide multimedia shows and exhibits for area businesses so they can showcase their products and services at trade shows and conventions. His most effective presentations use vintage images. When he is not installing a multimedia project, Roddy manages 10 employees in an office on the outskirts of Santa Fe, New Mexico. He has hired you to help him run the office. Because he just installed Windows 8, he asks you to personalize the Start screen and desktop on his computer to focus on multimedia and business tools. As you perform the following steps, note the original settings of the Start screen and desktop so you can restore them later. Complete the following steps:

1. Insert the USB flash drive or other removable media containing your Data Files in the appropriate drive, and then create a shortcut to this drive on the desktop. Use **Case1 Removable Disk Shortcut** as the name of the shortcut.
2. Use the Case1 Removable Disk Shortcut on the desktop to copy the five image files in the Windows3\Case1 folder provided with your Data Files to a new folder in the Public Pictures folder. Use **Vintage** as the name of the new folder.
3. Unpin the News, Weather, Sports, and Games tiles from the Start screen.
4. Pin the Paint and Windows Media Player desktop apps to the Start screen. (*Hint*: The Windows Media Player is a desktop accessory.)
5. Pin the Vintage folder (which you created in Step 2) to the Start screen.
6. Complete the following tasks to create and pin a custom shortcut to the Start screen:
   - On the desktop, create a custom shortcut to the Shut down command.
   - Name the shortcut **Shut down**.
   - Change the icon to display an appropriate image.
   - Pin the Shut down shortcut to the Start screen.
   - Delete the Shut down shortcut icon from the desktop.
7. Create an unnamed group for the Shut down tile. Use the name **Multimedia** for the group containing the Paint, Windows Media Player, and Vintage tiles.
8. Apply a different design to the Start screen background, and then change the color scheme to one that uses at least one shade of gray.
9. Change the user picture to display one of the images stored in the Vintage folder.

10. Display the Start screen, scroll to the right, and then press the Print Screen key to capture an image of the Start screen. Start Paint and then press the Ctrl+V keys to paste the image in the Paint file. Save the file as **Case1 Start XY**, where *XY* are your initials, in the Windows3\Case1 folder provided with your Data Files.

11. Complete the following tasks to add desktop icons to the desktop:

    • Change the desktop icon settings on your computer to display the Computer, User's Files, and Control Panel icons in addition to the default Recycle Bin icon.

    • Change the image for the User's Files icon so that it displays any other appropriate image.

12. Change the desktop theme to any other theme (including an online theme) that seems appropriate for Santa Fe Productions. Close Internet Explorer, if necessary.

13. Change the color of the window borders and taskbar to Color 14.

14. Open the Screen Saver Settings dialog box and select the Bubbles screen saver, if necessary. Move the dialog box so that some or all of the desktop items are clearly visible. Use a taskbar tool to minimize other open windows.

15. Press the Print Screen key to capture an image of the desktop. Make Paint the active window, and then press the Ctrl+V keys to paste the image in the Paint file. Save the file as **Case1 Desktop XY**, where *XY* are your initials, in the Windows3\Case1 folder provided with your Data Files.

16. Complete the following tasks to restore the settings on your computer:

    • Pin the News, Sports, Weather, and Games apps to the Start screen, and then add them to the groups of Windows 8 tiles.

    • Unpin the Paint, Windows Media Player, Vintage, and Shut down tiles from the Start screen.

    • Apply the original design and color scheme to the Start screen background.

    • Restore the original user picture.

    • Display the original set of icons on the desktop and then restore the original image for the User's Files icon.

    • Change the desktop theme to Windows, and then delete any themes you downloaded.

    • Delete the Vintage folder in the Public Pictures folder.

    • Delete the Case1 Removable Disk Shortcut icon from the desktop.

17. Close any open windows.

18. Submit the results of the preceding steps to your instructor, either in printed or electronic form, as requested.

Case Problem 2

CHALLENGE

See the Starting Data Files section at the beginning of this tutorial for a list of Data Files needed for this Case Problem.

Sennett-Hayes Restoration   Charlie Sennett and Lance Hayes own a furniture restoration company in New Haven, Connecticut. To promote their services, they provide computers in their showroom and invite people to browse their catalog, learn about furniture styles, and track the progress of their restoration project. You are the office manager for Sennett-Hayes Restoration and work with the staff and customers to help them use the company's resources. After installing Windows 8 on all of the office computers, Charlie asks you to personalize the desktop so it reflects the Sennett-Hayes company image. As you perform the following steps, note the original settings of the Start screen and desktop so you can restore them later. Complete the following steps:

1. Insert the USB flash drive or other removable media containing your Data Files in the appropriate drive, and then create a shortcut to this drive on the desktop. Use **Case2 Removable Disk Shortcut** as the name of the shortcut.

2. Use the Case2 Removable Disk Shortcut on the desktop to copy the five image files in the Windows3\Case2 folder provided with your Data Files to a new folder in the Public Pictures folder. Use **Furniture** as the name of the new folder.

3. Pin the following items to the Start screen: WordPad desktop app, Control Panel, and the Furniture folder.

✛ **Explore** 4. Make the Weather tile a live tile. (*Hint:* If necessary, start the Weather app, and then specify a location.)

5. Change the Start screen color scheme to one that uses black.

6. Change the user picture to display one of the images stored in the Furniture folder.

7. Display the Start screen, scroll to the right, and then press the Print Screen key to capture an image of the Start screen. Start Paint, and then press the Ctrl+V keys to paste the image in the Paint file. Save the file as **Case2 Start XY**, where *XY* are your initials, in the Windows3\Case2 folder provided with your Data Files.

8. Change the desktop icon settings on your computer to display the Network and Control Panel icons in addition to the default Recycle Bin icon. Change the image for the Network icon so that it displays any other appropriate image.

9. Change the desktop theme to any other available theme besides Windows. Select one image other than the first one to display as wallpaper.

10. Change the color of the window borders and taskbar to Color 8.

11. Save the current desktop settings as a theme for sharing. Name the theme **Sennett-Hayes**, and store it in the Windows3\Case2 folder.

12. Change the screen saver to Mystify. Leave the Personalization window open, but close any other open windows.

13. Auto-hide the taskbar.

14. Hide the taskbar and then press the Print Screen key to capture an image of the desktop. Make Paint the active window, and then press the Ctrl+V keys to paste the image in the Paint file. Save the file as **Case2 Desktop XY**, where *XY* are your initials, in the Windows3\Case2 folder provided with your Data Files.

✛ **Explore** 15. Complete the following tasks to restore the settings on your computer:
   • Delete the Furniture folder from the Public Pictures folder on your hard disk.
   • Unpin the WordPad, Control Panel, and Furniture tiles from the Start screen.
   • Apply the default color scheme to the Start screen background.
   • Restore the default image for the user picture.
   • Turn off the live tile feature for the Weather tile.
   • Display the original set of icons on the desktop and restore the default image for the Network icon.
   • Change the desktop theme to Windows, and then delete the Sennett-Hayes theme.
   • Restore the taskbar to its default state.
   • Delete the Case2 Removable Disk Shortcut icon from the desktop.

16. Close any open windows.

17. Submit the results of the preceding steps to your instructor, either in printed or electronic form, as requested.

Case Problem 3

See the Starting Data Files section at the beginning of this tutorial for a list of Data Files needed for this Case Problem.

Skyway Balloons   Brianna Sylvester is the manager of Skyway Balloons in Topeka, Kansas. Brianna provides piloted hot air balloons for people who enjoy the recreation of ballooning. Each balloon in the Skyway fleet is identified by color or design, and many have become attractions throughout the Topeka area. Brianna recently hired you as an assistant to provide customer service and general office support. She has a visual impairment and asks you to customize her computer so she can use it more effectively. As you perform the following steps, note the original settings of the desktop and other items so you can restore them later. Complete the following steps:

1. Insert the USB flash drive or other removable media containing your Data Files in the appropriate drive, and then create a shortcut to this drive on the desktop. Use **Case3 Removable Disk Shortcut** as the name of the shortcut.

2. Use the Removable Disk Shortcut on the desktop to copy the five image files in the Windows3\Case3 folder provided with your Data Files to a new folder in the Public Pictures library. Use **Balloons** as the name of the new folder.

3. Pin the following items to the Start screen: Paint desktop app, Magnifier desktop app, Narrator desktop app, and the Balloons folder.

Explore 4. Complete the following tasks to rearrange the tiles on the Start screen:
   - Unpin four small tiles for Windows 8 apps from the Start screen. (Note which tiles you remove so you can pin them later.)
   - Increase the size of two small tiles so that most Windows 8 apps have large tiles. (Note which tiles you expand so you can restore them to their original size later.)

Explore 5. Complete the following tasks to make the Start screen easier for Brianna to use:
   - Use the PC settings screen to display the Ease of Access settings.
   - Turn on high contrast.
   - Increase the cursor thickness to 5.

6. Display the Start screen, scroll to the far right, and then press the Print Screen key to capture an image of the Start screen. Start Paint, and then press the Ctrl+V keys to paste the image in the Paint file. Save the file as **Case3 Start XY**, where XY are your initials, in the Windows3\Case3 folder provided with your Data Files.

7. Change the desktop icon settings on your computer to display all of the built-in desktop icons. Change the image for the Computer icon so that it displays any other appropriate image.

Explore 8. Use the desktop shortcut menu to change the view of the desktop so it displays large icons. (*Hint*: Right-click the desktop, point to View, and then click Large icons.)

9. Change the desktop theme to a High Contrast theme of your choice.

10. Make Paint the active window and then pin Paint to the taskbar.

11. Use Paint to open the five images in the Balloons folder. Pin each image to the Paint Jump List.

Explore 12. Start the Magnifier desktop app and then use it to magnify any part of the desktop.

13. Right-click the Paint program button on the taskbar to display its Jump List. Press the Print Screen key to capture an image of the desktop. Make Paint the active window, and then press the Ctrl+V keys to paste the image in the Paint file. Save the file as **Case3 Desktop XY**, where XY are your initials, in the Windows3\Case3 folder provided with your Data Files. Click the magnifying glass icon and then click the Close button to close Magnifier.

14. Complete the following tasks to restore the settings on your computer:
   - Delete the Case3 Removable Disk Shortcut icon from the desktop.
   - Unpin the Paint, Magnifier, Narrator, and Balloons tiles from the Start screen.
   - Restore the Ease of Access options to their original settings.
   - Restore the original size of the tiles you expanded.
   - Pin the tiles you removed from the Start screen.
   - Move the Windows 8 tiles so they appear in two groups.
   - Unpin Paint from the taskbar, and then unpin the five balloon pictures from the Paint Jump List.
   - Display the original set of icons on the desktop and change the Computer icon to its default image.
   - Change the theme to Windows.
   - Change the view of the desktop so it displays Medium icons.
   - Delete the Balloons folder in the Public Pictures folder.

15. Close all open windows.

16. Submit the results of the preceding steps to your instructor, either in printed or electronic form, as requested.

Case Problem 4

There are no Data Files needed for this Case Problem.

Singh Satellite   After training to be a meteorologist, Dev Singh decided to start his own company providing satellite services to the airline industry in Houston, Texas. Dev recently upgraded all of the computers at Singh Satellite to Windows 8, and then hired you to manage the office. After working with a client in Dallas, Dev shows you a screen shot of that client's Start screen and another of his desktop. See Figure 3-48. He thinks the Start screen and desktop would be appropriate for the computers at Singh Satellite, and he asks you to re-create them on your computer.

Figure 3-48 | Model Start screen and desktop for Singh Satellite

To create this Start screen, complete the following:

1. Select the following settings for the Start screen:
   - Blue background with blue highlights
   - Make sure Travel, Bing, Weather, and Sports are live tiles (start each app and then turn on live tiles, if necessary)
   - Windows Media Player tile pinned to the Start screen
2. Select the following settings for the desktop:
   - Theme featuring abstract designs
   - Bubbles screen saver
3. Capture an image of the Start screen, and then save the image in a Paint file named **Case4 Start XY**, where *XY* are your initials, in the Windows3\Case4 folder provided with your Data Files.
4. Capture an image of the desktop with the Screen Saver Settings dialog box open, and then save the image in a Paint file named **Case4 Desktop XY**, where *XY* are your initials, in the Windows3\Case4 folder provided with your Data Files.
5. Restore the original settings, and then close all open windows.
6. Resubmit the results from the previous steps to your instructor either in printed or electronic form, as requested.

Working with the Internet and Email

Communicating with Others

OBJECTIVES

Session 4.1
- Define the relationship between the Internet and the Web
- Open, view, and navigate Web pages in Internet Explorer
- Revisit recently opened Web pages
- Organize links to your favorite Web pages
- Use RSS feeds and Accelerators

Session 4.2
- Explain how email works
- Send, receive, reply to, and delete email with Mail
- Attach a file to an email message
- Add a contact using People
- Create appointments with Calendar

Case | *San Antonio Historical Association*

Jason Rowley is the director of the San Antonio Historical Association (SAHA) in San Antonio, Texas. SAHA works to preserve historic structures, provides guided walking tours of San Antonio, and offers workshops to residents and visitors about San Antonio history, culture, and architecture. One of the organization's most popular workshops is on genealogy, which teaches participants how to begin genealogical research, where to search, and how to find information on family histories. Recently, Jason hired you as a project assistant to help him run the historical association. He wants to learn about using online resources to research ancestries so he can conduct sessions of the genealogy workshop. You regularly use Microsoft Internet Explorer to gather information for SAHA on the World Wide Web. You also use the Windows 8 Mail app to exchange email with SAHA's members and visitors. Jason has asked you to get him up to speed on using these programs.

In this tutorial, you'll explore how the Internet and the Web work, and use Internet Explorer to visit and organize Web pages. You'll examine email technology and use Mail to send, receive, and reply to email messages. You'll also use two Windows 8 apps to manage your contacts and your schedule.

STARTING DATA FILES

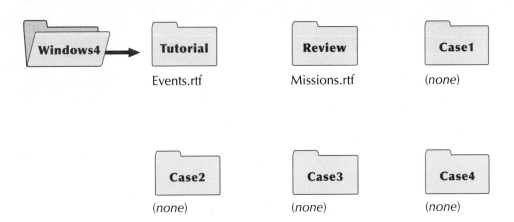

| Windows4 → | Tutorial | Review | Case1 |
| | Events.rtf | Missions.rtf | (*none*) |

| Case2 | Case3 | Case4 |
| (*none*) | (*none*) | (*none*) |

Session 4.1 Visual Overview:

In IE Windows 8, the **tab switcher** is an area that displays thumbnails of current or recently visited Web pages for easy navigation between them.

Windows 8 provides two versions of Internet Explorer: **IE Windows 8**, shown here on the left, and **IE Desktop**, shown here on the right.

Internet Explorer is a **Web browser**, a program that locates, retrieves, and displays Web pages.

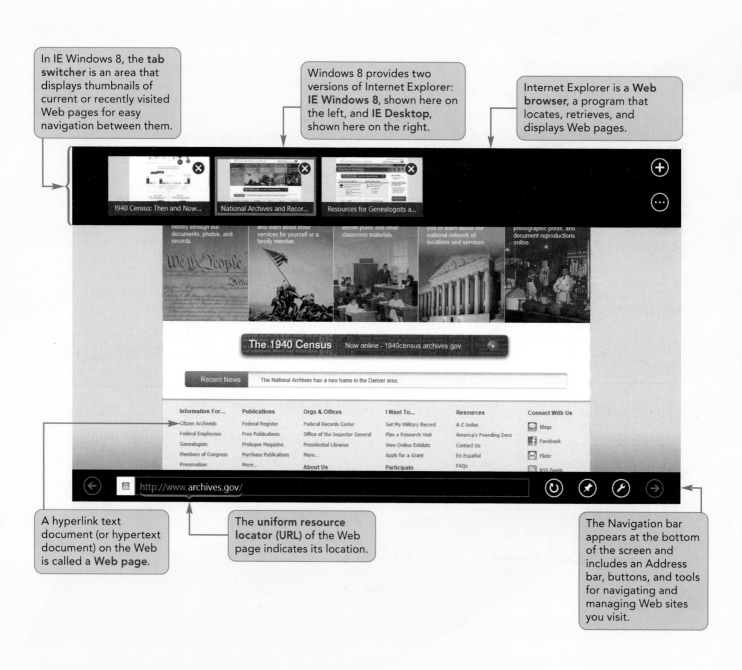

A hyperlink text document (or hypertext document) on the Web is called a **Web page**.

The **uniform resource locator (URL)** of the Web page indicates its location.

The Navigation bar appears at the bottom of the screen and includes an Address bar, buttons, and tools for navigating and managing Web sites you visit.

Courtesy of the National Archives and Records Administration; United States Census Bureau

Microsoft Internet Explorer

The **Favorites Center** displays links to your favorites, feeds, and recently visited Web pages.

The **Favorites bar** contains buttons for feeds and links to pages you view often.

A **hyperlink** (or **link**) is text or a graphic in a Web document that targets another part of the document or a different document altogether.

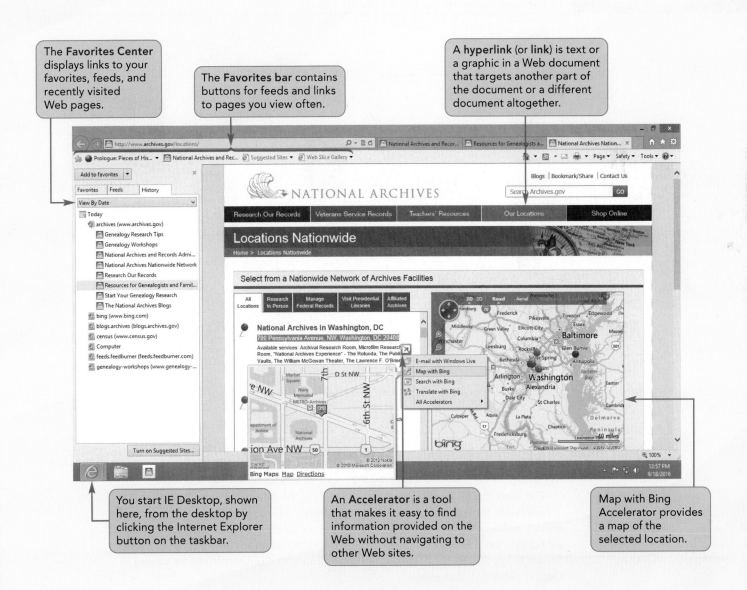

You start IE Desktop, shown here, from the desktop by clicking the Internet Explorer button on the taskbar.

An **Accelerator** is a tool that makes it easy to find information provided on the Web without navigating to other Web sites.

Map with Bing Accelerator provides a map of the selected location.

Exploring the Internet and the Web

When you connect two or more computers to exchange information and resources, they form a **network**. You can connect networks to each other to share information across a wide area. The worldwide, publicly accessible collection of networks is called the Internet, and it consists of millions of computers linked to networks all over the world. The Internet lets you access and exchange information via electronic mail (email), online newsgroups, file transfer, and the linked documents of the **World Wide Web**, better known as the **Web**. See Figure 4-1.

Figure 4-1	Connecting computers to the Internet

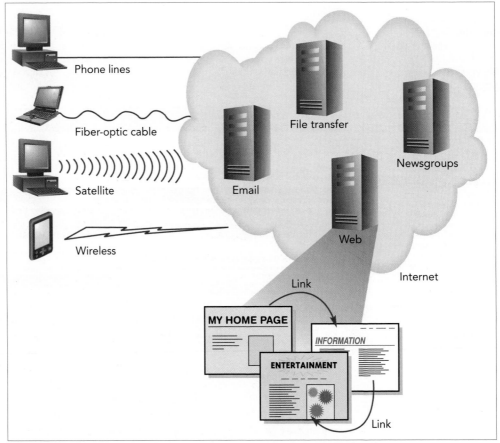

© 2014 Cengage Learning

The Web is a service that you can access via the Internet. While the Internet is a collection of networks connected by communication media such as fiber-optic cables and wireless connections, the Web is a collection of documents connected by hyperlinks. You click a link to display the targeted information. For example, in Figure 4-2, you can click links on the first Library of Congress Web document to display related documents.

| Figure 4-2 | Library of Congress Web page with links to other Web pages |

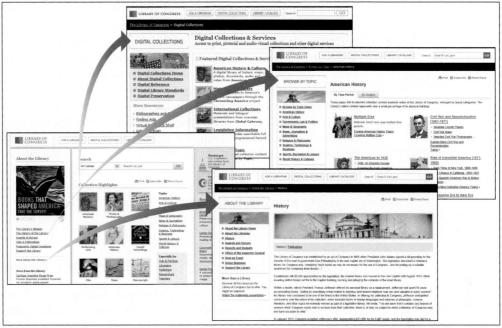

Courtesy of the Library of Congress

Web pages are stored on Internet computers called **Web servers**. A **Web site** is a collection of Web pages that have a common theme or focus, such as all pages containing information about the Library of Congress. The Web is appealing because it generally displays up-to-date information in a colorful, lively format that can use sound, video, and animation.

When you want to find information on the Web, you typically use a **search engine**, which is a program that conducts searches to retrieve Web pages. To work with a search engine, you enter a word or an expression as the search criteria. The search engine lists links to Web pages that fit your criteria. Popular general search engines include Google and Bing.

A recent innovation in Web technology is called **cloud computing**, which refers to providing and using computer tools, such as software, via the Internet (or the cloud). With cloud computing you can use your Web browser to access and work with software. You do not need to purchase and install a complete application. Instead, you use the software services you need for free or for a usage fee. For example, when you use a Web mapping service, such as MapQuest or Google Maps, to find directions from one location to another, you are using cloud computing. The software and data for the maps are not stored on your computer—they're on the cloud at the mapping service's Web site. This software is known as a **Web app**. For example, the Microsoft Office Web apps are provided on the cloud as simplified versions of the programs provided in Microsoft Office, such as Word and Excel.

Using Web Browsers

You use a Web browser, or browser, to visit Web sites around the world; interact with Web pages by clicking links; view multimedia documents; transfer files, images, videos, and sounds to and from your computer; conduct searches for specific topics; and run programs on other computers. The browser included with Windows 8 is called Internet Explorer.

When you attempt to view a Web page, your browser locates and retrieves the document from the Web server and displays its contents on your computer. The server stores the Web page in one location, and browsers anywhere in the world can display it.

For your browser to access the Web, you must have an Internet connection. In a university setting, your connection might come from your campus network. If you are working on a home computer, you have a few options for connecting to the Internet. Most likely, you are using a **broadband connection**, a high-capacity, high-speed medium for connecting to the Internet. Popular broadband technologies include a **digital subscriber line (DSL)**, which is a high-speed connection through your telephone line, and **digital cable**, which uses a cable modem attached to cable television lines. A **wireless connection** uses infrared light or radio-frequency signals to communicate with devices that are physically connected to a network or the Internet. Home connections also require an account with an **Internet service provider (ISP)**, a company that sells Internet access. The ISP provides instructions for connecting your computer to one of its servers, which is connected to the Internet. You can then use your browser to visit Web sites and access other Internet services.

Getting Started with Microsoft Internet Explorer

Microsoft Internet Explorer, the Web browser that comes with Windows 8, lets you communicate, access, and share information on the Web. Internet Explorer (IE) is available in two versions on your system: IE Windows 8 and IE Desktop. (See the Session 4.1 Visual Overview.) As its name suggests, IE Windows 8, which you open from the Start screen, uses the Windows 8 interface. Its clean design lets you focus on Web page content instead of browser controls. Large buttons, thumbnails, and horizontal scrolling make IE Windows 8 ideal if you are using a touchscreen device. IE Desktop, which you open from the desktop, includes toolbars, menus, and other controls designed for a pointing device such as a mouse. In general, you use IE Windows 8 when you are working with the Start screen or a Windows 8 app and want to quickly browse to a Web page or search for information. Choose IE Desktop when you are working on the desktop or with a desktop app and want to perform more extensive online tasks, such as saving a collection of sites as Favorites, viewing online media, or using Web apps.

When you start either version of Internet Explorer, it opens to a **home page**, which is the Web page a browser is set to open by default. The default home page for Internet Explorer is the Bing Web page, the Microsoft search engine. Your computer manufacturer or school might have set up a different home page.

Your first step in showing Jason how to research genealogy is to start Internet Explorer. Because your computer displays the Start screen after you sign in, you'll show Jason how to use IE Windows 8 first. You must be connected to the Internet to perform all of the steps in this session. Mute your speakers, if necessary, so the sounds that certain Web pages play do not disturb others.

To start IE Windows 8:

▶ **1.** Click the **Internet Explorer** tile on the Start screen. IE Windows 8 opens to its home page. Figure 4-3 shows the Bing main page in IE Windows 8. You might have a different home page.

Trouble? If a Network Connection dialog box opens, enter your user name and password, and then click the Connect button. If you do not know your user name or password, ask your instructor or technical support person for help; you must have an Internet connection to complete the steps in this tutorial.

Figure 4-3 IE Windows 8

When you start IE Windows 8, it displays your home page in the main part of the screen and a Navigation bar at the bottom. The Navigation bar includes the following tools:

- Address bar—View the address of the Web page; you can also type the address of a Web page you want to visit
- Back and Forward buttons—Browse to the previous or next Web page in a sequence of opened pages
- Page tools button—Download an app if the site provides one, find text on the page, or view the page in the desktop version of Internet Explorer
- Pin site button—Pin the current Web page to the Start screen
- Refresh button—Refresh the contents of the Web page

Now you're ready to use IE Windows 8 to open and view a Web page.

Opening a Page on the Web

To find a particular Web page among the billions stored on Web servers, your browser needs to know the uniform resource locator (URL) of the Web page. URLs are like addresses—they indicate the location of a Web page. As shown in Figure 4-4, a URL can consist of the following four parts:

- Protocol to use when transferring the Web page
- Address of the Web server storing the page
- Pathname of the folder containing the page
- Filename of the Web page

| Figure 4-4 | Parts of a URL |

© 2014 Cengage Learning

The URL for most Web pages starts with http, which stands for **Hypertext Transfer Protocol**, the most common way to transfer information around the Web. (A **protocol** is a standardized procedure computers use to exchange information.) When the URL for a Web page starts with http://, the Web browser uses Hypertext Transfer Protocol to retrieve the page.

The server address indicates the location of the Web server storing the Web page. In *www.loc.gov*, the *www* indicates that the server is a Web server, *loc* is the name the Library of Congress chose for this Web site, and *.gov* means that a government entity runs the Web server. Other common types of Web servers in the United States are .com (commercial), .net (network server providers or resources), .org (not-for-profit organizations), and .edu (educational institutions). The server address in a URL corresponds to an Internet Protocol (IP) address, which identifies every computer on the Internet. An **IP address** is a unique number that consists of four sets of numbers from 0 to 255 separated by periods, or dots, as in 216.35.148.4. Although computers can use IP addresses easily, they are difficult for people to remember, so domain names were created. A **domain name** identifies one or more IP addresses, such as loc.gov. URLs use the domain name in the server address part of the URL to identify a particular Web site.

In addition, each file stored on a Web server has a unique pathname, just like files stored on a disk. The pathname in a URL includes the names of the folders containing the file, the filename, and its extension. A common filename extension for Web pages is .html, or just .htm. For example, the pathname might be library/index.html, which specifies a file named index.html stored in a folder named library.

Not all URLs include a pathname. If you don't specify a pathname or filename in a URL, most Web browsers open a file named index.htm or index.html, which is the default name for a Web site's main page.

Opening a Web Page Using a URL

One way to open a Web page in Internet Explorer is to enter a URL, which you can often find in advertisements, in informational materials, and on the Web. You enter the URL in the Address bar of Internet Explorer.

In most cases, URLs are not case sensitive, so you can enter a URL using all lowercase or all uppercase text. However, if the Web server storing a Web page uses the UNIX operating system, the URL might be case sensitive. For mixed-case URLs, it's safer to enter them using the mixed case exactly as printed.

The first Web page you want to open for Jason is the home page of the U.S. Census Bureau, which has been providing statistics and information about the population and economy in the United States since 1790 and is a source of information for genealogists.

To open a page on the Web using a URL:

▶ **1.** Click the **Address bar** to select its contents, which should be the URL for your home page. Anything you now type replaces the selected URL. When you click the Address bar, the Navigation bar expands to show tiles for Web pages you've visited frequently and for any Web pages you pinned to the Start screen. You'll use the expanded Navigation bar in another set of steps.

> **Trouble?** If the contents of the Address bar are not selected, drag to select the entire address.

2. Type **www.census.gov** in the Address bar. As you type, Internet Explorer displays the names of other Web pages you've opened that have URLs starting with the same characters, a feature called AutoComplete.

3. Press the **Enter** key. Internet Explorer adds the http:// protocol to the URL for you, and then opens the main, or home, page for the U.S. Census Bureau Web site. See Figure 4-5.

> **Trouble?** If you receive a Not Found error message, you might have typed the URL incorrectly. Repeat Steps 1–3, making sure that the URL in the Address bar matches the URL in Step 2. If you still receive an error message, ask your instructor or technical support person for help.

> **Trouble?** If a window opens inviting you to download an app, click the Continue to Census.gov button.

| Figure 4-5 | Opening the U.S. Census Bureau home page |

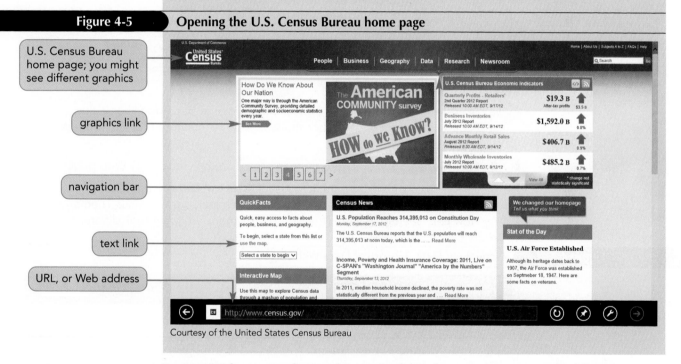

Courtesy of the United States Census Bureau

Because Web content changes frequently, the Web pages you open might differ from the figures in this tutorial.

A home page on the Web can have at least two meanings. It can be the Web page a browser is set to open by default. It can also be the main page for a Web site that provides links to other Web pages with related information.

Navigating with Links

The home page for a typical Web site includes plenty of links to help you navigate to its Web pages, and those pages also include links you can click to navigate from one page to another. Links can be text, images, or a combination of both. Text links are usually colored and underlined, though the exact style can vary from one Web site to another. To determine whether something on a Web page is a link, point to it. If the pointer changes to 🖑, the text or image is a link you can click to open a Web page. For some graphics links, a ScreenTip appears next to your pointer.

Jason's grandparents immigrated to the United States from northern England in 1940. You'll show Jason how to find information about the U.S. population in 1940 on the Census Bureau Web site.

To navigate a Web site using links:

1. Point to **People** on the site's Navigation bar. The pointer changes to 🖑 and a menu of links in the People category appears below the Navigation bar. See Figure 4-6.

Figure 4-6	Pointing to a link

People link on the Census Bureau home page

link pointer

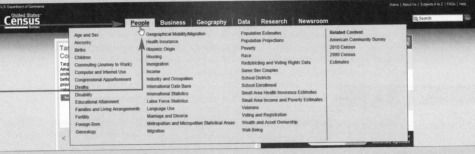

Courtesy of the United States Census Bureau

Trouble? If the current U.S Census Bureau home page does not include a People link, point to any other similar link and substitute that link when you perform Step 2.

2. Click **Genealogy** in the People menu to open the Genealogy Web page.

3. In the Quick Links list on the left, click **Historical Data** to open the Genealogy Data: Historical Data page, which includes a Census Then and Now link. See Figure 4-7. The Web page you open might look different.

Figure 4-7	Genealogy Data: Historical Data Web page

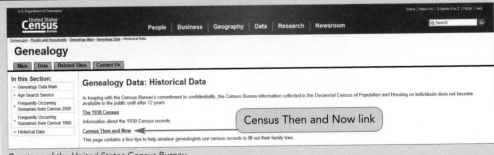

Courtesy of the United States Census Bureau

4. Click the **Census Then and Now** link to open the 1940 Census page, which illustrates how America has changed from 1940 to 2010.

   Trouble? If the Census Then and Now link does not appear on the current Web page, click any other link on the page.

5. Scroll to the bottom of the Census Then and Now page to review the entire illustration.

As you scroll the Census Then and Now page, Internet Explorer hides the tools on the Navigation bar so you can focus on the Web page content. You'll redisplay the Navigation bar and show other tools in IE Windows 8 shortly.

Displaying Web Pages Designed for Earlier Versions of Internet Explorer

IE Windows 8 and IE Desktop are versions of Internet Explorer 10. If you visit a Web site designed for earlier versions of Internet Explorer, the Web pages might not be formatted for Internet Explorer 10. For example, the Web page navigation bar, images, or text might appear out of place or the Web page might not scroll its full length. To improve the appearance of a Web site in your browser, you can turn on **Compatibility View**, which displays the page as it would appear in an earlier version of Internet Explorer. If Internet Explorer detects a Web page that might not appear correctly, the Compatibility View button appears on the Address bar. In IE Desktop, you can also click the Tools button on the Command bar and then click Compatibility View to reformat the current Web site. After turning on Compatibility View for a Web site, Internet Explorer displays the site in Compatibility View whenever you visit it unless the site is updated to appear correctly in Internet Explorer 10. In that case, Internet Explorer turns off Compatibility View and displays the site as designed.

Besides clicking links to navigate from one Web page to another, you can use tools that Internet Explorer provides.

Navigating with IE Windows 8 Tools

Recall that when you use File Explorer, you can click the Back and Forward buttons to navigate the devices and folders on your computer. IE Windows 8 includes similar buttons you can use to navigate from one Web page to another. IE Windows 8 keeps track of the pages you visited. To return to the previous page, you can click the left arrow button, which appears on your screen when you move the pointer to the left side of the screen. After you navigate to a previous page, you can click the right arrow button, which appears when you move the pointer to the right side of the screen, to continue to the next page in the sequence.

To return to previously viewed Web pages:

▶ **1.** Point to the left side of the screen, and then click the **left arrow button** |‹| to return to the Genealogy Data: Historical Data page.

▶ **2.** Point to the right side of the screen, and then click the **right arrow button** |›| to return to the Census Then and Now page.

Trouble? If you opened different Web pages in the previous set of steps, substitute the names of the pages as appropriate in Steps 1 and 2.

Besides using the arrow buttons in the middle of the screen to navigate Web pages, you can display the Navigation bar and use its Back and Forward buttons to navigate from one page to another. To display the Navigation bar, you right-click the background of a Web page. When you do so, the Navigation bar appears at the bottom of the screen and the tab switcher appears at the top of the screen, displaying thumbnails of currently opened Web pages. The tab switcher also provides tools for using **tabbed browsing**, a feature that lets you have more than one Web page open at the same time.

To display and use the IE Windows 8 Navigation bar:

▶ **1.** Right-click the background of the Web page to display the Navigation bar at the bottom of the screen and the tab switcher at the top of the screen. See Figure 4-8.

| Figure 4-8 | Navigation bar and tab switcher |

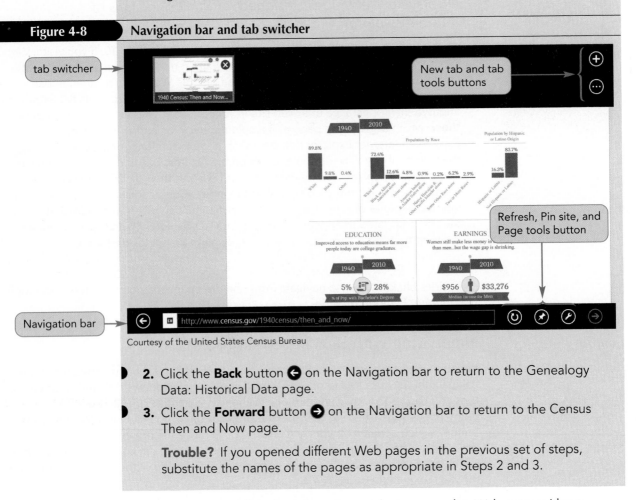

Courtesy of the United States Census Bureau

▶ **2.** Click the **Back** button ⊖ on the Navigation bar to return to the Genealogy Data: Historical Data page.

▶ **3.** Click the **Forward** button ⊖ on the Navigation bar to return to the Census Then and Now page.

Trouble? If you opened different Web pages in the previous set of steps, substitute the names of the pages as appropriate in Steps 2 and 3.

Next, you want to show Jason how to use tabs to open other Web pages without closing the Census Then and Now page.

Managing Web Pages in IE Windows 8

If you want to open a new Web page without closing the one you're currently viewing, you can use tabbed browsing to open more than one Web page at a time. To use tabbed browsing, you open a tab for each new page you want to view. To open a new tab, you can press the Ctrl key as you click a link on a Web page, or you can right-click the link and then click Open link in new tab on the shortcut menu. You can then switch from one Web page to another by clicking the tabs in the tab switcher. Each tab displays a thumbnail of its Web page so you can quickly identify the page you want to display. To close a tab, you click its Close Tab button in the Web page thumbnail on the tab switcher.

Now that you've explored a few pages on the Census Bureau Web site, you can compare that information to information on the National Archives Web site, which provides documents, photos, and records for people conducting family research. You'll show Jason how to open a new tab in IE Windows 8, and then use it to open the National Archives home page.

To open other Web pages on new tabs:

1. Right-click the background of the Web page to display the tab switcher, which includes a tab for the current Web page.

2. Click the **New Tab** button ⊕ on the tab switcher to open a blank page and to expand the Navigation bar to display lists of frequently visited and pinned pages.

3. Click in the **Address bar**, if necessary, type **www.archives.gov**, and then press the **Enter** key. The National Archives home page opens on the new tab. See Figure 4-9. The Web page you open might look different.

Figure 4-9   National Archives home page

National Archives home page

Genealogists link

URL entered in Address bar

Courtesy of the National Archives and Records Administration

4. Right-click the **Genealogists** link on the Web page, and then click **Open link in new tab** on the shortcut menu. The Resources for Genealogists Web page opens in a new tab, though the page is not visible yet. You need to display the tab switcher and then click the thumbnail for that page.

   Trouble? If the Genealogists link does not appear on the current Web page, right-click a different link on the page.

5. Right-click the background of the Web page to display the tab switcher, which includes thumbnails of each open Web page. See Figure 4-10.

Figure 4-10   Tabs for the open Web pages

three tabs open in IE Windows 8

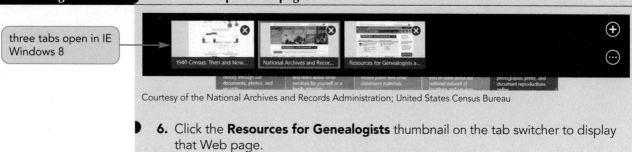

Courtesy of the National Archives and Records Administration; United States Census Bureau

6. Click the **Resources for Genealogists** thumbnail on the tab switcher to display that Web page.

Jason wants to be able to open the home pages for the Census Bureau and National Archives Web sites quickly, without entering the URL in the Address bar. You'll show him how to do so next.

Pinning Web Pages

When you find a Web site that you'll return to often, you can pin the site to the Start screen. Windows organizes all pinned sites into a group. However, you can further organize them into smaller groups if you pin many sites to the Start screen. To help you identify a pinned Web site at a glance, the tile for a pinned site reflects the site's color and icon. If you have an account on a Web site that displays messages or other account information, such as Twitter or Facebook, you can make the pinned site a live tile so it displays messages on the tile.

Pinning a site places a tile for the site on the Start screen and in the browser. When you click the Address bar, pinned sites appear on the left and tiles for sites you visit frequently appear on the right. In the browser, the tiles appear in the order you pinned them.

Because Jason wants to access the home pages for the Census Bureau and National Archives Web sites quickly, you'll pin the sites to the Start screen.

To pin Web sites to the Start screen:

▶ 1. Right-click the background of the Web page and then click the **National Archives** thumbnail on the tab switcher to display the National Archives home page.

▶ 2. Click the **Pin site** button ⊗ on the Navigation bar and then click **Pin to Start**. A text box appears, showing the name of the Web page. You can accept the default name, change it to a more meaningful name, or in this case, shorten it.

▶ 3. Select the text in the text box, type **National Archives**, and then click the **Pin site** button to pin the site to the Start screen.

TIP

You can also press the Backspace or Delete key to delete the text before typing a name for the pinned tile.

▶ 4. Right-click the background of the Web page, and then click the **1940 Census** thumbnail to display the 1940 Census Web page.

▶ 5. Click the **Address bar**, type **www.census.gov**, and then press the **Enter** key to display the home page for the Census Bureau Web site.

▶ 6. Click the **Pin site** button ⊗ on the Navigation bar, click **Pin to Start**, delete **Homepage** in the text box to shorten the name to "Census Bureau", and then click the **Pin to Start** button to pin the page to the Start screen.

   Trouble? If the Navigation bar is no longer open, right-click the background of the Web page to display the Navigation bar.

▶ 7. Drag the top of the IE Windows 8 app down until it shrinks to a thumbnail, and then continue dragging it to the very bottom of the screen to close IE Windows 8.

▶ 8. On the Start screen, scroll to the right to display the two tiles for the pinned sites. See Figure 4-11.

Figure 4-11   **Pinned sites on the Start screen**

9. Click the **National Archives** tile to open the site in IE Windows 8.

10. Click the **Address bar** to display tiles for frequently and recently visited Web pages and pinned sites. See Figure 4-12.

Figure 4-12   **Pinned sites in the browser**

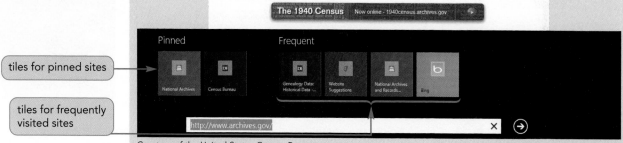

tiles for pinned sites

tiles for frequently visited sites

Courtesy of the United States Census Bureau

11. Click the **Census Bureau** tile to open the home page for the Census Bureau Web site.

Trouble? If a window opens inviting you to download an app, click Continue to Census.gov.

Now that Jason knows the basics of opening and navigating Web pages, he wants to learn how to search for a Web page and print it. He can do both using the Charms bar.

Using the Internet Explorer Charms Bar

You have already used the Charms bar to perform Windows tasks, such as searching for apps and accessing system settings. If you display the Charms bar while you are using IE Windows 8, you can perform Internet Explorer tasks, such as searching for Web sites, printing Web page content, and selecting IE Windows 8 settings. When you search the Web, IE Windows 8 uses the primary search engine, which is Bing by default. You can change the primary search engine if you prefer a different one.

Jason wants to find information about other genealogy workshops, so he asks you to search for Web pages that describe the workshops.

To search for and prepare to print a Web page:

1. Point to the upper-right corner of the screen to display the Charms bar.

2. Click the **Search** charm to display the Search Internet Explorer menu.

3. Type **genealogy workshops** in the Search box, and then press the **Enter** key. IE Windows 8 displays the results using your specified search engine. See Figure 4-13. Your results and search engine may differ.

Figure 4-13   **Search Internet Explorer menu and search results**

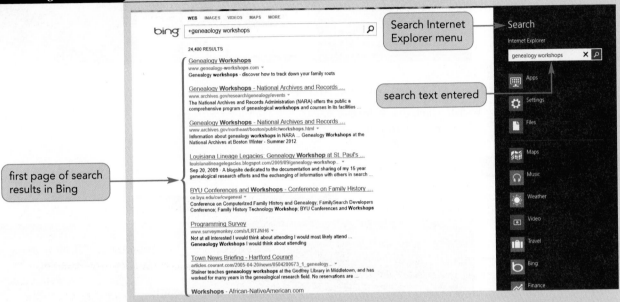

4. Click a link in the search results to display information about genealogy workshops.

5. Point to the upper-right corner of the screen to display the Charms bar again, and then click the **Devices** charm to display a list of devices Internet Explorer can use for printing. See Figure 4-14. Your list of devices will differ.

Figure 4-14   **IE Windows 8 Devices list**

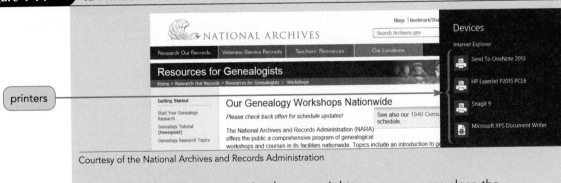

Courtesy of the National Archives and Records Administration

Jason doesn't want to print the page right now, so you can close the Devices menu.

6. Click a blank spot on the Web page to close the Devices menu.

You can also use the Charms bar to change IE Windows 8 settings and share a Web page via email.

Using Flip Ahead

If you find yourself visiting Web sites and then searching for a Next Page link to open the next page in a sequence, you can save time by using the **Flip ahead** feature. Flip ahead works with search results, articles printed on two or more Web pages, or any Web pages connected by Next Page buttons or links. For example, if you are browsing the results of a search in Google or Bing, you can use Flip ahead instead of scrolling to the bottom of the search results page and clicking a link to display the next page. You can also use Flip ahead if you are reading an online article, such as one published on a news Web site.

REFERENCE

Turning on Flip Ahead

- With IE Windows 8 open, display the Charms bar, and then click the Settings charm.
- Click Internet Options in the list of settings.
- Drag the Flip ahead slider from Off to On.

Flip ahead is turned off by default. To turn it on in IE Windows 8, you use the Internet Explorer Settings screen. When you view the first page of a multipage article, for example, or display the results of a Web search, the Forward button is activated in the Navigation bar. You can click the Forward button to display the next page of the article or search results.

Jason also wants to search for Web pages containing information about genealogy classes. You'll show him how to turn on Flip ahead and then use it to view search results.

To use Flip ahead:

1. Point to the upper-right corner of the screen to display the Charms bar, and then click the **Settings** charm to display a list of Internet Explorer settings.

2. Click **Internet Options** to display the Internet Explorer Settings screen. See Figure 4-15.

Figure 4-15   Internet Explorer Settings screen

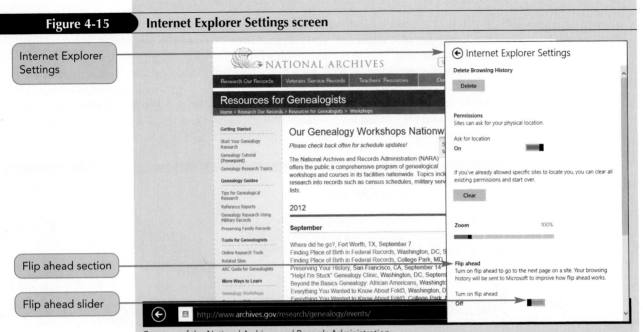

Internet Explorer
Settings

Flip ahead section

Flip ahead slider

Courtesy of the National Archives and Records Administration

3. In the Flip ahead section, drag the slider from Off to **On** to activate the Flip ahead feature.

4. Click a blank spot on the Web page to close the Internet Explorer Settings screen.

5. Display the Charms bar again, and then click the **Search** charm to display the Search Internet Explorer menu.

6. Type **genealogy classes** and then press the **Enter** key. Click the **Address bar** to close the Search menu but not the Navigation bar. Using the default search engine (Bing, in this case), IE Windows 8 displays the first page of links to Web pages about genealogy classes. Because this is the first of many pages of search results, the Forward button is active in the Navigation bar. See Figure 4-16. Your results and search engine may differ.

| Figure 4-16 | First page of search results |

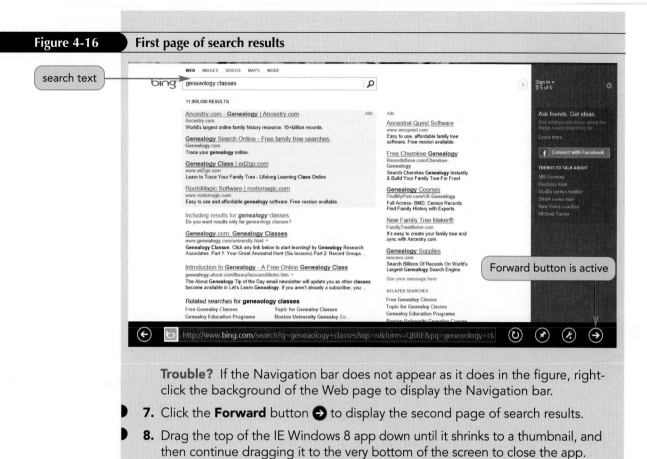

Trouble? If the Navigation bar does not appear as it does in the figure, right-click the background of the Web page to display the Navigation bar.

▶ **7.** Click the **Forward** button ➔ to display the second page of search results.

▶ **8.** Drag the top of the IE Windows 8 app down until it shrinks to a thumbnail, and then continue dragging it to the very bottom of the screen to close the app.

When you turn on the Flip ahead feature, you can still use the Back button on the Navigation bar as you usually do to navigate to the previous page you visited. To display the next page in a series of Web pages you visited during the current browser session, however, you use the right arrow button that appears in the middle of the screen when you move the mouse. The Forward button is reserved for navigating to the page a Web site designates as the next page in a sequence.

Next, you can switch to the desktop to use the other version of Internet Explorer 10—IE Desktop.

Using Internet Explorer on the Desktop

Using IE Desktop, you can perform all of the same tasks as you can with IE Windows 8, including opening Web pages, clicking links, navigating with Internet Explorer tools, and managing Web pages with tabbed browsing. The major difference between the two versions is the interface: IE Windows 8 is designed for touch browsing, while IE Desktop is designed for using a pointing device such as a mouse. IE Desktop features more controls and smaller buttons because you can make more precise selections with a pointer than you can with a fingertip. As mentioned earlier, the version you use depends on your current task. Usually, Windows starts the most appropriate version for you. For example, if you are working in a Windows 8 app and click a link to download a file or display information, Windows starts IE Windows 8. If you click a link while working in a desktop app, Windows starts IE Desktop.

IE Desktop provides more tools for Web browsing, especially if you are performing detailed work that requires precise control or lots of typing, such as using a Web app, completing forms, or conducting in-depth research. Jason asks you to start IE Desktop and give him a quick tour of its features.

To start Internet Explorer on the desktop:

1. Click the **Desktop** tile on the Start screen to display the desktop.

2. Click the **Internet Explorer** button 🅔 on the taskbar.

   Trouble? If a Connection dialog box opens, enter your user name and password, and then click the Connect button. If you do not know your user name or password, ask your instructor or technical support person for help; you must have an Internet connection to complete the steps in this tutorial.

3. If necessary, click the **Maximize** button ▢ to maximize the Internet Explorer window. Figure 4-17 shows the Bing home page in the Internet Explorer window. You might have a different home page.

Figure 4-17 IE Desktop window

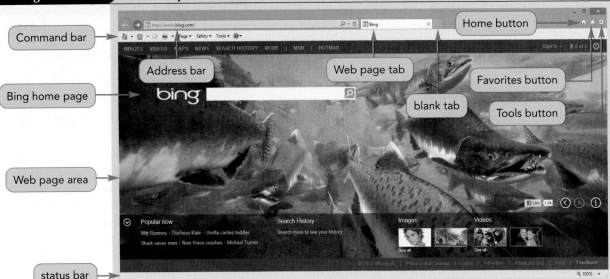

Trouble? If your IE Desktop window does not display the Command bar, right-click a blank area to the right of the tabs, and then click Command bar on the shortcut menu.

Trouble? If your Internet Explorer window does not display a status bar, click the Tools button on the Command bar, point to Toolbars, and then click Status bar.

The IE Desktop window includes the following elements:

- Address bar—Shows the address, or URL, of the Web page; you can also type an address here
- Command bar—Contains buttons you can click to perform common tasks, such as displaying the home page and printing a Web page

- Favorites button—Lets you open a pane displaying Web pages you've identified as favorites
- Home button—Lets you open the Web page specified as the home page for your browser
- Status bar— Shows information about the browser's actions; for example, indicates that a page is loading or is done loading
- Tab—Displays each Web page you open, letting you switch from one Web page to another
- Tools button—Lets you display a menu of options for working with IE Desktop
- Web page area—Shows the current Web page

Unlike IE Windows 8, IE Desktop includes a Command bar, a status bar, and a title bar, which are all typical elements in a window-based app. The Home and Tools buttons on the Command bar perform the same actions as the Home and Tools buttons on the right side of the Internet Explorer window.

Browsing Web Pages with IE Desktop

You browse Web pages using IE Desktop in the same way you do using IE Windows 8. Enter a URL or click a link to open a Web page and then use the browser tools to navigate from one page to another. Either version keeps track of the Web pages you visit so you can return to them quickly. The list of visited Web pages is called the **History list**. IE Desktop and IE Windows 8 share the same History list to make your Web browsing efficient no matter which version of Internet Explorer 10 you use. Instead of frequently entering the same URLs in the Address bar, you can begin to type an address and then let Internet Explorer's AutoComplete feature suggest the rest of the address, which it retrieves from the History list.

The National Archives Web site seemed to be the most promising resource for Jason as he prepares to teach workshops on researching family history. You'll show him how to explore that site using IE Desktop.

To browse Web pages and display them on separate tabs:

▶ **1.** Click the **Address bar** to select the URL for your home page, and then type **www.arch**. After Internet Explorer fills in the rest of the URL for you (*ives.gov*), press the **Enter** key to display the home page for the National Archives Web site.

Trouble? If Internet Explorer does not suggest the rest of the URL, type the complete address (www.archives.gov) and then press the Enter key.

▶ **2.** Click the **Research Our Records** button to open the Research Our Records Web page.

▶ **3.** Scroll down and then point to the **Research Your Ancestry** link to display the URL for the link in the status bar. See Figure 4-18. The Web page you open might look different. One way to tell if text or an image is a link in IE Desktop is to point to the item and then look in the status bar for the URL.

Figure 4-18   **Research Our Records Web page**

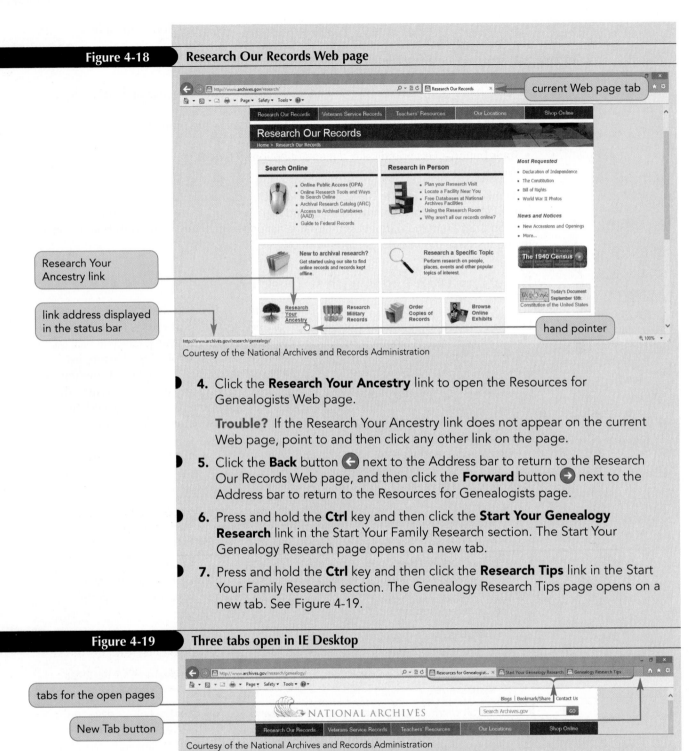

current Web page tab

Research Your Ancestry link

link address displayed in the status bar

hand pointer

Courtesy of the National Archives and Records Administration

4. Click the **Research Your Ancestry** link to open the Resources for Genealogists Web page.

Trouble? If the Research Your Ancestry link does not appear on the current Web page, point to and then click any other link on the page.

5. Click the **Back** button ⬅ next to the Address bar to return to the Research Our Records Web page, and then click the **Forward** button ➡ next to the Address bar to return to the Resources for Genealogists page.

6. Press and hold the **Ctrl** key and then click the **Start Your Genealogy Research** link in the Start Your Family Research section. The Start Your Genealogy Research page opens on a new tab.

7. Press and hold the **Ctrl** key and then click the **Research Tips** link in the Start Your Family Research section. The Genealogy Research Tips page opens on a new tab. See Figure 4-19.

Figure 4-19   **Three tabs open in IE Desktop**

tabs for the open pages

New Tab button

Blogs | Bookmark/Share | Contact Us

NATIONAL ARCHIVES

Courtesy of the National Archives and Records Administration

8. Point to the **Genealogy Research Tips** tab and then click its **Close Tab** button ❌ to close the page. Use the same technique to close the **Start Your Genealogy Research** tab.

9. Point to the **New Tab** button [ ] to display its icon, and then click the **New Tab** button [ ] to display a list of up to 10 Web sites you spend the most time using. This page is similar to the list of frequently visited sites displayed on the expanded Navigation bar in IE Windows 8. See Figure 4-20. The list of popular sites on your computer might differ.

| Figure 4-20 | New Tab page |

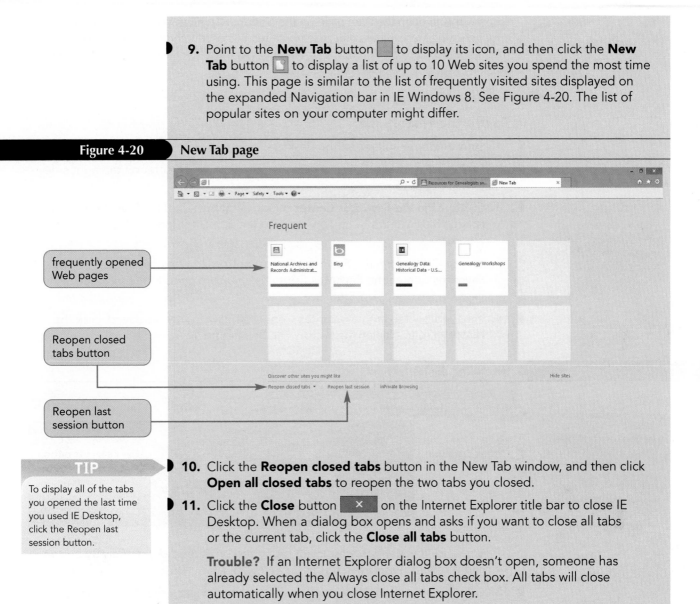

frequently opened Web pages

Reopen closed tabs button

Reopen last session button

TIP

To display all of the tabs you opened the last time you used IE Desktop, click the Reopen last session button.

10. Click the **Reopen closed tabs** button in the New Tab window, and then click **Open all closed tabs** to reopen the two tabs you closed.

11. Click the **Close** button [×] on the Internet Explorer title bar to close IE Desktop. When a dialog box opens and asks if you want to close all tabs or the current tab, click the **Close all tabs** button.

Trouble? If an Internet Explorer dialog box doesn't open, someone has already selected the Always close all tabs check box. All tabs will close automatically when you close Internet Explorer.

IE Desktop and IE Windows 8 share many of the same navigation features, including the Back and Forward buttons. One limitation of these buttons is that they apply only to your current session in the browser. If you close and then restart Internet Explorer, it starts keeping track of a fresh sequence of pages. To revisit Web pages you opened in previous sessions, you can use the History list.

Using the History List

To open any Web page you've recently visited, you can use the History list, which is available in the IE Desktop Favorites Center. The Favorites Center organizes Web page links and other information, including the History list. The History list includes the Web sites you visited today, last week, and up to three weeks ago by default. You can also click the View By Date button in the History list to change the default setup and view pages by date, by site, by the number of times visited, and in the order visited today. You can also search the pages in the History list to locate a specific Web site you've recently visited. Although both versions of Internet Explorer keep track of your browsing history, only IE Desktop lets you directly access the History list.

Jason wants to open the Web page on the National Archives Web site that provides tips for genealogy researchers. Because you already closed Internet Explorer, you can't use the Back button to return to that page. You'll use the History list to revisit the Genealogy Research Tips Web page.

To use the History list:

▶ **1.** Start Internet Explorer on the desktop.

▶ **2.** Click the **Favorites** button ⭐ to open the Favorites Center on the right side of the Internet Explorer window.

▶ **3.** Click the **Pin the Favorites Center** button 🖺 at the top of the Favorites Center to keep the Favorites Center open on the left side of the Internet Explorer window.

> Be sure to pin the Favorites Center to the Internet Explorer window so you can work with its features efficiently.

Trouble? If the Pin the Favorites Center button 🖺 does not appear in your Favorites Center, the Favorites Center is already pinned to the Internet Explorer window. Skip Step 3.

▶ **4.** If the History tab in the Favorites Center is not currently displayed, click the **History** tab to display the History list. See Figure 4-21.

| Figure 4-21 | Displaying the History list |

click a calendar icon to expand the list of Web sites visited

your History list might include additional dates

History tab

Favorites button

Trouble? If your History list is not organized by date, click the View By button and then click View By Date.

▶ **5.** Click **Today** in the History list. The list expands to show the Web sites you visited today.

▶ **6.** Click **archives (www.archives.gov)** to expand the list to show the pages you visited on the National Archives Web site.

▶ **7.** Click **Genealogy Research Tips**. The corresponding Web page opens in Internet Explorer. See Figure 4-22.

| Figure 4-22 | Revisiting a Web page |

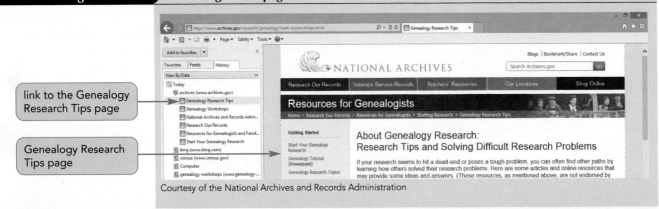

link to the Genealogy Research Tips page

Genealogy Research Tips page

Courtesy of the National Archives and Records Administration

Although the History list helps you access Web pages you opened recently, the Favorites Center helps you organize Web pages you open often, which you'll show Jason next.

Using Favorites

As you explore the Web, you'll find pages that are your favorites—those you visit frequently. When you use IE Desktop, you can save the location of your favorite Web pages in the Favorites list, a collection of links to the Web pages that you visit often. To display the Favorites list, you open the Favorites Center, where you can manage the Favorites list, Feeds, and the History list. The Favorites list initially includes a few folders of links, such as those to Microsoft Web sites. Your computer manufacturer might also include a few links in the Favorites list. If you find a Web page you want to visit often, you can add it to your Favorites list. When you want to retrieve one of your favorite Web pages, you can click its link in the Favorites list and display the page in your browser. As your list of favorite pages grows, you can organize the links into folders. For example, you could create a Favorites folder for travel Web sites and another for news Web sites.

To display the Favorites list:

▶ **1.** Click the **Favorites** tab in the Favorites Center to display the Favorites list. See Figure 4-23. Your Favorites list might be different.

Figure 4-23	Displaying the Favorites list

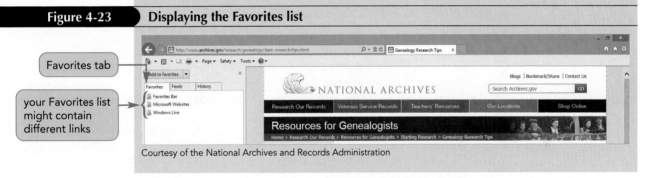

Favorites tab

your Favorites list might contain different links

Courtesy of the National Archives and Records Administration

The Genealogy Research Tips Web page provides the kind of information Jason will refer to often when preparing workshops for the San Antonio Historical Association. You'll add that page to the Favorites list.

Adding an Item to the Favorites List

To add a Web page to the Favorites list, you access the page in IE Desktop, and then you use the Add to favorites command. By default, IE Desktop adds the new page to the end of the Favorites list. If you organize the Web pages into folders, you can add a Web page to one of the folders. You can store the page using the title of the Web page as its name, or you can change the name so it is more descriptive or meaningful to you.

REFERENCE

Adding a Web Page to the Favorites List

- Open the Web page in IE Desktop.
- Open the Favorites Center.
- Click the Add to favorites button in the Favorites Center.
- Enter a new name for the Web page and select a folder, if necessary.
- Click the Add button.

If you are working on a school network, you might not be able to change the content of the Favorites list. In that case, read through the following steps and examine the figures, but do not perform the steps.

TIP

In IE Windows 8, right-click the Web page, click the Pin site button, and then click Add to favorites.

To add Web pages to your Favorites list:

1. With the Genealogy Research Tips page displayed in IE Desktop, click the **Add to favorites** button in the Favorites Center. The Add a Favorite dialog box opens, displaying the name of the Web page in the Name text box. You can change the name of the Web page, but the default name here makes the page easy to identify.

2. With Genealogy Research Tips displayed in the Name text box, click the **Add** button to add the Web page to the Favorites list.

Next, you can organize your favorite Web pages into folders.

Organizing the Favorites List

As you add more items to the Favorites list, you can organize its links by deleting some and moving others to new folders. Using folders is an excellent way to organize your favorite Web pages.

REFERENCE

Organizing the Favorites List

- Click the Add to favorites button arrow in the Favorites Center, and then click Organize favorites to open the Organize Favorites dialog box.
- To create a new folder, click the New Folder button, enter a folder name, and then press the Enter key.
- To move a link into a Favorites folder, drag the link to the folder, or select the item, click the Move button, select the new folder for the item, and then click the OK button.
- To remove an item from the Favorites list, select the item, and then click the Delete button.
- Click the Close button to close the Organize Favorites dialog box.

TIP

If you have many links and folders in the Favorites list, use the Move button in the Organize Favorites dialog box instead of dragging.

To organize your Favorites list:

1. Click the **Add to favorites button arrow** in the Favorites Center, and then click **Organize favorites**. The Organize Favorites dialog box opens.

   Trouble? If the Add a Favorite dialog box opens, you clicked the Add to favorites button instead of the arrow. Close the Add a Favorite dialog box, and then repeat Step 1.

2. Click the **New Folder** button, type **Ancestry Research** as the new folder name, and then press the **Enter** key.

3. In the Organize Favorites dialog box, drag the **Genealogy Research Tips** link to the Ancestry Research folder.

4. Click the **Close** button to close the Organize Favorites dialog box.

5. Click **Ancestry Research** in the Favorites list to display the contents of the folder. The new link you added is now stored in the Ancestry Research folder in the Favorites list.

Next, you want to show Jason another way to work with favorites—the Favorites bar.

Adding Pages and Feeds to the Favorites Bar

The Favorites bar provides another way to quickly access your favorite Web pages. The Favorites bar contains links to Web pages you view often and buttons for RSS feeds you subscribe to. An **RSS feed** (or **feed** for short) is frequently updated Web site content, such as news or commentary, delivered directly to your computing device when you are connected to the Internet. You can also use feeds to download audio content, such as a **podcast**, which is typically one of a series of audio files containing radio programs, comedy, or other information that you listen to on your computer or portable device.

When you visit a Web page that provides a feed or podcast, the Feeds button on the Favorites bar changes color to let you know that feeds are available. You can click the Feeds button and, if more than one feed is available, select one to subscribe to the feed. After you subscribe, you can add a feed to the Favorites bar so you can access the content quickly. When a feed publishes new information, Internet Explorer bolds the text in its button on the Favorites bar to alert you to the updated information.

First, you want to show Jason how to add the National Archives home page to the Favorites bar because you know he will use that page often. The Favorites bar is not open by default, so you need to open it before you can add links to it.

To display the Favorites bar and add a link to it:

▶ 1. Click the **Tools** button on the Command bar, point to **Toolbars**, and then click **Favorites bar**. The Favorites bar appears in the Internet Explorer window, shifting the Command bar to the right.

▶ 2. Click the **History** tab in the Favorites Center, and then click the **National Archives and Records Administration** link to display the National Archives home page.

▶ 3. Click the **Add to Favorites bar** button 📷 on the Favorites bar to add the National Archives home page to the Favorites bar. See Figure 4-24.

Figure 4-24   Adding a link to the Favorites bar

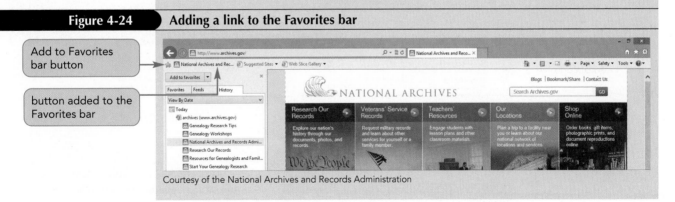

Add to Favorites bar button

button added to the Favorites bar

Courtesy of the National Archives and Records Administration

Jason wants to keep up with news and events at the National Archives. The Web site hosts a number of **blogs**, short for "Web logs," which are Web pages where an author or a group of authors post comments, articles, opinion, and other information on a regular basis. Each published piece of content is called a **blog post**. You can often subscribe to a blog as an RSS feed to access the changing information. You'll show Jason how to add a feed for a National Archives blog to the Favorites bar.

To add a feed to the Favorites bar:

▶ **1.** Scroll to display the lower-right part of the National Archives home page, and then click the **Blogs** link in the Connect With Us list to display a list of blogs the National Archives hosts.

▶ **2.** Scroll down the page and then click the **Prologue: Pieces of History** button to display the blog for Prologue, a magazine the National Archives publishes. The Feeds button on the Favorites bar is orange, indicating the page provides an RSS feed to which you can subscribe. See Figure 4-25.

Figure 4-25 ▶ **RSS feed detected on the Web page**

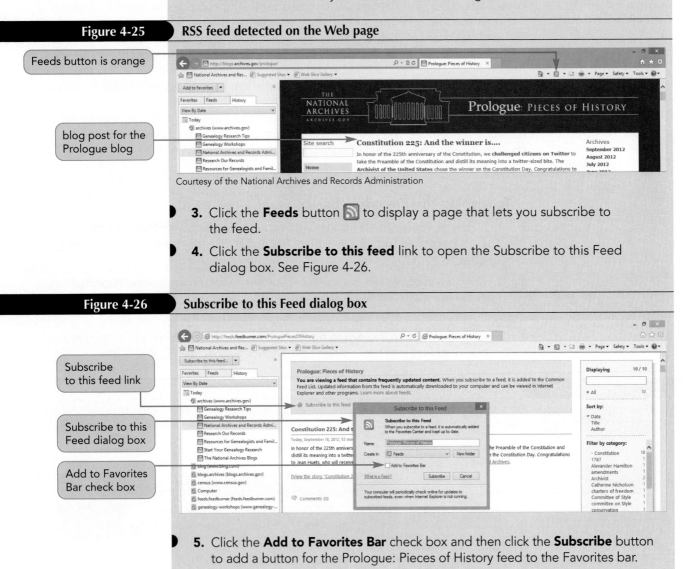

Feeds button is orange

blog post for the Prologue blog

Courtesy of the National Archives and Records Administration

▶ **3.** Click the **Feeds** button 🔊 to display a page that lets you subscribe to the feed.

▶ **4.** Click the **Subscribe to this feed** link to open the Subscribe to this Feed dialog box. See Figure 4-26.

Figure 4-26 ▶ **Subscribe to this Feed dialog box**

Subscribe to this feed link

Subscribe to this Feed dialog box

Add to Favorites Bar check box

▶ **5.** Click the **Add to Favorites Bar** check box and then click the **Subscribe** button to add a button for the Prologue: Pieces of History feed to the Favorites bar.

Another way to quickly access Web pages you open often is to pin them to the taskbar, which is similar to pinning them to the Start screen.

Pinning a Web Page to the Taskbar

If you want to open a Web page directly from the desktop without starting IE Desktop, you can pin the page to the taskbar. Doing so creates a shortcut to the Web page, which appears as a button on the taskbar. When you click the button for the pinned page, a streamlined IE Desktop window opens to display the page. Because you are probably using the pinned page for quick reference, this window contains fewer controls than the full version of IE Desktop. For example, it does not display the Command bar or Favorites bar.

Jason thinks he will often use the Resources for Genealogists page on the National Archives site. You'll pin this page to the taskbar and then show Jason how to open the page.

To pin a Web page to the taskbar:

1. On the History tab in the Favorites Center, click the **Resources for Genealogists and Family Historians** link to open the Web page.

2. Drag the **Resources for Genealogists and Family Historians** tab from the Internet Explorer window to the taskbar. When the Pin to Taskbar ScreenTip appears, release the mouse button to pin the page to the taskbar. See Figure 4-27.

| Figure 4-27 | Pinning a Web page to the taskbar |

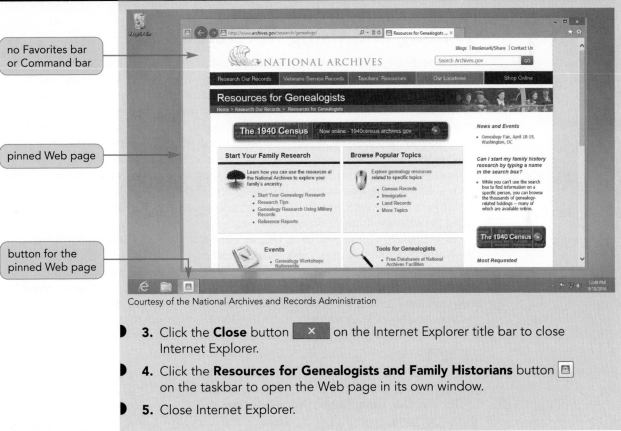

Courtesy of the National Archives and Records Administration

3. Click the **Close** button ✕ on the Internet Explorer title bar to close Internet Explorer.

4. Click the **Resources for Genealogists and Family Historians** button 🖼 on the taskbar to open the Web page in its own window.

5. Close Internet Explorer.

Now when Jason is working on the desktop, he can easily access the Web pages he needs in the Favorites list, on the Favorites bar, and on the taskbar.

INSIGHT

Letting Internet Explorer Suggest Sites

To help you discover Web sites that might interest you, you can use the Suggested Sites feature. When you turn on Suggested Sites, Internet Explorer reviews the Web pages open in your browser and those stored in your browsing history. Based on that information, it suggests other Web sites related to the content of the sites you visit most often. To view these suggestions, you click the See Suggested Sites button on the Favorites bar. When you use Suggested Sites, Internet Explorer sends your browsing history to Microsoft for analysis. Suggested Sites is turned off by default to protect your privacy. To turn it on, you can click the Tools button on the Command bar, point to File, click Suggested Sites, and then click the Yes button. When selected, this option appears with a check mark on the File menu. If you want to prevent Internet Explorer from sending your browsing history to Microsoft, turn off Suggested Sites by clicking the Tools button on the Command bar, pointing to File, and then clicking Suggested Sites to remove the check mark.

Finding and Using Accelerators

Accelerators are tools that make it easier to find information on the Web without navigating to other Web sites. For example, if you are viewing a Web page about a hotel in a city you plan to visit, you can select the hotel's address, and then use an Accelerator to quickly display a map showing the location of the hotel. Instead of copying the address, navigating to the Web page for a mapping service, pasting the address, and then viewing a map, you point to the Accelerator icon to display a preview of the map. In this case, you perform one step instead of four.

Accelerators are services provided by Web sites, so some sites have them and others do not. Internet Explorer comes with a selection of default Accelerators, including Map with Bing and Translate with Bing. You can add or remove Accelerators as necessary using the Manage Add-ons dialog box.

Jason plans to visit Washington, DC, in a few months. He wants to spend time at the National Archives and possibly attend a lecture or other event. He'd like to know where the National Archives building is located as he plans his trip. A colleague recommended a hotel in Washington, near the intersection of North Capitol Street NW and New York Avenue NE, and Jason wants to determine if the hotel is near the National Archives. You can use a button on the Favorites bar to open the home page for the National Archives, and then use the Bing Maps Accelerator to find the building on a map.

To use the Bing Maps Accelerator:

1. Start Internet Explorer on the desktop, and then click the **Close the Favorites Center** button ☒ to close the Favorites Center. Maximize the window.

2. Click the **National Archives and Records Administration** button on the Favorites bar to open the National Archives home page.

3. Click the **Our Locations** button near the top of the page to display a list of National Archives locations.

   Trouble? If a Select a Location window opens, click its close link to close the window.

4. On the Locations Nationwide page, select the address of the National Archives in Washington, DC. A blue Accelerator icon appears next to the selected text. See Figure 4-28. Your Accelerator might appear in a different location.

Figure 4-28 Displaying an Accelerator

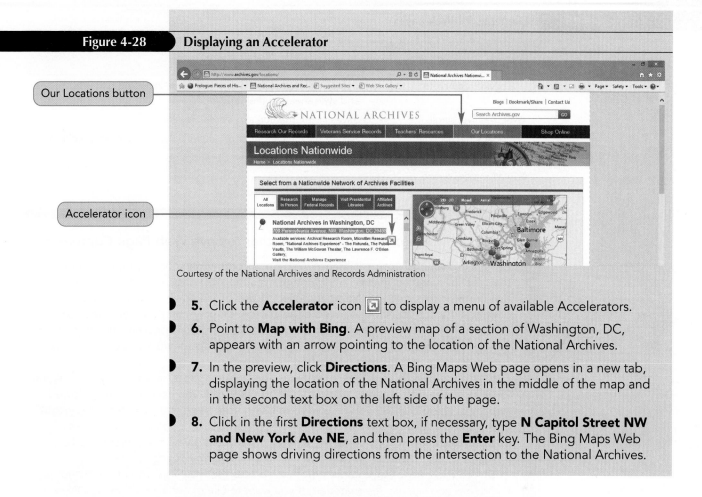

Our Locations button

Accelerator icon

Courtesy of the National Archives and Records Administration

5. Click the **Accelerator** icon 🔲 to display a menu of available Accelerators.

6. Point to **Map with Bing**. A preview map of a section of Washington, DC, appears with an arrow pointing to the location of the National Archives.

7. In the preview, click **Directions**. A Bing Maps Web page opens in a new tab, displaying the location of the National Archives in the middle of the map and in the second text box on the left side of the page.

8. Click in the first **Directions** text box, if necessary, type **N Capitol Street NW and New York Ave NE**, and then press the **Enter** key. The Bing Maps Web page shows driving directions from the intersection to the National Archives.

Printing and Saving Web Pages

If you find a page on the Web and want to refer to it when you don't have computer access, you can print the Web page. Sometimes, Web pages include a Printer-Friendly Format link or other similar link for printing a Web page, indicating that the Web site formats the page for a standard size sheet of paper before printing. However, not all Web pages provide such an option. Therefore, you should preview the page before you print it to see how it will look when printed. To preview a Web page, click the Print button arrow on the Command bar and then click Print preview. To print a page from Print preview, click the Print Document button on the Print Preview toolbar. To print a Web page without previewing it, you click the Print button on the Command bar.

You can also save Web pages and their content. To save a Web page as a file on your computer, click the Page button on the Command bar, and then click Save as. Enter a name for the file in the File name text box, and then select one of the four file types described in Figure 4-29 by clicking the Save as type button.

Figure 4-29   **File types for Web pages**

File Type	Description
Webpage, complete	Saves all files associated with the page, including graphics, frames, and style sheets in their original format
Web Archive, single file	Saves all information as a single file
Webpage, HTML only	Saves only the current page without graphics or other media files
Text File	Saves only the text on the current page

© 2014 Cengage Learning

PROSKILLS

Decision Making: Determining Whether to Save Web Page Content

Using a browser, you can easily save Web page content on your computer, including the graphic images displayed on the page, files the Web page provides, such as text or music files, and the Web page itself. However, doing so is not always legal or ethical. Before you save any Web page content on your computer, you need to determine whether you have the legal right to do so. This is especially important when you want to save and use images, video, and other media for work projects because commercial use of such content is often prohibited.

Web content such as software, video, music, and images is easy to copy in its digital form. However, if this material is protected by copyright, you usually are not allowed to copy or share it unless you receive permission from the owner. The term **copyright** refers to the originator's exclusive legal right to reproduce, publish, or sell works he or she creates. If you copy someone else's work without giving that person credit, you are committing plagiarism, and you may also be violating copyright laws.

Before you copy or save content from Web sites that you visit, you need to find out if and how you can use the materials. If you want to use material you find on a Web site, first get permission from the owner of the site. Often, Web sites include links to their copyright and permission-request information on their main pages. Even if you think that information or material you found is not copyrighted, you should always request permission to use it and give credit to any Web site that you use in your work or school projects.

Jason does not want to print or save any information you found for the National Archives because he can access it quickly using Internet Explorer tools. You can exit Internet Explorer.

To close tabs and exit Internet Explorer:

▶ **1.** Click the **Close** button [×] on the Internet Explorer title bar.

▶ **2.** Click the **Close all tabs** button in the Internet Explorer dialog box to close all tabs.

So far, you have learned about the structure of the Internet and the Web, and how to use the Windows 8 and desktop versions of Internet Explorer to open, navigate, and organize Web pages. In the next session, you'll use another service the Internet provides—email.

REVIEW

Session 4.1 Quick Check

1. A(n) _____ is a collection of Web pages that have a common theme or focus.
2. Explain the difference between IE Windows 8 and IE Desktop.
3. What are two definitions for the term *home page*?
4. When you use tabbed browsing in IE Windows 8, what does each tab display?
5. You can display the _____ while you are using IE Windows 8 to perform Internet Explorer tasks such as searching for Web sites, printing Web page content, and selecting IE Windows 8 settings.
6. In IE Desktop, you can open the _____ to display a list of Web sites you visited today.
7. Explain why you would use an Accelerator in Internet Explorer.
8. What is an RSS feed?

Session 4.2 Visual Overview:

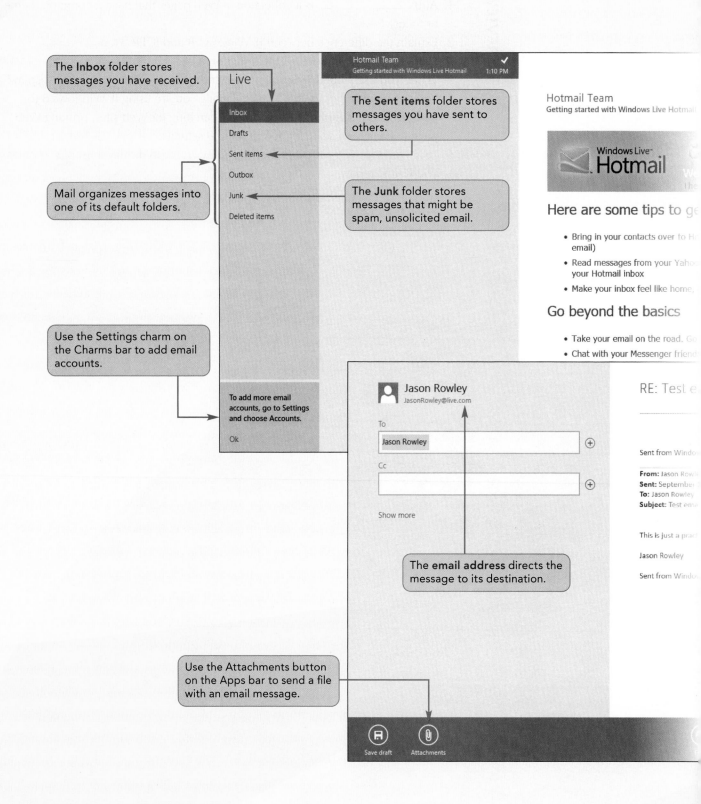

The **Inbox** folder stores messages you have received.

The **Sent items** folder stores messages you have sent to others.

Mail organizes messages into one of its default folders.

The **Junk** folder stores messages that might be spam, unsolicited email.

Use the Settings charm on the Charms bar to add email accounts.

The **email address** directs the message to its destination.

Use the Attachments button on the Apps bar to send a file with an email message.

Windows 8 Mail App

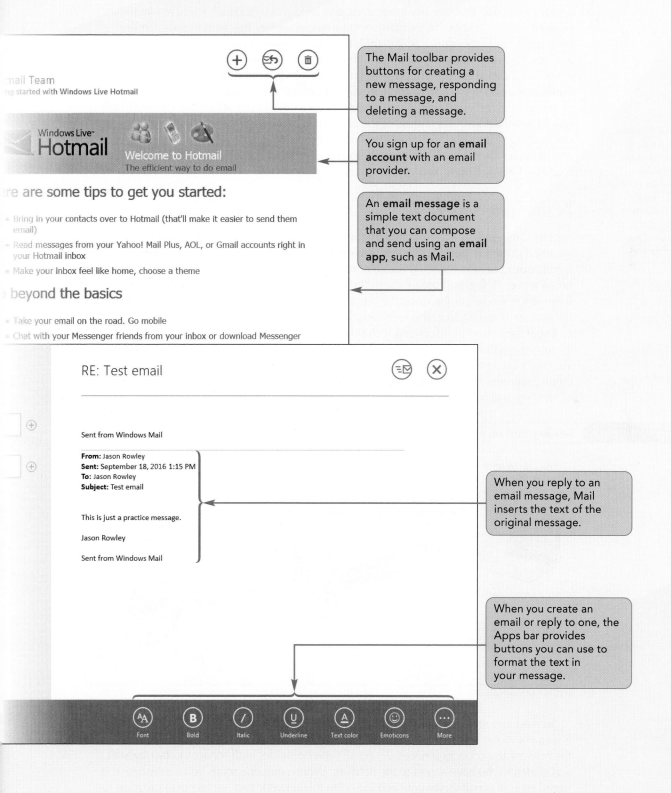

The Mail toolbar provides buttons for creating a new message, responding to a message, and deleting a message.

You sign up for an **email account** with an email provider.

An **email message** is a simple text document that you can compose and send using an **email app**, such as Mail.

When you reply to an email message, Mail inserts the text of the original message.

When you create an email or reply to one, the Apps bar provides buttons you can use to format the text in your message.

---

mail Team
ng started with **Windows Live Hotmail**

Welcome to Hotmail
The efficient way to do email

re are some tips to get you started:

- Bring in your contacts over to Hotmail (that'll make it easier to send them email)
- Read messages from your Yahoo! Mail Plus, AOL, or Gmail accounts right in your Hotmail inbox
- Make your inbox feel like home, choose a theme

beyond the basics

- Take your email on the road. Go mobile
- Chat with your Messenger friends from your inbox or download Messenger

---

RE: Test email

Sent from Windows Mail

From: Jason Rowley
Sent: September 18, 2016 1:15 PM
To: Jason Rowley
Subject: Test email

This is just a practice message.

Jason Rowley

Sent from Windows Mail

Font   Bold   Italic   Underline   Text color   Emoticons   More

Getting Started with Mail

As you learned, the Web is a service that the Internet provides. Another service is electronic mail, or email. Just as you use a browser, such as Internet Explorer, to use the Web, you can use an email application to work with email. Windows 8 includes Mail, a Windows 8 app that you use to send, receive, and manage email. If you're like most computer users, you exchange many email messages every day with friends, family, colleagues, and other contacts. You probably also receive newsletters, coupons, offers, and other types of messages from companies and organizations. You might start your email app as soon as you turn on your computer and leave it running until you shut down at the end of the day. In short, email is a central part of your computing activities.

Using Mail, you can send email to and receive email from anyone in the world who has an email address, regardless of the operating system or type of computer the person is using. Although this tutorial provides steps for using the Mail app, the concepts and activities the tutorial covers apply to any email application, including Microsoft Outlook, Outlook.com, and Windows Live Mail.

TIP

You can also download and install Windows Live Mail, a Windows Essentials application that runs on the desktop. Visit the Microsoft Windows Web site at windows.microsoft.com, and then search for *Windows Essentials*.

Examining How Email Works

An email message is a simple text document that you can compose and send using an email program, such as the Windows 8 Mail app. When you send a message, it travels from your computer, through a network, and arrives at a computer called an **email server**. The email server stores the email messages until the recipients request them. Then the server forwards the messages to the appropriate computers. Typically, the system administrator of your network or ISP manages the email server.

Email uses **store-and-forward technology**, which means you can send messages to anyone on the Internet or a network, even if a recipient's computer isn't turned on. When it's convenient, your recipients log on to the Internet or network and use their email programs to receive and read their messages. Figure 4-30 illustrates the process of sending and receiving email messages.

| Figure 4-30 | Sending and receiving email |

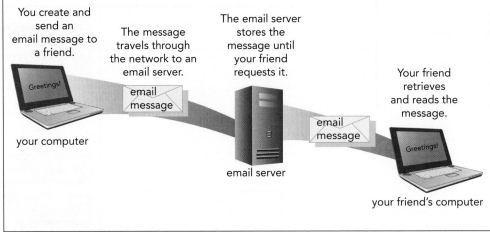

You create and send an email message to a friend.

The message travels through the network to an email server.

The email server stores the message until your friend requests it.

Your friend retrieves and reads the message.

your computer

email message

email server

email message

your friend's computer

© 2014 Cengage Learning

To send and receive email, you must be able to access an email server on the network. If your computer is part of a network at a college or university, for example, you log on to the network to access its services. An email server provides mail services to faculty, staff, and students who have access to the network. When someone sends you a message, it is stored on your email server until you log on to the network and use an email program to check your mail. The email server then transfers new messages to your electronic mailbox. You use an email program to open, read, print, delete, reply to, forward, and save the mail.

If your computer is not part of a network, you can access an email server on the Internet. To do so, you open an email account with a service that provides Internet access. For example, email accounts are included as part of the subscription fee for most ISPs. Email accounts are also provided free of charge by advertiser-supported Web sites, such as Outlook.com and Google. After you establish an email account, you can connect to the Internet to send and receive your email messages.

Addressing Email

Just as you must address a piece of ordinary mail, you need to supply an address for an email message. The email address you enter directs the message to its destination. Your email address is included in the message as the return address, so your recipients can easily respond to your message. Anyone who has an email address can send and receive electronic mail. If you work for a company or attend a school that provides email, a system administrator probably assigns an email address for you. Other times, you create your own email address, though it must follow a particular format. See Figure 4-31.

Figure 4-31 **Typical format of an email address**

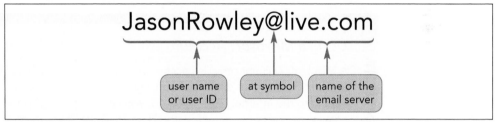

© 2014 Cengage Learning

The **user name**, or **user ID**, is the name entered when your email account is set up. The @ symbol signifies that the email server name is provided next. For example, "JasonRowley" is the user name and "live.com" is the email server.

The easiest way to learn a person's email address is to ask the person what it is. You can also look up an email address in a network or Internet directory. Most businesses and schools publish a directory listing email addresses of those who have email accounts on their network. Many Web sites also provide email directories for people with email accounts on the Internet, such as Yahoo! People Search at people.yahoo.com.

When you sign up for an email account, you can send your new email address to friends, colleagues, and clients. If your email address changes, such as when you change email services, you can subscribe to an email forwarding service so you don't miss any mail sent to your old address.

Setting Up Mail

To use email, you need an Internet connection, an email program, and an email address. Make sure you have an Internet connection and email address before performing the steps in this section. Having an email address means you have an email account, which is space on an email server reserved for your messages. You set up an account with an email service provider, which can be an ISP, an employer or school, or a Web service such as Outlook.com or Gmail.

You can set up the following types of email accounts in Mail:

- Hotmail—Microsoft offers Hotmail as a free Web-based email service.
- Outlook—This type of account can be an Exchange, Office 365, or Outlook.com account. Organizations such as a business or school typically offer Exchange accounts, which reside on an Exchange server. Home users usually do not have Exchange accounts.

- Google—Google provides Gmail, another free Web-based email service.
- Other—Account types other than Hotmail, Outlook, and Gmail, such as Internet Message Access Protocol (IMAP) accounts, which are often provided by ISPs.

If you already have one of these types of email accounts, you can set up Mail to send and receive email by starting Mail and then entering the user name and password you use for the account. If you use more than one of these email accounts, you can add them to Mail. For example, you might have an Exchange account at work or school and an Outlook.com account you use for personal email. Instead of switching from one email account to another, you can use Mail to receive email from your Exchange and Outlook.com accounts so you can manage all of your email from a single app.

If you do not have any of these types of email accounts, you can set up a free Outlook.com or Gmail account. To set up an Outlook.com account, use a browser to go to Outlook.com. Sign up for a Microsoft account by providing your name and other information and then selecting an account name (which is the same as a user name) and a password. If you start Mail before signing up for a Microsoft account, Mail lets you sign up as part of the email setup process. You can also set up a Gmail account in a similar way. Use a browser to go to mail.google.com, provide your name and other information, and then select a user name and password.

INSIGHT

Using a Microsoft Account

A Microsoft account provides access to online services such as SkyDrive for file storage and Outlook.com for email. You can sign in to a Microsoft account on any device connected to the Internet. When you do, you can read and respond to your Outlook.com email messages or access files stored on SkyDrive. If you access Outlook.com on a public computer, for example, and then return to your Windows 8 home computer, your email messages and responses also appear in Mail. Your Microsoft account synchronizes Outlook.com and Mail so your messages are up to date in either place.

Jason has an Outlook.com account, but he hasn't set up Mail to use it yet. Because this is the first time you're starting Mail on his Windows 8 computer, you'll show Jason how to set up Mail to use his Outlook.com account. The following steps assume that you have a Microsoft account.

To set up Mail:

1. If necessary, press the **Windows** key ⊞ to display the Start screen.

2. Click the **Mail** tile to start the Mail app. If this is the first time you started Mail, the Sign in with a Microsoft account screen opens, requesting your Microsoft account information.

   Trouble? If you have already set up Mail, the main Mail screen opens instead of the Sign in with a Microsoft account screen. Read but do not perform the rest of the steps.

   Trouble? If you do not have a Microsoft account, click the Don't have a Microsoft account? Sign up now link, follow the instructions on the Microsoft Web site to create a Microsoft account, and then repeat Step 2.

   Trouble? If a dialog box opens asking if you want Mail to be your default mail program, click the Yes button only if you are using your own computer and want to use Mail as your mail program. If you are using a school or institutional computer, click the No button or ask your technical support person for assistance.

> **3.** Enter the account name you use for your Hotmail or Outlook.com account, such as **JasonRowley@live.com**.

> **4.** Click the **Password** text box, and then enter the password for the account.

> **5.** Click the **Sign in** button. If this is the first time you are signing in to Mail, the app connects to your Hotmail account and displays messages received in that account.

Now you can show Jason how to send and receive email.

Sending and Receiving Email Using Mail

You can use the Mail app to compose, send, and receive email messages. After you set up an email account, you're ready to start using Mail to manage your email.

To start Mail:

> **1.** Start Mail, if necessary (click the **Mail** tile on the Start screen). Figure 4-32 shows the Mail screen. The email account shown in the figures in this tutorial belongs to Jason Rowley. Your screens will look different from the figures.

| Figure 4-32 | Mail app |

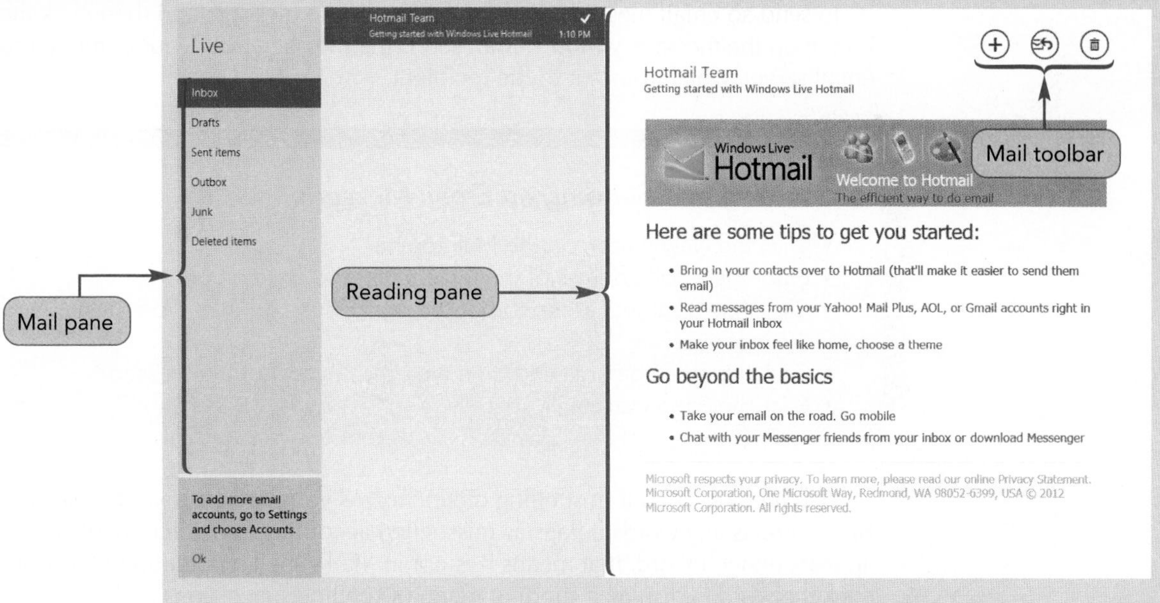

The Mail app includes the following tools and components:

- Mail pane—This part of the Mail screen lists your email accounts at the top followed by the default Mail folders, including the Inbox, Drafts, Sent items, Outbox, Junk, and Deleted items folders. Mail organizes your email into these folders automatically.
- Reading pane—This pane displays the contents of the selected message.
- Mail toolbar—The toolbar provides buttons for frequently performed commands, such as creating, replying to, and deleting email.

Creating and Sending Email Messages

An email message uses a format similar to a standard memo, which typically includes Date, To, and Subject lines, followed by the content of the message. The To line indicates who will receive the message. Windows 8 Mail automatically supplies the date you send the message (as set in your computer's clock). The Subject line, although optional, alerts the recipient to the topic of the message. You should always include a Subject line because people often delete messages without reading them if they do not contain subjects. Finally, the message area contains the content of your message. You can also include additional information, such as a Cc line, which indicates who will receive a copy of the message. The Mail screen separates this information into two panes, with the sender and receivers listed in the left pane and the subject and message content in the right pane.

INSIGHT

Using the Cc and Bcc Lines

In the To line, restrict the email addresses to those of your primary recipients. Use the Cc (courtesy copy) line for secondary recipients who should receive a copy of the message. If you are sending an email message to a large group of people, you can also use the Bcc (blind courtesy copy) line. (Right-click a blank spot on the Mail screen, click the More button on the Apps bar, and then click Show Bcc.) Mail sends an individual message to each person listed in the Bcc line, though the only other email address that appears is the sender's.

To send an email message, you first compose the message and then click the Send button on the message window. Mail sends the message from your computer to your email server, which routes it to the recipient.

REFERENCE

Creating and Sending an Email Message

- Click the New button on the Mail toolbar.
- Enter the email address of the recipient in the To text box.
- Click Add a subject at the top of the right pane and then type the subject of the message.
- Click the message area and then type the content of the message.
- Click the Send button.

Mail includes a built-in spelling dictionary. As you type the text of a message, Mail corrects any words it flags as misspelled according to its dictionary. If a red line appears under a word, that means it is not in Mail's spelling dictionary. You can right-click the word to display a shortcut menu of spelling suggestions and an option to add the word to the dictionary.

Now you can show Jason how to create and send an email message using Mail by sending a practice email to yourself.

To create and send an email message:

1. Click the **New** button ⊕ on the Mail toolbar. The screen for composing a new message opens. See Figure 4-33.

Figure 4-33	Composing a new message

enter the recipient's email address in the To text box

Jason Rowley
JasonRowley@live.com

To

Cc

Show more

Add a subject ← click to enter a subject

Add a message ←
Sent from Windows Mail

click to enter a message

Send button

TIP

To send this message to many people, you could type more than one email address in the To or Cc text boxes. Separate each address with a comma or semicolon.

2. Type your email address in the To text box.

   Trouble? If you're not sure what email address you should enter, check with your instructor or technical support person.

3. Click **Add a subject** in the right pane, and then type **Test email** as the subject.

4. Click **Add a message**, and then type **This is just a practice message**.

5. Press the **Enter** key twice, and then type your name.

6. Click the **Send** button 🖃 on the toolbar. Mail places the message in the Outbox. After a second or two, Mail removes the message from the Outbox, sends the message to your email server, and then places a copy of the sent message in the Sent items folder.

   To make sure your message has been sent, you can open the Sent items folder to see all of the messages you have sent.

   Trouble? After several seconds have passed, if Mail still displays the number 1 to the right of the Outbox folder in the Mail pane, indicating it contains one unsent message, then Mail is not configured to send messages immediately. In that case, right-click the middle of the screen and then click the Sync button on the Apps bar to send your message.

7. Click **Sent items** in the Mail pane. Your message appears in the Message list in the left pane, and the content of the message appears in the Reading pane.

   Trouble? If the content of your message does not appear in the Reading pane, click your message in the Message list.

When you clicked in the message area while composing a message, you might have noticed that the Apps bar displayed buttons for formatting the text. The buttons include Font, Font color, Highlight, Bold, Italic, Underline, Bulleted list, Emoticons, and More. To bold a word, for example, select the word and then click the Bold button on the Apps bar. To insert an emoticon such as a happy face, click in the message area, click the Emoticons button on the Apps bar, click a category icon, such as People or Travel, at the top of the panel, and then click an emoticon. You use the More button to apply options such as a priority (high, normal, or low) to the message, add the Bcc box, and undo or redo the most recent command.

Receiving and Reading Email Messages

TIP

If your computer is using a screen resolution of 1366 × 768 or higher, you can snap the Mail app to the screen so that it stays open as you work with other apps.

Mail automatically checks to see if you've received email whenever you start the program and periodically after that. (Every 30 minutes is the default.) Mail also checks for received email when you click the Sync button on the Apps bar. Email you receive appears in your Inbox. By default, the Inbox shows the name of the sender, the subject, and the date you received the message. Mail you have received but have not read yet appears in bold. To read a message, you click the message in the list to display its contents in the Reading pane.

To receive and read the Test email message:

  1. Click **Inbox** in the Mail pane to display the contents of the Inbox folder in the Message list.

  2. If necessary, right-click a blank area of the screen to display the Apps bar, and then click the **Sync** button. Mail retrieves your messages from your email server, routes them to your Inbox, and displays them in the Message list. Your Inbox folder might contain additional email messages from other people.

     Trouble? If the message you sent doesn't appear in the Inbox, wait a few minutes, and then click the Sync button again.

  3. If necessary, click the **Test email** message to display its contents in the Reading pane. See Figure 4-34.

Figure 4-34 Reading a message

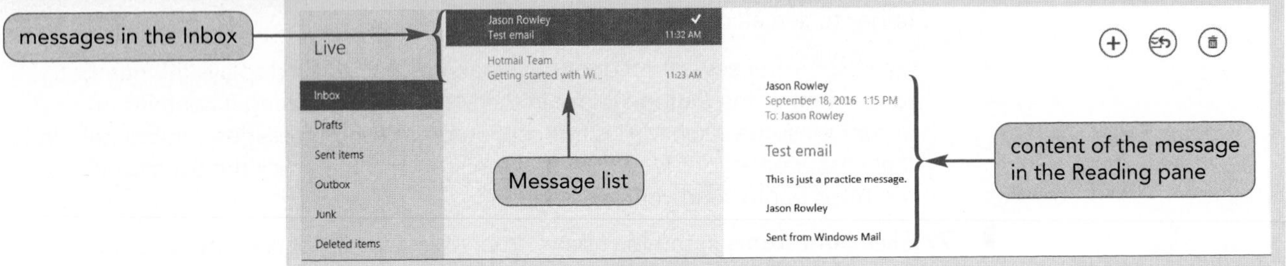

messages in the Inbox

Message list

content of the message in the Reading pane

Next, you'll show Jason how to perform another common email task—responding to the messages you receive.

Responding to Email Messages

Some of the email you receive may ask you to provide information, answer questions, or confirm decisions. Instead of creating a new email message, you can reply directly to a message that you receive. When you reply to a message, Mail inserts the email address of the sender and the subject into the proper places in the message screen, and includes the text of the original message.

You can respond to messages by using the Reply or Reply all command. If the original message was sent to more than one person, use the Reply command to respond to only the original sender. Use the Reply all command to respond to all other recipients as well. Use the Reply all command carefully so that the only messages people receive from you are those they need to read. You can also use the Forward command to create a message with the original message text, and then send the message to someone other than the original senders.

You will continue to show Jason the tools provided with Mail.

TIP

If you have added contacts to the People app, you can click the Add button (plus icon) next to the To text box, and then click a name to insert a contact's email address into the To text box.

To reply to the Test email message:

▶ **1.** With the Test email message selected in the Message list, click the **Respond** button 🔄 on the toolbar, and then click **Reply**. The screen displays the text of the original message, inserts the email address of the original recipient in the To text box, and displays RE: before the original subject text. See Figure 4-35.

| Figure 4-35 | Replying to a message |

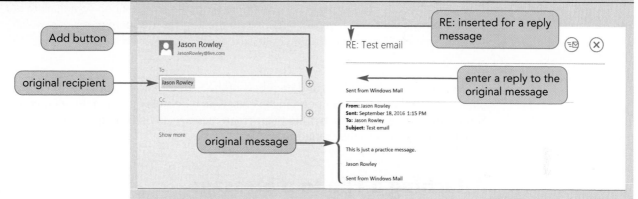

▶ **2.** Type **This test was successful.** in the message area, and then click the **Send** button 🖂 on the toolbar.

Trouble? If the message doesn't appear in the Sent items folder, right-click the screen and then click the Sync button on the Apps bar to send the message.

▶ **3.** When the RE: Test email message appears in your Inbox, click it to display its contents in the Reading pane.

Jason might want to delete the email messages he's read. You'll show him how to do so next.

Deleting Email Messages

After you read and respond to your messages, you can delete any message you no longer need. When you delete a message, it moves to the Deleted items folder. Messages remain in the Deleted items folder until you delete that folder's contents. This folder might be set up to permanently delete its contents when you close Mail. If not, you should delete them periodically by clicking the Deleted items folder in the Mail pane, selecting the messages, and then clicking the Delete button on the toolbar.

To delete the Test email messages:

▶ **1.** With the RE: Test email message selected in the Message list, hold down the **Shift** key, click the **Test email** message, and then click the **Delete** button 🗑 on the toolbar. The Inbox Message list no longer displays the Test messages.

Dealing with Junk Email

Junk email, or spam, is unsolicited email, often containing advertisements, fraudulent schemes, or legitimate offers. Mail includes a junk email filter that analyzes the content of the email messages you receive and moves suspicious messages to the Junk folder, where you can examine and manage them as necessary. To reduce the amount of junk email you receive, avoid posting your email address on Web sites or other public areas of the Internet. If a Web site requests your email address, read its privacy statement to make sure it doesn't disclose your email address to others. Finally, never respond to junk email—you're likely to receive even more spam. Be sure to open your Junk folder often to review the messages it contains, and then delete the spam messages, which are often from senders you don't recognize.

Jason mentions that visitors and members of the San Antonio Historical Association often request descriptions of upcoming events, which he stores in separate documents. You'll show him how to attach a file to an email message so he can reply to people and provide the documents they request.

Attaching a File to a Message

Besides sending email to others, you can also transfer files to them by attaching the files to messages. You can send any kind of file, including documents, pictures, music, or videos. Check the size of the files you attach before you send a message. If you attach a large file to an email message, it might take a long time for your recipient to download your message. Most email servers limit the size of the files you can attach; some allow files no larger than 3 MB. Check with your correspondents before sending large file attachments to find out about size restrictions and set up a convenient time to send the attachment.

You'll show Jason how to send and open an email message that includes an attachment. As before, you'll create a test message and send it to yourself.

To create and send a message with an attachment:

1. Copy the **Events** file from the Windows4\Tutorial folder provided with your Data Files to the Public Documents folder in the Documents library, and then return to the Mail app.

2. Click the **New** button ⊕ on the toolbar.

3. Type your email address in the To box.

4. Click **Add a subject** in the right pane, and then type **Events list you requested** as the message subject.

5. Right-click a blank spot on the Mail screen, and then click the **Attachments** button on the Apps bar. The Files screen opens.

6. If necessary, click the **Go up** link, click **Documents**, click **Events**, and then click the **Attach** button. Mail attaches the file to the message and displays the filename and size next to the file icon.

7. Type **This is a test email message with a file attachment.** in the message area.

8. Click the **Send** button ⬒ on the toolbar.

9. If necessary, right-click the screen and then click the **Sync** button on the Apps bar to send and receive the message.

When you receive a message that contains an attachment, you can choose to save or open the attached file. You should open files only after scanning them with antivirus software. Some people spread harmful software, called viruses, in email attachments. Before you open the file, you need to make sure the app used to create the attachment is installed on your computer. If it's not, you can sometimes use a text editor, such as WordPad or Notepad, to open and read the attached file.

To receive and open a message with an attachment:

▶ **1.** When the Events list you requested message appears in your Inbox, click the message so the contents appear in the Reading pane.

▶ **2.** Click the **Events.rtf** file icon in the Reading pane to display a shortcut menu, which lets you open, open with a specific program, or save the attachment.

▶ **3.** Click **Open** on the shortcut menu. The file opens in a desktop word-processing program, such as Word or WordPad. You could save the document now if necessary.

▶ **4.** Close the word-processing program.

PROSKILLS

Written Communication: Observing Email Etiquette

Because email is a widespread form of communication, you should follow standard guidelines and common sense when using it. For example, use language appropriate for the purpose of your message and your recipients. Following are a few guidelines to keep in mind when you are composing email messages so that you can communicate effectively, without offending or annoying your correspondents:

- Be concise and direct. People often read email messages while they are doing something else. As a courtesy to your correspondents and to make sure your message is read, get right to the point and keep your messages short.
- Include your response first. When you reply to an email, you can include text from the original message. If you do, make sure that your response is at the top of the message so your recipients can find it easily. If you respond to questions or insert comments in the original message, use a contrasting font color so your recipients can identify your additions.
- Don't email sensitive or confidential information. Email is not private, and your recipients can forward your message to others, either intentionally or accidentally. It's a good idea to be professional and careful about what you say to and about others.
- Avoid abbreviations. Although you should strive to be brief, don't overcompensate by using nonstandard abbreviations. Stick to the abbreviations that are common in business writing, such as FYI and ASAP.
- Don't use all capital letters. Using all capital letters, as in "SEND ME THE REPORT TODAY," can be difficult to read and makes it look like you're shouting.
- Pause and reread before sending. Be sure to reread the emails you write before you send them, and consider how they could be received. A message that you intend to be funny could be misinterpreted as rude. If you wrote an email in anger, calm down and revise your message before sending it. After you send an email message, you can't retrieve or stop it.

You're finished working with Mail for now, so you can close the app.

To close Mail:

▶ **1.** Press the **Windows** key ⊞ to return to the Start screen, and then click the **Mail** tile.

▶ **2.** Drag the top of the Mail app down until it shrinks to a thumbnail, and then continue dragging it to the very bottom of the screen to close the app.

If you were going to continue working on the desktop, you could use the Switch List to close the app: Point to the upper-left corner of the desktop, right-click the Mail window, and then click Close. However, you will continue using the Start screen to explore other new Windows 8 features with Jason.

Adding Information to the People App

Another communication app in Windows 8 is the People app, which you use to keep track of your contacts, including email correspondents. You can also use People on its own to save information about people and organizations. In addition to storing email addresses, you can store related information such as street addresses, home phone numbers, and personal information, such as anniversaries and birthdays. When you create an email message, you can click the Add button (a plus sign) next to the To text box to display a list of your contacts, and then click the name of the contact to insert the appropriate email address in the To text box.

You can add contact information to People by importing the information from social networking sites where you maintain contacts, such as Facebook, Google, LinkedIn, and Twitter. If you import the same contact information from two or more sources, the People app detects the duplicate contacts and combines them into a single entry called a linked contact. You can also create a new contact, and then enter as much information as you want about that contact on the New Contact screen.

If you import contact information from your accounts on social networking sites, People maintains a connection to those accounts so it can display updated contact information. If the People tile is a live tile on the Start screen, it also displays updated information as it becomes available.

REFERENCE

Adding a Contact in People

- Click the People tile on the Start screen.
- Click the New button on the Apps bar.
- Enter contact information on the New contact screen.
- Click the Save button.

Jason doesn't want to import his contacts from other services, so you'll show him how to use People to add a new contact.

To add a contact:

▶ **1.** Click the **People** tile on the Start screen. The People app opens, listing any contacts added to the app. Your People window might not contain any contacts. If this is the first time you are starting People, the main screen lists contact sources, including Facebook friends, Twitter contacts, Outlook contacts, and LinkedIn contacts.

▶ **2.** Right-click a blank spot on the screen, and then click the **New** button on the Apps bar to display the New contact screen. The type of online account you are using, such as Live, appears in the Account text box.

▶ **3.** Click the **First name** text box, type **Jason**, press the **Tab** key, and then type **Rowley** in the Last name text box.

▶ **4.** Press the **Tab** key, and then type **San Antonio Historical Association** in the Company text box.

TIP

You can click the Add button (plus icon) above a text box to enter additional names, email addresses, phone numbers, addresses, or other information for a contact.

▶ **5.** Click the **Email** text box to specify Jason's personal email address, and then type **JasonRowley@live.com**.

Trouble? If Personal does not appear under Email, click the option displayed (that is, Work or Other), click Personal, and then repeat Step 5.

▶ **6.** Click the **Save** button on the Apps bar.

▶ **7.** If the Jason Rowley contact information does not appear, click **Jason Rowley** on the People screen to display his contact information. See Figure 4-36.

Figure 4-36	New contact in People

ⓔ Jason Rowley

Email
JasonRowley@live.com
Personal

Other info
San Antonio Historical
Association
Company

Live

information entered for this contact

▶ **8.** Close the People app.

When you select a contact, you can click the Send email link to send that person an email message without starting the Mail app first. You can also view the contact's profile on a social networking site such as Facebook. If you have a photo of the contact, you can add it to the contact information to quickly identify the contact.

Next, you want to help Jason manage his schedule with the Calendar app.

Managing Your Schedule with Calendar

Calendar is another app that works with Mail. You use it to schedule appointments, track tasks, and stay on top of deadlines. Calendar also lets you schedule recurring events, such as weekly staff meetings, and set reminders so you don't miss an important appointment. When you schedule an event, Calendar blocks out the time in your schedule, helping you avoid scheduling conflicts. If the event is a meeting, you can invite contacts stored in the People app to attend the meeting. You can also adjust the Calendar view to display scheduled events in the Day, Week, or Month format. The Day format shows you the events for today and tomorrow.

Calendar actually includes more than one calendar. The Main calendar displays your user name and is designed for scheduling all of your appointments and events. Other calendars include Birthday, Personal, Holidays, and Work. If you want to keep your personal appointments separate from work events, for example, you can maintain two calendars—Personal and Work. On the Birthday calendar, add birthdays of your contacts and other people. Calendar will remind you about the upcoming birthday in a notification message as you are working anywhere in Windows 8. The same is true for the Holidays calendar. If you list national and personal holidays in the calendar, Calendar will remind you about each one.

Because Jason works so often at his computer, he is ready to use an electronic calendar. You'll show him how to start Calendar, which you did earlier.

To start Calendar:

1. Click the **Calendar** tile on the Start screen. The Calendar screen opens, showing a calendar for the current day, week, or month.

2. If the calendar shows the day or week view, right-click the screen and then click **Month** on the Apps bar to display your schedule for the month.

Now that you've opened Calendar, you can use it to schedule appointments.

Scheduling Appointments

In Calendar, you can schedule appointments such as meetings that occur for part of a day. You can also schedule events that last 24 hours or longer. An appointment appears as a colored block in your calendar, while a day-long event appears in a banner at the beginning of a day. When you schedule appointments, you can specify that they are recurring, such as training that takes place once a week, sales meetings scheduled once a month, or birthdays and other annual events. If you set a reminder for an event, a notification appears as you're working on another task in Windows 8, such as browsing the Internet.

REFERENCE

Scheduling an Appointment in Calendar

- Click the Calendar tile on the Start screen.
- Click the New button on the Apps bar.
- In the right pane, click Add a title and then enter a description of the appointment.
- In the When text boxes, enter or select the date of the appointment.
- In the Start text boxes, enter or select the time the appointment starts.
- In the How long text box, enter or select the length of the appointment.
- In the Where text box, enter the location of the appointment.
- If you have more than one calendar, click the Calendar arrow, and then select the calendar you want to use to schedule the appointment.
- Click the Save this event button on the toolbar.

The first appointment Jason wants to schedule is for a staff meeting later today, which is usually 30 minutes long.

To schedule an appointment:

▶ **1.** Double-click today's date. The Details pane opens on the left, displaying the details you can enter for the new appointment, such as the location and the start time.

▶ **2.** In the right pane, type **Staff meeting** as the event title.

Trouble? If the insertion point does not appear in the title area, click Add a title and then repeat Step 2.

▶ **3.** Click **Add a message** and then type **Be prepared to summarize the status of your latest projects.**

▶ **4.** Click each **Start** text box as necessary to select a time two hours from now.

▶ **5.** Click the **How long** text box, and then click **30 minutes**.

▶ **6.** Click the **Where** text box in the Details pane and then type **West conference room** as the location. You can accept the selection for the Calendar text box. See Figure 4-37.

Figure 4-37　　**Scheduling an appointment**

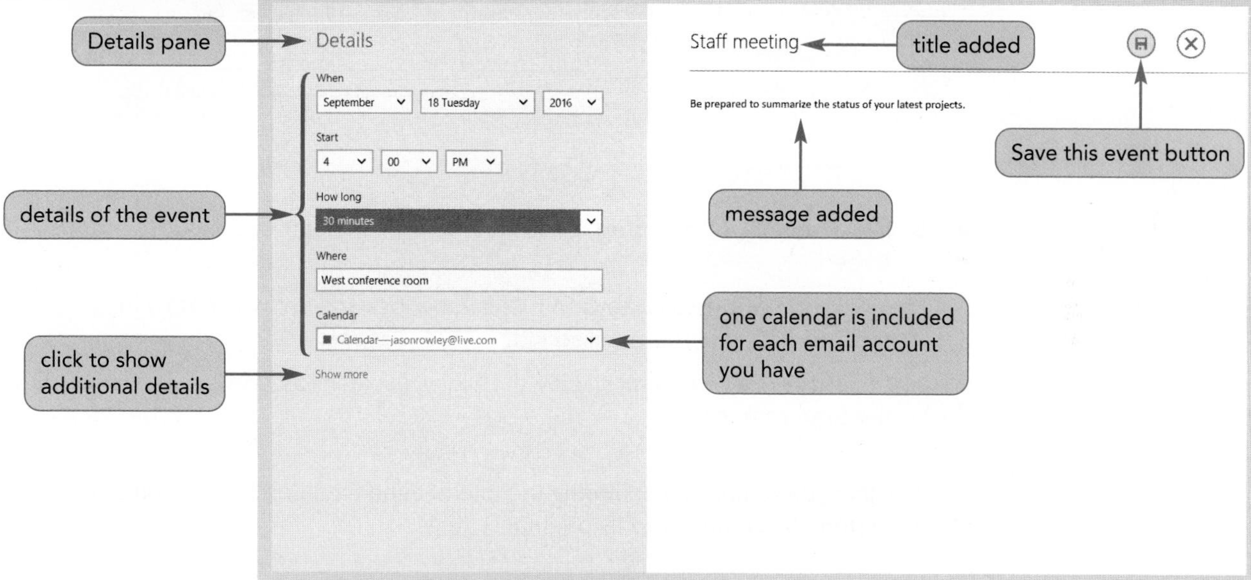

- Details pane
- Details

When
September ∨　18 Tuesday ∨　2016 ∨

Start
4 ∨　00 ∨　PM ∨

- details of the event

How long
30 minutes ∨

Where
West conference room

Calendar
■ Calendar—jasonrowley@live.com ∨

- click to show additional details
- Show more

Staff meeting ← title added

Be prepared to summarize the status of your latest projects.

- message added
- Save this event button
- one calendar is included for each email account you have

▶ **7.** Click the **Save this event** button Ⓗ on the toolbar.

▶ **8.** Close the Calendar app.

TIP

To edit an appointment already scheduled in the Calendar, double-click the appointment.

You've created an appointment for Jason's weekly staff meeting. Next, you can set appointment details to appear on your lock screen so you see them as soon as you turn on your computer or return to it after being away for awhile. You do so using the PC settings screen, which you've used in previous tutorials.

To display Calendar details on the lock screen:

▶ **1.** Display the Charms bar, and then click the **Settings** charm to display the Settings menu.

▶ **2.** Click the **Change PC settings** command to display the PC settings screen.

3. If necessary, click **Lock screen** to display the settings for the lock screen.

4. Scroll down to the Lock screen apps section. For the Choose an app to display detailed status setting, click the **Calendar** icon 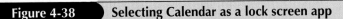 to display apps that can show detailed information on the lock screen. See Figure 4-38.

| Figure 4-38 | Selecting Calendar as a lock screen app |

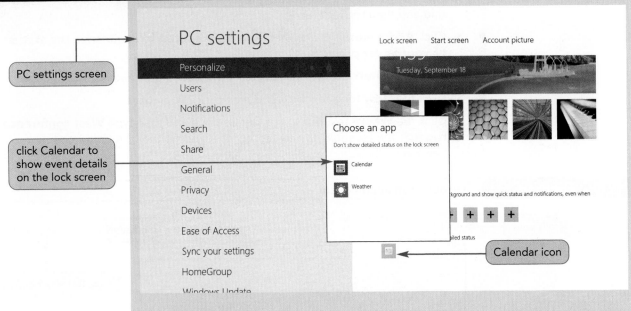

PC settings screen

click Calendar to show event details on the lock screen

Calendar icon

5. If Calendar is not selected, click **Calendar**, and then close the PC settings screen.

6. Press the **Windows+L** keys to display the lock screen, which now includes the appointment you entered in the Calendar app.

7. Clear the lock screen to display the Sign-in screen. Sign in as usual to display the Start screen.

Now that you've finished exploring the Internet and email on Jason's computer, you should restore the computer to its original settings.

Restoring Your Settings

If you are working in a computer lab or using a computer other than your own, complete the steps in this section to restore the original settings on the computer.

To restore your settings:

1. Click the **Desktop** tile to display the desktop.

2. Start Internet Explorer, click the **Safety** button on the Command bar, click **Delete browsing history**, click the **History** check box to select it (if necessary), deselect the other check boxes, and then click the **Delete** button. When a Notification bar appears at the bottom of the Internet Explorer window, click the **Close** button ⊠ to close the Notification bar.

3. Open the Favorites Center, click the **Add to favorites button arrow**, and then click **Organize favorites**.

▶ **4.** Click the **Ancestry Research** folder, and then click the **Delete** button. Click the **Close** button to close the Organize Favorites dialog box.

▶ **5.** Right-click the **Prologue: Pieces of History** button on the Favorites bar, and then click **Delete** on the shortcut menu.

▶ **6.** Use the same technique to delete the **National Archives and Records Administration** button on the Favorites bar.

▶ **7.** Click the **Tools** button on the Command bar, point to **Toolbars**, and then click **Favorites bar** to remove the Favorites bar from the Internet Explorer window.

▶ **8.** Close Internet Explorer.

▶ **9.** Right-click the **Resources for Genealogists and Family Historians** button on the taskbar, and then click **Unpin this program from taskbar**.

▶ **10.** Delete the **Events** file from the Public Documents folder in the Documents library.

▶ **11.** Press the **Windows** key ⊞ to return to the Start screen.

▶ **12.** Scroll to the right, right-click the **National Archives** tile, and then click **Unpin from Start** on the Apps bar.

▶ **13.** Right-click the **Census Bureau** tile and then click **Unpin from Start** on the Apps bar.

▶ **14.** Click the **Internet Explorer** tile to start IE Windows 8.

▶ **15.** Display the Charms bar, and then click the **Settings** button.

▶ **16.** Click **Internet Options** and then drag the Flip ahead slider from On to **Off**.

▶ **17.** Close the Settings screen and IE Windows 8.

▶ **18.** Start Mail, click the **No** button if a message appears asking if you want to set Mail as your default email program, click the **Events list you requested** message in the Inbox, and then click the **Delete** button ⓘ on the Mail toolbar.

▶ **19.** Click the **Sent items** folder in the Mail pane; select the **Events list you requested**, **Re: Test email**, and **Test email** messages; and then click the **Delete** button ⓘ on the Mail toolbar.

▶ **20.** Click the **Deleted items** folder in the Mail pane, select all messages in the Deleted items folder, and then click the **Delete** button ⓘ. Close the Mail app.

▶ **21.** Click the **People** tile on the Start screen. Click **Jason Rowley** in the list of contacts, right-click his name, click the **Delete** button on the Apps bar, and then click the **Delete** button to confirm. Close the People app.

▶ **22.** Click the **Calendar** tile on the Start screen. Click the appointment you added to the calendar, click the **Delete** button ⓘ, and then click the **Delete** button to confirm. Close the Calendar app.

▶ **23.** Display the Charms bar, click the **Settings** charm, click the **Change PC settings** command, click the **Calendar** icon ▦ in the Choose an app to display detailed status section, and then click **Don't show detailed status on the lock screen**.

▶ **24.** Close all apps and windows.

REVIEW

Session 4.2 Quick Check

1. When you send an email message, it travels from your computer, through a network, and then arrives at a computer called a(n) _____, which stores the message until the recipient requests it.
2. Where does Mail display the contents of a selected message?
3. Identify the user name and the email server name in the following email address: RosaMing@mail.net.
4. What information does Mail automatically provide for you when you reply to an email message?
5. What is the purpose of the Deleted items folder in the Mail app?
6. Describe two ways to add contact information to the People app.
7. If you set a reminder for a scheduled event, how does Calendar remind you?

Review Assignments

Data File needed for the Review Assignments: Missions.rtf

You already showed Jason how to conduct research on genealogy to prepare for his genealogy workshops at the San Antonio Historical Association. He also needs information about the San Antonio Missions, national historical parks in San Antonio, Texas, for a presentation he is giving to SAHA. You'll use Internet Explorer to research information about the missions. Complete the following steps:

1. Start IE Windows 8 on the Start screen, and then go to **www.nps.gov/saan**, which is the home page for the San Antonio Missions in the National Park Service Web site.
2. Click a link on this page to open the Plan Your Visit Web page for the San Antonio Missions.
3. Click the Things To Do link on the left to display visitor information.
4. Click a link on this page to display information about Mission Espada.
5. Pin the Web page about Mission Espada to the Start screen.
6. Open the Photos & Multimedia link on a new tab, and then display the Photos & Multimedia page.
7. Click the Address bar and then press the Print Screen key to capture an image of the screen. Start Paint, paste the screen image in a new file, and then save the file as **IE Windows 8 Missions** in the Windows4\Review folder provided with your Data Files.
8. Close IE Windows 8.
9. Open Internet Explorer on the desktop, and then go to **www.tshaonline.org**, which is the home page for the Texas State Historical Association.
10. Click The Handbook of Texas Online link, and then search for information about missions in Texas. Open two Web pages about the San Antonio missions on new tabs.
11. Open the Favorites Center and pin it to the Internet Explorer window. Use the History list or other Internet Explorer tools to navigate to a Web page you think will be especially useful to the San Antonio Historical Association, and then add it to your Favorites list.
12. Open the Favorites bar, go to **www.nps.gov/saan**, and then add a button for this Web page to the Favorites bar.
13. On any open Web page displaying information about a San Antonio mission, select the name of a location, and then use the Map with Bing Accelerator to preview a map of the location.
14. Press the Print Screen key to capture an image of the Internet Explorer window. In Paint, paste the screen image in a new file, and then save the file as **IE Desktop Missions** in the Windows4\Review folder provided with your Data Files.
15. Close Internet Explorer. Copy the **Missions** file from the Windows4\Review folder to the Public Documents folder in the Documents library.
16. Start Mail and create an email message. Enter your email address and your instructor's email address in the To text box and use **San Antonio mission** as the subject of the message.
17. In the message area, write a message describing one mission Jason should be sure to include in his presentation, based on your research.
18. Attach the **Missions** file to the message.
19. Send the message, and then add your email address and your instructor's email address to the People app.
20. Add an appointment to the Calendar for a 30-minute meeting with Jason at the San Antonio Historical Association today.

21. Complete the following tasks to restore your computer to its original settings:

- In IE Desktop, clear the History list, delete the Web page you added to the Favorites list, delete the button you added to the Favorites bar, close the Favorites bar, and then close the Favorites Center.
- Close Internet Explorer.
- Delete the Missions document from the Public Documents folder.
- On the Start screen, delete the tile for the pinned Web page.
- In Mail, delete the emails you sent and received, and then empty the Deleted items folder.
- In People, delete yourself and your instructor from the contacts list.
- In Calendar, delete the appointment you created.

22. Close all open windows and apps.

23. Submit the results of the preceding steps to your instructor, either in printed or electronic form, as requested.

Case Problem 1

There are no Data Files needed for this Case Problem.

Geology Central   Chad Marcus runs Geology Central, a nonprofit organization in Wichita, Kansas, that promotes geology education for students in grades 1 through 12. Chad runs a summer program on volcanoes, which is especially popular with students in all grades. He wants to take advantage of the volcano information posted on the Web by national geology organizations and use it in his program. Recently, Chad hired you to help administer the program. He asks you to find online information about volcanoes, especially information involving students. Complete the following steps:

1. Start Internet Explorer on the Start screen, and then go to the U.S. Geological Survey Education Web page at **education.usgs.gov**.

2. Using the tools on this page, look for information about volcanoes. (*Hint*: You might need to search for this information.) Open one of the pages you found.

3. On new tabs, open three other geology Web pages:
   - NASA Science: **kids.earth.nasa.gov**
   - The Dynamic Earth: **www.mnh.si.edu/earth**
   - Geology.com: **geology.com/volcanoes**

4. Click links on these Web pages and use the Charms bar to search for three other Web pages that provide information about volcanoes in the United States.

5. Pin the three Web pages you found to the Start screen.

6. Click the Address bar and then press the Print Screen key to capture an image of the screen. Start Paint, paste the screen image in a new file, and then save the file as **IE Windows 8 Volcanoes** in the Windows4\Case1 folder provided with your Data Files.

7. Close IE Windows 8.

8. Open Internet Explorer on the desktop, and then open The Dynamic Earth Web page at **www.mnh.si.edu/earth**, which is part of the Smithsonian National Museum of Natural History Web site. Turn down the volume on your speakers or use headphones before you click the Multimedia Version link, and then watch the Plate Tectonics and Volcanoes part of the multimedia presentation.

9. Pin The Dynamic Earth page to the taskbar. Close IE Desktop and then start it again.

10. Use Internet Explorer tools to explore the Smithsonian National Museum of Natural History Web site at **www.mnh.si.edu**, looking for pages on volcanoes. Save three Web pages about volcanoes in your Favorites list in a folder named **Volcanoes**.

11. Find a blog on the Smithsonian National Museum of Natural History home page, and then subscribe to its RSS feed. Add the feed to the Favorites bar, and then display the Favorites bar in the Internet Explorer window. Display the main page of the Natural History blog.

12. Pin the Favorites Center to the Internet Explorer window, if necessary, so that the Favorites list stays open. Open the Volcanoes folder in the Favorites list to display the Web pages you found.

13. Press the Print Screen key to capture an image of the desktop. In Paint, paste the screen image in a new file, and then save the file as **IE Desktop Volcanoes** in the Public Documents folder in the Documents library.

14. Close Internet Explorer.

15. Start Mail and create an email message. Enter your email address and your instructor's email address in the To text box and enter **Ideas for volcano program** as the subject of the message.

16. In the message area, write a message describing the volcano information provided on one of the Web pages you found.

17. Attach the **IE Desktop Volcanoes** file to the message, and then send it.

18. Restore your computer by completing the following tasks:
    - In IE Desktop, clear the History list, delete the folder you added to the Favorites list, delete the RSS feed you added to the Favorites bar, and then close the Favorites bar and the Favorites Center. Close IE Desktop.
    - Unpin the Web page from the taskbar.
    - Move the **IE Desktop Volcanoes** file to the Windows4\Case1 folder provided with your Data Files.
    - On the Start screen, delete the tiles for the pinned Web pages.
    - In Mail, delete the email you sent, and then delete the messages from the Deleted items folder.

19. Close all open windows and apps.

20. Submit the results of the preceding steps to your instructor, either in printed or electronic form, as requested.

Case Problem 2

APPLY

There are no Data Files needed for this Case Problem.

Folk Art Reproductions   Lorraine Rojas owns a company called Folk Art Reproductions in Bowling Green, Ohio. Lorraine's company acquires reproduction rights from museums and artists so it can create replicas of paintings, sculpture, quilts, and other decorative objects. Lorraine recently hired you as a research assistant. Your main responsibility is to learn about the folk art collections at American museums, which you can do by using Internet Explorer. Complete the following steps:

1. Start Internet Explorer on the Start screen, and then go to the American Folk Art Museum Web site at **folkartmuseum.org**.

2. On additional tabs, open the home pages for the following Web sites:
   - Museum of Craft and Folk Art: **www.mocfa.org**
   - Craft and Folk Art Museum: **www.cafam.org**

3. Click links and use the Internet Explorer tools to find a description of a current exhibition on each Web site.

4. Pin the three exhibition Web pages to the Start screen.

5. Click the Address bar and then press the Print Screen key to capture an image of the screen. Start Paint, paste the screen image in a new file, and then save the file as **IE Windows 8 Folk Art** in the Windows4\Case2 folder provided with your Data Files.

6. Close IE Windows 8.

7. Open Internet Explorer on the desktop, and then open the home page for the American Folk Art Museum.

8. Click links and use the Internet Explorer tools to find information about location and hours at the museum.

9. Pin the page you found to the taskbar. Close the Internet Explorer window and then start IE Desktop again.

10. Return to the American Folk Art Museum home page. (*Hint*: Use the History list.) On separate tabs, open three pages that show images of furniture, pottery, and quilts. Save these Web pages in your Favorites list in a folder named **Folk Art**.

11. Pin the Favorites Center to the Internet Explorer window, if necessary, so that the Favorites list stays open. Open the Folk Art folder in the Favorites list to display the Web pages you found.

12. Open the Web page pinned to the taskbar, and then select an address on the page. Use the Bing Maps Accelerator to preview a map of the location.

13. Press the Print Screen key to capture an image of the desktop. In Paint, paste the screen image in a new file, and then save the file as **IE Desktop Folk Art** in the Windows4\Case2 folder provided with your Data Files.

14. Close Internet Explorer.

15. Start Mail and create an email message addressed to you and your instructor. Enter **Folk Art Exhibition** as the subject.

16. In the message area, write a message describing the types of folk art objects collected by the museums you researched. Send the message to yourself and your instructor.

17. Restore your computer by completing the following tasks:
    - In IE Desktop, clear the History list, delete the folder you added to the Favorites list, and then close the Favorites Center.
    - Unpin the Web page from the taskbar.
    - Close Internet Explorer.
    - On the Start screen, delete the tiles for the pinned Web pages.
    - In Mail, delete the email you sent, and then empty the Deleted items folder.

18. Close all open windows and apps.

19. Submit the results of the preceding steps to your instructor, either in printed or electronic form, as requested.

Case Problem 3

There are no Data Files needed for this Case Problem.

Pro-Fit Chefs   Nicholas DeMars started Pro-Fit Chefs in Miami, Florida, to train chefs in preparing vegetarian dishes that are healthy and appealing. He also works in Miami public schools to create school lunches that feature produce from Florida farmers. Nicholas hired you as his project assistant, and asked you to find Web sites providing basic nutritional information for the chefs he trains. Complete the following steps:

1. Start Internet Explorer on the Start screen, and then go to the Choose My Plate Web site at **www.choosemyplate.gov**.
2. On additional tabs, open the following Web pages:
    - Nutrition.gov: **www.nutrition.gov**
    - Dietary Guidelines for Americans: **health.gov/dietaryguidelines**
3. Click links and use Internet Explorer tools to find at least one Web page from each site that provides lists of recommended foods to include in shopping and meal-planning lists or recipes.
4. Pin the three Web pages you found to the Start screen.

⊕ **Explore** 5. Use the Charms bar to send one of the Web pages you found to yourself and your instructor via email.

6. In IE Windows 8, click the Address bar and then press the Print Screen key to capture an image of the screen. Start Paint, paste the screen image in a new file, and then save the file as **IE Windows 8 Nutrition** in the Windows4\Case3 folder provided with your Data Files.
7. Close IE Windows 8.
8. Start Internet Explorer on the desktop. Open the home page for the Nutrition.gov Web site. (*Hint*: Use the History list.)

⊕ **Explore** 9. On separate tabs, open three Web pages that would be helpful to Pro-Fit Chefs. Save the group of open tabs in your Favorites list in a folder named **Nutrition**. (*Hint*: Open the Favorites Center, click the Add to favorites button arrow, click Add current tabs to favorites on the shortcut menu, name the folder **Nutrition**, and then click the Add button.)

⊕ **Explore** 10. Turn on Suggested Sites to allow Internet Explorer to discover Web sites you might like based on the Web sites you've visited. Display the Favorites bar, and then click the Suggested Sites button to display a list of Suggested Sites. Open two suggested sites on separate tabs.

11. Pin one of the suggested sites to the taskbar.

⊕ **Explore** 12. On the Nutrition.gov home page, click the En Español link on the navigation bar. Select the first paragraph on the page, click the Accelerator icon, and then point to Translate with Bing. Press the Print Screen key to capture an image of the desktop. In Paint, paste the screen image in a new file, and then save the file as **IE Desktop Nutrition** in the Windows4\Case3 folder provided with your Data Files.

⊕ **Explore** 13. Open the Dietary Guidelines for Americans Web page at **health.gov/dietaryguidelines**, and then click the links on the Web page to find a file you can download that provides nutritional guidelines. For example, look for a PDF link next to the name of an article. (Recall that PDFs, or Portable Document Format files, contain text and images that you can often download from a Web site and read with Windows Reader.) Right-click the link to a nutrition file, click Save target as, and then save the file as **Guidelines** in the Public Documents folder in the Documents library.

14. Start Mail and create an email message addressed to you and your instructor. Enter **Nutritional Guidelines** as the subject.

15. In the message area, write a message listing two guidelines for preparing nutritional meals.

16. Attach the **Guidelines** file to the message, and then send the message.

17. Restore your computer by completing the following tasks:

- In IE Desktop, clear the History list, delete the folder you added to the Favorites list, and then turn off Suggested Sites. Close the Favorites bar and the Favorites Center.

- Unpin the Web page from the taskbar.

- Move the **Guidelines** file from the Public Documents folder to the Windows4\Case3 folder provided with your Data Files.

- On the Start screen, delete the tiles for the pinned Web pages.

- In Mail, delete the email you sent, and then empty the Deleted items folder.

18. Close all open windows and apps.

19. Submit the results of the preceding steps to your instructor, either in printed or electronic form, as requested.

Case Problem 4

CHALLENGE

There are no Data Files needed for this Case Problem.

American Crew Club   The American Crew Club is a group of rowers in Bethesda, Maryland, that supports and promotes women's crew teams at colleges and universities in the United States. Maureen Upton, the club president, recently hired you as a part-time assistant. You help Maureen write the club newsletter and organize promotional events. Maureen wants you to visit college Web sites periodically to make sure they are promoting their women's crew teams. Complete the following steps:

1. Start Internet Explorer on the Start screen, and go to the women's crew page at the Wesleyan University Web site at **www.wesleyan.edu/athletics/wcrew**.

2. On additional tabs, open the following Web pages:

- Williams College Women's Crew page: **athletics.williams.edu/sports/wcrew**

- Sacramento State Women's Rowing page: **www.hornetsports.com/sports/wcrew**

3. Click links and use Internet Explorer tools to find at least one Web page from each site that shows the schedule for the current or upcoming season.

4. Pin the three Web pages you found to the Start screen.

Explore 5. Use the Charms bar to print one of the schedules you found.

6. In IE Windows 8, click the Address bar and then press the Print Screen key to capture an image of the screen. Start Paint, paste the screen image in a new file, and then save the file as **IE Windows 8 Crew** in the Windows4\Case4 folder provided with your Data Files.

7. Close IE Windows 8.

8. Open Internet Explorer on the desktop, and then on separate tabs, open the same three pages you opened in Steps 1 and 2.

Explore 9. Save all of the open tabs in your Favorites list in a folder named **Crew**. (*Hint*: Open the Favorites Center, click the Add to favorites button arrow, click Add current tabs to favorites, name the folder **Crew**, and then click the Add button.)

✪ **Explore** 10. On the Web site for any of the three colleges, find a Web page showing the results of a recent season. Click the Page button on the Command bar, click Save as to open the Save Webpage dialog box, navigate to the Windows4\Case4 folder provided with your Data Files, click the Save as type button, click Web Archive, single file (*.mht), and then type **Results** as the filename. Click the Save button.

✪ **Explore** 11. Turn on Suggested Sites to allow Internet Explorer to discover Web sites you might like based on the Web sites you've visited. Display the Favorites bar, and then click the Suggested Sites button to display a list of Suggested Sites.

12. Pin one of the suggested sites to the taskbar, and then close the window for the suggested site.

13. Press the Print Screen key to capture an image of the desktop. In Paint, paste the screen image in a new file, and then save the file as **IE Desktop Crew** in the Windows4\Case4 folder provided with your Data Files.

14. Restore your computer by completing the following tasks:
   - In IE Desktop, clear the History list, delete the folder you added to the Favorites list, turn off Suggested Sites, and then close the Favorites bar and the Favorites Center. Close IE Desktop.
   - Unpin the Web page from the taskbar.
   - On the Start screen, delete the tiles for the pinned Web pages.

15. Close all open windows and apps.

16. Submit the results of the preceding steps to your instructor, either in printed or electronic form, as requested.

OBJECTIVES

Session 5.1
- Use the Action Center
- Set up Windows Firewall and Windows Update
- Protect your computer from viruses and other malicious software
- Use Windows Defender to protect against spyware
- Examine Mail security

Session 5.2
- Manage Microsoft Internet Explorer security
- Protect privacy with InPrivate Browsing and Tracking Protection
- Set up user accounts
- Control access to your computer
- Examine other built-in security features

Protecting Your Computer

Managing Computer Security

Case | *Catapult Product Design*

A few years ago, Duane Ellison founded Catapult Product Design in Edison, New Jersey. Catapult designs, creates, and tests new products, ranging from industrial tools to consumer goods for corporate clients around the world. Recently, Duane has become concerned with the security of Catapult's computers. Many of Duane's product designers work at client offices using portable computers running Windows 8. Although these designers can access the Internet with their computers, they can't usually connect to the Catapult network, where an administrator oversees security. Instead, they must take advantage of the security tools in Windows 8 to prevent problems stemming from viruses, spyware, and other types of harmful software. Duane recently hired you to support the design staff. One of your first duties is to investigate the security features in Windows 8 and show Duane how to use them to address security threats.

In this tutorial, you'll explore the tools in the Action Center, including Windows Firewall and Windows Update. You'll learn how to set up Windows 8 to work with antivirus software and how to implement other security measures, including setting up user accounts. You will also examine Internet Explorer security settings so that you can use the Internet safely.

STARTING DATA FILES

There are no starting Data Files needed for this tutorial.

Session 5.1 Visual Overview:

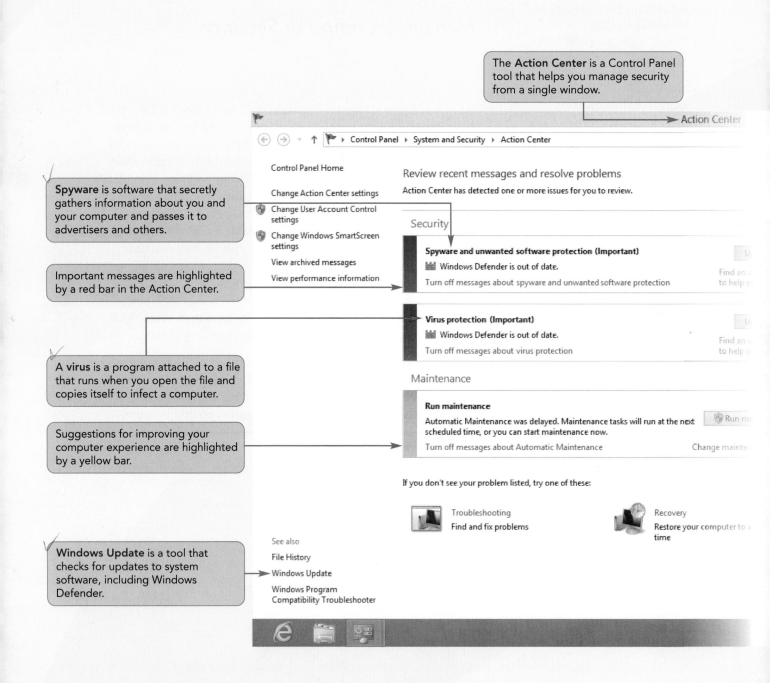

The **Action Center** is a Control Panel tool that helps you manage security from a single window.

Spyware is software that secretly gathers information about you and your computer and passes it to advertisers and others.

Important messages are highlighted by a red bar in the Action Center.

A **virus** is a program attached to a file that runs when you open the file and copies itself to infect a computer.

Suggestions for improving your computer experience are highlighted by a yellow bar.

Windows Update is a tool that checks for updates to system software, including Windows Defender.

Action Center

← → ∨ ↑ 🏳 › Control Panel › System and Security › Action Center

Control Panel Home

Change Action Center settings

Change User Account Control settings

Change Windows SmartScreen settings

View archived messages

View performance information

Review recent messages and resolve problems
Action Center has detected one or more issues for you to review.

Security

Spyware and unwanted software protection (Important)
📋 Windows Defender is out of date.
Turn off messages about spyware and unwanted software protection

Virus protection (Important)
📋 Windows Defender is out of date.
Turn off messages about virus protection

Maintenance

Run maintenance
Automatic Maintenance was delayed. Maintenance tasks will run at the next scheduled time, or you can start maintenance now.
Turn off messages about Automatic Maintenance

Change mainte

If you don't see your problem listed, try one of these:

Troubleshooting
Find and fix problems

Recovery
Restore your computer to time

See also

File History

Windows Update

Windows Program Compatibility Troubleshooter

The Action Center

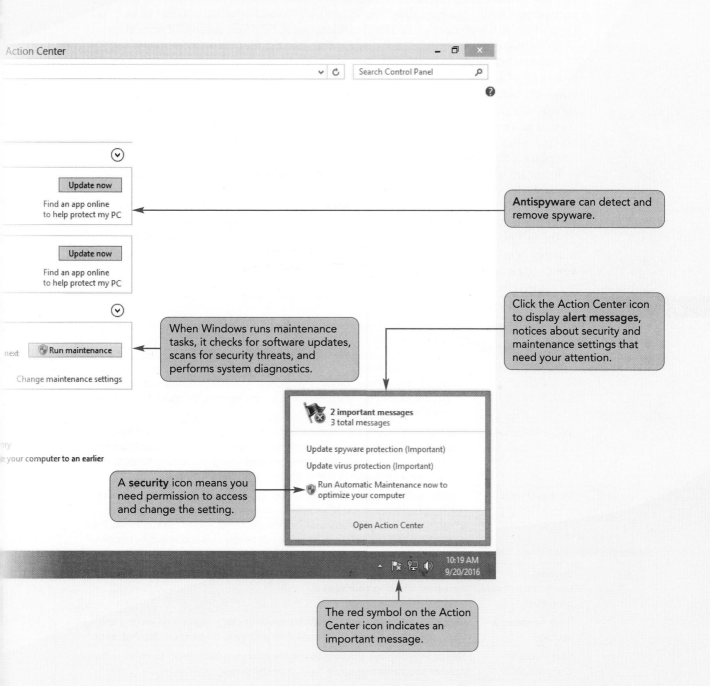

Antispyware can detect and remove spyware.

Click the Action Center icon to display **alert messages**, notices about security and maintenance settings that need your attention.

When Windows runs maintenance tasks, it checks for software updates, scans for security threats, and performs system diagnostics.

A **security** icon means you need permission to access and change the setting.

The red symbol on the Action Center icon indicates an important message.

Using the Action Center

Windows 8 provides many tools that help you keep your computer safe from threats such as harmful software, unsolicited email, and invasions of your privacy. When you connect to the Internet, send and receive email, or share your computer or files with others, your computer is vulnerable to harm from people who might attempt to steal your personal information, damage your files, or interrupt your work. You should use the Windows 8 security tools and other techniques to defend against these threats.

Harmful software (referred to as **malicious software**, or **malware**) includes viruses. By copying itself and triggering computer code, a virus can infect your computer. The damage a virus causes can range from changing your desktop settings to deleting or corrupting files on your hard disk. Viruses are often spread by email and run when you open an email attachment or the email message itself. Files you download from Web sites can also contain viruses that run when you save the files on your computer.

People who create and send malware are called **hackers**, a generic term that refers to anyone who intends to access a computer system without permission. (Hackers with criminal intent are sometimes called **crackers**, or black hat hackers.) Hackers can also invade your privacy by accessing your computer via the Internet to find information such as passwords and financial account numbers. Hackers sometimes access your computer using spyware, software that secretly gathers information about you and your computer actions, including sensitive information.

If you are working on a computer connected to a network, a network administrator probably defends the network against security threats such as viruses, worms, spyware, and hackers. Otherwise, if you are working on a home computer, for example, you should take advantage of the security features that Windows 8 provides.

The first place to go to secure your computer is the Action Center, a Control Panel tool that helps you manage security from a single window. Some of the security settings you can manage in the Action Center are listed in Figure 5-1.

| Figure 5-1 | Action Center features |

Security Feature	Description
Network Firewall	This feature uses Windows Firewall by default to monitor and restrict communication with the Internet, which helps protect your computer from hackers. Before an app can send or receive information via the Internet, Windows Firewall must allow it to do so.
Windows Update	This feature checks for the latest Windows updates on the Microsoft Web site, and then downloads and installs the updates for you. Because Windows updates often include security enhancements, using this feature helps to make sure that your computer is secure against most current threats.
Virus protection	Antivirus software is your best protection against viruses, worms, and other types of harmful software. If you have antivirus software, Windows reminds you to use it regularly to scan your computer for virus infections and to monitor email. If you do not have antivirus software, Windows Defender runs automatically to defend your computer against malware.
Spyware and unwanted software protection	Antispyware software, such as Windows Defender, prevents some types of malware from infecting your system.
Internet security settings	Action Center checks that your Web browser is using appropriate security settings to block malware from being installed on your system when you visit Web sites.
User Account Control (UAC)	This service displays a dialog box requesting your permission to install software or open programs that could harm your computer.
Windows SmartScreen	This tool protects your computer from unrecognized apps and files you download from the Internet.

© 2014 Cengage Learning

Most of the features listed in Figure 5-1 are considered essential—you should turn on all of these Action Center features to keep your computer secure. If Windows detects a problem with one of these essential security features, such as when your firewall is turned off, Windows displays an alert message. If you're working on the Start screen or in a Windows 8 app, the message appears and fades as you're working. If you're working on the desktop, the message appears near the Action Center icon in the notification area of your taskbar. For example, you might see the following alert message, "Solve PC issues: 1 message." You can click the alert message or click the Action Center icon and then click Open Action Center to open the Action Center on the desktop and find out how to address the problem. You can also see if the Action Center lists any new messages by pointing to the Action Center icon.

You'll start showing Duane how to use the security features in Windows 8 by opening the Action Center.

To open the Action Center:

▶ **1.** Click the **Desktop** tile on the Start screen to display the desktop.

▶ **2.** Click the **Action Center** icon 🏳 in the notification area of the taskbar. A message window opens.

Trouble? If the Action Center icon 🏳 does not appear in the notification area of the taskbar, display the Charms bar, click the Settings charm, click PC info, and then click Action Center in the System window.

▶ **3.** In the message window, click **Open Action Center** to open the Action Center.

▶ **4.** If necessary, click the **expand** button ⊙ to expand the Security section. See Figure 5-2.

| Figure 5-2 | Action Center |

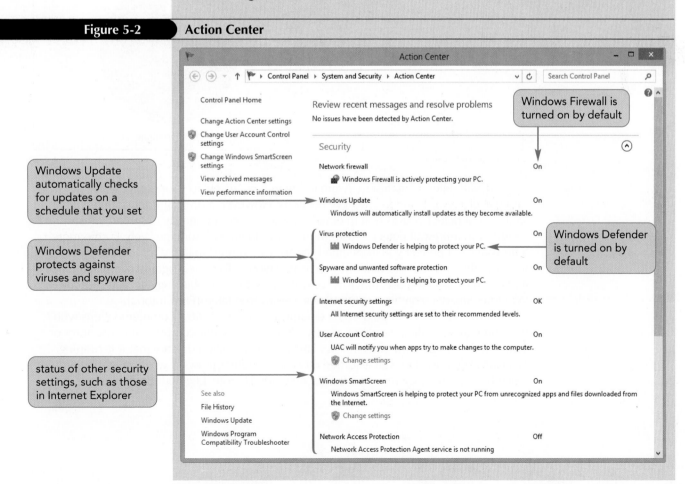

When you click the Action Center icon on the taskbar, the message window might list links to alert messages. If a security icon 🛡 appears next to a link, you might need permission to access and change the setting. You usually indicate that you have permission by entering an administrator password. Requiring a user to enter a password to change system settings is another way to protect your computer.

Leave the Action Center window open to perform the tasks described in the following sections.

Managing Windows Firewall

Windows Firewall is software that serves as a barrier between your computer and a network or the Internet. As shown in Figure 5-3, Windows Firewall checks information coming from the network or the Internet and either blocks it from your computer or allows it to pass, depending on your settings. In this way, Windows Firewall prevents unauthorized users from accessing your computer and is the first line of defense against malware. Many antivirus programs include a firewall that works in a similar way.

| Figure 5-3 | How Windows Firewall protects your computer |

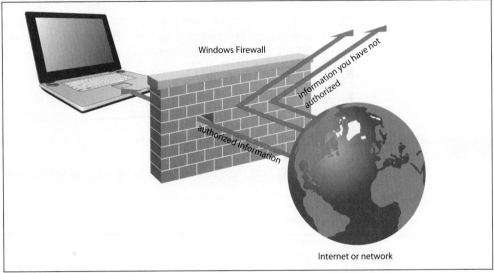

© 2014 Cengage Learning

A firewall defends against malware trying to gain access to your computer by monitoring your network and Internet connections. However, a firewall does not scan email, so it cannot detect viruses sent in email messages (a common way to spread viruses). Neither can a firewall detect viruses in files you download from the Web. Furthermore, a firewall can't protect you from email scams, called phishing, that try to deceive you into revealing private information such as passwords. To protect against viruses in email and downloaded files, use antivirus software. To minimize phishing attempts, use the Windows SmartScreen filter. (Both topics are covered later in this tutorial.)

Windows Firewall is turned on by default, so it doesn't allow communications with most programs via the Internet or a network. However, your computer manufacturer or someone else might turn off Windows Firewall, so you should verify that it is running. Typically, Windows Firewall is turned off only if another firewall, which might be provided by other security software or your network, is protecting your computer.

To turn on Windows Firewall:

▶ **1.** In the Action Center window, click **System and Security** in the Address bar to display the System and Security window.

▶ **2.** Click **Windows Firewall** to open the Windows Firewall window. See Figure 5-4.

Figure 5-4	Windows Firewall window

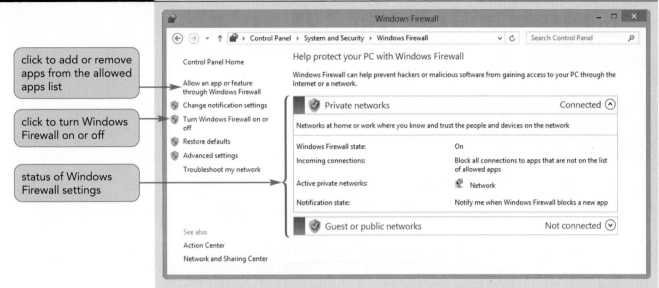

click to add or remove apps from the allowed apps list

click to turn Windows Firewall on or off

status of Windows Firewall settings

Trouble? If a different firewall is installed on your computer and is managing the firewall settings, your Windows Firewall window will look different from the figure, and you might not be able to change the settings. In that case, read but do not perform Steps 3–5.

▶ **3.** Click **Turn Windows Firewall on or off** in the left pane.

Trouble? If a User Account Control dialog box opens requesting an administrator password or your permission to continue, make sure you have permission to change Windows Firewall settings (check with your instructor, if necessary), and then enter the password or click the Yes button.

▶ **4.** In the Customize Settings window, click the first **Turn on Windows Firewall** option button (the one for Private network settings). See Figure 5-5.

Figure 5-5   **Customize Settings window**

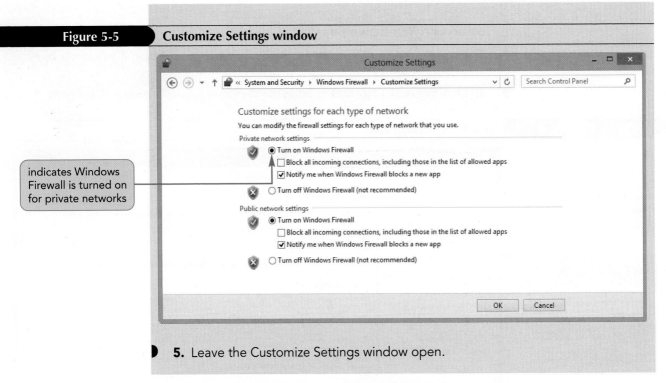

indicates Windows Firewall is turned on for private networks

5. Leave the Customize Settings window open.

When Windows Firewall is turned on and someone tries to connect to your computer from the Internet, Windows Firewall blocks the connection. Instead of turning off Windows Firewall every time you want to use a blocked program, you can customize the firewall by adding programs to its allowed list so that it maintains a level of security that's right for you.

In the Customize Settings window, you can specify firewall settings for each type of network location that you use. For example, you might use a private network at home or work and a public network in other locations. For each network location, you can select one of the following settings:

Turn on Windows Firewall—This setting is selected by default, meaning that most apps are blocked from communicating through the firewall.

Block all incoming connections, including those in the list of allowed apps—When you connect to a public network, such as in a hotel or an airport, you might want to select this setting. Windows blocks all apps, even those in the allowed list.

Notify me when Windows Firewall blocks a new app—When you select this check box, Windows Firewall informs you when it blocks a new app, giving you the option of adding the app to the allowed apps list.

• Turn off Windows Firewall (not recommended)—The only time you should select this setting is when another firewall is running on your computer.

Duane often uses network projectors to give presentations to potential clients in other locations. (A network projector is a video projector connected to a wireless or wired network, and it lets you give presentations using a network connection.) Before a network projector can communicate with a computer to indicate it is turned on and ready for the presentation, Windows Firewall must allow incoming connections from the network projector. You'll show Duane how to add the Connect to a Network Projector program to the allowed programs list so he can give network presentations without any problems.

If you are performing the following steps in a computer lab, you might not be allowed to change allowed programs. Check with your instructor or technical support person to determine whether you can specify Connect to a Network Projector as an allowed program in Windows Firewall. If you cannot, read but do not perform the following steps.

To add a program to the allowed programs list:

1. Click the **Back** button ⊕ to return to the Windows Firewall window.

2. In the left pane, click **Allow an app or feature through Windows Firewall** to open the Allowed apps window. See Figure 5-6.

   Trouble? If the Allow an app or feature through Windows Firewall link is inactive in the Windows Firewall window, click the Back button ⊕ to return to the System and Security window, and then click Allow an app or feature through Windows Firewall.

   Trouble? If a dialog box opens requesting an administrator password or your permission to continue, make sure you have permission to change the Windows Firewall settings (check with your instructor, if necessary), and then enter the password or click the Yes button.

Figure 5-6	Allowed apps window

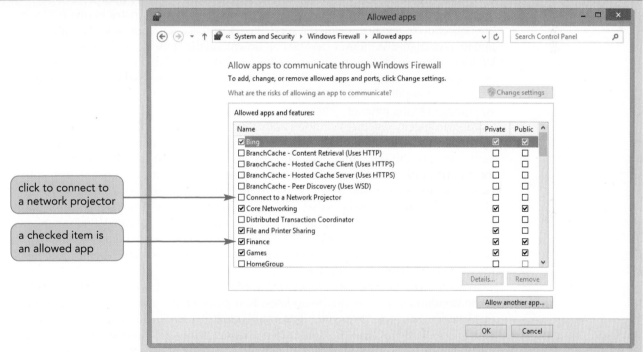

click to connect to a network projector

a checked item is an allowed app

3. Click the **Connect to a Network Projector** check box, if necessary, to select it. A check mark automatically appears in the Private column, indicating that Duane will be able to connect to the device within the company network.

   Trouble? If you cannot select an app in the list, click the Change settings button, and then repeat Step 3.

   Trouble? If you are not allowed to change the allowed apps in Windows Firewall, click the Cancel button in the Allowed apps window, and then skip Step 4.

4. Click the **OK** button to add Connect to a Network Projector to the allowed apps list and to return to the Windows Firewall window.

5. Click **System and Security** in the Address bar to return to the System and Security window.

Keep in mind that when you add an app to the Windows Firewall allowed apps list, you are making your computer easier for apps to access and therefore more vulnerable to malware infection. You should allow an app only when you really need it, and never allow an app that you don't recognize—it could be a virus or a worm. Finally, be sure to remove an app from the allowed apps list when you no longer need it.

Setting Up Windows Update

An **update** is a change to software that can prevent or repair problems, enhance the security of a computer, or improve a computer's performance. Microsoft regularly releases updates to Windows 8 and provides them for download from its Web site. You can look for, download, and install these updates any time you visit the Microsoft Web site. However, because updates often include critical security repairs and enhancements, Microsoft also makes them available to you through the Windows Update feature. Windows Update makes sure your operating system and its tools have the most recent software improvements and security enhancements.

When you use the Windows Update feature, Windows periodically checks for updates to the operating system from Microsoft, including security updates, critical updates, and service packs. (When Microsoft combines many updates in one package, the collection of updates is called a **service pack** and is often abbreviated as **SP**.) If an update is available, Windows Update can download the software and install it for you. Windows downloads the updates in the background according to a schedule you set, as long as you're connected to the Internet. If you are disconnected from the Internet before Windows finishes downloading, Windows continues downloading the next time you connect to the Internet.

You can specify whether Windows automatically downloads only important updates, downloads both important and recommended updates, or does not download automatically at all. Important updates are those you should install to maintain the security and reliability of Windows. Recommended updates usually enhance your computing experience and repair problems that are not considered critical. Microsoft also provides optional updates that don't apply to all Windows users. For example, if you use a particular piece of hardware, such as a digital music player, Windows might provide an optional update for the player's driver. Be sure to read the description of each optional update in the Windows Update window to determine whether you need to download and install the update.

In addition to the types of updates you want Windows to download, you can specify when Windows should install the updates. To notify you that updates are available or that Windows is ready to download or install updates, a notification appears on the Sign in screen. If you've set up automatic updating, Windows will download and install the update as you work on your computer. If restarting your computer is necessary to complete the update, Windows waits until you save data before restarting your computer. If your computer task takes up the entire screen, such as when you're watching a movie, Windows waits until you are finished with that task. You can also choose to have updates downloaded automatically but install them yourself: Click an update option on the Sign in screen or the Shutdown screen to install the updates.

To view your current update status and settings for Windows Update, you open the Windows Update window from the System and Security category of the Control Panel. You can also use this window to review your update history.

You recommend that Duane turn on automatic updating for important and recommended updates so he doesn't miss any of these updates for Windows 8. He wants to check for updates every morning at 8:00 while he is typically meeting with his staff. That way, Windows will not interrupt his work if it needs to install updates. Although he is not using his computer then, it is turned on and connected to the Internet.

As you perform the following steps, note your original settings so you can restore them later.

To set up Windows Update:

▶ **1.** In the System and Security window, click **Windows Update**. The Windows Update window opens. See Figure 5-7. Your settings might differ.

Figure 5-7 Windows Update window

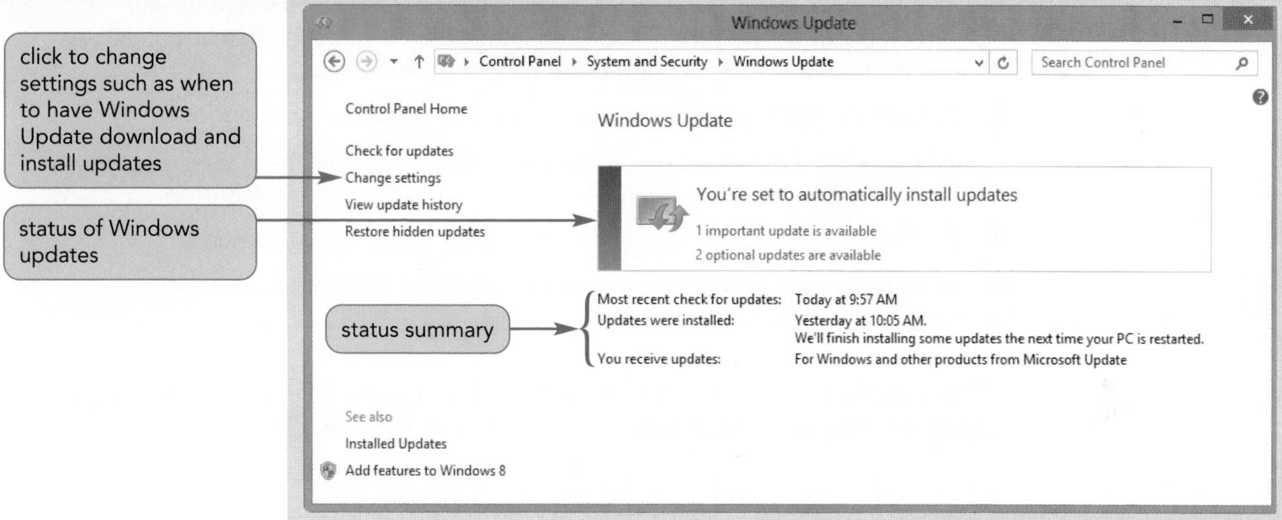

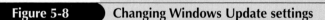

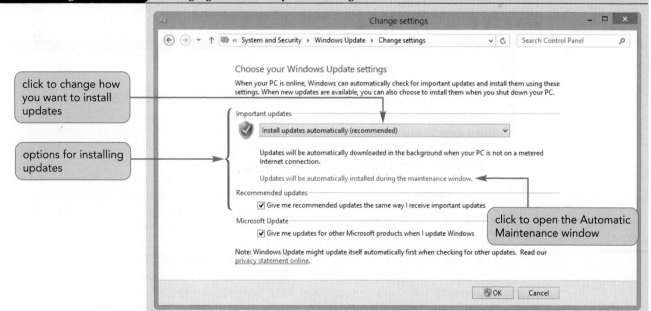

▶ **2.** In the left pane, click **Change settings**. The Change settings window opens. See Figure 5-8.

Figure 5-8 Changing Windows Update settings

▶ **3.** Make sure "Install updates automatically (recommended)" appears on the first button in the Important updates section. If it does not, click the button and then click **Install updates automatically (recommended)** in the list. Selecting this option means that Windows checks for updates according to a schedule, and then downloads and installs them for you when they are available.

TIP

To check for updates manually, click Check for updates in the left pane of the Windows Update window.

▶ 4. Click the **Updates will be automatically installed during the maintenance window**. link to open the Automatic Maintenance window so you can schedule the update check.

▶ 5. Click the **Run maintenance tasks daily at** button (which appears as 3:00 AM by default), and then click **8:00 AM**.

▶ 6. If necessary, click the **Allow scheduled maintenance to wake up my computer at the scheduled time** check box to select it. This option allows Windows to wake your computer for scheduled updates.

▶ 7. Click the **OK** button to close the Automatic Maintenance window.

   Trouble? If a dialog box opens requesting an administrator password or your permission to continue, enter the password or click the Yes button.

▶ 8. Click the **OK** button to accept the new Windows Update setting.

▶ 9. Click **System and Security** in the Address bar to return to the System and Security window.

Now that you know Duane's copy of Windows 8 is up to date, you can turn to protecting his computer from viruses and other types of malware.

Protecting Your Computer from Malware

Your best protection against malware is to use the current version of your antivirus software to scan email messages, attachments, and other files on your computer for viruses, worms, and other types of malware. Antivirus software locates a virus by comparing identifying characteristics of the files on your computer to the characteristics of a list of known viruses, which are called **virus definitions**. When it finds a virus, or any type of malware, the antivirus software notifies you about the virus.

INSIGHT

Recognizing Types of Malware

Recall that a virus is a program that replicates itself and attaches to files or programs, usually affects your computer's performance and stability, and sometimes damages or removes files. Viruses are often transmitted through email attachments or downloaded files, but they don't spread until you open the infected attachment or file. In contrast, a **worm** is harmful computer code that spreads without your interaction. A worm slips from one network connection to another, replicating itself on network computers. As it does, a worm consumes network resources, overwhelming computers until they become slow or unresponsive. Another type of malware is a **Trojan horse**, which is malware that hides inside another program, such as a photo-viewing program you download from the Web. When you install the program, the Trojan horse infects the operating system, allowing a hacker to access your computer. Trojan horses can't spread on their own; they depend on programs, including viruses and worms, to proliferate. If attackers access your system through a Trojan horse, they might install a **rootkit**, malware that gains administrator-level, or root-level, access to a computer or network without the system or users detecting its presence. Attackers use rootkits to monitor keystrokes (to learn passwords, for example), modify files, disable or alter tools that might detect the rootkit, and attack other devices on the network. Common symptoms of malware are when your computer runs much slower than normal, messages appear unexpectedly, programs start or close on their own, or Windows shuts down suddenly.

When you buy a new computer, most likely it comes with antivirus software already installed as a trial version so you can test it for a limited time. (Look for the antivirus software on the Apps screen.) Windows Defender is also installed on any Windows 8 computer to make sure the computer is protected from malware. To determine whether you should continue running the preinstalled antivirus software or Windows Defender, you should compare their features and read reviews from security experts to learn how well each app protects against viruses, spyware, Trojan horses, rootkits, and other malware.

Windows 8 can detect whether you have antivirus software installed on your computer. If you do not, Windows runs Windows Defender to protect your computer from malware. If you have antivirus software installed on your computer but the subscription has expired, Windows reminds you to renew the subscription, activate Windows Defender, or select another antivirus program from the Windows Store. If you have antivirus software installed and it's up to date, do not also run Windows Defender to scan for viruses because only one antivirus app should be running on your computer at any time.

Most vendors of antivirus software offer fee-based subscription services that provide regular updates for current virus definitions. You can refer to the antivirus software's help system to learn how to run the software and receive regular updates, or you can use the Action Center to check for updates. Besides Windows Defender, Windows recognizes most types of antivirus software and displays their status in the Action Center window. In most cases, you can use the Action Center to determine whether your antivirus software needs to be updated and then run the updating program. Windows Update keeps Windows Defender and its virus definitions up to date. Keeping the virus definition list current helps to protect your computer from new attacks. If your list of viruses is out of date, your computer is vulnerable to new threats.

Although Duane is certain that antivirus software is installed on his computer, he asks you to make sure it is up to date and that virus scanning is turned on.

To check for virus protection on your computer:

1. In the System and Security window, click **Action Center** to return to the Action Center window. If necessary, click **Security** to expand the Security section.

2. Examine the settings in the Virus protection section, which should report if an installed antivirus program is up to date and is protecting your computer. In Figure 5-9, the Action Center window reports that the antivirus program is out of date.

   Trouble? If the Action Center window reports that your virus protection is up to date and is protecting your computer, skip Step 3.

Figure 5-9	Antivirus software needs to be updated

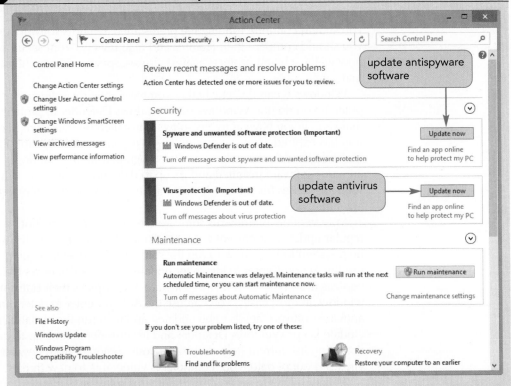

3. If necessary, click the **Update now** button. Your antivirus software starts and checks for updates on its manufacturer's Web site. When it is finished updating, close the antivirus software window, if necessary.

4. Close the Action Center.

PROSKILLS

Problem Solving: Avoiding and Removing Viruses

One of the most difficult computer problems to solve is removing a virus from your system. To avoid this problem, you can defend against viruses in the following ways so that they do not infect your computer:

- Do not open unexpected email attachments. If the message containing the attachment is from a trusted source, send an email to that person asking about the file and what it contains.
- Regularly scan your hard drive with an antivirus program. Most antivirus software includes an option to schedule a complete system scan. You only need to make sure your computer is turned on to perform the scan.
- Set your antivirus program to scan all *incoming email.*
- Keep your antivirus software up to date. New viruses are introduced frequently, and your antivirus software needs to use the latest virus definitions to protect your computer.
- Create backups of your work files periodically. Viruses can corrupt or destroy data files, which are the most valuable files on your computer.

When you notice symptoms such as your computer running slowly or turning off on its own, suspect a virus. You can try to remove a virus in the following ways:

- Update your antivirus software. Look for an update feature that connects with the Web site of your antivirus software developer to download the latest virus definitions.
- Use the antivirus software to scan your entire computer. The software might be able to remove the virus for you or identify the virus by name.
- Use an online scanner. If your antivirus software does not find or report a virus, visit the Microsoft Web site (www.microsoft.com) and search for "Windows security software providers". Look for vendors in the search results that provide free online virus scanners to help you find and remove the virus.
- Search for instructions on removing the virus. If your antivirus software or online scanner identifies but does not remove the virus, search an antivirus vendor's Web site to find information about removing the virus.

Another security concern is spyware, which can also affect your computing experience.

Defending Against Spyware

TIP

Before installing any software from a Web site, read the license agreement. Do not install software that requires you to accept pop-up ads and to let the program send data about you to the software publisher.

Spyware can install itself or run on your computer without your consent or control. It's called spyware because it monitors your computing actions, usually while you are online, to collect information about you. Spyware can change system settings, interrupt programs, and slow your computer's performance. Spyware may infect your computer when you visit a certain Web site or download a free program, such as a screen saver or search toolbar. Less frequently, spyware is distributed along with other programs on a CD, DVD, or other type of removable media. Sometimes, spyware passes information about your Web browsing habits to advertisers, who use it to improve their products or Web sites. Other times, a special type of spyware called **adware** changes your browser settings to open **pop-up ads**, which are windows that appear while you are viewing a Web page and advertise a product or service. Pop-up ads interrupt your online activities and can be difficult to close; they can also be vehicles for additional spyware or other types of malware.

Because spyware can download, install, and run on your computer without your knowledge or consent, it's often difficult to know if spyware is infecting your computer. If you are experiencing any of the following symptoms, they are most likely due to spyware:

New toolbars, links, or favorites appear in your Web browser unexpectedly.
Your home page, mouse pointer, or search program changes without your consent.

When you enter a URL for a Web site, such as a search engine, you go to a different Web site without notice.
Pop-up ads interrupt you, even when you're not on the Internet.
• Your computer suddenly restarts or runs slowly.

Be sure to scan your computer with a program, such as Windows Defender, to detect and remove any spyware on your computer.

Scanning Your Computer with Windows Defender

To protect your computer against spyware, you can run up-to-date antispyware software or antimalware software, such as Windows Defender, to check for both spyware and viruses. Windows Defender helps prevent malware from installing itself and running on your computer, and it periodically scans your computer to detect and remove malware.

REFERENCE

Performing a Quick Scan with Windows Defender

• On the Start screen, type *Windows Defender*.
• Click Windows Defender in the search results.
• Click the Quick option button on the Home tab.
• Click the Scan now button.

You need to keep the malware definitions in the antimalware up to date. Windows Defender refers to the definitions to determine if software it detects is a virus or spyware. When you update your computer, Windows Update installs any new virus and spyware definitions. You can also set Windows Defender to check for updated definitions before scanning your computer.

You'll show Duane how to start Windows Defender and scan for malware. You can run a quick scan, a full system scan, or a custom scan. A quick scan checks the locations on your computer that spyware is most likely to infect. A full scan checks all your files and programs, but takes longer and can make your computer run slowly. With a custom scan, you select the locations you want Windows Defender to check.

To start Windows Defender and perform a quick scan:

TIP

You can find Windows Defender in the Windows System category on the Apps screen.

1. Press the **Windows** key 🪟 to display the Start screen, type **Windows Defender**, and then click **Windows Defender** on the Apps screen. The Windows Defender window opens on the desktop. See Figure 5-10, which shows that Windows Defender is up to date. Your settings might differ.

   Trouble? If a dialog box opens indicating that Windows Defender is turned off, click the click here to turn it on link.

Figure 5-10   Windows Defender

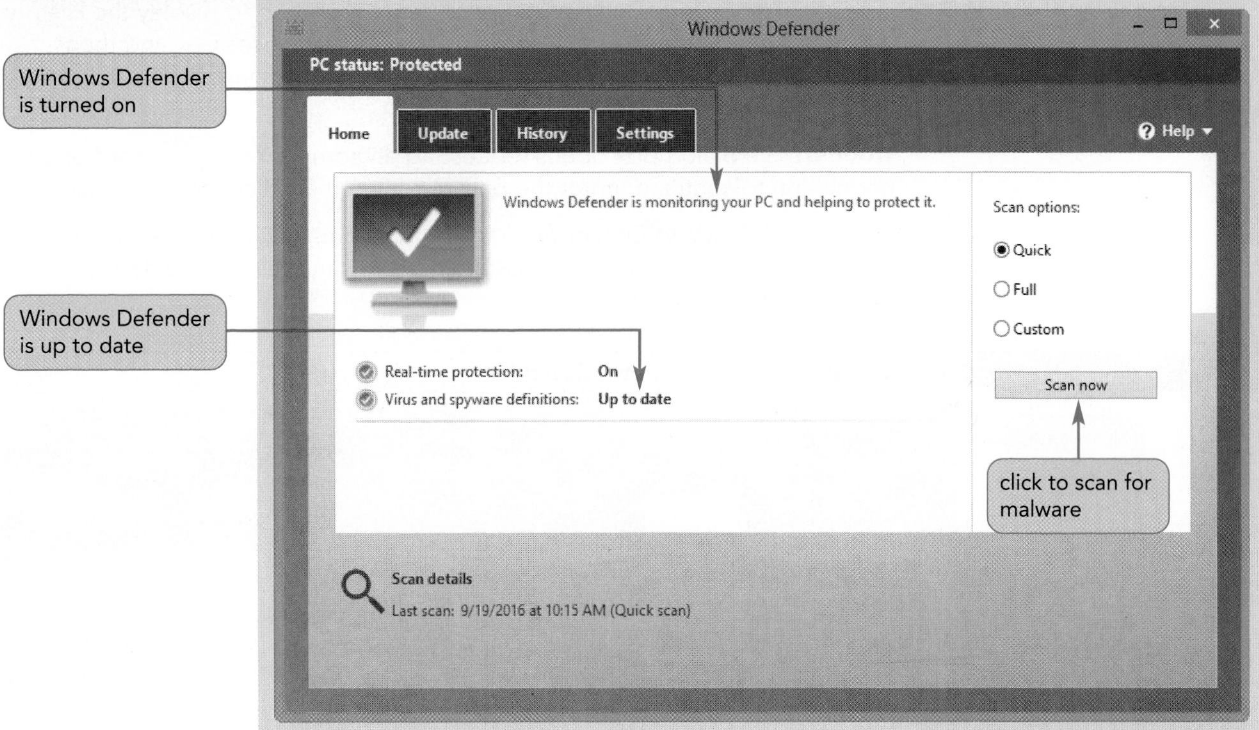

Windows Defender is turned on

Windows Defender is up to date

> **2.** If Windows Defender is not up to date, click the **Update** tab, and then click the **Update** button. Windows Defender checks for program and malware definition updates, downloads and installs any updates, and then reports the update status.

> **3.** If necessary, click the **Home** tab, click the **Quick** option button (if necessary), and then click the **Scan now** button. Windows Defender scans your computer, displaying first its progress and then the results of the scan. Depending on the number of programs on your computer, your scan might take a few minutes. Wait for the scan to finish and for Windows Defender to display the results before continuing.

If Windows Defender finds suspicious files, it alerts you that these files have been **quarantined**, which means Windows Defender moved them to another location on your computer to safely segregate them from other files. Quarantined files cannot run, so they cannot harm your computer. You can review all quarantined files to determine what to do with them. Open the History page in Windows Defender, click the Quarantined items option button, and then click the View details button to display a list of quarantined files. The file list includes the filename, alert level, and date of quarantine. The alert level can help you decide whether to remove or restore a file. Remove files with a Severe or High alert level. If you do not recognize or trust the publisher of files with Medium or Low alert levels, search the Web for information on those files to determine whether it is safe to restore them.

Windows Defender occasionally identifies a file as potential malware when the computer actually needs the file. If your computer has experienced problems since quarantining those files, start Windows Help and Support, and then click Microsoft Answers website on the Help home page to contact a Microsoft support person and determine what to do with the files. If you haven't had any computer problems since Windows Defender quarantined the files, you can remove the files or leave them in the quarantine location.

TIP

Most antivirus programs quarantine suspicious files so you can choose to restore or delete them.

To remove a quarantined file:

1. In the Windows Defender window, click the **History** tab to display the History page, click the **Quarantined items** option button, if necessary, and then click the **View details** button to display details about quarantined items. See Figure 5-11.

Trouble? If a dialog box opens requesting an administrator password or your permission to continue, enter the password and then click the Yes button.

Trouble? If Windows Defender did not quarantine any items after its quick scan, or if you do not have permission to work with quarantined items, read but do not perform Step 2.

Figure 5-11	Quarantined items in Windows Defender

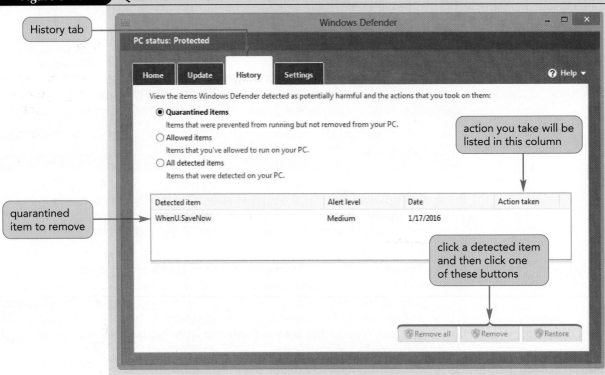

The quarantined item, WhenU.SaveNow, has a Medium alert level. Duane does not recognize the publisher of this program, so you will remove it.

2. In the Quarantined items list, click **WhenU.SaveNow** (or another item with a Severe, High, or Medium alert level and a publisher you do not recognize), and then click the **Remove** button.

Trouble? If a dialog box opens requesting an administrator password or your permission to continue, enter the password or click the Yes button.

Now that you've scanned Duane's computer and handled the items Windows Defender found, you can set an option to make sure Windows Defender runs effectively and then learn how to turn Windows Defender on and off.

Setting Windows Defender Options

To turn Windows Defender on or off, you use an option on the Settings page. If you have been using Windows Defender and then install a different antimalware app, you should turn Windows Defender off so it doesn't interfere with the other antivirus or antispyware program. If you remove other antimalware software or do not renew an antimalware subscription, Windows Defender runs automatically. To make sure your computer is being protected, you can verify Windows Defender's status on the Settings page.

Another option you can set for Windows Defender is whether to use Real-time protection. This setting is selected by default, which means Windows Defender is set to constantly monitor your computer for virus and spyware activity. Windows Defender then alerts you when suspicious software attempts to install itself or to run on your computer, and notifies you when programs try to change important Windows settings. As with quarantined items, when Windows Defender detects suspicious software, it assigns an alert level to the software and then displays a dialog box where you can choose one of the following actions:

Quarantine—Quarantine the software. Windows Defender prevents the software from running and allows you to restore it or remove it from your computer.

Remove—Permanently delete the software from your computer.

- Allow—Add the software to a list of allowed items so the software can run on your computer. Windows Defender does not alert you to risks that the software might pose to your privacy or your computer unless you remove the program from the Allowed items list.

You'll show Duane how to make sure Windows Defender is turned on and using real-time protection.

To verify Windows Defender options:

▌ **1.** In the Windows Defender window, click the **Settings** tab to display the Settings page. See Figure 5-12.

Figure 5-12   **Windows Defender Settings page**

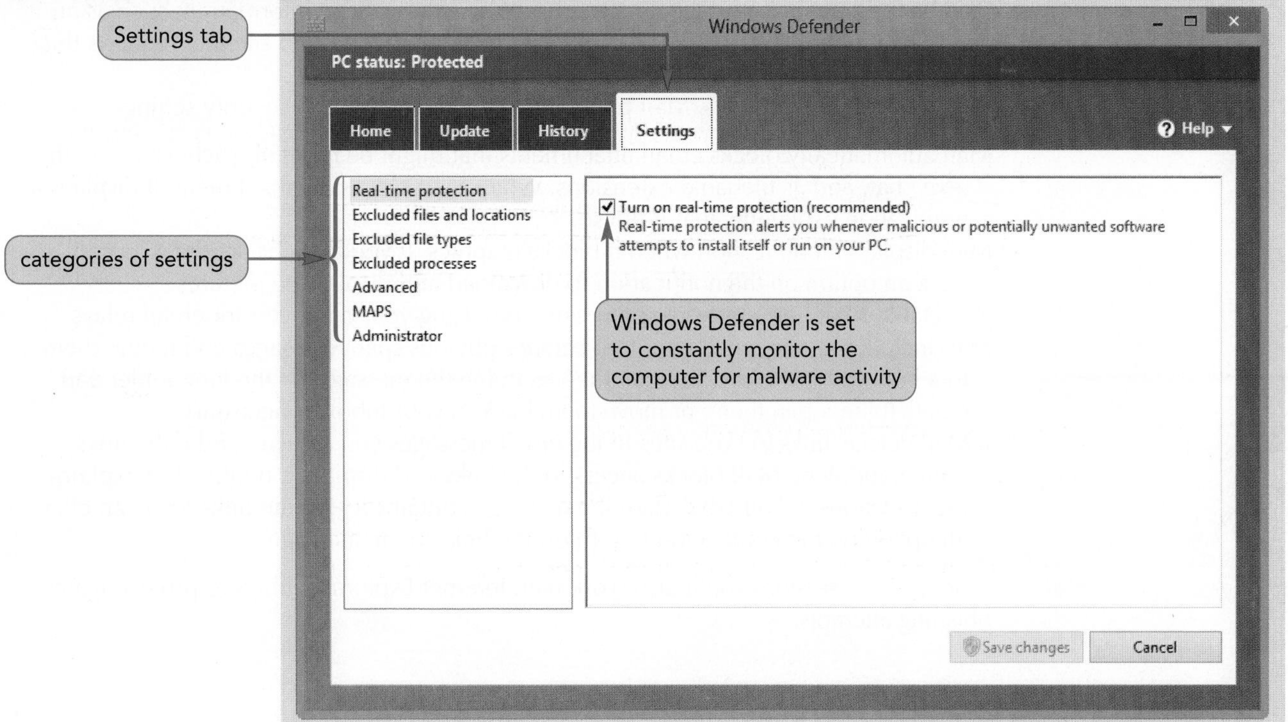

2. If necessary, click the **Turn on real-time protection (recommended)** check box to select it.

3. In the left pane, click **Administrator** to view the Administrator options. Make sure the Turn on Windows Defender check box is selected.

4. Click the **Save changes** button.

   Trouble? If you don't make any changes, the Save changes button is not available. Skip Step 4.

5. Close the Windows Defender window.

Defending Against Email Viruses

An annoying and potentially dangerous type of privacy invasion is **spam**, or junk email, messages offering products and services that are sometimes fake or misleading. Some users receive thousands of spam messages a day; the volume alone makes spam a nuisance. In addition, spam can be a vehicle for malware. Communicating via email is one of the most popular activities on the Internet, and email is the most common way for computer viruses to spread. Viruses and other security threats are often contained in email attachments, especially files with filename extensions such as .exe, .bat, and .js.

To help prevent spam and potentially offensive material, Mail does not download graphics with messages sent in HTML format. People sending spam (called spammers) often use graphics to access your email address. Spammers can also take advantage of vulnerabilities in your computer to use it to send spam to other computers without your permission, a practice known as an **email relay**. This lets spammers work without being detected and can seriously downgrade the performance of your computer.

Phishing (pronounced *fishing*) is an attempt to deceive you into revealing personal or financial information when you respond to an email message or visit a Web site. A typical phishing scam starts with an email message that looks like an official notice from a trusted person or business, such as a bank, credit card company, or reputable online merchant. The email message asks you to reply with sensitive information, such as an account number or password, or directs you to a fraudulent Web site that requests this information. Phishers often use the information for identity theft.

To combat these threats, Mail provides the following built-in security settings:

Mail automatically blocks email attachments that might be harmful, such as files with .exe, .bat, and .js filename extensions. When Mail blocks an attachment, it displays a notification explaining that it did so.

Mail displays a notification when it blocks graphics. If you trust the sender, you can click an option on the notification to download and display the pictures.

By default, Mail helps prevent spammers from using your computer for email relays.

Mail includes a junk email filter that catches obvious spam messages and moves them to a built-in Junk folder. You can then examine the messages in the Junk folder and delete them, open them, or move them back to your Inbox, if necessary.

If Mail detects links to Web sites in the email messages you receive, and if the links seem fraudulent, Mail blocks access to the links and displays a notification explaining its actions. If you are certain the message contains legitimate links, you can click an option on the notification to turn on the links in the message.

In the next session, you'll also work with Internet Explorer settings to protect against phishing attempts.

TIP

Viewing a picture in a junk email message might validate your email address and result in your receiving more junk email.

REVIEW

Session 5.1 Quick Check

1. What is malware? *224*
2. The _Action Center_ is a Control Panel tool that helps you manage security from a single window. *224*
3. _A Firewall_ checks communication coming from the Internet and either blocks it from your computer or allows it to pass.
4. What is Windows Update? *—230*
5. What does Windows 8 do if you do not have antivirus software installed on your computer? *runs Windows Defender*
6. If pop-up ads interrupt your computer work, even when you're not on the Internet, what should you suspect? *235 adware*
7. If Windows Defender finds files that might be spyware, it _quarantine_ the files, which means it moves them to another location on your computer and prevents them from running until you remove or restore the files.
8. _spam_ is a form of electronic direct mail, and can be a vehicle for malware.

Session 5.2 Visual Overview:

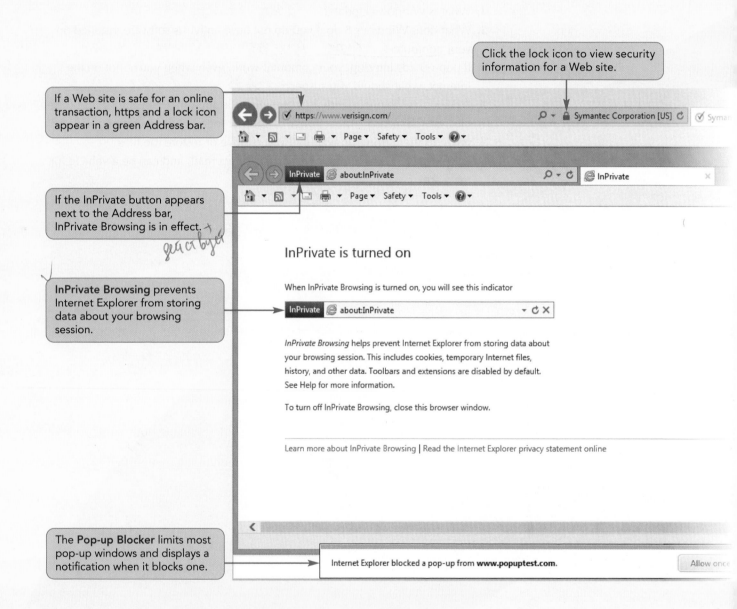

Click the lock icon to view security information for a Web site.

If a Web site is safe for an online transaction, https and a lock icon appear in a green Address bar.

If the InPrivate button appears next to the Address bar, InPrivate Browsing is in effect.

InPrivate Browsing prevents Internet Explorer from storing data about your browsing session.

The **Pop-up Blocker** limits most pop-up windows and displays a notification when it blocks one.

Internet Explorer Security Features

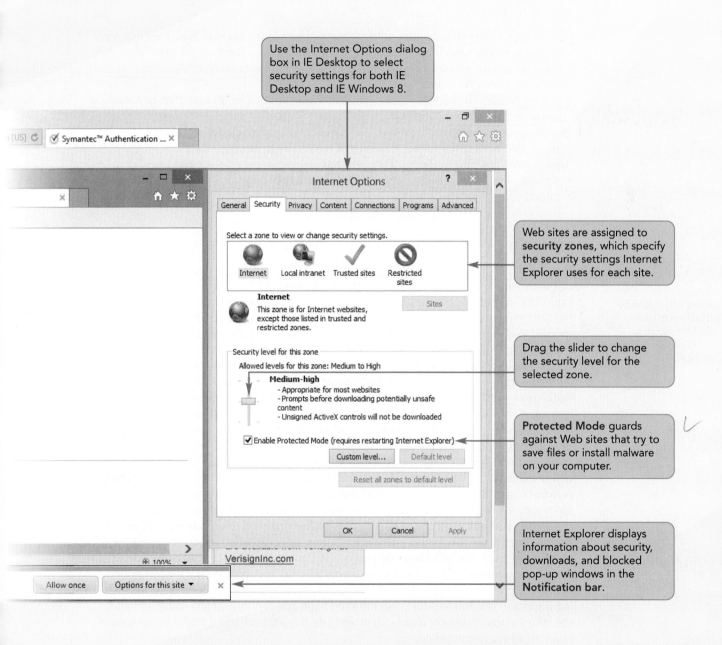

Use the Internet Options dialog box in IE Desktop to select security settings for both IE Desktop and IE Windows 8.

Web sites are assigned to **security zones**, which specify the security settings Internet Explorer uses for each site.

Drag the slider to change the security level for the selected zone.

Protected Mode guards against Web sites that try to save files or install malware on your computer.

Internet Explorer displays information about security, downloads, and blocked pop-up windows in the **Notification bar**.

Managing Microsoft Internet Explorer Security

Your computer is most vulnerable to security threats when you are connected to the Internet. You should therefore take advantage of the security settings in Internet Explorer to help protect your computer by identifying viruses and other security threats that are circulated over the Internet, making your computer and personal information more secure. Internet Explorer uses the security features provided in the following list. In general, you set options for these features using IE Desktop. When you do, they apply to IE Windows 8 as well.

SmartScreen Filter—This feature helps detect online scams, such as Web sites that try to trick you into revealing financial account information. The SmartScreen Filter also helps detect and block unknown and potentially malicious programs in files that you download from Web sites.

Protected Mode—This feature guards against Web sites that try to save files or install malware on your computer.

Digital signatures—Internet Explorer can detect and display **digital signatures**, which are electronic security marks added to files to verify their authenticity.

Pop-up Blocker—This tool allows you to limit or block most pop-up windows.

- Add-on Manager—This tool lets you disable or allow programs or controls that extend your browser's features.

Checking Web Sites with the SmartScreen Filter

Recall that phishing is an attempt to deceive you into revealing personal or financial information when you respond to an email message or visit a Web site. Internet Explorer can protect you from online scams by detecting possible phishing Web sites. The SmartScreen Filter helps to protect you from phishing attacks, online fraud, and spoofed Web sites. (A **spoofed Web site** is a fraudulent site posing as a legitimate one.) The SmartScreen Filter operates in the background to analyze a Web site you visit by comparing its address to a list of reported phishing and malicious software Web sites. If the SmartScreen Filter finds that the Web site you're visiting is on the list of known malware or phishing sites, Internet Explorer does not display the suspicious Web site. Instead, it shows a blocking Web page where you can choose to bypass the blocked Web site and go to your home page instead. If you are certain the blocked Web site is safe, you can continue to the site, though Microsoft does not recommend it.

If a spoofed site has not been reported as possibly malicious, the SmartScreen Filter will not detect it as a site to avoid. Commonly spoofed Web sites are those where you perform financial transactions, such as online banking or shopping sites. They often use phony Web addresses to mislead you into thinking you are visiting a legitimate site. When you visit a site that requests personal or financial information, look in the Address bar for the Web address. Internet Explorer displays the true domain you are visiting. For example, you might do your online banking at an Accounts Web page with the address *www.bank.com/accounts*. If you visit the Accounts Web page but notice that the Address bar displays the address *www.phony.com/accounts*, you are visiting a spoofed site and should close the Web page and report it as a possible phishing site. The Microsoft support team will investigate the site and add it to the list of known phishing sites as appropriate.

INSIGHT

Protecting Yourself from Phishing Attempts

In addition to using the SmartScreen Filter, use the following guidelines to protect yourself from online phishing:

- Never provide personal information in an email, an instant message, or a pop-up window.
- Do not click links in email and instant messages from senders you do not know or trust. Even messages that seem to be from friends and family can be faked. Therefore, check with the sender to make sure he or she actually sent the message (especially if the message contains only a link to a Web site).
- Only use Web sites that provide privacy statements or indicate how they use your personal information.

You can turn on the SmartScreen Filter to check Web sites and files automatically in both IE Desktop and IE Windows 8, or you can check them manually in IE Desktop by using the Tools button.

To turn on the SmartScreen Filter and check a Web site:

1. If necessary, click the **Desktop** tile on the Start screen to display the desktop.

2. Click the **Internet Explorer** button on the taskbar to start the browser.

3. Click the **Tools** button on the right side of the Internet Explorer window, point to **Safety**, and then click **Check this website**. Internet Explorer sends the URL of the page to Microsoft for verification.

   Trouble? If a dialog box opens explaining how the SmartScreen Filter works, click the OK button.

4. When the SmartScreen Filter dialog box opens to indicate it checked the Web site and does not report any threats, click the **OK** button.

5. Click the **Tools** button, point to **Safety**, and then click **Turn on SmartScreen Filter**. The Microsoft SmartScreen Filter dialog box opens. See Figure 5-13. Internet Explorer selects the Turn on SmartScreen Filter (recommended) option button for you.

   Trouble? If Turn off SmartScreen Filter appears when you point to Safety, the SmartScreen Filter is already turned on. Skip Steps 5 and 6.

Figure 5-13   Microsoft SmartScreen Filter dialog box

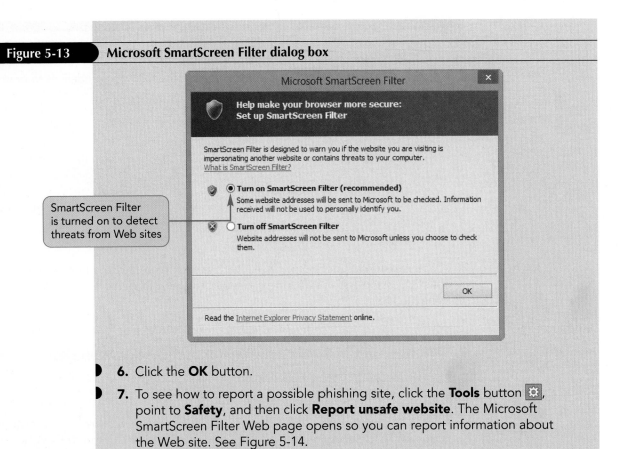

SmartScreen Filter is turned on to detect threats from Web sites

6. Click the **OK** button.

7. To see how to report a possible phishing site, click the **Tools** button ⚙,
point to **Safety**, and then click **Report unsafe website**. The Microsoft
SmartScreen Filter Web page opens so you can report information about
the Web site. See Figure 5-14.

Figure 5-14   Microsoft SmartScreen Filter Web page

select this check box if you think you encountered a phishing Web site

8. Close the Microsoft SmartScreen Filter Web page.

As you visit Web sites, Internet Explorer checks their certificates. A **certificate** is a digital document (similar to a digital signature) that verifies the security of a Web site you visit. Internet Explorer can detect certificate errors, which are signs that you are visiting a phishing site or one that uses spyware or other malware. If Internet Explorer detects a certificate error or other security problem, it identifies the problem type in the Address bar. For example, a certificate error message might appear in the Address bar. You can click the error message to learn about the problem. See Figure 5-15.

Figure 5-15	Security message in the Address bar

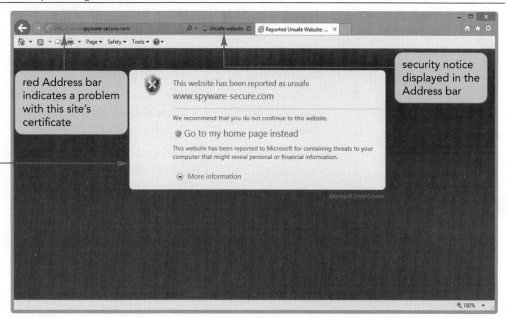

red Address bar indicates a problem with this site's certificate

security notice displayed in the Address bar

detailed message about the potentially unsafe Web site and the recommended action

The color of the Address bar also indicates the type of error or problem. Red means the certificate is out of date, is invalid, or has an error. Yellow signals that the certificate cannot be verified, which sometimes happens with a suspected phishing site. White means the certificate is normal, and green indicates sites that have high security, such as those for financial transactions.

Downloading Files Safely

The SmartScreen Filter also works with Internet Explorer's Download Manager to manage downloaded files. Download Manager lists the files you download from the Internet, keeps track of where they're stored on your computer, and lets you pause, open, run, delete, or save the downloaded files. The SmartScreen Filter analyzes files you want to download in a way similar to how it analyzes Web sites. When you select a file to download from a Web site, the SmartScreen filter refers to a list of files known to be malicious. If the file you want to download is on that list, the SmartScreen Filter blocks the download and explains the file is unsafe. If the file is not on the list of malicious files, the SmartScreen Filter refers to a list of programs downloaded by a significant number of other Internet Explorer users. The SmartScreen Filter notifies you if the file is not on the list of commonly downloaded files. In that case, you should not open or install the file unless you trust its publisher and the Web site that provided the file. You can use Download Manager to delete the program or run it if you know the file is safe.

If you download a file and later suspect it might be harmful, you can use Download Manager to run a set of security checks, including the SmartScreen Filter, before you open the file. The SmartScreen Filter checks to see if the file is on its updated list of malicious files. If you learn from another source that a downloaded file is unsafe, you can use Download Manager to report the file, which adds the file to the SmartScreen Filter list of malicious files.

You'll show Duane how to use Internet Explorer to display a list of downloaded files. Duane also wants to know where Download Manager stores downloaded files on his computer. If he suspects a downloaded file contains malicious software, he can quickly find the file and delete it using File Explorer. He can also use Download Manager to test, delete, and report suspicious files.

To display and test downloaded files:

▶ **1.** Click the **Tools** button ⚙ on the right side of the Internet Explorer window, and then click **View downloads** to display Download Manager. See Figure 5-16. The list of downloaded files on your computer will differ.

   Trouble? If Download Manager on your computer does not list any files, read but do not perform the remaining steps.

| Figure 5-16 | Download Manager |

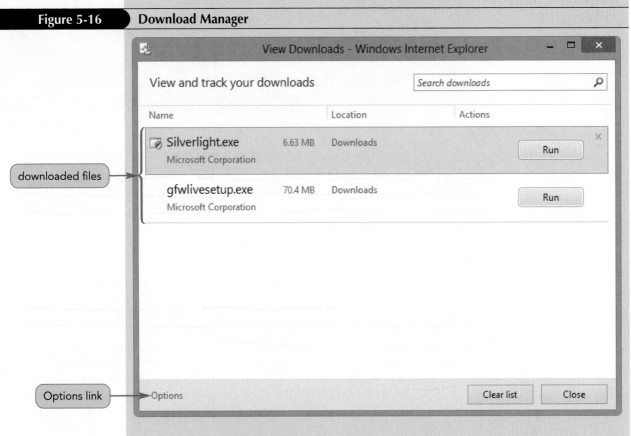

▶ **2.** Click the **Options** link to open the Download Options dialog box, which indicates the default location for downloaded files. By default, Windows 8 uses the Downloads folder for downloaded files. (If you wanted to change this location, you could click the Browse button in the Download Options dialog box.)

▶ **3.** Click the **OK** button to close the Download Options dialog box.

TIP

If you right-click a program file, the command on the shortcut menu is "Rerun security checks on this program."

▶ **4.** Right-click the first file listed in Download Manager, and then click **Rerun security checks on this file** on the shortcut menu. The SmartScreen Filter scans the file. If the file is safe, Download Manager displays only an Open button or a Run button. If the file is unsafe, Download Manager also displays a Delete button and indicates that the file could harm your computer.

▶ **5.** Close the View Downloads window.

Windows stores downloaded files in the Downloads folder on your hard disk by default. Therefore, if you use Download Manager to delete a downloaded file, Windows moves the file to the Recycle Bin. If you change the location to a removable disk that does not use a Recycle Bin, the file is permanently removed when you delete it.

Blocking Malware with Protected Mode and Security Zones

To install or run programs on your computer, hackers often take advantage of Web programming tools, such as scripts and ActiveX controls, that are designed to enhance your online experience. A **script** is programming code that performs a series of commands and can be embedded in a Web page. For example, a Web site designer might use a script to verify that you've completed all the necessary fields in an online form. In contrast, hackers use scripts on a Web page to automatically download programs to your computer that can collect and transmit information about you without your knowledge or authorization.

A common way for hackers to distribute adware and spyware is to download **ActiveX controls**, which are small, self-contained programs, from a Web page to your computer. Some ActiveX controls make it easier to perform tasks, such as submitting information to a Web site. Other ActiveX controls can harm your computer and files, especially those controls that lack digital signatures, meaning they are unverified. Recall that a digital signature is an electronic security mark that can be added to files, similar to a certificate added to Web sites. A digital signature identifies the publisher of a file and verifies that the file has not changed since it was signed. Internet Explorer offers a few ways to protect against malicious scripts and ActiveX controls, including Protected Mode and security zones. You can also specifically block a Web site from using ActiveX controls, which you do later in the tutorial.

INSIGHT

Digital Signatures

Internet Explorer (and other programs, including Windows 8) detects whether a file has a digital signature. A file without a valid digital signature might not be from the stated source or might have been tampered with (possibly by a virus) since it was published. Avoid opening an unsigned file unless you know for certain who created it and whether the contents are safe to open. However, even a valid digital signature does not guarantee that the contents of the file are harmless. When you download a file, determine whether to trust its contents based on the identity of the publisher and the site providing the file.

Internet Explorer runs in Protected Mode by default, making it difficult for hackers to install malware on your computer. If a Web page tries to install any type of software or run a script, Internet Explorer displays a message in the Notification bar warning you about the attempt. If you trust the program, you can allow it to run once or always. If you are not familiar with the program or don't want to run it, you can deny it once or always.

In addition to Protected Mode, Internet Explorer uses security zones so you can tailor your security settings to the kind of online computing you do. Internet Explorer classifies all Web sites in one of four security zones: Internet, Local intranet, Trusted sites, and Restricted sites. Each zone uses a certain level of security setting ranging from Low to High. When you visit a Web site that has been assigned to a security zone, the appropriate icon appears in the Internet Explorer status bar. Figure 5-17 summarizes the four security zones.

| Figure 5-17 | Internet Explorer security zones |

Security Zone	Description
Internet	Internet Explorer assigns all Internet Web sites to this zone by default and applies a Medium-high security level, which is appropriate for most sites. You can change the security level to Medium or High.
Local intranet	Internet Explorer assigns Web sites on your intranet (a corporate or business network) to this zone and applies a Medium-low security level. You can change this to any other level.
Trusted sites	You can assign Web sites to this zone that you trust not to damage your computer or files. This zone has a Medium level of security by default, but you can change it to any other level.
Restricted sites	You assign Web sites to this zone that might damage your computer or files. Adding sites to this zone does not block them, but it does prevent them from using scripts or active content. This zone has a High level of security by default and cannot be changed.

© 2014 Cengage Learning

You'll show Duane how to check the security level of his home page.

To check the security level of your home page:

1. With Internet Explorer open to your home page, click the **Tools** button ⚙ on the right side of the Internet Explorer window, and then click **Internet options** to open the Internet Options dialog box.

2. Click the **Security** tab to display the security settings. See Figure 5-18. Leave the dialog box open for now.

Figure 5-18 **Security tab in the Internet Options dialog box**

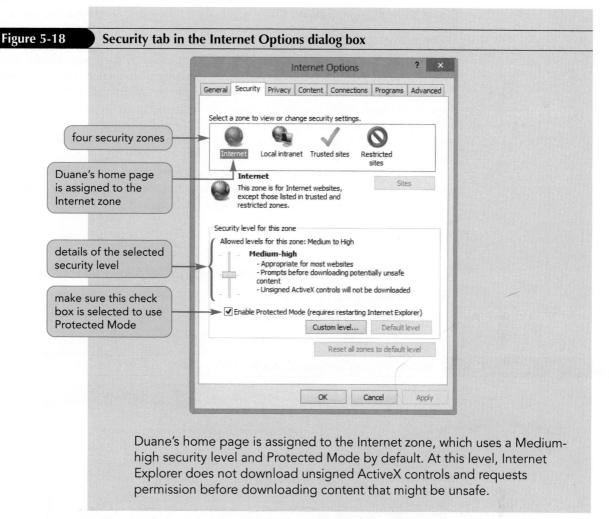

four security zones

Duane's home page is assigned to the Internet zone

details of the selected security level

make sure this check box is selected to use Protected Mode

Duane's home page is assigned to the Internet zone, which uses a Medium-high security level and Protected Mode by default. At this level, Internet Explorer does not download unsigned ActiveX controls and requests permission before downloading content that might be unsafe.

Next, you'll show Duane how to use the Pop-up Blocker to limit or block most pop-up windows when he visits Web sites. You use the Internet Options dialog box to select settings for the Pop-up Blocker.

Blocking Pop-Up Windows

A pop-up ad is a small Web browser window that appears when you visit a Web site and advertises a product or service. Many legitimate advertisers use pop-up ads because they effectively get your attention and provide information or services that might interest you. However, some pop-up ads are annoying because they repeatedly interrupt your online activities, are difficult to close, or display objectionable content. Other pop-up ads are dangerous because they can download spyware or **hijack** your browser—meaning they seize control of the browser, opening many more new windows each time you close one pop-up window until you have to close your browser or restart your computer.

To avoid the nuisance and danger of pop-up ads, Internet Explorer includes the Pop-up Blocker, which warns you about or blocks pop-up ads. The Pop-up Blocker is turned on by default, meaning that Internet Explorer blocks most pop-up windows. Not all pop-up windows are ads. If a pop-up window opens as soon as you visit a Web site, it probably contains an ad. However, many Web sites use pop-up windows to display tools such as calendars. For example, if you visit a travel Web site to make flight or hotel reservations, the site might provide a calendar in a pop-up window so you can select your travel dates. If you click a link or button to open the pop-up window,

Internet Explorer does not block it by default. However, it does block pop-up windows that appear automatically if you have not clicked a link or button.

To display a blocked pop-up window, you can use the Notification bar shown in the Session 5.2 Visual Overview. When you visit a Web site with pop-up windows and the Pop-up Blocker is turned on, the Notification bar opens to display a message informing you that it blocked a pop-up window. You can click the Options for this site button on the Notification bar to display a menu of settings, such as Temporarily Allow Pop-ups. To select long-term settings, you use the Pop-up Blocker Settings dialog box to block all pop-up ads, allow more pop-up ads, or specify which Web sites can display pop-up ads in your browser.

Duane has had problems with pop-up ads before, so he wants to block all pop-ups in Internet Explorer. You'll show him how to change the Pop-up Blocker settings to do so. As you perform the following steps, note your original settings so you can restore them later.

To change the Pop-up Blocker settings in Internet Explorer:

1. In the Internet Options dialog box, click the **Privacy** tab, and then click the **Settings** button. The Pop-up Blocker Settings dialog box opens. See Figure 5-19.

Figure 5-19　**Pop-up Blocker Settings dialog box**

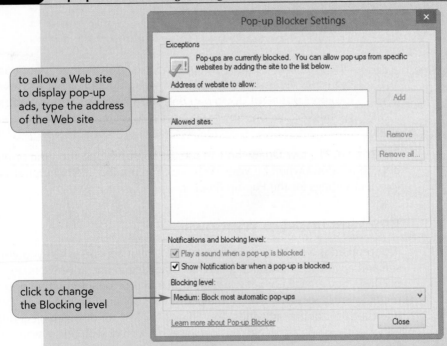

to allow a Web site to display pop-up ads, type the address of the Web site

click to change the Blocking level

2. Click the **Blocking level** button, and then click **High: Block all pop-ups (Ctrl+Alt to override)**.

   Trouble? If you are working in a computer lab, you might not have permission to change the Pop-up Blocker settings. In that case, skip Step 2.

3. Click the **Close** button to close the Pop-up Blocker Settings dialog box.

4. Click the **OK** button to close the Internet Options dialog box.

Next, you'll learn how to find out which add-on programs are installed to work with Internet Explorer.

Managing Add-On Programs

A browser **add-on** is a program offered by any software vendor that provides enhancements such as a toolbar or an improved search feature. For example, Microsoft Silverlight is a popular add-on that enhances the multimedia, animation, and other effects displayed in Internet Explorer. Some add-ons are safe and make your browser more effective; other add-ons, especially those that are installed without your permission, can affect the performance of Internet Explorer and even make it stop working. Internet Explorer provides an Add-on Manager so you can review, disable, update, or report add-ons to Microsoft. Other security features, such as Protected Mode, security levels, and the Notification bar, warn you when a Web site is trying to download add-on software to your computer.

You can usually install and use browser add-ons without any problems, but some cause Internet Explorer to shut down unexpectedly. If this happens, you can disable the add-on.

Internet Explorer usually asks for permission before running an add-on for the first time. If you don't recognize the program or its publisher, you can deny permission. Internet Explorer also maintains a list of preapproved add-ons that have been checked and digitally signed. It runs add-ons in this list without requesting your permission. You can view the list of preapproved add-ons in the Manage Add-ons dialog box.

Duane isn't aware of any add-ons his browser uses, so he wants to view the preapproved add-ons and any others that Internet Explorer is running.

To examine and manage add-ons:

▶ **1.** Click the **Tools** button 🔧 on the right side of the Internet Explorer window, and then click **Manage add-ons**. The Manage Add-ons dialog box opens. By default, this dialog box displays the toolbar and extension add-ons that are currently loaded in Internet Explorer.

▶ **2.** Click the **Currently loaded add-ons** button, and then click **Run without permission**. The preapproved add-ons appear in the list.

▶ **3.** Click the first add-on in the list to display details about it. See Figure 5-20.

Figure 5-20   Manage Add-ons window

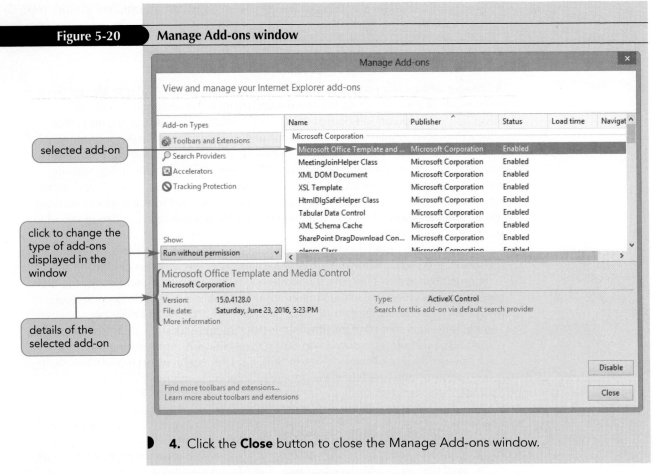

4. Click the **Close** button to close the Manage Add-ons window.

Now that you have explored the security settings in Internet Explorer, you can turn your attention to its privacy settings.

Selecting Internet Explorer Privacy Settings

In addition to security protection, Internet Explorer also includes the following tools and features to protect your privacy:

Privacy settings and alerts—These settings specify how to handle identifying information when you're online, and alert you when a Web site you're visiting doesn't meet your criteria.

InPrivate Browsing—This feature helps prevent Internet Explorer from storing data about your browsing session by opening a separate InPrivate Browsing Internet Explorer window to keep your browsing actions private.

Tracking Protection—This feature helps prevent Web site content providers from collecting information about sites you visit.

• Secure connections—Internet Explorer informs you when it is using a secure connection to communicate with Web sites that handle sensitive personal information.

Selecting Privacy Settings

- Click the Tools button, and then click Internet options.
- Click the Privacy tab in the Internet Options dialog box.
- Drag the slider to select a privacy setting ranging from Block All Cookies to Accept All Cookies.
- Click the OK button.

One privacy concern is cookies, which many Web sites store on your computer when you visit them. A **cookie** is a small file that records information about you, such as the type of browser you are using, your email address, and your preferences for using a Web site. Like other Web tools, cookies can enhance your online experience by helping trusted Web sites customize their service to you. However, they can also pose a security risk—hackers can retrieve cookies to search for private information such as passwords, or use cookies to track the Web sites you visit. In Internet Explorer, you can specify privacy settings to either allow Web sites to save cookies on your computer or prevent them from doing so.

One way to protect your privacy with Internet Explorer is to block cookies on some or all of the Web sites you visit. You should be selective about which Web sites you allow to store cookies on your computer. Blocking all cookies keeps your Web site visits private, but might also limit your experience or prove annoying. Allowing all cookies might compromise your privacy. Most users find that the default Medium-high privacy setting provides a good balance because it allows most **first-party cookies**, which are generated from the Web sites you visit and contain information the Web site reuses when you return. For example, to keep track of products you add to an electronic shopping cart or wish list, a Web site saves a first-party cookie on your computer. In contrast, the Medium-high privacy setting blocks most **third-party cookies**, which are generated from Web site advertisers, who might use them to track your Web use for marketing purposes.

Duane often visits his clients' Web sites for research as he prepares to develop products. He wants to protect the privacy of Catapult Product Design and his clients by blocking all cookies and then allowing only those issued by sites he trusts.

As you perform the following steps, note your original settings so you can restore them later.

To change privacy settings for saving cookies:

1. Click the **Tools** button ⚙ on the right side of the Internet Explorer window, and then click **Internet options**. The Internet Options dialog box opens.

2. Click the **Privacy** tab to view the privacy settings. See Figure 5-21. The Settings section describes how cookies are treated based on the security zone selected and the level of risk set.

Figure 5-21   **Privacy tab in the Internet Options dialog box**

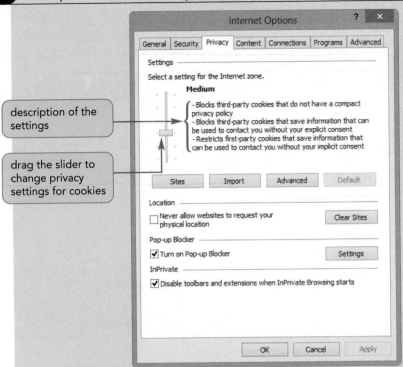

description of the settings

drag the slider to change privacy settings for cookies

Trouble? If you are working in a computer lab, you might not have permission to change the privacy settings. In that case, read but do not perform Steps 3–6.

3. Drag the slider up to the **Block All Cookies** setting. When you select this setting, Internet Explorer will not let a Web site store any cookies on your computer unless you explicitly allow it to do so.

4. Drag the slider back to **Medium**. This setting blocks cookies except for some first-party cookies and those created by Web sites you identify.

5. Click the **Sites** button to open the Per Site Privacy Actions dialog box. You use this dialog box to specify the Web sites you want to allow to store cookies on your computer. (If you had selected a lower privacy setting, you could also use this dialog box to block certain Web sites from storing cookies.)

6. Click the **OK** button to close the Per Site Privacy Actions dialog box. Leave the Internet Options dialog box open for the next set of steps.

TIP

To view temporary files before deleting them, click the Tools button, click Internet options, click the General tab, click the Settings button in the Browsing history section, and then click View files.

Internet Explorer will block most cookies on Duane's computer from now on. However, if Web sites stored cookies on his computer before you changed the privacy setting, they will remain there until you delete them. You can delete cookies by clearing your browsing history. In addition to cookies, Internet Explorer stores temporary Internet files, a history of the Web sites you've visited, information you've entered in the Address bar, and Web passwords you've saved. (A temporary Internet file is a copy of a Web page you viewed. Internet Explorer stores this file for a specified number of days, such as 20, so it can display the page quickly if you open it again.) Usually, maintaining this history information improves your Web browsing because it can fill in information that you would otherwise have to retype. If you have particular privacy concerns, however, such as when you are using a public computer, you can clear some or all of your browsing history to delete this information. Duane wants to delete all of the cookies and the list of Web sites he has visited.

To clear your browsing history:

▶ **1.** Click the **General** tab in the Internet Options dialog box, and then click the **Delete** button in the Browsing history section. The Delete Browsing History dialog box opens. See Figure 5-22.

Figure 5-22   Delete Browsing History dialog box

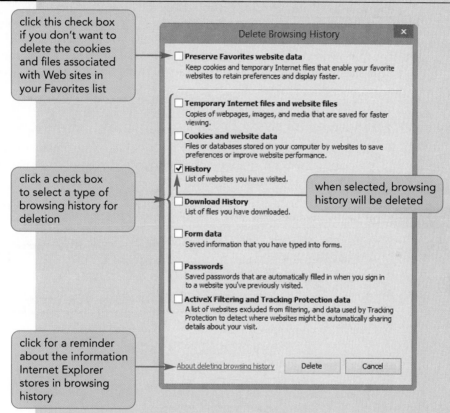

click this check box if you don't want to delete the cookies and files associated with Web sites in your Favorites list

click a check box to select a type of browsing history for deletion

when selected, browsing history will be deleted

click for a reminder about the information Internet Explorer stores in browsing history

Trouble? If you are working in a computer lab, you might not have permission to clear your browsing history. In that case, read but do not perform Steps 2–6.

TIP

When you delete all of your browsing history, you do not delete your list of favorites or subscribed feeds.

▶ **2.** If necessary, click the **Cookies and website data** check box to insert a check mark and indicate you want to delete all of the cookies stored on your computer.

▶ **3.** If necessary, click the **History** check box to insert a check mark and indicate you want to delete the list of Web sites you have visited.

▶ **4.** Click the **Delete** button to delete cookies and your browsing history.

▶ **5.** Click the **OK** button to close the Internet Options dialog box. A Notification bar appears on the bottom of the Internet Explorer window confirming that Internet Explorer deleted the selected browsing history.

▶ **6.** Click the **Close** button [X] to close the Notification bar.

Another privacy feature of Internet Explorer is InPrivate Browsing, which you'll explore next.

Protecting Your Privacy with InPrivate Browsing

TIP

To open an InPrivate window in IE Windows 8, right-click a blank spot on a Web page, click the Tab tools button, and then click New InPrivate tab.

If you want to keep information about your Web browsing private, you can use InPrivate Browsing. This feature prevents Internet Explorer from storing data about your browsing session. If you are searching online for a gift, for example, or want to prevent another user from retracing your steps to a Web site containing your financial information, use InPrivate Browsing to hide the history of the Web pages you visited. When you do, Internet Explorer opens a new window and displays InPrivate in the Address bar. As you work in the InPrivate window, Internet Explorer protects your privacy. To end your InPrivate Browsing session, close the browser window.

Keep in mind that InPrivate Browsing does not make you anonymous on the Internet. Web sites might still be able to identify you through your Web address, and any forms you complete and selections you make can be recorded and saved by those Web sites. You will show Duane how an InPrivate Browsing session works.

To turn on InPrivate Browsing:

▶ 1. Click the **Tools** button ⚙ on the right side of the Internet Explorer window, point to **Safety**, and then click **InPrivate Browsing** to open the InPrivate window. See Figure 5-23.

Figure 5-23	InPrivate window

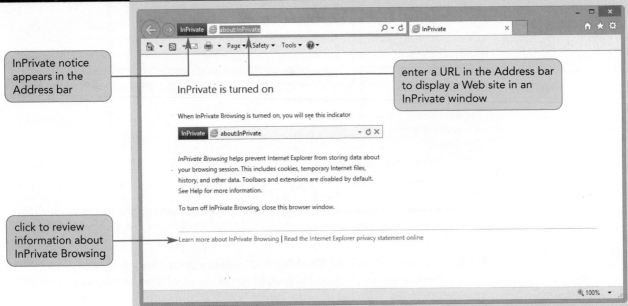

InPrivate notice appears in the Address bar

enter a URL in the Address bar to display a Web site in an InPrivate window

InPrivate is turned on

When InPrivate Browsing is turned on, you will see this indicator

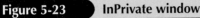

InPrivate Browsing helps prevent Internet Explorer from storing data about your browsing session. This includes cookies, temporary Internet files, history, and other data. Toolbars and extensions are disabled by default. See Help for more information.

To turn off InPrivate Browsing, close this browser window.

click to review information about InPrivate Browsing

Learn more about InPrivate Browsing | Read the Internet Explorer privacy statement online

▶ 2. In the Address bar, type **www.whitehouse.gov** and then press the **Enter** key. The home page for the White House Web site appears in the InPrivate browser window. Maximize the window.

Trouble? If a window opens other than the one for the White House home page, close the window or click a link to continue to the Web site.

▶ 3. Point to the **Briefing Room** link near the top of the page, and then click the **Your Weekly Address** link.

Trouble? If the Your Weekly Address link does not appear on the Web page you are viewing, click any other link.

▶ **4.** Click the **Show Address bar Autocomplete** button ▼ on the Address bar to display a list of recently visited Web sites and your favorite Web pages. Note that the White House Web pages you visited during your InPrivate Browsing session are not listed under History. When you close the InPrivate window, the list of recent Web pages in the regular Internet Explorer window will not include any of the White House pages either.

▶ **5.** Close the InPrivate window.

▶ **6.** In the regular Internet Explorer window, click the **Show Address bar Autocomplete** button ▼ on the Address bar to display a list of pages you visited recently except for those you visited during your InPrivate Browsing session.

Internet Explorer includes another privacy feature—Tracking Protection—which you'll learn about next.

Using Tracking Protection

Many Web pages use content such as ads, maps, or Web analysis tools that count the number of visitors to the Web site. This content is typically supplied by other Web sites called content providers or third-party Web sites. When you visit a Web site with third-party content, information that identifies your computer is sent to the content provider. For example, the content provider can learn your browser type, operating system, Web address, and screen resolution. If you visit many Web sites that the same content provider uses, the content provider can create a profile of your browsing preferences. The profile can be used to target ads that are likely to appeal to you, for example.

Web tracking tools, such as visitor counters, sometimes appear as visible content, but not always. For example, **Web beacons** are transparent images that invisibly track Web site usage. Web analysis tools often contain scripts that can track information such as the pages you visit and the selections you make. To control the information sent to content providers, you can use Tracking Protection.

Tracking Protection analyzes the content of Web pages you visit. If it finds content that is used on other Web sites, Tracking Protection blocks the content from Web sites that appear on Tracking Protection lists. Internet Explorer generates a personal Tracking Protection list based on sites you visit. You can also download Tracking Protection Lists created by software developers and have Internet Explorer block content from the providers on those lists.

By blocking content, Tracking Protection can protect your privacy on the Web. However, content providers often pay for Web site content that you can view or use for free. Blocking all third-party content can make Web pages load slowly and prevent Web sites you like from earning income they need. Instead of blocking all third-party content, you can use Tracking Protection to examine which content providers supply content to Web sites you've visited. The Web address of the content provider collecting information on a Web page is often displayed in the Internet Explorer status bar as the Web page opens. If you notice that you have trouble displaying Web pages when a content provider's address appears in the status bar, you can block that content provider to improve performance. Content providers who supply content to 30 or more Web pages might be collecting too much information about you, so you can block them as well.

Duane notices that when Web pages are slow to open, a Web address such as ads.doubleclick.net appears in the status bar. You suggest he block this content provider to see if that improves his browsing experience.

To block a content provider:

▶ **1.** Click the **Tools** button 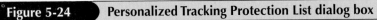 on the right side of the Internet Explorer window, point to **Safety**, and then click **Tracking Protection**. The Manage Add-ons dialog box opens with Tracking Protection selected in the Add-on Types pane.

▶ **2.** Click **Your Personalized List** in the right pane. If the status for this list is "Disabled," click the **Enable** button to turn on Tracking Protection. Note the original setting so you can restore it later.

▶ **3.** With Your Personalized List still selected, click the **Settings** button to open the Personalized Tracking Protection List dialog box. See Figure 5-24. The content providers in your dialog box will differ.

Figure 5-24 **Personalized Tracking Protection List dialog box**

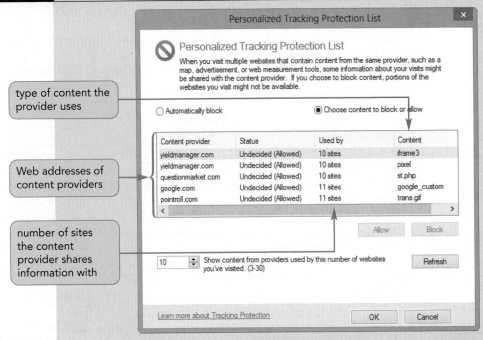

type of content the provider uses

Web addresses of content providers

number of sites the content provider shares information with

▶ **4.** Click the **Used by** column heading to sort the list in descending order by the number of sites that use each content provider. The providers that are used by the most sites appear at the top of the list.

Trouble? If no content providers appear in the list, skip Steps 4–6.

▶ **5.** If necessary, scroll the list and then click **doubleclick.net** where "test_domain.js" appears in the Content column. The .js file in this column indicates that this Web site provides a script file to other Web sites. Because the content is used by many sites, you can block the content to improve performance.

Trouble? If *doubleclick.net* does not appear in your Personalized Tracking Protection List dialog box, select any other content provider with content used by 20 or more sites.

▶ **6.** Click the **Block** button to block this content.

▶ **7.** Click the **OK** button to close the Personalized Tracking Protection List dialog box.

▶ **8.** Click the **Close** button to close the Manage Add-ons dialog box.

If Duane is having trouble displaying Web pages, he can return to the Personalized Tracking Protection List dialog box and allow content from *doubleclick.net*.

Blocking ActiveX Controls

Recall that ActiveX controls are small programs that allow Web sites to provide content such as videos. Hackers can also use ActiveX controls to collect information from your computer without your consent, damage applications and data, install software on your computer without your knowledge, or control your computer remotely. To prevent Web sites from installing and using ActiveX controls, you can turn on ActiveX Filtering in Internet Explorer. Because many Web sites provide ActiveX controls to extend the capabilities of the browser, you can turn on ActiveX Filtering for specific Web sites.

You'll show Duane how to turn on ActiveX Filtering and then turn it off for a trusted Web site.

To use ActiveX Filtering:

1. Click the **Tools** button ⚙ on the right side of the Internet Explorer window, point to **Safety**, and then click **ActiveX Filtering** to turn on ActiveX Filtering.

   Trouble? If ActiveX Filtering appears on the Safety list with a check mark, skip Step 1.

2. Click the **Tools** button ⚙ again, and then point to **Safety** to verify that ActiveX Filtering appears with a check mark on the Safety list.

3. Navigate to the Microsoft Web site at **www.microsoft.com**.

4. Click the **filter** icon 🚫 in the Address bar to display a dialog box notifying you that some content is filtered on this site. See Figure 5-25.

| Figure 5-25 | Filtering options for a Web site |

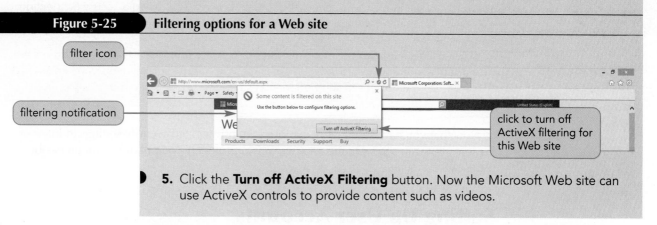

filter icon

filtering notification

click to turn off ActiveX filtering for this Web site

5. Click the **Turn off ActiveX Filtering** button. Now the Microsoft Web site can use ActiveX controls to provide content such as videos.

Although you have turned off ActiveX Filtering for the Microsoft Web site, this safety option is still enabled for other Web sites. To turn off ActiveX Filtering for all Web sites, use the Tools button on the right side of the Internet Explorer window.

PROSKILLS

Decision Making: Deciding Whether to Trust a Web Site

Your decision about whether to trust a Web site should be based on who publishes the Web site, what information the publisher wants from you, and what you want from the site. To make your Web browsing more efficient and productive, consider the following guidelines when deciding whether to trust a Web site with confidential information:

- Ensure you have a secure connection to the Web site. Look in the Address bar for a Web site address that begins with "https" rather than "http." Also, look for a security icon such as a padlock in the Address bar or status bar, which indicates that the Web site is secure.
- Confirm that you are familiar with the organization that sponsors the Web site. If you are a satisfied customer of a business that provides products in a physical location, you can probably trust its Web site. Read the Web site's privacy or terms of use statement to make sure you are comfortable with the terms. Avoid Web sites that require you to accept email offers or advertising from the Web site.
- Check to see if the Web site is certified by an Internet trust organization. An Internet trust organization verifies that a Web site has a privacy statement and gives you a choice about how it uses your information. Approved Web sites display one or more privacy certification seals, usually on their home page or order forms. However, unscrupulous Web sites sometimes fraudulently display these trust logos. You can contact the trust organization to see if the Web site is registered with it. Reputable trust organizations include TRUSTe (www.truste.com), the Better Business Bureau or BBBOnLine (www.bbb.org/online), and WebTrust (www.webtrust.org). On the Web site of each trust organization, you can display a list of certified Web sites.
- Stay away from sites that unnecessarily request confidential personal information. Provide personal or confidential information such as credit card numbers only when necessary and only on a secure form. Make sure you are using a secure connection when completing the form. Also, look for a message explaining that your information will be encrypted for security.
- Avoid sites that use untrustworthy ways to contact you. Untrustworthy Web sites are often referred to you through an email message from someone you don't know. Stay away from Web sites making offers that seem too good to be true.

Now that you have thoroughly explored the privacy and security settings in Internet Explorer, you can show Duane another way to protect his company's computers—by using user accounts.

Setting Up User Accounts

In Windows, a **user account** is a collection of information that indicates the files and folders you can access, the types of changes you can make to the computer, and your preferred appearance settings (such as your desktop background or color scheme). If you have a user account on a computer that you share with other people, you can maintain your own files and settings separate from the other users.

Setting Up a User Account

- Display the Charms bar, click the Settings charms, and then click Change PC settings.
- Click Users in the left pane of the PC settings screen.
- Click the Add a user button.
- Enter your email address.
- Enter a user name and password, and then click the Next button.
- Click the Finish button.

You can create two types of accounts in Windows 8:

- **Microsoft account**—This type of account provides access to Microsoft cloud computing services, such as Outlook.com for email, SkyDrive for file storage, and Xbox Live for games. With this type of user account, you can use Windows 8 and some Windows 8 apps to access files and other data stored in your online Microsoft account. For example, if you keep albums of photos on your SkyDrive, you can use the Photos app to display those photos on your PC. If you run Windows 8 on more than one PC, you can also **synchronize**, or **sync**, (that is, to make sure data on the two devices match) your settings, preferences, and some apps so that all your PCs are set up the same way. The advantage of a Microsoft account is that you provide one user name and one password to connect to the cloud and to sync settings.
- **Local-only user account**—This type of account accesses only resources on your computer.

In addition, a Microsoft account or a local-only user account is a Standard account or an Administrator account, which determines how much control the user has over the computer:

- **Standard account**—A Standard account is designed for everyday computing and can protect your computer and data by preventing users from changing settings that affect all users. To make changes such as installing software or changing security settings, Windows requests permission or a password for an Administrator account. Microsoft recommends that every regular user on a computer have a Standard account.
- **Administrator account**—An Administrator account is created when Windows 8 is installed and provides full access to the computer. The administrator can access the files of any user, install software, and change any settings. The intention is that when you install Windows 8, you first sign in to the computer as the administrator, and then create a Standard user account for yourself and for each person who will use the computer.

If someone needs temporary access to a computer, the administrator can turn on the **Guest account**, which is a built-in account that is inactive by default. The Guest account user cannot make any changes to settings or software.

When you install Windows 8, the setup program guides you through the steps of creating an Administrator account. During that process, you select whether you want to use your Microsoft account or a local-only user account as the Administrator account. If you don't have a Microsoft account, you can create one as you install Windows. After completing the installation, you can set up Standard accounts from the Start screen or the desktop. (You can turn on a Guest account or turn it off only from the desktop.) Any accounts you create after the initial Administrator account are Standard accounts by default. Standard accounts can be Microsoft or local-only user accounts.

Selecting a User Name and Password

When you create an Administrator account or a Standard account, Windows asks for your user credentials, which are a user name and a password. If you have a Microsoft account, you can provide the user name and password you use for that account. If you don't have a Microsoft account, you can create one as you set up a new Administrator or Standard account. To use a Microsoft account, you provide your email address and a password as your user credentials.

INSIGHT

Synchronizing Accounts

If you use your Microsoft account credentials for your user account on a Windows 8 laptop, for example, you can synchronize settings, preferences, and some apps that you use on other computers, such as a Windows 8 tablet. No matter which computer you use, the Start screen and desktop will look the same, and you'll have access to the same apps.

Before you can synchronize accounts, you need to trust each computer you use. (**Trusting** a computer means you verify that you have an account on that computer.) To trust a computer, open the PC settings screen and then select Users. If a message appears below your user name and picture indicating that your saved passwords for apps, Web sites, and networks won't sync until you trust the PC, click the Trust this PC link. Internet Explorer starts and opens a Manage your security info Web page on the Windows Live Web site to confirm you are adding the PC to your Microsoft account. The Web site sends you an email message with a confirmation link. When you receive the email message, open it and click the link to make the PC a trusted PC for your Microsoft account. The PC will then sync settings and data automatically.

If you set up a new Administrator or Standard account as a local-only user account, you must provide a user name, but the password is optional. However, Microsoft strongly recommends that you use a password for all accounts, which is one of the most effective ways you can keep your computer secure. When your computer is protected with a password, only someone who knows the password can sign in to Windows.

A **text password** is a series of letters, numbers, spaces, and symbols that you provide to access your files, applications, and other resources on the computer. Windows passwords are case sensitive, so *DnEllson18* is different from *dnellson18*. Passwords strengthen computer security because they help to make sure that no one can access the computer unless he or she is authorized to do so. Therefore, you should not give your passwords to others or write them in a place where others can see them.

When creating a text password, make sure you devise a strong password—one that is difficult to guess but easy for you to remember. Strong text passwords have the following characteristics:

Contain at least eight characters
Do not include your user name, real name, or company name
Are not words you can find in the dictionary
Are significantly different from your previous passwords
• Contain characters from each of the following categories: uppercase letters, lowercase letters, numbers, and symbols (not including spaces)

For any account that has a text password, you can also set up a four-digit **personal information number (PIN)** and a picture password to protect the account. Similar to a PIN you use for banking transactions, you can use a PIN for a Windows account as a fast way to sign in. (Keep in mind, however, that a PIN does not meet the requirements for a strong password.) A **picture password** involves an image and gestures, and is easiest to provide on a touchscreen device. You select a photo or another graphic stored in a location your computer can access, and then draw three gestures (that is, circles, lines, and taps or clicks) on the picture to create a password. You must remember the size, position, and direction of the gestures and the order you make them so you can repeat the gestures to gain access to your account. At times, Windows requests your text password, such as when you want to change system settings. At other times, you can use a PIN or picture password, such as to sign in to your account.

Creating a Microsoft Account

Duane is concerned that he and his staff at Catapult Product Design are all using the Administrator accounts that Windows created when it was installed. He wants to make sure that everyone creates a Standard user account with a password. Some part-time employees share a single computer, and Duane wants those employees to create separate Standard accounts on the same computer. To take advantage of cloud services and synchronization, he also wants the new accounts to be Microsoft accounts.

Duane wants to start by creating a Standard Microsoft user account on his computer. To do so, you provide his user name, which is the email address for his Microsoft account, and use the password for that account. Duane will also set up a PIN so he can sign in quickly and create a picture password as an alternate method for signing in to Windows.

Before you use a Microsoft account on your computer, you can create one at the Windows Live Web site to streamline the process. If you already have a Microsoft or Windows Live account, skip the following steps. You must be signed in using an Administrator account to perform the following steps. If you do not have access to an Administrator account, read but do not perform the following steps.

To set up a Microsoft account:

▶ 1. In IE Desktop, click the **Address bar**, type **https://signup.live.com**, and then press the **Enter** key. The Microsoft account Web page opens. Because you included "https" in the Web address, you can be confident this is a secure page.

▶ 2. Enter your name, birth date, and other requested information. For the Microsoft account name, you must provide an email address. Note your account name and password so you can use it with Windows 8.

▶ 3. Click the **I accept** button (or a similar button) to display the home page for your new Microsoft account.

▶ 4. Close Internet Explorer.

Next, you can create a Standard account using your Microsoft account credentials. You must be signed in using an Administrator account to perform the following steps. If you do not have access to an Administrator account, read but do not perform the following steps.

To create a Standard Microsoft user account:

▶ 1. Display the Charms bar, click the **Settings** charm, and then click **Change PC settings** to display the PC settings screen.

▶ 2. Click the **Users** category in the left pane to display a screen with your account information. See Figure 5-26. Your screen will differ.

Figure 5-26 **Your account screen**

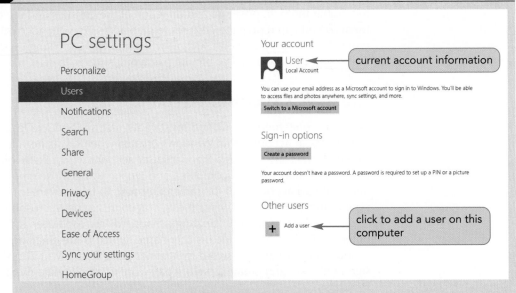

Trouble? If a message appears on your account screen about trusting the PC, disregard the message. You don't need to sync settings now.

3. Click the **Add a user** button to display the Add a user screen.

4. Enter the email address you use for your Microsoft account, and then click the **Next** button to display a screen confirming the email address.

   Trouble? If you do not have a Microsoft account, enter information for the new account, click the Next button, and then complete the setup steps.

5. Click the **Finish** button to create the account.

After you create an account, you can switch to that account and then change your text password, create a picture password, and create a PIN. You'll switch to the Standard account and then change its password. You'll use cPult!10 as the password, a combination of the name of Duane's company and the year it was founded.

To switch accounts and change a password:

1. Press the **Windows** key 🪟 to return to the Start screen.

2. Click the user icon in the upper-right corner of the screen, and then click **Sign out**. Windows signs out of your account and displays the lock screen.

3. Clear the lock screen, and then click the icon for the new account you just created.

4. Enter the password for your Microsoft account, and then press the **Enter** key. Windows takes a few minutes to set up the new account.

5. When the Start screen appears, display the Charms bar, click the **Settings** charm, click **Change PC settings**, and then click **Users** in the left pane.

6. In the Sign-in options section, click the **Change your password** button. The Change your Microsoft account password screen appears. See Figure 5-27.

| Figure 5-27 | Change your Microsoft account password screen |

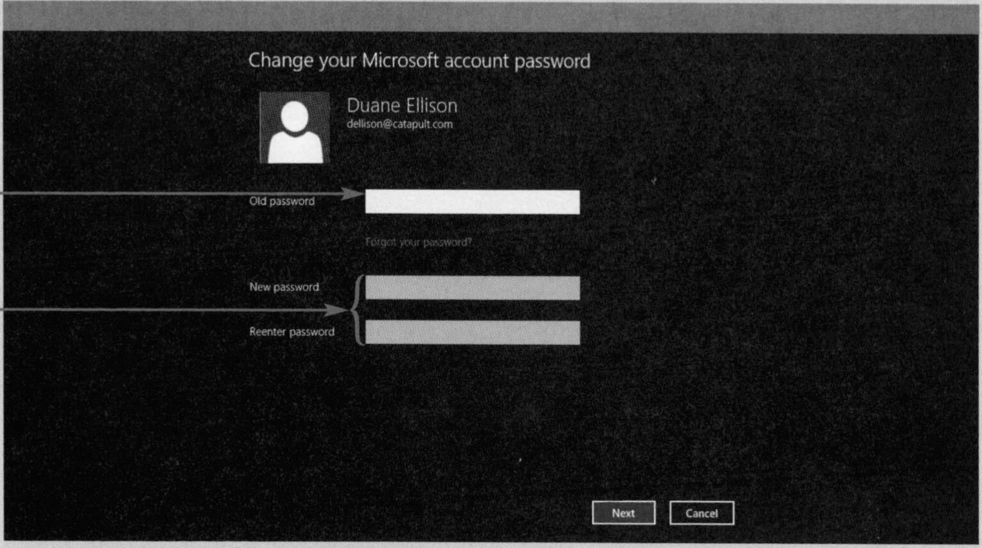

enter the password
for your email account

enter and confirm
the new password

TIP

If you forgot your password, click the Forgot your password link, and then go online to reset the password.

7. In the Old password text box, type your email password.

8. In the New password text box, type **cPult!10**. You must type the password again to confirm it.

9. Click the **Reenter password** text box, and then type **cPult!10**.

10. Click the **Next** button to confirm that you changed your password, and then click the **Finish** button.

If you forget your password and you're using a Microsoft account, you can reset your password online (go to https://signup.live.com and search for *reset password*). If you forget your password and you're using a local account, use your password hint as a reminder. You can also ask someone with an administrator account on your computer to change the password for you.

Next, you can create a PIN and a picture password. Duane wants to use 5410 as the PIN, the date he founded the company.

To create a PIN:

1. On the PC settings screen for Users, click the **Create a PIN** button to display a screen where you enter your account password.

2. Enter **cPult!10** as the password, and then click the **OK** button to display the Create a PIN screen. See Figure 5-28.

Figure 5-28 **Create a PIN**

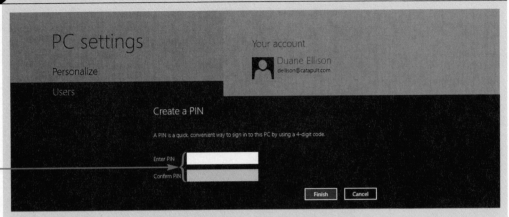

enter and confirm a four-digit PIN

PC settings

Personalize

Users

Your account

Duane Ellison
dellison@catapult.com

Create a PIN

A PIN is a quick, convenient way to sign in to this PC by using a 4-digit code.

Enter PIN

Confirm PIN

Finish   Cancel

▶ **3.** Enter **5410** in the Enter PIN text box.

▶ **4.** Click the **Confirm PIN** text box, type **5410**, and then click the **Finish** button to create the PIN. Note that a Remove button now appears next to the Change PIN button so you can delete the PIN if necessary.

▶ **5.** Close the PC settings screen.

Next, you can create a picture password for Duane's account. First, you'll take a screen shot of the White House home page and then use that image for the picture password.

To create a picture password:

▶ **1.** Start Internet Explorer, navigate to the White House Web site at **www.whitehouse.gov**, and then find a Web page you want to use for the picture password image.

▶ **2.** Press the **Print Screen** key to capture an image of the screen, and then close Internet Explorer.

▶ **3.** Right-click a blank spot on the Start screen to display the Apps bar, and then click the **All Apps** button to display the Apps screen.

▶ **4.** Click **Paint** under Windows Accessories to start Paint on the desktop, and then press the **Ctrl+V** keys to paste the screen image in a new Paint file.

▶ **5.** Click the **Save** button 🖫 on the Quick Access toolbar, and then save the screen image as a PNG file named **White House** in the Pictures library. Close Paint.

▶ **6.** Return to the PC settings screen for Users, and then click the **Create a picture password** button.

▶ **7.** Enter **cPult!10** as the password, and then click the **OK** button to display the Welcome to picture password screen. See Figure 5-29.

| Figure 5-29 | Welcome to picture password screen |

click to select an image

sample image

visual hint about how to draw a circle on this screen

 8. Click the **Choose picture** button, click the screen shot you saved in the Pictures library, and then click the **Open** button to select the picture.

 9. Click the **Use this picture** button. The Set up your gestures screen appears.

 10. Draw three gestures on the picture as described in the left pane of the screen. Select objects on the picture and use gestures you can remember easily.

 11. When the Confirm your gestures screen appears, repeat the gestures in the same order you used in Step 10.

 Trouble? If the "Something's not right" message appears, click the Try again button and repeat Step 11, carefully redrawing the gestures you created. If you are still having trouble, click the Start over button and repeat Steps 10 and 11, but make sure you use simple gestures (for example, draw a line under a word or picture) and note their placement on the screen.

 12. Click the **Finish** button, and then close the PC settings screen.

To perform the remaining steps in the tutorial, you need to sign out of the Standard account and sign in with your original (that is, Administrator) account.

 To switch accounts:

 1. On the Start screen, click the user icon, and then click **Sign out**. Windows signs out of your account and displays the lock screen.

 2. Clear the lock screen, and then click the icon for your Administrator account.

 3. If necessary, enter your password, and then press the **Enter** key.

Now you and Duane can show all of the Catapult Product Design employees how to create accounts and passwords on their computers.

Controlling Access to Your Computer

One way to manage access to your computer is to take advantage of **User Account Control (UAC)**, a feature that is turned on by default and can help prevent unauthorized changes to your computer. As you performed the previous steps, you might have seen UAC at work, asking for permission by providing an administrator password before performing actions that could affect your computer's settings. A UAC dialog box usually opens when a program or an action is about to start. The dialog box requests an administrator password as permission to start the program. By notifying you, UAC can help prevent malware from installing itself on or changing your computer without permission. Make sure the name of the action or program in the UAC dialog box is one that you intended to start. The dialog box indicates whether the program or action is part of Windows, is not part of Windows, is unidentified, or is blocked by the administrator. The dialog box also indicates whether the program has a digital certificate. If you are working on a computer on which you've set up an Administrator account and one or more Standard accounts, the UAC dialog box asks for an administrator password so that software can't be installed without the administrator's knowledge or permission.

The UAC feature is turned on by default and should not be turned off. You'll show Duane how to make sure UAC is turned on for all of the Catapult computers.

To verify that User Account Control is turned on:

▶ 1. On the Start screen, type **Control Panel** and then click **Control Panel** in the list of apps to open the Control Panel.

▶ 2. Click **User Accounts and Family Safety** to display the User Accounts and Family Safety window, and then click **User Accounts** to display the User Accounts window.

▶ 3. Click **Change User Account Control settings**. The User Account Control Settings window opens. See Figure 5-30.

| Figure 5-30 | User Account Control Settings window |

drag the slider to change when Windows notifies you about changes to your computer

describes the setting

> **4.** Drag the slider up and down to examine each setting, drag the slider to the **Notify me only when apps try to make changes to my computer (default)** setting, and then click the **OK** button.
>
> **Trouble?** If a User Account Control dialog box opens asking if you want to allow the program to make changes to this computer, click the Yes button.

Besides controlling access to your computer with passwords and UAC, you should be aware of security features that Windows provides at startup when installing apps.

Startup and App Security Features

Besides the tools and features covered so far in this tutorial, Windows provides behind-the-scenes security protections that don't require your intervention. One of these is a new boot method called **Unified Extensible Firmware Interface (UEFI)**. When you turn on the power to a computer, it performs a series of steps and checks as it loads the operating system and prepares for you to use it. This startup process is called **booting** the computer. UEFI boots a computer faster and in a more secure way than previous methods. Some malware is designed to start as the operating system loads. The computer is vulnerable at this point because antivirus software hasn't started yet. Rootkits in particular can interfere with operating system files and start before antivirus software can detect them. The Secure Boot feature in UEFI makes Windows 8 resistant to this type of malware. **Secure Boot** can detect when a file has interfered with the operating system and prevent that file from loading so it doesn't interfere with the operating system again.

After the operating system loads, the next application that starts is antivirus software. Malware sometimes tampers with antivirus software as it loads so it appears to be running but is in fact disabled. Windows 8 detects any tampering with the antivirus software and restores the unmodified version so it protects against malware.

Computers are also vulnerable to attack when you install new software. Malware can attach itself to legitimate files posted for download on Web sites, for example. When you download a new app, you might also be downloading a virus or worm. This scenario is very unlikely with apps you download from the Windows Store. Microsoft rigorously screens apps posted for download on the Windows Store to make sure they are free from malware. Microsoft provides a digital signature to verify the app is safe, and Windows tools such as the SmartScreen Filter and Windows Defender read the digital signature to make sure the file was not intercepted and changed during the download. Windows 8 also runs apps so they have only limited access to other resources on your computer, which minimizes the damage any malware could cause.

Restoring Your Settings

If you are working in a computer lab or on a computer other than your own, complete the steps in this section to restore the original settings on the computer. If a User Account Control dialog box opens requesting an Administrator password or confirmation after you perform any of the following steps, enter the password or click the Yes button.

To restore your settings:

> **1.** On the desktop, display the Control Panel Home page in Category view, click **System and Security**, and then click **Windows Firewall**.

▶ **2.** In the left pane of the Windows Firewall window, click **Allow an app or feature through Windows Firewall**, and then click the **Change settings** button.

▶ **3.** Click the **Connect to a Network Projector** check box to remove the check mark, and then click the **OK** button.

▶ **4.** Click **System and Security** in the Address bar, click **Windows Update**, and then click **Change settings** in the left pane. Click the **Updates will be automatically installed during the maintenance window** link, click the **Automatic Maintenance** button, click the original time set for installing updates, and then click the **OK** button. Minimize the Control Panel window.

▶ **5.** Start Internet Explorer on the desktop, click the **Tools** button 🔧 on the right side of the screen, and then click **Internet options**. Click the **Privacy** tab, and then click the **Settings** button. Click the **Blocking level** button, and then click your original setting. Click the **Close** button to close the Pop-up Blocker Settings dialog box.

▶ **6.** On the Privacy tab, drag the **Internet zone slider** to its original setting.

▶ **7.** Click the **General** tab in the Internet Options dialog box, and then click the **Delete** button in the Browsing history section. Click the **Cookies and website data** check box and the **History** check box to remove the check marks. Click **Cancel** in the Delete Browsing History dialog box. Click the **OK** button to close the Internet Options dialog box.

▶ **8.** Click the **Tools** button 🔧, point to **Safety**, and then click **Tracking Protection**. Click **Your Personalized List**, and then click the **Settings** button. Click **doubleclick.net** (or the name of the content provider you selected earlier) in the content provider list, click the **Allow** button, and then click the **OK** button. If Tracking Protection was disabled at the beginning of the tutorial, click the **Disable** button with Your Personalized List selected to turn off Tracking Protection. Close the Manage Add-ons window and Internet Explorer.

▶ **9.** Display the Control Panel window, return to the Control Panel home page, click **User Accounts and Family Safety**, and then click **Remove user accounts**. Click the icon for the Standard account you created, click **Delete the account**, click the **Delete Files** button, and then click the **Delete Account** button. Close the Control Panel window.

▶ **10.** Close all open windows.

REVIEW

Session 5.2 Quick Check

1. The _SmartScreen Filter_ ~~мульничество~~ helps detect online scams, such as Web sites that try to trick you into revealing financial account information.
2. What is the purpose of Protected Mode? —243 –244 –249
3. What is a Web site certificate? –247
4. Explain how you can use Download Manager to run a security check on a downloaded file. 248-249
5. By default, what types of pop-up windows does Internet Explorer block? — 251
6. If you don't want anyone to track the Web pages you visited, you can use _Tracking Protection_ — 258 — In Private Browsing.
7. What is the advantage of having a Microsoft account? 264–263
8. Name the three types of passwords you can use with Windows 8 and describe the purpose of each type.

5. Pop-up Blocker is turned on by default.
6.

PRACTICE

Review Assignments

There are no Data Files needed for the Review Assignments.

Duane Ellison, owner of Catapult Product Design, recently bought a new Windows 8 computer for you to share with Serena Olivera, one of his project managers. To market products, Serena specializes in using multimedia, which she plays using Windows Media Player. She is preparing to visit a client in Rockville, Maryland, and is concerned about the security of her computer during the visit. You'll show Serena how to keep the new computer secure. Complete the following steps, noting your original settings so you can restore them later:

1. Open the Action Center, and then perform the following tasks:

    Choose to allow an app through Windows Firewall.

    Change the settings to add Windows Media Player Network Sharing Service (Internet) to the allowed programs list.

    If the Allowed apps window is maximized, click the Restore Down button to resize it.

2. Open another Control Panel window and then change the settings in Windows Update to automatically check for and install updates every day at 7:00 AM. (*Hint*: Make sure you note the original time so you can restore the setting at the end of the exercise.) If the Automatic Maintenance window is maximized, click the Restore Down button to resize it.

3. Arrange the Allowed apps window and the Automatic Maintenance window to display the settings you changed. Press the Print Screen key to capture an image of the screen. Open Paint or WordPad, and then press the Ctrl+V keys to paste the image in a new file. Save the file as **Updated Settings** in the Windows5\Review folder provided with your Data Files.

4. Start Windows Defender, and then use it to perform a quick scan on your computer.

5. With the Windows Defender window open on your desktop and displaying the scan results, press the Print Screen key to capture an image of the window. Open Paint or WordPad, and then press the Ctrl+V keys to paste the image in a new file. Save the file as **Defender** in the Windows5\Review folder provided with your Data Files. Close all open windows.

6. In IE Desktop, open a Web page in your Favorites list or go to the home page of a popular search engine, such as Google (**www.google.com**) or Bing (**www.bing.com**). Use the SmartScreen Filter to verify this Web site is not a phishing Web site.

7. Make sure the Pop-up Blocker in Internet Explorer is turned on, and then visit a Web site that uses pop-up windows such as **www.merriam-webster.com** or **www.movies.com**. Enter a search term (for example, **dabble** or **The King's Speech**) to display a Notification bar explaining that Internet Explorer blocked a pop-up. Press the Print Screen key to capture an image of the desktop. Open Paint or WordPad, and then press the Ctrl+V keys to paste the image in a new file. Save the file as **Blocked** in the Windows5\Review folder provided with your Data Files.

8. Turn on InPrivate Browsing in Internet Explorer and then perform the following tasks:

    Visit the Maryland state Web site at **www.maryland.gov**.

    Click the VISITING tab.

    Click the Maryland Film Office link in the Arts & Culture section.

9. In the original Internet Explorer window you opened in Step 7 (that is, the dictionary or movie Web site), pin the Favorites Center to the window, click the History tab, if necessary, and then click the Today link to display Web sites you visited today except for those visited during your InPrivate Browsing session. (*Hint*: You can also click the Show Address bar Autocomplete button to display your browsing history.)

10. Perform the following tasks to capture an image of the windows:

   Arrange the InPrivate Browsing window so it appears on top of the dictionary or movie Web site window.

   Resize the windows so that the Favorites Center in the original Internet window is visible.

   Click the Show Address bar Autocomplete button in the Address bar of the InPrivate Browsing window to display a list of Web sites visited during this browsing session.

   Press the Print Screen key to capture an image of the desktop.

   Open Paint or WordPad, and then press the Ctrl+V keys to paste the image in a new file.

   Save the file as **InPrivate** in the Windows5\Review folder provided with your Data Files.

   Close all open windows.

11. Create a PIN for your user account using **6695** as the number.

12. With the Create a PIN (or Change your PIN) screen open, press the Print Screen key to capture an image of the screen. Open Paint or WordPad, and then press the Ctrl+V keys to paste the image in a new file. Save the file as **Pin** in the Windows5\Review folder provided with your Data Files. Return to the Start screen and then switch to your original account.

13. Restore the settings on your computer, including restoring the Pop-up Blocking level to its original setting. Remove Windows Media Player Network Sharing Service (Internet) from the Windows Firewall allowed programs list. Restore the settings in Windows Update and Windows Defender to install updates and scan at their original times. Close the Favorites Center in Internet Explorer and delete your browsing history. Remove the PIN you created for your user account.

14. Close all open windows.

15. Submit the results of the preceding steps to your instructor, either in printed or electronic form, as requested.

APPLY

Case Problem 1

There are no Data Files needed for this Case Problem.

Mulcahy Sports Medicine   Deanne Mulcahy runs a small business in Libertyville, Illinois, called Mulcahy Sports Medicine, which helps to train sports teams at small colleges and universities so the athletes avoid injury and work toward peak physical fitness. Deanne uses a laptop computer running Windows 8 to create most of her training plans, which she develops while visiting schools. She is concerned about maintaining security as she researches the latest in physical therapy and training programs on the Internet. In particular, she has experienced problems with pop-up ads and spyware and wants to know how to block pop-ups in Internet Explorer. You'll help her use the Windows 8 security settings to protect her computer. Complete the following steps, noting your original settings so you can restore them later:

1. Open the Action Center, and then add Wireless Portable Devices to the Windows Firewall allowed apps list. Leave the Allowed apps window open.

2. Change the settings in Windows Update to automatically check for and install updates every day at 5:00 AM. Leave the Automatic Maintenance window open.

3. Start Windows Defender, and then use it to perform a quick scan on your computer.

4. Arrange all windows to show the settings you changed, and then press the Print Screen key to capture an image of the desktop. Open Paint or WordPad, and then press the Ctrl+V keys to paste the image in a new file. Save the file as **Security** in the Windows5\Case1 folder provided with your Data Files. Close all open windows.

5. In IE Desktop, open the Internet Options dialog box to the Privacy tab. Open the Pop-up Blocker Settings dialog box. Set Internet Explorer to block all pop-ups. Press the Print Screen key to capture an image of the dialog box. Open Paint or WordPad, and then press the Ctrl+V keys to paste the image in a new file. Save the file as **Popups** in the Windows5\Case1 folder provided with your Data Files. Close the Pop-up Blocker Settings dialog box.

6. Change the security level for the Trusted sites zone to Low. Press the Print Screen key to capture an image of the window. Open Paint or WordPad, and then press the Ctrl+V keys to paste the image in a new file. Save the file as **SecurityZone** in the Windows5\Case1 folder provided with your Data Files. Close the Internet Options dialog box.

7. In the Manage Add-ons dialog box, display a list of the currently loaded add-ons for toolbars and extensions. Press the Print Screen key to capture an image of the window. Open Paint or WordPad, and then press the Ctrl+V keys to paste the image in a new file. Save the file as **AddOns** in the Windows5\Case1 folder provided with your Data Files. (*Hint*: If there are no add-ons listed, display the list of add-ons that run without permission.)

8. Enable Tracking Protection, if necessary, and then open the Personalized Tracking Protection List dialog box. Block a content provider, such as one that provides content with a .js extension. Press the Print Screen key to capture an image of the dialog box. Open Paint or WordPad, and then press the Ctrl+V keys to paste the image in a new file. Save the file as **Tracking** in the Windows5\Case1 folder provided with your Data Files.

9. Start a Windows 8 app and then capture the screen. Save the image as a file named **Windows 8 App** in the Pictures library. Close the Windows 8 app.

10. Create a picture password for your user account using the Windows 8 App picture. Enter the required three gestures.

11. Before you confirm the three gestures, press the Print Screen key to capture an image of the screen. Open Paint or WordPad, and then press the Ctrl+V keys to paste the image in a new file. Save the file as **PicPassword** in the Windows5\Case1 folder provided with your Data Files. Confirm the gestures and then close the PC settings screen. Switch to your original user account.

12. Restore the settings on your computer. Remove Wireless Portable Devices from the Windows Firewall allowed programs list. Restore the settings in Windows Update and Windows Defender to install updates and scan at their original times. Change the Pop-up Blocker setting to its default setting. Restore the security level for the Trusted sites zone to its original setting. Delete your browsing history. Remove the picture password from your user account, and then delete the Windows 8 App file from the Pictures library.

13. Close all open windows.

14. Submit the results of the preceding steps to your instructor, either in printed or electronic form, as requested.

Case Problem 2

There are no Data Files needed for this Case Problem.

St. Joseph City Center Brenda Gargano is the director of the St. Joseph City Center, a performing arts center in St. Joseph, Michigan. The City Center hosts a children's theater, and schedules theatrical and musical performances throughout the year. Because the City Center computers are not part of the municipal network, Brenda uses Remote Desktop to connect to other computers in the city, and regularly uses Mail and Internet Explorer to run the organization. She has experienced problems with spyware and viruses, and wants to know when to trust Web sites she visits. You'll help her use the Windows 8 security settings to protect her computer. Complete the following steps, noting your original settings so you can restore them later:

1. Change the settings to add Remote Desktop to the Windows Firewall allowed programs list. Capture an image of the Allowed apps window, and then save it in a Paint file named **Firewall** in the Windows5\Case2 folder provided with your Data Files.

⊕ **Explore** 2. In Windows Update, view your update history. (*Hint*: In the Windows Update window, click View update history in the left pane.) Capture an image of the View update history window, and save it as a Paint file named **Update History** in the Windows5\Case2 folder provided with your Data Files. Close all open windows.

3. In IE Desktop, open a Web page in your Favorites list or go to the home page of a popular search engine, such as Google (**www.google.com**) or Bing (**www.bing.com**). Use the SmartScreen Filter to verify this Web site is not a phishing Web site. Capture an image of the Internet Explorer window and SmartScreen Filter dialog box, and then save it in a Paint file named **Phishing** in the Windows5\Case2 folder provided with your Data Files.

4. In IE Desktop, change the security level for the Internet sites zone to High. Capture an image of the dialog box, and then save the image as a Paint file named **HighSecurity** in the Windows5\Case2 folder provided with your Data Files. Close all open windows.

⊕ **Explore** 5. Activate a guest account on the computer. (*Hint*: Open the Control Panel, click User Accounts and Family Safety, click User Accounts, and then click Manage another account. In the Manage Accounts window, click the Guest account, and then click the Turn On button.)

6. With the Manage Accounts window open on the desktop, capture an image of the window, and then save the image as a Paint file named **Guest** in the Windows5\Case2 folder provided with your Data Files.

7. Restore the settings on your computer. Remove Remote Desktop from the Windows Firewall allowed programs list. Restore the security level for the Internet sites zone to its original setting. Turn off the Guest account.

8. Close all open windows.

9. Submit the results of the preceding steps to your instructor, either in printed or electronic form, as requested.

CHALLENGE

CHALLENGE

Case Problem 3

There are no Data Files needed for this Case Problem.

Andiamo Caffé   Michael Monti owns the Andiamo Caffé in Providence, Rhode Island, and has designed the restaurant as a casual gathering place for the neighborhood. Besides Italian coffee and baked goods, Michael offers books, Internet connections, and computers to customers who want to use them. Michael is particularly concerned about the security of these computers. You'll help him use the Windows 8 security settings to protect a public computer. Complete the following steps, noting your original settings so you can restore them later:

✪ **Explore**   1. In Windows Firewall, block all incoming connections. (*Hint*: Select an option in the Customize Settings window.)

✪ **Explore**   2. Set Windows Defender to perform a custom scan of your removable disk.

3. Arrange the Windows Defender Options window and the Windows Firewall window to display the settings you changed, and then capture an image of the screen. Save the image as a Paint file named **Scan** in the Windows5\Case3 folder provided with your Data Files. Close all open windows.

4. In Internet Explorer, change the privacy level for the Internet zone to High. Capture an image of the dialog box, and then save it as a Paint file named **HighPrivacy** in the Windows5\Case3 folder provided with your Data Files.

5. Delete all temporary files and cookies in Internet Explorer.

✪ **Explore**   6. Set IE Desktop so that it does not store the browsing history. (*Hint*: On the General tab of the Internet Options dialog box, click the Delete browsing history on exit check box.) Capture an image of the dialog box, and then save it in a Paint file named **NoHistory** in the Windows5\Case3 folder provided with your Data Files.

✪ **Explore**   7. Activate a guest account on the computer. (*Hint*: Open the Control Panel, click User Accounts and Family Safety, click User Accounts, and then click Manage another account. In the Manage Accounts window, click the Guest account, and then click the Turn On button.)

8. With the Manage Accounts window open on the desktop, capture an image of the window, and then save it as a Paint file named **Account** in the Windows5\Case3 folder provided with your Data Files.

9. Restore the settings on your computer. Restore the original general settings in Windows Firewall. Restore the settings for a Windows Defender scan to their original settings. In Internet Explorer, restore the privacy level for the Internet zone to its original setting, and then restore the original setting of the Delete browsing history on exit check box. Turn off the Guest account.

10. Close all open windows.

11. Submit the results of the preceding steps to your instructor, either in printed or electronic form, as requested.

RESEARCH

Case Problem 4

There are no Data Files needed for this Case Problem.

Kapur Research   Martin Kapur is the president of Kapur Research, a firm in Des Moines, Iowa, that conducts plant and seed research for agricultural companies. Martin wants to protect the computers his researchers use against security threats. To do so, he first wants to understand who typically attacks computers and their data. He also wants to learn more about the types of attacks people use to access computers, and how much damage such attacks have caused. He asks you to research these topics and report your findings. Complete the following steps:

1. Use your favorite search engine to find information about the types of people behind attacks on desktop computers. (Attacks on networks are in a separate category.) Search for information about the following types of attackers:

    White hat hackers

    Black hat hackers

    Script kiddies

    Hacktivists

2. Use your favorite search engine to find information about the techniques attackers use to exploit a computer. Search for information about the following types of techniques:

    Key loggers

    Password cracking

    Social engineering

    Spoofing or phishing attacks

    Vulnerability scanners

3. Use a word processor to summarize your findings in one or two pages. Be sure to define any new terms and cite the Web sites where you found your information. Save the document as an RTF file named **Security**.

4. Submit the results of the preceding steps to your instructor, either in printed or electronic form, as requested.

WINDOWS

OBJECTIVES

Session 6.1
- Develop search strategies
- Search for apps and settings
- Find files by name, type, and category
- Filter the search results
- Add tags to files

Session 6.2
- Use Boolean filters in advanced searches
- Search within Windows 8 apps
- Search the Internet
- Narrow searches using advanced search features
- Select search providers in Internet Explorer

Searching for Information

Finding Apps, Settings, Files, and Information

Case | *Columbia Collectibles*

A few years ago, Jay Park opened Columbia Collectibles, a shop in Columbia, Missouri, that buys and sells collectible items, especially baseball cards, postcards, and posters. Jay wants to develop a Web site to showcase his collectibles and plans to feature valuable items for sale each week. He recently hired you to help him organize materials and keep the Web site up to date. Along with assisting Jay at the shop, your duties include taking digital photos of the collectible items, organizing them logically, and finding items for the Weekly Features Web page and the customer newsletter.

In this tutorial, you'll learn how to develop strategies for finding information, and then use the Windows 8 search tools to find files. You'll refine your searches by using advanced techniques such as Boolean filters and multiple criteria. You'll also learn how to apply these search strategies in Windows 8 apps and when using Internet Explorer to find information on the Web.

STARTING DATA FILES

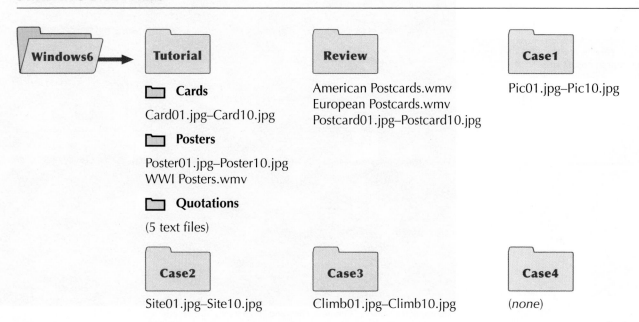

Windows6 → Tutorial

Cards
Card01.jpg–Card10.jpg

Posters
Poster01.jpg–Poster10.jpg
WWI Posters.wmv

Quotations
(5 text files)

Review
American Postcards.wmv
European Postcards.wmv
Postcard01.jpg–Postcard10.jpg

Case1
Pic01.jpg–Pic10.jpg

Case2
Site01.jpg–Site10.jpg

Case3
Climb01.jpg–Climb10.jpg

Case4
(*none*)

Session 6.1 Visual Overview:

Use the Search tab in a folder window to work with search results.

A search filter narrows a search to files that share a specified detail.

Select a condition when you use a search filter.

Saved searches are displayed in the Favorites list in the Navigation pane.

Click the Save search button to save the search criteria.

Search results are the files that meet your search conditions.

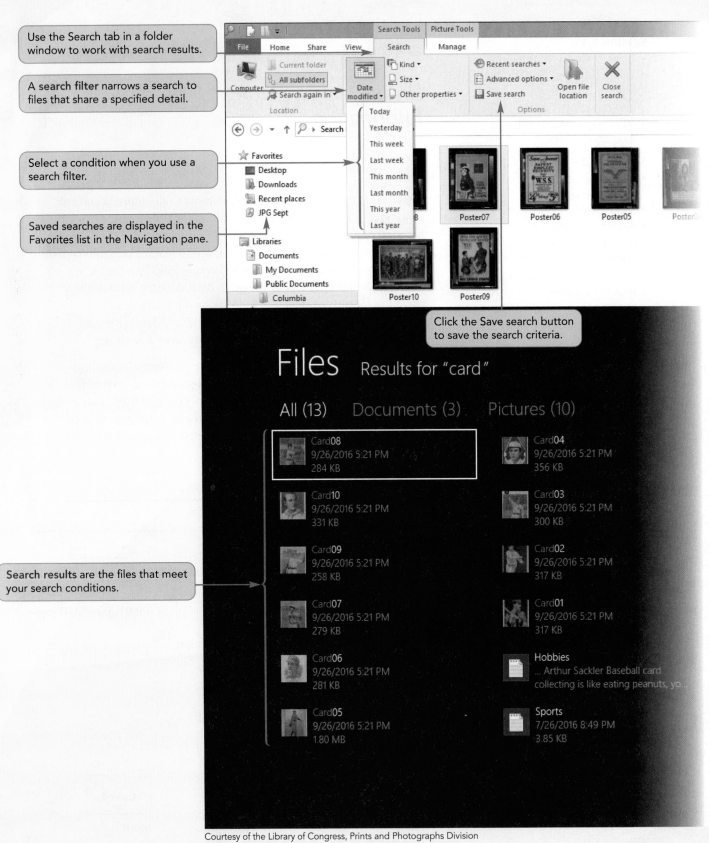

Searching for Files

Search for a type of file by using the filename extension as the search criterion.

A **tag** is text you add to photos and other types of files to describe them.

Search criteria are conditions that the file or folder must meet to have Windows find it.

Use the Search menu to search for apps, settings, and files.

Search for information stored in Windows 8 apps.

Developing Search Strategies

As you install programs and store data on your computer, the number of files and folders you have grows, and it becomes harder to locate a particular item. Using an efficient organization scheme helps you find files and folders when you need them. Knowing your way around the Start screen and the desktop makes it easier to find apps and settings. However, if pinpointing an item means browsing dozens or hundreds of files and folders, or if you don't know where to look, you can use a Windows 8 search tool. You have already used the Search menu to find apps and the Search text box in a folder window to find files. Figure 6-1 offers recommendations on when to choose one search tool over another.

Figure 6-1	Choosing a search tool

Search Tool	What to Find	What You Know	Technique to Use
Search menu (also called Start Search)	App	Some or all of the app name	Enter some or all of the app name
	Setting	Some or all of the setting name, description, or keyword	Enter some or all of the setting name, description, or keyword
	File anywhere on the computer, including system files	Some or all of the filename or a file detail	Enter some or all of the filename or enter a detail, an operator, and a filter
	Information in an app	Word or phrase appropriate for the app	Enter some or all of the word or phrase
Search text box in a folder window	File in the current folder or its subfolders	Some or all of the filename	Enter some or all of the filename
		Word or phrase in the file	Enter some or all of the word or phrase
		Details listed below the Search text box	Select a detail, such as size, and then select a filter, such as Large
		Details not listed below the Search text box	Enter a detail, an operator, and a filter
	File anywhere on the computer	Name, contents, or details	Expand the search, such as to libraries or the entire computer
Search text box in a Control Panel window	Control Panel tool	Some or all of the tool name, description, or keyword	Enter some or all of the tool name, description, or keyword

© 2014 Cengage Learning

To develop a search strategy, you need to know what you are looking for and you need to have some information about the item. Start by identifying what you want to find or what task you want to perform. The Search menu groups searches into three categories: Apps, Settings, and Files. Apps is selected by default. To search for settings or files, select the appropriate category on the Search menu. Folder windows also include a Search text box that makes it easy to find files. Likewise, Control Panel windows include a Search text box for finding Control Panel tools. For example, if you want to start Notepad, a text-editing application, to open a text file named Stamps.txt, you use the Apps category on the Search menu. If you want to find the Stamps.txt file and you're working on the Start screen, you can use the Files category on the Search menu. If you're working on the desktop, you can use the Search text box in a folder window.

Next, identify what you already know about the item you want to find. This information becomes your search criteria, which are conditions that the app, setting, or file must meet to have Windows find it. These conditions help you define and narrow your search so you can quickly find the item you want. For example, if you are searching for an app and using *explore* as the search condition, Windows locates and displays every app that matches that condition—in other words, all apps whose name contains a word starting with "explore," such as Internet Explorer and File Explorer. Note that case doesn't matter—you could type *explore*, *Explore*, or even *EXPLORE* to include Internet Explorer and File Explorer in the search results.

When you know what you want to find and what information you have about the item, you can choose the search tool that best fits your needs, and then use search criteria that are most likely to find the item. For example, suppose you want to find a photo that you took last New Year's Eve and stored somewhere in the Pictures library. Because you know the location of the photo, you can use the Search text box in the Pictures library window. You also know when you took the photo, so you can search for files created on 12/31/2015.

Searching for Apps

You have already used the Search menu to find apps installed on your computer. On the Start screen, you start typing a word that appears in the app's name. As you type, Windows displays the search results on the left and the Search menu on the right. Windows searches for apps by default, so the results include Windows 8 and desktop apps whose names contain a word starting with the text you typed. Because you start the search from the Start screen, this search method is also called Start Search.

When you use Start Search, Windows keeps track of the search text you use. As you enter text on the Search menu, Windows displays **search hints**, suggested words and phrases that begin with the letters you typed and have used previously as search text. You can click a search hint to search using that word or phrase again.

Jay often works with a stamp dealer in Berlin, Germany, to buy and sell stamps. He needs a quick way to convert the price of a stamp from U.S. dollars to euros when he's selling the stamp, and to convert from euros to U.S. dollars when he's buying the stamp. He asks you to find tools on his Windows 8 computer that let him perform these tasks.

You know that one app Jay can use to convert currencies is the Calculator app. You'll show him how to use Start Search to find the Calculator app.

To search for an app:

▶ **1.** On the Start screen, type **cal** to display the Apps screen and Search menu. See Figure 6-2.

Trouble? If the Start screen is not displayed on your computer, press the Windows key 🪟 and then repeat Step 1.

Figure 6-2   **Apps screen and Search menu**

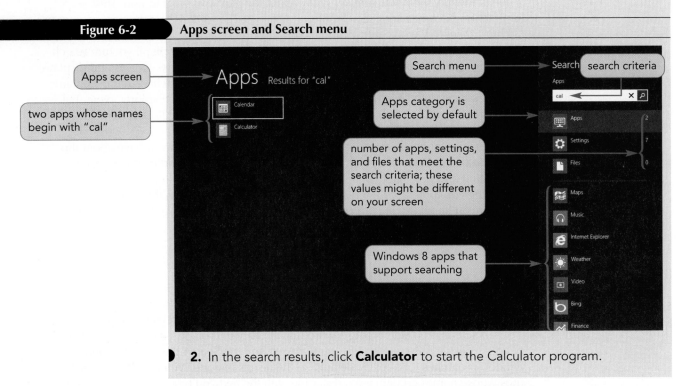

> **2.** In the search results, click **Calculator** to start the Calculator program.

When you use Start Search, the Search menu lists the number of apps, settings, and files that match your search criteria. Recall that you can display settings or files instead of apps by clicking Settings or Files on the Search menu. Below the Apps, Settings, and Files categories, the Search menu lists the Windows 8 apps that support searching. For example, you can search the Mail app to find email messages that match your search criteria. You'll search within an app later in this tutorial.

Jay has a stamp that he usually sells for $12. He knows that $1 currently equals 0.805 euros. You'll use the Calculator to determine the cost in euros of the $12 stamp.

To use the Calculator to convert dollars to euros:

TIP

Instead of typing the equation, you can also use the Calculator keypad.

> **1.** With Calculator as the active program, type **12 * .805** and then press the **Enter** key to display the results: 9.66.

> **2.** Click the **Close** button ⊠ to close the Calculator app.

> **3.** Press the **Windows** key ⊞ to return to the Start screen.

Besides converting between euros and dollars, Jay wants to display a clock that shows the current time in Germany. You'll use Start Search to look for such a tool on Jay's computer.

Searching for Settings

Windows settings include Control Panel tools, such as the Personalization tool, and items on the PC settings screen, such as your account picture. The Settings search results screen lists each PC settings item with a Settings icon ⚙ and each Control Panel tool with an icon identifying the tool, such as the Personalization icon 🖼.

To make searching more effective, each setting has a name, a description, and one or more keywords. For example, the Personalization tool on the Control Panel uses

"Personalization" as the name, "Change desktop background" as the description, and keywords such as "personalize" and "customize."

When you search for apps, Windows matches your search text to a word in the app name. For example, using *cal* as the search text produced two apps in the search results—Calendar and Calculator—because the names of both apps start with "cal." However, when you search for settings, Windows matches your search text to the setting name, description, and keywords. For example, when you search settings using "background" as the search text, the results include the Change desktop background setting, which you can click to open the Personalization tool in the Control Panel.

To find a tool that displays a clock in a different time zone, you can use the Settings category on the Search menu. (If you were already working in the Control Panel, you could use the Search text box in the Control Panel window.) You will use "clock" as the search text.

To search for a setting:

TIP

You can also press the Windows+W keys to search settings from the Start screen, Windows 8 app, or desktop.

1. On the Start screen, type **clock** to display the Apps screen and Search menu. Although no apps are displayed in the search results, a number of items appear in the Settings category. You can display the found items in the Settings category to see if one contains a tool you can use.

2. Click **Settings** on the Search menu to display the settings and tools on your computer that include a word beginning with "clock" in their name, description, or keywords. See Figure 6-3. Your results might differ.

| Figure 6-3 | Settings search results |

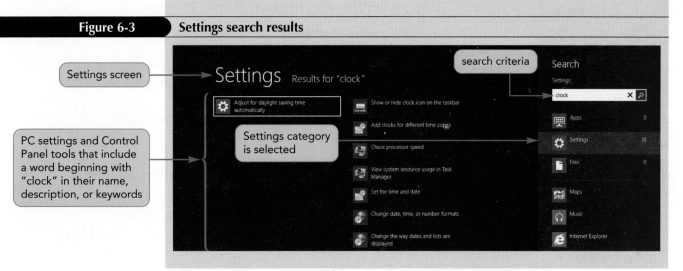

The results include one PC setting and nine Control Panel settings, as identified by the icon that appears next to each setting. How do you know if any of these settings will display a clock in another time zone? You can analyze the results by examining each item more carefully. The setting, "Add clocks for different time zones," sounds promising. To learn more about a setting, you can point to an item in the search results to display a ScreenTip that identifies the category of the setting and its description. To select a setting, you click it in the search results.

To examine and select a setting:

1. Click a blank spot in the search results to close the Settings menu, and then point to **Add clocks for different time zones**. The ScreenTip indicates that this setting is in the Date and Time category of the Control Panel and repeats the setting description.

2. Click **Add clocks for different time zones** to display the Date and Time dialog box, which is open to the Additional Clocks tab. See Figure 6-4.

Figure 6-4 **Date and Time dialog box**

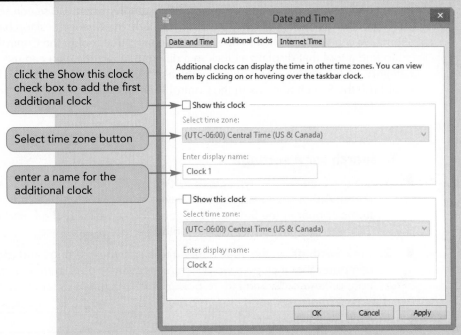

click the Show this clock check box to add the first additional clock

Select time zone button

enter a name for the additional clock

3. Click the first **Show this clock** check box to select it. The current time zone is selected for the additional clock, so you need to change it to show the time zone in Germany.

4. Click the **Select time zone** button, and then click **(UTC + 01:00) Amsterdam, Berlin, Bern, Rome, Stockholm, Vienna** to select the time zone for Germany.

5. Select the text in the Enter display name text box, and then type **Germany** to name the clock.

6. Click the **OK** button to close the Date and Time dialog box.

7. Point to the date and time control in the notification area of the taskbar to display the local time and the current time in Germany.

Jay is confident he will use the additional clock frequently when communicating with the German stamp dealer.

Searching for Files

You can search for files using Start Search or the Search text box in a folder window. Start Search looks for files stored anywhere on your computer, including system files stored in a system folder. The Search text box looks for files contained in the current folder or one of its subfolders. The tool you choose depends on your current task. If you just signed in to Windows or are working on the Start screen, use Start Search. If you are working on the desktop or in a folder window, use the Search text box.

When you search for files using either tool, you can conduct a basic search or an advanced search. If you use text from the filename or the file contents as search criteria, you are conducting a basic search. If you use other properties such as tags or file size as search criteria, you are conducting an advanced search. The other properties you can use as search criteria include any detail you can display as a column in a folder window. (Recall that you can display additional columns in a folder window by right-clicking any column heading, and then clicking a detail on the shortcut menu. If the detail you want to display does not appear on the shortcut menu, click More to open the Choose Details dialog box.) Figure 6-5 describes common criteria you can use when you conduct basic and advanced searches to find a file.

Figure 6-5 **Typical search criteria**

File Property	Description	What to Find	Search Criterion
Basic Searches			
Filename	All or part of the filename	File named April sales.docx	Apr or sales
File type	Filename extension	All of your photos	jpg
Contents	Text the file contains	File that uses "Baseball Card Sets" as a heading	Baseball Card Sets
Advanced Searches			
Date	Date the file was modified, created, or accessed	Document edited on May 15, 2016	datemodified:5/15/2016
Size	Size of the file	Files larger than 3 MB	size>3 MB
Tag	Word or phrase in the file properties	Photo with "winter," "vacation," and "ski" as tags	tag:winter vacation ski
Author	Name of the person who created the file	Document that Jay created	author:Jay

© 2014 Cengage Learning

When you combine criteria, such as to find a file named Agenda that you created last Monday, you are also conducting an advanced search. You'll learn how to combine search criteria later in the tutorial.

Finding Files by Name and Contents

Suppose you want to start working with a spreadsheet file named Poster Collection as soon as you sign in to Windows. On the Start screen, start typing a word in the filename, for example "poster," to display the Apps screen and the Search menu. Click Files on the Search menu to display all the files on your hard disk with filenames or contents that include a word beginning with the letters you typed. Performing this type of basic search using Start Search or a folder window is the most common way to find files on a Windows 8 computer.

A sales clerk for Columbia Collectibles created a short video that showcases the World War I posters in the shop's collection. Jay knows this video is stored somewhere on his computer, but isn't sure of the exact location or the complete filename. He does know that the filename includes the word "poster." You'll show him how to use Start Search to find the file.

First, however, you'll copy the Data Files for this tutorial to the Public Documents folder on your hard disk. The Windows6\Tutorial folder includes three subfolders: Cards, Posters, and Quotations. The Cards folder includes images of baseball cards and the Posters folder contains files related to the shop's poster collection. The Quotations folder contains text documents of quotations from authors, comedians, and other people on various subjects. Jay likes to include at least one quotation on the shop's Weekly Features Web page.

To search for files by name:

▶ **1.** Open File Explorer on the desktop, open the **Public Documents** folder in the Documents library, and then create a folder named **Columbia** in the Public Documents folder.

▶ **2.** If necessary, insert the USB flash drive containing your Data Files into a USB port on your computer.

▶ **3.** Right-click the **File Explorer** button 📁 on the taskbar, and then click **File Explorer** to open a second folder window. Display the contents of the Windows6\Tutorial folder provided with your Data Files. Copy the **Cards**, **Posters**, and **Quotations** folders from the Tutorial folder to the Columbia folder.

▶ **4.** Close the Tutorial folder window (the second window displaying the USB flash drive), but leave the Columbia folder window open on the desktop.

▶ **5.** Press the **Windows** key ⊞ to display the Start screen.

▶ **6.** Type **poster** to display the Search menu and the Apps screen.

▶ **7.** Click **Files** on the Search menu to display the files on the hard disk that meet the search criteria. See Figure 6-6.

| Figure 6-6 | Using Start Search to find files |

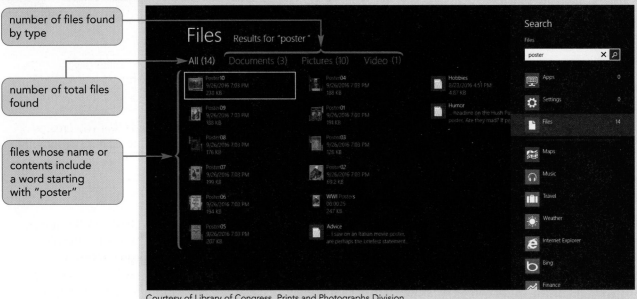

number of files found by type

number of total files found

files whose name or contents include a word starting with "poster"

Courtesy of Library of Congress, Prints and Photographs Division

TIP

You can also press the Windows+F keys to search for a file from the Start screen, Windows 8 app, or desktop.

▶ **8.** In the search results, click **Videos (1)** to display the video file Windows found: WWI Posters.

▶ **9.** Click the **WWI Posters** file to display a list of apps that can play this file, and then, if necessary, click **Video** to begin playing the file in the Video app.

Trouble? If a message appears advising you to create an account, close all open windows and screens and then press the Windows key ⊞ to return to the Start screen.

▶ **10.** When the video stops playing, close the Video app to return to the Start screen.

The search results for the previous steps included 11 files with names containing a word that starts with "poster." The results also included three text files named Advice, Hobbies, and Humor. To find out why, perform the same basic search again.

To search for files by contents:

▶ **1.** Type **poster** to display the Search menu and the Apps screen.

▶ **2.** Click **Files** on the Search menu to display the files and folders on the hard disk that meet the search criteria.

▶ **3.** Click a blank spot in the search results, and then point to the **Advice** text file to display its location in a ScreenTip. Next, point to the **Hobbies** and **Humor** files to display their ScreenTips.

▶ **4.** Click the **Advice** text file to open it in Notepad. This file contains quotations that provide advice from authors, comedians, and other people.

▶ **5.** Press the **Ctrl+F** keys to open the Find dialog box, type **poster** in the Find what text box, and then click the **Find Next** button. Notepad selects the first instance of "poster" in the Advice file.

▶ **6.** Close the Find dialog box and then close Notepad. The Columbia folder window is displayed on the desktop.

▶ **7.** In the Columbia folder window, double-click the **Quotations** folder, and then double-click the **Hobbies** text file to open it in Notepad.

▶ **8.** Repeat Step 5 to find the first instance of "poster" in the Hobbies file, and then close the Find dialog box and close Notepad. The Quotations folder window is still displayed.

▶ **9.** Open the **Humor** text file, find the first instance of "poster" in the file, and then close the Find dialog box and close Notepad.

Although the Advice, Hobbies, and Humor filenames do not include a word starting with *poster*, the file contents do. When you conduct a basic search to find files stored on a hard disk, Windows includes the file contents in the search. However, if you search files stored on a removable disk, such as a USB drive, Windows searches only the filenames, not the contents, by default.

Searching by File Type

Using the Search text box in a folder window to find files based on their filenames and contents is similar to using Start Search. You type text in the Search text box, and Windows displays only those files in the current folder or its subfolders that match the criterion: files whose contents or filename include a word starting with the text you typed.

You can also use a filename extension as the search criterion to find files by type. For example, you could enter *jpg* to find files with a JPG extension (also called JPGs), which are usually photo files. When you search for files by type, you can enter the filename extension on its own (*jpg*) or use an asterisk and a dot before the filename extension (**.jpg*). In this case, the asterisk is a **wildcard**, a symbol that stands for one or more unspecified characters in the search criterion.

Using a wildcard is a good idea if you want to search for certain types of files, such as those with a DOC extension. Suppose some of your filenames include words that start with the extension text, such as "Doctor Visit," "June Docket," or "Jay Docs." In this case, using a wildcard and a dot makes it clear that you are searching by filename extension only, and produces more accurate search results.

Jay is creating Web pages and printed marketing materials that feature notable baseball cards and posters in the shop's collection. He has been photographing these items and saving the photos on his computer. First, he wants to know how many card and poster photos he has saved. Because all of these photos are stored in two subfolders, you can provide the information Jay wants by conducting a basic search in a folder window using the filename extension .jpg as the search criterion.

To search for files by type:

1. In the folder window open on the desktop, display the contents of the Columbia folder in the Public Documents folder. If necessary, click the **Expand the Ribbon** button ⌄ to display the controls on the ribbon.

2. Click the **Search** text box, and then type **jpg**. Windows displays only the files with a .jpg extension in the folder window.

3. If necessary, click the **Large Icons** button 🖼 in the status bar to display the contents of the files. See Figure 6-7. Maximize the window, if necessary, to see all of the items, as shown in the figure.

| Figure 6-7 | Searching for files with a .jpg filename extension |

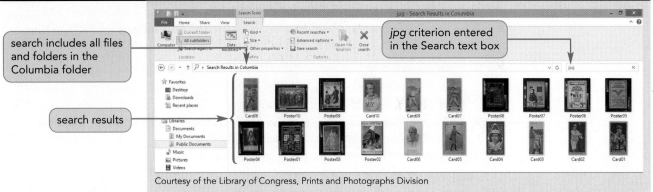

search includes all files and folders in the Columbia folder

jpg criterion entered in the Search text box

search results

Courtesy of the Library of Congress, Prints and Photographs Division

Decision Making: Searching vs. Sorting, Filtering, or Grouping

Recall that instead of using the Search text box, you can often quickly find files by sorting, filtering, or grouping files using the column headings or View menu in a folder window. The method you choose depends on the number of files you want to search, the location of the files, and their names. For example, suppose you need to find JPG files. If you want to search the current folder *and* its subfolders, use the Search text box—the other options find files only in the current folder.

If you're searching a single folder, the Search text box is also preferable if the folder contains similar filenames (because sorting would list many files that start with the same text) or many types of files (because grouping would produce many groups). If you want to find a particular file in a very large folder, it is often easier to use the Search text box rather than dealing with a long file list; however, if the folder doesn't contain too many files, then sorting, grouping, or filtering is usually a more efficient method.

Now that you found the photos of baseball cards and posters, Jay wants you to research the items so he can provide accurate information in the Web pages and printed brochure. Some of the JPG files you found have filenames starting with "Card" followed by a number, such as Card01 and Card02. The other JPG files have filenames starting with "Poster" followed by a number. Jay set his digital camera to assign these names so he could take the photos quickly. The camera used Card01 for the first photo Jay took of a baseball card and then automatically added 1 to the number each time he took another photo until he finished photographing the baseball cards. The camera used the same process to name the poster photos. Although this filenaming scheme worked well to save the photo files quickly, it poses challenges for your research because the filenames do not reveal anything about the content except that they show baseball cards or posters.

Filtering the Search Results by Size

Besides simply typing a few letters in the Search text box, you can also conduct more advanced searches using Start Search or a folder window. To search for files modified on a certain date or files of a certain size, for example, you can add a filter to narrow a search to files that share a specified detail. (Recall that a filter displays only files with a certain characteristic you specify.)

When you enter text in the Search text box of a folder window, Windows displays the results in the right pane and opens the Search tab on the ribbon. You use the buttons in the Refine group on the Search tab to narrow the results. For example, if you are searching the Pictures library for photos you took last week, you can click the Search text box in the Pictures library and then type *jpg* to display all the photos stored in the Pictures library. To narrow the results to display only the photos you took last week, click the Date modified button in the Refine group on the Search tab, and then click Last week. Windows displays only the files in the Pictures library that meet your criteria.

REFERENCE

Filtering Search Results

- Open the folder, library, or drive you want to search.
- Enter text in the Search text box.
- To specify a filter, click a button in the Refine group on the Search tab, and then click a criterion.

or

- On the Start screen, type a file property name, a colon, and the criterion.
- Click Files on the Search menu.

When you select a search filter, Windows automatically adds a file property name, a colon, and the criterion to the Search text box. The file property name is shorthand for the detail you want to use to narrow the search. The criterion determines how to narrow the search. For example, when you click the Date modified button on the Search tab and then click Last week, Windows inserts "datemodified:last week" in the Search text box.

To conduct an advanced search using Start Search, you enter the file property name, a colon, and the criterion directly in the text box on the Search menu.

Jay photographed one of the collectible items using a high resolution, which makes the image sharp and clear even when printed. He wants to use this photo in a printed brochure. However, he can't recall which photo has the high resolution. He mentions that high-resolution images are usually large files, often more than 1 MB in storage size. You can use this information to find the file Jay wants. Conducting a basic search using the jpg extension as the search text finds all the JPG files in the Cards and Posters folders. To narrow the search to large files only, you'll refine the results.

To narrow a search using a search filter:

▶ **1.** In the folder window displaying the results of the previous search, click the **Search Tools Search** tab, if necessary, and then click the **Size** button in the Refine group to display a list of size options. See Figure 6-8.

Trouble? If the folder window open on the desktop does not display the results of the previous search, type jpg in the Search text box.

Figure 6-8	Selecting a search filter

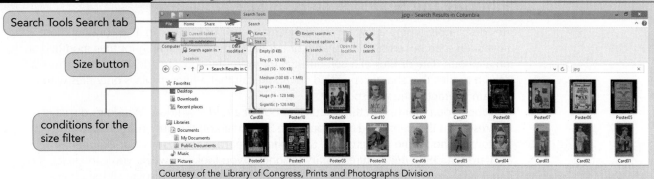

Courtesy of the Library of Congress, Prints and Photographs Division

▶ **2.** Click **Large (1–16 MB)** in the Size options list. Windows reduces the search results to files that meet both criteria—large JPG files.

Only one file meets the search criteria: Card05, which is a high-resolution photo of a Cy Young baseball card.

Filtering Search Results by Date Modified

приобрёт-ый ← *[handwritten margin note]*

Jay usually photographs a collectible item as soon as he receives it. On the shop's Weekly Features Web page, Jay wants you to display photos of collectible items he acquired recently, which are those photos taken after August 31, 2016. To find these files, you can start with the same criterion you used to find all the JPG files, and then narrow the results by specifying the date condition. When you use the Date modified button in the Refine group on the Search tab, you can select only predefined options such as Today, This week, or Last year. To use a specific date, you select one of these criteria and then click the Search text box to display a calendar where you can select a date or date range.

To find JPG files taken after August 31, 2016:

▶ **1.** In the folder window, click the **Back** button ⊙ until you return to the Columbia window.

▶ **2.** Click the **Search** text box, if necessary, and then type **jpg**. Windows displays all the JPG files in the search results.

▶ **3.** Click the **Date modified** button in the Refine group on the Search tab, and then click **Today** to select a date option. No results appear, so you need to modify the date further.

▶ **4.** Click in the text "today" in the Search text box to display a calendar control. See Figure 6-9.

TIP

Click the Search text box to display a list of recently used search text.

Figure 6-9	Using a date modified search condition

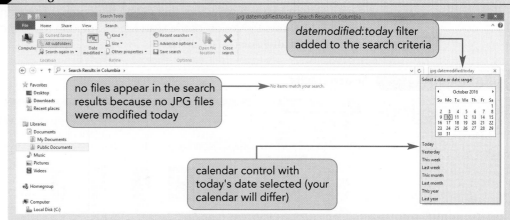

5. Use the calendar controls to display the **August 2016** page. To change the month, click the **left arrow** ◀ and **right arrow** ▶ buttons. When the calendar page for August 2016 appears, click **31**. See Figure 6-10.

Figure 6-10	Setting date criteria

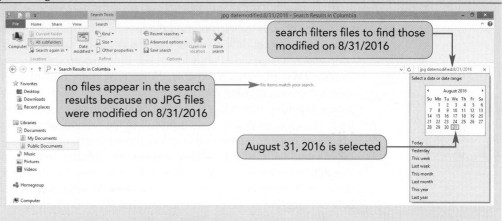

No files appear in the search results because no files in the Columbia folder were modified on August 31, 2016. You want to find files that were modified after that date. To do so, you use the greater than (>) operator. You can use the greater than operator with any property in the Search text box or the Search menu. For example, to find files that are larger than 500 KB, enter *size:>500KB*. (You can include a space after the colon or omit it—the space does not affect the search results.) You can also use the less than (<) operator in the same way. To find files less than 500 KB, enter *size:<500KB*. To find files modified after August 31, 2016, you use the greater than operator to enter *datemodified:>8/31/2016* in the Search text box.

To modify the search criteria:

▌ **1.** Click the **Search** text box.

▌ **2.** Move the insertion point after the colon (:) in datemodified, and then type **>**. Six files appear in the search results.

To make sure you find the files you need or to expand a search, you should examine the search results.

Examining the Search Results

After you enter search criteria using the Search text box, Windows filters the view of the folder window to display files that meet your criteria. These are your search results. Figure 6-11 shows the results of the search performed in the preceding set of steps: JPG files modified after August 31, 2016.

Figure 6-11	Search results

Courtesy of the Library of Congress, Prints and Photographs Division

Search results windows provide extra tools and information to help you work with the files you found. The title bar displays the search criteria. In Details view, the search results display the name, location, date modified, size, and other available properties of each file. If the results include text files, they preview their first two lines of text to help you identify the file contents.

Besides the buttons in the Refine group, the Search Tools Search tab contains other groups of controls to help you find the files or information you need. The Location group and Options group provide other search tools that you can use to broaden or narrow your search. Using the buttons in the Location group, you can change the default search location on your computer (that is, the current folder and all of its subfolders) or even search the Internet using your default Web browser (such as Internet Explorer) and **search provider**, which is a Web site that specializes in searching the Internet, such as Bing. The Options group stores a history of the criteria for your last eight searches. The Advanced options button in this group allows you to change how Windows uses the criteria entered to search for files using an exact match setting, for example. To speed up a search, you can set Windows to search an indexed location, such as the Documents library or Pictures library on your hard disk, so Windows searches the file contents. (An **indexed location** is one or more folders that Windows indexes so it can search them quickly. Libraries and other locations that contain your personal files—not system files— are indexed locations.) The Options group provides tools for saving the criteria and folder location of a search.

Jay occasionally works with files stored on a removable disk, so you want to show him how to search filenames and contents in that location.

To search for files on a removable disk:

▶ 1. If necessary, insert the USB flash drive containing your Data Files into a USB port on your computer.

▶ 2. In the folder window open on the desktop, display the contents of the Windows6\Tutorial folder on the USB flash drive.

▶ 3. Type **poster** in the Search text box to display files with filenames that contain a word beginning with *poster*.

▶ 4. Click the **Advanced options** button in the Options group on the Search Tools Search tab, and then click **File contents** under the In the non-indexed locations section (which includes the USB flash drive). Windows adds the three text files that contain a word beginning with "poster" to the search results.

> **Trouble?** If File contents is already selected, the text files are already displayed in the results for Step 3. Do not click File contents; this will deselect the option. Press the Esc key to close the list of advanced options.

In addition to the extra tools provided in a search results window, you can use the standard folder window tools to open, move, copy, rename, or delete a file.

Saving a Search

If you conduct a successful search that you are likely to conduct again, especially one that uses two or more criteria, you might want to save the search. Saving a search preserves your original criteria and folder location so you can perform the search again without reconstructing the criteria. By default, Windows saves the search in the Searches folder, which you can open from the Favorites list of any folder window's Navigation pane. You can double-click a saved search to use the same criteria in a new search. The search results display the most current files that match the original conditions, so the results might differ from other times when you conducted the same search.

To save a search and perform it again:

TIP

Click the Search text box to display the recent searches, and then click jpg datemodified:>8/31/2016.

1. In the search results window, click the **Back** button ⊙ to navigate back to the results of the jpg datemodified:>8/31/2016 search.

2. Click the **Save search** button in the Options group on the Search Tools Search tab. The Save As dialog box opens, providing jpg datemodified8-31-2016 as the filename. (Windows doesn't include the colon and greater than symbol because they are not allowed in filenames; Windows also replaces the forward slashes with dashes for the same reason.) See Figure 6-12.

| **Figure 6-12** | **Saving a search** |

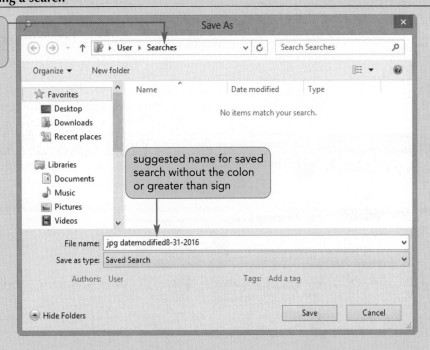

by default, Windows saves your searches in the Searches folder in your personal folder

suggested name for saved search without the colon or greater than sign

Be sure to save the search so you can use it again.

3. Change the filename to **JPG Sept**, and then click the **Save** button to save the search in the Searches folder.

4. To view the saved search, display the Favorites list in the Navigation pane, if necessary. The JPG Sept search appears in the Favorites list.

5. To test the search, click **Libraries** in the Navigation pane to change your current location, and then click **JPG Sept** in the Favorites list. Windows conducts the search again and finds the JPG files modified after August 31, 2016. See Figure 6-13.

Figure 6-13   **Performing a saved search**

shortcut to JPG Sept appears in the Navigation pane

Courtesy of the Library of Congress, Prints and Photographs Division

Jay asks if using tags would help him find and identify files. In fact, one of the most useful properties when searching for files is a file tag, which is one or more descriptive words you store with a file to help identify its purpose or contents. You are sure that adding tags to the photo files would save you and Jay a lot of time when searching for photos. You'll show him how to do so next.

Using Tags and Other Properties

As you know, properties are characteristics of files, such as names and sizes. When you create or modify a file, you automatically set some file properties, including the filename, location, and date created or modified. You can add other properties later, including tags, ratings, titles, and authors. Tags are often the most useful because they make finding similar files easier.

To add properties to a file, you can use the Details pane in a folder window or the file's Properties dialog box. (You can use the Details pane to add or modify the properties of only some types of files, such as Microsoft Office documents, but not TXT or RTF files.) To open the Details pane in a folder window, you click the Details pane button in the Panes group on the View tab. Figure 6-14 shows the Details pane when the Card05 file is selected in the Cards folder.

Figure 6-14   **File properties in the Details pane**

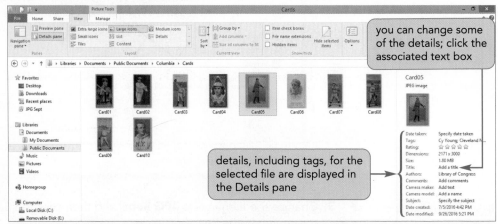

you can change some of the details; click the associated text box

details, including tags, for the selected file are displayed in the Details pane

Courtesy of the Library of Congress, Prints and Photographs Division

Properties you can add using the Details pane vary by file type. For photos, you can specify date taken, tags, and other properties by using the appropriate text box in the Details pane. You can also rate photos by clicking a star in a series of five stars. If you click the first star, you apply a one-star rating. If you click the fourth star, you apply a four-star rating.

If you want to specify file properties other than the ones that appear in the Details pane by default, you can open the Properties dialog box for a file. To do so, you right-click the file and then click Properties on the shortcut menu. On the Details tab, you can add or modify dozens of properties. Figure 6-15 shows the Properties dialog box for the Card05 file.

Figure 6-15   **File details in the Properties dialog box**

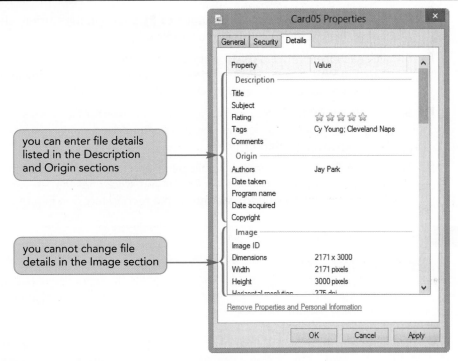

you can enter file details listed in the Description and Origin sections

you cannot change file details in the Image section

Adding Tags to Files

You can add a tag to a file by using the Save As dialog box when you save the file, or by using the Details pane or the file's Properties dialog box after you save the file. To use the Details pane, you select the file, click the Tags text box in the Details pane, and then type a word or phrase that will help you find the file later. To add more than one tag, separate each word or phrase with a semicolon (;). For example, if you have a photo of yourself on the peak of the Blackrock Mountain in Virginia, you could use *Blackrock; mountain; Virginia* as tags.

Jay has already added tags to most of the photo files in the Cards and Posters folders, but two recent files still need tags. Jay asks you to add descriptive tags to these files.

To add tags to files:

1. Open the **Posters** folder in the Public Documents\Columbia folder on your hard disk, and then switch to Details view. Maximize the window, if necessary.

2. Click the **Details pane** button in the Panes group on the View tab to display the Details pane.

3. Display the Tags column, if necessary, by right-clicking any column heading and then clicking **Tags** on the shortcut menu.

4. If necessary, click the **Size all columns to fit** button in the Current view group to display all of the columns in the window.

5. Click each file in the file list to examine its properties in the Details pane. Note that WWI Posters, Poster09, and Poster10 do not have any tags. WWI Posters is a video, so it's easy to identify that file without tags.

6. Click **Poster09** to display its image and text boxes for file details such as tags in the Details pane. Jay knows that this poster advertises World War I savings stamps and was printed in 1918.

7. Click the **Tags** text box in the Details pane, and then type **1918** as the first tag. Windows inserts an ending semicolon for you. Click after the ; (a semicolon), and then type **WWI savings stamps** as the second tag. See Figure 6-16.

| Figure 6-16 | Adding tags to a file |

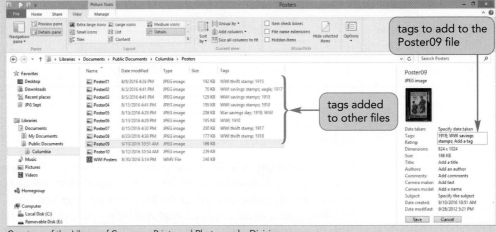

Courtesy of the Library of Congress, Prints and Photographs Division

8. Click the **Save** button in the Details pane. Windows saves the tags you added.

TIP

If Windows suggests tags as you begin to type, click the tag you want.

9. Add the tags **1917; WWI savings stamps; U.S. Treasury** to the Poster10 file, and then click the **Save** button. Note that after you save a tag in one file, that tag appears in the list of suggested tags for other files.

Selecting Tags for Files

To create tags that will help you find files later, keep the following guidelines in mind:

- Include the obvious. Use words or phrases that describe the overall purpose or content of the file. For photo files, use tags that list the people in the picture, the location of the photo, and the occasion. For documents, describe the type of document, such as a proposal or report, and its subject.
- Consider the sample tags. If you are working with files on a hard drive, you can find typical tags by typing a letter in the Tags text box in the Details pane. For example, type *p* to find sample tags that start with the letter *p*, such as people, pet owners, pets, and photography.
- Use complete words and phrases. Avoid abbreviations and codes because you might not remember them later. Assign complete words or use phrases to be as clear as possible. Feel free to use text that appears in the filename; doing so might help you find other related files with the same tag but a different filename.

You've already explored many ways to search for files on your computer. You conducted basic searches by searching filenames and contents. You also conducted advanced searches by using properties to filter the search results. In the next session, you'll build on these techniques by searching tags and combining criteria using short-hand notation and Boolean filters. You'll apply these new skills to search for information in Windows 8 apps and on the Internet.

Session 6.1 Quick Check

1. How do you search for an app from the Start screen? *286*
2. When you search for settings, what two groups of items does Windows search?
3. Explain when you typically use Start Search to search for files, and when you use the Search text box in a folder window.
4. When you conduct a basic search for files stored on a removable disk, what does Windows search by default? How does this differ from a basic search for files stored on a hard disk?
5. Explain how to search for TXT files in a folder window.
6. After searching for JPG files in the Pictures library, you can click the *date modified* button in the Refine group on the Search tab to narrow the results to display only the photos you took last week.
7. When you save a search, what exactly are you saving? *— saving search*

Session 6.2 Visual Overview:

Click a link to change the type of items displayed in the results.

Use the **Find toolbar** to find specific information on the page.

Bing is a **search engine**, a program that searches Web pages.

Each link in the search results is called a **hit**.

The **search expression** is the word or phrase that best describes the information you want to find.

The Find toolbar shows the number of matches on the page.

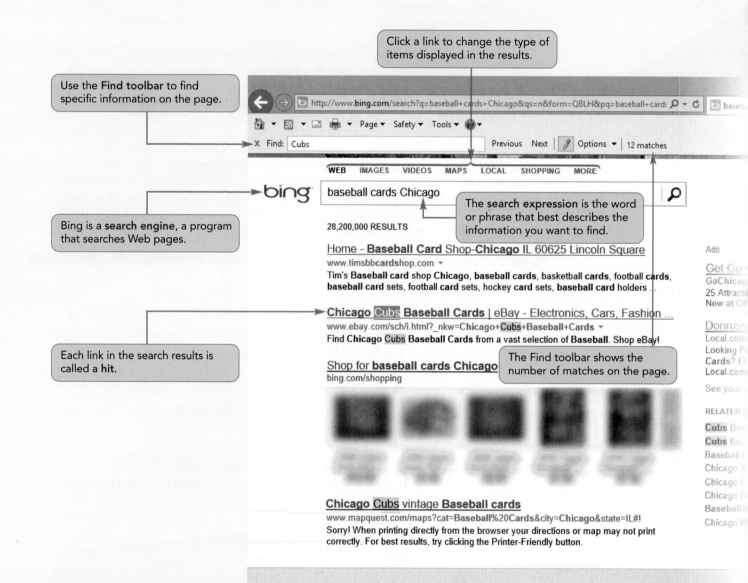

Searching the Internet

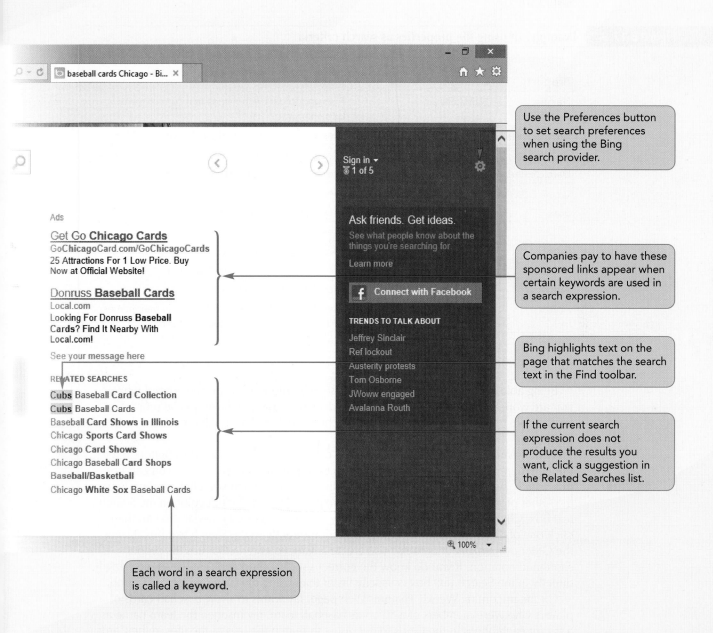

Use the Preferences button to set search preferences when using the Bing search provider.

Companies pay to have these sponsored links appear when certain keywords are used in a search expression.

Bing highlights text on the page that matches the search text in the Find toolbar.

If the current search expression does not produce the results you want, click a suggestion in the Related Searches list.

Each word in a search expression is called a **keyword**.

Using Advanced Search Criteria

In addition to searching for files using common properties such as file type or size, you can use the Search text box or the Search menu to search for other properties, including tags, title, and subject. To use any property as a criterion, you specify the property using the following shorthand notation: *property name:criterion*. (You can include or omit the space after the colon.) For example, if you want to search for files that include the word "Chicago" as a tag, you could enter *tag:chicago*. (The properties are not case sensitive, so you could also enter *Tag:Chicago*.) The properties you can use as search criteria include any detail you can display as a column in a folder window. Figure 6-17 provides examples of the shorthand notation you can use to specify file properties as search criteria.

| Figure 6-17 | Examples of using file properties as search criteria |

Property	Example	Finds
Name	Name:city	Files and folders with names that contain a word beginning with "city"
Date modified	DateModified:10/28/2016	Files and folders modified on October 28, 2016
	DateModified:<10/28/2016	Files and folders modified before October 28, 2016
Date created	DateCreated:>10/28/2016	Files and folders created after October 28, 2016
	DateCreated:2016	Files and folders created during the year 2016
Size	Size:200KB	Files with a size of 200 KB
	Size:>1MB	Files larger than 1 MB
Type	Type:docx	Files with a .docx filename extension
Tags	Tag:Chicago	Files that include "Chicago" as a tag
Authors	Author:Jay	Files that specify "Jay" as the author
Artists	Artist:Elvis	Files that specify artists with "Elvis" in their names, such as Elvis Presley and Elvis Costello
Rating	Rating:4 stars	Files with a rating of four stars

© 2014 Cengage Learning

Being able to include any file detail as a search criterion is especially useful when you are working with photos, music, and videos because they have special properties for their file types that are useful when searching, such as Artists, Album, Rating, and Length.

When searching in a folder window, you can use the Other properties button in the Refine group on the Search Tools Search tab to display a list of properties you can use in a search, such as authors, tags, and title. In each case, when you click a property on the Other properties list, Windows inserts the property name and a colon in the Search text box. Click the Search text box to display a list of suggested criteria. You can then click one of the suggestions or type the criterion directly in the Search text box. Using the Other properties button helps you create advanced criteria that use the proper shorthand notation. If you do know the correct shorthand notation, however, entering it directly in the Search text box is usually faster than using the Other properties button.

For the upcoming Weekly Features Web page, Jay wants to show baseball cards of players who were members of a St. Louis baseball team. Jay inserted the team name as a tag for each photo in the Cards folder. You can search the tags of the files in the Cards folder to find baseball card photos Jay can use.

To find files by specifying a property in the Search text box:

▶ **1.** Open the **Cards** folder in the Public Documents\Columbia folder on your hard disk.

▶ **2.** Click the **Search** text box, and then type **tag:St. Louis**. As you type, Windows filters the view of the files in the folder window, and then displays two files that contain the text "St. Louis" in their Tags property: Card06 and Card09.

▶ **3.** Click **Card06** and examine the information in the Details pane. This is a photo of a baseball card from 1887, showing Charles Comiskey when he played for the St. Louis Browns.

▶ **4.** Click **Card09** and examine its details. This is a photo of Ernest Lush, a member of the St. Louis Cardinals in 1911.

By searching for text in the Tags property, you found two photos to display on the Weekly Features Web page.

Combining Criteria When Searching File Contents

TIP

When you use two or more words as a search condition, Windows searches as if the condition includes the AND Boolean filter.

To perform a precise search, you can combine criteria in the Search text box or on the Search menu. For example, suppose you store your financial documents on your computer and need to find a list of charitable donations you made in 2016. You don't recall where you've stored this information, and scanning the filenames in your Financial folder doesn't reveal the file. If you search the contents of the files using *donation* as the search criterion, you'll find lists of donations for many years as well as other documents, including those with text such as "Thanks for your support! Every donation helps." If you search the contents of files using *2016* as the search criterion, you'll find dozens of documents that mention that year. To pinpoint your search, you can combine the criteria to find files that contain the word "donations" and the year "2016." When you search file contents, you can use **Boolean filters**, which are filters that let you search for specific information using the words AND, OR, and NOT to combine search criteria. You can use quotation marks and parentheses to refine the search conditions further. Figure 6-18 describes how to use AND, OR, and NOT along with quotation marks and parentheses when combining search criteria.

| **Figure 6-18** | **Combining search criteria** |

Word or Punctuation	Examples	When to Use
AND	donations AND 2016 donations 2016	To narrow the search to files that contain "donations" and "2016" even if the words are not next to each other
OR	donations OR 2016	To broaden the search to files that contain "donations" or "2016"
NOT	donations NOT 2016	To restrict the search to files that contain "donations" but not "2016"
" " (quotation marks)	"donations 2016"	To pinpoint the search to files that contain the exact phrase "donations 2016"
( ) (parentheses)	(donations 2016)	To open the search to files that contain both items next to each other in any order

© 2014 Cengage Learning

Note that when you use the words AND, OR, and NOT, you must enter them using all uppercase letters.

One of your ongoing projects for Columbia Collectibles is maintaining an archive of quotations, which Jay uses on the shop's Web pages and in the monthly customer newsletter. Jay, employees, and customers provide these quotations in various ways, such as in a word-processing document or an email message. You store the quotations ~ yutaon in TXT documents to make sure anyone at the shop can use the documents. However, this means that you cannot add tags or other properties to the files—you can add these details only to Microsoft Office documents.

Next week's Weekly Features Web page will showcase a few baseball cards from the shop's collection. To accompany photos of the cards, Jay wants to include at least one quotation about baseball card collecting. You can use Boolean logic to combine search criteria and search the contents of the Quotations folder to find suitable quotations.

INSIGHT

Preparing to Combine Search Criteria

Before you combine search criteria, select the search text, select the filter you plan to use, if any, and then select the condition. For example, choose *.txt as the search text to find text files. If you want to find text files modified after a certain date, use the datemodified: filter, and then select the appropriate date, such as >8/31/2016. Next, determine whether you should use AND, OR, or NOT to combine the criteria, and whether you need quotation marks or parentheses to find the files you want. For example, if you want to find files that use "Chicago" as a tag and have "Jay" as the author, you use the AND filter, whether you insert AND or not. In other words, *tag:Chicago AND author:Jay* is the same as *tag:Chicago author:Jay*.

If you want to find either text files or Word documents, you need to insert OR, as in *.txt OR *.doc*. (The search condition *.doc* finds Word documents that have a .doc or a .docx filename extension.) To determine the best criteria, test each method in order starting with AND. Keep in mind that AND narrows the search results, while OR broadens the results. For example, if you search for files that are photos and use "Chicago" as a tag, you find fewer files than searching for files that are photos or use "Chicago" as a tag.

Although you want to find quotations about baseball card collecting, using *baseball card* and *collecting* as search criteria won't find quotations that include "collection" or "collector" or even "collect," which might be appropriate quotations. A good rule of thumb when specifying search text is to use the root of the word; for example, use *collect* to find documents containing "collecting," "collection," "collector," and "collect". Using the root of a word is also called **stemming**. You can shorten the search text further by using "baseball" and "collect" as search criteria because cards are the most common items collected in baseball.

Next, determine the best way to combine the criteria, as shown in the following list:

- *Baseball collect* (or *baseball AND collect*) finds documents that include both words.
- *Baseball OR collect* finds documents that include at least one of the words.
- *Baseball NOT collect* finds documents that include "*baseball*" but not those that include "*collect.*"
- "*Baseball collect*" finds documents that include the exact phrase "*baseball collect.*"
- (*Baseball collect*) finds documents that include the exact words "baseball" and "collect" consecutively in either order.

Because the phrase *baseball collect* will produce the results you want, you'll use that as your search criteria to find quotations about baseball card collections.

To find files using AND criteria:

1. Open the **Quotations** folder in the Public Documents\Columbia folder on your hard disk.

2. Click the **Search** text box, and then type **baseball collect**. As you type, Windows searches filenames and file contents that meet your criteria and finds one file. See Figure 6-19.

Figure 6-19 Finding files that contain *baseball* AND *collect*

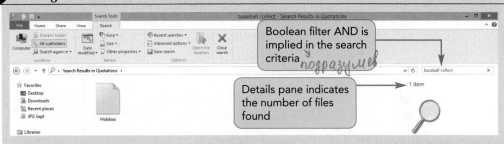

- Boolean filter AND is implied in the search criteria *подразумев*
- Details pane indicates the number of files found

3. To verify this file contains a quotation you can use, double-click **Hobbies** to open it in a text-editing program such as Notepad.

4. Press the **Ctrl+F** keys to open the Find dialog box, type **baseball** in the Find what text box, click the **Find Next** button until you find a quotation Jay can use, such as "Baseball card collecting is like eating peanuts, you just can't stop," and then close the Find dialog box and Notepad.

Jay plans to use that quotation, but says that he could also use quotations that mention baseball or mention collecting—he can work either type into the Web page. You can try your search again, this time using the Boolean filter OR to find files that contain either "baseball" or "collect."

To find files using OR criteria:

1. Display the contents of the Quotations folder again.

2. Click the **Search** text box, and then type **baseball OR collect**. Now Windows finds two files that contain the word "baseball" or "collect." See Figure 6-20.

Figure 6-20 Finding files that contain *baseball* OR *collect*

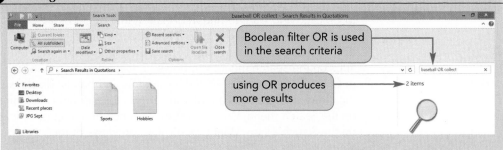

- Boolean filter OR is used in the search criteria
- using OR produces more results

To pinpoint what you want to find and to refine your search criteria, you can combine Boolean filters and file properties.

Combining Boolean Filters and File Properties

When you search files by file property, you can use Boolean filters to combine criteria. For example, suppose Jay is working on the baseball card Web page and requests a photo of a baseball card showing a Chicago baseball player in 1912. You can search the tags of the photo files to find those that contain this text. To search efficiently, you can use the Boolean filter AND to combine the criteria and search for photos that include the tags "Chicago" and "1912." (If you used the Boolean filter OR, you would find photos of baseball cards for Chicago players, but not necessarily those who played in 1912, and photos of baseball cards issued in 1912 that are not necessarily of Chicago players.) If you use *tag: Chicago 1912*, Windows searches for files that include "Chicago" as a tag and "1912" in any property. To restrict the search to tags only, enclose the criteria in parentheses.

To find files by combining file property criteria:

▶ **1.** Display the contents of the Public Documents\Columbia folder on your hard disk.

▶ **2.** Click the **Search** text box, and then type **tag: (Chicago 1912)**. Windows finds one file that meets your criteria. See Figure 6-21.

Figure 6-21   **Combining Boolean filters with file properties**

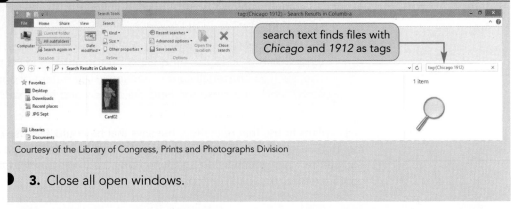

search text finds files with *Chicago* and *1912* as tags

Courtesy of the Library of Congress, Prints and Photographs Division

▶ **3.** Close all open windows.

You now know many expert techniques to search for files. One other type of search you can conduct is new to Windows 8: searching for information in Windows 8 apps.

Searching Within Windows 8 Apps

As you've learned, you can use Start Search to find apps installed on your computer by typing search text on the Search menu. Sometimes, however, the information you want to find is contained within an app. For example, suppose you are planning a trip to Chicago and want to find information that might be helpful for your trip. On the Start screen, you can type search text such as *Chicago* to display the Search menu. To display destination information about Chicago, click Travel in the list of Windows 8 apps on the Search menu. Windows starts the Travel app, which presents an overview of Chicago, lists recommended restaurants and hotels, displays photos of Chicago locations, and provides a tool you can use to find flights to Chicago. If you click Maps on the Search menu, Windows displays a detailed map of Chicago. If you click News on the Search menu, Windows displays previews of recent news stories about Chicago. You can click a preview to read the entire article.

Searching for Information in Windows 8 Apps

- On the Start screen, begin typing search text.
- Click a Windows 8 app on the Search menu.

Just as Windows keeps track of search text to display search hints, it keeps track of the Windows 8 apps you search. Windows rearranges the list of Windows 8 apps on the Search menu so that the apps you search the most often are near the top of the list.

The Search menu does not list all of the Windows 8 apps installed on your system—only those that are compatible with the Start Search feature. Figure 6-22 lists popular Windows 8 apps you can search and describes the types of information you can find.

| Figure 6-22 | Popular Windows 8 apps for searching |

Windows 8 App	Information to Find	Search Text
Bing	Information on the Web	Keywords for a Web page
Finance	Financial news and stock performance about a particular company	Company name or stock symbol
Internet Explorer	Information on the Web	Keywords for a Web page
Mail	Information in the subject line or body of an email message, sender name, and email address	Text in any part of an email message
Maps	Location or local business	Location or business name
News	Recent news stories	Text in a news story, source name, or author name
People	Contact name and other information such as email address	Any contact information, such as name, phone number, or email address
Photos	Photos on your computer or a service your computer can access, such as your Flickr account	Filename or tag
Sports	Sports scores and other information	Sport, team, or player name
Store	Windows 8 and desktop apps	App name or description
Travel	Information about a destination	Destination name
Weather	Weather in a specified location	Location name
Xbox apps	Videos, games, music, TV shows, and movies	Media name

© 2014 Cengage Learning

Next week, Jay is planning to travel to Chicago, Illinois, to meet with other baseball card dealers to exchange information and to buy and sell baseball cards. He asks you to find information about Chicago of general interest to travelers, including attractions, hotels, and restaurants. He also wants to know what kind of weather to expect in Chicago next week. You can find all of this information by searching Windows 8 apps.

To search for information in Windows 8 apps:

▶ **1.** Press the **Windows** key 🪟 to display the Start screen.

▶ **2.** Type **Chicago** to display the Apps screen and the Search menu with "Chicago" entered in the Search menu text box.

▶ **3.** Click **Travel** in the list of Windows 8 apps on the Search menu, scrolling down the menu if necessary. The Travel app starts and displays a photo of a Chicago location. See Figure 6-23. The Chicago photo in your Travel app might differ.

| Figure 6-23 | Searching for information in the Travel app |

search text entered

Travel is selected on the Search menu

Chicago, Illinois

▶ **4.** Move the pointer to display a horizontal scroll bar, and then drag the scroll bar to the right to display an overview of Chicago. Continue dragging the scroll bar to the right to display lists of attractions and hotels. Click **Art Institute of Chicago** in the Attractions list to display detailed information about the museum.

▶ **5.** Display the Charms bar and then click the **Search** charm on the Charms bar. The Search menu opens with "Chicago" still entered in the text box.

▶ **6.** Click **Weather** in the list of Windows 8 apps on the Search menu, scrolling as necessary. A Search Results screen appears listing locations that contain a word beginning with "Chicago." See Figure 6-24. Your search results might differ, but should include Chicago, Illinois.

| Figure 6-24 | Selecting a location in the search results |

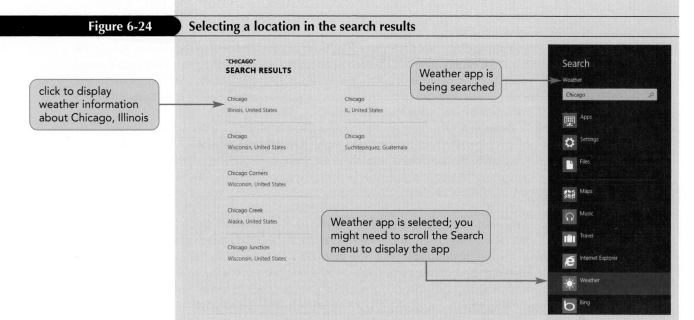

click to display weather information about Chicago, Illinois

Weather app is being searched

Weather app is selected; you might need to scroll the Search menu to display the app

7. Click **Chicago Illinois, United States** in the search results to display the weather conditions in Chicago for today and forecasts for the next few days.

8. Click the background of the Weather app, and then click the **right arrow** button ❯ to scroll the screen and show weather forecasts for next week.

9. Close the Weather app. You return to the Start screen.

Now that you've found general travel information about Chicago, Jay wants to find more specific information. He plans to visit a few baseball card shops so he can learn about their collections and any other goods or services they offer. This information is not available in any of the files on your computer or stored in a Windows 8 app. Instead, you can use Internet Explorer to search the Internet for the information.

Searching the Internet

The Internet provides access to a wealth of information; the challenge is to find the information you need or want. You have already learned how to develop search strategies and specific criteria to find files on your computer. You can use many of the same search strategies to find information on the Internet. Instead of using Windows tools such as the Search text box and Search menu, you use the search tools provided in Internet Explorer. Figure 6-25 summarizes the search tools you can use in IE Windows 8 and IE Desktop.

| Figure 6-25 | Internet Explorer search tools |

Search Tool	Description
Address bar	Enter search text in the Address bar to have your default search provider such as Google or Bing display the search results
Find on page	Search for text on the current Web page
Search provider	Add a search provider or select one to use its tools to search the Internet

The terminology that you use when searching the Internet is slightly different from the terminology you use to search for files on your computer. As shown in the Session 6.2 Visual Overview, the word or phrase you use to search the Internet is typically called a search expression. Each word in the search expression is called a keyword. After you enter a search expression using one of Internet Explorer's search tools, Internet Explorer displays the results, which are links to Web pages that meet your criteria. You can click these links, or hits, to access Web pages that contain the keywords in your search expression.

When you provide a search expression to Internet Explorer, it uses a search provider, which is a search engine such as Bing or Google or a reference Web site such as Wikipedia. Because searching all of the Web pages on the Internet to find those that contain your search expression would take a prohibitive amount of time, search providers typically search a database of indexed Web pages. These databases are updated periodically, though not often enough to keep all of the indexed Web pages up to date. This is why a page of search results might include inactive or broken links.

Web site designers and owners can make their Web pages easier for search providers to find by **optimizing** the site. In its Web page headings, an optimized site lists keywords and phrases that you and other Web users are likely to use to find the information on the Web page. Conversely, you are more likely to find the Web pages you want if you are aware of the types of keywords Web designers often use.

PROSKILLS

Problem Solving: Searching the Internet Effectively

Because the Internet provides access to a vast amount of information, finding the information you need can be a problem. Conducting a search that finds millions of results is inefficient, even if search providers list the Web pages most relevant to your search first. To work effectively, you need to use search techniques that provide a few high-quality results. Keep the following guidelines in mind to search the Internet efficiently:

- Be specific. If you search for general categories, you'll find an overwhelming number of pages. Searching for specific terms or details is more likely to provide results you can use. For example, instead of searching for "desserts," search for "pear cake recipe."
- Form a question. Think of your search expression as a question you want answered, such as "Are there restaurants in the Denver area that serve vegetarian food?" Eliminate the articles and common words to form a workable search expression, such as "restaurants Denver vegetarian."
- Search the results. Most search providers let you reduce the number of pages to review by searching your results. For example, suppose you search for "pear cake recipe" and find many thousands of results. If you want a recipe similar to the one your Swedish grandmother made, you can search the results using "Swedish" as your search expression.

Jay wants to know about the baseball card shops in Chicago, and you offer to search the Internet to find the information. You could use IE Windows 8 or IE Desktop to search for this information. (You could also use the Bing app to display search results in a tiled format; you click a tile to display the Web page in IE Windows 8.) In the following steps, you use IE Windows 8 because you are currently working on the Start screen. You'll start the search by using *Chicago baseball card shop* as the search expression to find Web pages describing baseball card shops in Chicago.

Because Web pages and search indexes change frequently, the search results you find when you perform the steps in this section will differ from those shown in the figures. The following steps use Bing as the search provider. If you are using a different search provider, your results will differ.

To search using a search expression:

▶ **1.** On the Start screen, click the **Internet Explorer** tile to start IE Windows 8.

▶ **2.** Click the **Address bar**, type **Chicago baseball card shop**, and then press the **Enter** key. Bing looks for Web pages containing the search expression you entered, and then displays the results. See Figure 6-26.

| Figure 6-26 | Search results for the search expression *Chicago baseball card shop* |

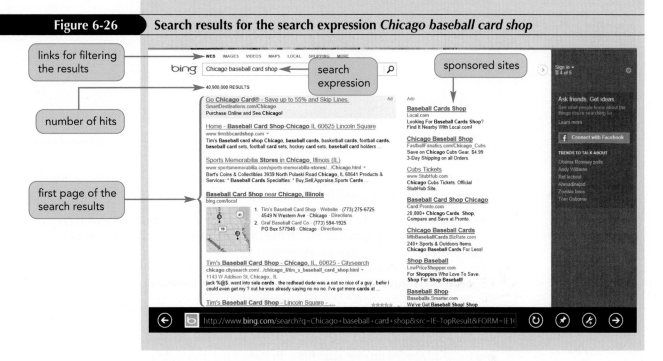

Using *Chicago baseball card shop* as the search expression produced more than 37 million results, which is not unusual and can change daily. Although the first few Web pages listed might provide the information you seek, you need to narrow your search to find more useful Web pages.

Narrowing Your Search

You can narrow your Internet search by modifying your search expression or by limiting the kinds of Web pages you want in your results. One way to modify your search expression is to use quotation marks to search for specific phrases. If you enclose a phrase in quotation marks, you restrict the results to Web pages that contain that exact phrase. For example, using a search expression such as *Stanford University Library* finds Web pages that include those three words anywhere on the page. If you enclose the search expression in quotation marks, as in *"Stanford University Library"*, you find only Web pages that include the exact text in the specified order.

Another way to modify your search expression is to use the advanced search features that search providers typically offer. Figure 6-27 shows the Advanced Search page from Google, a popular search provider.

Figure 6-27   Google Advanced Search page

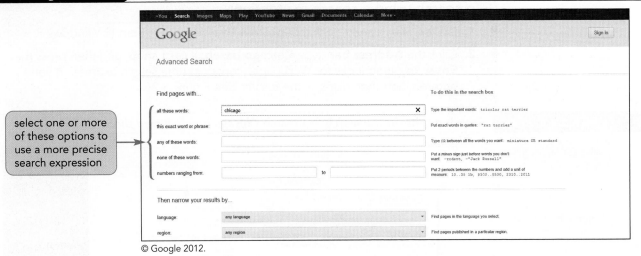

© Google 2012.

An advanced search page lets you specify and combine search conditions. Most advanced search pages provide the following types of options:

- Find pages that include all of the words. This is the default for most search providers.
- Limit the results to pages that match the exact phrase. This is the same as using quotation marks to enclose an expression.
- Find pages that include at least one of the words in the search expression.
- Specify keywords that you do not want included on the Web page.

Search engines often provide extensive help information. For example, enter a search term in Google, click the Options button, and then click Search Help to display the Google Inside Search Web page, which provides links to basic search information and more advanced tips for searching. In Bing, click the Help link at the bottom of the Bing home page to display the Bing Help page.

Besides providing an advanced search page for narrowing your search expression, most search providers include tabs or links that specify the kind of results you want. For example, the Bing results page shown earlier includes a navigation bar at the top of the page with links such as Web, Images, Videos, and Maps. By default, Bing displays Web pages in the results. If you are searching for images, such as photos and drawings, you can click the Images link before or after you enter a search expression to restrict the results to pages including images that meet your criteria.

Some of the Web pages you found when you used *Chicago baseball card shop* as a search expression described Chicago baseball, but didn't necessarily focus on baseball card shops. You can try narrowing your search by enclosing part of the expression in quotation marks to see if the results are more useful. You don't want to enclose the entire phrase in quotation marks because that would find only Web pages that contain that exact text in the same order, but not pages for Buck's Baseball Card Shop in Chicago, for example.

To narrow a search to an exact match:

▶ **1.** On the search results page, click in the search text box at the top of the page.

Trouble? If a message regarding the Flip Ahead feature appears at the bottom of the screen, click the Close button (unless your instructor requests that you click the Turn on flip ahead button).

2. Edit the text so it appears as **Chicago "baseball card shop"** and then press the **Enter** key. This time, you find fewer results because the search is restricted to only those Web pages that use *Chicago* as a keyword and include the exact phrase you entered in quotation marks. See Figure 6-28.

Figure 6-28   Search results for an exact phrase search expression

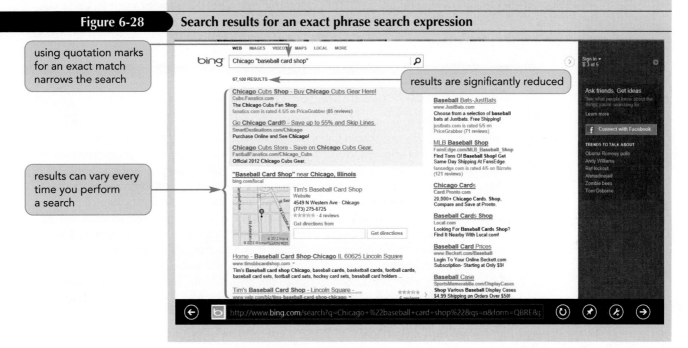

using quotation marks for an exact match narrows the search

results are significantly reduced

results can vary every time you perform a search

Including an exact phrase produced a list of baseball card shops in Chicago that is useful to you and Jay. Now he wonders if other places in Illinois have baseball card shops that he should know about. These are any baseball card shops that are not located in Chicago. To specify this kind of search condition, you can use a search provider's advanced search page. You can try this search using Google instead of Bing. You'll use Google's Advanced Search page to specify that you want to search for baseball card shops in Illinois, but not those in Chicago.

To narrow a search by excluding keywords:

1. Click the **Address bar**, type **www.google.com**, and then press the **Enter** key to open the main page on the Google Web site.

2. In the text box, type **Illinois** and then press the **Enter** key to display the results, which total millions of hits.

3. Click the **Options** button [⚙] on the right side of the page, and then click **Advanced search** to open the Advanced Search page with "Illinois" already entered in the first text box.

4. Click the **this exact word or phrase** text box, type **baseball card shop**, and then press the **Enter** key. The search results list several thousand Web pages, including many for baseball shops in Chicago, Illinois. Next, you'll exclude the keyword "Chicago" from the search.

   Trouble? If a message appears, asking whether you want AutoComplete to remember web form entries, click the No button.

5. Click the **Options** button ⚙ in the upper-right corner of the window, click **Advanced search** to open the Advanced Search page again, click the **none of these words** text box, type **Chicago**, and then press the **Enter** key. The search results page includes more hits with the best matches on the first page, which helps Jay identify baseball card shops he might want to visit outside of Chicago.

INSIGHT

Evaluating Web Pages in the Search Results

Although a Web page might be listed at the top of the search results, that doesn't guarantee the page provides reliable and up-to-date information that will meet your needs. On a search engine's Web page, the search results are usually organized into sections. At the top or in another prominent location on the page are sponsored links; companies pay to have these links appear when certain keywords are used in a search expression. The companies pay an additional fee when you click one of their sponsored links. Using sponsored links helps search engines offer their services free to the public. However, that doesn't mean a sponsored link will lead to the information you want. Before using a Web page or citing it as a source, review the content with a critical eye. At the bottom of the Web page, look for the author's name and evidence of the author's credentials. Look for links to the original source of quoted information, which tends to validate the information on a Web page. Also look for signs of bias, such as unsubstantiated claims or extreme points of view.

Jay wonders if you can quickly show where the shops are located outside of Chicago. To fulfill his request, you can use the Maps button on the Google toolbar. Recall that Bing and other search providers include a similar tool.

To display a map of shops in the search results:

TIP

The *-Chicago* in the search expression is a shorthand way of excluding "Chicago" from the search.

1. In the Google search results page, click the **Maps** button on the toolbar near the top of the page. Google lists the results on the left and shows a map on the right with markers for each location in the search results. See Figure 6-29.

| Figure 6-29 | Displaying locations in the search results |

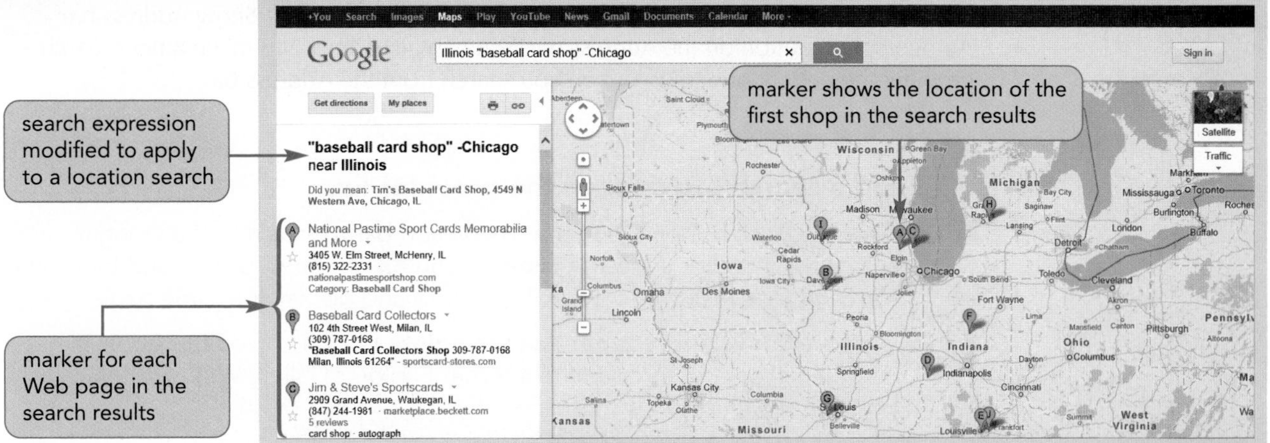

search expression modified to apply to a location search

marker shows the location of the first shop in the search results

marker for each Web page in the search results

© Google 2012.

Because you are now searching locations, Google modified the expression to specify shops near Illinois. Using *near* in the expression means Google is searching for locations near or in Illinois, not locations named Illinois.

Jay notes that one shop is right outside of Chicago, close enough that he could drop in during his visit next week.

Choosing Search Providers

In Internet Explorer, you can choose which provider you want to use when you search for information on the Internet. You can change the search provider for a specific search, and you can specify which search provider you prefer to use by default. When you first install Internet Explorer, only one provider might be available; however, you can add search providers to increase your searching options. You can only add a search provider in IE Desktop.

Keep in mind that you can use a search provider's Web site, such as google.com, to perform a search even if it is not selected as your search provider.

REFERENCE

Adding a Search Provider

- In IE Desktop, click the Show Address bar Autocomplete button on the Address bar, and then click Add.
- On the Internet Explorer Gallery Web page, click a search provider to select it, and then click the Add to Internet Explorer button.
- In the Add Search Provider dialog box, click the Add button.

You and Jay often use Wikipedia, an online encyclopedia, to search for information. Internet Explorer lets you use Wikipedia as a search provider, which is handy if you want to look up factual information about a topic. You'll add Wikipedia Visual Search to the provider list, which you can access by clicking the Show Address bar Autocomplete button on the Address bar. You can also choose to make a new search provider the default one to use when you search from the Address bar.

To add a search provider to the provider list:

▶ 1. Click the **Back** button ◉ on the Navigation bar to return to the Google search results, click the **Page tools** button ◉ on the Apps bar, and then click **View on the desktop** to open IE Desktop and display the same page.

▶ 2. Click the **Show Address bar Autocomplete** button ▼ on the Address bar, and then click **Add** to open the Internet Explorer Gallery Web site, which lists possible search providers. See Figure 6-30.

   Trouble? If you can't find the Show Address bar Autocomplete button ▼, point to the icons in the Address bar and view the ScreenTips to find the right one. Then repeat Step 2.

Figure 6-30   **Adding search providers**

scroll to display additional search providers

▶ 3. Scroll the page, looking for the Wikipedia Visual Search provider. If that search provider does not appear on the first Web page, click the **right arrow** button ◉ to display another page of search providers.

▶ 4. Click **Wikipedia Visual Search** to select it as a search provider, and then click the **Add to Internet Explorer** button to open the Add Search Provider dialog box.

▶ 5. Click the **Add** button.

▶ 6. Click the **Show Address bar Autocomplete** button ▼ on the Address bar to verify that Internet Explorer added Wikipedia W to the list of search providers.

TIP

To set the new search provider as the default, click the Make this my default search provider check box in the Add Search Provider dialog box.

One of Columbia Collectibles' most valuable baseball cards shows Johnny Evers, who was part of a famous double-play combination with Joe Tinker and Frank Chance known as Tinker-to-Evers-to-Chance. Jay is familiar with Evers' career as a player, but wants to review his career as a coach. You can use Wikipedia as the search provider to find a summary of Johnny Evers' coaching career.

To use Wikipedia as the search provider:

▶ 1. If necessary, click the **Show Address bar Autocomplete** button ▼ on the Address bar to display the list of search providers, and then click **Wikipedia** W to make Wikipedia the current search provider.

▶ 2. On the Wikipedia Web page, select the text in the Search text box, type **Johnny Evers**, and then press the **Enter** key. Wikipedia displays a page of search results, with an entry for Johnny Evers at the top.

▶ 3. Click **Johnny Evers** to display his page in Wikipedia.

When you are displaying a Web page, you can use the Find toolbar in IE Windows 8 or IE Desktop to find specific information on the page. To open the Find toolbar in IE Windows 8, display the Apps bar, click the Page tools button, and then click Find on page. To open the Find toolbar in IE Desktop, press the Ctrl+F keys. You'll show Jay how to search for information about Johnny Evers' coaching career using the Find toolbar in IE Desktop.

To find information on a Web page:

▶ 1. Press the **Ctrl+F** keys to display the Find toolbar at the top of the Internet Explorer window.

▶ 2. In the Find text box, type **coach**. Internet Explorer highlights all instances of "coach," selects the first instance, and displays the number of matches on the page. See Figure 6-31.

| Figure 6-31 | Using the Find toolbar |

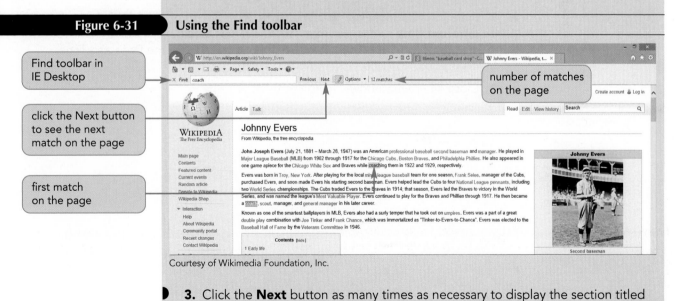

- Find toolbar in IE Desktop
- click the Next button to see the next match on the page
- first match on the page
- number of matches on the page

Courtesy of Wikimedia Foundation, Inc.

▶ 3. Click the **Next** button as many times as necessary to display the section titled "Coaching and managing career," which summarizes the positions Johnny Evers held as a baseball coach.

▶ 4. Click the **Close the Find bar** button X to close the Find toolbar.

▶ 5. Close Internet Explorer.

If you use a particular search provider often, you can make it the default search provider. You use IE Desktop to set the default search provider. When you do, you automatically set the default search provider for IE Windows 8 as well. To change the default search provider, click the Tools button on the right side of the IE Desktop window, and then click Manage add-ons. In the Add-on Types list, click Search Providers. Click the search provider you want to use, and then click the Set as default button.

Restoring Your Settings

If you are working in a computer lab or on a computer other than your own, complete the steps in this section to restore the original settings on the computer.

To restore your settings:

1. Open File Explorer, and then click **JPG Sept** in the Favorites list on the Navigation pane to conduct the saved search.

2. Click the **Search** text box to display the Search Tools Search tab, click the **Advanced options** button in the Options group, and then click **File contents** under the In the non-indexed locations section to remove the check mark.

3. Cut the **JPG Sept** search file from the Navigation pane, and then paste it in the **Columbia** folder in the Public Documents folder.

4. Move the **Columbia** folder to the **Windows6\Tutorial** folder provided with your Data Files.

5. Close the Details pane in the folder window, and then close File Explorer.

6. Start IE Desktop, click the **Tools** button ⚙ on the right side of the window, and then click **Manage add-ons**. In the Add-on Types list, click **Search Providers**, click **Wikipedia (en)**, and then click the **Remove** button.

7. Press the **Windows** key ⊞, type **clock**, click **Settings**, click **Add clocks for different time zones**, click the first **Show this clock** check box to remove the check mark, and then click the **OK** button to close the Date and Time dialog box.

8. Close all open windows.

REVIEW

Session 6.2 Quick Check

p 304

1. What shorthand notation would you use to find files that include the word "stamp" in the Title property?   *title: stamp*

2. If you use *tag: Chicago OR 1912* as search criteria, what files would you find?

3. Explain how you would use the Search menu to find news stories about Columbia, Missouri.

4. When you enter a search expression to search the Internet, each word in the search expression is called a(n) ___*keyword*___.   *filters*

5. How can you narrow a Web search to search for a specific phrase? – *boolean*

6. After using a search expression to search the Web, how can you specify that you want to display only images in the results?   *use toolbar*

7. Explain how to find search providers to add to Internet Explorer.   *on the Address bar click show Address bar Auto complete*

PRACTICE

Review Assignments

Data Files needed for the Review Assignments: American Postcards.wmv, European Postcards.wmv, Postcard01.jpg–Postcard10.jpg

You are now working with Jay Park on developing and showcasing the postcard collection at Columbia Collectibles. You have taken photographs of his most recently acquired postcards and created two videos featuring American and European postcards. Jay wants to post the videos and some photos on the shop's Web site. Jay wants you to help him search for apps that can play videos and find postcards for specific Web pages. Complete the following steps:

1. In the Public Documents folder on your hard disk, create a folder named **Postcards**. Copy all of the files in the Windows6\Review folder provided with your Data Files to the Postcards folder.

2. Display the Start screen. Search for a file that contains the word "European" in its filename. Play the file in the Video app.

3. Press the Print Screen key to capture an image of the screen, and then paste the image in a new Paint or WordPad file. Save the file as **Video App** in the Windows6\Review folder provided with your Data Files. Minimize Paint or WordPad, and then close the Video app.

4. Search for an app you can use to play media files, and then start the app. (*Hint*: If a dialog box opens where you can select initial settings, click the Recommended settings option button, and then click the Finish button.) Click Videos in the left pane of the app window, drag the American Postcards video stored in the Postcards folder to the app's window, and then play the video.

5. Press the Print Screen key to capture an image of the screen, and then paste the image in a new Paint or WordPad file. Save the file as **Media App** in the Windows6\Review folder provided with your Data Files. Close the media app.

6. Search for a setting on your computer related to media files. Display a setting for using AutoPlay with all media and devices. Press the Print Screen key to capture an image of the window, and then paste the image in a new Paint or WordPad file. Save the file as **Media Setting** in the Windows6\Review folder provided with your Data Files. Close the AutoPlay window. Minimize the Paint or WordPad window.

7. Search for all of the **JPG** files in the Postcards folder.

8. Add the following tags to Postcard02: **Statue of Liberty; 1905**. Change the filename to **Statue of Liberty**.

9. Add the following tags to Postcard09: **Eiffel Tower; Paris; France; 1900**. Change the filename to **Eiffel Tower**.

10. In the Postcards folder, search for photos that have **France** as a tag. Move the files you found to a new subfolder named **French Postcards** in the Postcards folder.

11. In the Postcards folder, find a photo that has **New York** and **1904** as tags. Change the name of this file to **1904**. Close File Explorer. Minimize the Paint or WordPad window, and then close all other open windows.

12. Start IE Desktop and use Bing to find Web pages providing information about postcard collections. Narrow the search to find Web pages about vintage postcard collections. Narrow the search again by finding only images of vintage postcard collections. (*Hint*: Click the Images link on the results page.) Press the Print Screen key to capture an image of the first screen of search results, and then paste the image in a new Paint or WordPad file. Save the file as **Vintage1** in the Windows6\Review folder provided with your Data Files.

13. Add a new search provider to Internet Explorer, and then use it to search for vintage postcard collections. (*Hint*: Add a search provider not used in the tutorial.) With the search results displayed, press the Print Screen key to capture an image of the first screen of search results, and then paste the image in a new Paint or WordPad file. Save the file as **Vintage2** in the Windows6\Review folder provided with your Data Files.

14. Using the new search provider, display Web pages for postcards from the 1960s. Open one of the Web pages on the first page of search results, and then find a postcard on the page associated with the Kennedy family. (*Hint*: If you are having difficulty finding a Web page associated with the Kennedy family, go to www.zazzle.com/1960s.) Press the Print Screen key to capture an image of the Web page, and then paste the image in a new Paint or WordPad file. Save the file as **1960s** in the Windows6\Review folder provided with your Data Files.

15. Restore your computer by removing the new search provider from Internet Explorer. Move the Postcards folder from the Public Documents folder on your hard disk to the Windows6\Review folder provided with your Data Files. Close the Details pane in the folder window, and then close all open windows.

16. Submit the results of the preceding steps to your instructor, either in printed or electronic form, as requested.

Case Problem 1

APPLY

Data Files needed for this Case Problem: Pic01.jpg–Pic10.jpg

Farm to Table   Bernie and Sarah Underwood started a Web site called Farm to Table, which is devoted to providing information about farmer's markets, farm stands, and community supported agriculture (CSA) services in the Hudson River Valley in New York. They primarily serve as content editors, selecting articles, reviews, and photos from contributors in the area. You work as an all-around assistant to Bernie and Sarah. Currently, they want you to help them find photos from contributors for their Web pages on summer fruits and vegetables. They also want to back up their files online, and ask you to find information about programs they can use to do so. Complete the following steps:

1. Search for an app you can use to read news stories. Start the app and then scroll to the far right to display news on health or technology.

2. Press the Print Screen key to capture an image of the app, and then paste the image in a new Paint or WordPad file. Save the file as **News App** in the Windows6\Case1 folder provided with your Data Files. Close the app.

3. Search for a setting on your computer related to backups. Display the setting or tool for saving backup copies of files.

4. Press the Print Screen key to capture an image of the tool, and then paste the image in a new Paint or WordPad file. Save the file as **Backups** in the Windows6\Case1 folder provided with your Data Files. Close the window or screen.

5. On the Start screen, search for information about Hudson, New York, and then display the information in the Maps app. Zoom in to display the city. Press the Print Screen key to capture an image of the tool, and then paste the image in a new Paint or WordPad file. Save the file as **Hudson** in the Windows6\Case1 folder provided with your Data Files.

6. Open File Explorer and then review the tags and other properties already assigned to the files in the Windows6\Case1 folder. Add the tag **fruit** or **vegetable** to files as appropriate.

7. Using the Details pane, add **Lori Scott** as the author of the following photos: Pic01, Pic06, and Pic07.

8. Use the Search text box to find a photo that includes the tag **grapes** and has **Sharon Nikas** as the author. Rename the file **Summer Fruit**.

9. Start IE Desktop and use Bing to find Web pages providing information on farms in the Hudson River Valley. Narrow the search to find Web pages on organic farms in the Hudson River Valley. Display images of the farms. (*Hint*: Click the Images link on the results page.) Press the Print Screen key to capture an image of the screen, and then paste the image in a new Paint or WordPad file. Save the file as **Organic Farms** in the Windows6\Case1 folder provided with your Data Files.

10. If necessary, add Google as a search provider in Internet Explorer, and then use Google to show a map of organic farms near Hudson, New York. Modify the search to show information about organic farms in the state of New York in the Hudson River Valley. Press the Print Screen key to capture an image of the screen, and then paste the image in a new Paint or WordPad file. Save the file as **Organic Map** in the Windows6\Case1 folder provided with your Data Files.

11. Restore your computer by removing the new search provider from Internet Explorer. Close all open windows.

12. Submit the results of the preceding steps to your instructor, either in printed or electronic form, as requested.

Case Problem 2

Data Files needed for this Case Problem: Site01.jpg–Site10.jpg

Salem Architectural Society   Tiffany Garrity is the director of the Salem Architectural Society (SAS) in Salem, Oregon. She is developing a presentation to give to local groups about the services and activities the society offers, such as architectural tours and walks, workshops on historical preservation, and information about architectural styles and periods. As an intern at the SAS, you help Tiffany prepare for presentations and workshops. She asks you to help her organize the pictures she has of sites in Salem and to research general information about architectural styles and terms. Tiffany would like to play appropriate music during her presentations, so she wants information about music-playing apps. She also wants to minimize the file size of the presentation so she can email it on request. Complete the following steps:

1. Search for an app you can use to play music. Start the app and then display the my music screen. (*Hint*: Scroll the music app screen to the left.)

2. Press the Print Screen key to capture an image of the app, and then paste the image in a new Paint or WordPad file. Save the file as **Music App** in the Windows6\Case2 folder provided with your Data Files. Close the music app.

3. Search for a setting that lets you adjust the system volume. Open the setting window, and then press the Print Screen key to capture an image of the window. Paste the image in a new Paint or WordPad file. Save the file as **Volume** in the Windows6\Case2 folder provided with your Data Files. Close the volume setting window.

4. Add a tag to each JPG file in the Windows6\Case2 folder to identify the type of site shown in the photo. Use **bridge**, **building**, **church**, **fountain**, **gargoyle**, and **window** as tags. Add more than one tag as appropriate to fully describe the site.

5. Using the Details pane, add **Historic site** as a comment in the following photos: Site01, Site02, Site07, Site09, and Site10.

✪ **Explore**   6. Search for historic sites that have gargoyles. (*Hint*: Start your search using **comment** as the property name in the Search text box.) Move the files you found to a new subfolder named **Gargoyles** in the Windows6\Case2 folder.

✪ **Explore**   7. Using **dimensions** as the property name in the Search text box, find files in the Windows6\Case2 folder that have 484 pixels as one of their dimensions. Press the Print Screen key to capture an image of the search results showing the files you found. Paste the image in a new Paint or WordPad file, and save the file as **Dim 484** in the Windows6\Case2 folder provided with your Data Files.

8. In the Windows6\Case2 folder, search for files that are less than 100 KB in size. (*Hint*: Add **KB** to the search text.) Press the Print Screen key to capture an image of the search results showing the files you found. Paste the image in a new Paint or WordPad file, and save the file as **100 KB** in the Windows6\Case2 folder provided with your Data Files.

306

9. Start IE Desktop, and use Bing to find Web pages providing information on architectural styles. Narrow the search to Web pages that provide this information only about Salem, Oregon. Press the Print Screen key to capture an image of the screen, and then paste the image in a new Paint or WordPad file. Save the file as **Salem** in the Windows6\Case2 folder provided with your Data Files.

10. Use any other search provider to conduct a search for information about architectural styles. Open a page displaying information about this topic. Use the Find toolbar to find information on the page about architectural styles in the Victorian era. Press the Print Screen key to capture an image of the screen showing the Find toolbar, and then paste the image in a new Paint or WordPad file. Save the file as **Victorian** in the Windows6\Case2 folder provided with your Data Files. Close all open windows.

11. Submit the results of the preceding steps to your instructor, either in printed or electronic form, as requested.

Case Problem 3

CREATE

Data Files needed for this Case Problem: Climb01.jpg–Climb10.jpg

Peak Performers   Derek Cruz started a club called Peak Performers in Salt Lake City, Utah, for mountain-climbing enthusiasts. The club has grown in popularity and now has hundreds of active members around the country. In his online newsletter, Derek is starting a feature called Top Ten Climbs. He wants to kick off the feature by posting photos and writing descriptions of his 10 favorite climbs. He also wants to follow current sports news to learn about climbers around the world. As his editorial assistant, you offer to help him find this information and produce the description text. Complete the following steps:

1. Search for an app you can use to follow sports events. Start the app and then display sports news.

2. Press the Print Screen key to capture an image of the app, and then paste the image in a new Paint or WordPad file. Save the file as **Sports App** in the Windows6\Case3 folder provided with your Data Files.

3. Search within any Windows 8 app for information about Yosemite National Park. With information that clearly identifies Yosemite National Park displayed, press the Print Screen key to capture an image of the opening window. Paste the image in a new Paint or WordPad file. Save the file as **Yosemite** in the Windows6\Case3 folder provided with your Data Files. Close the app.

4. Working in the Windows6\Case3 folder, add **El Capitan; Yosemite** as tags to the Climb08 file. Add the tag **Hoffman Peak** to the Climb09 file.

5. Conduct a search in the Case3 folder to find photo files with **glacier** as a tag or **Derek** as an author.

6. Press the Print Screen key to capture an image of the search results, and then paste the image in a new Paint or WordPad file. Save the file as **Search1** in the Windows6\Case3 folder provided with your Data Files.

7. Conduct another search in the Case3 folder to find files with **glacier** as a tag and **Derek** as an author.

8. Press the Print Screen key to capture an image of the search results, and then paste the image in a new Paint or WordPad file. Save the file as **Search2** in the Windows6\Case3 folder provided with your Data Files.

9. Conduct another search in the Case3 folder to find files with **park** or **mountain** as a tag.

10. Press the Print Screen key to capture an image of the search results, and then paste the image in a new Paint or WordPad file. Save the file as **Search3** in the Windows6\Case3 folder provided with your Data Files.

11. Start IE Desktop and conduct a search to produce the results shown in Figure 6-32.

| Figure 6-32 | Bing search results |

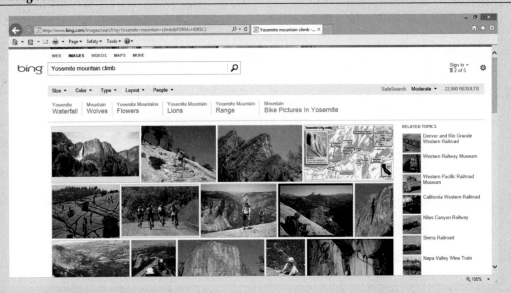

12. Press the Print Screen key to capture an image of the first screen of search results, and then paste the image in a new Paint or WordPad file. Save the file as **Search4** in the Windows6\Case3 folder provided with your Data Files. Close all open windows.

13. Submit the results of the preceding steps to your instructor, either in printed or electronic form, as requested.

Case Problem 4

There are no Data Files needed for this Case Problem.

Thornton Research Lindsey and Sam Thornton are starting a company called Thornton Research. They plan to provide research services for businesses and others, especially those who need marketing and demographic information. They learned their research techniques using print materials and through casual Internet use. They hired you as an assistant to help them learn how to take full advantage of the Internet. Complete the following steps:

1. Start Internet Explorer and use any search provider to research the following terms:

   Web 2.0

   Web 3.0

   Deep Web

   Metasearch engine

   Subject directory

2. Use WordPad or another word-processing program to create a document that lists these terms and provides a definition for each one. Save the document as **Research** in the Windows6\Case4 folder.

3. Search providers such as Google and Bing offer many tools for online research. For example, Bing has a social search tool that lets you collaborate with others to find information. After you enter a search term, Google displays a list of search tools to the left of the search results including Sites with images, Related searches, and Dictionary. Learn how to use one of these specialty search tools.

4. In the Research document, describe the search tool you selected and then explain how to use it. Be sure to mention the purpose of the tool and the steps for using it. Save the document.

5. Submit the results of the preceding steps to your instructor, either in printed or electronic form, as requested.

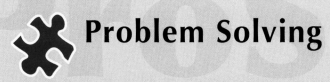

Problem Solving

Selecting the Best Settings for Efficient Computer Work

When you solve problems, you work through a series of stages to gather information about the problem and its possible solutions. Problem solving in general involves the following tasks:

1. Recognize and define the problem.
2. Determine possible courses of action.
3. Collect information needed to evaluate alternative courses of action.
4. Evaluate each alternative's merits and drawbacks.
5. Select an alternative.
6. Implement the decision.
7. Monitor and evaluate performance to provide feedback and take corrective action.

If you are involved in solving a complex problem with many possible causes, you perform all seven steps in the process. If you are solving a simpler problem or have limited time to explore solutions, you can condense the steps. For example, you might recognize the problem in one step; determine possible actions, and evaluate and select an alternative in the next step; and then implement and evaluate your decision in another step.

Recognize and Define the Problem

A problem is an obstacle that prevents you from reaching a goal. This definition is especially fitting for work with a computer. For example, suppose your goal is to create a report containing text and graphics, but you don't know which program to use. In this case, your lack of familiarity with the programs on your computer is an obstacle preventing you from reaching your goal of efficiently creating a report with text and graphics.

After identifying a simple problem, such as which computer program to use, you can focus on solutions. Start by considering any possible solution. For example, start each program on your computer related to text and graphics and examine its features. Next, compare and evaluate those alternatives. Which programs help you meet your goal most effectively? Select the best solution and then try it, observing the results to make sure it actually solves the problem. Can you efficiently create the report with the program you selected? If not, try a different program until you find the best possible solution.

PROSKILLS

Set Up Your Computer to Work Efficiently

The way you set up your computer can help you avoid problems and work with efficiency. Two common problems for Windows users are not being familiar with the programs installed on their computers, and not being able to quickly access folders, files, devices, and information they use often. You can avoid or solve these problems by personalizing your computer and using a few Windows programs that let you work efficiently and securely. As you select settings, capture and save images of your computer so you can document what you've done. Complete the following tasks:

1. Start Windows 8 and sign in, if necessary.

2. Change the Start screen, account picture, lock screen, desktop icons, and taskbar to suit your preferences.

3. Use IE Windows 8 or IE Desktop to research themes you can use on your computer. If you find a theme you like, download and install it on your computer.

4. Pin tiles to the Start screen for the apps you use often. Pin apps you use often to the taskbar. Add files you use often to the Jump Lists for these programs.

5. Set up shortcuts on your desktop to the folders and devices you use often. Capture an image of the desktop and of the Start screen.

6. In IE Windows 8, pin Web pages you visit often to the Apps bar. In IE Desktop, add the Web pages that you visit often to your Favorites list. Open the Favorites Center, and then capture an image of the Internet Explorer window.

7. Using the People app, create contacts for your correspondents. Capture an image of the contact list in the People app.

8. Using the Calendar app, set up your appointments and tasks for the upcoming week. Capture an image of the event calendar.

9. Open the Windows 8 Action Center, and make sure you are using all of the recommended security settings. In particular, make sure you are using an up-to-date antivirus program and that Windows Update is set to check for updates regularly. Both settings help you avoid the problems of security threats to your computer. Capture an image of the Action Center window.

10. Submit the images you captured to your instructor, either in printed or electronic form, as requested.

WINDOWS

Managing Multimedia Files

Working with Graphics, Photos, Music, and Videos

Case | *Grove Village Veterinary Pet Clinic*

Doug Weston and Carl Patel own the Grove Village Veterinary Pet Clinic, which provides veterinary services for pets in Grove Village, Indiana, and surrounding areas. As an intern at the clinic, you greet the animals and owners before they see the veterinarians and help the front-desk staff with check-in and billing. Because you have a special interest in graphic design, you are also working with the marketing manager to create graphics the clinic can use to market and sell its services. Your first projects are to create a logo for the clinic's Web site and email stationery, and to assemble a multimedia presentation to promote pet care and showcase the pets that visit the clinic.

получить

In this tutorial, you'll learn how to create, acquire, and modify multimedia files, including graphics, photos, music, and videos. You'll also explore how to organize and play audio files. Finally, you'll learn how to share media files with others and set up a multimedia slide show.

STARTING DATA FILES

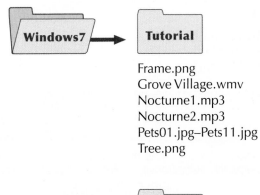

Windows7 → **Tutorial**

Frame.png
Grove Village.wmv
Nocturne1.mp3
Nocturne2.mp3
Pets01.jpg–Pets11.jpg
Tree.png

Review

Animal01.jpg–Animal07.jpg
Bugle.wav
Cat.png
Dog.png
Frame.png
Jazz.wav
Paw Print.png

Case1

Border.png
Mountains.png
Rocks.wav
Stream.wav
Trek01.jpg–Trek10.jpg

Case2

Boat1.jpg–Boat5.jpg
Sailboat.png
Waves.wav

Case3

Bird.wav
Bouquet1.jpg–Bouquet5.jpg
Crickets.wav
Flower.jpg

Case4

Beads.jpg
Sculpture.jpg

Session 7.1 Visual Overview:

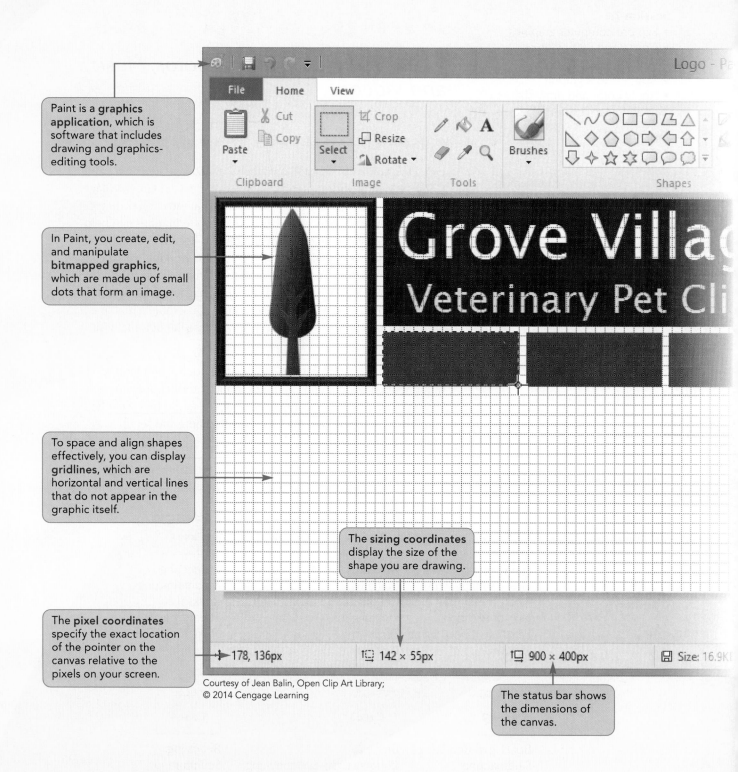

Paint is a **graphics application**, which is software that includes drawing and graphics-editing tools.

In Paint, you create, edit, and manipulate **bitmapped graphics**, which are made up of small dots that form an image.

To space and align shapes effectively, you can display **gridlines**, which are horizontal and vertical lines that do not appear in the graphic itself.

The **sizing coordinates** display the size of the shape you are drawing.

The **pixel coordinates** specify the exact location of the pointer on the canvas relative to the pixels on your screen.

The **status bar** shows the dimensions of the canvas.

Logo - P

File   Home   View

Paste   Cut   Copy   Select   Crop   Resize   Rotate   A   Brushes

Clipboard   Image   Tools   Shapes

Grove Villag
Veterinary Pet Cli

178, 136px   142 × 55px   900 × 400px   Size: 16.9K

Courtesy of Jean Balin, Open Clip Art Library;
© 2014 Cengage Learning

Creating Graphics in Paint

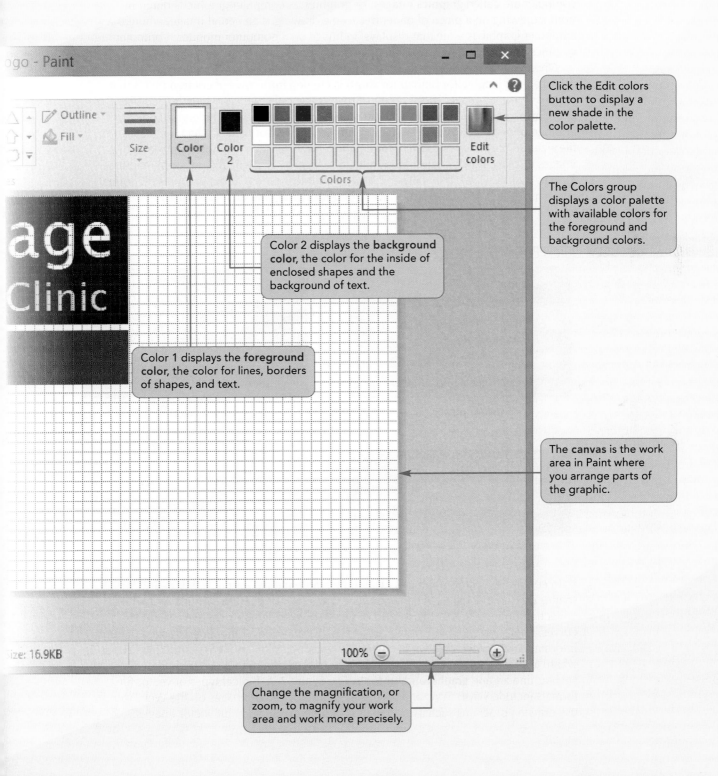

Click the Edit colors button to display a new shade in the color palette.

The Colors group displays a color palette with available colors for the foreground and background colors.

Color 2 displays the **background color**, the color for the inside of enclosed shapes and the background of text.

Color 1 displays the **foreground color**, the color for lines, borders of shapes, and text.

The **canvas** is the work area in Paint where you arrange parts of the graphic.

Change the magnification, or zoom, to magnify your work area and work more precisely.

Exploring Computer Graphics

Pictures and other images enhance your experience of working on a computer and make the documents you produce more appealing and engaging. Pictures on a computer are called **graphics images**, or **graphics**. A computer graphic is different from a drawing on a piece of paper because a drawing is an actual image, whereas a computer graphic is a file that displays an image on a computer monitor. Computer graphics come in two fundamental types: bitmapped and vector.

When you manipulate a bitmap graphic, you work with a grid of dots, called pixels. A bitmapped graphic (or bitmap for short) is created from rows of colored pixels that together form an image. The simplest bitmaps have only two colors, with each pixel being black or white. Bitmaps become more complex as they include more colors. Photographs or pictures with shading can have millions of colors, which increases file size. Bitmaps are appropriate for detailed graphics, such as photographs and the images displayed on a computer monitor. See Figure 7-1. Typical types of bitmap file formats include PNG, JPG, GIF, and BMP. (You'll learn more about graphics file formats later.) You create and edit bitmaps using graphics programs such as Adobe Photoshop and Windows Paint. Bitmap-editing programs are also called painting programs.

Figure 7-1 ▶ **Bitmapped graphics**

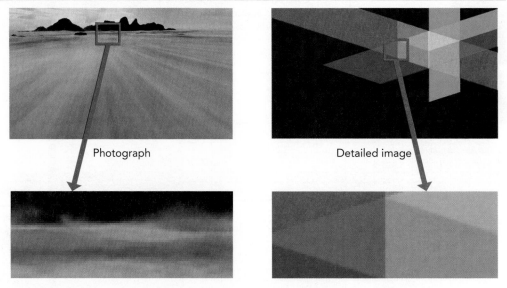

Photograph

Detailed image

Pixels in bitmapped images

In contrast, a **vector graphic** is created by mathematical formulas that define the shapes used in the image. When you work with a vector graphic, you interact with a collection of lines. Rather than a grid of pixels, a vector graphic consists of shapes, curves, lines, and text that together make a picture. While a bitmapped image contains information about the color of each pixel, a vector graphic contains instructions about where to place each component. Vector images are appropriate for simple drawings, such as line art and graphs, and for fonts. See Figure 7-2. Typical types of vector file formats include WMF, SWF, and SVG, a standard for vector images on the Web. You use drawing programs such as Adobe Illustrator to create and edit vector images.

Figure 7-2   **Vector graphics**

Aa Bb Cc

Aa Bb Cc

Fonts are a kind of vector image

A vector shape is a collection of points, lines, and curves

Edges stay smooth when a vector image is enlarged

Courtesy of jogdragoon, Open Clip Art Library

Decision Making: Selecting Bitmapped or Vector Graphics

If you're designing materials that include graphics, such as a Web page or flyer, one of your first decisions is whether to use bitmapped or vector graphics. Keep the following guidelines in mind as you make this decision:

- In general, a bitmap file is much larger than a similar vector file, making vector files more suitable for displaying graphics on Web pages.
- Avoid resizing bitmapped graphics because resolution (the number of pixels in an image) affects their quality. If you enlarge a bitmapped graphic, it often looks jagged because you are redistributing the pixels in the image. If you reduce the size of a bitmapped graphic, its features might be indistinct and fuzzy. On the other hand, you can resize vector graphics without affecting quality because vectors redraw their shapes when you resize them.
- To edit vector graphics, you often need to use the same drawing program that was used to create them. Before you acquire vector graphics from various sources, make sure you have the program that created them in case you need to edit them. In contrast, most painting programs can open many types of bitmapped graphic formats.
- Bitmaps are suitable for photographs and photorealistic images, while vector graphics are more practical for typesetting or graphic design.

You can add graphics files to your computer in a few ways. One way is to use a **scanner**, which is a device that converts an existing paper image into an electronic file that you can open and work with on your computer. Another popular method is to use an external or built-in digital camera to take photos and then store the images on your computer. You can also capture images displayed on your computer monitor and save them as graphics. You have already captured screen images using the Print Screen key on your keyboard. In addition, Windows 8 provides the Snipping Tool as an accessory. Instead of capturing the full screen, you can use the Snipping Tool to capture a window, tile, or any other part of the screen. Software and Web sites also provide graphics you can use, often as **clip art**, or completed pictures and symbols you can add to electronic documents. The clip art images Web sites provide are usually line drawings and therefore vector images. Many Web sites maintain online catalogs of drawings, images, and photographs that are available for download. Some of these sites charge a membership fee, some charge per image, and others provide copyright-free images that are also free of charge.

To edit a graphic or create one from scratch, you use a graphics program. Windows 8 includes a basic graphics program called Paint, which lets you create, edit, and manipulate bitmap graphics, though not vector graphics. Many programs designed for Windows 8, including Microsoft Office, include tools for creating and editing vector graphics such as charts, flowcharts, and other drawings in a document or worksheet, for example. Doug wants to combine two images to create the clinic logo; because they are both bitmapped graphics, you can use Paint for this project.

Creating Graphics in Paint

As you already know, Paint is a Windows 8 accessory application that you can use to create and modify bitmapped graphics. Using Paint, you can draw shapes, add and change colors, insert text, remove parts of a picture, and copy and paste images, including those you capture on your computer screen. Doug is ready to learn about Paint, so you can start the application and introduce him to its graphic tools.

To start Paint:

▶ **1.** On the Start screen, type **Paint** to display the Apps screen and Search menu with "Paint" entered in the Search text box.

Trouble? If the Start screen is not displayed on your monitor, press the Windows key ⊞ to display the Start screen.

▶ **2.** Click **Paint** on the Apps screen to start Paint on the desktop. If necessary, resize the Paint window to display all of the tools on the Home tab.

When you start Paint without opening a picture, the Paint window is mostly blank, providing a few tools for drawing and painting. The white area in the Paint window is the canvas, where you work with your graphic. Above the canvas is the ribbon, which opens to the Home tab by default. The status bar at the bottom of the window provides information about the tools you select and about the location of the pointer when it's in the canvas. See Figure 7-3.

Figure 7-3 ▶ **Paint window**

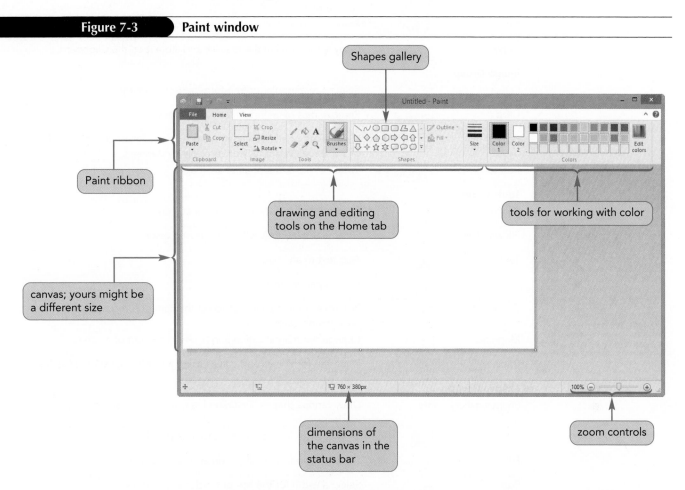

Figure 7-4 describes the tools on the Home tab you can use to create and edit graphics.

Figure 7-4	Paint tools

Tool	Icon	Description
Clipboard Group		
Paste		Insert an image from the Clipboard or one stored on your computer.
Cut	Cut	Remove some or all of the graphic and store it on the Clipboard.
Copy	Copy	Copy some or all of the graphic and store it on the Clipboard.
Image Group		
Select		Select a rectangular or free-form part of an image.
Crop	Crop	Remove part of an image from the sides.
Resize	Resize	Make some or all of an image larger or smaller, or change the slant of an image horizontally or vertically by degrees.
Rotate	Rotate ▾	Rotate or flip some or all of an image.
Tools Group		
Pencil		Draw a free-form line or one pixel at a time.
Fill with color		Fill an enclosed area with the selected color.
Text	A	Add text to an image.
Eraser		Erase a part of an image.
Color picker		Pick up a color in an image to set the current foreground or background color.
Magnifier		Change the magnification and zoom into or out of an image.
Brushes		Paint free-form lines and curves using a brush in a variety of styles.
Shapes Group		
Shapes gallery	n/a	Draw various shapes, including lines, rectangles, and ellipses (circles).
Outline		Select a style for the line or border as you draw.
Fill	Fill ▾	Select a style for the fill (inside area) as you draw.
Size		Select a width for the line or border as you draw.
Colors Group		
Color 1		Select the foreground color (the color for lines, borders of shapes, and text).
Color 2		Select the background color (the color for the inside of enclosed shapes and the background of text).
Color palette	n/a	Select a color to change the foreground or background color.
Edit colors		Select a color that does not appear on the palette.

© 2014 Cengage Learning

Opening a Graphic in Paint

You open a graphic in Paint the same way you open a file in any Windows 8 program—use the Open dialog box to navigate to where you store the image file, select the file, and then open it. Paint can keep only one graphic open at a time, similar to the way Notepad handles files. If you are working with a graphic and then try to open another one, Paint closes the first graphic and gives you a chance to save your changes before opening the new graphic. If you want to work with a second image at the same time as the first image, you can start another session of Paint and open the second image.

Doug asks you to show him how to open the two PNG files he found so you can discuss how to combine them to create a single image.

To open the two image files:

1. Click the **File** tab on the ribbon, and then click **Open**. The Open dialog box opens.

2. Navigate to the Tutorial folder in the Windows7 folder provided with your Data Files.

3. Click **Tree** in the list of files, and then click the **Open** button. The tree image opens in the Paint window. See Figure 7-5.

| Figure 7-5 | Tree image open in Paint |

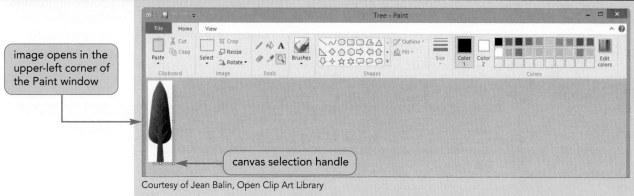

image opens in the upper-left corner of the Paint window

canvas selection handle

Courtesy of Jean Balin, Open Clip Art Library

4. To examine the second image, click the **File** tab, and then click **Open**.

5. In the file list, click **Frame** and then click the **Open** button. Paint closes the tree image so only the frame image appears in the Paint window.

Now that you've seen the two images Doug wants to use, you can plan the logo graphic. Clearly, the best way to combine these images is to insert the tree image inside the frame. You also need to add the name of the clinic—Grove Village Veterinary Pet Clinic—to the graphic. After making a few sketches, you and Doug agree on the design shown in Figure 7-6.

| Figure 7-6 | Design for the logo |

green frame

tree image

colored background

© 2014 Cengage Learning

To start creating this design, you need to add the tree image to the center of the frame. You'll show Doug how to do this shortly. Before you do, you should save the Frame file with a new name in case you need the original again in its unchanged state.

Saving a Graphics File

When you save a graphics file with a new name, you use the Save As dialog box, as you do in other Windows 8 applications. In the Save As dialog box, you select a location for the file, provide a filename, and select a file type, or format, if necessary. Paint can save and open images in many bitmap formats, and each format has its pros and cons. To work effectively with graphics, you should understand the basics of the most popular Paint file bitmap formats: PNG, JPG, GIF, and BMP. A fifth file format—TIF—is useful if you are creating images for print. PNG is the default format in Windows 8.

When you create a graphics file, you choose its format based on what you intend to do with the image and where you want to display it. If you want to use the image on a Web site or send it via email, for example, you need an image with a small file size. In this case, you should choose a file format that compresses color information. For example, if a picture has an area of solid color, it doesn't need to store the same color information for each pixel. Instead, the file can store an instruction to repeat the color until it changes. This space-saving technique is called **compression**. Some compression methods save space without sacrificing image quality, and others are designed to save as much space as possible, even if the image is degraded. Figure 7-7 summarizes the pros and cons of five bitmapped graphics formats.

| Figure 7-7 | Graphics file formats |

File Format	Advantages	Disadvantages	Use for
Graphics Interchange Format (GIF)	Compresses images without losing quality and allows animation	Not suitable for photographs	Graphics such as logos, line drawings, and icons
Joint Photographic Experts Group (JPG or JPEG)	Efficiently compresses photographic images	Can reduce quality	Photographs and images with fine detail
Portable Network Graphics (PNG)	Compresses images without losing quality	Does not allow transparency	Nonphotographic images designed for the Web
Tagged Image File Format (TIF or TIFF)	Maintains image quality in print and on screen	Some Web browsers cannot display TIF images	Images used in desktop publishing, faxes, and medical imaging
Windows Bitmap (BMP)	Simplest way to store a bitmapped graphic	Can waste large amounts of storage space	Basic shapes and images with few colors

© 2014 Cengage Learning

The Frame and Tree files are both PNG files, which is an appropriate file format for displaying graphics on a Web page or distributing graphics via email. You'll save a copy of the Frame file as a PNG file. However, if you need to provide a graphic in a different file format, you can convert it in Paint by choosing that format when you save the file.

To save the Frame image with a new name:

1. Click the **File** tab, and then click **Save as**. The Save As dialog box opens.

2. If necessary, click the **Browse Folders** button to open the Navigation pane, and then navigate to the Windows7\Tutorial folder provided with your Data Files.

3. In the File name text box, type **Logo**. The file type is already displayed as PNG (*.png) in the Save As dialog box. See Figure 7-8.

TIP

To save a file as a different type, point to Save as and then click a different file type, such as JPEG picture.

Figure 7-8   Saving the Frame file with a new name

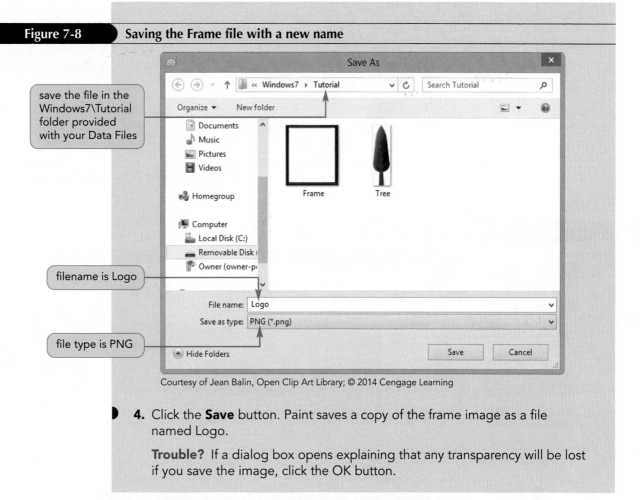

save the file in the Windows7\Tutorial folder provided with your Data Files

filename is Logo

file type is PNG

Courtesy of Jean Balin, Open Clip Art Library; © 2014 Cengage Learning

4. Click the **Save** button. Paint saves a copy of the frame image as a file named Logo.

   Trouble? If a dialog box opens explaining that any transparency will be lost if you save the image, click the OK button.

Saving a Bitmapped Graphic in a Different File Type

In general, you cannot improve the quality of a compressed image by saving it in a different file format. For example, suppose you convert a JPG graphic, which omits some color information to compress the file, to a format such as TIF, which doesn't sacrifice quality to reduce file size. The colors from the original JPG file remain the same, but the file size increases because the TIF file provides an expanded color palette that includes colors not used in the image.

Now you are ready to create the clinic logo by combining the picture of the tree with the frame image.

Copying and Pasting to Create a Graphic

One way to insert the tree image inside the frame is to open the Tree file again, select the entire image, cut or copy it, open the Logo file with the frame image, and then paste the tree image in the frame. To reduce the number of steps you need to perform, Paint provides a shortcut method—the Paste from command on the Paste button. You can use this command when you want to copy an entire image from another file and paste it in your current image.

To paste the tree image in the Logo file:

1. Click the **Paste button arrow** in the Clipboard group, and then click **Paste from**. The Paste From dialog box opens, which has the same controls as the Open dialog box.

   Trouble? If the Paste From dialog box did not open, you probably clicked the Paste button instead of the Paste button arrow. Click the Undo button on the Quick Access toolbar, and then repeat Step 1.

2. In the file list, click **Tree** and then click the **Open** button. The tree image appears in the upper-left corner of the logo picture in a selection box. See Figure 7-9.

Figure 7-9 ▶ Pasting the tree image in the Logo file

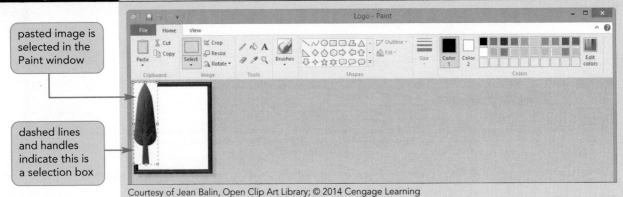

pasted image is selected in the Paint window

dashed lines and handles indicate this is a selection box

Courtesy of Jean Balin, Open Clip Art Library; © 2014 Cengage Learning

Because you need to move the tree image, do not click anywhere in the Paint window. If you do, you remove the selection box from the tree image and its pixels replace the ones from the logo picture underneath it.

Trouble? If you click in the Paint window and remove the selection box from the tree image, click the Undo button on the Quick Access toolbar, and then repeat Steps 1 and 2.

If you make a mistake while working in Paint, click the Undo button on the Quick Access toolbar. You can reverse up to your last three actions.

The selection box around the tree image indicates that you can manipulate the image by moving, copying, resizing, or deleting it. You can think of the selected image as floating on top of the frame picture because any changes you make to the tree image do not affect the Logo file until you click to remove the selection box. You want to show Doug how to move the tree image to the center of the frame. You can do so by dragging the selected tree image.

To move the selected tree image:

1. Point to the selected **tree image**. The pointer changes to ✛.

2. Drag the **tree image** near the center of the frame as shown in Figure 7-10, and then release the mouse button. The tree image is still selected, but it now appears in the middle of the frame.

Figure 7-10 Moving the tree image

move the tree image to the center of the frame

Courtesy of Jean Balin, Open Clip Art Library; © 2014 Cengage Learning

> **3.** Click anywhere outside of the selected image to remove the selection box. The tree image is now part of the Logo file.

Now that you have created the first major part of the graphic, you should save the Logo file so you don't inadvertently lose your changes.

To save the Logo graphic:

> **1.** Click the **Save** button 🖫 on the Quick Access toolbar. Paint saves the current image using the same name and location you used the last time you saved the graphic.

Next, you need to add the name of the clinic to the graphic to make it a true logo. According to your sketch, the clinic name should appear in a colored rectangle that extends to the right of the frame. Right now, there's not enough room in the graphic to accommodate this rectangle. You need to modify the graphic by resizing the canvas and then moving the image to create space for the clinic name.

Modifying Graphics in Paint

After you create and save an image in Paint, you can modify it by adding graphic elements, such as lines, shapes, and text; changing colors; and cropping, or removing, parts. According to your sketch for the clinic logo, you need to add a text box to the right of the framed tree image. To provide enough work space for creating the text box, you should first resize the canvas.

Resizing the Canvas and Moving an Image

When you open a graphic, it fills the canvas if the graphic is the same size as or larger than the canvas. If the graphic is smaller than the canvas, you can resize the canvas to fit snugly around the image. Doing so reduces file size and eliminates a border around your picture. Reducing the width or height of the canvas is one way to **crop**, or remove, a row or column of pixels from an edge of a graphic. You can also resize the canvas if you want to make it larger than the image so you can add more graphic elements to the picture. When you enlarge the canvas, the image remains in the upper-left corner of the Paint window as you drag a selection handle on the canvas to make it longer, wider, or both.

TIP

You can also select an entire image by pressing the Ctrl+A keys.

After increasing the size of the canvas, you often need to move the image to provide room to work or so that the image fits more aesthetically within the enlarged space. To move all or part of an image in Paint, you first select the image using the Rectangular selection tool or the Free-form selection tool. With the Rectangular selection tool, you draw a selection box around the area you want to select. With the Free-form selection tool, you draw a line of any shape around the area. To select the entire graphic, you can click the Select button arrow in the Image group on the Home tab and then click Select all.

When you move a graphic, part of the selection box can extend past the edges of the canvas. Because Paint saves only the part of the graphic that appears on the canvas, make sure all parts of a moved graphic appear on the canvas before you remove the selection box. You lose any part that extends past the canvas when you remove the selection box. The measurements in the following steps depend on a screen resolution of 1366 x 768. If necessary, change to the same resolution by right-clicking a blank spot on the desktop, clicking Resolution on the shortcut menu, clicking the Resolution button, and then dragging the slider to 1366 × 768.

To resize the canvas and then move the logo graphic:

1. Point to the selection handle on the lower-right corner of the canvas so that the pointer changes to ⬉, and then begin to drag down and to the right, watching the dimensions in the middle of the status bar. See Figure 7-11.

Figure 7-11 **Resizing the canvas**

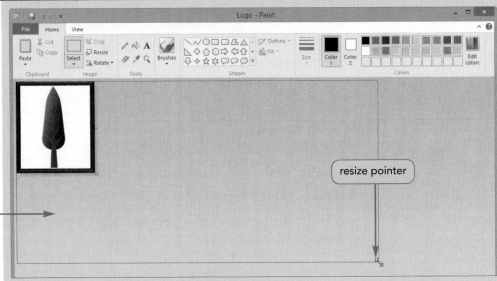

canvas will expand to fill this area

resize pointer

Courtesy of Jean Balin, Open Clip Art Library; © 2014 Cengage Learning

2. When the dimensions are about 900 × 400px, release the mouse button.

3. Click the **Select button arrow** in the Image group, and then click **Select all** to select the entire graphic.

4. Drag the graphic down and to the right as shown in Figure 7-12 to create room to work on the logo.

Figure 7-12 Moving the graphic

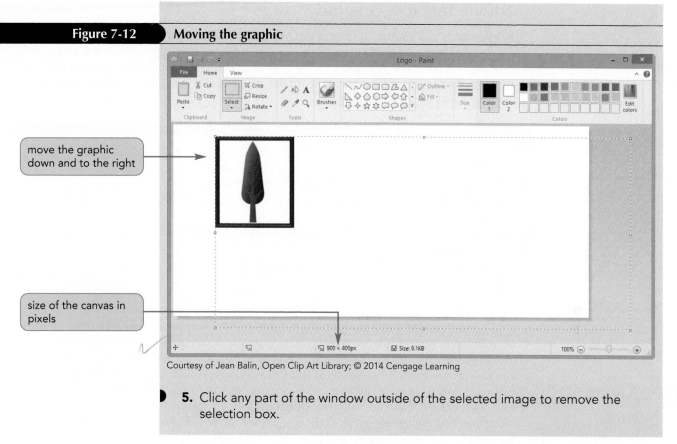

move the graphic down and to the right

size of the canvas in pixels

Courtesy of Jean Balin, Open Clip Art Library; © 2014 Cengage Learning

▶ **5.** Click any part of the window outside of the selected image to remove the selection box.

You can resize the canvas to any dimensions you need for your graphic, including those that extend beyond the boundaries of the Paint window. If you do, you can scroll horizontally and vertically to display the entire graphic or you can enlarge the Paint window. When you are working with a large canvas and plan to print the graphic, be sure to use Print Preview to see how the graphic will look when printed. To do so, click the File tab, point to Print, and then click Print Preview. Click the Page setup button in the Print group on the Print Preview tab to open the Page Setup dialog box, where you select print settings such as paper size. If you want to print the graphic on a single page, be sure the Fit to option button is selected and is set to 1 by 1 pages.

As you've already noticed, Paint helps you identify and control your location while you are drawing shapes or dragging selections. The pixel coordinates in the status bar specify the exact location of the pointer on the canvas relative to the pixels on your screen. Paint displays the pixel coordinates in an (x,y) format (x represents the horizontal location and y represents the vertical location). Pixel coordinates of 150 × 25, for example, indicate that the center of the pointer is 150 pixels from the left edge of the screen and 25 pixels from the top. Using these coordinates helps you position a shape or an image on the canvas, and position graphic elements in relation to one another. In addition, when you draw a shape, you can use the sizing coordinates, which appear immediately to the right of the pixel coordinates, to determine the size of the shape you are dragging. For example, when you draw a text box, you might start at pixel coordinates 15 × 15 and drag to sizing coordinates of 300 × 30—so your text box is long and narrow and appears in the upper-left corner of the graphic.

Resizing the canvas and moving the image provides plenty of room to work as you perform the next step—adding the clinic name to the graphic.

Adding Text to a Graphic

To add words to a graphic in Paint, you use the Text tool. You first use the Text tool to create a text box, and then you type your text in this box. When you select the Text tool, the Text Tools Text tab opens on the ribbon so you can select a font, a size, and attributes for the text. If your text exceeds the length and width of the text box, you can drag the sizing handles to enlarge the box.

REFERENCE

Adding Text to a Graphic

- Click the Text tool, and then drag a text box on the canvas.
- On the Text Tools Text tab, select a font, a font size, and attributes (bold, italic, or underline).
- Type the text in the text box, and use the sizing handles to resize the text box, if necessary.
- Adjust the font, font size, and attributes, as necessary.
- Click outside the text box.

When you add text to a graphic, Paint displays black text on a white rectangle, by default. If you want to change the colors, you should do so before you use the Text tool. (Changing colors after you complete your work with the Text tool is tricky.) You can change the Color 1 (foreground) and Color 2 (background) colors, which appear to the left of the color palette in the Colors group on the Home tab. Paint uses Color 1 for lines, borders of shapes, and text. Paint uses Color 2 for the background of text rectangles and the inside, or fill, color of enclosed shapes. To set a color, you click the Color 1 or Color 2 button, and then click a color in the palette. If the color palette does not contain a color you want to use, you can select one from your image using the Color picker tool. Click the Color picker tool in the Tools group on the Home tab, and then click a color in the image to change Color 1 to the color you clicked. Do the same with the right mouse button to change Color 2.

REFERENCE

Magnifying a Graphic

- To zoom in, click the Magnifier tool, and then click the graphic one or more times, or drag the magnification slider to the right to increase the magnification.
- To zoom out, click the Magnifier tool, and then right-click the graphic one or more times, or drag the magnification slider to the left to decrease the magnification.

TIP

You can also change the magnification by clicking the View tab and then clicking the Zoom in or Zoom out button.

According to your sketch, "Grove Village Veterinary Pet Clinic" should appear on two lines in a colored rectangle to the right of the frame. The words "Grove Village" should be in a large white font on one line and the words "Veterinary Pet Clinic" should appear in light green on the next line. To match the font and style that Doug and Carl use for other promotional materials, you'll use Lucida Sans as the font of the text. You suggest picking a color from the tree image as the background color of the text box and using white as the foreground color for the first line of text. When you use the Color picker tool to change a color, it is often helpful to zoom in, or increase the magnification of the image, so you can see the pixels of color more clearly. To do so, you can use the Magnifier tool or you can use the magnification control on the status bar. Increase the magnification by dragging the slider to the right or by clicking the Zoom in button. You can decrease the magnification, or zoom out, by dragging the slider to the left or by clicking the Zoom out button.

To zoom in and pick a color:

▶ **1.** Click the **Magnifier** tool 🔍 in the Tools group, and then click the center of the tree image twice to increase the magnification to 300% and center the Paint window on the tree. See Figure 7-13.

| Figure 7-13 | Changing the magnification of the image |

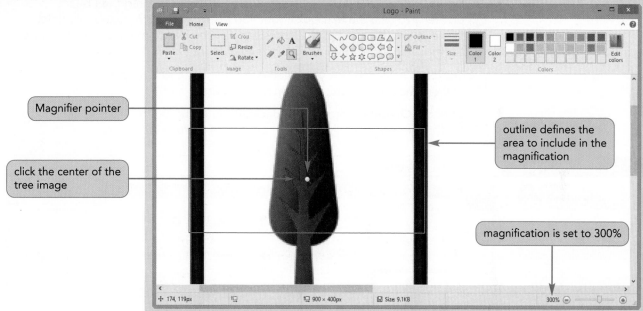

Magnifier pointer

click the center of the tree image

outline defines the area to include in the magnification

magnification is set to 300%

Courtesy of Jean Balin, Open Clip Art Library; © 2014 Cengage Learning

Trouble? If you magnified a different area of the graphic, use the scroll bars to display the center of the tree as shown in Figure 7-13.

▶ **2.** Click the **Color picker** tool 🖊 in the Tools group, and then right-click a **dark-green pixel** in the tree image. The Color 2 button displays the color you clicked.

Trouble? If you clicked the dark-green pixel with the left mouse button instead of the right, repeat Step 2.

▶ **3.** Click the **Color 1** button in the Colors group, and then click the **white color square** in the color palette (middle row, first column). The Color 1 button displays white.

▶ **4.** Click the **Zoom out** button ⊖ on the status bar twice so the graphic appears at 100% zoom.

Now you are ready to use the Text tool to add the clinic name to the graphic. To avoid making mistakes in the current logo graphic, you'll create the text box below the framed tree and then move it to a more precise position later. The text box you draw will be dark green, and the text you type will be white. In addition, the text will appear with the font, size, and attributes shown on the Text Tools Text tab. The font size of the letters is measured in points, where a single point is 1/72 inch. That means a one-inch-tall character is 72 points, and a half-inch-tall character is 36 points. Attributes are characteristics of the font, including bold, italic, underline, and strike-through. You can change the font, size, and attributes before you type, after you select the text you type, or as you edit the text. When you are satisfied with the text and its appearance, you click outside the text box so that Paint anchors the text into place, making it part of the bitmapped graphic. After the text is anchored in a graphic, you can change the font or its attributes only by deleting the text and starting over with the Text tool.

To add text to the graphic:

▶ **1.** Click the **Text** tool [A] in the Tools group.

▶ **2.** Below and to the left of the tree image on the canvas, drag the I beam pointer [to create a text box about 430 pixels wide by 90 pixels tall. Refer to the left-middle part of the status bar for the size coordinates. Then release the mouse button. The Text Tools Text tab appears on the ribbon.

   Trouble? If the text box you created is not about 430 × 90 pixels, click outside of the selected text box, and then repeat Steps 1 and 2.

▶ **3.** Click the **Opaque** button in the Background group on the Text Tools Text tab to display the green fill in the text box. See Figure 7-14.

Figure 7-14	Creating a text box

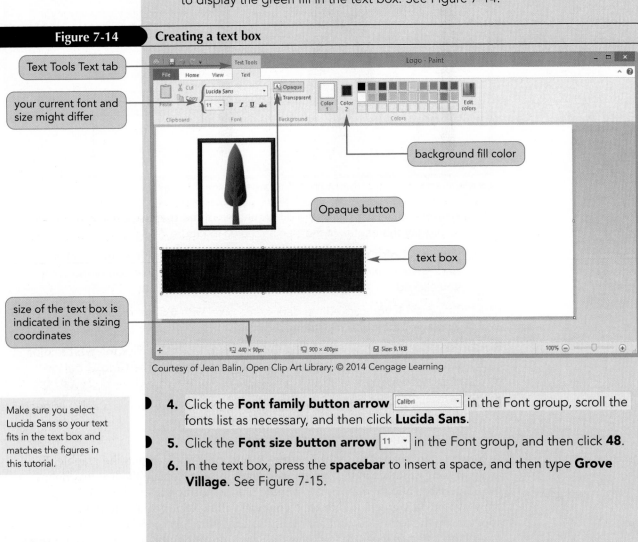

Courtesy of Jean Balin, Open Clip Art Library; © 2014 Cengage Learning

Make sure you select Lucida Sans so your text fits in the text box and matches the figures in this tutorial.

▶ **4.** Click the **Font family button arrow** [Calibri ▾] in the Font group, scroll the fonts list as necessary, and then click **Lucida Sans**.

▶ **5.** Click the **Font size button arrow** [11 ▾] in the Font group, and then click **48**.

▶ **6.** In the text box, press the **spacebar** to insert a space, and then type **Grove Village**. See Figure 7-15.

Figure 7-15	Adding text with the Text tool

Courtesy of Jean Balin, Open Clip Art Library; © 2014 Cengage Learning

> **Trouble?** If the text wraps within the text box or does not fill the text box as shown in the figure, drag the lower-right sizing handle to increase the size of the text box.

▶ **7.** Click a blank area of the canvas outside the text box to anchor the text.

▶ **8.** Click the **Save** button 🖫 on the Quick Access toolbar to save your work.

Now you need to use the same techniques to create a text box with a dark-green background and light-green text that displays the rest of the clinic's name. This time, however, you'll use the Color picker tool to select dark green as the foreground color, and then edit the color to make it a light shade of green. Later, you will move this text below the "Grove Village" text you just created.

To add a second line of text to the graphic:

▶ **1.** Click the **Color picker** tool 🖉 in the Tools group, and then click the background of the text box. Both the Color 1 button and the Color 2 button display dark green.

▶ **2.** Click the **Edit colors** button in the Colors group to open the Edit Colors dialog box.

▶ **3.** To select a shade of light green, click near the top of the narrow bar on the right that shows colors ranging from very light green to very dark green. See Figure 7-16.

Figure 7-16   Selecting light green in the Edit Colors dialog box

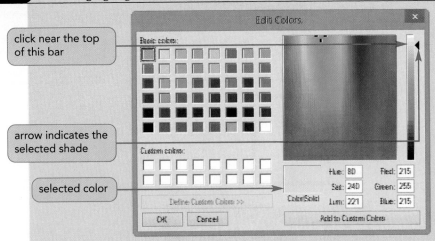

click near the top of this bar

arrow indicates the selected shade

selected color

4. Click the **OK** button to change Color 1 to light green. Now the text you add to the graphic will appear in light green with a dark-green background.

5. Click the **Text** tool **A** in the Tools group, and then click to the right of the "Grove Village" text to insert a text box.

   Trouble? If the text box appears too far to the right, use the move pointer and drag the text box closer to the other text box.

6. Click the **Font size button arrow** in the Font group, type **30**, and then press the **Enter** key.

7. In the new dark-green text box, press the **spacebar** to insert a space, and then type **Veterinary Pet Clinic**. See Figure 7-17.

Figure 7-17   Adding a second line of text

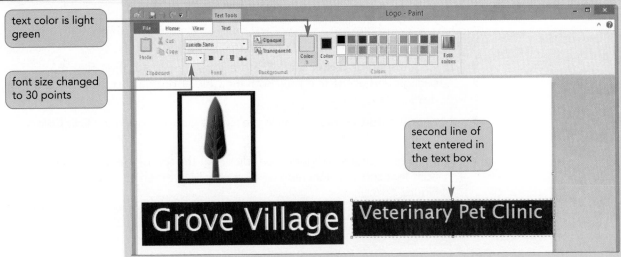

text color is light green

font size changed to 30 points

second line of text entered in the text box

Courtesy of Jean Balin, Open Clip Art Library; © 2014 Cengage Learning

Trouble? If the text wraps within the text box or does not fill the text box as shown in the figure, resize the text box.

> **8.** Click a blank area of the canvas outside the text box to anchor the text.

> **9.** Click the **Save** button 🖫 on the Quick Access toolbar to save your work.

Next, you'll show Doug how to draw a rectangle next to the framed tree image. When you finish, you'll move the two lines of text to the new rectangle.

Drawing Shapes

To draw closed shapes, such as squares and circles, you select a shape from the Shapes gallery, and then draw the shape on the canvas. Before or after you draw a shape, you can set the following options:

- Outline—Select a style for the shape's outline. You can use solid color, crayon, marker, oil, natural pencil, watercolor, or no outline.
- Fill—Select a style for the shape's fill, or inside area. You can use solid color, crayon, marker, oil, natural pencil, watercolor, or no fill.
- Size—Select a width for the outline, ranging from thin to thick.
- Color 1—Select a color for the shape's outline.
- Color 2—Select a color for the shape's fill.

TIP

Holding down the Shift key while dragging to create a shape keeps the proportions equal.

For example, to draw a rectangle, click the Shapes button, click the Rectangle tool, and then drag the drawing pointer diagonally to create the shape. To draw a square, you hold down the Shift key while dragging. Similarly, you draw an ellipse, or oval, by selecting the Ellipse tool and then dragging to create the shape. To draw a circle, hold down the Shift key while dragging. While the shape is selected, you can select an outline and fill style, an outline size, and an outline and fill color. You can also set these options before you draw.

Now you can draw a dark-green rectangle next to the framed tree graphic. Later, you'll move the two lines of text you created to this rectangle to match the logo's design.

To draw a rectangle:

> **1.** Click the **Color picker** tool 🖊 in the Tools group, and then click the dark-green background of the text box to change Color 1 to dark green. Color 2 is already dark green, which is the color you want for the fill of the rectangle.

> **2.** Click the **Rectangle** tool ☐ in the Shapes gallery. See Figure 7-18.

Figure 7-18 **Preparing to use the Rectangle tool**

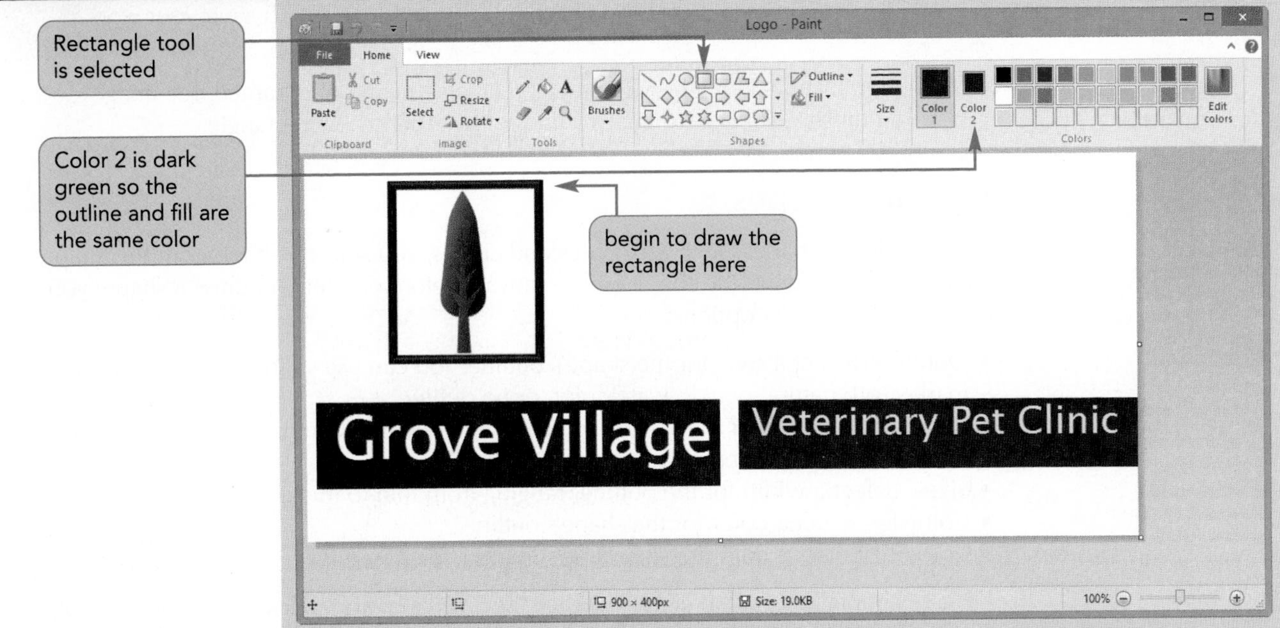

Rectangle tool is selected

Color 2 is dark green so the outline and fill are the same color

begin to draw the rectangle here

Grove Village   Veterinary Pet Clinic

Courtesy of Jean Balin, Open Clip Art Library; © 2014 Cengage Learning

> 3. Click the **Outline** button in the Shapes group, and then click **Solid color**.

> 4. Click the **Fill** button in the Shapes group, and then click **Solid color**.

> 5. Click the **Size** button, and then click the first size, if necessary, which draws a 1-pixel line.

TIP

Watch the sizing coordinates in the second section on the status bar as you draw the rectangle.

> 6. Place the drawing pointer ┼ a few pixels to the right of the framed tree, drag to draw a rectangle about 440 pixels wide and 160 pixels tall, and then release the mouse button. Figure 7-19 shows the rectangle before releasing the mouse button. Your pixel coordinates may differ.

Figure 7-19 **Drawing a rectangle**

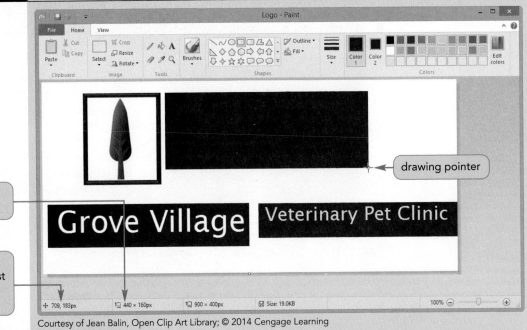

drawing pointer

sizing coordinates in the status bar

Grove Village   Veterinary Pet Clinic

pixel coordinates in the status bar; the first number is the horizontal position

709, 183px   440 × 160px   900 × 400px   Size: 19.0KB   100%

Courtesy of Jean Balin, Open Clip Art Library; © 2014 Cengage Learning

> **Trouble?** If the shape you drew is not similar to the one in the figure, click the Undo button ▇ on the Quick Access toolbar, and then repeat steps as necessary to redraw the rectangle.
>
> **7.** Click outside the rectangle to deselect it.

Now you can move the two lines of text you created into the rectangle.

Moving Part of a Graphic

To move part of a graphic, you select the area you want to move, and then drag the selection to a new location. You can also move or copy part of a graphic using the options in the Clipboard group on the Home tab: Select an area, click the Cut or Copy button in the Clipboard group, and then click the Paste button to paste the selection into the graphic. The graphic appears in a selection box in the upper-left corner of the canvas until you drag the selected image to the desired location.

Before you move part of a graphic, you might need to change Color 2 so it matches the surrounding area. For example, you would leave Color 2 as dark green if you wanted to adjust the placement of the text within a text box so the background remains dark green. However, you would change Color 2 to white before moving the entire text box so the area it occupies changes to white after you move it.

When you move or copy part of a graphic using a selection tool, you can select the image with a solid background (the default) or a transparent background. Choose the Transparent selection command on the Select button list to omit the background color from the selection, so any areas using that color become transparent and allow the colors in the underlying picture to appear in its place when you move or copy the selected image. For example, if you use the Transparent selection command when you select and move a shape with a white background, the background becomes transparent when you move it to a colored area of the graphic. When the Transparent selection command is selected, it appears with a check mark on the Select button list. Remove the check mark to include the background color in your selection when you move or paste it somewhere else in the picture.

TIP

To delete an area of a graphic, select the area using a selection tool, and then press the Delete key.

INSIGHT

Using a Solid or Transparent Background

Using the Transparent selection command in Paint can be an effective way to move an image so it does not appear with a rectangular border. For example, the top of the tree in the logo graphic has a curved outline. If you select the tree without using the Transparent selection option and move it to a green area of the graphic, the tree image remains in a white rectangle. If you select the tree using the Transparent selection command, however, the tree image appears against a green background when you move it into a green area, emphasizing the curved outline of the treetop. The Transparent selection command works best in a graphic that does not use thousands or millions of colors. A white background in a JPG file, for example, often includes hundreds of shades of white, and only one of those shades is set to be transparent when you use the Transparent selection command.

You'll show Doug how to move first the "Grove Village" text and then the "Veterinary Pet Clinic" text to the dark-green rectangle.

To move the text into the rectangle:

1. Click the **Select button arrow** in the Image group. If the Transparent selection command appears with a check mark, click **Transparent selection** to remove the check mark, and then click the **Select button arrow** again.

2. Click **Rectangular selection**. The pointer changes to ╬. The Select button displays the Rectangular selection tool and will do so until you change the type of selection.

3. Drag to select all of the **Grove Village** text in the first text box, but only select as much background as necessary.

4. Point to the selected text, and then use the move pointer ✛ to drag the text up to the new rectangle, centering the text in the upper part of the rectangle.

   Trouble? If part of the text remains in its original location, click the Undo button ▨ on the Quick Access toolbar, and then repeat Steps 3 and 4.

5. Click a blank spot on the canvas to deselect the text.

6. Select the **Veterinary Pet Clinic** text, and then drag the selected text so it is close to the first line of text but not overlapping it. See Figure 7-20.

Figure 7-20 | **Moving text to the rectangle**

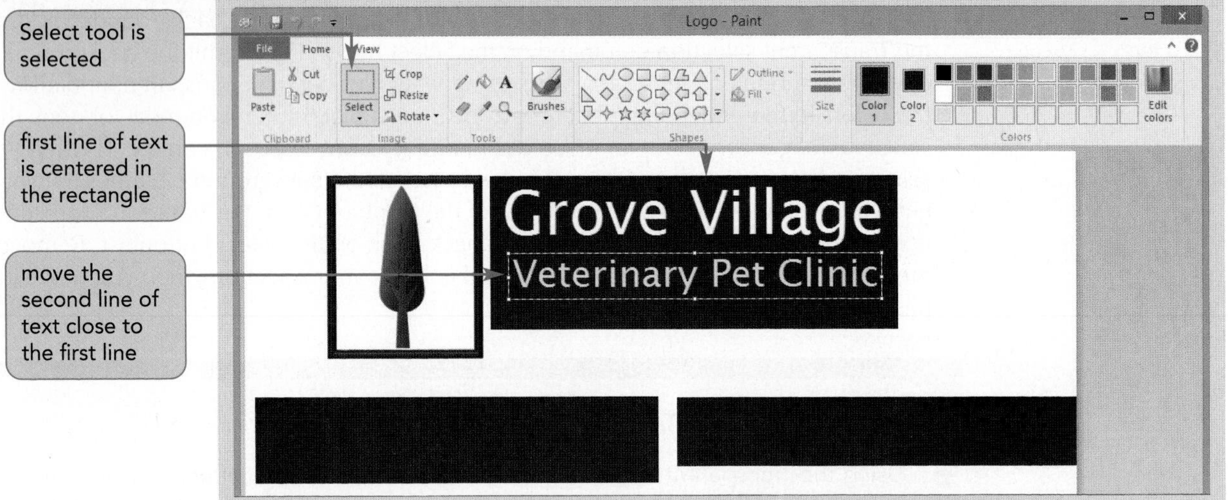

Select tool is selected

first line of text is centered in the rectangle

move the second line of text close to the first line

Courtesy of Jean Balin, Open Clip Art Library; © 2014 Cengage Learning

7. Click outside the selection to complete the move. Now both lines of text are part of the rectangle.

8. If you need to adjust the placement of the text, drag to select a line of text, and then use the arrow keys to fine-tune its placement in the rectangle.

Because Color 2 (the background color) is still set to green, moving the text within the rectangle does not introduce new colors into the text box. Now you want to align the top of the rectangle with the top of the frame, which involves moving the entire rectangle. Before doing so, however, you need to change Color 2 to white so the area the rectangle now occupies doesn't remain green after you move the rectangle.

To move the text box:

1. Click the **Color 2** button in the Colors group, and then click the **white color box** in the color palette to change the background color to white.

2. If necessary, click the **Select** button in the Image group to use the Rectangular selection tool.

3. Drag to select the rectangle containing the "Grove Village Veterinary Pet Clinic" text and as little of the white background as possible. A dashed outline appears around the rectangle.

   Trouble? If the selection box you created contains some of the frame on the left or does not contain all of the rectangle, click outside of the selection, and then repeat Steps 2 and 3.

4. If necessary, use the move pointer ✛ to drag the rectangle so that it appears a few pixels to the right of the frame and aligned with the top edge of the frame. See Figure 7-21.

| Figure 7-21 | **Moving the rectangle** |

make sure Color 2 is white

move the rectangle so it is top-aligned with the frame

Courtesy of Jean Balin, Open Clip Art Library; © 2014 Cengage Learning

Trouble? If the rectangle does not move when you drag it, but the selection box changes size, you probably dragged a sizing handle instead of the entire selection. Click the Undo button 🔲 on the Quick Access toolbar, and then repeat Step 4.

Trouble? If the rectangle is already a few pixels to the right of and top-aligned with the frame, skip Step 4.

5. When the rectangle is in a position similar to the one shown in the figure, click a blank area of the canvas to anchor the text box into place.

6. Click the **Save** button 🔲 on the Quick Access toolbar to save your work.

The entire image is now similar to your original sketch, but you and Doug discuss adding other graphic elements to enhance the logo. In particular, you suggest adding a row of rectangles below the text box to balance the image and draw the eye to the clinic name. Before adding the rectangles, you need to delete part of the large green rectangle containing the logo text.

Deleting Part of a Graphic

To delete part of a graphic, you use a selection tool to select the elements you want to remove, and then press the Delete key on the keyboard. Before deleting part of a graphic, check the Color 2 tool on the Home tab. When you press the Delete key, the selected area will be filled with the color displayed on the Color 2 tool.

To create enough white space for the rectangles you want to add to the logo graphic, you need to delete part of the green text box.

To delete part of the green text box:

▶ **1.** If necessary, click the **Select** button in the Image group to use the Rectangular selection tool.

▶ **2.** Drag to select a green area at the bottom of the rectangle that does not contain any text. Your goal is to create about an inch (72 pixels) of white space from the bottom of the rectangle to the bottom of the frame on the left. See Figure 7-22.

Figure 7-22   **Selecting an area for deletion**

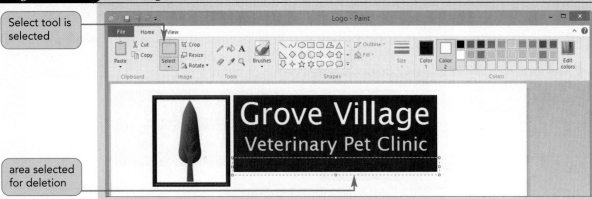

Select tool is selected

area selected for deletion

Courtesy of Jean Balin, Open Clip Art Library; © 2014 Cengage Learning

> **Trouble?** If the selection box contains part of the text in the rectangle, click outside of the selection, and then repeat Step 2.

▶ **3.** Press the **Delete** key to delete the selected area.

Now you have enough room to insert the three rectangles below the text box. You want to add three filled rectangles below the text box. You can use the same shade of dark green as in the large rectangle for the foreground and background colors. You also want to zoom in on the graphic so you can work accurately.

To draw a rectangle:

▶ **1.** Click the **Magnifier** tool 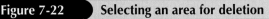 in the Tools group, and then click below the **V** in "Veterinary" to magnify the graphic by 200%.

▶ **2.** Click the **Color picker** tool in the Tools group, and then right-click the dark-green background of the rectangle to change Color 2 to dark green.

Trouble? If you clicked the background instead of right-clicking it, click the Color picker tool 🖋 again, and then right-click the dark-green background.

3. Click the **Rectangle** tool ☐ in the Shapes gallery. The settings you chose earlier for the Outline, Fill, and Size buttons still apply, so you don't need to change those settings.

TIP

Refer to the coordinates in the second section from the left on the status bar as you draw the rectangle.

4. Place the drawing pointer ─┼─ a few pixels below the text box, and then drag to draw a rectangle about 142 pixels wide and 55 pixels tall, and then release the mouse button.

   Trouble? If the shape you drew is not about 142 pixels wide and 55 pixels tall, click the Undo button ▦ on the Quick Access toolbar, and then repeat Step 4 as necessary to redraw the rectangle.

5. Click outside the rectangle to deselect it.

6. With Color 2 selected in the Colors group, click the **white square** in the color palette to change the background color to white.

7. If necessary, click the **Select** button in the Image group, drag to select the rectangle you just drew, and then move it so it is left-aligned with the large green rectangle and bottom-aligned with the frame.

The element you added is the right size and shape and is in the right position, but repeating the color from the text box doesn't create enough of a contrast. You can change the color of the new rectangle to a different one in the tree image to determine if that suits the design of the logo.

Changing Colors

TIP

You can also add color to an image by using a Brush tool and then choosing a style, such as Airbrush.

You can add color to a graphic by choosing colors as you draw or applying color to shapes after you finish drawing them. Before you use a drawing tool, you can select a color for the line or shape, as you did when you drew the rectangles. If you want to add color to an existing image or color a large area of an image, you use the Fill with color tool. When you use the Fill with color tool to click a pixel in a graphic, Paint changes the color of that pixel to Color 1. To change the color to Color 2, right-click a pixel with the Fill with color tool. If adjacent pixels are the same color as the one you clicked, Paint also changes those colors to Color 1. In this way, you can use the Fill with color tool to fill any enclosed area with color. Make sure the area you click is a fully enclosed space. If it has any openings, the new color will extend past the boundaries of the area you are trying to color.

REFERENCE

Filling an Area with Color

- Click the Fill with color tool.
- Click the Color 1 button, and then click the desired color in the color palette.
- Click inside the border of the area you want to color.

You suggest to Doug that a contrasting color, such as the brown that appears in the trunk of the tree image, would make the rectangles more appealing, and you offer to show him how to quickly change the color of the rectangle you drew.

To change the color of the rectangle:

1. Click the **Color picker** tool 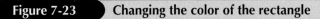 in the Tools group, and then click a brown pixel in the tree image to change the foreground color (Color 1) to brown.

2. Click the **Fill with color** tool in the Tools group, and then move the pointer into the graphic. The pointer changes to a paint can, indicating that any pixel you click will change to the foreground color.

3. Click inside the **rectangle** to change its color from dark green to brown. See Figure 7-23.

Figure 7-23	Changing the color of the rectangle

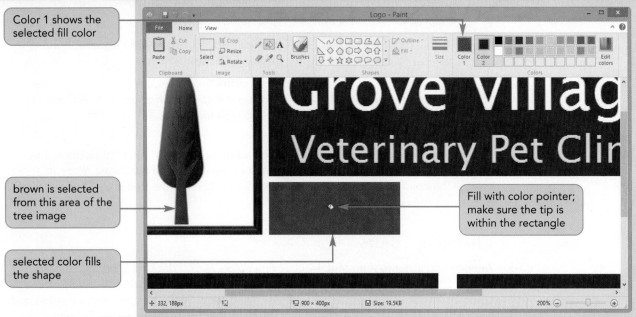

Color 1 shows the selected fill color

brown is selected from this area of the tree image

selected color fills the shape

Fill with color pointer; make sure the tip is within the rectangle

Courtesy of Jean Balin, Open Clip Art Library; © 2014 Cengage Learning

Trouble? If your rectangle is a different shade of brown from the one shown in the figure, continue with the steps. If your rectangle is not brown at all, however, click the Undo button on the Quick Access toolbar, and then repeat Steps 1–3.

Trouble? If the background of the logo graphic turns brown instead of the rectangle, you clicked the background instead of the rectangle. Click the Undo button on the Quick Access toolbar, and then repeat Step 3, making sure the tip of the paint can pointer is within the border of the rectangle.

4. To view the entire image with the new color, click the **Magnifier** tool in the Tools group, and then right-click the graphic to return to 100% magnification.

5. Click the **Save** button on the Quick Access toolbar to save your work.

Coloring the square brown creates contrast, which makes that graphic element more interesting. Now you can complete the logo graphic by copying the rectangle so three brown rectangles appear below the dark green one.

Copying an Image

Recall that to copy an image, you use a method similar to the one used for moving an image: You select the area you want to copy, copy it to the Clipboard, and then paste it in your graphic. Because the pasted image appears in a selection box in the upper-left corner of the graphic, you must drag the image to a new location. You'll show Doug how to copy the brown rectangle and then paste it to create a row of three rectangles below the text box. To create an appealing arrangement, you must make sure that the rectangles are evenly spaced and that their tops and bottoms are aligned. To space and align shapes effectively, you can display gridlines on the canvas to position the shapes accurately. The gridlines do not become a part of the graphic—they are only a visual guide that appears in the Paint window. You'll show Doug how to display gridlines to aid in positioning the brown rectangles in a row.

To copy and paste the rectangle:

▶ **1.** Click the **Magnifier** tool 🔍 in the Tools group, and then click the center of the brown rectangle twice to magnify the image 300%.

▶ **2.** Click the **View** tab, and then click the **Gridlines** check box in the Show or hide group to display the gridlines in the Paint window.

▶ **3.** Click the **Home** tab, click the **Select** button in the Image group, and then drag to select only the **brown rectangle**.

   Trouble? If the selection box includes part of the frame or the dark-green rectangle, or does not include the entire brown rectangle, click outside the selection box and repeat Step 3.

▶ **4.** Click the **Copy** button in the Clipboard group to copy the brown rectangle to the Clipboard.

▶ **5.** Click the **Paste** button in the Clipboard to paste the brown rectangle in the upper-left corner of the Paint window.

▶ **6.** Drag the selected rectangle next to the first brown rectangle, leaving one and a half squares of white space on the grid between the two shapes. If necessary, use the arrow keys on your keyboard to adjust the vertical position of the rectangle and its alignment with the first rectangle. The lower edge of the new rectangle should be on the same row of the grid as the lower edge of the first rectangle.

▶ **7.** Click outside the selection, and then scroll to the right to display the right edge of the second rectangle.

▶ **8.** Click the **Paste** button again to paste another copy of the rectangle in the upper-left corner of the Paint window.

▶ **9.** Drag the selected rectangle to align its right edge with the right edge of the dark-green rectangle and its top with the top edges of the other two brown rectangles. See Figure 7-24.

Figure 7-24   **Pasting and positioning copies of the rectangle**

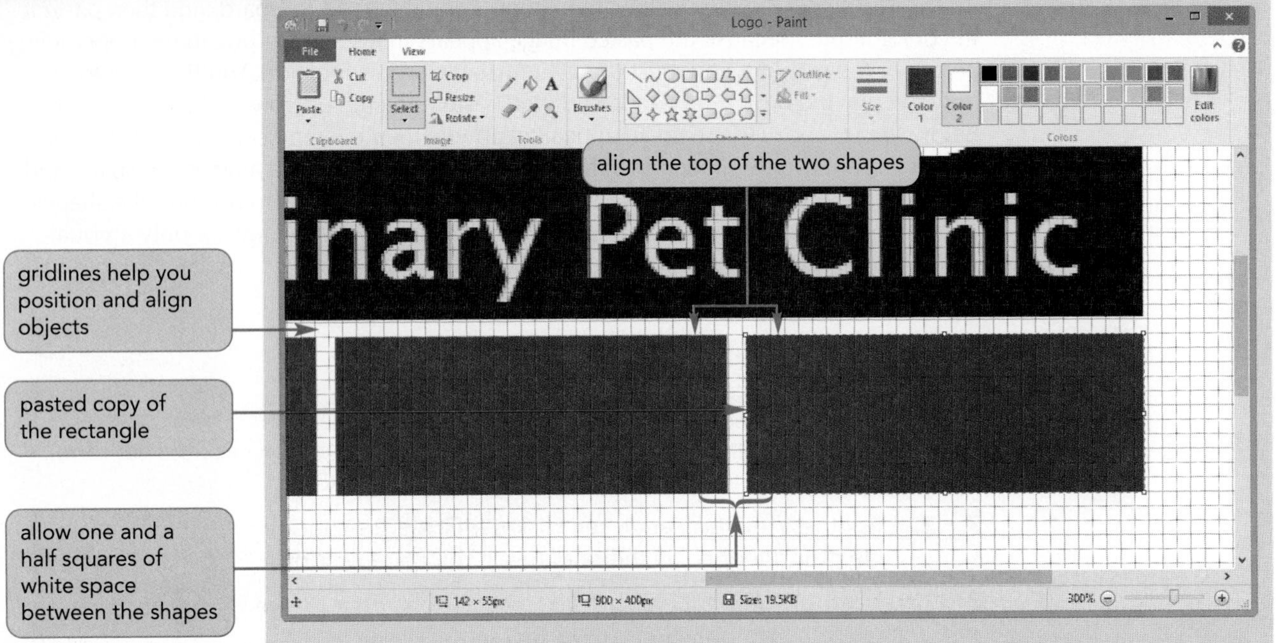

gridlines help you position and align objects

align the top of the two shapes

pasted copy of the rectangle

allow one and a half squares of white space between the shapes

Trouble? If the three rectangles are not evenly spaced or bottom-aligned, use the Select tool to select a rectangle, and then drag it to change its position so it is evenly spaced and aligned with the other rectangles.

▶ **10.** Click outside the selection to deselect the rectangle.

▶ **11.** To view the entire image with the three rectangles, click the **Zoom out** button ⊝ on the status bar twice to return to 100% magnification.

Your last task is to position the image on the canvas to minimize the amount of unnecessary white space in the graphic.

Cropping a Graphic

Recall that you can crop an image to remove one or more rows or columns of pixels from the edge of a picture. When you crop a graphic to eliminate unnecessary white space by resizing the canvas, you reduce file size and prevent a border from appearing around your picture when you paste it into another file. You can also crop a graphic using the Crop tool in the Image group on the Home tab. To do so, you select the area you want to retain in the graphic, and then click the Crop tool to remove all parts of the graphic beyond the selection.

To crop the logo graphic:

▶ **1.** Click the **Select** button in the Image group.

▶ **2.** Using the selection pointer ✛, drag to select the frame, the dark-green rectangle with text, and the three brown rectangles, as shown in Figure 7-25.

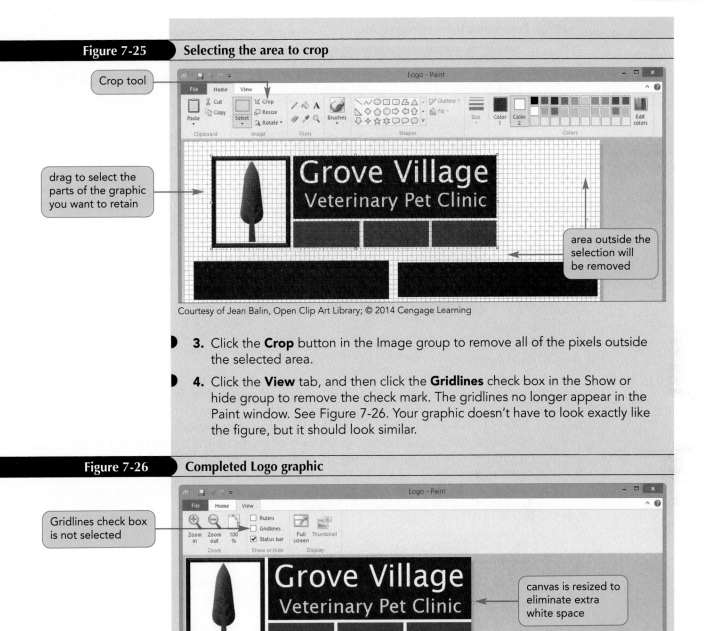

Figure 7-25   **Selecting the area to crop**

Courtesy of Jean Balin, Open Clip Art Library; © 2014 Cengage Learning

> **3.** Click the **Crop** button in the Image group to remove all of the pixels outside the selected area.

> **4.** Click the **View** tab, and then click the **Gridlines** check box in the Show or hide group to remove the check mark. The gridlines no longer appear in the Paint window. See Figure 7-26. Your graphic doesn't have to look exactly like the figure, but it should look similar.

Figure 7-26   **Completed Logo graphic**

Courtesy of Jean Balin, Open Clip Art Library; © 2014 Cengage Learning

Trouble? If you cropped the image so that parts of the logo image are cut off, click the Undo button ⬜ on the Quick Access toolbar, and then repeat Steps 2 and 3.

Cropping is the best way to resize a bitmapped graphic. Although you can resize a graphic in Paint to make the entire image larger or smaller, the results are often disappointing. Because you cannot change the size of an individual pixel, resizing the overall image tends to distort it. For example, when you try to enlarge a bitmapped graphic, Paint duplicates the pixels to approximate the original shape as best it can—often resulting in jagged edges. On the other hand, when you shrink a bitmapped graphic, Paint removes pixels and the graphic loses detail. In either case, you distort the original graphic. For example, Figure 7-27 shows how the current logo image looks when it's enlarged.

Figure 7-27   **Enlarging a bitmapped graphic**

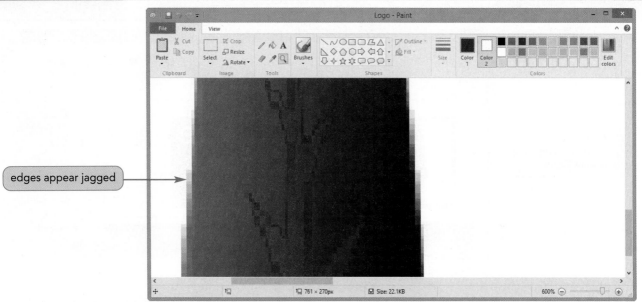

edges appear jagged

Courtesy of Jean Balin, Open Clip Art Library

How do you bypass this problem? In Paint, there is no easy solution to resizing graphics because they are all bitmapped. If your work with graphics requires resizing—for example, if you want a graphic that looks good on a small business card and a large poster—using vector graphics is a better choice. Because vector graphics are mathematically based, you can resize them as necessary without sacrificing image quality. However, you need to buy a graphics program that allows you to work with vector graphics.

You've completed the graphic for Grove Village Veterinary Pet Clinic, so you can save the Logo file and close Paint.

To save the file and close Paint:

1. Click the **Save** button on the Quick Access toolbar.

2. Close the Paint window.

Now that you've shown Doug how to use Paint to create and modify bitmapped graphics, you can get ready to work with Carl to develop a multimedia presentation.

Session 7.1 Quick Check   ~~JPG~~ *bitmapped (photographs)* [handwritten]

REVIEW

1. What type of computer graphic is appropriate for detailed images, such as photographs and the images displayed on a computer monitor?   *BMP* *PNG, JPG, GIF* [handwritten]

2. What type of computer graphic is created by mathematical formulas that define the shapes used in the image?   *rector graphic - WMF, SWF, SVG* [handwritten]

3. Name five graphics file formats you can use in Paint.

   ③ GIF [handwritten]
   JPG (JPEG) [handwritten]
   PNG [handwritten]
   TIF (TIFF) [handwritten]
   BMP [handwritten]

4. If Color 1 is yellow and Color 2 is blue when you use the Text tool to add text to an image, what colors are the text and the background?   *yel   blue* [handwritten]

5. Explain what happens when you use the Transparent selection command to select and move a shape with a white background into a colored area of the graphic.   *It becomes transparent* [handwritten]

6. If you want to change a color in an image, you can use the ___*Fill with color*___ tool.

7. When you crop a graphic to eliminate unnecessary white space, do you increase or reduce the file size?

Session 7.2 Visual Overview:

The Pictures library contains tools for working with photos.

Click the Slide show button in the View group to play a slide show.

Apps such as the Photos app detect and display photos stored in the Pictures library and its folders.

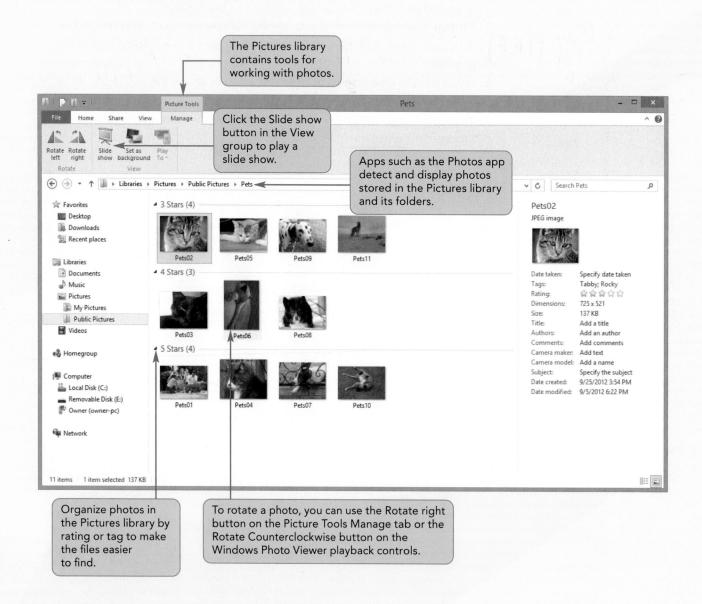

Organize photos in the Pictures library by rating or tag to make the files easier to find.

To rotate a photo, you can use the Rotate right button on the Picture Tools Manage tab or the Rotate Counterclockwise button on the Windows Photo Viewer playback controls.

Photos courtesy of Cade Martin; C. E. Price; Jon Sullivan; Carolina Vigna-Marú; Dusan Bicanski; Michelle Buntin; Ina Meyer; www.public-domain-image.com

Viewing and Sharing Photos

SkyDrive is a Microsoft service that provides online, or cloud, storage space for your files.

Anyone can access files you post in the SkyDrive Public folder.

The Photos app also displays photos stored in your SkyDrive.

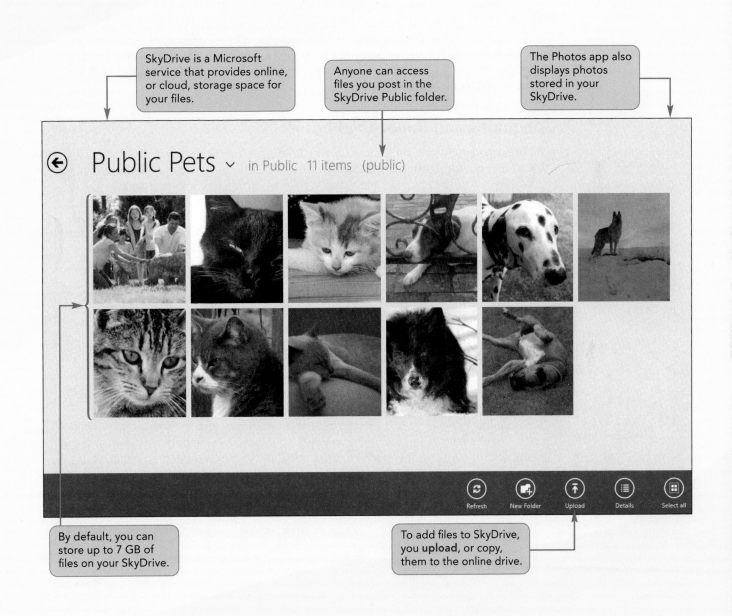

By default, you can store up to 7 GB of files on your SkyDrive.

To add files to SkyDrive, you **upload**, or copy, them to the online drive.

Working with Photos

Innovations in digital cameras and computers have transformed the field of photography, letting anyone edit and print photos without using a darkroom or professional photo lab. Instead, you can take photos with your computer, or transfer them from your digital camera or phone to your Windows 8 computer, where you can fine-tune the images, display them in a slide show, use them as a screen saver or wallpaper, and share them with others.

As an intern for Grove Village Veterinary Pet Clinic, you are preparing to work with Carl Patel, one of the clinic owners. Carl wants to create a multimedia presentation that the clinic can use to promote pet adoption and animal health. He'd like to include a slide show of photos with a musical accompaniment in the presentation. Carl has already transferred photos of pets from his digital camera to his computer. You'll show him how to view, organize, and edit the photos so he can assemble them into a slide show to play in the clinic waiting room.

Acquiring and Importing Photos

Before you can create a slide show on your computer, you need to acquire and possibly import photos. The most popular way to acquire photos is to use a digital camera to take the photos. The camera can be a single electronic device or part of another device such as a smartphone or computer. (Cameras built into computers are usually called **Webcams**.) Cameras store photos as JPG image files, so you can work with them using any photo editor or painting graphics program. Using a digital camera lets you control the subject matter and maintain the legal rights to the images—two notable advantages. Unless you're a trained photographer, the main disadvantage is that your images are not professional quality, though you often can improve them using digital editing tools. If you are using the photos for the enjoyment of family and friends, you might not need to do more than snap the photos on your digital camera and then transfer them to your Windows 8 computer.

If you need professional photos, such as for a product brochure or Web site, you have a few options. Hiring a photographer to create and prepare the images can be effective, though expensive. You can also purchase photos from stock collections, typically provided online, by paying a licensing fee. These collections usually contain royalty-free images that you can use for any purpose, and cost anywhere from thousands of dollars to under $20 for hundreds or thousands of images. You can download photos free of charge and copyright only if the photos are in the public domain and are freely available for use. If you have conventional photographs printed on paper, you can use a scanner to convert the photos into digital pictures if you own the copyright or the photos are in the public domain.

PROSKILLS

Decision Making: Using Copyright-Protected, Royalty-Free, and Public-Domain Photos

Many school and work projects involve graphics. Where and how to acquire graphics is often a decision you need to make early in the project—one that can have legal consequences. Although you can easily copy photos displayed on Web sites, that doesn't mean that you should. Most photos and other media on the Web are protected by copyright law. A copyright gives photographers (and other types of graphic artists and creators) the exclusive right to control their images. They can decide who can copy, distribute, or derive material from their photographs. Before you can use a copyrighted photo, you must receive permission from the photographer.

Some Web sites and services offer royalty-free photos, meaning that the photographers do not receive payment each time their photos are used. However, the photographers still retain the rights to the photos even if they don't receive royalties for each use. Photos in the public domain are the only ones not protected by copyright law. These include photos for which the copyright has expired, some government images, and those explicitly identified as being in the public domain.

If you want to copy photos from the Web or another digital source, the following guidelines help you respect the photographer's rights:

• Ask the owner of the copyright for permission.
• Find out if the photographer has any stipulations on how the material may be used.
• If explicit guidelines are given, follow them, and credit the source of your material.
• Keep a copy of your request and the permission received.

If you acquire photos from a Web site or other digital source, you only have to copy them to a folder on your computer so you can edit and organize them. However, if you are using a digital camera, including one in your cell phone, you need to perform an additional step of importing the photo files from the device to your computer. One way to do this is to connect the device directly to the computer using a cable that plugs into the computer's USB port. Another way is to import pictures using a memory card reader, a device that plugs into your computer's USB port. In either case, Windows 8 should recognize your camera or card (it recognizes most makes and models of digital cameras and cards), and guide you through the steps of importing pictures. After importing the images, Windows 8 stores them in the Pictures library by default.

INSIGHT

Using the Camera App

The Windows 8 Camera app lets you use your Webcam to take photos and record videos. Start the Camera app by clicking its tile on the Start screen. The Camera app displays the Webcam image in a full-screen view. Click the screen to capture the image and store it in the Camera Roll folder in the Pictures library on your computer. You can also use the Camera app to record videos with your Webcam. To do so, click the Video mode button on the Apps bar to switch to video mode. Click the screen to start recording. As you record, a timer appears so you can keep track of how much video you are recording. When you're finished, click the screen again to stop recording. You can use the Photos app to display photos you take with the Camera app, and use the Videos app to play videos you record with the Camera app.

Viewing and Organizing Photos

Windows 8 provides a number of tools for working with photos. Although some of these tools have features in common, each one is designed to serve a particular purpose, as explained in the following descriptions:

- Pictures library—The Pictures library and its folders are the best places to store your digital photos because they offer tools that are not available in other folders. For example, you can use the Slide show button to play the photos in the current folder as a full-screen slide show. You can also use the Search box in the Pictures library to quickly find photos stored anywhere on your computer, which is particularly helpful if you have dozens or hundreds of photos, as many people do. Other apps, such as the Windows 8 Photos app, detect the photos stored in the Pictures library so you can quickly create a slide show or share photos with others.

- Photos app—You have already worked with the Windows 8 Photos app to view photos stored in your Pictures library, SkyDrive, Facebook account, or Flickr account. You can play a slide show of photos stored in a single location, show a collage of the photos, or display each photo one at a time.

- Windows Photo Viewer—Although Windows Photo Viewer is not a separate program you can open from the Start screen or Apps menu, it is a full-featured tool you can open from the Pictures library. If you click a photo file in the Pictures library and then click the Open button arrow in the Open group on the Home tab, you can select Windows Photo Viewer as the tool you want to use to open the file. The Pictures library and Windows Photo Viewer share many features. For example, you can view, rotate, and print photos and see a slide show from either the Pictures library or Windows Photo Viewer. However, while the Pictures library is designed to help you find and organize photos by displaying all of them in one place, Windows Photo Viewer lets you concentrate on each photo one at a time. Besides rotating photos, you can zoom in and view photos at full size.

You might have additional photo-editing tools installed on your computer. These tools are often provided by digital camera and computer manufacturers.

Your first task in developing a presentation with Carl is to review the photos he has taken of cats and dogs that come to the veterinary clinic, for which he has obtained permission from the owners. Start by copying the photos in your Tutorial folder to a subfolder of the Pictures library.

To copy photo files to the Pictures library:

▸ **1.** Open a folder window that displays the contents of the Windows7\Tutorial folder provided with your Data Files.

▸ **2.** Create a new folder in the Public Pictures folder named **Pets**, and then copy the 11 pet photos (**Pets01–Pets11**) to the Pets folder.

▸ **3.** If necessary, display the files in the Pets folder, and then resize the Pets folder window to display all of the tools on the Home tab.

Be sure to create the Pets folder in the Public Pictures folder so you can use the photo tools provided in the Pictures library.

Now you can show Carl how to use the Pictures library and Windows Photo Viewer to display, examine, and organize photos.

To examine photos using the Pictures library:

1. In the Pets folder window, switch to Details view, if necessary, to view the photo ratings.

2. Make sure the Name, Date, Tags, Size, and Rating columns are displayed in the Pets folder window. If necessary, right-click a column heading and then click to check or uncheck column names so they match the ones shown in Figure 7-28.

| Figure 7-28 | Displaying the Pets folder photos in the Pictures library |

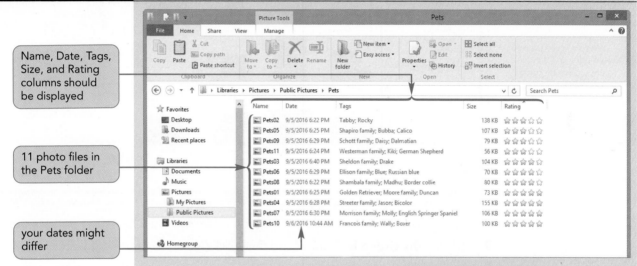

Name, Date, Tags, Size, and Rating columns should be displayed

11 photo files in the Pets folder

your dates might differ

3. Click the **View** tab, and then click the **Details pane** button in the Panes group to open the Details pane.

4. Click **Large icons** in the Layout group to switch to Large icons view.

Carl added tags and ratings to these photos when he imported them to the computer. You can use the tags, ratings, and other details to arrange the photos so they are easier to reference. For example, Carl often needs to refer to pet photos by tag so he can see the pet names and breed. He might also want to select all of the photos he rated with five stars. You'll show him how to use the Pictures library to arrange the photos.

To arrange the pet photos:

1. Click the **Group by** button in the Current view group, and then click **Rating**. The photos are arranged into three sections: 3 Stars, 4 Stars, and 5 Stars. See Figure 7-29.

Figure 7-29 Arranging photos by Rating

Large icons view is selected

files are grouped according to rating

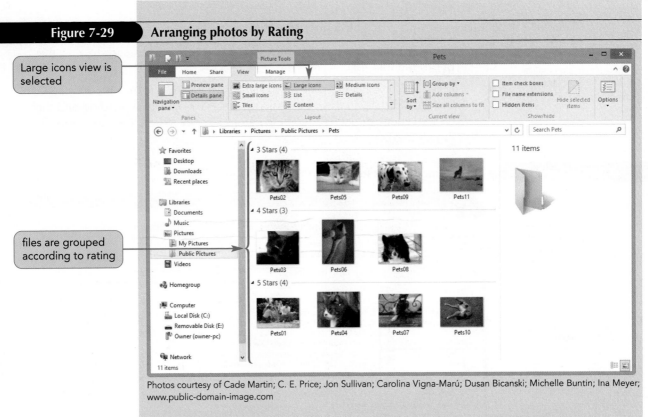

Photos courtesy of Cade Martin; C. E. Price; Jon Sullivan; Carolina Vigna-Marú; Dusan Bicanski; Michelle Buntin; Ina Meyer; www.public-domain-image.com

▶ **2.** Click the **Group by** button, and then click **(None)** to return to folder view.

▶ **3.** Click the **Sort by** button in the Current view group, and then click **Name** to sort the files by name.

As you've seen, the Pictures library lets you see all of your photos in one place and then arrange them by date, rating, or other criteria. Now you want to show Carl how to use Windows Photo Viewer so he can compare the two tools.

To view photos using Windows Photo Viewer:

▶ **1.** In the Pets folder window, click the **Pets01** photo, click the **Home** tab, click the **Open button arrow** in the Open group, and then click **Windows Photo Viewer**. The photo opens in Windows Photo Viewer. See Figure 7-30.

Trouble? If the photo opens in a different app, you clicked the Open button instead of the Open button arrow. Close the app window, return to the desktop, and then repeat Step 1.

Figure 7-30 Windows Photo Viewer

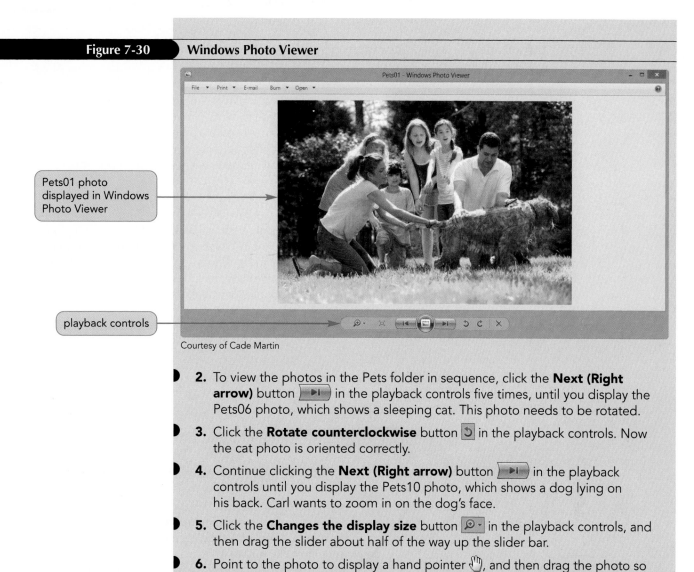

Pets01 photo displayed in Windows Photo Viewer

playback controls

Courtesy of Cade Martin

2. To view the photos in the Pets folder in sequence, click the **Next (Right arrow)** button  in the playback controls five times, until you display the Pets06 photo, which shows a sleeping cat. This photo needs to be rotated.

3. Click the **Rotate counterclockwise** button in the playback controls. Now the cat photo is oriented correctly.

4. Continue clicking the **Next (Right arrow)** button in the playback controls until you display the Pets10 photo, which shows a dog lying on his back. Carl wants to zoom in on the dog's face.

5. Click the **Changes the display size** button in the playback controls, and then drag the slider about half of the way up the slider bar.

6. Point to the photo to display a hand pointer , and then drag the photo so the dog's head is in the middle of the image. See Figure 7-31.

Figure 7-31 Magnified view of Pets10 photo

hand pointer in Windows Photo Viewer; drag the image to scroll

Fit to window button

Changes the display size button

Courtesy of Ina Meyer

▶ **7.** To display this photo at its original size, click the **Fit to window** button ⊡ in the playback controls.

Besides examining and rotating photos, you can play a simple slide show in Windows Photo Viewer. Carl wants to play a slide show of Grove Village Veterinary Pet Clinic projects when he and Doug attend veterinary conferences and career fairs, or when they are invited to a school to talk about what veterinarians do. Also, it will be nice to have a slide show playing in the office while pet owners wait for appointments.

Playing a Simple Slide Show

You can play a simple slide show in the Pictures library by clicking the Slide show button on the Picture Tools Manage tab; in Windows Photo Viewer by clicking the round Play slide show button in the playback controls; or in the Photos app by clicking the Slide show button on the Apps bar. In any case, the slide show includes all of the photos in the current folder and its subfolders, and plays the photos one after another at various speeds.

REFERENCE

Playing a Slide Show

- In the Pictures library window, click the Slide show button on the Picture Tools Manage tab.
  or
- In Windows Photo Viewer, click the Play slide show button in the playback controls.
  or
- In the Photos app, click the Slide show button on the Apps bar.

During a slide show, all three Windows tools automatically display a series of full-screen photos. The slide show plays all of the photos in the current folder, starting with the selected photo or the first one if none is selected. While a slide show is running in Windows Photo Viewer, you can right-click a photo to pause the show, adjust the speed, go forward or backward, and choose whether pictures are shown randomly or sequentially.

TIP

To play a slide show with only a few photos, select the photos before you click the Play slide show button.

To play a simple slide show:

▶ **1.** In Windows Photo Viewer, click the **Play slide show** button ⊙ in the playback controls. The monitor darkens, and Windows Photo Viewer fills the screen with the current photo, displays it for a few seconds, and then displays the next photo.

▶ **2.** To slow the slide show so you can examine the photos, right-click a slide, and then click **Slide Show Speed - Slow** on the shortcut menu.

▶ **3.** After viewing one photo that could be cropped (Pets11, the German Shepherd), right-click a slide, click **Slide Show Speed - Medium** on the shortcut menu to return to the default speed, and then press the **Esc** key to end the slide show.

▶ **4.** Close Windows Photo Viewer.

Carl says that a simple slide show isn't catchy enough to attract new patients. He also wants to play music while displaying the photos. You'll show him how to create such a slide show later. Right now, you want to edit a photo you found to improve its composition. You'll show Carl how to use Paint to edit the photo next.

Editing a Photo

For basic photo editing such as cropping, adding text, or drawing a border, you can open a photo in Paint and use the techniques you learned in the previous session to fine-tune the image. Camera manufacturers often provide software for removing red eye (a common problem when using a flash to snap photos of people) and adjusting brightness and contrast. Microsoft also provides this type of photo touch-up software on its Windows Live site (http://windows.microsoft.com/en-US/windows-live/essentials-home) and in the Windows Store.

To crop the photo of the German Shepherd, you can open the image in Paint and then crop it.

To crop a photo:

1. In the Pets folder window, right-click the **Pets11** photo, point to **Open with**, and then click **Paint** on the shortcut menu. The photo opens in the Paint window.

TIP

You can also use the Crop tool to crop photos.

2. Click the **Select button arrow** in the Image group, and then click **Select all** to select the entire photo. You want to remove some of the background image above and to the left of the dog.

3. Drag the selection up and to the left of the Paint window to remove about an inch from the left and the top of the photo. See Figure 7-32.

| Figure 7-32 | Cropping a photo in Paint |

drag the entire image to remove about an inch from the left and top of the photo

Courtesy of www.public-domain-image.com

4. Click outside of the selection box to deselect the image.

▶ **5.** Drag the lower-right selection handle on the canvas up and to the left to remove the unnecessary white space.

▶ **6.** Click the **Save** button 🔲 on the Quick Access toolbar to save the photo with the same name.

▶ **7.** Close the Paint window.

Carl wonders if he could make the photos available to any patient who has a Windows 8 computer. You'll show him how to quickly share the photos with others next.

Sharing Photos

When you share your photos, you make them available for other people to view on their computers. The most popular way to share photos is to post them on a photo-sharing Web site or another type of site where you have an account, such as Facebook or SkyDrive. You can also send photos to others in email messages. A photo-sharing Web site lets you share and store pictures, often free of charge. (Check the Web site's policies before copying your files to an online album.) You can then invite others to visit the Web site and view your photo albums.

The easiest way to share photos with SkyDrive or email is to use the Share charm on the Charms bar. You can also start the SkyDrive or Mail app and then share the files, which is a good alternative if you are planning to do additional work in either app. You'll use both techniques in the following steps.

Sharing Photos Using SkyDrive

SkyDrive is a Microsoft service that provides online, or cloud, storage space for your files. You can use the Windows 8 SkyDrive app or the SkyDrive Web site (https://skydrive.live.com or SkyDrive.com) to store up to 7 GB of files in a secure online location that you can access any time you have an Internet connection. (You can purchase additional storage space as necessary.) After posting, or uploading, the files, you can organize them so that some files are private, meaning that only you and others you specify can access them. You can also designate files as public, which means anyone can view and open them. One advantage of using SkyDrive is that you can use a Web browser to open and, in some cases, edit a file—you don't need to start the app that was used to create the file. In addition, you can use any device to access the files, such as a Windows 8 computer, a tablet running a different operating system, or a smartphone.

SkyDrive provides a standard set of folders for each user: Documents, Pictures, and Public. You can add others as you need them. The Documents folder is designed for storing files such as text documents and spreadsheets. The Pictures folder includes tools for organizing and sharing photos. For example, you can arrange photos into albums. The Public folder is for files that anyone else can access, though you can share other files and folders as well.

Carl wants to post all of the photos in the Pets folder on his SkyDrive so that anyone with a Web browser can view them. You'll show him how to upload the files to the Public folder on his SkyDrive. Because he wants to keep these pet photos separate from other files in the Public folder, you'll also show him how to create a folder in the Public folder on his SkyDrive. To do so, you'll use the SkyDrive app. In this case, you can't use the Share charm on the Charms bar because you can't create folders when you use that technique.

To perform the following steps, you need to have a Microsoft account. If you don't have a Microsoft account, use a Web browser to go to https://signup.live.com, and then provide the requested information, including a user name (your email address) and password. Note your user name and password so you can use it to access SkyDrive.

To upload photos using SkyDrive:

▶ **1.** Press the **Windows** key ⊞ to display the Start screen.

▶ **2.** Click the **SkyDrive** tile to open the SkyDrive app. If necessary, sign in by providing your user name and password. Your SkyDrive opens and displays a tile for each default folder and those you might have already created.

▶ **3.** Click the **Public** folder to open it.

▶ **4.** Right-click a blank area of the screen to display the Apps bar, and then click the **New Folder** button to create a folder for the pet photos.

▶ **5.** Type **Public Pets** as the name of the folder, and then click the **Create folder** button.

▶ **6.** Click the **Public Pets** folder to open the folder.

▶ **7.** Right-click a blank area of the screen to display the Apps bar, and then click the **Upload** button to display the Files screen, where you can select the files you want to upload to SkyDrive.

▶ **8.** Click **Files** to display a list of locations that contain files, click **Pictures**, click the **Pets** folder, and then click **Select all**. The photos in the Pets folder appear on the Files screen, each with a check mark to indicate it is selected. See Figure 7-33.

Figure 7-33	Selecting files to upload

files in the Pets folder

check mark indicates a selected file

Add to SkyDrive button

Photos courtesy of Cade Martin; C. E. Price; Jon Sullivan; Carolina Vigna-Marú; Dusan Bicanski; Michelle Buntin; Ina Meyer, www.public-domain-image.com

▶ **9.** Click the **Add to SkyDrive** button on the Files screen. It takes a few seconds for Windows to add the photos to the Public Pets folder on your SkyDrive.

▶ **10.** Close SkyDrive.

Now anyone with a Web browser can sign in to SkyDrive and view the pet photos. Carl can use a feature on SkyDrive to send email invitations to the clinic's clients. When clients receive such an email, they can click a link in the message to view the photos on Carl's SkyDrive.

Distributing Photos via Email

If you have an account set up in the Windows 8 Mail app, you can use the Share charm on the Charms bar to share photos via email. When you use the Share charm, you share information or files from one Windows 8 app to another (not from the desktop or the Start screen). For example, you can start Windows 8 Internet Explorer and then use the Share charm to send the URL and a preview of the current Web page using Mail or another Windows 8 app that's available for sharing. To share photos, you start the Photos app and then click the Share charm on the Charms bar to display a list of Windows 8 apps to which you can send photos, including Mail and SkyDrive.

Patients often ask Carl about the proper way to wash a dog. Carl has a photo that illustrates how to do so using a backyard hose. You'll show Carl how to display this photo in the Photos app and then use the Share charm on the Charms bar to email the photo.

You must have an account set up in the Mail app to share photos via email. If you do not have an account set up yet, open the Mail app, which will guide you to set up an account.

To share a photo via email:

▶ 1. On the Start screen, click the **Photos** tile to open the Photos app.

▶ 2. Click **Pictures library** at the bottom of the screen to display the photos stored in your Pictures library.

▶ 3. Click the **Pets** folder to open it, and then right-click the first photo, **Pets01**, to select it (a check mark appears in the upper-right corner of the photo). Now you are ready to share the selected photo.

▶ 4. Display the Charms bar, and then click the **Share** charm to display the Share menu. See Figure 7-34.

| Figure 7-34 | Share menu for sharing photos |

Courtesy of Cade Martin

▶ 5. Click **Mail** on the Share menu. Your email address, the To text box, and other controls for sharing the selected photo via email appear in the Mail app window on the right of the screen.

TIP

To include more than one email address in the To text box, insert a semicolon between each email address.

▶ **6.** Type your email address to send yourself a copy of the photo.

▶ **7.** Click **Add a subject**, and then type **How to wash a dog**.

▶ **8.** Click the **Send** button ⊜ to send the photo and message to your email account. The Mail app closes automatically.

▶ **9.** Close the Photos app.

Now you are ready to show Carl how to find and play music to accompany his slide show.

Finding and Playing Music

To play digital music files on your computer, you can use the Windows 8 Music app or the Windows Media Player desktop application. The Music app is similar to the Photos app—you use it to play any music files stored in the Music library on your computer. In addition, you can visit an online marketplace that provides albums and songs for purchase and download. You can generally preview the music free of charge. For music files stored on your computer, you can create **playlists**, which are lists of media files, such as songs, that you want to play in a specified order.

You can also use Windows Media Player to play music stored on your computer, CDs, or Web sites; download music files you've purchased from online stores; and create your own albums of songs and burn them onto CDs or sync them to a portable music player, such as an MP3 player or your cell phone.

Before you purchase and download music files from an online store using either app, make sure you understand the usage rights that the store grants you. The content that stores provide is typically protected by media usage rights, which specify what you can do with the content. For example, these rights might specify that you cannot burn the file to an audio CD, or they might limit the number of times you can burn or sync the file.

Carl wants to find music he can use with his slide show of pet photos, but he's not sure what music would work best. He does know that most animals respond to classical music, so he wants to use piano or orchestral music from that genre. You suggest using the Music app to visit the online store where you can preview music free of charge.

Before performing the following steps, make sure that your computer has a sound card and speakers, and that the speakers are plugged into a power source, turned on, and connected to your computer. Also, make sure that the speaker volume is not muted, but is low enough to hear without disturbing others. If you don't have speakers but do have a sound card, you might be able to plug headphones into a headphone jack to listen to music. If your computer does not have the hardware necessary to play music, you can still perform the following steps, though you won't be able to hear the music.

To use the Music app to preview music:

▶ **1.** On the Start screen, click the **Music** tile to open the Music app.

   Trouble? If this is the first time you are running the Music app, you might be requested to sign in to your Microsoft account. Enter the user name and password for your Microsoft account to continue.

▶ **2.** Scroll to the right and then click the **xbox music store** link to display a list of musical genres on the left and a list of featured albums for sale on the right.

▶ **3.** Click **Classical** in the list of musical genres, which displays a list of featured albums for sale currently.

4. Click an album in the list on the right to display options for playing or purchasing the music. See Figure 7-35. The album you selected might differ.

Figure 7-35 **Selecting an album**

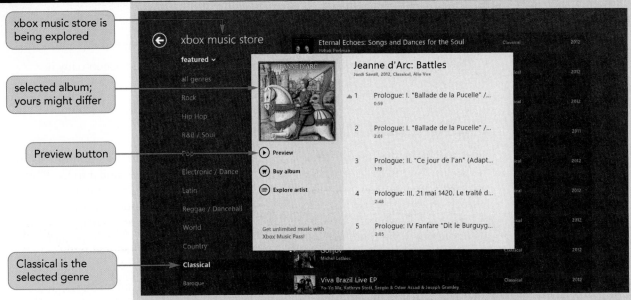

xbox music store is being explored

selected album; yours might differ

Preview button

Classical is the selected genre

TIP

To search for music by keyword or phrase, display the Charms bar, click the Search button, and then enter the keyword or phrase.

5. Click the **Preview** button to play excerpts of the musical pieces on the album.

Trouble? If you do not hear any music, your speakers might be muted. If you have permission to do so, turn up the speaker volume slightly.

6. Click the **Pause** button on the Apps bar to stop playing the music.

7. Click a blank spot on the screen to close the list of options, and then close the Music app.

Carl does have a couple of music files that might work with the slide show. You can copy these files to the Music library and then use Windows Media Player to create a playlist of this music to manage the files.

To copy music files and start Windows Media Player:

1. On the Start screen, click the **Desktop** tile to display the desktop, and then open a folder window that displays the contents of the Windows7\Tutorial folder provided with your Data Files.

2. Create a folder in the Public Music folder named **Grove Village**, and then copy the **Nocturne1** and **Nocturne2** files to the Grove Village folder.

3. Press the **Windows** key 🪟 to display the Start screen.

4. Type **Media** to display the Apps screen and Search menu, and then click **Windows Media Player** in the search results to start Windows Media Player.

Trouble? If this is the first time you are running Windows Media Player, a dialog box opens before the main program window does, giving you the option to choose Recommended settings or Custom settings. Unless your instructor specifies otherwise, click Recommended settings, and then click the Finish button.

5. If necessary, maximize the window. See Figure 7-36. Your window might contain different music or might not contain any music yet.

Figure 7-36 **Windows Media Player window**

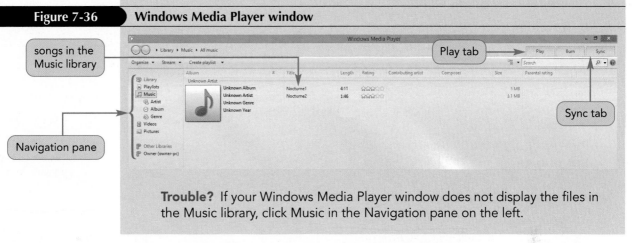

songs in the
Music library

Play tab

Sync tab

Navigation pane

Trouble? If your Windows Media Player window does not display the files in the Music library, click Music in the Navigation pane on the left.

Although Windows Media Player initially displays the songs in the Music library, it monitors the Music library and updates your collection when you add or remove files. (This is a good reason to store your music files in the Music library or its subfolders.) It also adds any music files you play on your computer or the Internet, and music that you rip from a CD or download from an online store.

Using Windows Media Player

To play music in Windows Media Player, double-click a song, an album, or a playlist. While a song is playing, Windows Media Player provides information and controls at the bottom of the window. A progress bar and timer track the progress of the song, and information such as the song title, album title, musician name, and composer name flashes in the lower-left corner of the window as the song plays. You can use the playback controls, which are similar to the controls on a CD player, to play, stop, rewind, fast-forward, mute, or change the volume.

You offer to play the two music files in the Grove Village folder so that Carl can determine whether they are appropriate for the slide show.

As you did earlier, before you perform the following steps, turn down the volume of your computer speakers or use headphones so you do not disturb others in the room. If your computer does not have the hardware necessary to play music, you can still perform the following steps, though you won't be able to hear the music.

To play a song:

1. Locate the **Nocturne1** song, and then double-click it. The song begins to play and playback controls appear at the bottom of the window. See Figure 7-37.

| Figure 7-37 | Playing music in Windows Media Player |

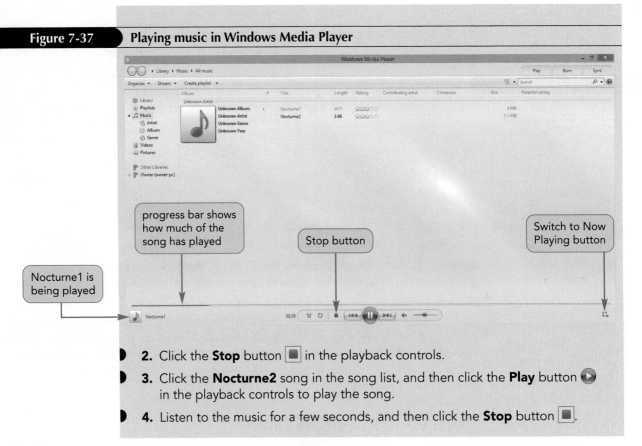

progress bar shows how much of the song has played

Stop button

Switch to Now Playing button

Nocturne1 is being played

2. Click the **Stop** button ■ in the playback controls.

3. Click the **Nocturne2** song in the song list, and then click the **Play** button ▶ in the playback controls to play the song.

4. Listen to the music for a few seconds, and then click the **Stop** button ■.

Carl thinks both of those songs are good options to use in his slide show, but he wants Doug to listen to the songs as well. Doug often listens to a portable player as he walks to work, so Carl wants to sync those songs to Doug's portable player. Then Doug can choose one of the songs for the slide show. You'll show Carl how to add the songs to a new playlist so they are easy to sync.

Creating a Playlist

A playlist contains one or more digital media files and provides a way to organize files that you want to work with as a group. For example, you can create a playlist of lively songs that you play to wake up in the morning, or a playlist of your favorite songs you burn on a CD or transfer to a portable music player so you can take them with you. By default, items in a playlist are played in the order they appear in the list. You can change the order of the items by dragging them within the list, or you can shuffle the items in the list, which means they play in a random order.

REFERENCE

Creating a Playlist

- In Windows Media Player, click the Create playlist button on the toolbar.
- Enter a name for the playlist.
- Drag albums, songs, and other music from the file list to the List pane.
- Click the Save list button.

or

- Make sure the music you want to add to a playlist is stored in the Music library.
- In the Music app, select the songs you want to add to the playlist.
- Click the Add to playlist button on the Apps bar.
- Click the Create playlist button on the Apps bar, and then enter a name to add the selected songs to the new playlist.

You can create two types of playlists in Windows Media Player—regular and auto. A regular playlist does not change unless you add or delete songs or other items in the list. As its name implies, an auto playlist changes automatically according to criteria you specify. For example, you could add any song rated four stars or more to an auto playlist. As Windows Media Player monitors your folders for new songs, it adds any with at least a four-star rating to that auto playlist.

Now that you and Carl have listened to two songs, you'll add these songs to a new regular playlist.

To create a regular playlist:

1. Click the **Play** tab, if necessary, to open the list pane on the right side of the window.

   Trouble? If songs or playlists are already listed in the pane, click the Clear list button at the top of the pane.

2. Drag the **Nocturne1** and **Nocturne2** songs from the song list to the bottom portion of the list pane. Nocturne1 appears in the new playlist.

   Trouble? If a song you added to the playlist begins to play, click the Stop button ■ on the playback controls.

3. Click the **Save list** button at the top of the pane.

4. Type **Pet Slide Show** and then press the **Enter** key. See Figure 7-38.

Figure 7-38   Saved playlist

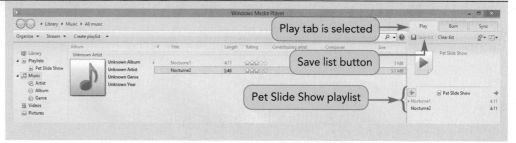

By default, playlists are saved with a .wpl extension in the Playlists folder, which is located in the My Music folder in the Music library.

If you want to change the order of the songs in the playlist, you can drag a song to a new position in the list pane. To play the songs in a playlist in order, right-click the playlist in the Navigation pane and then click Play. To play the songs in random order after you click Play, click the Turn shuffle on button 🔀 in the playback controls.

Next, you can sync the songs in the Pet Slide Show playlist to a portable music device.

Syncing Files to a Portable Device

When you connect a device to your computer for the first time, Windows Media Player selects the sync method that works best for your device, depending on the storage capacity of the device and the size of your library in Windows Media Player. If your portable music device has a storage capacity of more than 4 GB and your entire Media Player library can fit on the device, Windows Media Player offers to sync automatically. If you accept this option, your entire Media Player library is copied to your device. Every time you connect your device to your computer while Windows Media Player is running, Windows updates the contents of the portable music device to match the contents of the Media Player library. If you add songs to the Media Player library, Windows automatically copies the songs to your device the next time you connect it to your computer. If you delete songs from the Media Player library, Windows deletes those songs from your device the next time you connect it to your computer. You can also choose what to sync automatically by specifying the playlists you want to sync.

To perform the following steps, you can use a USB flash drive or a portable music device. If you are not equipped with the proper hardware, read but do not perform the following steps.

To sync files to a portable device:

1. If you are using a portable music device, turn it on and then connect it to your computer. If you are using a USB flash drive, connect it to your computer.

2. In Windows Media Player, click the **Sync** tab to open the Sync tab in the list pane.

3. Click the **Sync 'Pet Slide Show'** link in the list pane. The two songs in the Pet Slide Show playlist appear in the Sync list, and Windows 8 displays how much free space is available on the drive.

4. Click **Start sync** at the top of the pane. A progress bar appears in the Sync tab.

5. When Windows 8 is finished syncing, close Windows Media Player.

Carl gives Doug his portable music player and asks him to listen to the new songs. Doug says that the songs are ideal, and he would like to play both during the slide show. To do so, you can start playing the Pet Slide Show playlist in the Music app, set it to repeat, and then play the pet photos as a slide show in the Photos app.

Playing a Slide Show with Music

The Music app and Windows Media Player can access playlists that you created and saved in the Music library. Both apps let you set a playlist to play through once and then repeat by replaying the songs in the playlist. While the songs are playing, you can use the Photos app to play a slide show of the photos in the Pets folder.

To play a slide show with music:

▶ **1.** In a folder window, navigate to the Playlists folder in the Music library.

▶ **2.** Right-click the **Pet Slide Show** file, point to **Open with**, and then click **Music** to open the playlist in the Music app.

▶ **3.** Right-click the screen to display the Apps bar. See Figure 7-39.

Figure 7-39 Playing a playlist in the Music app

Pet Slide Show is the selected playlist

Apps bar in the Music app

▶ **4.** Click the **Repeat** button to play the songs repeatedly during the slide show.

▶ **5.** Press the **Windows** key ⊞ to redisplay the Start screen. Note that the music continues to play.

▶ **6.** Click the **Photos** tile to open the Photos app, navigate to the Pets folder in the Pictures library, if necessary, and then click the **Pets** folder.

▶ **7.** Display the Apps bar, and then click **Slide show** to display the photos in a slide show while the music continues to play.

▶ **8.** Close all open apps.

Carl can perform the same steps to play the music and slide show on the computer in the clinic waiting room. Now that the slide show is complete, Carl asks you to preview a video he created of the pet photos. He wants to burn the video on a DVD so he can send it to patients who request it. You'll show him how to do so next.

Working with Videos

The Windows 8 Video app is designed to play videos created in popular video formats—including MPEG-4, WMV, and WMA. All of the copyright and other rules that apply to downloading graphics and photos from the Web apply to videos—you need permission from the video owner to download and use a video unless it's in the public domain.

The easiest way to play a video in the Video app is to copy the video file to the Videos library or one of its folders. The Video app displays all of the video files in the Videos library by default, so you will be able to find them easily.

As you saw when you played videos in earlier tutorials, after you begin playing a video file, you can use the playback controls to control the video. Move the mouse to display the playback controls. You can also use the Video app to purchase and download videos and recorded TV from an online store, similar to the way you can purchase and download music. You can use the Search charm on the Charms bar to search for a video by keyword or phrase.

Carl's video is named Grove Village. To prepare to play this video, you need to copy it to a folder in the Videos library.

To copy the Grove Village video to the Videos library:

▶ 1. On the Start screen, click the **Desktop** tile to display the desktop, and then open a folder window that displays the contents of the Windows7\Tutorial folder provided with your Data Files.

▶ 2. Create a new folder in the Public Videos folder named **Pet Videos**, and then copy the **Grove Village** file to the Pet Videos folder.

▶ 3. In the Pet Videos folder, right-click the **Grove Village** file, point to **Open with**, and then click **Video** to start playing the file in the Video app.

   Trouble? If Windows asks you for a user name and password, enter the user name and password you use for your Microsoft account.

   Trouble? If a message appears regarding other apps you can use to play the file, continue with Step 4. The message is just a reminder that will close shortly.

▶ 4. After watching the video for a few seconds, right-click the screen to display the Apps bar, and then click the **Pause** button.

▶ 5. Close the Video app.

Next, you'll show Carl how to burn the Grove Village video to a DVD so he can send it to patients.

Burning a Video onto a DVD

If you want to share videos with others (and have permission to do so), you can burn a video file onto a CD or DVD. To **burn** a file means to use a computer to copy the file to an optical disc, such as a CD or DVD, so you can later play the file on a media player, such as a home theater system. Because video files are often quite large, burning them onto a disc is usually the best way to transfer them to other people. To do so, you need the right kind of drive on your computer and a recordable CD or DVD.

To burn a CD, you must have a rewritable CD drive or a CD burner connected to or installed in your computer. The type of recordable CD you should use depends on the types your CD burner supports and the type of disc you prefer. For instance, you can use either a blank CD-Recordable (CD-R) or CD-Rewritable (CD-RW) disc for burning CDs, though not all CD players can play CD-RW discs.

A DVD can hold much more data than a CD. To burn a DVD, you must have a rewritable DVD drive or a DVD burner connected to or installed in your computer. Many Windows 8 computers come with rewritable DVD drives. Some DVD burners work with a DVD-Recordable (DVD-R or DVD+R) or a DVD-Rewritable (DVD-RW or DVD+RW) disc, while others support only certain ones. Check the information about your DVD drive that came with your computer to learn what your DVD burner can use.

Carl's computer includes a rewritable DVD drive, and you have a recordable DVD. You're ready to burn the Grove Village video onto the DVD.

To perform the following steps, you need a recordable DVD and a rewritable DVD drive on your computer. If you do not have this equipment, read but do not perform the following steps.

To burn a video onto a DVD:

▶ **1.** On the Start screen, click the **Desktop** tile to display the desktop.

▶ **2.** If necessary, open a folder window, and then navigate to the Pet Videos folder in the Videos library.

▶ **3.** Insert a recordable DVD into your DVD drive. When a notification appears, read the notification and then wait until it fades from the screen.

▶ **4.** Click the **Grove Video** file to select it.

▶ **5.** Click the **Share** tab, and then click the **Burn to disc** button in the Send group. The Burn a Disc dialog box opens.

▶ **6.** Click the **With a CD/DVD player** option button, and then click the **Next** button.

▶ **7.** When a folder window opens displaying the contents of the DVD, right-click a blank spot in the folder window, and then click **Burn to disc** on the shortcut menu to open the Burn to Disc dialog box.

▶ **8.** Click the **Next** button to copy the file to the DVD so it can be played on a video player.

▶ **9.** Click the **Finish** button, remove the DVD from the drive, and close all open windows.

You hand the DVD to Carl so he can give it to an interested patient. He can easily burn other DVDs as necessary when patients request them.

Restoring Your Settings

If you are working in a computer lab or on a computer other than your own, complete the steps in this section to restore the original settings on your computer.

To restore your computer:

▶ **1.** Navigate to the **Pictures** library on your computer, and then move the **Pets** folder to the Windows7\Tutorial folder provided with your Data Files.

▶ **2.** Navigate to the **Music** library on your computer, and then move the **Grove Village** folder to the Windows7\Tutorial folder provided with your Data Files.

▶ **3.** Open the **Playlists** folder in the Music library, and then move the **Pet Slide Show** file to the Windows7\Tutorial folder provided with your Data Files.

▶ **4.** Navigate to the **Videos** library on your computer, and then move the **Pet Videos** folder to the Windows7\Tutorial folder provided with your Data Files.

▶ **5.** If you do not want to store copies of the pet photos on your SkyDrive, display the Start screen and then click the **SkyDrive** tile. Open the Public folder, right-click the **Public Pets** folder, and then click **Delete** on the shortcut menu.

REVIEW

Session 7.2 Quick Check

1. Name three tools you can use to view photos as a slide show in Windows 8. *[handwritten: 372]*

2. _OneDrive_ is a Microsoft service that provides online, or cloud, storage space for your files. *[handwritten: use share charm on the charm bar]*

3. If you are viewing a photo in the Photos app, what is the easiest way to share the photo with someone else via email? *[handwritten: 374]*

4. A(n) _playlist_ is a list of media files, such as songs, that you want to play in a specified order. *[handwritten: - 378]*

5. What two apps can you use in Windows 8 to listen to music files stored in the Music library? *[handwritten: Music and W media player]*

6. What does it mean to sync the files in the Windows Media Player library with a portable music device? *[handwritten: 380]*

7. If you are working in the Videos library, how can you quickly play a video file in the Video app? *[handwritten: - 381]*

Review Assignments

See the Starting Data Files section at the beginning of this tutorial for a list of Data Files needed for the Review Assignments.

Grove Village Veterinary Pet Clinic is creating a postcard to mail to patients to remind them about upcoming appointments. Doug Weston wants to design a graphic that includes the Web address and phone number for the clinic. Your goal is to create the postcard shown in Figure 7-40. In addition, Carl Patel is working on a slide show featuring pets other than cats and dogs. He has a few photos and asks you to assemble these into a slide show. He also wants a musical accompaniment to the slide show. Complete the following steps:

Figure 7-40   **Completed postcard**

Courtesy of Booyabazooka, Open Clip Art Library; Rob, Open Clip Art Library; © 2014 Cengage Learning

1. Start Paint, open the **Frame** picture from the Windows7\Review folder provided with your Data Files, and then save it as **Postcard** in the same folder. (*Hint*: Accept that transparency will be lost when you save the image.)

2. Paste the **Paw Print** picture into the Postcard picture, and center it within the frame.

3. Increase the size of the canvas to at least 900 × 500 pixels to create a larger work area. Move the graphic down and to the right so that it is easier to work with.

4. Select white as Color 1 and a dark-green color from the frame graphic as Color 2, the background color. (*Hint*: Remember to use the right mouse button to change Color 2.)

5. Using the Text tool with an Opaque background, create a text box of about 600 × 70 pixels below the frame. Choose Lucida Sans as the font and 36 as the point size. (*Hint*: If necessary, choose another font and font size.) Type **Grove Village Pet Clinic** in the text box.

6. Change Color 1 to the same shade of light green as used in the paw print image.

7. Create another text box of about 600 × 70 pixels. Choose Lucida Sans as the font and 26 as the point size. Type **gcpets.course.com** as the Web address. Press the spacebar twice, and then type **(317) 555-2600** as the phone number.

8. To the right of the frame, draw a dark-green rectangle 620 pixels wide and 115 pixels tall.

9. Move the first line of text to center it in the upper part of the rectangle. Move the second line of text to center it below the first line. Save your work.

10. Change Color 1 and Color 2 to the same shade of light green as used in the paw print image.

11. Use the Rectangle tool to draw a light-green rectangle the same width as the dark-green rectangle and 6 pixels high. Position the light-green rectangle so it is left-aligned with the dark-green rectangle and bottom-aligned with the frame.

12. Paste the **Dog** picture into the Postcard picture, and then position it in the lower-right corner of the graphic, just above the light-green rectangle. Save your work.

13. Change Color 1 to the same light purple used in the dog image. (On some monitors, this shade of light purple appears as gray.)

14. Use the Line tool to draw a 1-pixel vertical line from the top to the bottom of the light-green rectangle slightly to the left of the dog image. (*Hint*: Refer to the figure showing the completed postcard, if necessary.)

15. Fill the left side of the vertical line with light purple. Change Color 2 to white. Save your work.

16. Paste the **Cat** picture into the Postcard picture, and then position it to the left of the dog image.

17. Crop the graphic to remove the white space around the graphic.

18. Compare your graphic to the figure shown at the beginning of the Review Assignments, make any final modifications as necessary, save your work, and then close Paint.

19. Copy the seven pet photos (Animal01–Animal07) from the Windows7\Review folder provided with your Data Files to a new folder in the Pictures library named **GV Clinic**. (*Hint*: Don't copy the Cat, Dog, Frame, Paw Print, and Postcard files.)

20. In the GV Clinic folder window, use a tool on the Picture Tools Manage tab to rotate the Animal05 photo.

21. Crop the Animal01 photo so that the bird is in the middle of the photo by removing about one-third of the photo on the right and one-third on the bottom.

22. Copy the Bugle and Jazz files from the Windows7\Review folder provided with your Data Files to a new folder in the Music library named **Soundtrack**.

23. Create a playlist named **GV Slide Show** consisting of the Bugle and Jazz music (in that order). Start playing the GV Slide Show playlist in an appropriate app.

24. Play a slide show of the photos in the GV Clinic folder. (*Hint*: If necessary, lower the volume of your speakers.)

25. Press the Print Screen key to capture an image of the slide show, and then paste the image in a new Paint or WordPad file. Save the file as **PetShow** in the Windows7\Review folder provided with your Data Files.

26. Move the GV Slide Show playlist file from the Playlists folder in the Music library to the Windows7\Review folder provided with your Data Files.

27. Delete the Soundtrack folder from the Music library.

28. Move the GV Clinic folder from the Pictures library to the Windows7\Review folder provided with your Data Files.

29. Submit the results of the preceding steps to your instructor, either in printed or electronic form, as requested.

Case Problem 1

APPLY

See the Starting Data Files section at the beginning of this tutorial for a list of Data Files needed for this Case Problem.

Adventure Treks   Rosie Keyes owns Adventure Treks in Golden, Colorado, a travel company that organizes ecological and adventure tours for hikers, skiers, and other outdoor enthusiasts. As Rosie's assistant, you help her serve customers, scout locations, and create promotional materials. Rosie asks you to work with two images to develop a logo for the company. She also wants to create a slide show of tour locations. Your goal is to create the logo shown in Figure 7-41. Refer to the figure as you complete the following steps:

Figure 7-41   Completed Adventure Treks logo

Courtesy of Open Clip Art Library

1. Start Paint, open the **Border** picture from the Windows7\Case1 folder provided with your Data Files, and then save it as **Trek Logo** in the same folder.
2. Paste the **Mountains** picture into the Trek Logo picture, and center it within the border.
3. Increase the size of the canvas to at least 900 × 525 pixels to create a larger work area.
4. Select white as Color 1, and then select a bright green color from the mountain image as Color 2, the background color.
5. Using the Text tool with an Opaque background, create a text box of about 634 x 70 pixels below the border. Choose Arial Black as the font and 36 as the point size. Press the spacebar, and then type **Adventure Treks** in the text box.
6. Move the text to right-align it in the rectangle. Save your work.
7. Change Color 2 to white, and then move the green rectangle so it's about 10 pixels below the border graphic. Make sure no part of the green rectangle extends to the right of the border graphic.
8. If necessary, crop the graphic to remove any white space below or to its right.
9. Make any final modifications as necessary, save your work, and then close Paint.
10. Copy the 10 photos of outdoor settings (in other words, all the JPG files) from the Windows7\Case1 folder provided with your Data Files to a new folder in the Pictures library named **Outdoors**.
11. Rotate the Trek09 photo so it appears in the correct orientation.
12. Copy the Rocks and Stream files from the Windows7\Case1 folder provided with your Data Files to a new folder in the Music library named **Sounds**.
13. Create a playlist named **Treks Sounds** consisting of the Rocks and Stream sounds (in that order). Start playing the Treks Sounds playlist in an appropriate app, and set the playlist to repeat.
14. Play a slide show of the photos in the Outdoors folder.
15. Press the Print Screen key to capture an image of the slide show, and then paste the image in a new Paint or WordPad file. Save the file as **AT Show** in the Windows7\Case1 folder provided with your Data Files.
16. Move the Treks Sounds playlist file from the Playlists folder in the Music library to the Windows7\Case1 folder provided with your Data Files.
17. Move the Sounds folder from the Music library to the Windows7\Case1 folder provided with your Data Files.

18. Move the Outdoors folder from the Pictures library to the Windows7\Case1 folder provided with your Data Files.

19. Submit the results of the preceding steps to your instructor, either in printed or electronic form, as requested.

CHALLENGE

Case Problem 2

See the Starting Data Files section at the beginning of this tutorial for a list of Data Files needed for this Case Problem.

Savannah Marina   The Savannah Marina in Savannah, Georgia, rents boats and slips to recreational sailors and boat owners. Todd and Abbie Peckham manage the marina and recently hired you to help them create marketing materials. Your goal is to create the logo shown in Figure 7-42. Todd also asks you to show him how to use Paint to create an image for the marina's Web site and to create a slide show they can make available for download. Complete the following steps.

Figure 7-42   **Completed Savannah Marina logo**

Courtesy of Open Clip Art Library

1. Start Paint, open the **Sailboat** file from the Windows7\Case2 folder provided with your Data Files, and then save it as **Marina** in the same folder. (*Hint*: Accept that transparency will be lost when you save the image.)

2. Increase the size of the canvas to at least 600 × 525 pixels to create a larger work area.

3. Change Color 1 and Color 2 to a shade of pale yellow that appears in the sail. Select the Oval shape tool, and then change the Outline and Fill settings to Solid color.

4. Near the top of the canvas and to the right of the boat, draw a perfect circle about 200 × 200 pixels round with a pale yellow solid outline and a pale yellow solid fill. (*Hint*: Hold down the Shift key as you drag to draw the circle.)

5. Deselect the circle, and then change Color 1 and Color 2 to white.

6. If necessary, move the yellow circle so that its top edge touches the top of the canvas. Save your work.

7. Choose the Transparent selection command, select the boat, and then move the boat to the circle so that the top of the boat is centered in the yellow circle.

8. Change Color 1 to a shade of light blue selected from the boat, and then change Color 2 to a shade of dark red selected from the boat.

9. Below the boat image, create a text box about 350 pixels wide and about 50 pixels tall. Choose an Opaque background and 32-point Book Antiqua for the text. Type **Savannah Marina** in the text box. Make sure the text appears on one line. Center the text within the dark-red rectangle. Save your work.

10. Change Color 2 to white. If necessary, move the dark-red rectangle so it is centered just a few pixels below the boat.

11. Move the entire image so that the left edge of the rectangle touches the left edge of the canvas. (The top edge of the yellow circle should still touch the top edge of the canvas.)

⊕ **Explore** 12. Use the Rectangular selection tool to point to the lower-right corner of the rectangle, and then note its pixel coordinates. Click the File tab on the Paint ribbon, and then click Properties to open the Image Properties dialog box. If the pixel coordinates are different from what you found when using the Rectangular selection tool, enter the pixel coordinates in the appropriate text boxes. Click the OK button.

13. Compare your graphic to the figure shown at the beginning of this Case Problem, and then make any final modifications as necessary. Save your work, and then close Paint.

14. Copy the five boat photos and the Marina graphic from the Windows7\Case2 folder provided with your Data Files to a new folder in the Pictures library named **Savannah**.

15. Crop the Boat4 image to focus more closely on the sailboat.

16. Copy the Waves sound file to a new folder in the Music library named **Ocean Sounds**.

⊕ **Explore** 17. Right-click the Waves sound file and then play the sound using Windows Media Player. Turn repeat on so the sound plays continuously.

18. Play a slide show of the photos in the Savannah folder.

19. Press the Print Screen key to capture an image of the slide show, and then paste the image in a new Paint or WordPad file. Save the file as **Marina Show** in the Windows7\Case2 folder provided with your Data Files.

20. Email the Boat1 photo to your instructor.

⊕ **Explore** 21. Use the Music app to search the online store for classical music related to ships. (*Hint*: Use **classical ships** as the search text.) Select an album and then preview its music. As the music plays, press the Print Screen key to capture an image of the Music app, and then paste the image in a new Paint or WordPad file. Save the file as **Ship Music** in the Windows7\Case2 folder provided with your Data Files.

⊕ **Explore** 22. Use the Video app to search the online store for movies related to boats. Select a movie, explore the movie, and then play the trailer. As the trailer plays, press the Print Screen key to capture an image of the Video app, and then paste the image in a new Paint or WordPad file. Save the file as **Boat Movie** in the Windows7\Case2 folder provided with your Data Files.

23. Move the Savannah folder from the Pictures library to the Windows7\Case2 folder provided with your Data Files.

24. Move the Ocean Sounds folder from the Music library to the Windows7\Case2 folder provided with your Data Files.

25. Submit the results of the preceding steps to your instructor, either in printed or electronic form, as requested.

CHALLENGE

Case Problem 3

See the Starting Data Files section at the beginning of this tutorial for a list of Data Files needed for this Case Problem.

Fleur de Lis   Ingrid Whitcomb is the owner and principal designer for Fleur de Lis, a florist shop in Portland, Oregon. Ingrid specializes in using native plants in distinctive designs for her clients, who typically hire her for weddings and other memorable occasions. Ingrid recently hired you as a part-time sales associate at the shop. When she learned that you have some graphic design training, she asked you to help her design a graphic she can use on her Web site to attract interest and new business. Your goal is to create the graphic shown in Figure 7-43. She also wants you to develop a slide show high-lighting floral bouquets and arrangements in natural settings. Complete the following steps:

Figure 7-43   **Fleur de Lis graphic**

Courtesy of Dr. Thomas G. Barnes, U.S. Fish and Wildlife Service

1. Start Paint, open the **Flower** picture from the Windows7\Case3 folder provided with your Data Files, and then save it as **Fleur de Lis** in the same folder.
2. Increase the width of the canvas to at least 900 pixels to create a larger work area.
⊕ **Explore**   3. Select the image only (not the white background), and then rotate the image to the right by 90 degrees. (*Hint*: Click the Rotate button in the Image group, and then click Rotate right 90°.) If necessary, drag the selected image so the entire image appears on the canvas.
4. Change Color 1 to a shade of white in a flower petal.
5. Change Color 2 to the same shade of black as in the background of the image.
6. Crop the image so that the large green leaf nearly touches the left edge of the canvas and the white flower is near the top of the canvas.

⊕ **Explore** 7. Change the image properties to a width of **725** and a height of **459**. (*Hint*: Click the File menu, and then click Properties to open the Image Properties dialog box.) Fill any white background with Color 2. Save your work.

8. In a blank spot in the lower-right corner of the image, create a text box of about 250 × 40 pixels. Select 24-point Copperplate Gothic Light for the text. Type **Fleur de Lis** in the text box.

9. Move the text to the left to leave about 1.5 inches between the end of the text and the right edge of the image. Save your work.

10. Copy the lower-right petal in the flower image to a blank area in the lower-right corner of the image, next to the text. When you select the petal, you will probably include some pixels from another part of the flower.

⊕ **Explore** 11. In the copy of the petal, erase the unnecessary pixels by clicking the Eraser tool, clicking the smallest size in the Size button list, and then clicking the pixels you want to erase from the leaf. Increase the magnification to work effectively. Save your work when you finish.

12. Compare your graphic to the figure shown at the beginning of this Case Problem, and then make any final modifications as necessary. Save your work, and then close Paint.

13. Copy the Fleur de Lis graphic and the five bouquet photos from the Windows7\Case3 folder provided with your Data Files to a new folder in the Pictures library named **Flowers**. Copy the sound files to a new folder in the Music library named **Nature**.

14. Rotate the Bouquet3 photo.

15. Navigate to the Nature folder in your Music library. Right-click a sound file, point to Open with, and then click Windows Media Player. Click the Switch to Library button, if necessary, to open the library. Add the Bird and Crickets sounds to a new playlist named **Natural Sounds**.

⊕ **Explore** 16. Start playing the Natural Sounds playlist, and then set the playlist to repeat so the sounds play continuously.

17. Play a slide show of the photos in the Flowers folder.

18. Press the Print Screen key to capture an image of the slide show window, and then paste the image in a new Paint or WordPad file. Save the file as **Fleur** in the Windows7\Case3 folder provided with your Data Files.

19. Open the **Playlists folder** in the Music library, and then move the Natural Sounds file to the Windows7\Case3 folder provided with your Data Files.

20. Move the Nature folder from the Music library to the Windows7\Case3 folder provided with your Data Files.

21. Move the Flowers folder from the Pictures library to the Windows7\Case3 folder provided with your Data Files.

22. Submit the results of the preceding steps to your instructor, either in printed or electronic form, as requested.

CREATE

Case Problem 4

Data Files needed for this Case Problem: Beads.jpg and Sculpture.jpg

Woodside Antiques Gayle Snyder is the manager of Woodside Antiques in Scranton, Pennsylvania. Gayle hired you as her assistant to provide marketing and graphic design services to the store. She asks you to design a logo she can use in print and online. Your goal is to create the logo shown in Figure 7-44. Refer to the figure as you complete the following steps:

Figure 7-44 Creating a logo for Woodside Antiques

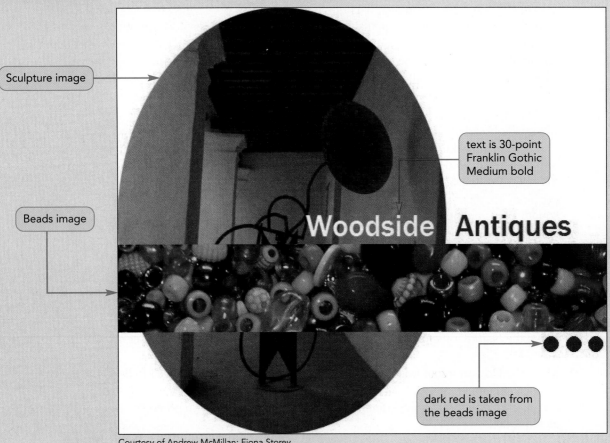

Courtesy of Andrew McMillan; Fiona Storey

1. Create a logo for Woodside Antiques using the figure and the following information as guides:
   - The oval image is named Sculpture and is stored in the Windows7\Case4 folder provided with your Data Files.
   - The beads image is named Beads and is stored in the Windows7\Case4 folder provided with your Data Files.
   - The text uses 30-point Franklin Gothic Medium bold font.
   - The word *Woodside* uses a white foreground color and a transparent background.
   - The word *Antiques* uses a dark-red foreground color taken from the beads image.
   - The three circles on the right side of the image use the same shade of dark red as the word *Antiques*.

2. Save the graphic as **Woodside** in the Windows7\Case4 folder provided with your Data Files.

3. Be sure to save your work after making a significant change to the graphic.

4. Submit the results of the preceding steps to your instructor, either in printed or electronic form, as requested.

OBJECTIVES

Session 8.1
- Manage mobile computing devices
- Select and modify power plans
- Present information to an audience
- Explore network concepts
- Manage network connections

Session 8.2
- Set up and use a homegroup
- Access shared network folders
- Synchronize desktop settings
- Allow remote access to your computer

Connecting to Networks with Mobile Computing

Accessing Network Resources

WINDOWS

Case | *Virginia Business Innovation Center*

Phil Mendoza is the director of the Virginia Business Innovation Center (VBIC), an agency in Richmond, Virginia, that provides assistance to new and growing businesses in the state. VBIC helps people launch businesses and apply for start-up funding, and then set up accounting, marketing, and sales processes. You have been working for VBIC as a project assistant for a few months, specializing in helping clients upgrade to Microsoft Windows 8. Phil is preparing to configure a wireless network for Visual Impact, a graphics design firm in Newport News, Virginia, and he asks you to help him. Phil knows how to perform networking tasks in earlier versions of Windows, but not in Windows 8. Because Phil often works on his notebook when he travels around the state to visit businesses, he also asks you to adjust mobility settings on his computer so he can use it while traveling without worrying about losing power or disturbing his travel companions.

In this tutorial, you will explore mobile computing, including maintaining power and accessing other computing resources. You will also examine network concepts and learn how to connect two or more computers in a network, and then use the network to share files, folders, and resources.

STARTING DATA FILES

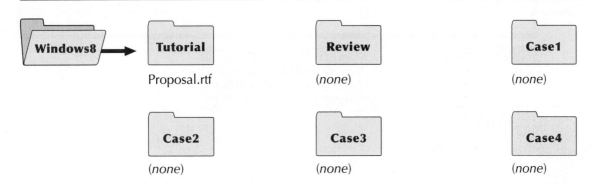

Windows8 →	Tutorial	Review	Case1
	Proposal.rtf	(*none*)	(*none*)
	Case2	Case3	Case4
	(*none*)	(*none*)	(*none*)

Session 8.1 Visual Overview:

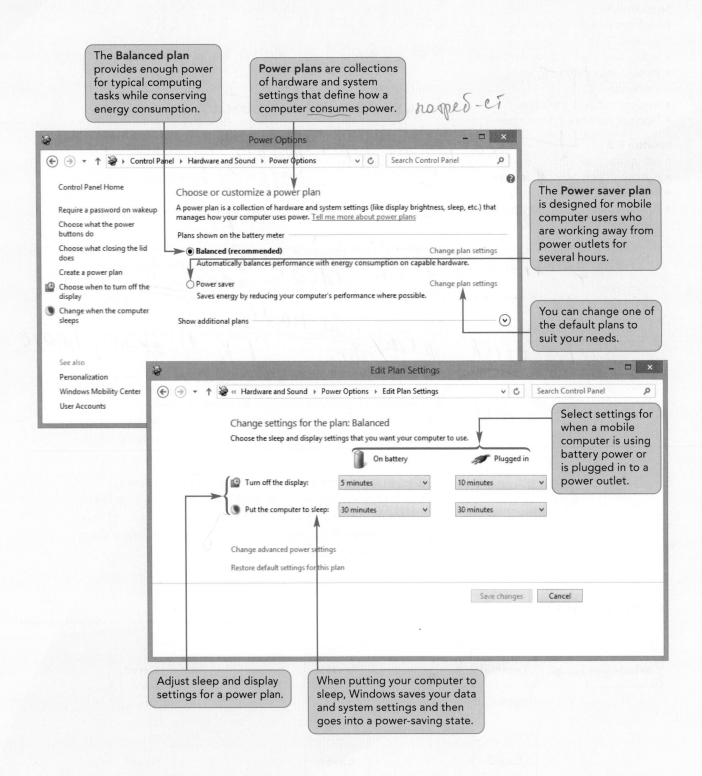

The **Balanced plan** provides enough power for typical computing tasks while conserving energy consumption.

Power plans are collections of hardware and system settings that define how a computer consumes power.

The **Power saver plan** is designed for mobile computer users who are working away from power outlets for several hours.

You can change one of the default plans to suit your needs.

Select settings for when a mobile computer is using battery power or is plugged in to a power outlet.

Adjust sleep and display settings for a power plan.

When putting your computer to sleep, Windows saves your data and system settings and then goes into a power-saving state.

Windows Mobility Center

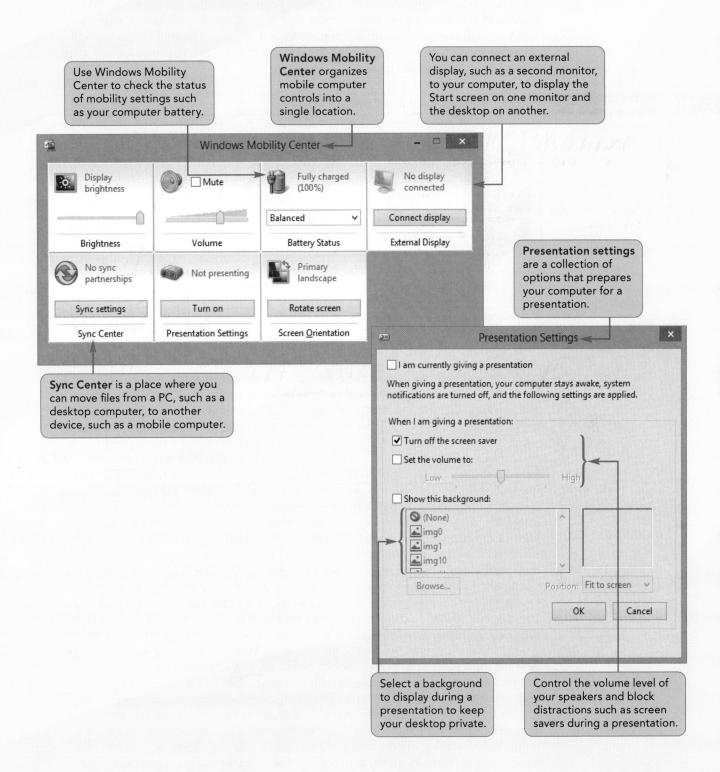

Use Windows Mobility Center to check the status of mobility settings such as your computer battery.

Windows Mobility Center organizes mobile computer controls into a single location.

You can connect an external display, such as a second monitor, to your computer, to display the Start screen on one monitor and the desktop on another.

Presentation settings are a collection of options that prepares your computer for a presentation.

Sync Center is a place where you can move files from a PC, such as a desktop computer, to another device, such as a mobile computer.

Select a background to display during a presentation to keep your desktop private.

Control the volume level of your speakers and block distractions such as screen savers during a presentation.

Managing Mobile Computing Devices

A **mobile computer**, or a **mobile personal computer (PC)**, is a mobile computing device you can easily carry, such as a laptop, notebook, or tablet PC. Currently, more people are buying mobile PCs, preferring their portability and flexibility, than desktop PCs. Although a desktop PC must always be plugged into a power source and uses cables to connect most of its components and devices, a mobile PC contains all of its necessary parts in a single package, including a display screen, processor, keyboard, and pointing device. See Figure 8-1.

Figure 8-1   **Comparing desktop and mobile PCs**

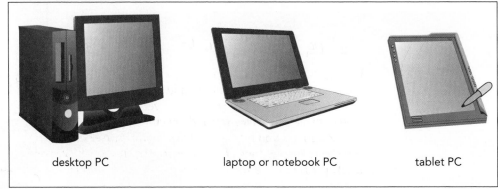

| desktop PC | laptop or notebook PC | tablet PC |

© 2014 Cengage Learning

The terms **notebook computer** and **laptop computer** are interchangeable, although *laptop* is the older term and *notebook* is sometimes associated with a smaller, lighter computer. Both refer to mobile computers that are smaller than the average briefcase and light enough to carry comfortably. A notebook or laptop has a flat-screen display and keyboard that fold together, and a battery pack that provides power for a few hours so that you don't have to plug the device into a wall outlet. A special type of notebook computer called a **netbook** is a mobile computer used primarily to access the Internet and email services. A **tablet PC**, or **tablet** for short, is smaller than a notebook or laptop and has a touchscreen and sometimes a pointing device, such as a stylus. With most tablets today, you can use your fingertip to make selections and enter information instead of using a keyboard or a pointing device.

Mobile computers are just as powerful as desktop computers; but more importantly, they let you take your computer almost anywhere, including while traveling and meeting with others. However, the portability of mobile computers introduces two problems that desktop computers typically do not have: managing power and keeping your files synchronized. When you're using a notebook computer while traveling, for example, you need a way to preserve battery power so you don't lose data or have to shut down unexpectedly. If you do some of your work on a mobile computer, such as at a client meeting, and other work at a desktop computer, especially one connected to a network, you need a way to update the files stored on your desktop computer or network with the work you saved on your mobile computer, and vice versa.

Windows 8 solves these problems with Windows Mobility Center, power plans, and sync settings. Windows Mobility Center organizes mobile computer controls in a single location. These controls let you view and adjust the settings you use most often on a mobile computer, including the screen brightness, speaker volume, and battery status. While working in Windows Mobility Center, you can also select a power plan, a collection of hardware and system settings that define how a computer consumes power. For example, you can choose a plan designed to minimize power consumption, maximize system performance, or strike a balance between the two. If you work on more than one computer, you can access Sync Center from Windows Mobility Center to move files from a PC, such as a notebook computer, to another device, such as a desktop computer, network computer, tablet, portable music player, digital camera, or mobile phone. By synchronizing the files, Sync Center helps you maintain consistency among two or more versions of the same file stored in different locations, so you don't use an out-of-date file on a portable device, for example, when you have a more current version on your desktop PC. Besides files, you can sync settings such as the desktop theme, File Explorer preferences, and browser and app settings. By using a Microsoft account and SkyDrive, you can also sync files stored in more than one location.

Using Windows Mobility Center

Windows Mobility Center provides a control panel for managing a mobile computer. Although hardware vendors can add and change features in Windows Mobility Center, by default Windows 8 lets you adjust power settings such as the brightness of the computer screen, the speaker volume, and the current power-saving scheme. Windows Mobility Center also lets you manage settings you often need when you are working away from your desk, such as those for synchronizing files, using an external display, and controlling what appears on the screen when you give a presentation. See Figure 8-2.

| Figure 8-2 | Windows Mobility Center |

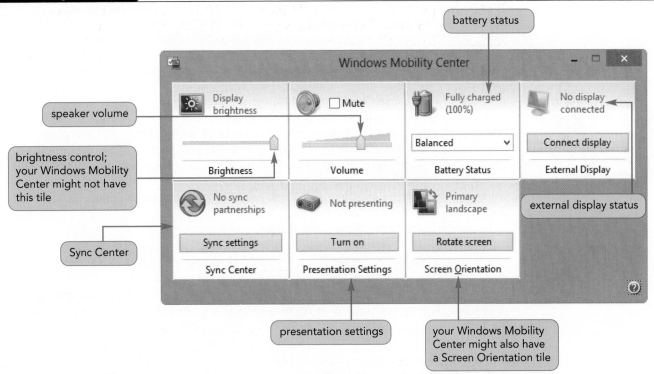

Each control in Windows Mobility Center is represented by a tile. If your computer includes hardware that controls display brightness, your Windows Mobility Center might not include the Brightness tile. Windows Mobility Center typically includes a Screen Orientation tile for tablet PCs. Figure 8-3 describes the purpose of each tile.

Figure 8-3   Settings in Windows Mobility Center

Tile	Icon	Description
Brightness		Dim or increase the brightness of your screen.
Volume		Use the slider to control the volume of the computer's speakers or mute the speakers to turn off the sound completely.
Battery Status		Select a power scheme that suits how you are working with your computer.
External Display		Connect your computer to another monitor or projector.
Sync Center		Open Sync Center to identify devices containing files to synchronize and then exchange information.
Presentation Settings		Control what appears on a projector when your computer is connected to one.
Screen Orientation		Set the screen orientation on a tablet PC to portrait or landscape.

© 2014 Cengage Learning

Setting Speaker Volume

You can set the speaker volume in three ways: using the Volume tile in Windows Mobility Center, using the speaker icon in the notification area of the taskbar, and using the speaker icon on the Settings menu. In any of these cases, you drag a slider to increase or decrease the volume. As you drag, a ScreenTip displays the current volume setting, which ranges from a low of 0 to a high of 100. When you stop dragging, Windows plays a sound at the current volume so you can hear how loud or soft it is. You can also use any of these methods to mute sound, which effectively turns off the speakers. You use the same controls to turn the sound back on.

As you help Phil prepare for the trip to the Visual Impact offices in Newport News, Phil reminds you that he wants to work on his notebook during the drive. He is planning to review the presentation he will give to Visual Impact staff. Because the presentation includes audio, he wants to turn off the speakers on his notebook during the trip so that the presentation does not distract anyone else. You'll show Phil how to test the volume of the speakers and then mute them using Windows Mobility Center. Note the original volume setting so you can restore it later.

To perform most of the steps in this session, you must be working on a mobile computing device; or if instructed to do so, you can use a desktop computer on which Windows Mobility Center has been enabled—a process that involves changing Windows registry settings and is beyond the scope of this tutorial (check with your instructor or technical support person). If you are not working on a mobile computing device or a desktop computer with Windows Mobility Center, read but do not perform the steps.

To open Windows Mobility Center and adjust the speaker volume:

1. On the Start screen, type **Control Panel** to display the Search menu and Apps screen, and then click **Control Panel** in the search results to open the Control Panel window.

2. Click **Hardware and Sound** to open the Hardware and Sound window, and then click **Windows Mobility Center** to open Windows Mobility Center. Minimize the Hardware and Sound window.

> **Trouble?** If your Control Panel window opens to Large icons view or Small icons view, click the View by button, click Category, and then repeat Step 2.
>
> **3.** To test the speaker volume, drag the **Volume** slider to **30**. Windows plays a sound at that volume.
>
>   **Trouble?** If your speakers are already set to 30, drag the Volume slider to 40.
>
> **4.** Click the **Mute** check box to insert a check mark. The Volume tile changes to indicate that Windows has turned the speakers off. The Volume icon in the notification area of the taskbar also changes to indicate the Mute setting.

Now that you've shown Phil how to control the volume of his notebook speakers, you'll demonstrate how to manage battery power with power plans.

Selecting a Power Plan

One advantage of mobile computers over desktop computers is mobile computers get the power they need from a battery, which is installed within the computer case. However, even with recent improvements in battery cell technology, you can use a mobile computer powered by a battery for only a limited time before you need to recharge the battery. To help you manage your mobile computer's power, you can track the status of the battery charge in Windows Mobility Center, in the status box that appears when you display the Charms bar, and in the notification area of the taskbar. All three places display a battery meter icon that shows how much charge remains in the battery. See Figure 8-4.

Figure 8-4	Battery status

Although a battery meter icon always appears on the taskbar of a mobile computer, it can also appear on a desktop computer that is plugged into an uninterruptible power supply (UPS) or other short-term battery device. If your computer has more than one battery, you can click the battery meter icon in the notification area of the taskbar to display the charge remaining on one battery, click it again to see the charge remaining on the second battery, and so on. Point to the battery meter icon to see the combined charge.

You can also point to the battery meter icon to display the amount of time and percentage of battery power remaining. The appearance of the battery meter icon changes to display the current state of the battery so that you can see how much charge remains even when you are not pointing to the icon. When the battery charge is higher than 25 percent, the battery image in the icon is completely or mostly white. When the battery charge reaches 25 percent, a yellow warning sign appears on the icon. When the charge is 10 percent or lower, a critical sign appears and Windows displays a notification so you can recharge the battery. See Figure 8-5.

Figure 8-5 **Changes in the battery meter icon**

your mobile PC is plugged in and the battery is charging	battery is fully charged	your mobile PC is running on battery power	battery charge is low	battery charge is critical

© 2014 Cengage Learning

Besides displaying the percentage of charge remaining in the battery, the battery meter icon and the Battery Status tile in Windows Mobility Center display your current power plan. As defined in the Session 8.1 Visual Overview, a power plan is a collection of hardware and system settings that manages how your computer uses and conserves power. To match how you are using your mobile computer with how it consumes energy, you select a power plan. Windows 8 provides three default plans that let you save energy, maximize system performance, or balance energy conservation with system performance. The three default plans are called Balanced, Power saver, and **High performance**, and are described in Figure 8-6. Some computer manufacturers set up additional power plans, so your computer might have different plans.

Figure 8-6 **Default power plans**

Power Plan	Description
Balanced	Balances energy consumption and system performance by adjusting your computer's processor speed to match your activity
Power saver	Saves power on your mobile computer by reducing system performance and extending battery life
High performance	Provides the highest level of performance on your mobile computer but consumes the most energy

© 2014 Cengage Learning

You can select a power plan by clicking the Battery Status button arrow in Windows Mobility Center, or by clicking the battery meter icon in the notification area of the taskbar and then clicking a power plan option button. (You can also select Power Options in the Hardware and Sound category of the Control Panel.) Most mobile computers include the kind of hardware Windows 8 expects to support power management settings. However, if your computer does not have the proper kind of hardware or if Windows cannot identify it, the Battery Status button arrow or battery meter icon menu displays only the plans your computer supports.

REFERENCE

Selecting a Power Plan

- Open Windows Mobility Center.
- Click the Battery Status button arrow, and then click a power plan.

or

- Click the battery meter icon in the notification area of the taskbar.
- Click a power plan option button.

Because Phil will have to run his laptop computer on battery power during the trip to Newport News, you show him how to monitor his power consumption by pointing to the battery meter icon in the notification area of the taskbar. Next, you'll show him how to change his power plan to Power saver, which is designed for mobile computer users who are working away from power outlets for several hours. Note your original settings so you can restore them later.

To perform the following steps, you must be working on a PC with a battery power source, such as a notebook. If you are not working on such a computer, read but do not perform the steps.

To change the power plan:

1. In Windows Mobility Center, click the **Battery Status button arrow**, and then click **Power saver**.

   Trouble? If your Battery Status is already set to Power saver, skip Step 1.

2. Minimize the Windows Mobility Center window.

To extend battery life, the Power saver plan slows system performance (which you might notice only when you are performing a power-intensive task, such as editing a video) and lowers the brightness of the display.

INSIGHT

Choosing a Power Plan

When working with computers that are connected to a battery, choose a battery plan that best fits your current activities to conserve battery power and to save energy in general. If you are engaging in activities that don't require a lot of power, such as reading email messages or listening to music, switch to the Power saver plan. If you need a lot of computing power, such as when you are working with complex spreadsheets or creating movies, use the High performance plan. If you are performing a variety of tasks, select the Balanced power plan so that the processor can run at full speed when you are playing a game or watching a video, but slow down to save power when you are checking your email.

Phil thinks the Power saver plan is perfect for conserving the battery charge while he's traveling. He can then change to the Balanced plan when he arrives in Newport News, though he wants to fine-tune that plan to suit his needs. During his presentation, he wants to use power settings that are not offered in any of the default plans, so you'll show him how to modify a default plan.

Customizing Power Options

If the default power plans provided by Windows 8 or your computer manufacturer do not address your power needs, you can change one of the default plans. All of the plans specify how long the computer can be idle before Windows turns off the display and how long to wait before Windows puts the computer to sleep when you are using battery power or a wall outlet. When putting your computer to sleep, Windows saves your data and system settings in temporary memory and then suspends operations as it goes into a power-saving state. During sleep, the screen is blank and the computer does not perform any activities, which conserves power. In fact, while a mobile computer is asleep, it typically uses 1 to 2 percent of battery power per hour, which is a fraction of what it uses when running on full power. When you wake a computer by moving the mouse or pressing a key, for example, Windows displays the Start screen or desktop in its presleep state, including open windows and running programs.

Besides changing sleep settings and displaying turn-off times for each default power plan, you can specify advanced settings such as whether to hibernate and how long to wait before hibernating. **Hibernation** is a power-saving state that saves your work to your hard disk, puts your computer into a low-power state, and then turns off your computer. Of the three power-saving states in Windows 8, hibernation uses the least amount of power. Because the sleep states require some power, Windows automatically puts a mobile computer into hibernation after a specified period of time. Windows also puts a mobile PC into hibernation when the battery charge is critically low. If your computer does not hibernate by default, you can enable hibernation using the power options, which you work with shortly.

Hybrid sleep is an alternative to sleep designed for desktop computers. As its name suggests, hybrid sleep is a combination of sleep and hibernation. Windows saves your open documents and programs to temporary memory and to your hard disk, and then goes into a low-power state without turning off the power. You resume from hybrid sleep in the same way and almost as quickly as from standard sleep. The advantage of hybrid sleep is that if a power failure occurs while your computer is asleep, Windows can restore your documents because it saved them to your hard disk. If you turn on hybrid sleep and click the Sleep option on the Power button menu, Windows puts your computer into hybrid sleep instead of standard sleep.

Windows 8 also has a setting called **hybrid boot**, or fast startup, which starts a computer quickly after it's been shut down. You can manage the fast startup and other shutdown settings, which include sleep, hibernate, and lock, using the System Settings window. By default, the lock screen appears after you restore your computer from sleep or hibernation. You can use the System Settings window to show or hide the lock screen after any type of shutdown.

PROSKILLS

Decision Making: Choosing a Power-Saving State

Sleep, hybrid sleep, and hibernation are three power-saving states Windows uses to conserve power on mobile and desktop computers. Selecting the right option for your computer and your usage style can help you work more efficiently. Keep the following guidelines in mind when choosing a power-saving state:

- Sleep—If you do not plan to use your computer for several hours, Microsoft recommends putting it to sleep rather than turning it off. Sleep is preferable to turning off your computer because when you're ready to use your computer again, it wakes quickly so you can resume your work where you left it. If you put a computer to sleep yourself, be sure to save your data first so you don't lose it in case of a power failure. Even if you let Windows put your computer to sleep after a specified amount of idle time, standard sleep is the best power-saving state for average computing because it resumes operations faster than hybrid sleep or hibernation.
- Hibernation—When you are finished working and know you won't use your mobile computer for up to a day, and that you won't have a chance to recharge the battery on a mobile computer during that time, put the computer into hibernation yourself. Otherwise, you can generally let Windows determine when to use hibernation. If you don't plan to use the computer for more than a day, you save wear and tear on your electronic components and conserve energy by turning the computer off. Hibernation is safer than sleep, but slower to return to a full-power state.
- Hybrid sleep—If you are concerned that you might lose power while your desktop computer is asleep, such as during electrical storms, turn on hybrid sleep so that Windows saves your data on the hard disk before it puts your computer to sleep. Using hybrid sleep, your computer quickly resumes running and avoids the risk of losing data.

Not all computers are set to display Sleep or Hibernate on the **Power menu**, which is the list of shutdown options that appears when you click the Power button on the Settings menu. You can use the System Settings window to include Sleep and Hibernate on the Power menu. Some computers can use one of these shutdown options but not both, so your System Settings window might display only one of these power-saving options.

Phil wants to make sure that the fast startup, sleep, hibernate, and lock settings are enabled on his mobile computer because each option is useful to him depending on his work environment.

To turn on all shutdown settings:

1. Display the Hardware and Sound window, and then click **Power Options**. The Power Options window opens. See Figure 8-7.

TIP

You can also open the Power Options window by clicking the battery meter icon in the notification area of the taskbar and then clicking More power options.

Figure 8-7 Power Options window

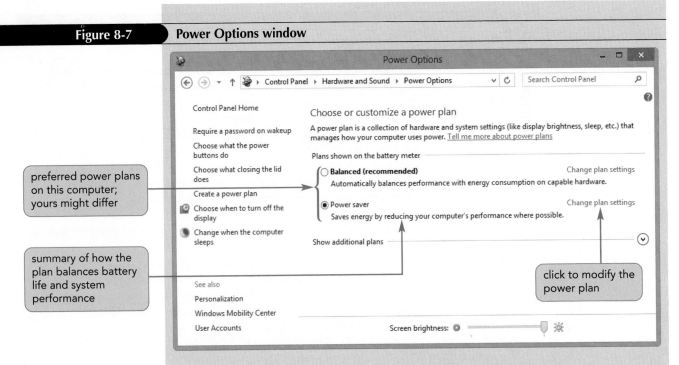

preferred power plans on this computer; yours might differ

summary of how the plan balances battery life and system performance

click to modify the power plan

This window lists power plans and summarizes how each plan balances battery life with system performance.

2. Click **Choose what the power buttons do** in the left pane to open the System Settings window.

   Trouble? If the left pane displays a link titled "Choose what the power button does," click that link instead.

3. If some options are inactive (gray), click the **Change settings that are currently unavailable** link to activate the options.

4. Scroll down to display the Shutdown settings section, if necessary. See Figure 8-8. Your settings might differ.

| Figure 8-8 | System Settings window |

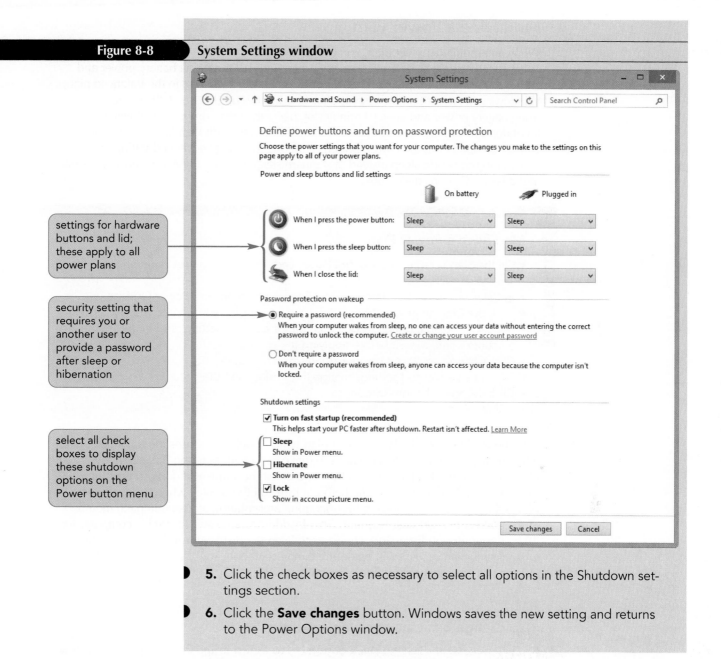

settings for hardware buttons and lid; these apply to all power plans

security setting that requires you or another user to provide a password after sleep or hibernation

select all check boxes to display these shutdown options on the Power button menu

5. Click the check boxes as necessary to select all options in the Shutdown settings section.

6. Click the **Save changes** button. Windows saves the new setting and returns to the Power Options window.

Now when Phil clicks the Power button on the Settings menu, Sleep and Hibernate will be listed along with Shutdown and Restart. Note that the System Settings window also determines the settings for the hardware power buttons (one or more buttons included on your computer case) and other items for all power plans. You work with these settings later in this session. To select power settings that affect only one power plan, which is what you want to do for Phil, you modify the power plan.

Modifying a Power Plan

When you modify a power plan, you can adjust up to two basic settings and dozens of advanced settings that apply when your computer is running on battery power and when your computer is plugged into a power outlet. For example, in the Balanced plan, Windows is set to turn off the display after five minutes of idle time if the computer is using battery power and after 10 minutes of inactivity if the computer is plugged into an outlet. You can increase or decrease these times in the Edit Plan Settings window, which you open from the Power Options window. To change advanced settings, such as whether to use hybrid sleep instead of standard sleep, you use the Advanced settings tab in the Power Options dialog box.

REFERENCE

Modifying a Power Plan

- On the Start screen, type Control Panel, and then click Control Panel on the Apps screen.
- In Category view, click Hardware and Sound, and then click Power Options.
- Click the Change plan settings link for the power plan you want to modify.
- For each available option, click its button for a power setting, and then click the amount of time to wait before applying the setting.
- Click Change advanced power settings.
- Expand an advanced setting, change the setting, and then click the OK button.
- Click the Save changes button.

Although Phil uses the Power saver plan while traveling, he uses the Balanced plan when he meets with clients. He wants to make two changes to the Balanced power plan so he can work effectively at client sites. First, he wants Windows to wait for more than 10 minutes of idle time before it turns off the display when his computer is plugged in. For example, during his upcoming presentation at Visual Impact, members of the audience might raise questions that lead him to step away from his computer for 20 to 30 minutes of discussion. He wants to keep the display turned on for 30 minutes when it's plugged in, as it will be during the presentation. You'll show Phil how to change this basic setting for the Balanced power plan.

To change basic power plan settings:

1. If necessary, click the **Back** button ⊖ to return to the Power Options window.

2. Click the **Change plan settings** link for the Balanced power plan. The Edit Plan Settings window opens for the Balanced plan. See Figure 8-9. Your settings might differ. If you are using a desktop computer, your options might also differ.

Figure 8-9   Edit Plan Settings window

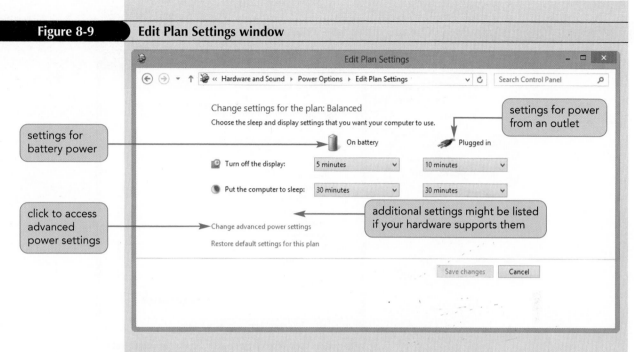

settings for battery power

settings for power from an outlet

click to access advanced power settings

additional settings might be listed if your hardware supports them

3. For the Turn off the display setting, click the **button** in the Plugged in column, and then click **30 minutes**.

Trouble? If you are working on a desktop computer, the window probably includes only one column of settings. Click the button for the Turn off the display setting, and then click 30 minutes.

4. Click the **Save changes** button. Windows saves the new setting and returns to the Power Options window.

You can change the other basic power plan settings the same way—click a button for the Turn off the display or the Put the computer to sleep setting while on battery or plugged in, and then select an amount of idle time Windows should wait before activating that setting. You can turn off the setting by selecting Never. For example, if you do not want Windows to put the computer to sleep when it's plugged in, click the button in the Plugged in column for the Put the computer to sleep setting, and then click Never. However, you might lose data if you prevent a mobile computer from sleeping or hibernating and the battery runs out of power.

Next, you'll show Phil how to set multimedia power settings. He occasionally shows videos during client visits. Playing videos can consume a lot of power, so Phil typically plugs his notebook into a power source when he shows videos. In that case, he can use as much power as necessary to optimize video quality. When he plays videos on battery power using the Balanced plan, he is typically just quickly reviewing the video himself, so he can optimize power rather than quality when using battery power. To select these multimedia power settings, you need to change an advanced power option.

To change advanced power plan settings:

1. In the Power Options window, click the **Change plan settings** link for the Balanced power plan to open the Edit Plan Settings window again.

2. Click the **Change advanced power settings** link to open the Power Options dialog box. See Figure 8-10.

Figure 8-10   Power Options dialog box

click to change the
advanced settings for a
different power plan

click to expand a setting

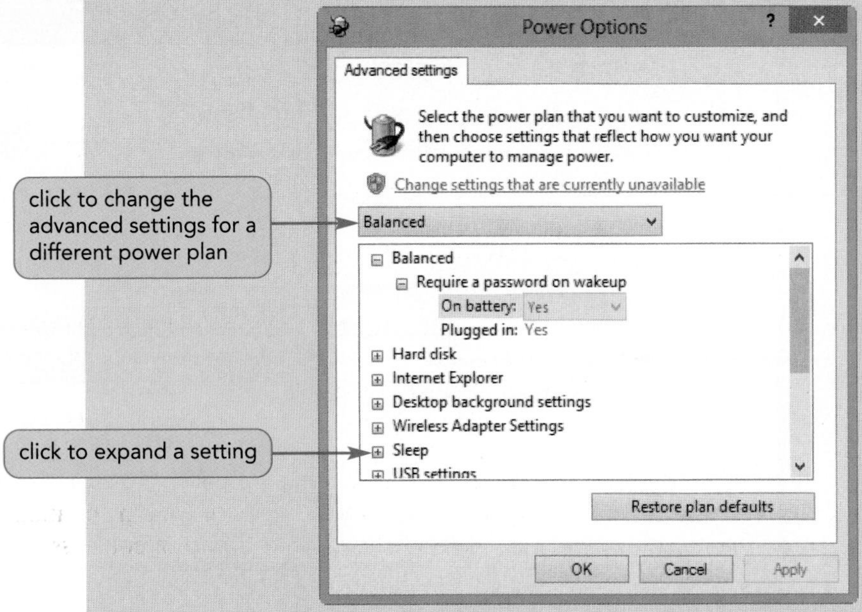

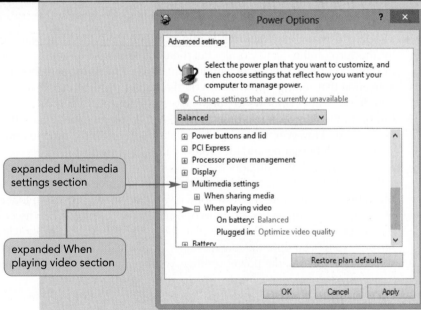

3. Scroll down, click the **expand** button ⊞ for the Multimedia settings option, and then click the **expand** button ⊞ for the When playing video setting. See Figure 8-11. The Plugged in option is already using the setting Phil wants (Optimize video quality), so you only need to change the On battery option.

Figure 8-11   Specifying Multimedia settings

expanded Multimedia
settings section

expanded When
playing video section

4. In the When playing video section, click **On battery**, click the **Balanced** button, and then click **Optimize power savings**.

5. Click the **OK** button to close the Power Options dialog box.

6. Click the **Back** button ⊖ to return to the Power Options window.

You've changed basic and advanced settings in Phil's Balanced power plan. Next, you'll show him how to change other power options.

Selecting Other Power Options

Besides using power plans, you can control other power settings, such as what Windows should do when you press a hardware power button or close the lid on your mobile PC. You can apply the following settings to all of your power plans or only to a specific plan.

- Define power button and lid settings. Recall that by default, Windows puts a mobile computer to sleep when you press a hardware power button or close the lid. It also puts the computer to sleep when you press the hardware sleep button (if your computer has one). You can change the power button, sleep button, and lid settings for all power plans to hibernate, shut down, or do nothing when your computer is running on battery power or is plugged in.
- Require a password on wakeup. If you sign in to your computer by providing a password, Windows locks your computer for security when it sleeps and requires that password to unlock the computer when it wakes from sleep. This is especially helpful if you need to protect confidential information on your computer. However, if you're the only one who uses your computer and you use it at home or another private place, you can change this setting if you don't want to enter a password every time your computer wakes.

Phil is in the habit of using the Sleep command on the Power button menu to put his notebook computer to sleep and likes having the computer go to sleep when he closes the lid. However, if his computer is running on battery power, he wants to save the battery charge by having the computer hibernate and eventually turn off when he presses the hardware power button on the computer case. In addition, although he wants to maintain password protection during the trip to Newport News, he wants to know how to turn off the password protection on wake-up setting so he doesn't need to provide the password when he works from home. You'll show Phil how to change the power button and password protection on wake-up settings. Because he wants these settings to apply no matter which power plan he is using, you'll use the System Settings window to make these selections so they apply system-wide.

To change power options:

▶ **1.** In the Power Options window, click **Choose what the power buttons do** in the left pane. The System Settings window opens.

 Trouble? If the left pane displays a link titled "Choose what the power button does," click that link instead.

▶ **2.** For the When I press the power button setting, click the **button** in the On battery column, and then click **Hibernate**.

 Trouble? If you are using a desktop computer, your window does not have two columns of buttons. Click the button for the When I press the power button setting, and then click Hibernate.

▶ **3.** Click the **Change settings that are currently unavailable** link, if necessary, to make the Password protection on wakeup settings available.

 Trouble? If a dialog box opens requesting an administrator password or your permission to continue, enter the password and then click the Yes button.

▶ **4.** Click the **Don't require a password** option button. This means that when your computer wakes from sleep, it is unlocked and anyone can access your data and settings.

TIP

If you don't have a password, you can click the Create or change your user account password link to create one.

5. Click the **Require a password (recommended)** option button. This means that when your computer wakes from sleep, it is locked and you or another user must enter your Windows password to unlock it.

Trouble? If the original Password protection on wakeup setting did not require a password, click the Don't require a password option button to restore that setting.

6. Click the **Save changes** button.

7. Close the Power Options window.

The change you made to the power button now applies to all of the power plans on Phil's computer. To make these changes to only a particular power plan, you open the Advanced settings tab in the Power Options dialog box as you did earlier (that is, in the Edit Plan Settings window for the Balanced power plan), and then change the Require a password on wakeup for the Power buttons and lid settings.

If you turn off the setting to require a password to wake your computer from sleep, you should also turn off your screen saver password. (A screen saver password locks your computer when the screen saver is on. The screen saver password is the same as the one you use to sign in to Windows and to wake your computer from sleep.) To turn off the screen saver password, open the Control Panel, click Appearance and Personalization, click Change screen saver, and then click the On resume, display logon screen check box to remove the check mark.

Now that you've shown Phil how to control the power state of his mobile PC, you're ready for the trip to Newport News. When you arrive, you can help him prepare his computer for the presentation to Visual Impact.

Presenting Information to an Audience

Giving a presentation is a common practice in business and education. When you use a computer to give a presentation to an audience, you can combine images, text, animation, sound and visual effects, and audio to educate, inform, or train others. You can give a presentation to a small or large group of people while you are all in the same room, or you can present the information remotely to people with whom you share a network connection. To create a presentation, you can use apps such as the slide show feature in the Pictures folder, Microsoft PowerPoint, or any other presentation program. You can then connect your computer to a projector to broadcast the presentation. To start and control the presentation, you use the keyboard and pointing device on your computer and the tools provided in the presentation program to perform tasks such as switching from one image or slide to another and ending the presentation.

Before you give a presentation, you can use Windows Mobility Center to adjust presentation settings, which are a collection of options that prepare your computer for a presentation. For example, you can control the volume level of your computer and block distractions such as notifications and reminders. You can also use Windows Mobility Center to connect your computer to an external display, such as a larger monitor or projector.

Preparing a Computer for a Presentation

TIP

You can also hide notifications by displaying the Charms bar, clicking the Settings charm, clicking Notifications, and then selecting a time.

Using Windows Mobility Center, you can specify the settings that Windows 8 uses as you are giving a presentation. When you turn on presentation settings, your computer stays awake and Windows blocks system notifications, such as notices about available software updates. You can also choose to turn off the screen saver, adjust the speaker volume, and change your desktop background image. Windows saves these settings and applies them when you turn on presentation settings in Windows Mobility Center. To turn on presentation settings, you can click the Turn on button in the Presentation Settings tile of Windows Mobility Center. Windows also turns on presentation settings when you connect your mobile PC to a projector. To turn off presentation settings, you can click the Turn off button in Windows Mobility Center. Windows also turns off presentation settings when you disconnect your computer from a projector or when you shut down or sign out of your PC.

Now that you and Phil have arrived in Newport News, you have some time to prepare for his presentation, which he'll give in the Visual Impact conference room. First, you'll customize the presentation settings to turn off the screen saver, turn up the volume, and change the desktop background to black. Then you'll show Phil how to turn the presentation settings on and off. Note your original settings so you can restore them later.

To customize presentation settings:

1. Open the Windows Mobility Center window.

2. In the Presentation Settings tile, click the **Change presentation settings** icon. The Presentation Settings dialog box opens. See Figure 8-12.

Figure 8-12 **Presentation Settings dialog box**

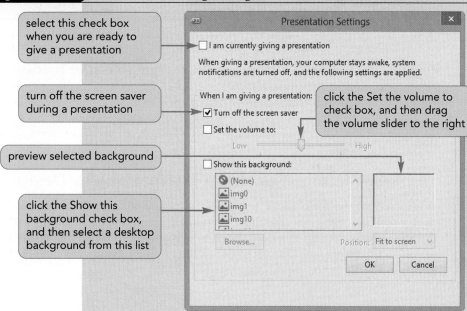

select this check box when you are ready to give a presentation

turn off the screen saver during a presentation

preview selected background

click the Show this background check box, and then select a desktop background from this list

click the Set the volume to check box, and then drag the volume slider to the right

3. If necessary, click the **Turn off the screen saver** check box to insert a check mark.

Trouble? If you inadvertently click the I am currently giving a presentation check box, click it again to remove the check mark.

▶ **4.** Click the **Set the volume to** check box, and then drag the slider to **85**. As you drag the slider, numbers appear above it to indicate the volume.

▶ **5.** Click the **Show this background** check box, and then click **(None)**, if necessary. A preview of the background, in this case, a black background, appears to the right.

▶ **6.** Click the **OK** button.

Now Windows will turn off the screen saver, turn up the speaker volume, and display a black desktop background when Phil turns on the presentation settings, which you'll show him how to do next.

To turn presentation settings on and off:

▶ **1.** In the Presentation Settings tile, click the **Turn on** button. The desktop, taskbar, and window borders turn black, and the Turn on button toggles to the Turn off button. See Figure 8-13.

Figure 8-13	**Turning on presentation settings**

black desktop background

Presentation Settings tile indicates that you are presenting

It's not yet time for Phil's presentation, so you can turn off the settings for now.

▶ **2.** In the Presentation Settings tile, click the **Turn off** button. The desktop returns to its pre-presentation state.

Next, you'll help Phil select display settings when he connects his notebook computer to a projector.

Displaying Information on an External Display Device

When you connect a mobile PC to a projector or any other type of additional display device such as a flat-screen monitor, Windows 8 detects the extra display and recommends the video settings that correspond to that device. To select settings for the additional device, display the Charms bar, click the Devices charm, and then click Second screen to display the options shown in Figure 8-14.

Figure 8-14 Selecting a display option

Figure 8-15 describes what each option in this panel means.

Figure 8-15 Second screen display options

Display Option	Description	When to Use
PC screen only	Does not extend your desktop to another display device	When you are using your computer as usual
Duplicate	Duplicates your desktop on each display device	When you are giving a presentation on a projector or a fixed display, such as a TV-type monitor
Extend	Extends your desktop across all of your display devices	When you want to increase your work space, such as by displaying one program window on your primary monitor and another window on a secondary monitor
Second screen only	Shows your desktop on the external display devices, but not on your mobile PC screen	When you want to conserve battery power

© 2014 Cengage Learning

When you disconnect the external display device, Windows restores the original display settings to your main computer monitor. The next time that you connect the same monitor, Windows automatically applies the display settings that you used the last time that you connected that monitor.

REFERENCE

Connecting to an External Display Device

- Connect your mobile computer to an external display device, such as a projector or secondary monitor.
- If Windows does not automatically detect the external display and open a dialog box with display options, open Windows Mobility Center, and then click the Connect display button in the External Display tile.
- Display the Charms bar, click the Devices charm, click Second screen, and then click the appropriate option to duplicate, extend, or show your desktop on the external display only.

Before adding a second display device to your computer, make sure that you have a video card that supports multiple monitors or that your computer has more than one video card. A video card that supports multiple monitors has two video ports—check the back of your computer to find ports labeled as "Video" or with an icon of a monitor.

When you connect the second display device, Windows should recognize the secondary monitor and open the panel with options for duplicating, extending, or showing your screen on the second screen only. One way to use a second display is to show the Start screen on one monitor and the desktop on another.

Phil connects his notebook computer to the projector in the conference room, uses the Devices charm to display options for the second screen, and selects the Duplicate setting. Phil's desktop is now displayed on his notebook and is projected on a large white screen in the conference room.

Exploring Network Concepts

As you know, a network is a collection of computers and other hardware devices linked together so they can exchange data and share hardware and software. Networks offer many advantages. Groups of computers on a network can use the same printer, so you don't have to purchase a printer for each computer. Network computers can also share an Internet connection, so you don't need to purchase and install a broadband modem for each computer. Networks also facilitate group projects because one person can save a document in a folder that other users on other computers can access. A network also improves communication in a company because coworkers can easily share news and information.

Large companies that want to connect their computers on a network usually hire a team of network specialists to determine what type of hardware the company should purchase and how to connect the devices to form a **local area network (LAN)**, a network of computers and other hardware devices that reside in the same physical space, such as an office building. Small office and home users can set up a simplified LAN to enjoy the advantages of networking. Like large companies, you also need to decide what type of network technology and hardware you will use if you want to set up a small network. (**Network technology** is the way computers connect to one another.) The most common types of network technology for a small office or home network are wireless, Ethernet, and Powerline. Figure 8-16 compares network technologies.

Figure 8-16 Comparing network technologies

Network Technology	How It Sends Information Between Computers	Pros	Cons
Wireless	Uses radio waves, microwaves, or infrared light	Setting up the network and moving computers are easy because there are no cables.	Wireless technology is more expensive and often slower than Ethernet. Wireless connections can be interrupted by interference.
Ethernet	Uses Ethernet cables	Ethernet is a proven and reliable technology, and Ethernet networks are inexpensive and fast.	Ethernet cables must connect each computer to a hub, switch, or router, which can be time consuming and difficult when the computers are in different rooms.
Powerline	Uses existing home electrical wiring to send information between computers	You don't need hubs or switches to connect more than two computers in a Powerline network.	You need an electrical outlet in each room where you want to have a computer, and Powerline networks can be affected by interference and noise on the line.

© 2014 Cengage Learning

Small office and home networks use a variety of special hardware, including the following devices:

- Network adapters—Also called **network interface cards (NICs)**, **network adapters** connect computers to a network. Network adapters are usually installed inside your computer, though you can also plug one into a USB port. See Figure 8-17.

Figure 8-17 Network interface card

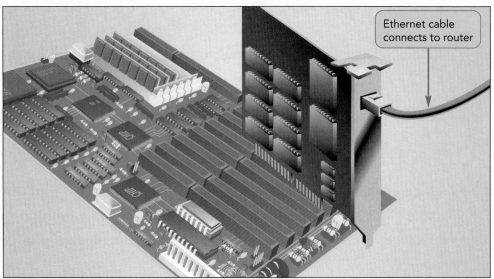

Ethernet cable connects to router

© 2014 Cengage Learning

- Network hubs and switches—Used on an Ethernet network, **network hubs** or **network switches** connect two or more computers to the network.
- Routers or access points—**Routers** connect computers and networks to each other and let you share a single Internet connection among several computers. They are called routers because they direct network traffic. An **access point** provides wireless access to a wired Ethernet network. An access point plugs into a wired router and sends out a wireless signal, which other wireless computers and devices use to connect to the wired network. Most home networks share access to the Internet by connecting a wireless router to a modem and to a computer with an Internet connection.
- Modems—To connect your computer to the Internet, you need a **modem**, which sends and receives information over telephone or cable lines.
- Cables—On an Ethernet or Powerline network, **cables** connect computers to each other and to other devices, such as hubs and routers.

Figure 8-18 describes the hardware required for each type of network technology.

| Figure 8-18 | Hardware needed for each type of network technology |

Network Technology	Hardware Required
Wireless	• Wireless network adapter installed on each computer in the network • Wireless access point or router
Ethernet	• Ethernet network adapter on each computer in the network • Ethernet hub or switch if you only want to connect more than two computers • Ethernet router if you want to connect more than two computers and share an Internet connection • Ethernet cables
Powerline	• Powerline network adapter for each computer on your network • Ethernet router to share an Internet connection • One electrical outlet for each computer on your network

© 2014 Cengage Learning

Setting Up a Small Office or Home Network

After you determine what type of network you want and acquire the hardware you need, you typically set up a small office or home network by performing the following tasks:

- Install the hardware. Install the network adapters in the computers that need them, if necessary.
- Set up an Internet connection. If you want the network computers to access the Internet, set up a connection to the Internet, usually through a modem.
- Connect the computers. On an Ethernet network, you need a hub, switch, or router to connect the computers. Use a router to share an Internet connection. Connect the router to the computer that is connected to the modem.

If you only want to share an Internet connection on a wireless network, you need to complete two steps:

- Configure the wireless router to broadcast signals.
- Set up Windows 8 on each computer to receive the signals.

In the first step, you install a wireless router and configure it to start broadcasting information to and receiving information from your computer. To have the router broadcast radio signals, you need to run the setup software provided with your router. The steps to run this software vary depending on your router, but usually you need to provide a network name, or **service set identifier (SSID)**, which is a name you use to identify your wireless network. You'll see this name later when you use Windows 8 to connect to your wireless network. The setup software also lets you turn on security settings to encrypt your data when you transmit it, which helps to prevent unauthorized people from accessing your data or your network. To do so, you need to provide a password so that you can access the network. See Figure 8-19.

Figure 8-19   **Wireless network sharing an Internet connection**

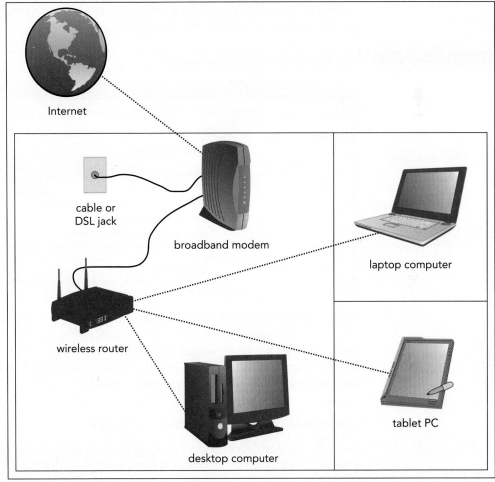

Internet

cable or
DSL jack

broadband modem

wireless router

desktop computer

laptop computer

tablet PC

© 2014 Cengage Learning

The following section shows you how to set up Windows 8 to receive the wireless signals.

If you want to share files and printers as well as an Internet connection on a wireless network, you can set up a homegroup, which is discussed later in this tutorial.

Managing Network Connections

After you connect two or more computers through cables or wireless connections, you can use Windows 8 to monitor and manage your network connections. If your network is set up to share a network printer or an Internet connection, Windows works behind the scenes to organize requests to use these resources. For example, if two people want to print documents at the same time on the network printer, Windows lines up the printer requests in a queue and prints the documents one after the other. It also lets all the network users share a single Internet connection so they can visit Web sites and exchange email without interrupting each other. You can check your network connection by displaying the Charms bar, clicking the Settings charm, and then clicking the name of your network connection. For other networking tasks, such as verifying you are connected to a network, finding and connecting to a wireless network, and setting up a new connection or network, you use the Network and Sharing Center window. See Figure 8-20.

Figure 8-20	Network and Sharing Center window

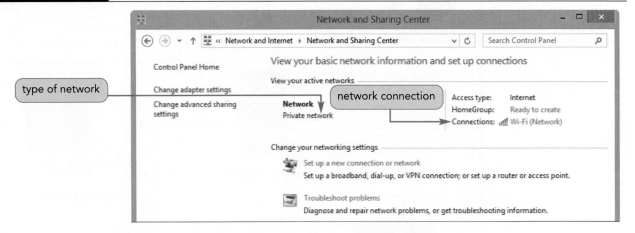

You can now show Phil how to connect his mobile PC to the Visual Impact wireless network. He has prepared some sample network policy documents and wants to copy them to a folder on the network that the Visual Impact partners can access. Phil might also need to retrieve a document stored on their network. Before he can perform those tasks, he needs to connect to the wireless network.

Connecting to a Wireless Network

TIP

You can also connect to or disconnect from a network in the Network and Sharing Center window.

If your PC has a wireless network adapter, you can display a list of available wireless networks and then connect to one of those networks, whether it's your own private wireless network or a public one. You can display a list of available wireless networks from the desktop by clicking the network icon in the notification area of the taskbar. To display a list of wireless networks from the Start screen, display the Charms bar, click the Settings charm, and then click the network icon (which appears with the name of the network to which your computer is currently connected). Windows displays the following information about each available wireless network:

 • Network name—This is the SSID you or someone else provided when the network was set up. Because wireless signals extend past the boundaries of your home or office, the wireless adapter in your computer often detects more than one network within its range.

- Security—Unsecured networks don't require a password, whereas security-enabled networks do. Security-enabled networks also encrypt data before transmitting it, meaning that unauthorized people cannot intercept sensitive information such as a credit card number when you send it across the network. When you set up a wireless network, you should create a strong password or **passphrase** (more than one word). A strong passphrase has at least 20 characters, including spaces, and is not a common phrase that other people are likely to know. If you don't create a passphrase, the network is protected with a **network security key**, which is usually a series of hexadecimal numbers assigned by Windows.
- Signal strength—Windows displays a series of bars that indicate the strength of the signal; the more bars highlighted, the stronger the connection. Having the strongest signal (five bars highlighted) means that the wireless network is nearby or has no interference. To improve the signal strength, you can move your computer closer to the wireless router or access point, or move the router or access point away from sources of interference such as brick walls or walls that contain metal support beams.

If you use a wireless network regularly, you can choose to connect to the network automatically any time your computer is within range. Unless you are accessing a public network, such as in an airport or a hotel, be sure to connect only to the wireless network you are authorized to use, even if you can access an unsecured private network. If you are authorized to connect to more than one wireless network, you should generally use the one with the strongest signal. However, even if an unsecured network has a stronger signal than a security-enabled one, keep in mind that it's safer for your data to connect to the security-enabled network, as long as you are an authorized user of that network.

Visual Impact already has a wireless network set up in its offices. Phil asks you to help him perform some basic tasks to manage the Visual Impact network by connecting his mobile computer to the company's wireless network. The passphrase to access the network is VIuser12 newport Design.

The following steps assume you are equipped to connect to a wireless network named VImpact. Substitute the name of your network and your network password when you perform the following steps. If you are not equipped to connect to a wireless network, read but do not perform the following steps.

To connect to a wireless network:

▶ **1.** Display the Charms bar, click the **Settings** charm, and then click the network icon, which is labeled with the name of your network. The Networks panel opens. See Figure 8-21.

| Figure 8-21 | Networks panel |

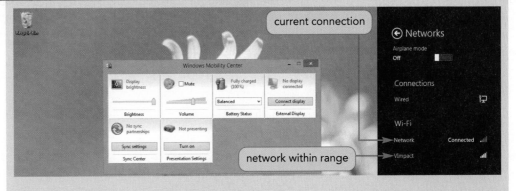

Make sure you are connected to a network to perform the rest of the steps in this tutorial.

2. Click your **network name**, such as VImpact, in the list of available networks, and then click the **Connect** button. If a Disconnect button appears, you are already connected to the network. Read but do not perform the remaining steps.

Trouble? If your network is not listed in the Networks panel, the signal strength might be low. Move your computer closer to the wireless router or access point, if possible, close the Networks panel, and then repeat Steps 1 and 2.

Trouble? If your network is not listed in the Networks panel, but one or more networks are listed as "Unnamed network," click an Unnamed network, click the Connect button, and then enter your network name.

3. If a text box opens requesting your network security key, enter your passphrase, such as VIuser12 newport Design, and then click the **Next** button. Windows connects to the network.

4. When asked if you want to turn on sharing between PCs and connect to devices on this network, click **Yes, turn on sharing and connect to devices** if you are working on a home or work network.

Trouble? If you are connecting to a network in a public place such as an airport, click No, don't turn on sharing or connect to devices.

5. If necessary, click the desktop to close the Networks panel.

Phil's mobile computer is now connected to the Visual Impact wireless network. Because older cordless phones and other devices can interfere with a wireless connection, you should periodically check the status of the connection. You can do so by opening the Network and Sharing Center, or by using the network icon in the notification area of the status bar or the Settings menu. You'll show Phil how to check the status using the network icon on the taskbar.

To check the status of a wireless connection:

1. Point to the **network** icon ▥ in the notification area of the taskbar. A small notification window shows the status of your network connection.

2. Close all open windows.

Now that you've helped Phil connect to the Visual Impact wireless network, you are ready to perform some typical network tasks, which involve connecting to and sharing files with other computers on the network. You'll do that in the next session.

REVIEW

Session 8.1 Quick Check

1. A(n) _Tablet PC_ computer is smaller than a notebook or laptop and has a touchscreen and a pointing device, such as a stylus.

2. What is Windows Mobility Center?

3. Explain how to use Windows Mobility Center to set the speaker volume.

4. A(n) _power plan_ is a collection of hardware and system settings that manages how your computer uses and conserves power.

5. Why does Windows automatically put a mobile computer into hibernation −402 rather than sleep after a specified amount of time?

6. What three settings should you specify when giving a presentation? − 411

7. How does a wireless network send information between computers?

Session 8.2 Visual Overview:

A **homegroup** is a group of computers on a home network that can share files and devices.

When you are connected to a network, you can display the contents of another computer using File Explorer.

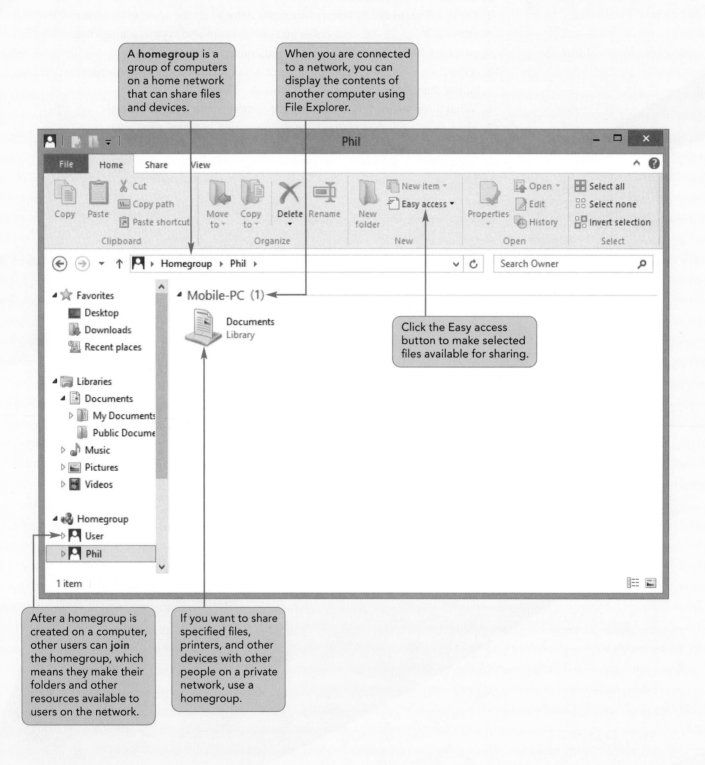

Click the Easy access button to make selected files available for sharing.

After a homegroup is created on a computer, other users can **join** the homegroup, which means they make their folders and other resources available to users on the network.

If you want to share specified files, printers, and other devices with other people on a private network, use a homegroup.

Sharing Files

A **sync partnership** is a set of rules specifying which files and folders you want to sync, where to sync them, and when.

You use Sync Center to identify devices containing files to synchronize and then exchange information.

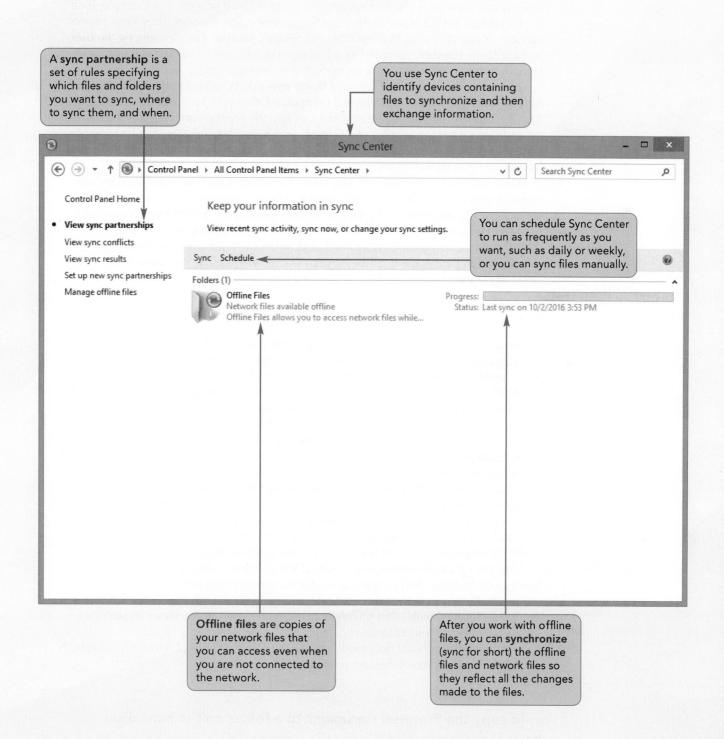

You can schedule Sync Center to run as frequently as you want, such as daily or weekly, or you can sync files manually.

Offline files are copies of your network files that you can access even when you are not connected to the network.

After you work with offline files, you can **synchronize** (*sync* for short) the offline files and network files so they reflect all the changes made to the files.

Using a Windows Homegroup

Like so many others today, you probably have more than one computing device in your home, including desktop computers, notebooks, and tablets. To make managing those devices easier and to share files and resources among them, you can create a **home network**, a small private network specifically designed for communication among the devices in a home or a small office (usually fewer than 10 people). For example, if all the computers in your house connect to the same wireless network, they form a home network. If you also want to share files and devices, such as a printer, among the users on your home network, you can use a homegroup. Medium or large companies with Windows computers will have a network, but no homegroup.

To broaden the capabilities within a home network, Windows creates a homegroup for you when you set up a Windows 8 computer. Other user accounts on Windows 8 or 7 computers on your home network can join the homegroup, which is the easiest and safest way to share files and printers on a home network. You can let someone connect to your home network to provide access to the Internet, but you don't have to let that user join the homegroup.

When setting up a homegroup, you select the libraries that you want to share with others. If you want to keep some files private, you can prevent certain files and folders in those libraries from being shared. You can protect the entire homegroup with a password, which each user must enter to connect to other computers.

Only computers running Windows 8 or Windows 7 (not earlier versions of Windows) can participate in a homegroup. Computers running Windows 8 RT, Windows 7 Starter, or Home Basic can join a homegroup, but cannot create one.

Creating a Homegroup

Although Windows 8 creates a homegroup when you first set up your computer, you can create one manually if necessary. Now that Phil's notebook is connected to the wireless network at Visual Impact, you suggest he create a homegroup on his notebook, and then, using the desktop computer in the conference room, join the homegroup so he can easily share files between the two computers while working at the Visual Impact offices. Because Phil's notebook is a member of the VBIC homegroup in Richmond, he must first leave that homegroup. (A computer can belong to only one homegroup at a time.) You'll show Phil how to leave the VBIC homegroup and then create a homegroup to use at Visual Impact. When he returns to VBIC, he can easily leave the Visual Impact homegroup and rejoin the VBIC homegroup.

As you create a homegroup for Phil, you can select the libraries and devices he can share with other members of the homegroup. In particular, Phil has a document named Proposal that outlines the services VBIC will provide to Visual Impact. He wants to share the Proposal document with other people at Visual Impact.

After you create the homegroup, users of Visual Impact computers can join Phil's homegroup because their computers are on the same private network as Phil's notebook. As they join, these users also select the libraries and devices on their computers to share with other members of the homegroup. Later, they can select individual files and folders to share.

First, copy the Proposal document from the Windows8\Tutorial folder provided with your Data Files to a new folder on your hard disk.

To copy the Proposal document to a folder on the hard disk:

▶ **1.** Start File Explorer on the desktop, and then navigate to the Documents library on the hard disk of your computer.

▶ **2.** Click the **New folder** button in the New group on the Home tab.

▶ **3.** Type **VBIC** as the name of the folder, and then press the **Enter** key.

4. Copy the **Proposal** file from the Windows8\Tutorial folder provided with your Data Files to the VBIC folder.

5. Close all open folder windows.

Next, leave the homegroup that your computer belongs to so you can create a new one.

To leave a homegroup:

1. Display the Charms bar on the desktop, click the **Settings** charm, and then click **Control Panel** to open the Control Panel window.

2. In the Search text box, type **homegroup**, and then click **HomeGroup** in the Control Panel window. See Figure 8-22.

| Figure 8-22 | HomeGroup window |

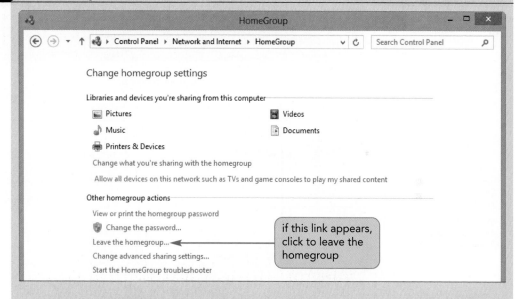

Trouble? If Windows indicates that your network does not have a homegroup, read but do not perform the remaining steps.

Trouble? If Windows indicates that you have been invited to join a homegroup, close the HomeGroup window. Read but do not perform the remaining steps.

3. Click **Leave the homegroup**. The Leave the Homegroup window opens with options for leaving or remaining in the homegroup.

4. Click **Leave the homegroup** to confirm you do not want to belong to this homegroup. Windows removes your computer from the homegroup.

5. When Windows indicates that you have successfully left the homegroup, click the **Finish** button.

Now you can create a homegroup on your mobile computer.

If the HomeGroup window now indicates that someone else on your home network has created a homegroup, you can join that homegroup shortly. In that case, your computer is playing the role of a Visual Impact user's computer joining Phil's homegroup. Read but do not perform the following steps.

If the HomeGroup window now indicates that there is currently no homegroup on the network, you can create one. In that case, your computer is playing the role of Phil's notebook computer. Complete the following steps. You will share the Documents library and printers and devices connected to your computer so that other members of the homegroup can access the Proposal document and print it.

To create a homegroup:

▶ **1.** In the HomeGroup window, click the **Create a homegroup** button. A window opens explaining how to use a homegroup.

▶ **2.** Click the **Next** button. A window opens where you select the libraries and devices you want to share with the other computers in the homegroup.

▶ **3.** Click the buttons in the Permissions list as necessary to select only the Documents library and the Printers & Devices resource, as shown in Figure 8-23.

Figure 8-23   Selecting libraries and resources to share

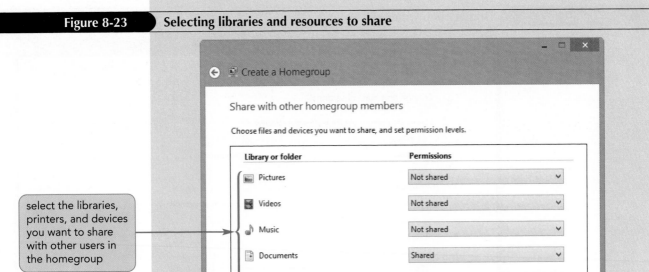

select the libraries, printers, and devices you want to share with other users in the homegroup

▶ **4.** Click the **Next** button. Windows creates the homegroup and generates a password. Other users on the network need this password to join the homegroup, so you should print it.

▶ **5.** Click the **Print password and instructions** link, and then click the **Print this page** button to print the password, if requested by your instructor.

▶ **6.** Click the **Print** button in the Print dialog box to print the information, and then close the View and print your homegroup password window.

▶ **7.** Click the **Finish** button.

GQ 38 dr6BG4

You can change the password to one that's easier to remember. In the HomeGroup window, click the Change the password link, and then follow the steps in the wizard to change the password.

Adding Other Computers to a Homegroup

After you create a homegroup, other computers on your network can join the homegroup. You must give users the homegroup password so they can join. Joining involves using the HomeGroup window to select files and resources for sharing, just as you did when you created the homegroup, and then entering the homegroup password. After other users join the homegroup, you can access the files they've selected for sharing and vice versa.

If you did not create a homegroup on your computer because someone else already created a homegroup on the network, perform the following steps. You will share only the Documents library with other members of the homegroup. In the figures, the name of the homegroup creator is Phil and his computer is named Mobile-PC.

If you created a homegroup in the previous set of steps, read but do not perform the following steps.

To join a homegroup:

▶ **1.** Display the HomeGroup window, which includes a message indicating that a user created a homegroup on the network. See Figure 8-24.

Figure 8-24	Joining a homegroup

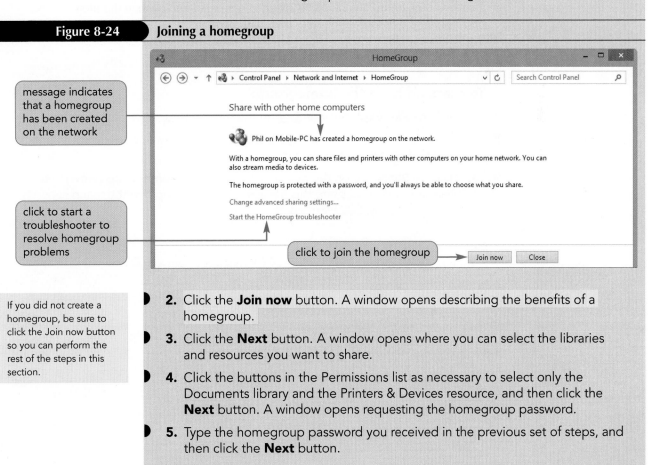

message indicates that a homegroup has been created on the network

click to start a troubleshooter to resolve homegroup problems

Share with other home computers

Phil on Mobile-PC has created a homegroup on the network.

With a homegroup, you can share files and printers with other computers on your home network. You can also stream media to devices.

The homegroup is protected with a password, and you'll always be able to choose what you share.

Change advanced sharing settings...

Start the HomeGroup troubleshooter

click to join the homegroup → Join now   Close

If you did not create a homegroup, be sure to click the Join now button so you can perform the rest of the steps in this section.

▶ **2.** Click the **Join now** button. A window opens describing the benefits of a homegroup.

▶ **3.** Click the **Next** button. A window opens where you can select the libraries and resources you want to share.

▶ **4.** Click the buttons in the Permissions list as necessary to select only the Documents library and the Printers & Devices resource, and then click the **Next** button. A window opens requesting the homegroup password.

▶ **5.** Type the homegroup password you received in the previous set of steps, and then click the **Next** button.

Trouble? If you do not remember the password, click the Where can I find the homegroup password? link, follow the instructions for retrieving it, and then repeat Step 5.

Trouble? If you rejoined the homegroup, you do not have to enter the password again. Skip Step 5.

▶ **6.** When a window appears indicating you successfully joined the homegroup, click the **Finish** button, and then minimize the HomeGroup window.

Next, you'll access the Documents library available for sharing on the homegroup.

Sharing Files with a Homegroup

After you set up a homegroup with two or more computers, you can share files using File Explorer. First, you can specify which files and folders you want to share in the library you selected for sharing. You can share files and folders with everyone in your homegroup, with only specific people in your homegroup, or with accounts on your computer. You can also prevent a file or folder from being shared with anyone, even if it's stored in a library you selected for sharing.

When you share files or folders with other people in your homegroup, you can provide two types of access to the file or folder. **View access** means the homegroup members you specified can read the file(s) but not change them. **View and edit access** means the homegroup members you specified can read and change the file(s).

You'll share the Proposal document with all members of your homegroup, but only allow them view access so they don't change the file.

To share a file on the homegroup:

▶ **1.** Click the **File Explorer** icon ▣ on the taskbar to open a folder window.

▶ **2.** Navigate to the VBIC folder in the Documents library, and then click the **Proposal** document to select it.

▶ **3.** Click the **Share** tab on the ribbon, and then click **Homegroup (view)** in the Share with group to share this file with all homegroup members and allow view access only. See Figure 8-25.

Figure 8-25 **Sharing a file with other homegroup members**

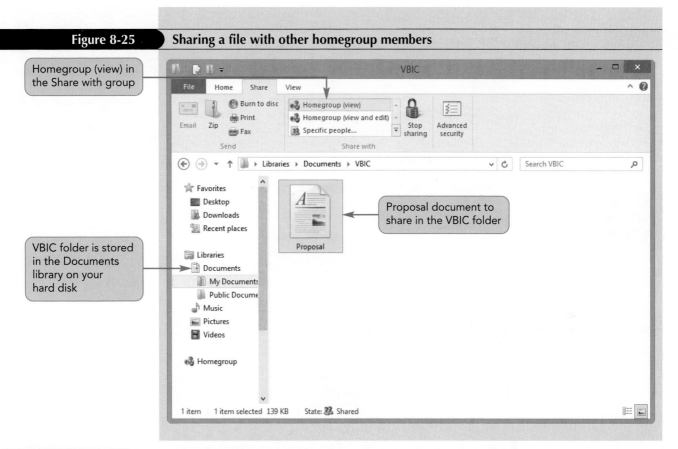

Homegroup (view) in the Share with group

VBIC folder is stored in the Documents library on your hard disk

Proposal document to share in the VBIC folder

To access files on a homegroup member's computer, you click or expand Homegroup in the Navigation pane to display the other users in your homegroup. Click or expand a user icon to display the libraries that the user selected for sharing. Then, navigate the libraries and folders as you usually do to find the file you want to access.

If you can work on a homegroup computer other than the one where you just shared the Proposal file, perform the following steps on that computer. Otherwise, read but do not perform the steps.

In the following steps, the name of the computer you want to access is Mobile-PC and the user account is named Phil. When you perform the following steps, substitute the name of the computer you are using and your user account on that device for *Mobile-PC* and *Phil*.

To access shared files on a homegroup:

▸ **1.** On a computer in the homegroup (other than the computer where you shared the Proposal document), click the **File Explorer** icon ▨ on the taskbar to open a folder window.

▸ **2.** In the Navigation pane, click **Homegroup**. The Navigation pane displays the users in your homegroup.

▸ **3.** In the Navigation pane, click the **Phil** user (or any user in the homegroup) to display the libraries available for sharing on the computer you are using. See Figure 8-26.

| **Figure 8-26** | **Displaying libraries available for sharing** |

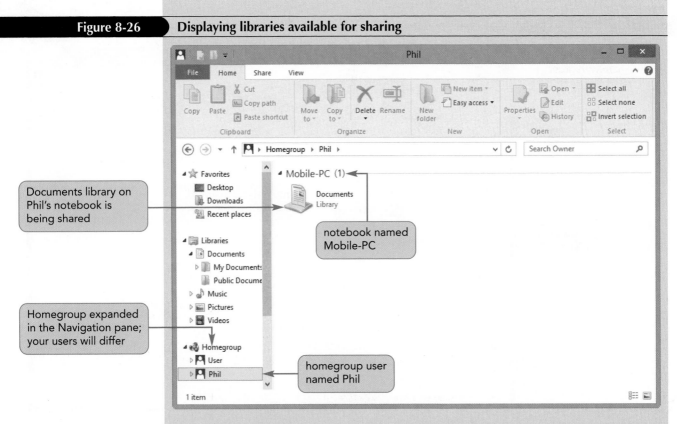

Documents library on Phil's notebook is being shared

notebook named Mobile-PC

Homegroup expanded in the Navigation pane; your users will differ

homegroup user named Phil

4. Navigate to the VBIC folder in the Documents library, and then double-click the **Proposal** document to open it. The document opens in WordPad or another program that can open RTF files, such as Word.

5. Type your name at the beginning of the document, and then click the **Save** button on the Quick Access toolbar to save the document with the same name and in the same location. If you are using WordPad, a dialog box opens indicating that access was denied. If you are using Word, a dialog box asks if you want to replace the existing file. Click the **Yes** button. A Microsoft Word dialog box indicates this file is read-only. In either case, the view access set on the document prevents you from saving changes to the file. If the document had view and edit access, you would be able to save the file with your changes.

6. Click the **OK** button to close the dialog box, click the **Cancel** button, if necessary, to close the Save As dialog box, and then close the document without saving your changes.

If you no longer want to share a file or folder on your computer, select the file or folder, and then click the Stop sharing button in the Share with group on the Share tab.

When you click the Stop sharing button, you prevent the file or folder from being shared with anyone in the homegroup. If you want to share the file or folder with some people but not others, click the More button in the Share with group on the Share tab, if necessary, click Specific people, and then select the users who can share access to the file or folder.

Sharing a Printer with a Homegroup

If a printer is connected to a homegroup computer using a USB cable or wireless connection, the printer can be shared with the homegroup. After the printer is shared, you can access it through the Print dialog box in any application, just like any printer directly connected to your computer.

The following steps assume that a printer is connected to a computer in your homegroup but not to your computer directly. If that is not the case, read but do not perform the following steps. Both the printer and the homegroup computer connected to it should be turned on. If you performed the previous steps on a computer other than your own, return to your computer to perform the remaining steps in this section.

To connect to a homegroup printer:

▶ **1.** Display the Control Panel, and then click **View devices and printers** in the Hardware and Sound category. If Windows can automatically connect to the printer, it appears in the Devices and Printers window.

▶ **2.** If the homegroup printer is not listed in the Devices and Printers window, click the **Windows found a homegroup printer** message to connect to the printer.

   Trouble? If the Devices and Printers window does not display a message or the homegroup printer, the printer needs to be installed on the computer hosting the homegroup. Skip Step 2.

▶ **3.** Close the Devices and Printers window.

Phil mentions that he might need to use homegroup files even when he's not connected to the homegroup. You'll show him how to do so next.

Accessing Offline Files

After setting up and sharing files and folders on a homegroup or other network, you might need to work with those files, but you might not be able to access them because your network connection is slow or not available. To avoid this problem, you can create **offline files**, which are copies of your network files that you store on your computer and use when you are not connected to the network.

To create offline files, you first enable offline files on your computer, and then navigate to the folder or file stored on a network computer other than your own. After you choose the network files you want to make available offline, Windows creates copies of these files for you on your computer. If you change the network copies of the offline files, Windows updates, or synchronizes, the offline files so they remain exact duplicates of the network files. When you are not connected to the network, you can open the offline files on your computer knowing that they have the same content as the network files. When you're finished working with the offline files and reconnect to the network, you can use Sync Center to synchronize the offline files and network files yourself, or you can wait for Windows to do it the next time you access the network files.

You can synchronize files whenever you copy and save network files to your computer. When you first create offline files, Windows 8 transfers the files from the network to a specified folder on your hard disk. After that, when you connect to the network folder that contains the files you've also stored offline, Windows makes sure that both the folder containing the offline files and the network folder contain the most recent versions of the files.

You explain to Phil that offline files are especially popular with mobile computer users. You'll show him how to set up his notebook to use offline files, and then you'll make a Public folder on the Visual Impact network available to him offline.

Setting Up a Computer to Use Offline Files

Before you specify that a network file or folder should be available offline, make sure that offline files are enabled on your computer. When this feature is turned on, Windows synchronizes the offline files on your computer with the network files as soon as you reconnect to the network.

To make sure offline files are enabled on your computer:

▶ **1.** Open the Control Panel, type **Offline** in the Search text box, and then click **Manage offline files** in the Sync Center category. The Offline Files dialog box opens. See Figure 8-27.

Figure 8-27   **Offline Files dialog box**

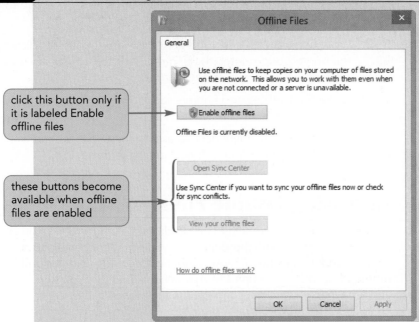

click this button only if it is labeled Enable offline files

these buttons become available when offline files are enabled

▶ **2.** Click the **Enable offline files** button. The other options to open Sync Center and view your offline files become available.

▶ **3.** Click the **OK** button to close the dialog box.

Before you share files or folders in one of the Public folders, you should make sure that Public folder sharing is turned on. To do so, you use the Advanced sharing settings window, which you open from the Network and Sharing Center.

To make sure Public folder sharing is turned on:

▶ **1.** In the Control Panel window, click the **Search** text box, type **Network**, and then click **Network and Sharing Center**. The Network and Sharing Center window opens.

> **2.** In the left pane, click **Change advanced sharing settings**. The Advanced sharing settings window opens. See Figure 8-28.

Figure 8-28	Advanced sharing settings window

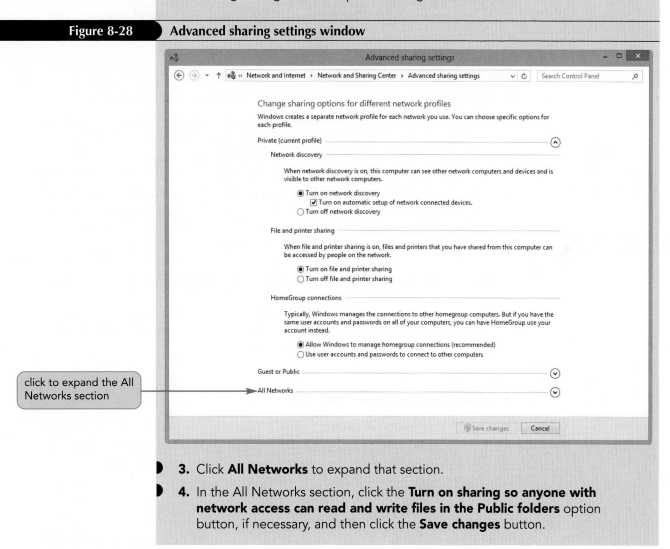

click to expand the All Networks section

> **3.** Click **All Networks** to expand that section.

> **4.** In the All Networks section, click the **Turn on sharing so anyone with network access can read and write files in the Public folders** option button, if necessary, and then click the **Save changes** button.

Next, you'll access a network folder and make it available to Phil offline.

Making a File or Folder Available Offline

To use a file or folder offline from the homegroup, you specify that it is always available offline. (When you make a folder available offline, all the files in the folder are also available offline.) Afterwards, you will be able to open the file or folder even if the network version is unavailable. You'll show Phil how to use offline files and folders by making the Public Documents folder on the conference room computer available offline.

The following steps assume that a computer named Conference-PC is connected to your network. If your network does not include a computer named Conference-PC, substitute the name of a different network computer that you can access in the following steps. The steps also assume that you have permission to access the Public Documents folder on the network computer. If you do not have permission to access this folder, ask your instructor which folder you can make available offline. Perform the following steps on a homegroup computer (other than the notebook where you created the homegroup).

To make network files available offline:

▶ **1.** In the Address bar of the Network and Sharing Center window, click **Network and Internet** to display the Network and Internet window.

▶ **2.** Click **View network computers and devices** to open the Network window.

▶ **3.** Double-click the **Conference-PC** computer (or any computer listed on your network) to display the users and resources on the computer.

▶ **4.** Double-click the **Users** folder, and then double-click the **Public** folder.

▶ **5.** Right-click the **Public Documents** folder, and then click **Always available offline** on the shortcut menu if this command is not checked. Windows prepares the files in the Public Documents folder so they are available offline. Depending on the number of files in the folder, this could take a few minutes.

   Trouble? If the Always available offline command does not appear on the shortcut menu, navigate to and right-click a folder you have permission to access offline. If you do not have permission to access any folders offline, read but do not perform the remaining steps.

TIP

To view all of your offline files, open the Offline Files dialog box again, and then click the View your offline files button.

Now you can show Phil how to work with the files in the Public Documents folder offline.

If you made a different folder available offline, substitute that folder for the Public Documents folder in the following steps. If you did not make any folders available offline, read but do not perform the following steps.

To work with offline files:

▶ **1.** Click the **Public Documents** folder to select it, if necessary.

▶ **2.** Click the **Easy access** button in the New group on the Home tab, and then click **Work offline**. This option appears only if you have already made this folder available offline.

▶ **3.** Close the folder window.

TIP

When you are finished working offline, click the Easy access button in the New group, and then click Work offline to deselect the option and sync the changes you made with the files on the network.

Any changes you or Phil makes to the files in the Public Documents folder on the Visual Impact computer will now be made offline. In addition, if you lose your network connection, Windows turns on offline files and copies to your computer the files you designate as offline files so you can work on them. When you deselect the Work offline option or reconnect to the network, Windows syncs the two copies. You can find out if you're working offline by opening the network folder that contains the file you are working on, and then looking in the status of the folder window. If the status is Offline (working offline), you are working with a copy of the file on your computer. If the status is Online, you are working with the file on the network. You can also use Sync Center to sync all of your offline files at the same time so they match the network copies.

Synchronizing Folders

If you use more than one computer, such as a desktop computer and a mobile PC, it can be difficult to keep track of all your files. To make sure that you have the most recent versions of your files on your mobile PC before you travel, for example, you can synchronize information on your mobile PC, desktop computer, and other devices by using Sync Center. To do so, you create a set of rules that tells Sync Center what files you want to sync, where to sync them, and when. Sync Center makes it easy to move files from a computer to another device, such as another computer or a network server, portable music player, digital camera, or smartphone. Besides copying files from one device to another, Sync Center can maintain consistency among two or more versions of the same file stored in different locations. If you add, change, or delete a file in one location, you can use Sync Center to add, overwrite, or delete an earlier version of the file in other locations.

You can also use Sync Center to manage offline files. In this case, Sync Center compares the size and time stamp of an offline file with a network file to see if they are different. For example, suppose you changed an offline file, but have not made the same changes in the network copy. Sync Center copies the offline file to the network so both versions are identical. If Sync Center finds a new file in an offline folder, for example, it copies the file to the network folder. The same is true for deleted files. If Sync Center finds that a file has been deleted from the network folder, for example, it deletes the same file in the offline folder.

Sometimes Sync Center discovers a conflict, which means that both a network file and its offline copy have been changed. A sync conflict occurs whenever differences can't be reconciled between a file stored in one location and a version of the same file in another location. A sync conflict stops the sync from being completed. This usually happens when a file has changed in both locations since its last sync, making it difficult to determine which version should be left unchanged (or kept as the master copy) and which should be updated. In this case, Sync Center asks you to select the version you want to keep.

When you are synchronizing a mobile device and your computer, you can use Sync Center to set up a one-way or two-way sync. In a one-way sync, every time you add, change, or delete a file or other information in one location, such as the Music folder on your hard disk, the same information is added, changed, or deleted in the other location, such as your mobile device. Windows does not change the files in the original location, such as the Music folder on your hard disk, because the sync is only one way. In a two-way sync, Windows copies files in both directions, keeping files in sync in two locations. Every time you add, change, or delete a file in either location, the same change is made in the other sync location.

Using Sync Center

You use Sync Center to set up a sync by specifying which files and folders you want to sync, where to sync them, and when. This set of rules—which represents a partnership between two or more sync locations—is called a sync partnership.

To perform the following steps, you must be working on a mobile computer. If you are not working on a mobile computer, read but do not perform the following steps. Perform the following steps on the notebook you used to create the homegroup.

TIP

To sync only one file or folder, select the file or folder, click the Easy access button in the New group, and then click Sync.

To open Sync Center and sync offline files:

▶ **1.** Open the Windows Mobility Center window.

▶ **2.** Click the **Sync settings** button in the Sync Center tile. The Sync Center window opens. See Figure 8-29.

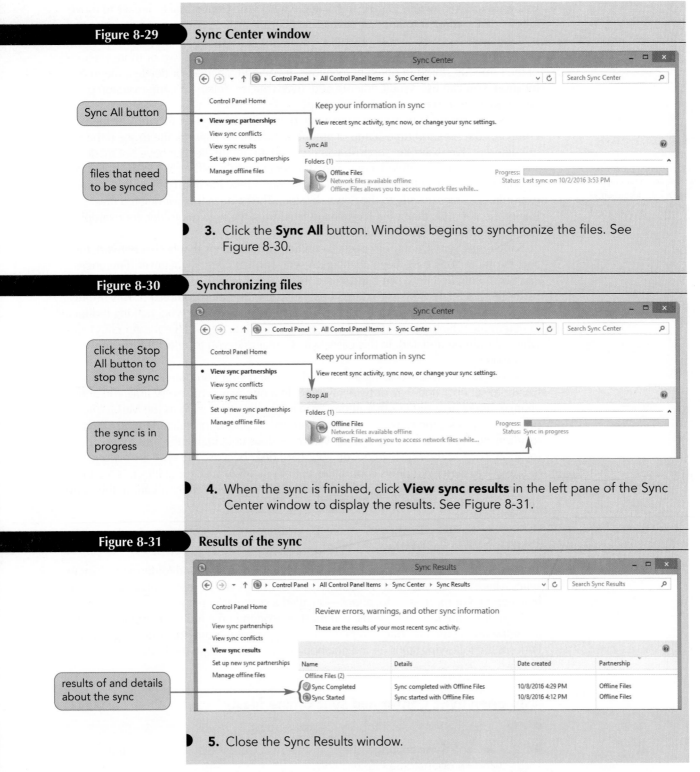

Figure 8-29   **Sync Center window**

Sync All button

files that need to be synced

3. Click the **Sync All** button. Windows begins to synchronize the files. See Figure 8-30.

Figure 8-30   **Synchronizing files**

click the Stop All button to stop the sync

the sync is in progress

4. When the sync is finished, click **View sync results** in the left pane of the Sync Center window to display the results. See Figure 8-31.

Figure 8-31   **Results of the sync**

results of and details about the sync

5. Close the Sync Results window.

During the sync, if Sync Center finds that the offline file is identical to the network file, Sync Center does nothing because the files are already in sync. If Sync Center finds that an offline file differs from its network version, Sync Center determines which version of each file to keep and copies that version to the other location. It selects the most recent version to keep unless you have set up the sync partnership to sync differently. If you added a new file in one location but not the other, Sync Center copies the file to the other location. If you deleted a file from one location but not the other, Sync Center deletes the file from the other location. If Sync Center finds a conflict, however, you should know how to resolve it.

Resolving Synchronization Conflicts

If Windows performs a sync and Sync Center finds that a file has changed in both locations since the last sync, Sync Center flags this as a sync conflict and asks you to choose which version to keep. You must resolve this conflict so that Sync Center can keep the files in sync. When Sync Center detects one or more conflicts, it displays a message similar to the one shown in Figure 8-32.

| Figure 8-32 | Sync Center shows a conflict |

a yellow progress bar indicates a conflict; a red progress bar indicates an error

click to display details about the conflict

To resolve the conflicts, you click the conflict link, select the offline files, and then click the Resolve button. When you do, the Resolve Conflict dialog box opens for each file in conflict and asks if you want to keep this version and copy it to the other location, or if you want to keep both copies. See Figure 8-33.

| Figure 8-33 | Resolving sync conflicts |

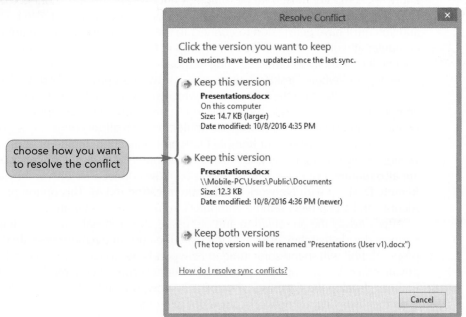

choose how you want to resolve the conflict

Click the appropriate option, and then click the OK button.

PROSKILLS

Problem Solving: Synchronizing Files on SkyDrive and a PC

If you store files on your SkyDrive, you might need to synchronize your SkyDrive with your PC. For example, suppose you store one version of a Word document named Report on SkyDrive and another version of the Report document on your PC. If you edit the Report document on your PC, you need to sync the SkyDrive files so Report includes the same changes. The SkyDrive app provided on the Start screen does not include a synchronize feature. Instead, you can download and install the SkyDrive desktop application, which uses an interface similar to File Explorer to display your SkyDrive folders and files. (You can download the SkyDrive desktop app from the SkyDrive Web site at apps.live.com/skydrive.) The best way to use the SkyDrive app to sync files is to store files on your PC in subfolders of the built-in libraries, such as the Documents and Pictures libraries. Duplicate these subfolders on your SkyDrive and store files in the same locations. If you use more than one computer, you can use the SkyDrive app to sync files on all of your computers.

Using Remote Desktop Connection

Another way to share information among computers is to use **Remote Desktop Connection**, a technology that allows you to use one computer to connect to a remote computer in a different location. For example, you can connect to your school or work computer from your home computer so you can access all of the programs, files, and network resources that you normally use at school or work. If you leave programs running at work, you can see your work computer's desktop displayed on your home computer, with the same programs running.

Suppose you are planning to use a mobile computer at home and want to connect to your computer at work. To use Remote Desktop Connection, the mobile computer and work computer must both be running Windows and must be connected to the same network or to the Internet. Remote Desktop Connection must also be turned on, and you must have permission to connect to the work computer. If you are using a computer at work or school, firewall settings at those locations may prevent you from connecting to another computer using Remote Desktop Connection.

Setting up Remote Desktop Connection is a two-part process. First, you allow remote connections on the computer to which you want to connect, such as your work computer. Next, you start Remote Desktop Connection on the computer you want to connect from, such as your mobile computer. You can allow connections from computers running any version of Remote Desktop Connection, including those in earlier versions of Windows. If you know that the computers connecting to your computer are also running Windows 7 or Windows 8, allow connections only if they are running **Remote Desktop with Network Level Authentication (NLA)**. This option provides more security and can protect remote computers from hackers and malware.

After viewing the presentation and discussing the proposal, the Visual Impact partners decide that they want Phil to create the custom database described in the proposal. Phil will spend some time in Newport News to work on the database. In a private office, Visual Impact is providing a desktop computer named Office-PC where Phil can develop the database when he is in Newport News. This Office-PC computer is on the Visual Impact network, but is not part of the homegroup. Phil anticipates that he will also need to access the Office-PC computer when he is not in Newport News. You'll show him how to allow remote connections on the Office-PC computer.

First, you need to determine whether the Office-PC computer is running a version of Remote Desktop with NLA. Perform the following steps on a network computer other than your computer. If you do not have access to such a computer, read but do not perform the following steps.

To see if the computer is running a version of Remote Desktop with NLA:

▶ **1.** Press the **Windows** key 🎴 to display the Start screen, start typing **Remote Desktop Connection**, and then click **Remote Desktop Connection** on the Apps screen. The Remote Desktop Connection dialog box opens. See Figure 8-34.

Figure 8-34	Remote Desktop Connection dialog box

▶ **2.** Click the **Remote Desktop Connection** icon in the title bar, and then click **About**. A window opens describing Remote Desktop Connection. See Figure 8-35. Look for the phrase "Network Level Authentication supported," which indicates whether the computer is running a version of Remote Desktop with NLA.

Figure 8-35	About Remote Desktop Connection window

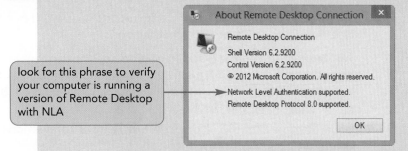

▶ **3.** Click the **OK** button to close the About Remote Desktop Connection window.

▶ **4.** Click the **Close** button ❌ to close the Remote Desktop Connection dialog box.

Now you are ready to set up your computer to allow a remote desktop connection from another computer. Before performing the following steps, sign in to your computer as an Administrator. If you are not allowed to use an Administrator account on your computer, read but do not perform the following steps.

To set up Remote Desktop Connection:

▶ **1.** Open the Control Panel, click **System and Security**, and then click **System**. The System window opens.

▶ **2.** In the left pane, click **Remote settings**. The System Properties dialog box opens to the Remote tab. See Figure 8-36.

Figure 8-36   Remote tab in the System Properties dialog box

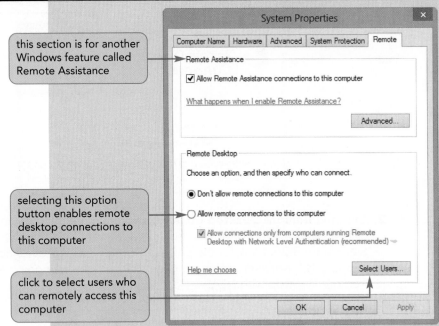

this section is for another Windows feature called Remote Assistance

selecting this option button enables remote desktop connections to this computer

click to select users who can remotely access this computer

Trouble? If you are asked for an administrator password or confirmation, type the password or provide confirmation.

Trouble? If the Remote Desktop section does not appear in your System Properties dialog box, a firewall setting might prevent you from connecting to a remote computer. Close the dialog box, and then read but do not perform the remaining steps.

▶ **3.** Under Remote Desktop, click the **Allow remote connections to this computer** option button, if necessary.

Trouble? If a dialog box opens regarding your power settings, click the OK button.

Trouble? If the check box below the Allow remote connections to this computer option button does not contain a check mark, click the check box.

▶ **4.** Click the **Select Users** button. The Remote Desktop Users dialog box opens.

▶ **5.** Make sure a message indicates that the Administrator account already has access on the computer, and then click the **OK** button to close the Remote Desktop Users dialog box.

▶ **6.** Click the **OK** button to close the System Properties dialog box. Close the System window.

To allow users other than the Administrator to use a remote desktop connection to your computer, click the Add button in the Remote Desktop Users dialog box, enter the name of the user, or computer, who can access your computer, and then click the OK button. The name you entered appears in the list of users in the Remote Desktop Users dialog box. You can remove any user who should not have remote access.

After you set up Remote Desktop Connection on your remote computer, such as the one at work, you can start Remote Desktop Connection on the computer you want to work from, such as the mobile computer. Before you do, you need to know the name of the computer to which you want to connect. To find the name of a computer, you open the System window by opening the Control Panel, click System and Security, and then click System. The computer name is listed in the Computer name, domain, and workgroup settings section.

The following steps assume that you are set up to connect to a remote computer. To do so, you need to know the name of the computer to which you want to connect. If you are not set up to connect to a remote computer, read but do not perform the following steps. Perform the following steps using the notebook you used to create the homegroup.

To start Remote Desktop Connection to connect to a remote computer:

▶ **1.** Use the Search charm to open the Remote Desktop Connection dialog box again.

▶ **2.** In the Computer text box, type **Office-PC**. This is the name of the desktop computer Phil will use at Visual Impact.

   Trouble? If the name of the remote computer to which you want to connect is not named Office-PC, enter its name instead of Office-PC in the Computer text box.

▶ **3.** Click the **Connect** button to connect to that computer on your network.

   Trouble? If a Remote Desktop Connection dialog box opens asking if you want to connect even though the identity of the remote computer cannot be verified, click the Yes button.

▶ **4.** If necessary, enter your user name and password, and then click the **OK** button to establish the connection.

▶ **5.** Click the **Close** button, and then click the **OK** button to disconnect.

Now Phil can access the Office-PC computer at Visual Impact when he is working in the VBIC offices in Richmond.

Restoring Your Settings

If you are working in a computer lab or on a computer other than your own, complete the steps in this section to restore the original settings on your computer.

To restore your settings:

▶ **1.** Open Windows Mobility Center, and then drag the **Volume** slider to its original setting.

▶ **2.** If necessary, click the **Mute** check box to remove the check mark and turn the speakers on.

    Trouble? If your speakers were turned off when you originally opened Windows Mobility Center in Session 8.1, skip Step 2.

▶ **3.** Click the **Change power settings** icon 📦 in the Battery Status tile to open the Power Options window, and then click the **Balanced** option button, if necessary.

▶ **4.** Click **Change plan settings** for the Balanced power plan, click **Restore default settings for this plan** in the Edit Plan Settings window, and then click the **Yes** button to restore the settings. Close the Edit Plan Settings window.

▶ **5.** In the Windows Mobility Center window, click the **Change presentation settings** icon 🖥️ in the Presentation Settings tile, and then restore the screen saver, volume, and background controls to their original settings. Click the **OK** button. Close the Windows Mobility Center window.

▶ **6.** Open the Network folder window, and then navigate to the Public Documents folder on the network. Click the **Public Documents** folder, click the **Easy access** button in the New group on the Home tab, and then click **Work offline** to deselect the option.

▶ **7.** Open the HomeGroup folder window from the Navigation pane. Click the **Homegroup** tab, if necessary, click the **Change homegroup settings** button in the Manage group, click the **Leave the homegroup** link, and then click **Leave the homegroup** to confirm you want to leave. Click the **Finish** button. Close all windows.

▶ **8.** Open the Remote Desktop Connection dialog box. In the Computer text box, select the name of the computer to which you have a remote desktop connection, such as Conference, and then click the **Disconnect** button, if necessary.

▶ **9.** Delete the **VBIC** folder from the Documents folder, and then close all open windows.

In this session, you learned how to create and join a homegroup and then share files with other members of the homegroup. You also learned how to access offline files and then synchronize them with network files. Finally, you learned how to use Remote Desktop Connection to connect to a remote computer.

REVIEW

Session 8.2 Quick Check

1. A(n) _Homegroup_ is a group of computers on a home network that can share files and printers.
2. After setting up a homegroup with two or more computers, how can you share files?
3. How can you tell if Windows can automatically connect to a homegroup printer?
4. A(n) _offline files_ is a copy of a network file that you can access even when you are not connected to the network.
5. Sync Center can keep files in sync in two circumstances. What are these two circumstances?
6. If you want to connect to your work computer from your home computer, you could use _____.
7. What can you use to keep files on your SkyDrive in sync with files on your PC?

PRACTICE

Review Assignments

There are no Data Files needed for the Review Assignments.

You are now working with Phil Mendoza's partner, Lily Hammond, to help her prepare for a meeting with a client in Norfolk, Virginia—a small video production studio named Norfolk Video. Lily asks you to help her prepare her mobile computer for the trip and for a presentation she plans to make to Norfolk Video when she arrives. Lily also requests your help with connecting her Windows 8 notebook to the Norfolk Video wireless network and sharing some of its resources. Complete the following steps, noting your original settings so you can restore them later:

1. Open Windows Mobility Center, and then change the speaker volume to 25.

2. In the Power Options window, change the plan settings for the Power saver plan so that the display turns off after 10 minutes of idle time when running on battery power and after 15 minutes when plugged in. (If you are not using a mobile computer, set the Power saver plan to turn off the display after 15 minutes of idle time.) Save your changes. Use the advanced settings to have the plan hibernate after 45 minutes of idle time on any type of power. (*Hint*: Use the Change advanced power settings link to open the Power Options dialog box.)

3. Display the settings for the Power saver plan with the Power Options dialog box clearly visible as well, and then press the Print Screen key to capture an image of the window. Paste the image in a new Paint file, and then save the file as **Saver** in the Windows8\Review folder provided with your Data Files.

4. Change what the hardware power buttons do so that when you press a power button when running on battery power, your computer hibernates. (If you are not using a mobile computer, do the same for the default type of power.) Press the Print Screen key to capture an image of the window. Paste the image in a new Paint file, and then save the file as **Power Button** in the Windows8\Review folder provided with your Data Files. Save your changes, and then close the Power Options window.

5. Change the presentation settings so that when you give a presentation, you turn off the screen saver, set the volume to 75, and show img11 as the desktop background. Press the Print Screen key to capture an image of the window. Paste the image in a new Paint file, and then save the file as **Presentation** in the Windows8\Review folder provided with your Data Files.

6. Connect to an available wireless network, entering a security key or passphrase as necessary. (If you are not equipped to connect to a wireless network, connect to a wired network.) Open the Network and Sharing Center window, and then capture an image of the screen. Paste the image in a new Paint file, and then save the file as **Wireless** in the Windows8\Review folder provided with your Data Files.

7. If necessary, connect to an available homegroup or create a new homegroup. Change the home-group settings to share all libraries, printers, and devices. Press the Print Screen key to capture an image of the window. Paste the image in a new Paint file, and then save the file as **Homegroup** in the Windows8\Review folder provided with your Data Files.

8. From the Network window, navigate to the Public Downloads folder on a homegroup computer, if possible, and then make that folder always available offline. As Windows is making the files available, press the Print Screen key to capture an image of the screen. Paste the image in a new Paint file, and then save the file as **Offline** in the Windows8\Review folder provided with your Data Files.

9. Copy a file from the My Documents folder on your computer to the Public Downloads folder on a homegroup computer, if possible.

10. Open Sync Center and synchronize the offline files. When the sync is finished, view the sync results and then press the Print Screen key to capture an image of the window. Paste the image in a new Paint file, and then save the file as **Sync** in the Windows8\Review folder provided with your Data Files.

11. Open the Remote tab in the System Properties dialog box, and then allow connections only from computers running Remote Desktop with NLA. Press the Print Screen key to capture an image of the dialog box with this setting. Paste the image in a new Paint file, and then save the file as **Remote Desktop** in the Windows8\Review folder provided with your Data Files. Close all open dialog boxes.

12. Restore your original settings. Change the speaker volume to its original setting. Change the Power saver plan to its default settings, and then select your original plan. Restore the original action to the hardware power button. Restore the presentation settings to their original form. Deselect the option to make offline files available for the Public Downloads folder on the network computer. Disconnect from the network, if necessary, and then close all open windows.

13. Submit the results of the preceding steps to your instructor, either in printed or electronic form, as requested.

Case Problem 1

APPLY

There are no Data Files needed for this Case Problem.

Over the Moon Theater   Graham Hanlon is the director of the Over the Moon Theater in Boulder, Colorado. The theater provides a traveling troupe of actors and puppeteers who give educational performances to children around the country. Graham recently hired you to train him and the traveling troupe members in using Windows 8 to perform mobile computing tasks, including managing power options and connecting to wireless networks when working at theaters outside of Boulder. Complete the following steps, noting your original settings so you can restore them later:

1. Open Windows Mobility Center, and then mute the speakers.

2. Change the plan settings for the Balanced plan so that the display turns off after 10 minutes of idle time when running on battery power, and after 1 hour when plugged in.

3. Set the Balanced plan to hibernate after 60 minutes whether running on battery or another type of power. Arrange the Power Options dialog box and the Edit Plan Settings window so you can see the settings in both windows, and then press the Print Screen key to capture an image of the desktop. Paste the image in a new Paint file, and then save the file as **Edited Plan** in the Windows8\Case1 folder provided with your Data Files. Save your changes.

4. Set the computer to require a password when waking from sleep. Press the Print Screen key to capture an image of the window. Paste the image in a new Paint file, and then save the file as **Wakeup** in the Windows8\Case1 folder provided with your Data Files. Save your changes, and then close the Power Options window.

5. Change the presentation settings so that when you give a presentation, the volume is set to High, the screen saver is turned off, and the background displays img4. Press the Print Screen key to capture an image of the Presentation Settings dialog box. Paste the image in a new Paint file, and then save the file as **Settings** in the Windows8\Case1 folder provided with your Data Files. Save your changes.

6. Display a list of wireless networks within range of your computer. Capture an image of the screen. Paste the image in a new Paint file, and then save the file as **Networks** in the Windows8\Case1 folder provided with your Data Files.

7. Open the HomeGroup window, and then open the Advanced sharing settings window. Expand the Private section, if necessary. Press the Print Screen key to capture an image of the window. Paste the image in a new Paint file, and then save the file as **Private** in the Windows8\Case1 folder provided with your Data Files.

8. Open the Remote Desktop Connection dialog box, and then determine whether your computer supports Network Level Authentication. Press the Print Screen key to capture an image of the window that provides this information. Paste the image in a new Paint file, and then save the file as **RDC** in the Windows8\Case1 folder provided with your Data Files. Close all Control Panel windows.

9. Restore your original settings by turning on the speakers. Change the Balanced power plan to its default settings, and then select your original plan. Remove password protection on wakeup. Restore the presentation settings to their original form. Close all open windows.

10. Submit the results of the preceding steps to your instructor, either in printed or electronic form, as requested.

Case Problem 2

There are no Data Files needed for this Case Problem.

Open-Air Rooms Jessica Underwood started Open-Air Rooms in Birmingham, Alabama, to create spaces where homeowners can entertain and enjoy the outdoors. Jessica often travels around the Birmingham area to meet with potential clients and vendors, so she wants to know more about the Windows 8 mobile computing features. During many meetings, she plays slide shows that run on a notebook computer to showcase her designs. As Jessica's assistant, you help her with a wide range of tasks, including managing the company's computers. She asks you to help her use Windows 8 to perform mobile computing tasks, including managing power options and giving presentations. Complete the following steps, noting your original settings so you can restore them later:

1. Open Windows Mobility Center and then change the speaker volume to 30.

2. Change the plan settings for the Power saver plan so that the display turns off after five minutes of idle time when running on battery power and after 30 minutes when plugged in. (If you are not using a mobile computer, set the display to turn off after 30 minutes of idle time.)

⊕ **Explore** 3. For the Power saver plan, enable adaptive brightness for all types of power, which is an advanced setting. Arrange the Power Options dialog box and the Edit Plan Settings window so you can see the settings in both windows, and then press the Print Screen key to capture an image of the desktop. Paste the image in a new Paint file, and then save the file as **Display** in the Windows8\Case2 folder provided with your Data Files.

4. Set the computer to hibernate when you press a hardware power button while using any type of power. Make sure a password is required to access your computer when it wakes up. Press the Print Screen key to capture an image of the window. Paste the image in a new Paint file, and then save the file as **Hibernate** in the Windows8\Case2 folder provided with your Data Files. Save your changes, and then close the Power Options window.

5. Change the presentation settings so that when you give a presentation, the volume is set to 80, the screen saver is turned off, and a black background is displayed. Press the Print Screen key to capture an image of the Presentation Settings dialog box. Paste the image in a new Paint file, and then save the file as **Black** in the Windows8\Case2 folder provided with your Data Files. Save your changes.

CHALLENGE

⊕ **Explore** 6. Open the HomeGroup window, and then open the Advanced sharing settings window. In the settings for All Networks, display the media streaming options. Press the Print Screen key to capture an image of the window. Paste the image in a new Paint file, and then save the file as **Media** in the Windows8\Case2 folder provided with your Data Files.

⊕ **Explore** 7. From the HomeGroup window, start the HomeGroup troubleshooter. Follow the steps in the Troubleshooter until the results are displayed, and then press the Print Screen key to capture an image of the screen. Paste the image in a new Paint file, and then save the file as **Trouble** in the Windows8\Case2 folder provided with your Data Files.

8. Open a window that displays devices on your network. Press the Print Screen key to capture an image of the screen. Paste the image in a new Paint file, and then save the file as **Network Devices** in the Windows8\Case2 folder provided with your Data Files.

9. Restore your original settings. Change the speaker volume to its original setting. Change the Power saver plan to its default settings, and then select your original plan. Restore the presentation settings to their original form. Close all open windows.

10. Submit the results of the preceding steps to your instructor, either in printed or electronic form, as requested.

Case Problem 3

TROUBLESHOOT

There are no Data Files needed for this Case Problem.

Kenyon Polling   Max Kenyon is a polling specialist who consults with companies, political candidates, and other public personalities who need to refer to poll results to make decisions. His company, Kenyon Polling in Barrington, Illinois, employs people who often work on mobile computers at their clients' offices. As a project assistant, part of your job is to make sure the employees are using their computers effectively. Max asks you to show him how to use Windows 8 to perform mobile computing tasks, including conserving battery power, connecting to networks, and sharing files. Complete the following steps, noting your original settings so you can restore them later:

1. Open the Power Options window, click a link to learn more about power plans, and then click a link to learn about fast startup. Read the information about fast startup. Leave the Help and Support window open.

2. Use the Power Options window to define power buttons, set the computer to hibernate on battery power for all power buttons and closing the computer lid, and make sure fast startup is turned on. Arrange the windows to display the help topic and the Power Options setting. Press the Print Screen key to capture an image of the screen. Paste the image in a new Paint file, and then save the file as **Save Power** in the Windows8\Case3 folder provided with your Data Files.

3. In the Power Options window, show additional plans. Change the High performance power plan to turn off the display after five minutes of idle time when running on battery power, and after 15 minutes when plugged in. (If you are not using a mobile computer, set the display to turn off after 15 minutes of idle time.) Use advanced settings to have the plan hibernate after 120 minutes of idle time when using any type of power. Press the Print Screen key to capture an image of the window. Paste the image in a new Paint file, and then save the file as **Kenyon** in the Windows8\Case3 folder provided with your Data Files.

4. Change the presentation settings so that when you give a presentation, the volume is set to 75, the screen saver is turned off, and img12 is shown as the desktop background. Press the Print Screen key to capture an image of the screen. Paste the image in a new Paint file, and then save the file as **Present** in the Windows8\Case3 folder provided with your Data Files.

5. Connect to an available wireless network, entering a security key or passphrase as necessary. (If you are not equipped to connect to a wireless network, connect to a wired network.)

⚙ **Troubleshoot** 6. Use the Search text box in the Control Panel window to search for trouble-shooting computer problems. Start a wizard that troubleshoots Internet connections, and then capture an image of the desktop. Paste the image in a new Paint file, and then save the file as **Connections** in the Windows8\Case3 folder provided with your Data Files.

7. Make a folder in the Public folder always available offline. Display the menu indicating this setting is turned on, and then press the Print Screen key to capture an image of the screen. Paste the image in a new Paint file, and then save the file as **Public** in the Windows8\Case3 folder provided with your Data Files. Close all open windows.

⚙ **Troubleshoot** 8. Start a troubleshooting wizard that can find and fix problems with accessing files and folders on other computers. Run the wizard. After Windows finishes detecting problems, capture an image of the screen. Paste the image in a new Paint file, and then save the file as **Shared Folders** in the Windows8\Case3 folder provided with your Data Files.

9. Open Sync Center and synchronize the offline files. When the sync is finished, view the sync results, resize the columns to show the date of the sync, and then press the Print Screen key to capture an image of the window. Paste the image in a new Paint file, and then save the file as **Sync** in the Windows8\Case3 folder provided with your Data Files.

10. Change the homegroup settings on your computer to share only documents. Capture an image of the window. Paste the image in a new Paint file, and then save the file as **Homegroup** in the Windows8\Case3 folder provided with your Data Files.

11. Restore your original settings. Restore the High performance power plan to its default settings, and then select your original plan. Restore the presentation settings to their original form. Restore the original sharing setting for the Public Documents folder on the network computer. Close all open windows.

12. Submit the results of the preceding steps to your instructor, either in printed or electronic form, as requested.

RESEARCH

Case Problem 4

There are no Data Files needed for this Case Problem.

Monroe Day School   The faculty and staff of the Monroe Day School in Monroe, Louisiana, are considering connecting their computers on a network. The school has the following characteristics and requirements:

- There are 12 users—eight on mobile computers and four on desktop computers.
- All computers are running Windows 8.
- Most of the faculty use their computers outside of the office.
- All users often distribute large files to other users.

Wilson Thibodeau is the technology manager at the school, and he asks you, an administrative assistant, to help him research small office networks using the Internet and Windows Help and Support. Complete the following steps:

1. Use the Internet to research appropriate networks for the Monroe Day School. Choose two types of networks to recommend. Create a document with four column headings: **Network Technology**, **Hardware Requirements**, **Speed**, and **Cost**. Complete the columns according to the following descriptions:

Network Technology	Hardware Requirements	Speed	Cost
List two types of networks.	List devices and other hardware required.	List speed considerations or rates.	List cost considerations.

2. Save the document as **Monroe** in the Windows8\Case4 folder provided with your Data Files.

3. Submit the results of the preceding steps to your instructor, either in printed or electronic form, as requested.

Maintaining Hardware and Software

Managing Software, Disks, and Devices

OBJECTIVES

Session 9.1
- Back up and restore files
- Create a system restore point
- Install and uninstall software
- Explore Windows To Go drives

Session 9.2
- Maintain hard disks
- Enable and disable hardware devices
- Install and update device drivers
- Adjust monitor settings
- Install and set up printers

Case | Arlington Wellness Center

The Arlington Wellness Center in St. Paul, Minnesota, provides fitness training and classes for people who want to improve their health through nutrition and exercise and for others who are rehabilitating from illness or injury. Andrea Keenan is the director of the Arlington Wellness Center. When she needs to complete office work, she conducts much of her business on a Windows 8 PC. As her assistant office manager, you are responsible for maintaining the hardware and software at the center.

In this tutorial, you will set up the File History feature to back up files and folders automatically and to restore files you've backed up. You will also create a system recovery drive and then learn how to refresh and reset Windows 8. After preparing to install new apps, you will install software from the Windows Store and view your updates. You will also learn how employees can work efficiently at home or the office using Windows To Go. To improve system performance, you will check for problems on a hard disk and learn how to maintain the devices attached to a computer, including your monitor and printer.

STARTING DATA FILES

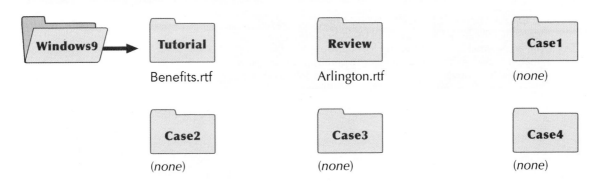

Windows9 → Tutorial
Benefits.rtf

Review
Arlington.rtf

Case1
(*none*)

Case2
(*none*)

Case3
(*none*)

Case4
(*none*)

Session 9.1 Visual Overview:

When you **restore** a file, you use Windows to recover a saved version of the file from File History and to copy it to a location you specify.

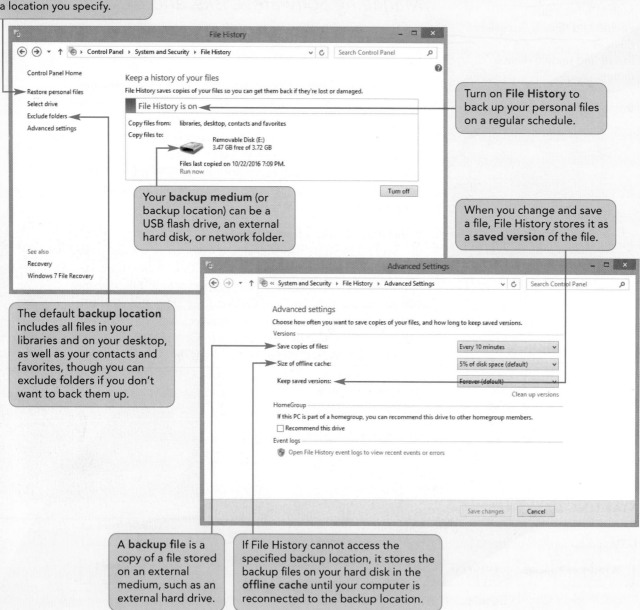

Turn on **File History** to back up your personal files on a regular schedule.

Your **backup medium** (or backup location) can be a USB flash drive, an external hard disk, or network folder.

When you change and save a file, File History stores it as a **saved version** of the file.

The default **backup location** includes all files in your libraries and on your desktop, as well as your contacts and favorites, though you can exclude folders if you don't want to back them up.

A **backup file** is a copy of a file stored on an external medium, such as an external hard drive.

If File History cannot access the specified backup location, it stores the backup files on your hard disk in the **offline cache** until your computer is reconnected to the backup location.

Managing Data and Software

Installed programs have been set up on your computer so that you can run them.

If a program is not running correctly, you can change or repair the installation.

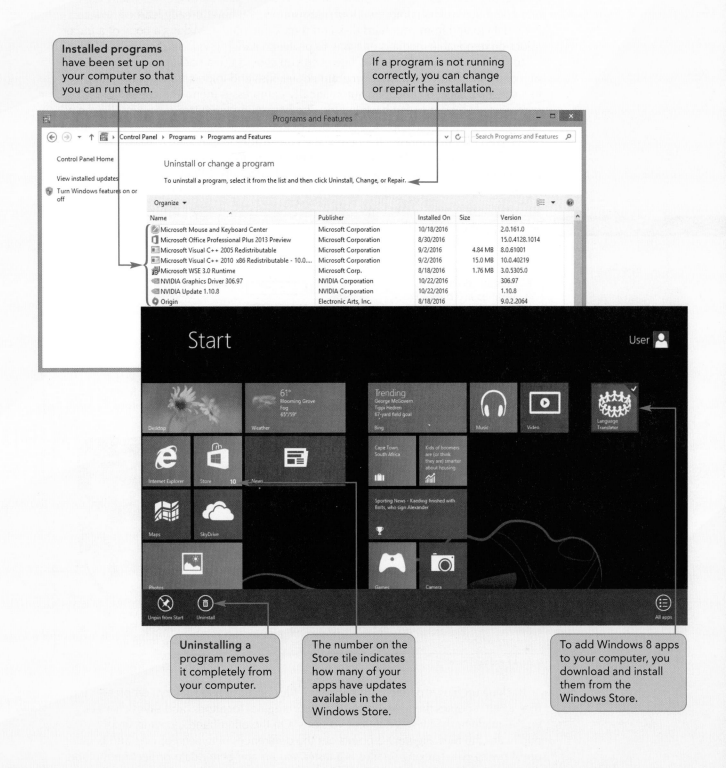

Uninstalling a program removes it completely from your computer.

The number on the Store tile indicates how many of your apps have updates available in the Windows Store.

To add Windows 8 apps to your computer, you download and install them from the Windows Store.

Backing Up and Restoring Files

No one is safe from computer problems that result in data loss. Problems such as a power surge, a power loss, a failed section of a hard disk, or a computer virus can strike at any time. Rather than risk disaster, you should make copies of your important files regularly. By doing so, if disaster strikes, you will be able to recover your files and continue working almost without interruption. You have already learned how to copy data to and from your hard disk and removable media. Making a copy of a file or folder on removable media is one way to protect data.

To protect data on a hard disk, however, you should use a backup program instead of a copy procedure. A **backup program** copies files and folders from a hard disk to a specified location and then automatically compresses them. The copied and compressed files are called backup files. The backup program stores backup files on a backup medium (or backup location) such as an external hard disk or a network drive. To back up files in Windows 8, you use the File History feature.

To illustrate how File History works, suppose you store all of your important files in the Documents library in three folders named Accounts, Clients, and Projects. Figure 9-1 shows how File History backs up the files in these folders.

| Figure 9-1 | Backing up data using File History |

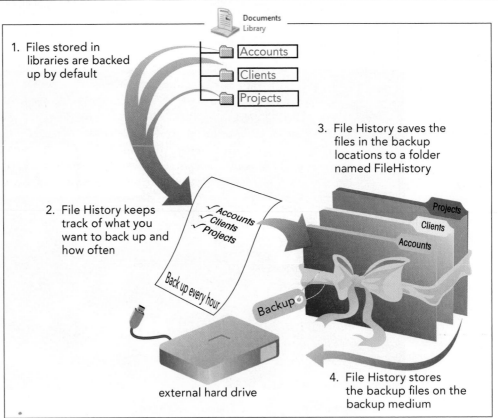

© 2014 Cengage Learning

Backing up files is different from copying files because File History compresses the files when it copies them, keeps track of their original locations, and saves changes you've made to the files as different versions. On the other hand, copying simply duplicates the files. Figure 9-2 points out the differences between copying and backing up, showing why backing up files is a faster, easier, and better data-protection method than copying files.

| Figure 9-2 | Comparing copying and backing up files |

Copy	Back Up
Copying your files can be time consuming and tedious because you must navigate to and select each file and folder that you want to copy.	Using File History is faster because you select folders in one step, and File History automatically backs up the files in those folders every hour.
Because a copy of a file occupies the same amount of space as the original file, making a copy of all the files on a hard disk is impractical.	When File History backs up your files, it compresses them so they take up much less space than the original files.
You need to manually track which files and folders have changed since your last backup.	File History keeps track of which files and folders are new or modified, and then backs up only the files that have changed since your last backup.
You need to set reminders on your own to create backups periodically.	File History regularly backs up your files and folders so that you don't have to remember to do it.
If you do lose data because of a computer failure, it is not easy to locate a file you need in your backups.	File History keeps track of the files you have backed up, and makes it easy to find and recover a file.

© 2014 Cengage Learning

By using File History to back up your files, you don't have to worry if you lose an important file or damage your hard disk. You can use File History to restore a particular version of a file. For example, suppose you start writing a report on Monday, add information to it on Tuesday and Wednesday, and then complete the report on Thursday. You've saved the report in a folder in the Documents library. File History is turned on, so Windows is backing up the report file every hour. Several days later, you realize that you accidentally deleted a table of important information that you want to include in the report. Instead of trying to re-create the table, you can use File History to restore a version of the report file that still includes the table. By copying the table from the backup file to the current version of the report, you save a lot of time and anguish.

REFERENCE

Setting Up File History to Back Up Files

- Open the Control Panel, click System and Security, and then click File History.
- Select a backup location (or medium).
- Select folders and files you want to back up.
- Specify the advanced options, including how often the backup should occur and how much of the disk space you want to allot.
- Click the Turn on button.

If you back up files using Windows 7, you can use Windows Backup to back up and restore your files. Windows Backup is considered a **legacy program**, which means it is designed for earlier versions of Windows and is being phased out of use.

Setting Up File History

By default, File History is turned off because it needs information from you before it can start backing up your files. Backing up files with File History involves the following general tasks:

- Selecting a backup location (or medium)
- Selecting folders and files you want to back up

- Specifying the advanced options, including how often the backup should occur, how much of the disk space you want to assign to backups, and how long you want to keep the different versions of the backups

Once you set up File History, you can turn it on so it automatically begins backing up your files every hour to your specified backup medium, which you will explore next, and keeps all copies of the files indefinitely. By default, File History backs up all the files in the libraries, desktop, favorites, and contacts for your user account. You can change the frequency of the backups, the backup location, how long File History keeps the backup files, and the folders to include in the backup.

Selecting the Backup Location

With Windows 8, you can create backups on an external hard drive, a USB flash drive, or a network folder. To select the location that is best for you, consider the hardware installed on your computer as well as the number and size of files that you want to back up. You can back up files to any of the following locations:

- External hard drive—If your computer has a USB port, you can attach an external hard drive to it and then back up files to the external drive. If you plan to back up all of your libraries, desktop, favorites, and contacts, use an external hard drive with plenty of space. The capacity of external hard drives ranges from 320 GB to a few terabytes. (A **terabyte (TB)** is equivalent to 1,000 gigabytes.) Because of its portability, capacity, and ease of use, backing up to an external hard drive is the option experienced computer users prefer.
- USB flash drive—If you are backing up a limited amount of data, you can use a USB flash drive. Capacities typically range from 4 GB to 128 GB of data. USB flash drives are inexpensive and convenient, so they are a good choice for documents and other personal files. However, they are less reliable than external hard disks, so they are not suitable for long-term file storage.
- Network folder—If your computer is on a network, you can create a backup on a network folder. You need to have permission to save files in the folder and set sharing options so that unauthorized users cannot access the backup.

If your computer is not equipped with a USB port or if you are not connected to a network, you can use an Internet-based file storage service instead of File History. These services let you store personal, password-protected backups, usually on a server you can access via the Internet. File History does not support these types of online backup locations.

Selecting Folders to Back Up

By default, File History backs up all the files in your libraries and their folders, including libraries you created yourself, desktop files, browser favorites, and contact records. These locations should include all of your documents, pictures, music, videos, compressed folders, and other personal files. File History does not back up files stored in any other locations. For example, File History does not let you back up system files, program files, Web email not stored on your hard disk, files in the Recycle Bin, temporary files, or user profile settings. In addition, you cannot back up files that have been encrypted using the Encrypting File System (EFS), which is a Windows feature that allows you to store information on your hard disk in an encrypted format. Furthermore, you can back up only files stored on hard disks formatted with the NT File System (NTFS), not the earlier versions of the file allocation table (FAT) file system. Nearly all hard disks in contemporary computers use NTFS.

Determining Which Files to Back Up

The most valuable files on your computer are your data files—the documents, pictures, videos, projects, and financial records that you create and edit. You should back up any data files that would be difficult or impossible to replace, and regularly back up files that you change frequently. You should also back up browser favorites and contact records, which File History does by default, because this information would be time consuming and difficult to re-create manually. You don't need to back up programs because you can download them from the vendor's Web site again or use the original product discs to reinstall them, and programs typically take up a lot of space on backup media.

In some cases, you might want to exclude folders from the backup. For example, if you've stored many large files in the Videos library that you could download from a Web site, you can conserve storage space by excluding the Videos library from the backup.

Changing Advanced Settings

By default, File History backs up copies of files every hour, which is considered a continuous backup cycle. It also keeps saved versions of files forever, so you can restore any saved copy of a document if necessary. You use the Advanced Settings window to change these and other settings as follows:

- Save copies of files—If you are working on an important project and can't afford to lose even a few minutes of work, you can change this setting from every hour to every 10, 15, 20, or 25 minutes. If you work at your computer infrequently and notice the system slows during backups, you can increase the amount of time between backups to every 3, 6, or 12 hours or to once a day.
- Size of offline cache—If File History cannot access the external drive or network folder that you specified for backups, it stores the backup files in a temporary area of storage on your hard disk called the offline cache. When your computer is reconnected to the backup location, File History moves the backup files from the offline cache to the backup location. This feature is especially convenient if you are using a mobile computer because File History continues to create backups even when you are disconnected from your backup location. By default, File History uses up to 5 percent of disk space for the offline cache. You can decrease this to 2 percent or increase it to 10 or 20 percent of hard disk space, depending on how long your computer is disconnected from the backup medium and the amount of files you change.
- Keep saved versions—By default, File History keeps saved versions of files forever so you can access every version of a saved file when necessary. However, if the backup location is quickly running out of space, you can change this setting to 1, 3, 6, or 9 months; 1 or 2 years; or until space is needed. You can also click the Clean up versions link and then select which versions to delete, such as those older than 1 year.

Using File History with a Homegroup

If you are a member of a homegroup, you can use File History to invite other members of the homegroup to back up files in a central backup location. To do so, select the Recommend this drive check box in the Advanced Settings window. File History sends a message to the other members of the homegroup asking if they want to back up their personal files. If they accept the invitation, their files are backed up according to your File History settings.

Backing Up Files

After you set up File History, specify a backup location, select folders to back up, and change any advanced settings as necessary, you are ready to start backing up files. Before you do so for Andrea, you should copy files to a library on Andrea's computer so that File History includes them in the backup. You'll store the files in a folder named Andrea so that you can find them easily later.

To copy files to the Andrea folder:

▶ **1.** Open File Explorer on the desktop, and then navigate to the Public Documents folder in the Documents library on the hard disk of your computer.

▶ **2.** Click the **New folder** button in the New group on the Home tab.

▶ **3.** Type **Andrea** as the name of the folder, and then press the **Enter** key.

▶ **4.** Copy the **Benefits** file from the Windows9\Tutorial folder provided with your Data Files to the Andrea folder.

▶ **5.** Close all open folder windows.

> Make sure you are creating the new folder in the Public Documents folder, not the My Documents folder.

To back up Andrea's file, your computer needs access to a USB flash drive. In the following steps, this drive is named Removable Disk on drive E. Substitute the name of your backup location for Removable Disk (E:) as necessary. Keep in mind that when you use File History to back up your personal files, you can choose an external hard drive or a network folder instead.

To start File History:

▶ **1.** Open the Control Panel window in Category view.

▶ **2.** Click **System and Security,** and then click **File History** to open the File History window.

> **Trouble?** If System and Security does not appear in your Control Panel window, click the View by button, click Category, and then repeat Step 2.

▶ **3.** Insert a USB flash drive in a USB port, and then press the **F5** key to refresh the File History window, which now identifies the USB flash drive as a backup location. See Figure 9-3.

> **Trouble?** If a folder window for the USB drive opens, click the Close button ✕.

> **Trouble?** If your USB flash drive does not appear in the File History window, click Select drive in the left pane, and then select your USB flash drive.

Figure 9-3   File History window

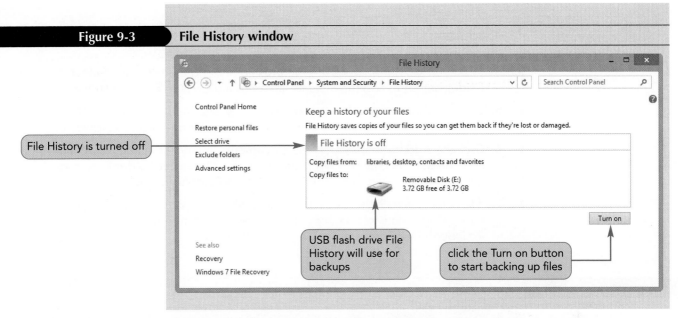

If you wanted to save backup copies of all of the files in the libraries and desktop of your computer as well as all of your favorites and contacts, you could click the Turn on button to start backing up those files. In this case, you want to back up only the files in the Public Documents folder, which includes the Andrea folder, so you must exclude the other default locations.

To exclude folders from the backup:

1. Click **Exclude folders** in the left pane of the File History window to open the Exclude Folders window.

2. Click the **Add** button to open the Select Folder window, where you select the folders you do not want to include in the backup. See Figure 9-4.

Figure 9-4   Select Folder window

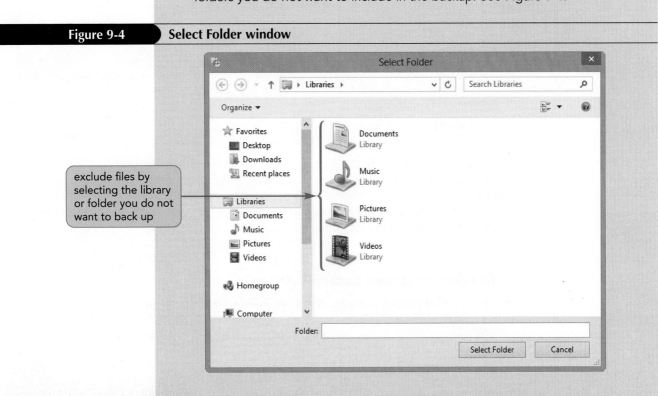

TIP

When you specify a folder to exclude, File History also excludes all of its subfolders.

▶ **3.** Click the **Music** library, and then click the **Select Folder** button to add the Music library to the Exclude Folders window.

▶ **4.** Click the **Add** button, click the **Pictures** library, and then click the **Select Folder** button to add the Pictures library to the Exclude Folders window.

▶ **5.** Click the **Add** button, click the **Videos** library, and then click the **Select Folder** button to add the Videos library to the Exclude Folders window.

▶ **6.** Click the **Add** button, expand the **Documents** library in the Navigation pane, click the **My Documents** folder, and then click the **Select Folder** button to add the My Documents folder to the Exclude Folders window.

▶ **7.** If the Documents library contains folders other than the My Documents and Public Documents folders, repeat Step 6 as many times as necessary to exclude those folders from the backup. The Exclude Folders window should look similar to Figure 9-5.

Figure 9-5	Exclude Folders window with excluded folders

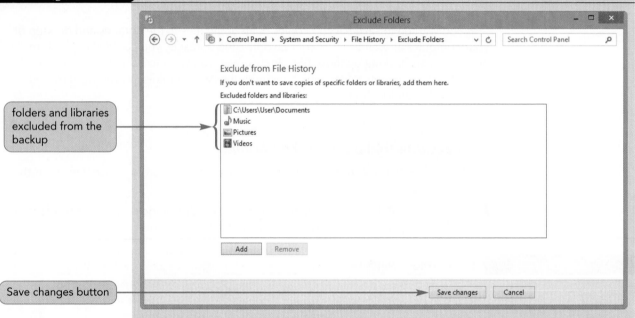

folders and libraries excluded from the backup

Save changes button

▶ **8.** Click the **Save changes** button to save your selections and return to the File History window.

Now File History will back up only files stored in the Public Documents folder, including those in the Andrea folder. It will also back up any desktop, favorite, and contact files.

To show Andrea how File History saves versions of files, you can set File History to back up more often than every hour.

To select advanced backup settings:

▶ **1.** Click **Advanced settings** in the left pane of the File History window to open the Advanced Settings window. See Figure 9-6.

| Figure 9-6 | Advanced Settings window |

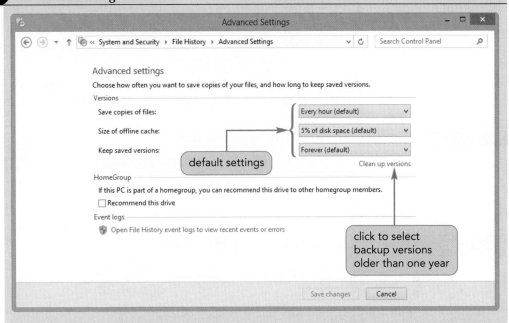

2. Click the **Every hour (default)** button to display a list of time intervals, and then click **Every 10 minutes** to have File History back up files in the specified locations every 10 minutes.

3. Click the **Save changes** button to save your setting change and return to the File History window.

Decision Making: Creating a Backup Strategy

Before you back up files, develop a backup strategy that you can follow throughout the life of your computer. A backup strategy is a routine you develop for creating backups regularly. The most effective strategy balances security, efficiency, and storage space. Consider the following scenarios:

- Security—If your only concern is security, you could set File History to back up all the files in the default locations more frequently than every hour and store the backup file indefinitely. However, this approach devotes many resources to creating backups and consumes a lot of storage space on the backup medium.
- Efficiency—If your main concern is efficiency, you could save time and money by backing up only your most important files occasionally, such as once a day, and storing them for a limited amount of time. The drawback is that you risk losing many hours of work with this strategy. Instead, you should set a backup routine that secures your data without costing you too much time and money.
- Low computer usage—If you create and modify only a few documents a week, you could back up all of your personal files less frequently than every hour, but store them forever in case you need them.
- High computer usage—If you create and modify many important documents each day, and losing any of those documents would be a hardship, you should back up all of your personal files at least every hour and store them forever.

Now you are ready to turn on File History and back up files.

To start backing up files:

1. Click the **Turn on** button in the File History window. File History reports that it is saving copies of your files for the first time. See Figure 9-7. Keep in mind that these are backup copies of your files, not copies you could create your-self using the Copy command.

Trouble? If a dialog box opens asking if you want to recommend this drive to other members of your homegroup, click the No button.

Figure 9-7 **Using File History to back up files**

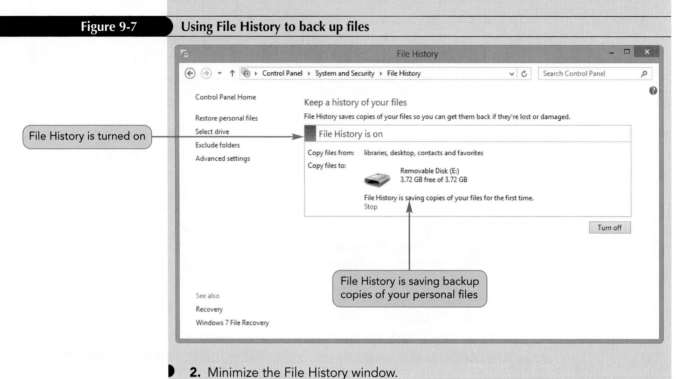

2. Minimize the File History window.

The first time File History backs up your files, it creates a folder named **FileHistory** in your backup location, and then copies all of the files saved in libraries, on the desktop, and as favorites or contacts, except for those folders you excluded from the backup. This is considered a full backup of your files. Do not delete or move the FileHistory folder in your backup location. If you delete the FileHistory folder, you will lose your backup files. If you move the folder, File History can no longer use it to track the files that have changed on your computer.

After making the first full backup, File History works in the background to back up only files that have changed since your last backup. That means it doesn't need as much storage space to create the subsequent backups. If the backup medium runs out of storage space, File History asks you to replace the drive with a bigger one or change the setting that tells File History how long to keep saved versions. If you replace the drive, File History continues to back up only files that have changed since your last backup. Be sure to store the original drive in a safe place in case you need to restore files it contains.

To demonstrate to Andrea how File History maintains separate versions of backup files, you can change the file stored in the Andrea folder. The Benefits file lists the benefits of becoming a member of the Arlington Wellness Center. You can research the benefits of any fitness center and then add a benefit to the list in the Benefits file.

To modify the Benefits file:

▶ **1.** Click the **File Explorer** button 📁 on the taskbar to open a folder window, and then navigate to the **Andrea** folder in the Public Documents folder.

▶ **2.** Double-click the **Benefits** document in the Andrea folder to open the document in an application such as WordPad or Microsoft Word, and then read the list of benefits.

▶ **3.** Click the **Internet Explorer** button 🅔 on the taskbar to start IE Desktop.

▶ **4.** Use a search engine and your searching skills to find information about fitness centers like the Arlington Wellness Center and the benefits they offer to members.

▶ **5.** In the Benefits document, select the text in the first bullet ("Group exercise studios"), and then replace it with text describing a benefit you found.

▶ **6.** Save the Benefits document, and then close the application window.

▶ **7.** Close Internet Explorer.

When you saved the Benefits document, you saved a different version of the document. The original version includes "Group exercise studios" as the text for the first bullet, and the updated version contains your replacement text.

Restoring Files and Folders

All hard disks eventually fail, even if you maintain them conscientiously. When a hard disk fails, you can no longer access the files it contains. For that reason alone, you should back up your personal files regularly. If your hard disk does fail and a computer maintenance expert believes data recovery is nearly impossible, you'll need to install a new hard disk or reformat the one that you have. Practically everyone who has been using computers for a long time has a data loss story to tell. Many computer owners who now make regular backups learned the hard way how important it is to protect data. Backing up your files is one of the most effective ways to save time and maintain data integrity when you are working on a computer. Create the first backup file, and then let File History regularly create backup copies of updated files. If you do lose data, File History allows you to easily restore the files you lost.

In earlier versions of Windows backup applications, you restored files by first selecting a set of backups created on a certain date. Next, you navigated the backup set to find a folder and then the file you want. To determine the contents of the file, you restored it to the hard disk, and then opened it. If the file you selected was not the version you needed, you closed the file, returned to the backup set, and then restored a different file.

> **TIP**
>
> Another way to restore a file is to click Restore personal files in the left pane of the File History window, and then navigate to the file you want to restore.

File History makes it much easier to restore the right version of a file because you use File Explorer and its familiar interface to find the file you want. Suppose you created a poster for a presentation on Windows 8 and saved this graphics file with the name Poster in the Presentations folder in the Pictures library. The Poster file originally included images of the Start screen and the desktop, and then later you removed the desktop image from the file. Now you want to restore the version of the Poster file with the Start screen and the desktop. To do so, you use File Explorer to navigate to the Presentations folder in the Pictures library, which contains only the latest saved copy of the Poster file. Click the History button in the Open group on the Home tab to display the most recently saved files in the Presentations folder. See Figure 9-8.

Figure 9-8   Displaying a folder's history

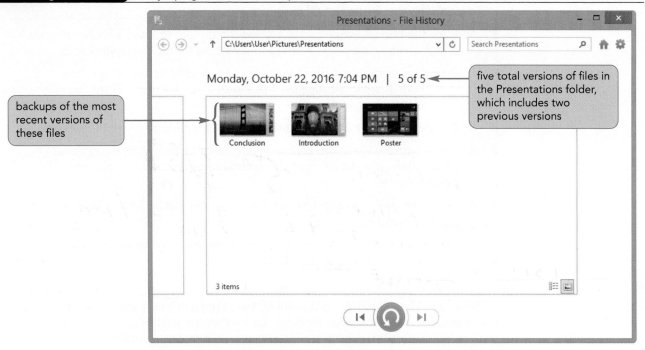

To display the file's history, which comprises all of the saved versions of the file, including the one displaying the Start screen and desktop, you double-click the Poster file. See Figure 9-9.

Figure 9-9   Displaying a file's history

You click the Previous version and Next version buttons in the Poster.png - File History window until you find the version you want. Once you find the correct version, click the Restore button to restore the file to its original location. File History lets you choose to replace the current file with the backup or to skip the replacement. If you want to save both the older version and the current one, you can move the current version to a different folder or rename it before restoring the older version.

You'll show Andrea how to restore the original version of the Benefits file.

To restore a file from File History:

▶ **1.** Display the contents of the Andrea folder, if necessary.

▶ **2.** Click the **History** button in the Open group on the Home tab. If 10 or more minutes have passed since File History made the first backup, the folder window shows the latest version of the file, which is the one containing text you wrote based on your research.

▶ **3.** Click the **Previous version** button 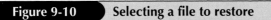 to display the previous version of the file. If necessary, continue clicking the **Previous version** button ◄ until you display the original version of the file, which contains "Group exercise studios" as the text for the first bullet. See Figure 9-10.

Trouble? If your computer does not include an application that can preview the contents of .rtf files, an icon appears for each version of the file instead of the file contents. Double-click the file icon to open the file, and then close the file when you find the correct version.

| Figure 9-10 | Selecting a file to restore |

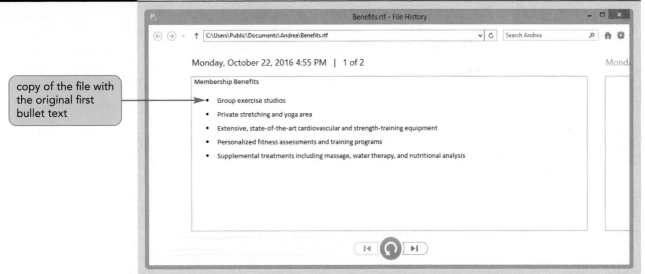

copy of the file with the original first bullet text

▶ **4.** Click the **Restore** button to restore the file to its original location, which is the Andrea folder. The Replace or Skip Files dialog box opens because you are restoring an older version of the Benefits file into a folder that already contains a file named Benefits.

▶ **5.** Click **Replace the file in the destination** to finish restoring the Benefits file.

▶ **6.** Close all open windows.

If you did not want to restore the older file, you could click the Skip this file option in the Replace or Skip Files dialog box. To examine file details more carefully, you could click the Compare info for both files option, also in the Replace or Skip Files dialog box. If you restored the file to a folder that did not already contain a file with the same name, File History would restore the file without opening the Replace or Skip Files dialog box.

Managing System Software

Although your personal files are the most valuable files you have on a computer, they are useful to you only if you have the right software to open, edit, and otherwise enhance those files, including system software. If your hard disk or system suffers damage so that Windows cannot start, you need a **system recovery drive**, which is removable media containing system recovery tools to help restore a computer if a serious system error occurs. If you use an optical disc such as a DVD, this tool is called a **system repair disc**.

If you can start Windows but discover other system problems as you are working on the computer, you can save system files without affecting your personal files by using **System Restore**, a Windows tool that helps you restore your computer's system files to an earlier point when your system was working reliably. If your system becomes unstable or starts to act unpredictably after installing software, you can try uninstalling the software to see if that solves your problem. If uninstalling does not solve your problem, you can undo system changes by restoring your computer to an earlier date when the system worked correctly.

Windows 8 also introduces two tools called Refresh and Reset, which can help you avoid problems with the operating system. Using Refresh, you reinstall Windows 8 while keeping all of your settings, personal files, and Windows 8 apps. You do need to reinstall all of your desktop applications, which you can typically do using the software publisher's Web site or your original installation CD or DVD. The Reset tool returns your system to its original state before you installed any apps or created any files. The Reset tool is ideal when you are selling, donating, or recycling your computer because it removes all traces of your identity. Both tools complete their work quickly, often in less than 10 minutes.

Creating a System Recovery Drive

To make sure you can start Windows and access recovery tools if something goes wrong with your operating system, you should create a system recovery drive. Most people create a system recovery drive right after they install or upgrade to Windows 8, or when they purchase a new Windows 8 computer. You can use a USB flash drive, CD, or DVD to create a recovery drive that contains files Windows needs to start and then provide you with troubleshooting and system repair tools even when it cannot start as normal. The system recovery drive does not contain a full version of Windows, but only enough files to start your computer.

You'll show Andrea how to create a system recovery drive. To do so, you need a USB flash drive that can hold at least 256 MB of data. If the drive contains any data, Windows deletes the data as it creates the recovery drive, so be sure to select an unused (or clean) USB flash drive or one that contains files you no longer need. If you do not have a USB flash drive that meets these requirements, read but do not perform the following steps.

To create a system recovery drive:

▶ **1.** Insert a USB flash drive into a USB port on your computer, making sure the USB flash drive can hold at least 256 MB of data and does not contain any data you need. Close any dialog boxes that open.

Trouble? If you have a USB flash drive connected to your computer and do not want to use it as a system recovery drive, click the Show hidden icons ▲ on the taskbar, click the Safely Remove Hardware icon 🔌 and then click Eject for the drive that you want to remove (for example, Eject E:\Removable Disk). When Windows displays a Safe to Remove Hardware message, remove the USB flash drive from the computer, and then close the message.

▶ **2.** Press the **Windows** key 🪟 to display the Start screen, type **recovery**, and then click **Settings** on the Search menu. The Settings screen displays a list of recovery settings.

▶ **3.** Click **Create a recovery drive** in the search results to start the Recovery Drive Wizard, which guides you through the steps of creating a system recovery drive.

Trouble? If a User Account Control dialog box opens requesting a password or your permission to continue, enter the password or click the Yes button.

▶ **4.** Click the **Next** button to display the next wizard dialog box, which lists the USB flash drives connected to your computer.

▶ **5.** Click the name of the USB flash drive, such as E:\Removable Disk, and then click the **Next** button to display a dialog box warning you that Windows will delete everything on the USB flash drive as it creates the recovery drive.

▶ **6.** Click the **Create** button. Windows copies utilities and other files to the USB flash drive so you can use the drive to troubleshoot and repair a start-up problem in Windows 8.

▶ **7.** When the recovery drive is ready, click the **Finish** button.

TIP

If you use an optical disc instead of a USB drive, click Create a system repair disc with a CD or DVD instead.

Store the system recovery drive in a safe place. If your computer does not start properly, you can insert the USB flash drive in a USB port, and then restart the computer to display the Troubleshoot screen shown in Figure 9-11.

Figure 9-11   Troubleshoot screen

click to display additional system recovery options

You'll learn about the Refresh your PC and Reset your PC options later in this session. You can click Advanced options to display a screen with additional system recovery options, including Automatic Repair, which attempts to fix the problems that keep Windows from loading.

Creating a System Restore Point

System Restore tracks changes to your computer's system files and uses a feature called System Protection to create a **restore point**, which is a snapshot of your computer's system files. A restore point contains information about these system files and settings in the **registry**, which is a database of information about your computer's configuration. If your system becomes unstable, use System Restore to return your computer settings to a particular restore point. System Restore creates restore points at regular intervals (typically once a day) and when it detects the beginning of a change to your computer, such as a Windows Update. You can also create a restore point yourself at any time, such as before playing an online game.

Creating a System Restore Point

REFERENCE

- Open the Control Panel, click System and Security, and then click System.
- In the left pane, click System protection to open the System Properties dialog box.
- Click the System Protection tab, and then click the Create button.
- Enter a description to help you identify the restore point, and then click the Create button.
- Click the Close button.

Although Windows 8 automatically creates system restore points periodically and before a significant system event such as installing new software, you can create a restore point yourself at any time. When a restore point is created, Windows saves images of its system files, programs, and registry settings. It might also save images of files that help to run programs, such as scripts and batch files. As with backup files, Windows can only create restore points on NTFS disks, not FAT disks. To create restore points, you need at least 300 MB of free space on a hard disk that has at least 1 GB of storage space. System Restore might use from 3 to 5 percent of the space on each disk. As this space fills up with restore points, System Restore deletes older restore points to make room for new ones.

Because System Restore reverts to previous system settings without affecting your personal files, it usually cannot help you recover a personal file that has been lost or damaged. Use File History to recover a working version of a personal file.

Andrea's computer is working well right now, so you'll show her how to create a restore point to protect her system. Before you do, you want to make sure that System Protection is turned on for her computer.

To make sure System Protection is turned on:

1. Point to the lower-left hot corner until the Start screen thumbnail appears, right-click the **Start screen** thumbnail to display the System menu, click **Control Panel**, click **System and Security**, and then click **System**. The System window opens.

2. In the left pane, click **System protection**. The System Properties dialog box opens. See Figure 9-12. The Available Drives list shows for which drives System Protection is turned on. Make sure that System Protection is turned on for the system drive, the internal hard drive where Windows 8 is installed on your computer, which is most likely drive C.

Figure 9-12   **System Properties dialog box**

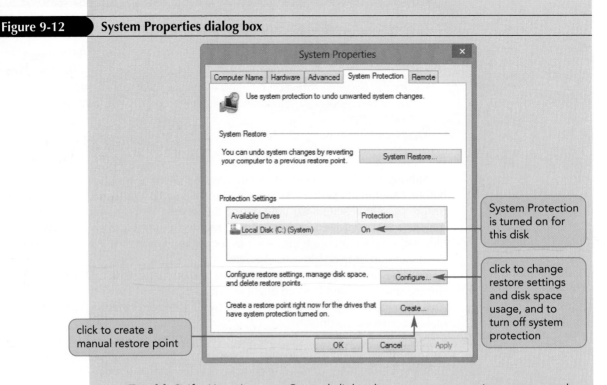

Trouble? If a User Account Control dialog box opens requesting a password or your permission to continue, enter the password or click the Yes button.

You can use this dialog box to create a restore point yourself.

To create a restore point:

1. In the System Properties dialog box, click the **Create** button. The System Protection dialog box opens.

2. Type **Andrea** as the description for this restore point. Windows will add the current date and time automatically.

3. Click the **Create** button. Windows creates a restore point, which might take a few minutes, and then displays a message indicating it was created successfully.

4. Click the **Close** button.

At any point after you or Windows 8 creates a restore point, you can select one to undo changes made to your system up to that restore point. Every time you use System Restore, Windows creates a restore point before proceeding, so you can undo the changes if reverting to a restore point doesn't fix your problem. If you need to restore your computer, Windows recommends using the most recent restore point created before a significant change, such as installing a program. You can also choose from a list of restore points. It's a good idea to select restore points in descending order, starting with the most recent. If that doesn't solve your problem, try the next most recent, and so on. Although System Restore doesn't delete any of your personal files, it removes programs installed after the restore point you select, requiring you to reinstall those programs. The System Restore Wizard includes a Scan for affected programs option so you can see which programs will be removed when you restore the system.

You'll show Andrea how to restore her computer in case she has system problems and wants to revert to a previous point. You won't actually restore her computer in the following steps because it doesn't need it right now. You'll work as far as you can through the System Restore dialog boxes, and then click the Cancel button instead of the Finish button. You also inform Andrea that she should always save and close any open files and close any running programs before using System Restore.

To begin restoring a computer:

▶ **1.** In the System Properties dialog box, click the **System Restore** button. The System Restore Wizard starts.

▶ **2.** Click the **Next** button. The next System Restore dialog box opens, where you can choose a restore point. See Figure 9-13.

| Figure 9-13 | Choosing a restore point |

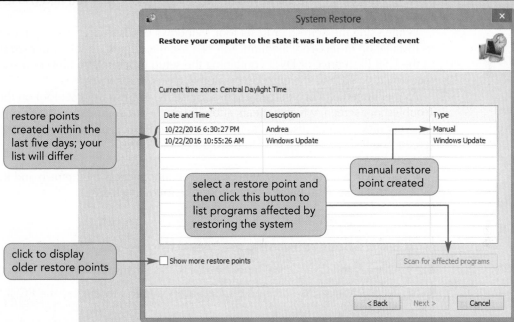

▶ **3.** Click the **second restore point** in the list, which might be for a recent Windows update, and then click the **Next** button. The last System Restore dialog box opens so you can confirm your restore point.

Trouble? If only one restore point appears in the list, click the Show more restore points check box to display earlier restore points.

▶ **4.** Click the **Cancel** button to close the dialog box without restoring the computer.

Trouble? If you clicked the Finish button instead of the Cancel button, confirm that you want to restore your computer, and then wait until System Restore finishes and restarts your computer. Open the System Properties dialog box, click the System Restore button, click the Undo System Restore option button, click the Next button, click the Finish button, and then click the Yes button.

▶ **5.** Close all open windows.

TIP

After selecting a restore point, you can scan for affected programs to identify the programs added since Windows created that restore point.

Recall that Windows 8 saves restore points until they fill up the hard disk space reserved by System Restore. (You can change the amount of space allocated for System Restore in the System Protection dialog box.) As you and Windows create new restore points, System Restore deletes old ones. If you turn off System Protection on a disk, Windows deletes all the restore points from that disk. When you turn System Protection back on, Windows starts creating new restore points.

Refreshing or Resetting a System

If an electrical storm, a power surge, a virus, or another threat causes system problems severe enough to prevent Windows from running normally, you can refresh your installation of Windows. While System Restore returns your system to an earlier state, the Refresh tool installs a fresh copy of Windows on your computer and retains your data, settings, and Windows 8 apps (but not desktop applications). As a more drastic alternative, you can use the Reset tool to remove all of your files and apps, reinstall Windows, and then change all of your system settings to their defaults. You should use the Reset tool only if you are disposing of your computer, or if you haven't created any files or installed any apps that you want to preserve.

While using the Refresh or Reset tool, Windows needs to access setup files stored on its installation or recovery medium. You can use the original installation medium (such as the USB flash drive or DVD containing the setup program and files) or a system recovery disk, such as the one you created in a previous section.

As mentioned earlier, you can choose to use the Refresh or Reset tool on the Troubleshoot screen, which appears after you start your computer using the system recovery disk. You can also access the Refresh and Reset tools on the PC settings screen. You'll show Andrea how to learn about the Refresh and Reset tools using the PC settings screen.

If you are in a computer lab, you probably cannot access the Refresh and Reset tools. In that case, read but do not perform the following steps.

To learn about refreshing and resetting your system:

▶ **1.** Display the Charms bar, and then click the **Settings** charm.

▶ **2.** Click **Change PC settings** on the Settings menu to display the PC settings screen.

▶ **3.** Click **General** in the left pane, and then scroll the right pane to display the Refresh tool, which is titled "Refresh your PC without affecting your files." See Figure 9-14.

Figure 9-14	Refresh and Reset tools

PC settings

- Personalize
- Users
- Notifications
- Search
- Share
- General
- Privacy
- Devices
- Ease of Access
- Sync your settings
- HomeGroup
- Windows Update

Language preferences

Available storage

You have 371 GB available. See how much space your apps are using.

View app sizes

Refresh your PC without affecting your files

If your PC isn't running well, you can refresh it without losing your photos, music, videos, and other personal files.

Get started — *click to start refreshing Windows*

Remove everything and reinstall Windows

If you want to recycle your PC or start over completely, you can reset it to its factory settings.

Get started — *click to start resetting Windows*

Advanced startup

Start up from a device or disc (such as a USB drive or DVD), change Windows startup settings, or restore Windows from a system image. This will restart your PC.

Restart now

4. Close the PC settings screen.

Be sure to close the PC settings screen without making any selections. Starting the refresh or reset process could make your system unusable.

If you decide that you do want to reset your system, make sure you have been creating backups with File History, and have the File History drive or network folder handy so you can restore your files.

Managing Application Software

When you buy a new Windows 8 computer, it comes with the operating system and other system software already installed, along with a few useful Windows 8 apps. The computer manufacturer might also install Windows 8 or desktop apps such as entertainment or utility software. To add other software to your system, you **install** it, which means you copy files from a Web site, a hard disk, or removable media to your system to make the software ready to run and use. To install Windows 8 apps, you must download them first from the Windows Store. You can also install desktop applications from the Windows Store or the publisher's Web site, or by using removable media. When you no longer need or want the software, you can uninstall it, which removes the software from your system.

Installing Apps from the Windows Store

If you want to install a Windows 8 app on your system, you must first visit the Windows Store, the online marketplace for Windows 8 apps and tools. By providing apps exclusively in the Windows Store, Microsoft can enforce strict guidelines to make sure that Windows 8 apps are secure, perform reliably, work as advertised, and protect your privacy. The Windows Store features three types of apps: free, paid, and trial versions of paid apps. (A trial version lets you try out the software before you buy it. Usually, without any initial cost, you can install and use the software for a limited time or you can use only some features.) These apps are organized into categories such as Social, Entertainment, Games, and Productivity.

You know that the Windows Store provides a translation app that translates words, phrases, and paragraphs from one language to another. You think Andrea might find the app useful to communicate with Arlington's Spanish-speaking members. You'll show Andrea how to download and install this free app from the Windows Store.

To perform the following steps, make sure you have permission to download and install software from a Web site. If your school does not allow you to download files or install software, read but do not perform the following steps. You also need a Microsoft (or Windows Live) account to download and install apps from the Windows Store.

TIP

A number in the lower-right corner of the Store tile indicates how many of your Windows 8 apps have updates available.

To install an app from the Windows Store:

▶ **1.** On the Start screen, click the **Store** tile to visit the Windows Store.

▶ **2.** Scroll to the right, and then click **Productivity** to display the Productivity apps. See Figure 9-15. The apps in the Windows Store change frequently, so the apps displayed on your screen most likely differ from the figure.

Figure 9-15   **Productivity apps in the Windows Store**

▶ **3.** If necessary, scroll to the right, and then click the **Language Translator** app to select it and display information about this free app. See Figure 9-16.

Trouble? If the Language Translator app does not appear in the Productivity category, click any other free app.

| Figure 9-16 | Language Translator app information |

preview of the Language Translator app

click to install the Language Translator app

4. Click the **Install** button to begin downloading and installing the app. A notification appears in the upper-right corner of your screen when the app is installed.

Trouble? If a screen appears requesting your Microsoft account information, enter the user name and password for your Microsoft account.

Microsoft and other developers often continue to improve apps in the Windows Store even after you've installed them. You can download updates for your apps by visiting the Windows Store. If an Updates link appears in the upper-right corner of the Windows Store screen, click the link to select all of the updates available for your apps. You can then click the Install button to update your apps.

Now you can show Andrea how to start the Language Translator app. Like any other Windows 8 program, it is available on the Start screen. After starting this app, you can demonstrate it to Andrea and see if she wants to keep it on her computer. You'll show her how to use the app to translate a membership benefit from English to Spanish.

To start the Language Translator app:

1. Press the **Alt+F4** keys to close the Windows Store, scroll the Start screen to the right, and then click the **Language Translator** tile to start the Language Translator app.

2. In the box on the left, type **area for private stretching and yoga**, and then click the **Translate** button to display the phrase in Spanish.

3. Click the **speaker** icon below the Spanish text box to hear a Spanish speaker pronounce the phrase.

4. Close the Language Translator app.

TIP

Click the buttons with the default languages (English and Spanish) to select other languages to translate.

Andrea isn't sure that she'd use the new app, so you'll show her how to uninstall it.

Uninstalling Software

You can uninstall software from your computer if you no longer use it. Doing so frees up space on your hard disk, sometimes a significant amount of space, depending on the app. To uninstall Windows 8 apps, you right-click the appropriate tile on the Start screen or Apps screen, and then click the Uninstall button on the Apps bar. To uninstall desktop applications, you use the Programs and Features window. In either case, uninstalling removes the program's files and any changes made to Windows system settings, such as in the registry.

To use the Programs and Features window, you first open the Control Panel in Category view, and then click the Uninstall a program link on the Home page. The Programs and Features window lists all the desktop applications and other software tools installed on your computer. Click an application and then click the Uninstall button on the toolbar to uninstall the application. You can also use the Programs and Features window to change a program's configuration by adding or removing certain options. Usually this means that you turn optional features of the program on or off. Not all programs let you change their features. To determine whether you can, click the program name in the Programs and Features window, and then look for the Change or Repair button on the toolbar.

You'll show Andrea how to uninstall the Language Translator app and remove its tile from the Start screen.

To uninstall a Windows 8 app:

▶ 1. Scroll the Start screen to the right, and then right-click the **Language Translator** tile to select the tile and display the Apps bar. See Figure 9-17.

Figure 9-17   **Preparing to uninstall an app**

Language Translator is the selected app

Uninstall button on the Apps bar

▶ 2. Click the **Uninstall** button on the Apps bar. Windows indicates that the app and its related info will be removed from the computer.

▶ 3. Click the **Uninstall** button in the dialog box to confirm you want to uninstall the app. Windows removes the app from the computer, which could take a few minutes.

TIP

You can also right-click an app on the Apps screen and then click the Uninstall button on the Apps bar.

Setting Up a Program for Compatibility

If you install programs written for earlier versions of Windows, such as Windows Vista or Windows XP, chances are that they will run properly. However, some older programs might run poorly or not run at all. When you run an older program, the Program Compatibility Assistant dialog box might open if it detects known compatibility issues. The dialog box notifies you about the problem and offers to fix it the next time you run the program.

If the Program Compatibility Assistant dialog box does not appear when you run an older program, you can use the Program Compatibility Troubleshooter to select and test compatibility settings that might fix the problems in the older program. You can let Windows apply recommended settings or you can troubleshoot the program manually. When you troubleshoot manually, you can choose an operating system recommended for the program or one that previously supported the program correctly. After you apply recommended settings or select an operating system, you can start the older program to see if the new settings solve the problem. If they don't, you can return to the troubleshooter and try other settings.

Microsoft advises that you should not use the Program Compatibility Troubleshooter on older antivirus programs, disk utilities, or other system programs because it might remove data or create a security risk.

Andrea installed a Windows XP program called E-Organizer on her Windows 8 computer, and it has not displayed menus or title bars correctly since she installed it. You'll run the Program Compatibility Troubleshooter, select the E-Organizer program to run it with compatibility settings, and see if that solves the problem.

The following steps select compatibility settings for a program named E-Organizer. Ask your instructor to identify a program on your computer that you can use instead of E-Organizer. The program should not be an antivirus program, a disk utility, or another system program. Substitute the name of that program for E-Organizer when you perform the following steps.

To use the Program Compatibility Troubleshooter:

▶ 1. Open the Control Panel in Category view, and then click **Programs** to display the Programs window.

▶ 2. Click **Run programs made for previous versions of Windows** in the Programs and Features category. The Program Compatibility Troubleshooter starts.

▶ 3. Click the **Next** button. The next dialog box lists programs installed on your computer and instructs you to select the program that is causing problems.

▶ 4. Click **E-Organizer** (or the program name recommended by your instructor), and then click the **Next** button. Windows 8 gives you two options: Try recommended settings or Troubleshoot program.

▶ 5. Click **Try recommended settings**. Windows detects which operating system the program is designed for and then applies settings, if possible. See Figure 9-18.

TIP

To test a program that is not listed, you can click Not Listed and then browse for the program you want to troubleshoot.

Figure 9-18   **Program Compatibility Troubleshooter window**

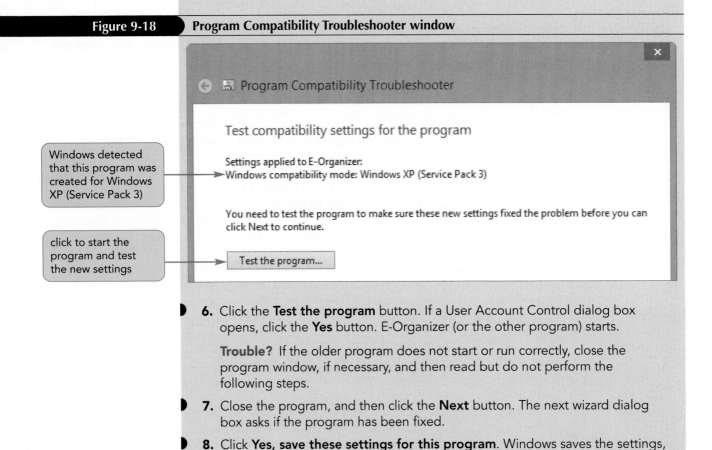

Windows detected that this program was created for Windows XP (Service Pack 3)

click to start the program and test the new settings

6. Click the **Test the program** button. If a User Account Control dialog box opens, click the **Yes** button. E-Organizer (or the other program) starts.

   Trouble? If the older program does not start or run correctly, close the program window, if necessary, and then read but do not perform the following steps.

7. Close the program, and then click the **Next** button. The next wizard dialog box asks if the program has been fixed.

8. Click **Yes, save these settings for this program**. Windows saves the settings, generating a report that provides a summary.

9. Click the **Close** button to close the Program Compatibility window.

10. Close all open windows.

Exploring Windows To Go

Windows To Go is a feature new to Windows 8 that is designed for businesses and other organizations to use with their employees. These organizations often use Windows computers on a network and specify the appearance and content of the Start screen and desktop on each computer, including security policies and custom applications developed or modified specifically for the organization. Employees who travel or work from home want to replicate the setup on their office computers so they can work in a familiar environment even when they are out of the office. At the same time, businesses might discourage employees from connecting their personal computers to the company network because they don't want to risk introducing malware to the network.

Windows To Go solves these problems by allowing businesses to install all of the software employees need on a USB 3.0 flash drive. (USB 3.0 is the current version of USB flash drive technology.) The Windows To Go drive includes Windows 8 and the organization's settings, security policies, and software. Employees can then plug the Windows To Go drive into a computer that they use away from the office to access Windows 8 and the computing environment they use at work, including applications and settings. They can store files on the organization's network folders. When employees remove the Windows To Go drive from their computers, the computers resume their original state, which might be a personalized Windows 7 or Windows 8 environment.

Creating a Windows To Go drive involves advanced computing tasks that are typically performed by a technical expert.

You're finished showing Andrea how to back up and restore files, and manage her software. In the next session, you'll examine how to maintain hard disks and monitors, and work with device drivers.

REVIEW

Session 9.1 Quick Check

1. After you set up _____File History_____ by turning it on for the first time, it automatically backs up your files every hour.

2. Explain how using File History to back up files differs from copying files.

3. After making the first full backup, which files does File History continue to back up?

4. Which button do you click in the File Explorer window to display all of the versions of a selected file?

5. What is a system recovery drive?   466

6. A(n) _Restore point_ is a snapshot of your computer's system files.

7. If an older program doesn't run correctly in Windows 8, what can you do?

Session 9.2 Visual Overview:

Hardware is any physical piece of equipment, called a **device**, that is connected to your computer and controlled by your computer.

A **local disk** is installed in your computer.

Windows 8 must be installed on a disk using the **NTFS file system**, which is the underlying structure a computer uses to organize data on the hard disk.

As part of a regular maintenance program, you should be familiar with the properties of your hard disk, including how much free space it has.

The **Disk Cleanup tool** frees disk space by deleting unnecessary files such as temporary files.

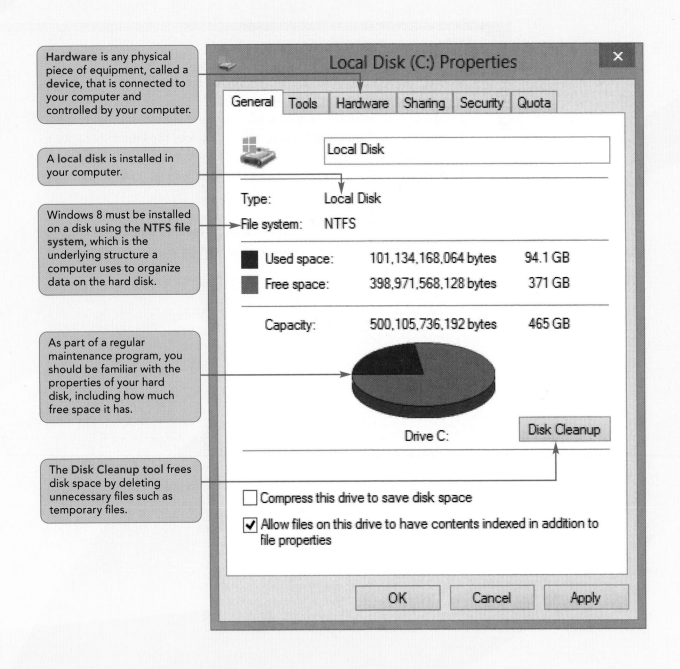

Local Disk (C:) Properties

| General | Tools | Hardware | Sharing | Security | Quota |

Local Disk

Type: Local Disk
File system: NTFS

Used space: 101,134,168,064 bytes   94.1 GB
Free space: 398,971,568,128 bytes   371 GB

Capacity: 500,105,736,192 bytes   465 GB

Drive C: Disk Cleanup

☐ Compress this drive to save disk space

☑ Allow files on this drive to have contents indexed in addition to file properties

OK   Cancel   Apply

Managing Hardware

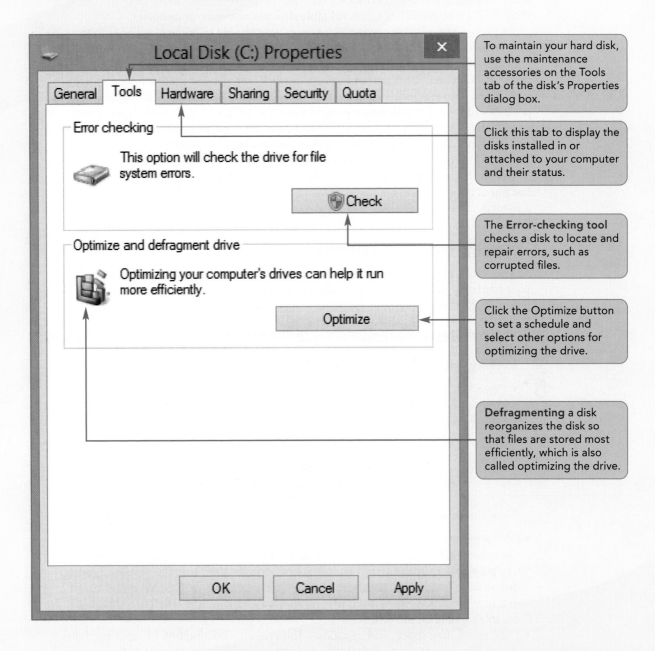

To maintain your hard disk, use the maintenance accessories on the Tools tab of the disk's Properties dialog box.

Click this tab to display the disks installed in or attached to your computer and their status.

The **Error-checking tool** checks a disk to locate and repair errors, such as corrupted files.

Click the Optimize button to set a schedule and select other options for optimizing the drive.

Defragmenting a disk reorganizes the disk so that files are stored most efficiently, which is also called optimizing the drive.

Maintaining Hard Disks

As a computer owner, one of your most important responsibilities is to maintain your hard disk by keeping it free of problems that could prevent you from accessing your data. The failure of a hard disk can be a headache if you have backups of your data, and a disaster if you don't. Windows 8 helps you prevent disk failure from occurring in the first place by providing some valuable disk maintenance accessories.

As part of a regular maintenance program, you should become familiar with the properties of your hard disk, including whether it is partitioned. Next, you should check each disk on your computer to locate and repair errors, such as parts of corrupted files and damaged sections on the disk. Then you should defragment each disk. If you are responsible for maintaining a computer that is used all day, you should probably run these maintenance procedures on a weekly or even daily basis. On the other hand, if you use your computer less frequently—for example, you use a home computer only for correspondence, games, and maintaining your finances—you might only need to run disk maintenance procedures once every month or so.

Andrea has not performed any maintenance tasks on her computer, so you'll guide her through the cleanup tasks and show her how to make sure they are completed on a regular basis.

Viewing Hard Disk Properties

As you know, all of the applications and system files on your computer are stored on your hard disk. You should periodically check the amount of free space on your hard disk to make sure the computer does not run out of room.

REFERENCE

Viewing Hard Disk Properties

- Open File Explorer, and then click the Computer icon in the Navigation pane.
- Right-click a hard disk in the Computer window.
- Click Properties on the shortcut menu.

View the properties of your hard disk to learn the following information:

- File system—Recall that Windows 8 must be installed on a hard disk using the NTFS file system. NTFS supports file system recovery (in the case of a hard disk failure) and can access disk drives up to 2 TB in size. NTFS is the preferred file system if your disk drive is larger than 32 GB. Your computer might also be able to access a disk that uses the FAT32 file system, which employs an older, less efficient method of organizing data on the disk.
- Used space, free space, and capacity—The Properties dialog box for your hard disk shows the amount of space that files and other data use, the amount of free space remaining, and the total capacity of the disk.
- All disk drives—The Hardware tab of a disk's Properties dialog box lists all of the disks installed in or attached to your computer. If you are having trouble with a disk, you can view more details about it, such as its status, which indicates whether it is working properly.

You'll start your maintenance session with Andrea by viewing the properties of her hard disk. In the following steps, the hard disk is named Local Disk (C:). Substitute the name of your hard disk if it is different.

To view the properties of a hard disk:

TIP

You can also click a hard disk icon to view its total size and available free space in the Details pane of the folder window.

1. Display the desktop, click the **File Explorer** button on the taskbar, and then click **Computer** in the Navigation pane to open the Computer window.

2. Right-click **Local Disk (C:)**, and then click **Properties** on the shortcut menu to open the Local Disk (C:) Properties dialog box. See Figure 9-19. The space details on your computer will differ.

Figure 9-19 | **Local Disk (C:) Properties dialog box**

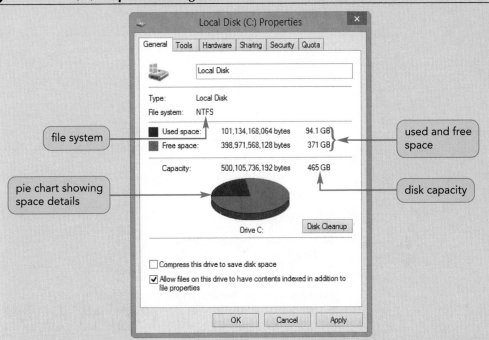

Trouble? If the hard disk where Windows 8 is installed has a different name, right-click that disk icon, and then click Properties.

3. Click the **Hardware** tab to display the disks attached to your computer. See Figure 9-20.

Figure 9-20   Hardware tab of the Local Disk (C:) Properties dialog box

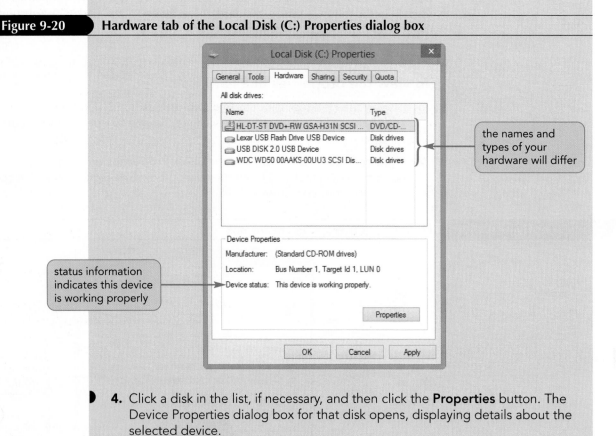

the names and types of your hardware will differ

status information indicates this device is working properly

4. Click a disk in the list, if necessary, and then click the **Properties** button. The Device Properties dialog box for that disk opens, displaying details about the selected device.

5. Click the **OK** button to close the Device Properties dialog box.

6. Close the Computer window, but leave the Local Disk (C:) Properties dialog box open.

You want to show Andrea another way to learn more about her hard disk.

Checking for Partitions

A **partition** (sometimes called a **volume**) is part of a hard disk that works like a separate disk—it can be formatted with a file system and identified with a letter of the alphabet. A hard disk needs to be partitioned and formatted before you can store data on it. Computer manufacturers usually perform this task for you, and set up the hard disk as a single partition that equals the size of the hard disk. You are not required to partition a hard disk into several smaller partitions, but you can do so if you want to use partitions to organize data on your hard disk or if you want to install more than one operating system on your computer. Some users prefer to have separate partitions for Windows operating system files, apps, and personal data.

You can use Disk Management, which is an Administrative tool, to view the partitions on your system. Windows computers must have a **system partition**, which contains the hardware-related files that tell a computer where to look to find the files that start Windows. They must also have a **boot partition**, which contains the Windows operating system files. These files are located in the Windows file folder. Usually, the system partition files and boot partition files are located in the same main (or primary) partition, especially if you have only one operating system installed on your computer.

If you have more than one operating system on your computer, such as Windows 8 and Windows 7 (called a **dual-boot** or **multiboot computer**), you have more than one boot partition. In this case, a single system partition remains and serves as the primary partition. The other partitions are for your programs and data.

You'll show Andrea how to view the partitions on her hard disk and identify the system partition in the Disk Management window. Usually, only experienced computer administrators work in this window, but you can open it to view basic information about your hard disk and any other disks attached to your computer.

You need to sign in to Windows using an Administrator account to perform the following steps. If you are not allowed to sign in as an Administrator, read but do not perform the following steps.

To view the partitions on a hard disk:

▶ **1.** Open the Control Panel in Category view, and then click **System and Security**.

▶ **2.** Scroll to the Administrative Tools category, and then click **Create and format hard disk partitions**. The Disk Management window opens. See Figure 9-21. You can resize or scroll the window to see information for all the disks on your computer. The information in your Disk Management window will differ.

| Figure 9-21 | Disk Management window |

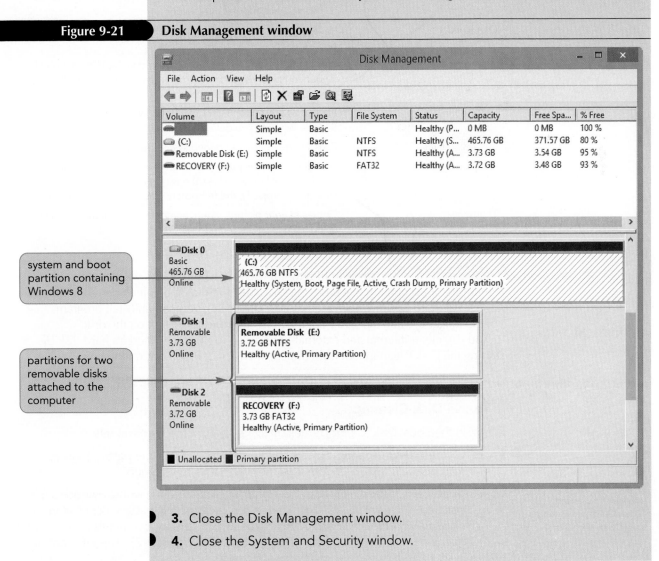

system and boot partition containing Windows 8

partitions for two removable disks attached to the computer

▶ **3.** Close the Disk Management window.

▶ **4.** Close the System and Security window.

Now that you and Andrea are acquainted with her hard disk, you can start performing maintenance tasks. The first task is to remove unnecessary files using Disk Cleanup.

Deleting Unnecessary Files with Disk Cleanup

When you work with applications and files in Windows 8, unnecessary files, such as temporary Internet and setup files, accumulate on your hard disk and impair system performance. The Disk Cleanup tool helps you free disk space by permanently deleting these files. When you start Disk Cleanup, it searches your disk for unnecessary files, and then lists the types of files it found in the Disk Cleanup dialog box. Figure 9-22 describes the typical types of files Disk Cleanup can remove when you choose to clean your files to free space on your hard disk. Your Disk Cleanup dialog box might include a different set of files depending on your computer activity.

Figure 9-22	Typical types of files to remove when using Disk Cleanup

Category	Description
Downloaded Program Files	Program files downloaded automatically from the Internet when you view certain Web pages
Temporary Internet files	Web pages stored on your hard disk for quick viewing, stored in the Temporary Internet Files folder
Offline webpages	Web pages stored on your computer so you can view them without being connected to the Internet
Hibernation File Cleaner	Information about your computer stored in the Hibernation file if your computer is set to hibernate; removing this file disables hibernation
Recycle Bin	Files you deleted from your computer, which are stored in the Recycle Bin until you delete them
Setup Log Files	Files Windows created during system setup
Temporary files	Files generated by programs to be used temporarily; usually these are deleted when you close the program; but if the program isn't shut down properly, the temporary files remain on your disk
Thumbnails	Copies of your picture, video, and document thumbnails if you are using file and folder thumbnails

© 2014 Cengage Learning

You can also choose to clean files for all users on a computer if you are using an Administrator account. In that case, the Disk Cleanup dialog box includes an additional tab named More Options. Using the More Options tab, you can uninstall programs that you no longer use and delete all but the most recent restore point on the disk.

You can clean internal and external hard disks. You'll clean Andrea's hard disk by starting the Disk Cleanup tool from the Local Disk (C:) Properties dialog box.

To use Disk Cleanup:

1. In the Local Disk (C:) Properties dialog box, click the **General** tab.

2. Click the **Disk Cleanup** button. If you have more than one partition on your hard disk, a dialog box opens asking which files to clean up.

3. If necessary, click the **Drives** arrow button, click the drive where Windows 8 is installed, such as Local Disk (C:), and then click the **OK** button. Disk Cleanup calculates how much space you can free (which takes a few minutes), and then opens the Disk Cleanup for (C:) dialog box. See Figure 9-23. The information in your Disk Cleanup dialog box will differ.

TIP

You can also start Disk Cleanup by typing *Disk Cleanup* on the Start screen, and then clicking Disk Cleanup on the Apps screen in the search results.

Figure 9-23	Disk Cleanup for (C:) dialog box

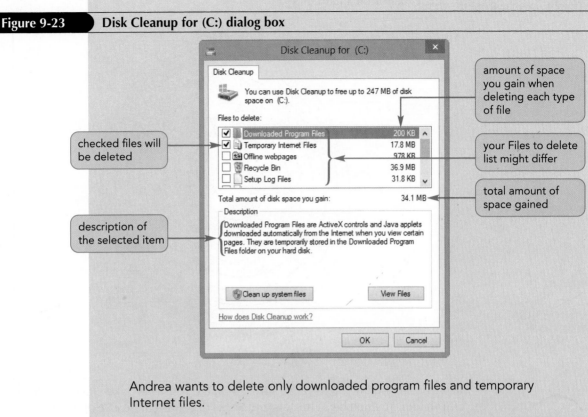

Andrea wants to delete only downloaded program files and temporary Internet files.

▶ **4.** If the Downloaded Program Files and Temporary Internet Files check boxes are not selected, click to select them.

▶ **5.** Scroll the list and then click to remove check marks from any other boxes.

▶ **6.** Click the **OK** button. A dialog box opens asking if you're sure you want to permanently delete these files.

▶ **7.** Click the **Delete Files** button. It might take a few minutes to clean the files from your hard disk.

Next, you'll check Andrea's hard disk for errors and other problems.

Checking a Hard Disk for Errors

A computer hard disk is a magnetic storage device that contains one or more metal platters that are usually sealed in your computer. Sections of the magnetic surface of a disk sometimes get damaged. Regularly scanning your disks for errors can be an effective way to prevent potential problems that would make data inaccessible. The Windows Error-checking tool not only locates errors on a disk, but also attempts to repair them. If it can't repair them, the tool marks the defective portions of the disk so that Windows doesn't try to store data there. In some earlier versions of Windows, the Error-checking tool was called Check Disk or ScanDisk.

To understand what problems the Error-checking tool looks for and how it repairs them, you need to understand the structure of a disk. A hard disk is organized as a concentric stack of disks or platters. Each platter has two surfaces, and each has its own read/write head, which are the small parts of a disk drive that move above the disk platter, and read and write data magnetically on the surface of the platters. The data is stored on concentric circles on the surfaces called **tracks**. An individual block of data is one **sector** of a track, as shown in Figure 9-24.

Figure 9-24   Single platter on a hard disk

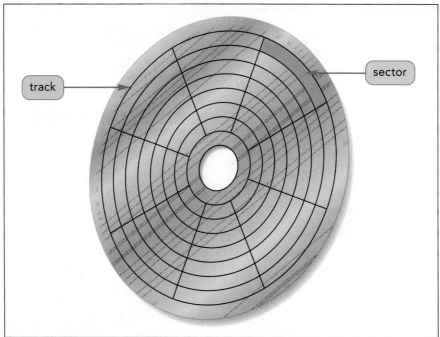

© 2014 Cengage Learning

Corresponding tracks on all surfaces on a drive, when taken together, make up a **cylinder**. The number of sectors and tracks depends on the size of the disk. A 400 GB hard disk, for example, has 160,384 cylinders. Each cylinder has 80 heads, with one head per track. Each track has 63 sectors, with 512 bytes per sector. That makes 420,278,584,320 bytes, which is considered 400 GB.

Although the physical surface of a disk is made up of tracks and sectors, a file is stored in clusters. A **cluster** is one or more sectors of storage space—it represents the minimum amount of space that an operating system reserves when saving the contents of a file to a disk. Most files are larger than 512 bytes (the size of one sector). That means a file is often stored in more than one cluster. A file system error known as a **lost cluster** occurs if Windows loses track of which clusters contain the data that belongs to a single file. The Error-checking tool identifies file system errors and can repair them if necessary.

INSIGHT

Checking for Errors After Power Failures

If your computer suffers a power surge, a power failure, or any problem that locks it up, Windows might lose one or more clusters from a file that was open when the problem occurred. This means that you could lose the data stored in those clusters. The presence of lost clusters on a disk is not damaging, but lost clusters do take up valuable space. Having too many lost clusters can lead to other types of file system errors. To prevent an accumulation of file system errors, you should check your hard disk for errors immediately after a power failure. The Error-checking tool can remove lost clusters and their data automatically.

When you use the Windows 8 Error-checking tool to scan your disk for errors, you can specify whether you want it to automatically repair problems with files that the scan detects, such as lost clusters, or only report problems and not fix them. You can also perform a thorough disk check by scanning for and repairing physical errors on the hard disk itself, including **bad sectors**, which are areas of the disk that do not record data reliably. Performing a thorough disk check can take much longer to complete.

You'll show Andrea how to check her hard disk for file system errors. Because her computer is still relatively new, it's unlikely the hard disk has any bad sectors. After using her computer for a while, she should check the hard disk on a regular basis for bad sectors and file system errors. To perform the following steps, you must be using an Administrator account. If you are not using an Administrator account, read but do not perform the steps.

To check the hard disk for errors:

▶ **1.** In the Local Disk (C:) Properties dialog box, click the **Tools** tab. See Figure 9-25.

| Figure 9-25 | Tools tab of the Local Disk (C:) Properties dialog box |

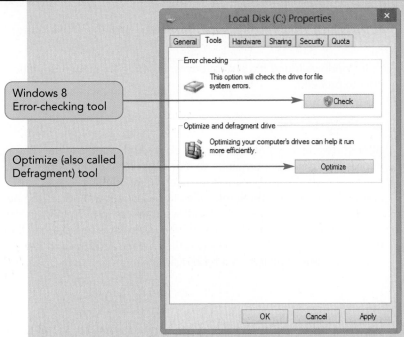

Windows 8 Error-checking tool

Optimize (also called Defragment) tool

▶ **2.** Click the **Check** button to open the Error Checking (Local Disk (C:)) dialog box. See Figure 9-26.

Figure 9-26	Error Checking (Local Disk (C:)) dialog box

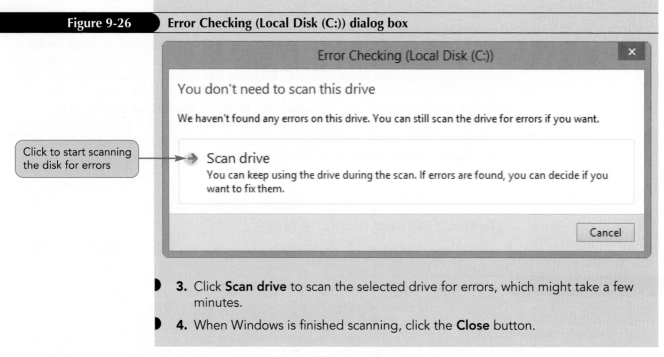

Click to start scanning the disk for errors

3. Click **Scan drive** to scan the selected drive for errors, which might take a few minutes.

4. When Windows is finished scanning, click the **Close** button.

If Windows found file system errors, it would fix them automatically or advise you how to proceed.

Defragmenting a Disk

After correcting any errors on your hard disk, you can use the Optimize Drives tool to improve the disk's performance so that apps start and files open more quickly. When you save a file, Windows stores as much of the file as possible in the first available cluster. If the file doesn't fit into one cluster, Windows locates the next available cluster and puts more of the file in it. Windows attempts to place files in contiguous clusters whenever possible. The file is saved when Windows has placed all of the file data into clusters. Figure 9-27 shows two files named Address and Recipes saved on an otherwise unused platter on a hard disk.

Figure 9-27   **Two files saved on a hard disk**

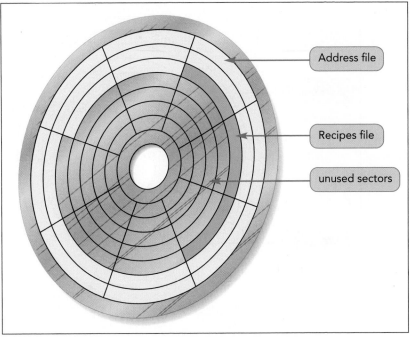

Address file

Recipes file

unused sectors

© 2014 Cengage Learning

As you create and save new files, Windows uses more clusters. If you delete a file or two, Windows frees those clusters. Figure 9-28 shows the disk after you save a new file named Memo and then delete the Recipes file.

Figure 9-28   **Adding one file and deleting another file**

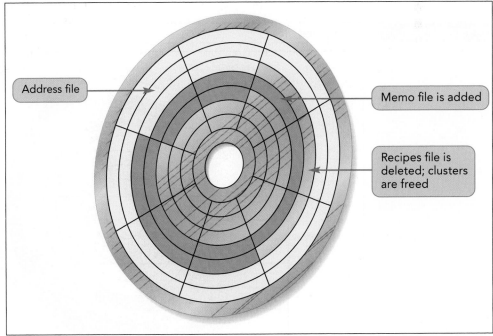

Address file

Memo file is added

Recipes file is deleted; clusters are freed

© 2014 Cengage Learning

The next time you save a file, Windows searches for the first available cluster, which is now between two files. Figure 9-29 shows what happens when you save a fourth file named Schedule—it is saved to clusters that are not adjacent.

Figure 9-29   Adding a new file in fragmented clusters

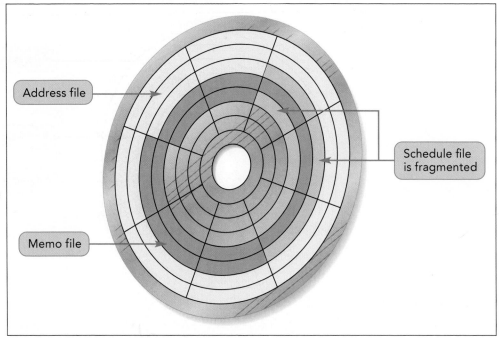

© 2014 Cengage Learning

The more files you save and delete, the more scattered the clusters for a file become. A disk that contains files whose clusters are not next to each other is said to be **fragmented**. The more fragmented the disk, the longer Windows takes to retrieve the file, and the more likely you are to have problems with the file. Figure 9-30 shows a fragmented disk. When an app tries to access a file on this disk, file retrieval takes longer than necessary because the app must locate clusters that aren't adjacent.

Figure 9-30   Fragmented files

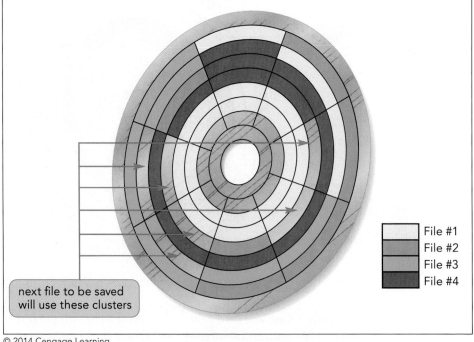

© 2014 Cengage Learning

Whenever a disk has been used for a long time, it's a good idea to defragment it. Defragmenting rearranges the clusters on the disk so each file's clusters are adjacent to one another. When a disk is in this state, it is said to be optimized. To defragment a disk, you use the Optimize Drives tool, which rearranges the data on your hard disk and reunites fragmented files so your computer can run more efficiently. In Windows 8, Optimize Drives runs on a schedule so you don't have to remember to run it, although you can still run it manually or change the schedule it uses.

You'll show Andrea how to start Optimize Drives and examine its schedule. Because defragmenting a hard disk can take a long time and you must close all apps, including antivirus software, before defragmenting, you won't defragment now.

To start Optimize Drives:

1. On the Tools tab of the Local Disk (C:) Properties dialog box, click the **Optimize** button. The Optimize Drives dialog box opens. See Figure 9-31.

    Trouble? If a dialog box opens with a message that Optimize Drives was scheduled using a different program, click the Cancel button, and then read but do not perform the remaining steps.

Figure 9-31	Optimize Drives dialog box

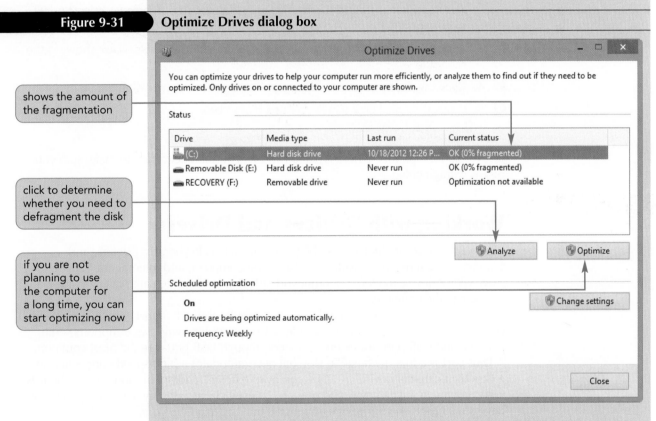

shows the amount of the fragmentation

click to determine whether you need to defragment the disk

if you are not planning to use the computer for a long time, you can start optimizing now

2. Click the **Change settings** button to examine the defragmenting schedule. Another Optimize Drives dialog box opens showing the optimization schedule. See Figure 9-32.

Figure 9-32   Optimization schedule

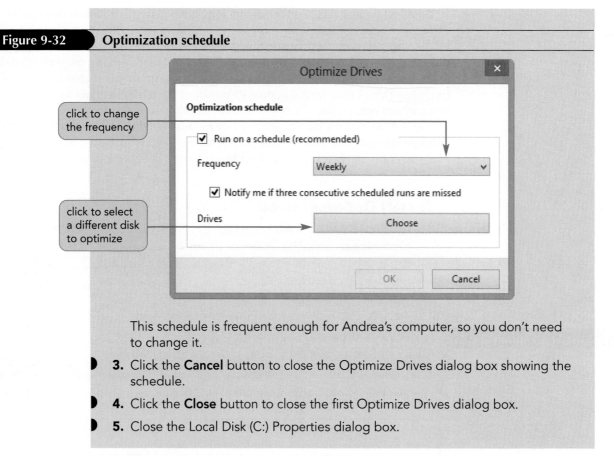

This schedule is frequent enough for Andrea's computer, so you don't need to change it.

▶ **3.** Click the **Cancel** button to close the Optimize Drives dialog box showing the schedule.

▶ **4.** Click the **Close** button to close the first Optimize Drives dialog box.

▶ **5.** Close the Local Disk (C:) Properties dialog box.

By default, Optimize Drives is set to run every week if necessary to make sure your disk is defragmented.

Working with Devices and Drivers

Hardware devices include external equipment such as keyboards, printers, and scanners, which remain outside the case of the computer, and internal equipment, such as disk drives, modems, and network adapter cards, which are placed inside the case of the computer.

External devices are connected to your computer through a **port**, which is a physical connection that is visible on the outside of the computer. Windows 8 supports serial, parallel, and USB ports for external devices, though USB ports are the most common. A **USB port** is a thin, rectangular slot that accommodates a high-speed connection to a variety of external devices, such as removable drives, additional monitors, keyboards, video conferencing cameras, and printers. To use USB technology, your computer must have a USB port, and the device you install must have a USB connector, which is a small, rectangular plug. See Figure 9-33. The location of ports varies depending on the device and its manufacturer. Some tablet computers might not include USB ports because they rely on wireless network technology to transfer data.

| Figure 9-33 | USB ports on a notebook computer |

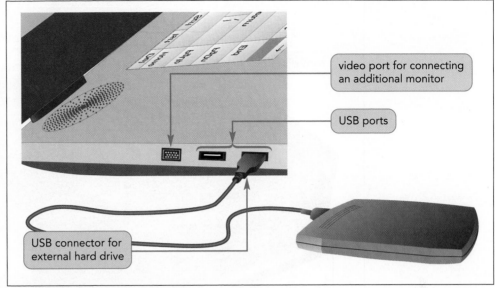

video port for connecting an additional monitor

USB ports

USB connector for external hard drive

© 2014 Cengage Learning

When you plug the USB connector into the USB port, Windows recognizes the device and allows you to use it immediately. The current version of USB technology is USB 3.0, which is faster and more efficient than earlier versions (USB 1.1 and USB 2.0).

You can also **daisy-chain** up to 127 devices together, meaning that you plug one device, such as a scanner, into the USB port, and then plug a second device, such as a microphone, into the scanner, so you are no longer limited by the number of ports on your computer. Instead of daisy-chaining devices, you can also connect multiple devices to a single inexpensive **USB hub**. A hub is a box that contains many USB ports—you plug the hub into your computer, and then plug your USB devices into the hub. USB devices communicate with your computer more efficiently—a USB port transfers data many times faster than other types of ports. You can also connect and disconnect USB devices without shutting down or restarting your computer.

Internal devices are connected to the **motherboard**, a circuit board inside your computer that contains the **microprocessor** (the "brains" of your computer), the computer memory, and other internal hardware devices. Internal devices are connected either directly to the motherboard (such as the microprocessor and your memory chips) or via a socket in the motherboard called an **expansion slot**. You can insert devices such as network adapter cards or sound cards into expansion slots. Devices that you insert into expansion slots are often called **expansion cards** or **adapter cards** because they "expand" or "adapt" your computer, and they look like large cards. See Figure 9-34.

Figure 9-34 **Internal devices in a desktop computer**

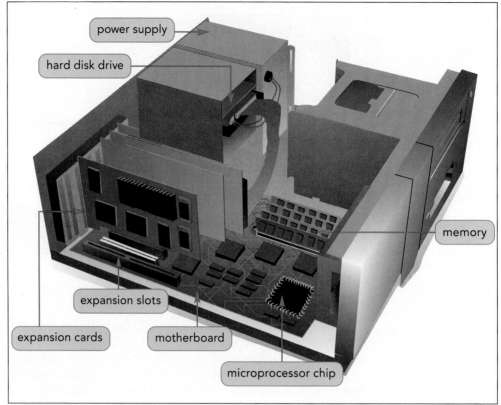

© 2014 Cengage Learning

Understanding Device Resources

Windows assigns each device a set of system resources to help it work with the computer. Windows can assign up to four resources to a device: an IRQ, a DMA channel, an I/O address, and a memory range. When two devices share a particular resource, a **device conflict** can occur, rendering one or both of the devices unusable.

A hardware device often needs to use the microprocessor in the computer to send or receive information. When you are trying to complete several computer tasks at once (for example, when you search for a Web page while you are printing a document and playing an audio CD), Windows needs a way to handle these simultaneous requests. It does so by assigning each device an **interrupt request (IRQ) line** number that signals the microprocessor that the device is requesting an action. Windows 8 makes available 16 IRQ numbers, numbered from 0 to 15, to hardware devices. Lower numbers have higher priority and receive attention first. One common hardware headache is to have more devices than available IRQs, resulting in an IRQ conflict. If you use USB devices, however, Windows 8 only uses one set of resources for all USB devices, meaning you don't have to resolve these types of IRQ conflicts.

If the device does not need to use the microprocessor, information can be transferred directly between the device and the system's memory. This channel for transferring data is called the **direct memory access (DMA) channel**. Most computers have four DMA channels, numbered from 0 to 3, available for your devices.

When the computer receives information from one of its devices, it needs a place to store that data in the computer's memory. It does this by reserving a specific section of the computer's memory for each device. The section of the computer's memory devoted to the different devices on a computer is called the **I/O address**. Each device requires a different I/O (input/output) address.

Finally, some devices, such as video cards, require additional computer memory for their own use (not related to communicating with the microprocessor). For example, a video card needs additional memory to manage video and graphics that are not essential to the operating system. This resource is called the **memory address** or **memory range**.

Your computer uses all four types of system resources—IRQs, DMA channels, I/O addresses, and memory addresses—to communicate between hardware and software.

Understanding Device Drivers

Each hardware device requires a **driver**, a software file that enables Windows to communicate with and control the operation of the device. In most cases, drivers come with Windows 8. If not, you can find them by going to Windows Update in the Control Panel window and checking for updates. If Windows doesn't have the driver you need, you can find it on the media that came with the hardware or device you want to use, or on the manufacturer's Web site. Hardware manufacturers update drivers on a regular basis to improve device performance and speed. If you are having trouble with a device, you can use Windows Update or check the manufacturer's Web site to download and install an updated driver.

A **signed driver** is a device driver that includes a digital signature. Recall that a digital signature is an electronic security mark that identifies the publisher of the software and whether someone has changed the original contents of the driver package. If a publisher signed a driver by verifying its identity with a certification authority, you can be confident that the driver actually comes from that publisher and hasn't been altered. Windows alerts you if a driver is not signed, was signed by a publisher that has not verified its identity with a certification authority, or has been altered since it was released.

Installing a Device

Before installing new hardware, check the instructions included with the device to determine whether you need to install a driver before you connect the device. Typically, Windows detects a new device after you connect it and then installs the driver automatically. However, some devices require you to install the driver before plugging the device in. Although most devices that have power switches should be turned on before you connect them, others require that you turn them on during the installation process. Because of differences like this one, it is a good idea to read the instructions included with a new device before you connect it.

To install new devices of any type, you typically can plug the device into a port or install a new add-on card in your computer, and then Windows 8 detects the hardware, automatically installs the correct driver, and notifies you when installation begins and when it's complete. The first time you plug a USB device into a USB port, for example, Windows installs a driver for that device. After that, you can disconnect and reconnect the device without performing additional steps.

Enabling and Disabling Devices

Device Manager is a Windows tool that lets you manage the external and internal devices your computer uses. Using Device Manager, you can determine which devices are installed on your computer, update driver software for your devices, check to see if hardware is working properly, and modify hardware settings.

REFERENCE

Enabling and Disabling Devices

- Open the Control Panel in Category view, click System and Security, and then click Device Manager in the System category. If you are prompted for an administrator password or confirmation, type the password or provide confirmation.
- Expand the list of devices as necessary, and then click a device.
- If the device is disabled, click the Enable button on the toolbar to enable it. If the device is enabled, click the Disable button on the toolbar to disable it.

You can use Device Manager to change how your hardware is configured and interacts with your programs. Advanced users can use the diagnostic features in Device Manager to resolve device conflicts and change resource settings. Typically, however, you use Device Manager to update device drivers and troubleshoot problems by checking the status of your devices. Suppose you occasionally have trouble burning files to a disc in your CD/DVD drive. You can check the status of that drive in Device Manager and try to repair it by disabling it and then enabling it. When troubleshooting, you might also disable a device instead of uninstalling it to see if that device is causing a larger system problem. If the problem persists, you can enable the device and disable a different device. When you disable a device, you turn it off. When you enable a device, you turn it on.

You'll start Device Manager and show Andrea how to disable and then enable a USB flash drive.

To perform the following steps, you need to log on using an Administrator account. You also need a USB flash drive, such as the one you used to create backups in Session 9.1. Disabling a USB flash drive does not affect any existing data on the drive. If you cannot sign in using an Administrator account or if you do not have a USB flash drive, read but do not perform the following steps.

To disable a USB flash drive:

1. If necessary, plug a USB flash drive into a USB port on your computer. Close any dialog boxes that open.

2. Display the System and Security window in the Control Panel, and then click **Device Manager** in the System category. The Device Manager window opens. See Figure 9-35.

Figure 9-35   **Device Manager window**

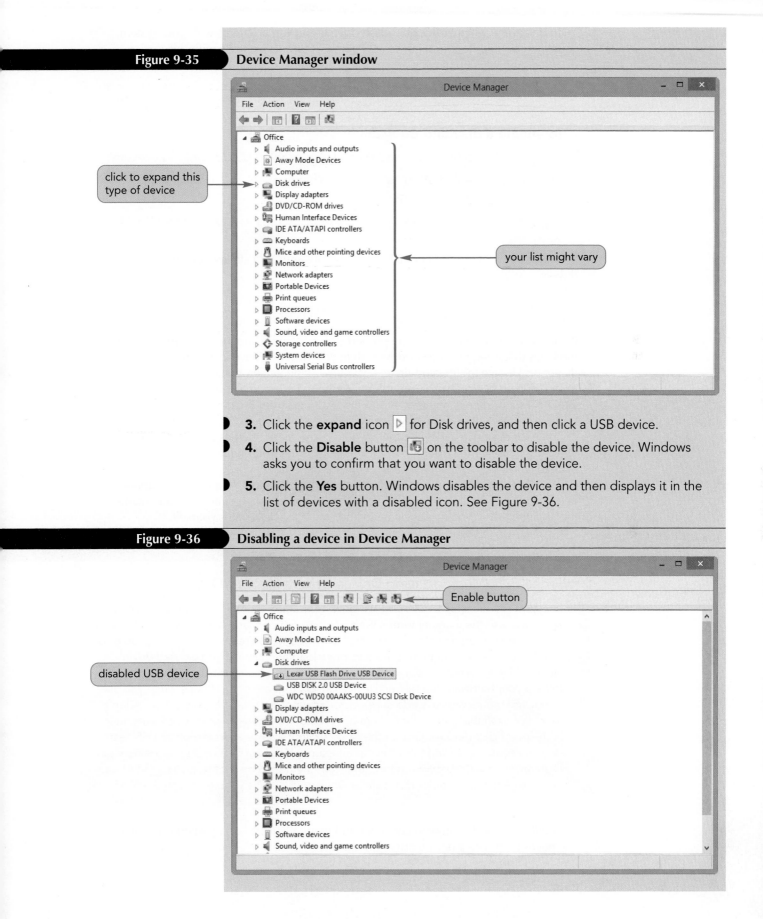

click to expand this type of device

your list might vary

3. Click the **expand** icon ▷ for Disk drives, and then click a USB device.

4. Click the **Disable** button 🔲 on the toolbar to disable the device. Windows asks you to confirm that you want to disable the device.

5. Click the **Yes** button. Windows disables the device and then displays it in the list of devices with a disabled icon. See Figure 9-36.

Figure 9-36   **Disabling a device in Device Manager**

Enable button

disabled USB device

To determine whether this USB flash drive is causing problems with your system, you could troubleshoot to see if your system now works properly with this device disabled. Andrea is not having any problems with this USB flash drive, so you can enable it again.

To enable a disabled device:

▶ **1.** In the Device Manager window, click the disabled **USB device**, if necessary.

▶ **2.** Click the **Enable** button on the toolbar to enable the device. Windows turns on the device so you can use it.

Trouble? If an AutoPlay dialog box or a Recovery window opens, close it.

Another way to troubleshoot a hardware problem is to install or update device drivers.

Installing and Updating Device Drivers

If a hardware device isn't working properly, or if an application that you're installing indicates that it requires newer drivers than you currently have installed, first check Windows Update for updated drivers. Windows Update automatically installs the device drivers you need as it updates your computer. In some cases, such as when technical support personnel ask you to install drivers from the device manufacturer's Web site, you can also manually update drivers for your device using Device Manager.

To install or update a device driver, you can use the Properties dialog box for the hardware device. The Driver tab in this dialog box lets you update the driver, roll it back to a previous version, disable it, or uninstall it. You can also find out if a driver is signed. If you want to update a driver, you can have Windows search your computer and the Internet for the appropriate files. If you have removable media that contains the updated driver, you can navigate to and install the driver files yourself.

PROSKILLS

Problem Solving: Installing Device Drivers on Your Own

Sometimes you install a device in Windows 8 and find that it is working well. Then, when you visit the manufacturer's Web site, you notice that it has provided a newer driver that you can download and install. However, if you're not having any problems with the device, you might not need to download and install that updated driver. Newer drivers are not necessarily better. They might not include any improvements to help your hardware run better. Device drivers that are not available when you use Windows Update typically add support for new products or technologies you don't have. For example, a manufacturer might provide new drivers when it releases new high-speed USB devices. One of the drivers might also support the older USB flash drive that you purchased from the manufacturer. Unless you have one of the new USB flash drives, you probably won't benefit from the new driver. If the driver hasn't been fully tested with your older USB flash drive, it might cause problems with the hardware.

You'll show Andrea how to check for and manually install an updated driver in case she needs to update a device driver on her own.

To perform the following steps, you need to sign in to Windows using an Administrator account. The USB flash drive that you worked with in the preceding set of steps should also be available and plugged into a USB port. If you cannot sign in using an Administrator account or if you do not have a USB flash drive, read but do not perform the following steps.

To update and install a device driver:

▶ **1.** In the Device Manager window, double-click the **USB device** to open its Properties dialog box. See Figure 9-37.

| Figure 9-37 | Properties dialog box for a USB device |

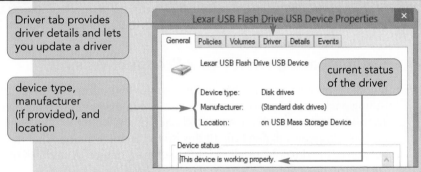

Driver tab provides driver details and lets you update a driver

device type, manufacturer (if provided), and location

current status of the driver

▶ **2.** Click the **Driver** tab. You can use this tab to find out if a driver is signed, update the driver, roll it back, disable it, or uninstall it. See Figure 9-38.

| Figure 9-38 | Driver tab in the device's Properties dialog box |

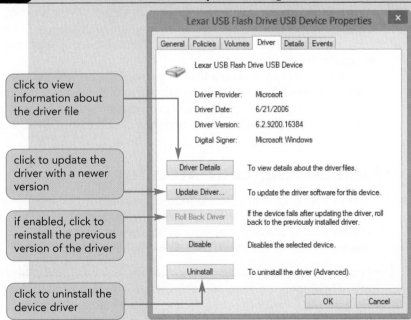

click to view information about the driver file

click to update the driver with a newer version

if enabled, click to reinstall the previous version of the driver

click to uninstall the device driver

▶ **3.** Click the **Driver Details** button. The Driver File Details dialog box opens, displaying the name, location, and other details about the driver file.

▶ **4.** Click the **OK** button to close the Driver File Details dialog box.

▶ **5.** Click the **Update Driver** button. A dialog box opens asking how you want to search for driver software.

> **6.** Click **Search automatically for updated driver software**. Windows searches your computer and the Internet for the latest version of the driver software. For Andrea's USB flash drive, it determines that the best driver software for the device is already installed.
>
>   **Trouble?** If Windows determines that you need to update the driver software for your device, it asks if you want to install the software now. Click the No button.
>
> **7.** Click the **Close** button to close the Update Driver Software dialog box.
>
> **8.** Close all open windows.

Sometimes, installing an updated driver can cause more problems than it solves. In that case, you can restore the driver to a previous version.

Rolling Back a Driver to a Previous Version

If your computer or device has problems after you upgrade a driver, try restoring, or rolling back, the driver to a previous version. In many cases, that solves the problem. To roll back a driver, you use the Roll Back Driver button on the Driver tab of the device's Properties dialog box. (If this button is not available, that means no previous version of the driver is installed for the selected device.) Windows restores the previous version of the driver.

Safely Removing Devices

You can remove, or unplug, most USB devices whenever you like. The same is true for PC cards, which some mobile computers use to connect to a network or the Internet. When unplugging storage devices, such as USB flash drives, make sure that the computer has finished saving any information to the device before removing it. If the device has an activity light, wait a few seconds after the light stops flashing before unplugging the device.

You know you can remove a USB device or PC card when you see the Safely Remove Hardware icon in the notification area of the taskbar. This means that all devices have finished all operations in progress and are ready for you to remove. Click the icon to display a list of devices, and then click the device you want to remove.

Maintaining Your Monitor

When your monitor is installed, Windows chooses the best display settings for that monitor, including screen resolution, refresh rate, and color. If you start having display problems with your monitor or want to improve its display, you can change the following settings or restore them to their defaults:

- Brightness and contrast—For the best results, you can use a calibration device to adjust brightness, contrast, and color settings. You usually attach the device to the front of your monitor to read light and color levels, and then use a program that came with the device to optimize your monitor's display. You can also adjust brightness and contrast manually (though not as precisely) by using the hardware controls, which are usually placed on the front of the monitor.
- Color settings—The number of colors determines how realistic the images look. However, the higher the resolution and color setting, the more resources your monitor needs; the best settings for your computer balance sharpness and color quality

with computer resources. Windows colors and themes work best when you have your monitor set to 32-bit color.

- Display resolution—You can adjust the screen resolution to improve the clarity of the text and images on your screen. Recall that at higher resolutions, computer images appear sharper. They also appear smaller, so more items fit on the screen. At lower resolutions, fewer items fit on the screen, but they are larger and easier to see. At very low resolutions, however, images might have jagged edges. Recall that for an LCD monitor, you should use its native resolution.
- Screen refresh rate—To reduce or eliminate flicker, you can adjust the screen refresh rate. If the refresh rate is too low, the monitor can flicker. Most monitor manufacturers recommend a refresh rate of at least 75 hertz.

Andrea already knows how to adjust the brightness, contrast, and screen resolution. You'll show her how to maintain her monitor by adjusting the screen refresh rate and selecting color settings.

Adjusting the Screen Refresh Rate

A flickering monitor can contribute to eyestrain and headaches. You can reduce or eliminate flickering by increasing the **screen refresh rate**, which determines how frequently the monitor redraws the images on the screen. The refresh rate is measured in hertz. A refresh rate of at least 75 hertz generally produces less flicker.

Adjusting the Screen Refresh Rate

- Right-click the desktop, and then click Screen resolution on the shortcut menu.
- Click the Advanced settings link.
- Click the Monitor tab.
- Click the Screen refresh rate button, and then click a refresh rate.

You might need to change your screen resolution before changing the refresh rate because not every screen resolution is compatible with every refresh rate. The higher the resolution, the higher your refresh rate should be. Recall that to change your screen resolution, you can right-click the desktop, click Screen resolution on the shortcut menu, click the Resolution button, and then drag the slider.

Andrea recently increased the screen resolution on her monitor from 1280 x 720 to 1366 x 768 to improve the clarity of her icons. However, the screen flickers slightly since she changed that setting. You'll show her how to increase the screen refresh rate to reduce monitor flicker.

TIP

You can also open the Screen Resolution window by opening the Control Panel, clicking Adjust screen resolution, and then clicking Advanced settings.

To change the screen refresh rate:

1. Right-click the desktop, and then click **Screen resolution** on the shortcut menu. The Screen Resolution window opens.

2. Click the **Advanced settings** link. The Properties dialog box for your monitor opens.

3. Click the **Monitor** tab to display the monitor properties. See Figure 9-39.

Figure 9-39   **Monitor tab in the monitor's Properties dialog box**

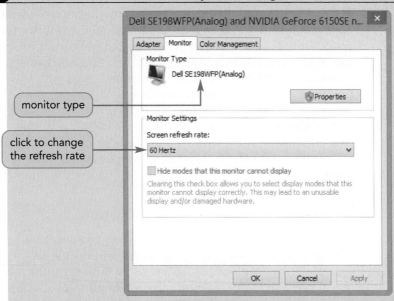

4. Click the **Screen refresh rate** button, and then click **75 Hertz**.

Trouble? If your list of refresh rates does not include 75, click any other refresh rate that is higher than your current refresh rate.

Trouble? If you cannot change the screen refresh rate, click a blank spot in the dialog box to close the Screen refresh list, and then skip Steps 4, 5, and 6. Leave the monitor's Properties dialog box open.

5. Click the **Apply** button to apply the new setting. Windows asks if you want to keep these display settings.

6. Click the **Keep changes** button and leave the monitor's Properties dialog box open.

Next, you'll show Andrea how to manage the color settings on her computer. She is planning to update and print a four-color ad for the Arlington Wellness Center, and she wants to make sure the colors she sees on her monitor are the same colors that print in the ad.

Selecting Color Settings

You can use the Properties dialog box for your monitor to make sure that the colors displayed on your monitor match the colors produced on a color printer, for example. To do so, you use the Windows 8 color management settings.

Hardware devices that produce color, such as monitors and printers, often have different color characteristics and capabilities. Monitors can't display the same set of colors that a printer can print because they use different techniques to produce color on a screen or on paper. Scanners and cameras also have different color characteristics. Even two devices of the same type can display color differently. For example, the LCD monitor built into a laptop computer might display shades of color that are different from those displayed on the LCD monitor attached to a desktop computer.

To overcome these differences, Windows 8 uses color management settings and color profiles to maintain consistent colors no matter which device produces the color content. Hardware manufacturers can create a color profile, which is a file that describes the color characteristics of a device. Profiles can also define viewing conditions, such as low light or natural light. When you add a new device to your computer, the color profile for that device is included with the other installation files, so you don't need to add or remove a color profile. In addition, the default color management settings almost always produce the best results; therefore, only color professionals, such as compositors and typographers, should change them. However, you can use the Properties dialog box for your monitor to verify that your computer is using the default color management settings.

Before Andrea updates and prints her four-color ad for the Arlington Wellness Center, you'll show her how to make sure her computer is using the default settings for color management.

To verify the color management settings:

▶ **1.** In the Properties dialog box for your monitor, click the **Color Management** tab, and then click the **Color Management** button. The Color Management dialog box opens to the Devices tab, which identifies your hardware display and lists its color profiles, if any.

▶ **2.** Click the **Advanced** tab to display the color management settings. See Figure 9-40, which shows all of these settings set to the system default. Your settings might differ.

| Figure 9-40 | Advanced tab in the Color Management dialog box |

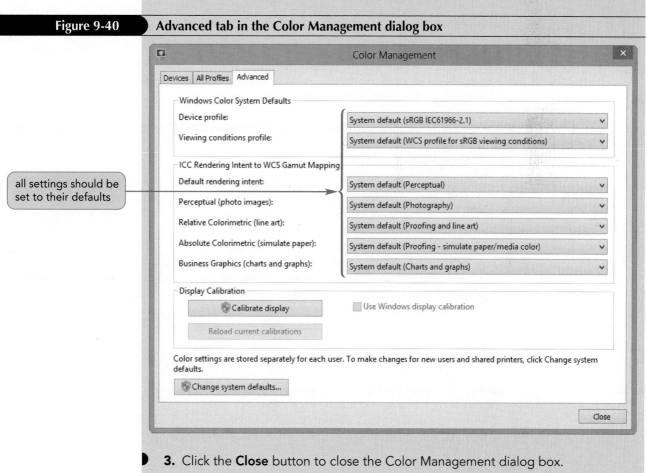

▶ **3.** Click the **Close** button to close the Color Management dialog box.

▶ **4.** Click the **OK** button to close the Properties dialog box for your monitor.

Now you can turn to the final hardware task: installing and setting up a printer.

Installing and Setting Up a Printer

Before you can print anything from your computer, you need to connect a printer directly to your computer, making it a **local printer**, or create a connection to a network or shared printer. Before using Windows 8 to install a printer, check the manual that came with your printer. For some printers, you plug the printer into your computer, usually using a USB port, and then you turn on the printer. Once the printer is on, Windows 8 detects the new printer and installs its driver. For other printers, you need to install their software first, and then plug in and turn on the printer.

Most printers that you buy today are USB printers, meaning you connect them by plugging the printer's cable into a USB port on your computer. Most also have wireless capabilities, so you can share a printer on your homegroup or wireless Internet connection. Older printers use a parallel cable that connects to your computer's printer port (also called the LPT1 port). If you are installing a second or third printer, you might need to use a parallel cable if you are using the computer's USB ports for other devices.

After you physically connect a local printer, you open the Devices and Printers window and start the Add Printer Wizard, which guides you through the steps of installing the printer and its drivers. You use the same wizard to set up a network printer for which you've turned on printer sharing.

Installing a Local Printer

Using the printer manufacturer's directions, you attach or connect the printer to your computer. Windows usually installs the printer without further action from you. If Windows does not recognize the printer, you can open the Devices and Printers window from the Control Panel to install it yourself.

REFERENCE

Installing a Local Printer

- Follow the printer manufacturer's instructions to connect the printer to your computer.
- If Windows does not automatically detect the printer and install its drivers, open the Control Panel, click Hardware and Sound, and then click Devices and Printers.
- Click the Add a printer button on the toolbar.
- In the Add Printer Wizard, click Add a local printer.
- Click the Next button to accept the existing printer port.
- Select the printer manufacturer and the printer name, and then click the Next button.
- Enter a printer name, and then click the Next button.
- Click the Finish button.

Andrea already uses a laser printer that is connected to her network, and she needs to connect a color printer to her computer using a USB cable plugged into the printer port. You'll show Andrea how to install her Hewlett-Packard color laser printer, which is called HP Color LaserJet 2800 Series PS.

If you are working on a school or institutional network, you probably cannot install a printer on your computer. In that case, read but do not perform the following steps.

To install a local printer:

1. Physically connect your printer to your computer. The Devices and Printers window opens. See Figure 9-41.

Figure 9-41 Devices and Printers window

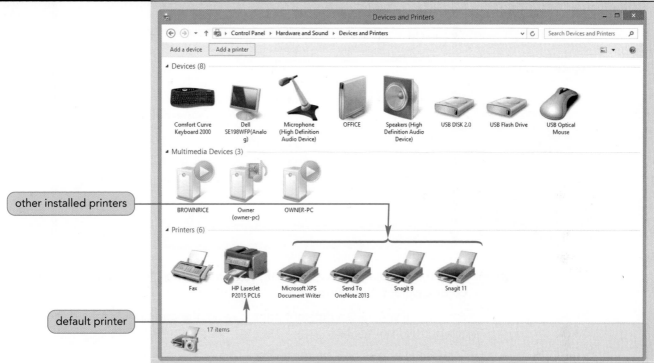

other installed printers

default printer

Trouble? If you plugged the printer into a USB port, Windows might detect the printer and install the drivers automatically. In that case, the printer is ready to use. Read but do not perform the following steps.

Trouble? If the Devices and Printers window does not open, display the Control Panel Home page, and then click View devices and printers in the Hardware and Sound category.

2. Click the **Add a printer** button on the toolbar. The Add Printer Wizard starts and lets you choose whether to add a local or network printer.

3. Click **Add a local printer**. The next wizard dialog box opens, where you can choose a printer port.

4. Make sure the Use an existing port option button is selected, and then click the **Next** button. The next wizard dialog box opens, where you can select the manufacturer and model of your printer. See Figure 9-42.

Figure 9-42 **Installing the printer driver**

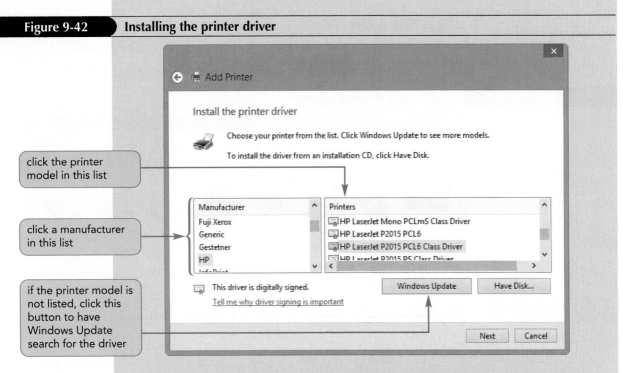

click the printer model in this list

click a manufacturer in this list

if the printer model is not listed, click this button to have Windows Update search for the driver

5. Scroll the Manufacturer list, click **HP**, scroll the Printers list, and then click **HP Color LaserJet 2800 Series PS**.

Trouble? If you have a different printer, select the appropriate manufacturer and printer from the list.

6. Click the **Next** button. The next wizard dialog box asks you to confirm the printer's name or enter a different one.

TIP

To verify that the printer works correctly, click the Print a test page button before clicking the Finish button.

7. Click the **Next** button to accept the default name. The final wizard dialog box confirms that the printer is installed and lets you print a test page, if necessary.

Trouble? If the Printer Sharing window opens, click the Do not share this printer option button, and then click the Next button.

8. Click the **Finish** button.

After you successfully install the color laser printer for Andrea, she notices that it is now the default printer, meaning that all of the documents she prints will be directed to that printer unless she changes that setting using the Print dialog box. She prints far more often on the black-and-white laser printer. You'll show her how to specify that printer as the default.

Changing the Default Printer

If you have more than one printer connected to your computer, you can select the one you want to use by default. When you use Windows or your apps to print, a Print dialog box opens and lets you select settings, including a printer. The Print dialog box selects the default printer automatically, though you can change it if you like. In some apps, when you click a Print button, the content prints on the default printer without opening a Print dialog box. Therefore, you should select the printer you use most often as your default printer. You can do so in the Devices and Printers window.

Andrea wants to make her black-and-white laser printer the default instead of her color printer. You'll show her how to change her default printer using the Devices and Printers window.

To change the default printer:

▶ **1.** In the Devices and Printers window, right-click the **HP LaserJet** printer icon, and then click **Set as default printer** on the shortcut menu. Windows displays a default icon ✅ on the HP LaserJet.

   Trouble? If you have a different printer to set as the default, right-click that printer and then click Set as default on the shortcut menu.

   Trouble? If you are not allowed to change the default printer, read but do not perform Step 1.

Restoring Your Settings

If you are working in a computer lab or on a computer other than your own, complete the steps in this section to restore the original settings on your computer. If a User Account Control dialog box opens requesting an Administrator password or confirmation after you perform any of the following steps, enter the password or click the Continue button.

To restore your settings:

▶ **1.** Open the Control Panel in Category view, click **System and Security**, click **File History** to open the File History window, and then click the **Turn off** button to disable automatic backups. Leave the Control Panel open.

▶ **2.** Move the **Andrea** folder in your Documents library to the Windows9\Tutorial folder provided with your Data Files.

▶ **3.** Right-click the desktop, and then click **Screen resolution** on the shortcut menu.

▶ **4.** Click the **Advanced settings** link, and then click the **Monitor** tab. Click the **Screen refresh rate** button, and then click your original refresh rate, such as **60 Hertz**. (Your refresh rates might differ.) Click the **OK** button, and then click the **Keep changes** button to close the Properties dialog box for your monitor. Click the **OK** button to close the Screen Resolution window.

▶ **5.** Open the Devices and Printers window, right-click the extra printer you installed in this tutorial, and then click **Remove device** on the shortcut menu. Click the **Yes** button to confirm that you want to remove the device.

▶ **6.** Close all open windows.

8.1
512MB
8 - 256. 512MB

Session 9.2 Quick Check

REVIEW

1. How do you display the properties of your hard disk?
2. On a hard disk, the boot _partition_ contains the Windows operating system files.
3. Why should you occasionally use the Disk Cleanup tool to maintain your system?
4. _defragmentation_ rearranges the clusters on a disk so each file's clusters are adjacent to one another.
5. What is a device driver?   *487*
6. Why might you need to change the screen refresh rate for your monitor?   *503*
7. How do you set a printer as the default printer?

Review Assignments

PRACTICE

Data File needed for the Review Assignments: Arlington.rtf

You are now working with Mark Salisbury, the sales manager of the Arlington Wellness Center. He has recently acquired a new Windows 8 computer, and he asks you to show him how to maintain its hardware and software. He is particularly concerned about protecting the photos he uses to promote the center and its products. Complete the following steps, noting your original settings so you can restore them later:

1. Use File Explorer to create a folder named **Mark** in the Public Documents folder on your computer, and then copy the Arlington file Windows9\Review folder provided with your Data Files to the Mark folder.

2. Attach a USB flash drive or an external hard drive you can use for backups by plugging the drive into a USB port on your computer.

3. Open the File History window, and then select the USB flash drive or external hard drive you attached in Step 2 as the drive to use for backups.

4. Exclude all locations from the backup except the Public Documents folder, and then set File History to make backups every 10 minutes.

5. Turn on File History. Press the Print Screen key to capture an image of the screen. Paste the image in a new Paint file, and then save the file as **File History** in the Windows9\Review folder provided with your Data Files.

6. Open the **Arlington** document, add your name to the beginning of the document, format your name in red, save the document, and then close the application window.

7. Download and install a free Spotlight app from the Windows Store. When a notification appears indicating the app has been installed, press the Print Screen key to capture an image of the screen. Paste the image into a new Paint file, and then save the file as **Installed App** in the Windows9\Review folder provided with your Data Files.

8. Open the System window, and then create a restore point named **Salisbury**. Open the System Restore window, navigate to the dialog box displaying the restore points on your computer, and then press the Print Screen key to capture an image of the screen. Paste the image in a new Paint file, and then save the file as **Restore Points** in the Windows9\Review folder provided with your Data Files.

9. Display the amount of free space and used space on your hard disk. With the dialog box open showing this information, press the Print Screen key to capture an image of the screen. Paste the image in a new Paint file, and then save the file as **Free Space** in the Windows9\Review folder provided with your Data Files.

10. Open the Disk Cleanup dialog box for your hard disk, and then choose to clean up only your temporary files (not temporary Internet files). Press the Print Screen key to capture an image of the screen. Paste the image in a new Paint file, and then save the file as **Temporary** in the Windows9\Review folder provided with your Data Files. Close the Disk Cleanup dialog box without deleting files.

11. Display the schedule for defragmenting your hard disk. Press the Print Screen key to capture an image of the screen. Paste the image in a new Paint file, and then save the file as **Optimize** in the Windows9\Review folder provided with your Data Files. Close the Optimize Drives dialog boxes.

12. Open the Device Manager window and expand devices as necessary to display the drives attached to your computer. Disable the USB flash drive. With the Device Manager window open, press the Print Screen key to capture an image of the screen. Paste the image in a new Paint file, and then save the file as **Disable** in the Windows9\Review folder provided with your Data Files. Enable the USB flash drive.

13. Open the **Arlington** document in the Mark folder, add your school's name to the beginning of the document, format your name and the school's name in blue, save the document, and then close the application window.

14. Display the refresh rate of your monitor. With the Properties dialog box for your monitor open, press the Print Screen key to capture an image of the screen. Paste the image in a new Paint file, and then save the file as **Refresh Rate** in the Windows9\Review folder provided with your Data Files.

15. Install a local printer named **Office** in the Devices and Printers window. (*Hint*: You can install a local printer even if it is not connected to your computer.) Do not share the printer or set it as the default. With the Devices and Printers window open, press the Print Screen key to capture an image of the screen. Paste the image in a new Paint file, and then save the file as **Office Printer** in the Windows9\Review folder provided with your Data Files.

16. Display the history of the files in the Mark folder. Restore the file that displays your name in red (and does not include your school's name) to the Mark folder.

17. Turn off File History, and then move the Mark folder to the Windows9\Review folder provided with your Data Files.

18. Restore your settings by removing the Office printer from the Devices and Printers window. Close all open windows. Display the Start screen, and then uninstall the productivity app you installed in Step 7.

19. Submit the results of the preceding steps to your instructor, either in printed or electronic form, as requested.

Case Problem 1

APPLY

There are no Data Files needed for this Case Problem.

Wildman Art Gallery   Horace Wildman is the owner of the Wildman Art Gallery in Montpelier, Vermont. He recently hired you to help him automate the gallery's business operations and marketing efforts. Horace has been using a Windows 8 mobile computer for a few months, and he asks you to help him properly maintain its hardware and software. Complete the following steps, noting your original settings so you can restore them later:

1. Start Bing in IE Windows 8, and then press the Windows+Print Screen keys to capture an image of the Bing window. The image is automatically saved in the Screenshots folder in the Pictures library as a file named Screenshot (x), where x is a number, as in Screenshot (1). (*Hint*: You can open File Explorer and navigate to the Pictures library to make sure the file has been saved.)

2. Attach a USB flash drive or an external hard drive you can use for backups by plugging the drive into a USB port on your computer.

3. Open the File History window, and then select the USB flash drive you attached in Step 2 as the drive to use for backups.

4. Exclude all locations from the backup except the Pictures library.

5. Turn on File History. Press the Print Screen key to capture an image of the screen. Paste the image in a new Paint file, and then save the file as **Pictures Backup** in the Windows9\Case1 folder provided with your Data Files.

6. Download and install a free photo app from the Windows Store. When a notification appears indicating the app has been installed, press the Print Screen key to capture an image of the screen. Paste the image in a new Paint file, and then save the file as **Photo App** in the Windows9\Case1 folder provided with your Data Files.

7. Create a restore point named **Horace**. With the System Restore window open and displaying the restore points on your computer, press the Print Screen key to capture an image of the screen. Paste the image in a new Paint file, and then save the file as **Horace Restore** in the Windows9\ Case1 folder provided with your Data Files. Close the System Restore window without restoring your system.

8. Open the Properties dialog box for your local hard disk. Display all of the disk drives attached to your computer. With the dialog box open showing this information, press the Print Screen key to capture an image of the screen. Paste the image in a new Paint file, and then save the file as **Disk Drives** in the Windows9\Case1 folder provided with your Data Files.

9. Use Device Manager to check for an updated driver for any device on your computer. After checking, press the Print Screen key to capture an image of the dialog box showing the results. Paste the image in a new Paint file, and then save the file as **Updated Driver** in the Windows9\ Case1 folder provided with your Data Files. If Windows found an updated driver, do not install it.

10. Increase the resolution of your monitor, and then increase the screen refresh rate, if possible. With the Screen Resolution window open, press the Print Screen key to capture an image of the screen. Paste the image in a new Paint file, and then save the file as **Screen Res** in the Windows9\Case1 folder provided with your Data Files.

11. Install a local printer named **Gallery** in the Devices and Printers window. (*Hint*: You can install a local printer even if it is not connected to your computer.) Do not share the printer or set it as the default. With the Devices and Printers window open, press the Print Screen key to capture an image of the screen. Paste the image in a new Paint file, and then save the file as **Gallery Printer** in the Windows9\Case1 folder provided with your Data Files.

12. Turn off File History, and then move the Screenshot (x) file from the Screenshots folder in the Pictures library to the Windows9\Case1 folder provided with your Data Files.

13. Restore your settings by removing the Gallery printer from the Devices and Printers window and restoring your original screen resolution. Close all open windows. Display the Start screen, and then uninstall the photo app you installed in Step 6.

14. Submit the results of the preceding steps to your instructor, either in printed or electronic form, as requested.

CHALLENGE

Case Problem 2

There are no Data Files needed for this Case Problem.

Cape Coral Literacy Agency   Jason Mancini is the director of the Cape Coral Literacy Agency, an organization dedicated to improving adult literacy in Cape Coral, Florida. You are a part-time assistant for the agency and primarily help Jason perform computer tasks using his Windows 8 computer. Jason recently lost some data during a power failure, so he asks you to help him back up the files in his libraries. He is also concerned about maintaining the software on his computer. You'll show him how to complete these maintenance tasks. Complete the following steps, noting your original settings so you can restore them later:

1. Attach a USB flash drive or an external hard drive you can use for backups by plugging the drive into a USB port on your computer.

2. Open the File History window, and then select the USB flash drive you attached in Step 1 as the drive to use for backups.

3. Turn on File History, and then set it to back up files every 3 hours. Press the Print Screen key to capture an image of the screen. Paste the image in a new Paint file, and then save the file as **Full Backup** in the Windows9\Case2 folder provided with your Data Files. To save time and disk space, click the Stop link to stop creating a backup.

4. Download and install a free electronic reader app from the Windows Store. When a notification appears indicating the app has been installed, press the Print Screen key to capture an image of the screen. Paste the image in a new Paint file, and then save the file as **E-reader App** in the Windows9\Case2 folder provided with your Data Files.

5. Open the System Restore window, and then select the first automatic restore point in the list. With the System Restore window open and displaying the restore points on your computer, press the Print Screen key to capture an image of the window. Paste the image in a new Paint file, and then save the file as **Auto Restore** in the Windows9\Case2 folder provided with your Data Files. Close the System Restore window without restoring your system.

⊕ **Explore** 6. Use Windows Update to check for optional updates to your computer, including device drivers. (*Hint*: Open the Windows Update window, click Check for updates, and then wait while Windows looks for the latest updates for your computer.) Display the optional updates available, and then press the Print Screen key to capture an image of the window. Paste the image in a new Paint file, and then save the file as **Driver Updates** in the Windows9\Case2 folder provided with your Data Files. Close the Windows Update window without installing any updates.

⊕ **Explore** 7. Open the Programs and Features window, and then select the first application in the list. (*Hint*: Open the Programs category in the Control Panel, and then click Programs and Features.) Press the Print Screen key to capture an image of the screen. Paste the image in a new Paint file, and then save the file as **Installed** in the Windows9\Case2 folder provided with your Data Files.

⊕ **Explore** 8. Display the partitions on your computer. Press the Print Screen key to capture an image of the page. Paste the image in a new Paint file, and then save the file as **Partitions** in the Windows9\Case2 folder provided with your Data Files.

9. Display the Start screen, and then uninstall the electronic reader app you installed in Step 4.

10. Submit the results of the preceding steps to your instructor, either in printed or electronic form, as requested.

CHALLENGE

Case Problem 3

There are no Data Files needed for this Case Problem.

Burnett Production Group   Cilla Burnett is the founder of the Burnett Production Group in Memphis, Tennessee. Cilla and her associates represent Memphis musicians and book performances for them throughout the United States. Cilla hired you to help her maintain the computer hardware for her company. Complete the following steps, noting your original settings so you can restore them later:

1. Install a USB flash drive or an external hard disk on your computer.

2. Display the amount of free space and used space on the removable disk. With the dialog box open showing this information, press the Print Screen key to capture an image of the window. Paste the image in a new Paint file, and then save the file as **USB Space** in the Windows9\Case3 folder provided with your Data Files.

3. Open the Error Checking dialog box for the removable disk. Press the Print Screen key to capture an image of the screen. Paste the image in a new Paint file, and then save the file as **Scan** in the Windows9\Case3 folder provided with your Data Files.

⊕ **Explore** 4. Display the schedule for defragmenting your removable disk, and then click the Analyze button. When the analysis is complete, press the Print Screen key to capture an image of the window. Paste the image in a new Paint file, and then save the file as **Analysis** in the Windows9\Case3 folder provided with your Data Files.

⊕ **Explore** 5. Click the ReadyBoost tab in the Properties dialog box for the removable disk. Settings on this tab let you use a USB flash drive to boost your available memory. Test the device, if possible. Even if you cannot test the device, press the Print Screen key to capture an image of the screen. Paste the image in a new Paint file, and then save the file as **ReadyBoost** in the Windows9\Case3 folder provided with your Data Files.

⊕ **Explore** 6. Open the Device Manager window, and then display all of the devices by connection. (*Hint*: Click View on the menu bar, and then click Devices by connection if it is not selected.) Press the Print Screen key to capture an image of the screen. Paste the image in a new Paint file, and then save the file as **Device Manager** in the Windows9\Case3 folder provided with your Data Files. Return the view to Devices by type.

⊕ **Explore** 7. In the System and Security window, click Schedule tasks in the Administrative Tools category to explore the settings you can use to start a program according to a schedule (rather than manually from the Apps screen, for example). Press the Print Screen key to capture an image of the screen with the Task Scheduler window open. Paste the image in a new Paint file, and then save the file as **Scheduler** in the Windows9\Case3 folder provided with your Data Files.

8. Install a local printer named **Burnett** in the Devices and Printers window. Do not share the printer or make it the default. With the Devices and Printers window open, press the Print Screen key to capture an image of the window. Paste the image in a new Paint file, and then save the file as **Cilla** in the Windows9\Case3 folder provided with your Data Files.

9. Restore your settings by removing the Burnett printer from the Devices and Printers window and removing the USB device from your computer. Close all open windows.

10. Submit the results of the preceding steps to your instructor, either in printed or electronic form, as requested.

RESEARCH

Case Problem 4

There are no Data Files needed for this Case Problem.

Brightview Academy   Natalie Linder is the director of the Accessibility Department at Brightview College in Tucson, Arizona. Brightview is an independent coeducational boarding school for adolescents and young adults with complex language, learning, and cognitive disabilities. It is committed to developing student competence and confidence in academic, social and independent living skills. You work part-time for Natalie and usually perform data entry, computer hardware maintenance, and other computer-related tasks. Natalie is interested in learning more about making computers accessible to special needs students, and she asks you to research the hardware and software accessibility features of Windows 8. Complete the following steps:

1. Use your favorite search engine to find information about how to make a computer easier to use for the hearing and visually impaired. Try searching for information about the following types of information:
   - Accessible computing
   - Assistive technology
   - Accessibility features
2. Use Windows Help and Support and your favorite search engine to find information about the features Windows 8 provides for the hearing and visually impaired.
3. Select two or three features that interest you, and then write a paragraph about each feature. Be sure to explain how to use the feature and how to change the settings, if any, in Windows 8. Also describe the benefits the feature provides to the hearing and visually impaired.
4. Save the paragraphs in a document named **Accessibility** in the Windows9\Case4 folder provided with your Data Files.
5. Submit the results of the preceding steps to your instructor, either in printed or electronic form, as requested.

WINDOWS

OBJECTIVES

Session 10.1
- Optimize computer performance
- Monitor system tasks
- Examine system information
- Increase memory capacity with ReadyBoost

Session 10.2
- Troubleshoot typical computer problems
- Respond to software and operating system errors
- Use the Problem Steps Recorder
- Manage Remote Assistance

Improving Your Computer's Performance

Enhancing Your System and Troubleshooting Computer Problems

Case | *Fab Homes*

Fab Homes in Santa Rosa, California, manufactures prefabricated, environmentally friendly buildings, and then delivers them in modules to people who want to build their own homes. Fab Homes also contracts with local construction crews, designers, and project experts to make sure home building proceeds smoothly and quickly. You work for Fab Homes as a computer specialist, and your supervisor is Kenny Shen, the company's system administrator. Your job is to help Kenny keep the computers at Fab Homes running at peak performance. Kenny is familiar with system maintenance and troubleshooting tools in earlier versions of Windows, but he is new to Windows 8.

In this tutorial, you will improve your computer's performance by optimizing system settings and increasing memory capacity. You'll monitor system performance, and diagnose and repair computer problems using the Problem Steps Recorder and Remote Assistance.

STARTING DATA FILES

There are no starting Data Files needed for this tutorial.

Session 10.1 Visual Overview:

If a subscore for a graphics component is less than 4, adjust the visual effects, such as displaying thumbnails instead of icons.

Windows calculates **subscores** by rating each hardware component that can affect performance.

Your computer's **Windows Experience Index** grades each hardware component and assigns it a score.

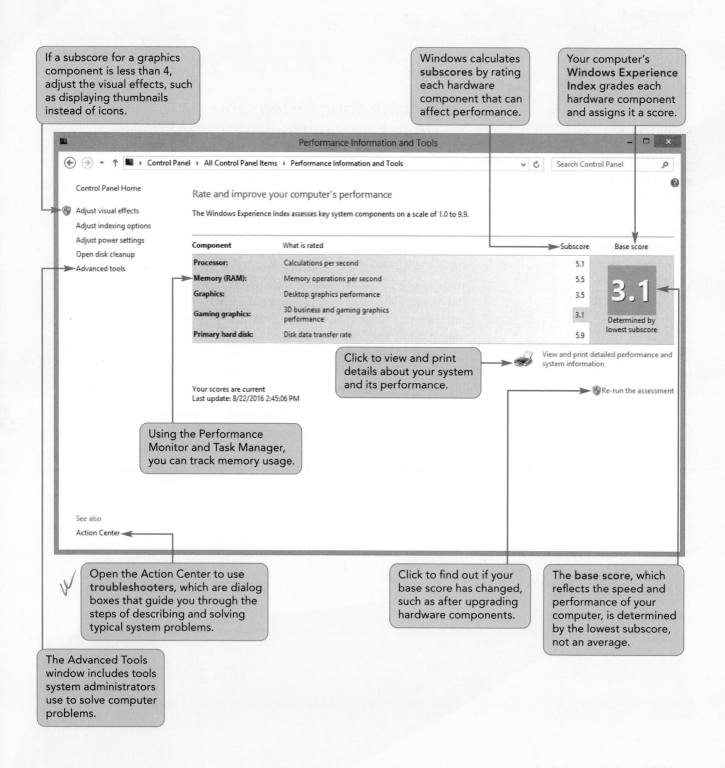

Click to view and print details about your system and its performance.

Using the Performance Monitor and Task Manager, you can track memory usage.

Open the Action Center to use **troubleshooters**, which are dialog boxes that guide you through the steps of describing and solving typical system problems.

Click to find out if your base score has changed, such as after upgrading hardware components.

The **base score**, which reflects the speed and performance of your computer, is determined by the lowest subscore, not an average.

The Advanced Tools window includes tools system administrators use to solve computer problems.

Tracking System Performance

Click to open **Event Viewer**, a performance tool that tracks system events such as critical errors and warnings.

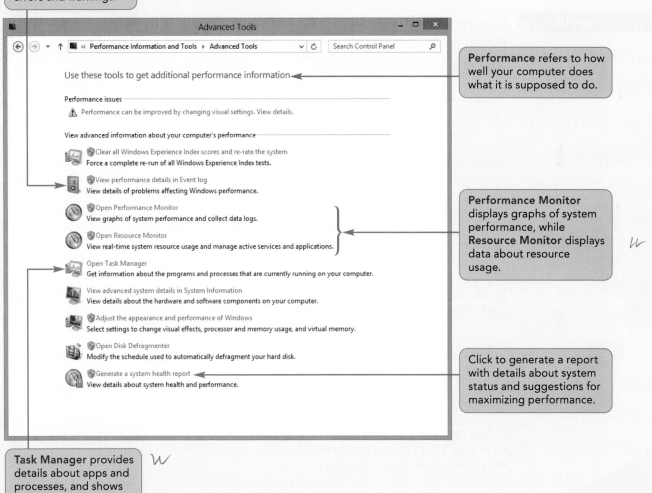

Advanced Tools

« Performance Information and Tools ▸ Advanced Tools   Search Control Panel

Use these tools to get additional performance information

Performance refers to how well your computer does what it is supposed to do.

Performance issues

⚠ Performance can be improved by changing visual settings. View details.

View advanced information about your computer's performance

Clear all Windows Experience Index scores and re-rate the system
Force a complete re-run of all Windows Experience Index tests.

View performance details in Event log
View details of problems affecting Windows performance.

Open Performance Monitor
View graphs of system performance and collect data logs.

Open Resource Monitor
View real-time system resource usage and manage active services and applications.

Performance Monitor displays graphs of system performance, while **Resource Monitor** displays data about resource usage.

Open Task Manager
Get information about the programs and processes that are currently running on your computer.

View advanced system details in System Information
View details about the hardware and software components on your computer.

Adjust the appearance and performance of Windows
Select settings to change visual effects, processor and memory usage, and virtual memory.

Open Disk Defragmenter
Modify the schedule used to automatically defragment your hard disk.

Generate a system health report
View details about system health and performance.

Click to generate a report with details about system status and suggestions for maximizing performance.

Task Manager provides details about apps and processes, and shows how your computer is using system resources, such as RAM.

Improving System Performance

After using your computer for a while, and especially after installing software or saving and deleting files, you might notice changes in your system performance. These changes usually mean that your computer is not as quick to respond to your actions or to perform system tasks as it was when Windows 8 was first installed. In that case, you can improve system performance by completing certain maintenance tasks. Start by opening the Performance Information and Tools window from the Control Panel, shown in the Visual Overview for this session.

The Performance Information and Tools window lets you view and complete the information and performance tasks described in Figure 10-1.

| Figure 10-1 | Tasks and information provided in the Performance Information and Tools window |

Task or Information	Description	How to Use
Windows Experience Index base score	View your score to learn the capability of your computer's hardware and software to run Windows 8 and perform computing tasks	Click the Rate this computer button or the Re-run the assessment link to calculate your base score.
Adjust visual effects	Modify how Windows displays menus and windows to improve performance	Use the Performance Options dialog box to optimize how Windows displays menus and windows.
Adjust indexing options	Set indexing options to help you quickly find files on your computer	Use the Indexing Options dialog box to specify which locations to index.
Adjust power settings	Modify how Windows consumes or conserves power, which directly affects performance, especially for mobile computers	Use the Power Options window to change power plans and their settings.
Open disk cleanup	Remove temporary or unnecessary files that can take up too much storage space	Use the Disk Cleanup tool to delete unnecessary files.
Advanced tools	Examine advanced performance information to avoid related problems	Use the Advanced Tools window to view notifications about performance problems and how to solve them.

© 2014 Cengage Learning

You have already explored some of these tools in earlier tutorials. This tutorial discusses each item in the Performance Information and Tools window to help improve the performance of your computer.

Rating Your Computer's Performance

Your computer's Windows Experience Index base score reflects the speed and performance of your computer's components, including the processor, random access memory (RAM), graphics card, and hard disk. A higher base score generally means that your computer performs better and faster than a computer with a lower base score, especially when working on more advanced and resource-intensive tasks. Windows 8 calculates the base score by rating each hardware component that can affect performance and giving it a subscore. The base score is the lowest subscore, not an average. If the subscore for your general graphics component is 4.1 but all of the other subscores are 6.5 or higher, the base score for your computer is 4.1. Using this type of rating system helps you identify the system component that might be a performance bottleneck. ~janepn

Viewing and Calculating Your Base Score

- Open the Control Panel in Category view, click System and Security, click System, and then click the Windows Experience Index link.
- In the Performance Information and Tools window, view the Windows Experience Index base score and subscores for your computer. If these scores are not displayed, click the Rate this computer button.
- To find out if your score has changed, click the Re-run the assessment link.

When you open the Performance Information and Tools window, it displays the base score calculated the last time Windows 8 rated the hardware components on your computer. If it has never rated the components, you can click the Rate this computer button to score the computer. After you install new hardware, you can recalculate the rating by clicking the Re-run the assessment link to update the score.

Software publishers other than Microsoft might identify the minimum base score your computer needs to run their software. You can therefore use the base score to make decisions when purchasing software. For example, if your computer has a base score of 6.1, you can confidently purchase software designed for Windows 8 that requires a computer with a base score of 6 or lower. If you want to use a particular program or feature of Windows 8 that requires a higher score than your base score, note the lowest subscore in the Performance Information and Tools window. You might need to upgrade the component with that subscore to meet the necessary base score.

You can generally interpret your computer's base score according to the descriptions in Figure 10-2.

Figure 10-2	Interpreting base scores

Base Score	What the Computer Can Do
1–2	Complete general computing tasks, such as running office productivity programs and searching the Internet, but not use advanced multimedia features of Windows 8 apps
3	Respond more quickly than computers in the 1–2 range while running the same types of applications
4–5	Run Windows 8 features at a level adequate for most computer users
6–9.9	Play HDTV content, and run high-end, graphics-intensive programs, such as multiplayer games

© 2014 Cengage Learning

In addition, consider how you use your computer when interpreting the subscores. If you use your computer primarily to perform office productivity tasks by working with word processing, spreadsheet, email, and Web browsing software, then your processor and memory components should have high subscores. If you use your computer to play games or run high-end graphics programs, such as a video editor, then your RAM, graphics, and gaming graphics components should have high subscores. If you use your computer as a media center, such as to play multimedia slide shows or record digital TV programs, then your processor, hard disk, and graphics components need high subscores.

Fab Homes mostly uses office productivity apps and custom databases to track its building plans, supplies, and contacts. Kenny wants to make sure that the base score on his notebook computer is high enough to use the apps, and that his subscores are appropriate for his typical tasks, which involve producing spreadsheets and reports that analyze Fab Homes' inventory. You'll show Kenny how to view and calculate the Windows Experience Index base score for the first time on his Windows 8 notebook.

To view and calculate a computer's base score:

▶ 1. Display the Charms bar from the desktop, click the **Settings** charm, and then click **Control Panel** on the Settings menu to open the Control Panel window. Switch to Category view, if necessary.

▶ 2. Click the **System and Security** category, click **System** to open the System window, and then click the **Windows Experience Index** link in the System section. The Performance Information and Tools window opens.

▶ 3. If necessary, click the **Rate this computer** button to assess the hardware and calculate a base score, which might take a few minutes. Windows displays the subscores and the base score in the Performance Information and Tools window. See Figure 10-3.

   Trouble? If Windows 8 has already calculated a base score, the Rate this computer button does not appear. Click the Re-run the assessment link to have Windows recalculate the base score.

| Figure 10-3 | Results of calculating the base score |

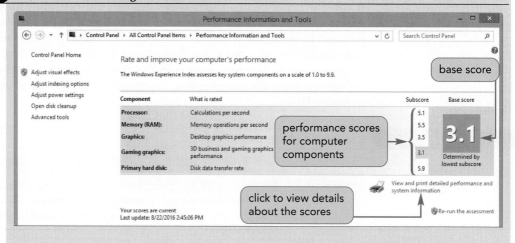

The subscores for Kenny's computer are average for the processor, memory, and hard disk, which is appropriate for the types of tasks he performs. His gaming graphics score of 3.1 is the lowest subscore, and is therefore his base score. This is an appropriate score for his current computing needs. However, he is considering attaching a second monitor when he needs to improve his productivity. Before he sets up a second monitor, he will need to increase the graphics score by upgrading his graphics components. You suggest that Kenny view the details about those components so he knows what to upgrade.

To view system details:

▶ 1. In the Performance Information and Tools window, click the **View and print detailed performance and system information** link. The More details about my computer page opens, displaying detailed information about Kenny's system. See Figure 10-4.

Figure 10-4   Displaying system details

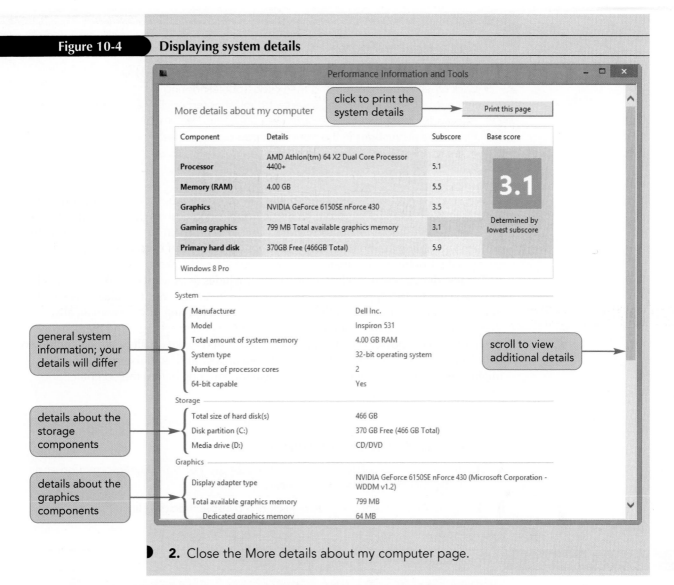

2. Close the More details about my computer page.

Kenny has noticed that his notebook computer is using more battery power than it did at first, though he switches to the Power saver plan when his computer is not plugged into a wall outlet. The increase in power consumption limits the amount of time he can be mobile with his notebook. You'll help him identify ways to improve his computer's power usage.

Using Troubleshooters to Find and Fix Computer Problems

Recall that you can use the security tools in the Action Center to keep your computer and its data secure. The Action Center also includes tools for maintaining your computer, including a collection of troubleshooters. Although troubleshooters are not designed to address every computer problem, they are a good place to start to keep your computer in excellent running condition.

Using a Troubleshooter

- Click the Action Center icon in the notification area of the taskbar.
- Click Open Action Center, and then click Troubleshooting.
- In the list of troubleshooters, select a troubleshooter; or click a category, and then select a troubleshooter.
- Follow the instructions in the troubleshooter dialog boxes.

When you run a troubleshooter, it might ask you some questions or reset common settings as it works to fix the problem. If the troubleshooter fixes the problem, you can close the troubleshooter dialog box. If it can't fix the problem, you can display options and then go online to find an answer. In either case, you can display a complete list of changes the troubleshooter made.

The first dialog box in each troubleshooter includes an Advanced link. Click this link to display a selected Apply repairs automatically check box. You can clear this check box to select a solution from a list of fixes instead of applying them automatically.

You can use the Power troubleshooter to analyze power settings, and then change them to conserve power on all types of computers and extend battery life on computers with batteries. The Power troubleshooter automatically finds and fixes problems that might affect power consumption, such as waiting too long before the computer goes to sleep.

To use the Power troubleshooter:

1. In the See also section of the left pane of the Performance Information and Tools window, click **Action Center**.

2. In the Action Center window, click the **Troubleshooting** link. The Troubleshooting window opens. See Figure 10-5.

Figure 10-5   **Troubleshooting window**

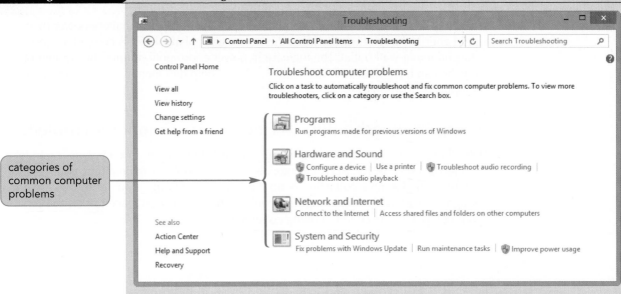

categories of common computer problems

3. Click the **Improve power usage** link in the System and Security category to start the Power troubleshooter. The first dialog box in the troubleshooter opens. See Figure 10-6.

Figure 10-6   **Power troubleshooter**

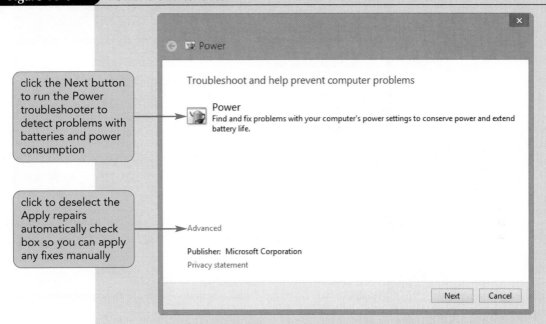

click the Next button to run the Power troubleshooter to detect problems with batteries and power consumption

click to deselect the Apply repairs automatically check box so you can apply any fixes manually

4. Click the **Next** button. Windows checks for problems that might affect system performance. It finds two problems on Kenny's computer. See Figure 10-7.

Trouble? If Windows does not detect any problems on your computer, continue to Step 5. By viewing the Troubleshooting report you can see the kinds of checks that were performed.

Figure 10-7   **Issues found**

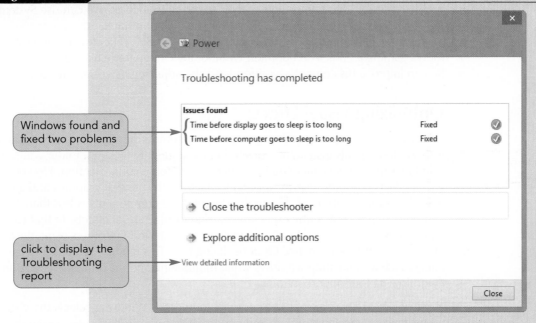

Windows found and fixed two problems

click to display the Troubleshooting report

▶ **5.** Click the **View detailed information** link to display the Troubleshooting report. See Figure 10-8.

Figure 10-8   **Troubleshooting report**

details about how Windows solved the problems

▶ **6.** Scroll down to read about the issues Windows found, if any, and potential issues that were checked.

▶ **7.** Click the **Next** button, if necessary, and then click the **Close** button.

Windows found problems with Kenny's computer and then automatically applied solutions. If Windows does not detect any problems, you can explore other options. These include using Windows Help and Support, searching for answers or posting a question in a Windows online community, or finding related troubleshooters. If the problem persists, you can use other tools to get assistance or you can use System Recovery to revert your computer to a previous working state.

Recall that the base score for Kenny's computer is 3.1, reflecting the lowest subscore for his gaming graphics component. Until Kenny can upgrade his graphics hardware, he can improve his computer's performance by adjusting its visual effects.

Optimizing Visual Effects

Windows 8 uses visual effects to enhance your computing experience. For example, it shows thumbnails instead of icons to help you identify files in a folder window. It also fades menu items after you click them to reinforce your selection. However, these visual effects consume system resources related to the general graphics and gaming graphics components. If a subscore for one of these components is less than 4, your computer might be working especially hard to display visual effects. In that case, you can improve performance by displaying some effects and not others using the Visual Effects tab in the Performance Options dialog box. This tab lists settings for visual effects such as animating windows when minimizing and maximizing. It also provides the following four option buttons:

• Let Windows choose what's best for my computer—Windows selects the visual effects to balance appearance and performance for your computer hardware.

- Adjust for best appearance—Use all of the visual effects listed.
- Adjust for best performance—Use none of the visual effects listed.
- Custom—Select only the visual effects you want to use.

Note that selecting one of the first three options automatically selects or deselects the features listed in the box under Custom.

You'll show Kenny how to turn off window animation to improve performance.

To adjust visual effect settings:

1. Click the **Back** button ⬅ in the Troubleshooting window until you display the Performance Information and Tools window again.

2. In the left pane, click **Adjust visual effects**. The Performance Options dialog box opens to the Visual Effects tab. See Figure 10-9. Note the default settings so you can restore them later.

   Trouble? If a User Account Control dialog box opens requesting a password or your permission to continue, enter the password or click the Yes button.

Figure 10-9 Performance Options dialog box

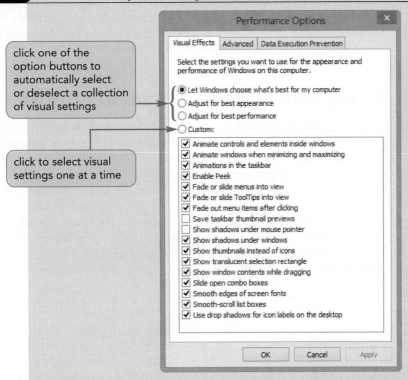

click one of the option buttons to automatically select or deselect a collection of visual settings

click to select visual settings one at a time

3. Click the **Animate controls and elements inside windows** box to remove the check mark. This automatically selects the Custom option button at the top of the Visual Effects tab.

4. Click the **Animate windows when minimizing and maximizing** box to remove the check mark.

5. Click the **OK** button to change the visual effects Windows uses.

The Performance Information and Tools window also includes other tools you can use to improve performance. Recall that you can set indexing options to help you find files on your computer. When Windows indexes a folder, it keeps track of details for the files the folder contains. Windows can then scan the indexed information rather than the file contents so it can find files quickly. In addition, Windows indexes only some locations, such as the built-in libraries, and not others, such as system folders and removable drives. To specify which folders to include in your indexed locations, click Adjust indexing options in the left pane of the Performance Information and Tools window to open the Indexing Options dialog box. You can search more efficiently and improve performance by excluding folders from your indexed locations and including only those that you commonly use. To remove a folder from the indexed locations, click the folder name in the Indexing Options dialog box, click the Modify button, clear the check box for the folder in the Change selected locations list, and then click OK.

Changing your power settings also affects performance. In the left pane of the Performance Information and Tools window, click Adjust power settings to select a default power plan or create a new one. Kenny should avoid the High performance plan, which uses settings that optimize performance and minimize battery life.

You can use the Disk Cleanup tool to delete temporary and other unnecessary files. In the left pane of the Performance Information and Tools window, click Open disk cleanup. Windows 8 calculates how much space you can free by permanently deleting files such as temporary Internet files and downloaded program files. You can also select other types of files, such as those in the Recycle Bin. After you select the files to remove, click the OK button to delete the files.

Using Advanced Performance Tools

To put together a complete picture of your computer's performance, you can use advanced system tools, such as Event Viewer and System Information. These performance tools are listed in the Advanced Tools window, which notifies you about performance issues and suggests how to address them. For example, if Windows detects that a driver is reducing performance, the Advanced Tools window displays a notification you can click to learn which driver is causing the problem, and to view help on how to update the driver. Performance issues are listed at the top of the Advanced Tools window in order of importance. In other words, issues at the beginning of the list affect the system more than issues at the end of the list. The Advanced Tools window also provides access to the advanced performance tools described in Figure 10-10.

| Figure 10-10 | Advanced performance tools |

Advanced Tool	Description
Windows Experience Index	This index reflects the performance capacity of your computer in various categories.
Event Viewer	Event Viewer tracks details of system events captured in event logs that might affect your computer's performance.
Performance Monitor	This monitor displays graphs of system performance.
Resource Monitor	This monitor collects data about resource usage.
Task Manager	Task Manager provides details about apps and processes, and shows how your computer is using system resources, such as RAM.
System Information	This tool displays details about the hardware and software components on your computer.
Performance Options	This dialog box is the same one used to adjust visual effects. You can also use it to manage memory and Data Execution Prevention (DEP), a Windows 8 tool that protects against damage from viruses and other security threats.
Disk Defragmenter	Use the Disk Defragmenter window to schedule disk defragmentation or to immediately start defragmenting.
System Diagnostics	This tool generates a report about the status, or health, of hardware resources, system response times, and other system information, and provides suggestions for maximizing performance.

© 2014 Cengage Learning

[handwritten notes: "Type Event Viewer"; checkmarks and page numbers — Event Viewer 531, Performance Monitor 533, Resource Monitor 538, Task Manager 539, System Information 545]

You have already used the Windows Experience Index to rate Kenny's computer. You'll explore the other advanced performance tools with Kenny shortly. Right now, you want to open the Advanced Tools window to see if it detects any performance issues.

To view performance issues:

1. In the Performance Information and Tools window, click **Advanced tools** in the left pane. The Advanced Tools window opens. See Figure 10-11. Windows identifies one issue that might affect the performance of Kenny's computer.

Figure 10-11 Advanced Tools window

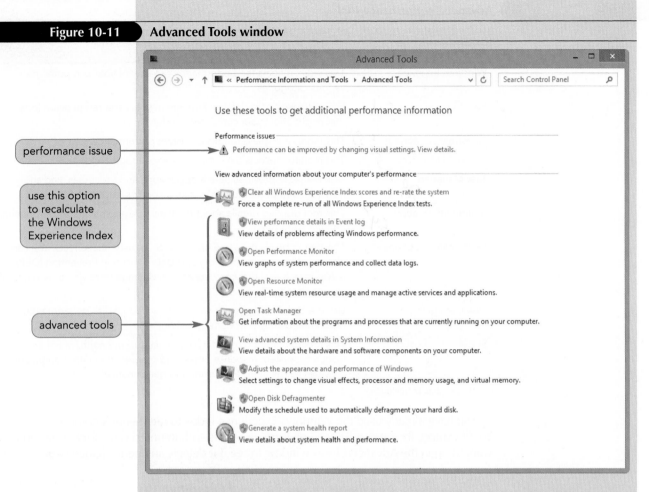

performance issue

use this option to recalculate the Windows Experience Index

advanced tools

2. Under Performance issues, click the **Performance can be improved by changing visual settings. View details.** link. A Performance Information and Tools dialog box opens to suggest how to address the issue. See Figure 10-12.

Trouble? If a different performance issue is listed first in your Advanced Tools window, click that issue. If no issues are listed in your Advanced Tools window, read but do not perform the remaining steps.

Trouble? If the Performance Information and Tools dialog box opens as a minimized window, click its button on the taskbar to open the window on the desktop.

| Figure 10-12 | Suggested resolution for performance issue |

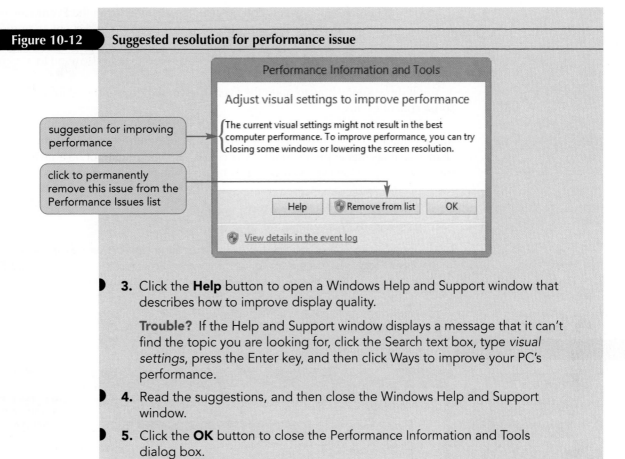

suggestion for improving performance

click to permanently remove this issue from the Performance Issues list

> **3.** Click the **Help** button to open a Windows Help and Support window that describes how to improve display quality.
>
> **Trouble?** If the Help and Support window displays a message that it can't find the topic you are looking for, click the Search text box, type *visual settings*, press the Enter key, and then click Ways to improve your PC's performance.
>
> **4.** Read the suggestions, and then close the Windows Help and Support window.
>
> **5.** Click the **OK** button to close the Performance Information and Tools dialog box.

Next, you will explore some of the advanced performance tools that Kenny has not used before.

Viewing Details About System Events

When you are troubleshooting problems with Windows and other programs, it is often helpful to view details about system events, such as a program closing unexpectedly. Windows records these system events in an **event log**, a special text file that contains details about the event. You can read event logs by using Event Viewer, an advanced performance tool that tracks system events, including the following types:

- Program events—Windows classifies the severity of each program event as critical, error, warning, or information. A **critical event** indicates that a failure has occurred from which the application or component cannot automatically recover. An **error** indicates a significant problem, such as loss of data. A **warning** is an event that indicates a potential problem. An **information event** indicates that a program, driver, or service performed successfully.
- Security events—These events are called **audits** and are either successful or failed. For example, when you sign in to Windows, Event Viewer records that as a successful audit.
- System events—Similar to program events, Windows classifies each system event as critical, error, warning, or information.

To view details about an event, double-click the event listed in the Event Viewer window to open the Event Properties window, which describes the event and provides details that are helpful to a PC professional. You can copy the event properties to the Clipboard, and then paste them in a text file or an email message to send to a computer technician, for example.

You'll show Kenny how to open the Event Viewer window and find information about critical events.

To perform the following steps, you must be signed in to Windows using an Administrator account. If you are not signed in as an Administrator, you can only change settings that apply to your user account, and you might not be able to access some event logs. However, you can still complete the following steps.

To use Event Viewer:

▶ **1.** In the Advanced Tools window, click the **View performance details in Event log** link. A message might appear indicating that Windows is adding a snap-in, which is a tool installed in a window, and then the Event Viewer window opens. See Figure 10-13. The layout of your Event Viewer window might differ.

| Figure 10-13 | Event Viewer window |

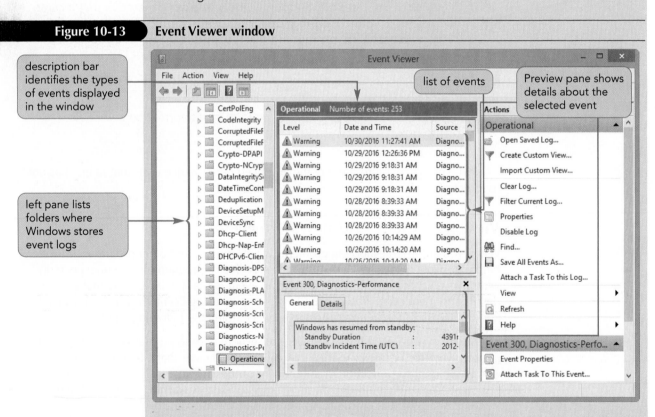

description bar identifies the types of events displayed in the window

list of events

Preview pane shows details about the selected event

left pane lists folders where Windows stores event logs

▶ **2.** Scroll the list of events, and then double-click a **Critical** event. The Event Properties window opens. See Figure 10-14. Note that this particular event has an Event ID of 351 and is associated with the NVIDIA Windows Kernel Mode Driver. If necessary, you could provide the Event ID to a PC technician or a Microsoft Web site to troubleshoot your computer.

Trouble? If no Critical events are listed in your Event Viewer window, double-click any type of event.

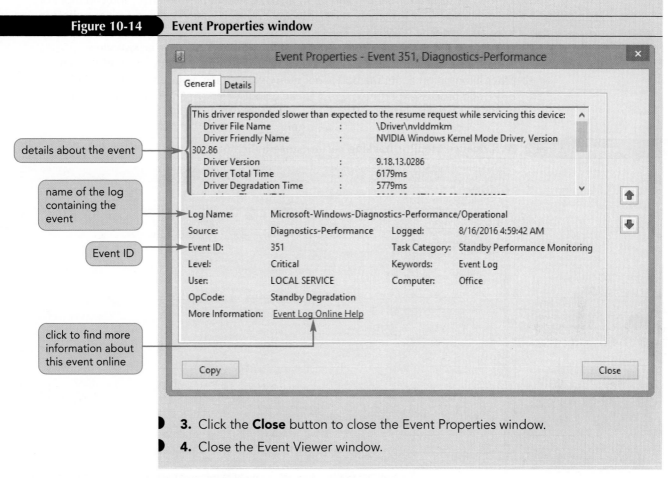

Figure 10-14   **Event Properties window**

details about the event

name of the log containing the event

Event ID

click to find more information about this event online

> 3. Click the **Close** button to close the Event Properties window.
>
> 4. Close the Event Viewer window.

Events often involve drivers, which are the files that help connect hardware devices to a computer. If a Critical or Warning event indicates a problem with a driver, such as one that caused a delay during startup or standby (sleep), you can try updating or reinstalling the driver to improve performance.

Monitoring System Performance

A common complaint from computer users is that their computer seems to be running more slowly than usual. If you are experiencing this same symptom, too many programs might be running at the same time, causing a loss of performance, or the computer might be low on memory or require an upgrade to a faster processor. To determine the cause, you need to measure the performance of the system in numerical terms.

REFERENCE

Monitoring System Performance

Administ Tool → Performance (& monitor)

- Open the Control Panel in Category view, click System and Security, click System, and then click the Windows Experience Index link.
- Click Advanced tools.
- Click Open Performance Monitor.
- Expand the Monitoring Tools folder.
- Click Performance Monitor to graph system performance.

You can use Performance Monitor to analyze system performance. You can monitor the performance of programs and hardware, customize the data you want to collect in logs, and generate reports.

When you open the Performance Monitor window, it displays an overview describing the Performance Monitor tool. A system summary provides statistics and other information about memory, your network interface, your physical disk (or hard disk), and processor performance. You can also use Performance Monitor to produce a graph that reflects system performance. See Figure 10-15.

Figure 10-15 **Performance Monitor tracking performance indicators**

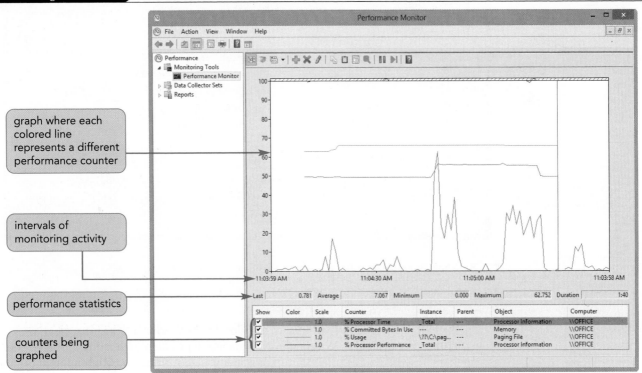

graph where each colored line represents a different performance counter

intervals of monitoring activity

performance statistics

counters being graphed

By default, Performance Monitor tracks the percentage of time your processor is working, which is one measure of how busy your system is. You can also track other performance indicators, such as how fast your computer retrieves data from the hard disk. Tracking performance information can locate the source of trouble in a slow system, and can help you determine what needs to be done to speed up the system.

To track performance indicators other than processor time, you add an item, called a **counter**, to measure a particular part of the system performance and track the values of the counter in the graph. The counter is updated at intervals you specify—usually every few seconds. To add a counter to the graph, you click the Add button on the Performance Monitor toolbar to open the Add Counters window. This window lists performance counters that are included with Windows 8.

Another common problem that affects performance is low memory. Your computer has two types of memory—RAM and virtual memory. All programs use RAM (random access memory); so if you have many programs running or are using a program that requires a lot of RAM, Windows might not have enough RAM to run a program. In that case, Windows temporarily moves information that it would normally store in RAM to a file on your hard disk called a **paging file**. The paging file is a hidden file on the hard disk that Windows uses to hold parts of programs and data files that do not fit in RAM. Windows moves data from the paging file to RAM as needed and moves data from RAM to the paging file to make room for new data. Because Windows swaps data in and out of the paging file, it is also known as a swap file. The amount of information temporarily stored in a paging file is called **virtual memory**. Using virtual memory—in other words, moving information to and from the paging file—frees up enough RAM for programs to run correctly.

Preventing and Solving Low Memory Problems

If you try to open a dialog box or make a selection in an application and the application responds slowly or seems to stop working, your computer is probably low on memory. You can prevent or solve low memory problems by observing the following guidelines:

- Run fewer applications at the same time, especially those that run at startup and those that show signs of requiring lots of memory.
- Increase the size of the paging file. Windows increases virtual memory the first time your computer becomes low on memory, but you can increase it up to the amount of RAM installed. However, this might cause your applications to run more slowly overall.
- Determine if an application uses too much memory. Track the paging file usage in Performance Monitor or Task Manager when you are running a particular application. If these tools show frequent activity, check for updates to the application and install them.
- Install more RAM. Open the System window to view the amount of RAM your computer has installed, and then look on the computer manufacturer's Web site to find out if you can install more. Because this solution involves purchasing and installing RAM, try the other solutions first.

You'll show Kenny how to use Performance Monitor to track processor time. In this case, the graph in the Performance Monitor window measures the percentage of time that the processor is not idle. A value near 100% suggests that the processor is almost never idle. If so, that indicates the processor might be so busy that it can't perform tasks efficiently. If a Fab Homes employee reports that a computer is working slowly, you can track the processor time to see if the employee is running too many programs or processes at the same time.

Besides tracking processor time on Kenny's computer, you'll also track the paging file usage to diagnose memory problems. If a Fab Homes employee indicates that a program is responding slowly or that Windows reports a low memory problem, you can track the paging file usage and increase its size, if necessary. (You'll learn how to increase the size of the paging file shortly.)

To perform the following steps, you must be signed in to Windows using an Administrator account. If you are not signed in as an Administrator, read but do not perform the following steps.

To track processor time:

1. In the Advanced Tools window, click **Open Performance Monitor**. The Performance Monitor window opens.

2. In the left pane of the Performance Monitor window, expand the **Monitoring Tools** folder, if necessary, and then click **Performance Monitor**. The Performance Monitor graph appears in the right pane, tracking the percentage of time that the processor is in use each second. See Figure 10-16. The graph on your computer will show different activity.

Figure 10-16   Tracking processor time

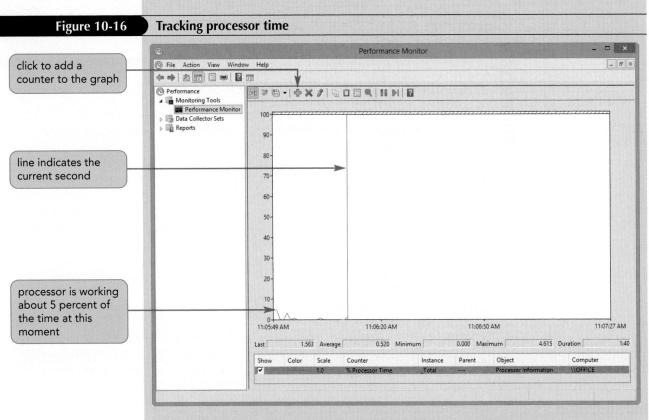

click to add a
counter to the graph

line indicates the
current second

processor is working
about 5 percent of
the time at this
moment

3. Click the **Add** button 🔲 on the Performance Monitor toolbar. The Add
Counters dialog box opens. See Figure 10-17.

Figure 10-17   Adding a counter to the Performance Monitor

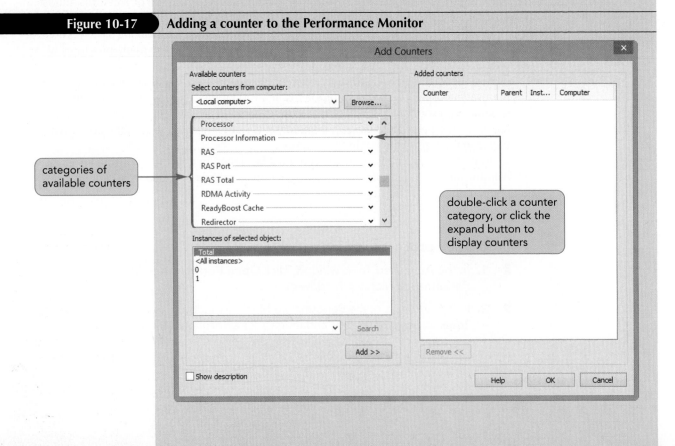

categories of
available counters

double-click a counter
category, or click the
expand button to
display counters

4. Scroll the Available counters list, and then double-click **Paging File**. Details you can track appear below the Paging File entry.

5. Click **% Usage**, and then click the **Add** button to use that counter.

6. Click the **OK** button. The Performance Monitor begins tracking paging file usage. See Figure 10-18.

Figure 10-18	Tracking paging file usage

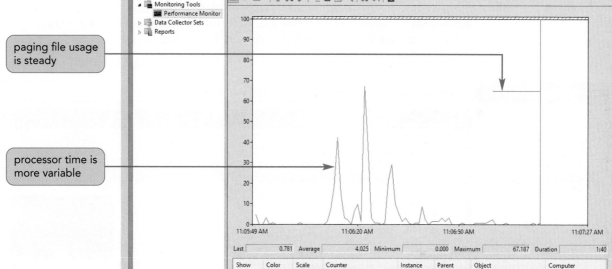

The graph shows that the paging file usage is steady. This number usually increases significantly when you start a program that uses many system resources, such as a Microsoft Office program. If the paging file usage does not decrease by that same amount when you close the program, the program leaves temporary files or processes open in memory, which can cause problems. Windows usually recovers that memory after a few minutes of idle time. If it does not, a temporary solution is to restart your computer to clear everything from RAM and make the maximum amount of memory available to your computer. The long-term solution is to install updates to the program that is not handling memory efficiently.

The Performance Monitor on Kenny's computer is tracking two system indicators, but both lines in the graph are red. You'll show Kenny how to change the % Usage counter to a contrasting color so he can distinguish one counter from the other.

To change the color of the % Usage counter:

1. Below the graph, right-click the **% Usage** counter, and then click **Properties** on the shortcut menu. The Performance Monitor Properties dialog box opens to the Data tab.

2. Click the **Color** button, and then click **blue** (the third color from the top of the list).

> **3.** Click the **OK** button. The % Usage indicator line is now displayed in blue.

> **4.** Close the Performance Monitor window.

Next, you'll show Kenny how to use another advanced tool to track system performance—Resource Monitor.

Using Resource Monitor

Another tool you can use to measure system performance is Resource Monitor. On the Overview tab of the Resource Monitor window, you can view four graphs to track the usage of the **central processing unit (CPU)**, disk, network, and memory as your computer is using these resources. The Overview tab also includes four bars—one for each system resource. You can click a bar or an expand button to display details about each resource. For example, click the Memory bar to display a summary of memory usage. See Figure 10-19.

Figure 10-19	Overview tab in the Resource Monitor window

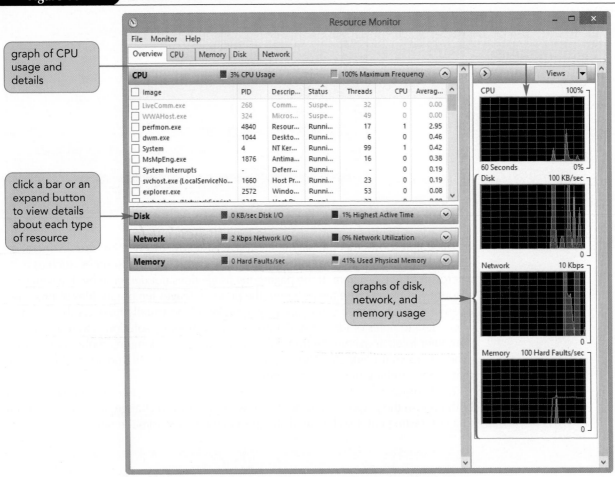

The CPU graph shows how much of the CPU is being used at any given moment. The CPU is the main circuit chip in a computer and performs most of the calculations necessary to run the computer. A high percentage of CPU usage means that the currently running programs or processes are consuming most of the available CPU resources, which can slow the performance of your computer. If the CPU usage appears frozen at or near 100%, some programs might not be responding. (You can use Task Manager to stop running the program, which you'll do shortly.) Click the CPU bar to view the processes, or images, that are using CPU resources. (A **process** is a task performed by a program and usually contains information about starting the program.)

The Disk graph and bar reflect program activity on your hard disk, measured by the number of times a program reads (retrieves) data from the hard disk or writes (stores) data on the hard disk. Click the Disk bar to see which files are reading or writing data to your hard disk.

The Network graph and bar indicate the amount of network activity your computer is experiencing, measured in kilobytes per second (Kbps). Click the Network bar to see the network address of the programs exchanging information with your computer.

The Memory graph and bar display the percentage of RAM currently being used and the number of hard faults occurring per second. A **hard fault**, or **page fault**, occurs when a program retrieves data from RAM and stores it on the hard disk. When you run a program, Windows stores only part of it in RAM. If you perform a task such as a calculation in a program, Windows frees up RAM so the program can complete the task. If enough RAM is not available, Windows moves some data from RAM to the hard disk. In this case, the program can still complete the task, but it must wait while Windows swaps data from RAM to the hard disk. If a program is responding slowly to your commands, look in the Memory graph and bar for a high number of hard faults, which indicates that the program is continually reading data from disk rather than RAM.

Fab Homes employees occasionally report that their computers are suddenly running more slowly than normal. You'll show Kenny how to open the Resource Monitor window and view the resources Windows is currently using to diagnose the problem with an employee's computer.

To perform the following steps, you must be signed in to Windows using an Administrator account. If you are not signed in to Windows as an Administrator, read but do not perform the following steps.

To examine an overview of resource usage:

1. In the Advanced Tools window, click the **Open Resource Monitor** link. The Resource Monitor window opens to the Overview tab.

2. Click the **Memory** bar, if necessary, to display details about memory usage. For example, explorer.exe is File Explorer, which typically uses more memory than other processes. It should appear near the top of the Memory list.

3. Close the Resource Monitor window.

The resources on Kenny's computer do not indicate any performance problems. However, you and Kenny can track these resources to diagnose problems for the Fab Homes employees.

Using Task Manager to Examine System Information

Besides using Performance Monitor to track system information, you can also use Task Manager to view information about the programs and processes running on your computer. Task Manager does not provide as much information as the Performance and Resource Monitors. However, any user can open Task Manager, whereas only Administrators can use the Performance and Resource Monitors.

You can use Task Manager to monitor your computer's performance or to close an application that is not responding. When you start Task Manager, it shows only the Windows 8 apps and desktop applications running on your computer. You can expand the Task Manager window to display more details, as shown in Figure 10-20.

Figure 10-20 Expanded Task Manager window

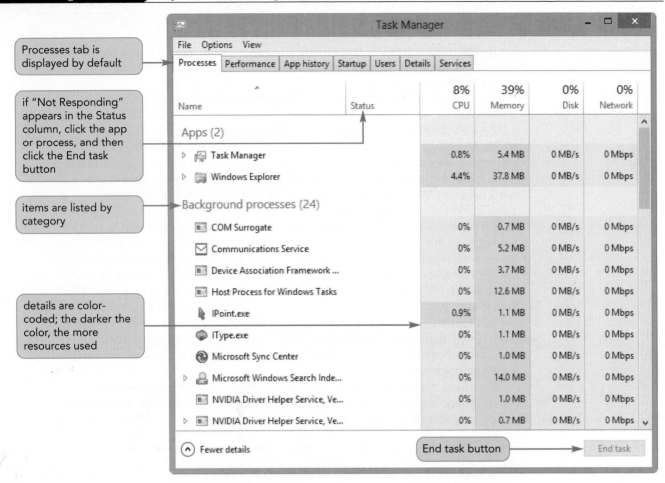

Processes tab is displayed by default

if "Not Responding" appears in the Status column, click the app or process, and then click the End task button

items are listed by category

details are color-coded; the darker the color, the more resources used

The expanded Task Manager window contains the tabs described in Figure 10-21.

Figure 10-21 Tabs in the Task Manager window

Task Manager Tab	Description
Processes	Lists the apps and processes running on your computer, including apps that are not responding, and provides resource-usage statistics, which are color coded (the darker the color, the more resources used)
Performance	Provides graphs and statistics about how your computer is using system resources, such as memory and the CPU
App history	Lists details about how apps have used resources such as CPU time and network bandwidth in the past few days
Startup	Lists programs that start when Windows starts and allows you to enable or disable the programs
Users	Identifies the users that are currently signed in to the computer and their status
Details	Provides details about the running apps and processes
Services	Lists current services, which are the background programs or processes that support other programs

You can use some of the tabs in the Task Manager window to troubleshoot system problems and improve performance. For example, the Processes tab displays each active application, background process, and Windows process and groups them by type. If "Not Responding" appears in the Status column for an app, you can close the app by clicking it and then clicking the End task button. However, closing an application this way discards any unsaved changes you made with that app.

Although viruses and other malware rarely appear as apps or processes on the Processes tab, they sometimes appear as processes on the Details tab. To learn more about a process, you can right-click it on the Details tab, and then click Properties on the shortcut menu. Click the Details tab in the Properties dialog box to view a description of the file, the program it's associated with, and its copyright information. Often, the Details tab for malware files does not provide any information. You can also search the Web for more information about the files listed on the Processes tab and the Details tab. To do so, right-click the file, and then click Search online on the shortcut menu. If you are certain a process is associated with malware, click the file, and then click the End task button. If you don't know the purpose of a process, don't end it. If you end a process associated with an open program, such as a word-processing program, the program closes without saving your data. If you end a process associated with a system service, some part of the system might not function properly.

Recall that a **service** is a program or process running in the background that supports other programs; currently running services appear on the Services tab in the Task Manager window. If a process is associated with a service, you can right-click a service on the Services tab, and then click Go to details on the shortcut menu. (This command is available only for services associated with an active process.) The Details tab opens and selects the process associated with that service.

Similar to the Performance Monitor window, the Performance tab displays graphs to illustrate how your computer is using system resources, including CPU and RAM. You can also open Resource Monitor on the Performance tab of the Task Manager window. Recall that if the CPU Usage percentage appears frozen at or near 100%, a program might not be responding. In that case, you should open the Processes tab and end that app as previously described.

PROSKILLS

Decision Making: Selecting a Tool to Solve Performance Problems

The term *performance* refers to how efficiently your computer is working and how quickly Windows responds to your requests and commands. If your computer is performing poorly, you waste time waiting for it to complete tasks such as opening files and folders. A computer's performance normally decreases over time as you install programs and save files. However, if a computer is performing so slowly that it significantly affects your productivity, you need to know how to identify and solve the problem. You might need to add memory, remove a troublesome device driver, or replace the entire system. How do you know what to do to fix the problem? Start by using Performance Monitor and Task Manager. Each one is designed to provide certain types of information.

Performance Monitor is the main tool you use to diagnose problems with system performance. System administrators typically use Performance Monitor with a new system to set **baselines**, which are starting points used for comparisons. System administrators select key counters for memory, the network interface, the paging file, the physical disk, and the processor. They graph them a few times during a typical day, and then save the graph and data. You can also set baselines to create a record of your computer when it is performing well. If you notice your computer is working more slowly than normal, select the same counters and graph them again. Then, compare the baseline information to the new information to diagnose the problem. For example, the **Pages/Sec counter** shows how often the system accesses the paging file. In a high-performing system, this value is zero or close to zero. Having consistently high values probably means that your system does not have enough RAM, so adding RAM could solve the performance problem. Performance Monitor's drawback is that it includes hundreds of counters. Although you can search online for information about each one, you need to understand what each counter measures to accurately interpret the data, which takes time and technical knowledge.

Task Manager provides a simplified version of Performance Monitor. Although Task Manager does not save information so you can compare it later, the Performance tab provides immediate and clear information related to system performance. For example, click Memory on the Performance tab to display details about how your program is using RAM. The Committed values show how many demands programs and files are making on available memory resources. If the first Committed value is close to the second one, close applications and large files to improve performance. As with the Performance Monitor counters, you can search online for more information about the values on the Performance tab.

You'll explore Task Manager with Kenny to show him the kinds of information it provides. First, start an application so you can track information about it.

To start and use an application:

▶ **1.** Start Internet Explorer, and then open a new tab.

▶ **2.** Use the Address bar to display the Microsoft Web site at **www.microsoft.com** on the new tab.

Next, open the Task Manager window.

To explore Task Manager:

1. In the Advanced Tools window, click **Open Task Manager** to open the Task Manager window.

2. If the Task Manager window includes a More details button, click the **More details** button to display all of the tabs, options, and information in a larger Task Manager window.

3. On the Processes tab, click the **expand** icon 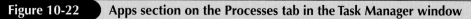 next to Internet Explorer in the Apps section to display the tabs open in Internet Explorer. See Figure 10-22. The Apps section lists both Windows 8 and desktop apps. Your list of apps might differ.

| Figure 10-22 | Apps section on the Processes tab in the Task Manager window |

amount of memory Internet Explorer is using

Internet Explorer is expanded, showing two tabs

click to show fewer details

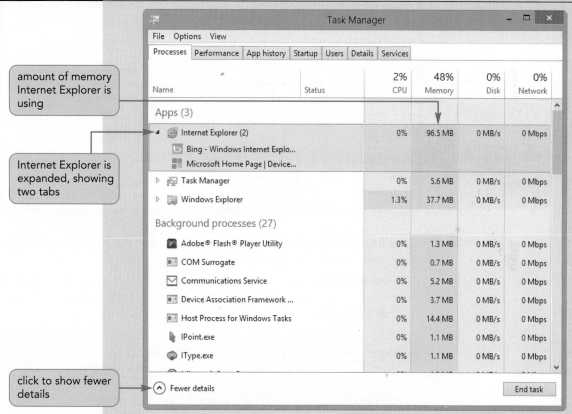

Trouble? If your Task Manager window does not group processes in sections such as the Apps and Background processes, click View on the menu bar, and then click Group by type to select the option.

4. In the Memory column, note the background color and the value for Internet Explorer, and then scroll down to see if a background process or Windows process is using a similar amount.

5. Click the **Performance** tab to display system performance information, including a graph. By default, this tab displays a CPU graph and statistics.

6. Click **Memory** in the left pane to display memory details. See Figure 10-23. Note the amount of memory in use and available.

Figure 10-23   **Memory details on the Performance tab**

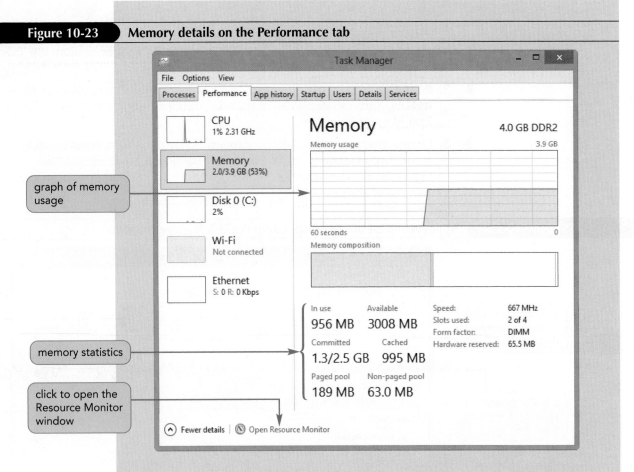

graph of memory usage

memory statistics

click to open the Resource Monitor window

7. Close Internet Explorer, and then watch the change in the Memory usage graph and corresponding statistics.

8. Click the **Processes** tab to view the total amount of memory that apps and processes are using, which is smaller than the total amount used when Internet Explorer was open.

9. Scroll down to the Windows processes section, right-click **Desktop Window Manager**, and then click **Go to details**. The Details tab opens and highlights the dwm.exe file. This file helps to manage the desktop and its windows. If you ended this task, your desktop would become unstable. Therefore, you should not disable this process, even if it uses a lot of memory.

10. Close the Task Manager window.

Before ending a task or process, research the filename on the Web to learn its purpose and whether it's safe to end manually.

Although Task Manager provides information about software running on your computer and displays some resource information also included in Performance Monitor, you can use another window to examine a summary of hardware on your computer.

Examining System Information

The System Information window collects detailed information about your computer system, some of which is also provided in other windows, including Device Manager. Advanced users often find it more convenient to use the System Information window to learn details such as the computer name, operating system version, processor type, and total amount of RAM.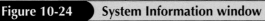

Although Kenny is comfortable using Device Manager to view hardware information, including device conflicts, drivers, and component names, you'll show him how to use the System Information window to view this same hardware information as well as other system details that computer administrators often need to know.

To examine system information:

▶ **1.** In the Advanced Tools window, click **View advanced system details in System Information** to open the System Information window. By default, this window opens to show a system summary. See Figure 10-24.

   Trouble? If your System Information window does not open showing a system summary, click System Summary in the left pane.

Figure 10-24	System Information window

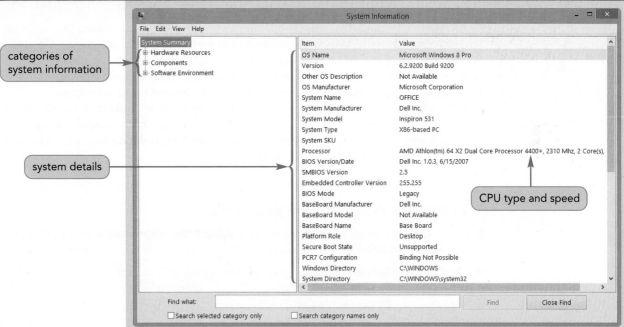

▶ **2.** Click the **expand** icon ⊞ next to Hardware Resources, and then click **IRQs** to display a list of hardware resources, including the IRQ (interrupt request) number, device, and status. (Recall that Windows assigns each hardware device an IRQ number and ranks the devices, giving lower numbers higher priority so they receive attention first.)

▶ **3.** Click the **expand** icon ⊞ next to Components to display in the left pane a list of the types of devices installed on your computer.

▶ **4.** Click the **expand** icon ⊞ next to Storage, and then click **Drives** to display details about the drives on your computer, such as their drive letter, size, and free space.

TIP

You can search for the device name and error code on the Web to troubleshoot the device.

5. Click **Problem Devices** in the Components list to display details about devices experiencing problems on your computer, if any.

6. Click the **expand** icon ⊞ next to Software Environment to display a list of software details.

7. Click **Running Tasks** in the Software Environment list to display a list of running processes, similar to the one displayed on the Details tab in the Task Manager window.

8. Click **System Drivers** in the left pane to display details about drivers that Windows uses. Recall that the Event Viewer window displayed earlier listed a critical event with a driver named \Driver\nvlddmkm. You can learn more about that driver in the System Information window, which indicates its file location and whether it's running, for example.

9. Close the System Information window.

Instead of selecting items in the left pane of the System Information window, you can also search for a component such as "running tasks" to display details about that component.

Increasing Memory Capacity

If you receive warnings that your virtual memory is low, you can increase the minimum size of your paging file. Windows sets the initial minimum size of the paging file at the amount of RAM installed on your computer plus 300 MB. It sets the maximum size at three times the amount of RAM installed on your computer. If you see warnings at these recommended levels, then increase the minimum and maximum sizes.

Although Kenny's computer has enough virtual memory to perform efficiently, you'll show him how to increase the minimum and maximum size of the paging file for future reference. To do so, you use the Performance Options dialog box, which is the same dialog box you used to select visual effects.

To increase the size of the paging file:

1. In the Advanced Tools window, click **Adjust the appearance and performance of Windows** to open the Performance Options dialog box.

2. Click the **Advanced** tab to display paging file information. See Figure 10-25.

Figure 10-25   **Advanced tab in the Performance Options dialog box**

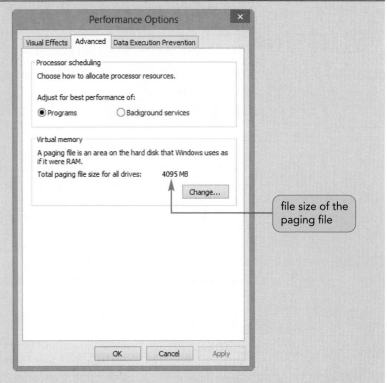

file size of the paging file

▶ **3.** Click the **Change** button to open the Virtual Memory dialog box. See Figure 10-26.

Figure 10-26   **Virtual Memory dialog box**

when this box is checked, Windows manages your paging file

summary of the total paging file size for all drives

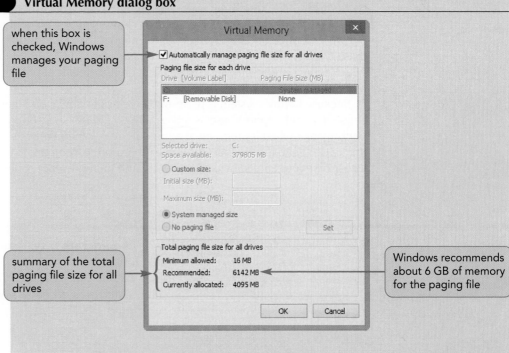

Windows recommends about 6 GB of memory for the paging file

> If Kenny wanted to manage the paging file size himself, he could click the Automatically manage paging file size for all drives box to remove the check mark, click the drive he wants to manage, click the Custom size option button, enter the initial (minimum) and maximum size for the paging file, and then click the Set button.
>
> ▶ **4.** Click the **Cancel** button to close the Virtual Memory dialog box without making any changes.
>
> ▶ **5.** Click the **OK** button to close the Performance Options dialog box.

The Virtual Memory dialog box shows that Kenny has about 4 GB of RAM on his computer, but Windows recommends about 6 GB for the paging file on all drives. If Kenny notices a decline in performance on his computer, the first solution he should try is adding at least 2 GB of RAM.

Two tools remain in the Advanced Tools window: Disk Defragmenter and a system health report. You and Kenny already know how to defragment a disk. You click Open Disk Defragmenter to display the Optimize Drives dialog box and then click the Optimize button, or you can let Windows defragment the hard disk according to a schedule you can set. You'll show Kenny how to generate a system health report next.

Generating a System Health Report

To have Windows collect data about your system and diagnose any problems, you can generate a system health report titled "System Diagnostics Report." This report includes a number of sections. The first section identifies the computer, the date of the report, and the length of time Windows spent collecting the data for the report. The second section, Diagnostic Results, is especially helpful to system administrators. This section has two subsections: The Warnings section lists problems found on the computer, if any, and assigns them a severity level, such as Critical or Warning. The Performance section shows the results of basic system checks, such as a survey of the attributes of the operating system, and a resource overview, such as CPU and network usage. The Software Configuration and Hardware Configuration sections provide details about these checks. Also included are the CPU, Network, Disk, and Memory sections, with Report Statistics, the last section, which lists details about the computer, files, and events.

Because Kenny's system is performing well right now, you'll generate and save a system health report to use as a baseline, which is a snapshot of the computer's performance when it's running at a normal level. When the system has problems, Kenny can generate another system health report to compare to the baseline report. Using baseline reports, he can anticipate and then prevent problems.

To generate a system health report:

▶ **1.** In the Advanced Tools window, click **Generate a system health report**. The Resource and Performance Monitor window opens and displays a progress bar as Windows collects data about your system for 60 seconds. When it's finished collecting data, Windows generates and displays the System Diagnostics Report. See Figure 10-27.

| Figure 10-27 | System Diagnostics Report |

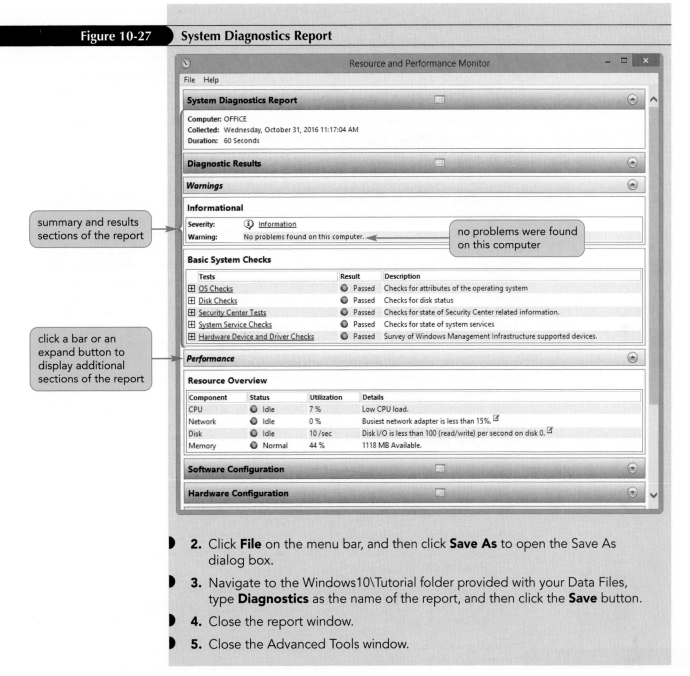

summary and results sections of the report

no problems were found on this computer

click a bar or an expand button to display additional sections of the report

2. Click **File** on the menu bar, and then click **Save As** to open the Save As dialog box.

3. Navigate to the Windows10\Tutorial folder provided with your Data Files, type **Diagnostics** as the name of the report, and then click the **Save** button.

4. Close the report window.

5. Close the Advanced Tools window.

You now want to show Kenny another useful way to increase memory capacity using a USB flash drive and a feature called ReadyBoost.

Using ReadyBoost to Increase Memory Capacity

ReadyBoost is a Windows tool that can use storage space on some removable media devices, including USB flash drives, to speed up your computer. When you insert a device with this capability, the AutoPlay dialog box offers you the option to speed up your system using ReadyBoost. If you select this option, you can then choose how much memory to use for this purpose, up to a maximum of 256 GB of additional memory on one or more removable media devices.

In some situations, you might not be able to use all of the memory on your storage device to speed up your computer. If your computer has a hard disk that uses solid-state drive (SSD) technology, it might be too fast to benefit from ReadyBoost. In this case, the AutoPlay dialog box does not provide a Windows ReadyBoost option. Some USB storage devices contain both slow and fast flash memory, and Windows can only use fast flash memory to speed up your computer. If your device contains both slow and fast memory, keep in mind that you can only use the fast memory portion for this purpose. USB flash drives eventually wear out after a certain number of uses, so using ReadyBoost can wear out the USB drive, although it generally takes a few years.

Keep in mind that ReadyBoost is not a replacement for an adequate amount of system memory. The surest way to improve computer performance is to invest in additional RAM. In addition, ReadyBoost is not a replacement for the paging file. ReadyBoost works with the paging file to maximize the amount of memory your computer can use. For certain types of tasks, ReadyBoost provides extra memory that the computer can access much more quickly than it can access data on the hard drive. For other types of tasks, Windows uses the paging file more efficiently.

The recommended amount of memory to use for ReadyBoost acceleration is one to four times the amount of RAM installed in your computer. For instance, if your computer has 2 GB of RAM and you plug in an 8 GB USB flash drive, dedicating from 2 GB to 6 GB of that drive to ReadyBoost offers the best performance boost. If you reserve less than the total capacity of the removable drive for ReadyBoost, you can use the remaining space for storing files.

You can turn ReadyBoost on or off for a flash drive or other removable storage device, as long as the removable media device contains at least 256 MB of space to work with ReadyBoost. The USB flash drive must also support USB 2.0 or higher. Windows indicates whether the USB flash drive you want to use is suitable for ReadyBoost.

You will show Kenny how he can get extra storage when he is on the road using ReadyBoost. To perform the following steps, you need a USB flash drive that has at least 1 GB of free space. If you do not have such a device, read but do not perform the following steps.

To use ReadyBoost:

1. Plug a USB flash drive into an available USB port on your computer. A notification appears asking what should happen with removable drives. See Figure 10-28.

   Trouble? If a notification does not appear, open File Explorer, if necessary, right-click the USB flash drive, click Properties, and then click the ReadyBoost tab. Skip Step 2.

Figure 10-28 Removable drive notification

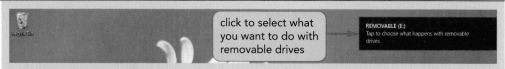

2. Click the notification, and then click **Speed up my system** to open the Properties dialog box for the USB flash drive. If necessary, click the **ReadyBoost** tab. See Figure 10-29.

   Trouble? If the Speed up my system option does not appear on the notification, the USB flash drive might not have the required performance characteristics for boosting memory. Find a different USB flash drive and repeat Step 1.

Figure 10-29 ReadyBoost tab in the Properties dialog box for a USB flash drive

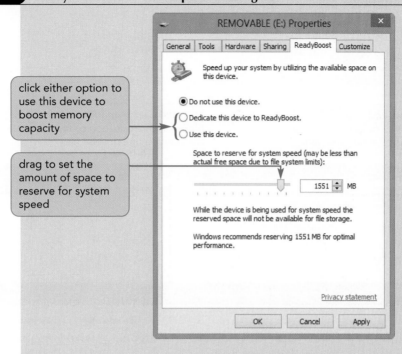

click either option to use this device to boost memory capacity

drag to set the amount of space to reserve for system speed

▶ **3.** Click the **Use this device** option button to turn on ReadyBoost.

▶ **4.** Drag the slider to the far right, if possible, to select the maximum amount of available space on your USB flash drive to reserve for boosting your system speed.

▶ **5.** Click the **OK** button. A ReadyBoost icon, indicating the size of the increased memory, appears in the File Explorer window.

▶ **6.** Close all open windows.

Each time Kenny attaches that USB flash drive to his computer, he will have more than 2 GB of extra memory that Windows can use to improve system performance. The settings you select on the ReadyBoost tab apply to that USB flash drive until you change them.

Session 10.1 Quick Check

REVIEW

1. If your Windows Experience Index subscores are 5.5 for all components except graphics, which has a 4.1 subscore, what is the base score?
2. What can you use to have Windows guide you through the steps of finding and fixing typical system problems? *Troubleshooters*
3. If the graphics or gaming graphics subscores in the Windows Experience Index are low, what settings can you change to improve system performance?
4. In the Event Viewer window, a(n) _Warning_ is an event that indicates a potential problem.
5. What does the main part of the Performance Monitor window display? *534*
6. The _processes_ tab in the Task Manager window lists the apps and processes running on your computer and their color-coded resource-usage statistics.
7. What does ReadyBoost do?

Session 10.2 Visual Overview:

The **Microsoft Community** is a Web site that hosts forums of users and Microsoft experts where you can search, browse, and post questions and answers.

A **forum** is an online location where questions and answers are exchanged.

Search the forum for an answer to a question or for a solution to a problem.

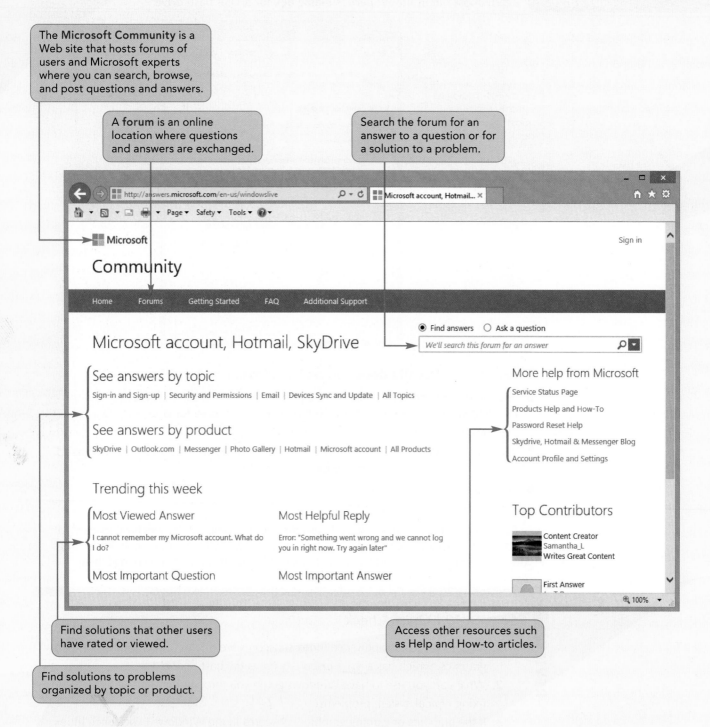

Find solutions that other users have rated or viewed.

Access other resources such as Help and How-to articles.

Find solutions to problems organized by topic or product.

Solving System Problems

Windows stores unresolved problem messages in an **archive**, a collection of records about system problems.

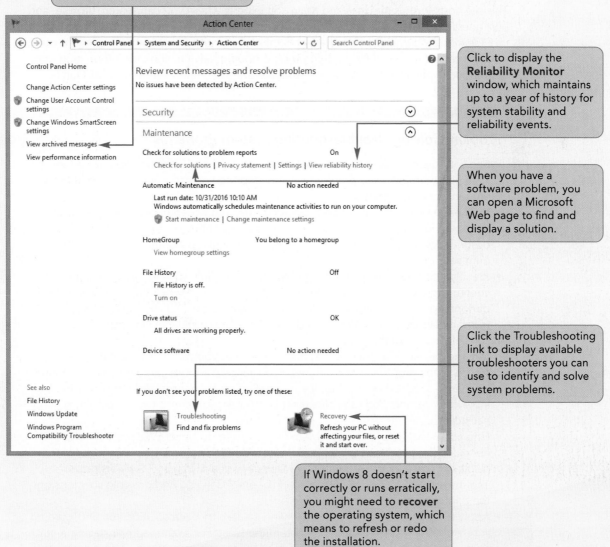

Click to display the **Reliability Monitor** window, which maintains up to a year of history for system stability and reliability events.

When you have a software problem, you can open a Microsoft Web page to find and display a solution.

Click the Troubleshooting link to display available troubleshooters you can use to identify and solve system problems.

If Windows 8 doesn't start correctly or runs erratically, you might need to **recover** the operating system, which means to refresh or redo the installation.

Finding Troubleshooting Information

When you have problems with Windows, its programs, your computer, or other hardware, you can find troubleshooting information in at least two resources: the Troubleshooting window in the Control Panel and the Microsoft Solution Centers on the Web. You have already used a troubleshooter to identify and solve power problems. You can use similar troubleshooters if you have problems with programs, hardware devices, networking and the Internet, and system and security tools.

You can also use Windows Help and Support to find Help topics designed to guide you while troubleshooting and solving problems. On the Windows Help and Support home page, you can click Contact support to open a page listing ways to get customer support or other kinds of help, including access to the Microsoft Community Web site. This site hosts forums for users and Microsoft experts where you can search, browse, and post questions and answers. It also provides access to support articles and videos that provide troubleshooting steps to help you solve or identify a problem. You can also use a search engine to search the Web for troubleshooting advice. Look for information from established experts, and never download a file unless you know and trust the source.

PROSKILLS

Problem Solving: Troubleshooting System Problems

When you suspect a problem on your computer, take a systematic approach to solving it. Complete the following problem-solving steps so you can troubleshoot problems thoroughly and consistently.

- Define the problem—Describe the trouble that you observe, being as specific as possible. For example, if you are having trouble printing, note when the trouble occurs, such as when you try to print from a particular program or with a certain print setting.
- Identify possible causes—Look for obvious causes first, such as a loose cable connecting a printer to your computer. Next, determine when the system was last performing normally and what has changed since then. Did you download and install a new driver from Windows Update? Did you install new hardware? These are possible causes of the problem.
- Test the causes—For each cause, determine what you can do to see if it is the source of the problem. For example, if you suspect a loose cable is causing printing problems, reconnect the cable. If you installed a new printer driver, try reverting to a previous version. You can solve most computer problems by systematically testing each cause.
- Find additional help—If the problem persists, refer to other resources for solutions. For example, does the Devices and Printers window or the Device Manager window display a message about the printer? Does Windows Help and Support provide information about the problem or a similar one? Can you find possible solutions on the printer manufacturer's Web site?
- Apply solutions—As you did when testing causes, try each solution you find, starting with the solutions that affect your system the least. For example, try installing a new printer driver before using System Restore to restore your system. Before you make any major changes to your computer, set a system restore point and back up your data so you don't lose important work.

Kenny wants Fab Homes employees trained to use Windows Help and Support to troubleshoot typical computer problems, such as those involving network connections and hardware. With training, employees can be proactive when addressing computer problems and knowledgeable if they have to escalate issues to the technical support team. You'll show him how to find troubleshooters that employees can use to solve these problems.

To troubleshoot Internet problems:

1. Click the **Action Center** icon 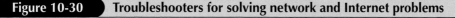 in the notification area of the taskbar, and then click **Open Action Center** to open the Action Center window.

2. Scroll down, if necessary, click **Troubleshooting** to open the Troubleshooting window, and then click **Network and Internet** to open the Network and Internet window. See Figure 10-30.

| Figure 10-30 | Troubleshooters for solving network and Internet problems |

network and Internet troubleshooters

troubleshooter for the network printer

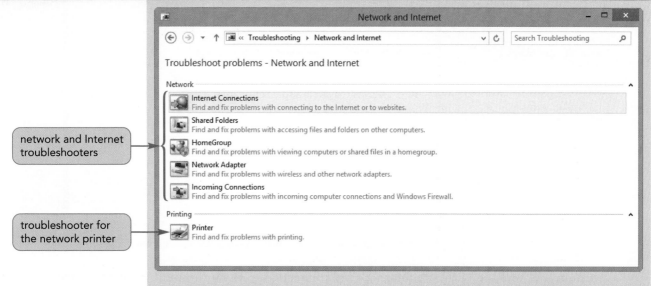

3. Click **Internet Connections** to start the Internet Connections wizard.

Kenny wants to review changes and repairs before Windows applies them, so you need to display an advanced option.

4. Click the **Advanced** link to display advanced options. See Figure 10-31.

| Figure 10-31 | Troubleshooter for Internet connection problem |

remove this check mark so Windows will not apply solutions automatically

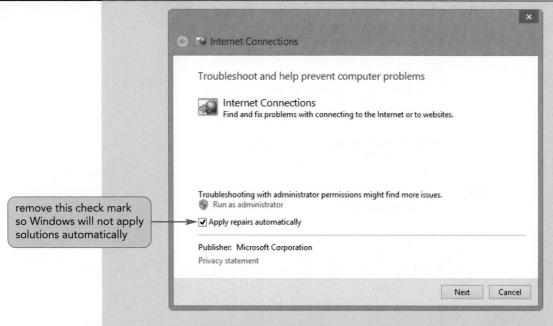

▶ **5.** Click the **Apply repairs automatically** check box to remove the check mark, and then click the **Next** button. The next dialog box displays possible Internet connection problems that need troubleshooting. See Figure 10-32.

Figure 10-32   **Possible problems**

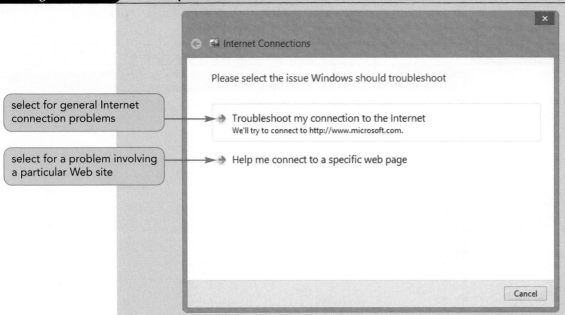

select for general Internet connection problems

select for a problem involving a particular Web site

▶ **6.** Click **Troubleshoot my connection to the Internet**. Windows tests the Internet connection and reports that it couldn't identify the problem.

Trouble? If Windows identifies a problem with your Internet connection, you can still perform the next step.

▶ **7.** Click **Explore additional options**. Windows displays other resources for solving the problem. See Figure 10-33. Your Additional Information window might contain other options.

Figure 10-33	Additional resources

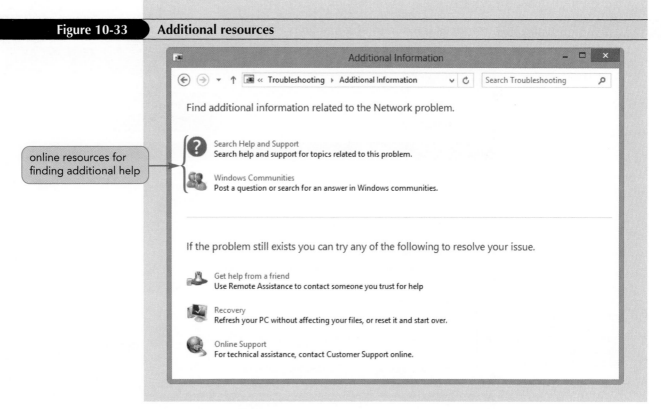

online resources for
finding additional help

You'll show Kenny the next step to take if employees can't find solutions to their problems using a troubleshooter.

Searching the Microsoft Community

The Microsoft Community is a Web site that provides support information for Microsoft product users. Because the Microsoft Community supports all Microsoft software products, it is a valuable resource when you are troubleshooting computer problems. However, it can sometimes be difficult to pinpoint the answer to your question. Just as you search for information on the Internet, you can search the Microsoft Community for answers by entering one or more keywords. The Web page then displays the answer or support articles associated with those keywords.

Fab Homes employees can have problems with their Microsoft accounts. You'll show Kenny how to use the Microsoft Community forum to find answers to questions other users have about Microsoft accounts.

To find information on the Microsoft Community Web site:

TIP

You can also click the Microsoft Community website link on the Help and Support home page.

1. In the Additional Information window, click **Windows Communities**. Internet Explorer starts and opens the Microsoft Community Web page for Windows.

2. Click the **Forums** link on the navigation bar, and then click **Microsoft account, Hotmail, SkyDrive**. The Microsoft account, Hotmail, SkyDrive page opens, listing questions and answers related to those topics. See Figure 10-34. Information on the Web changes frequently, so when you open the Web page, it might differ from the one shown in the figure.

Figure 10-34	Forum on the Microsoft Community

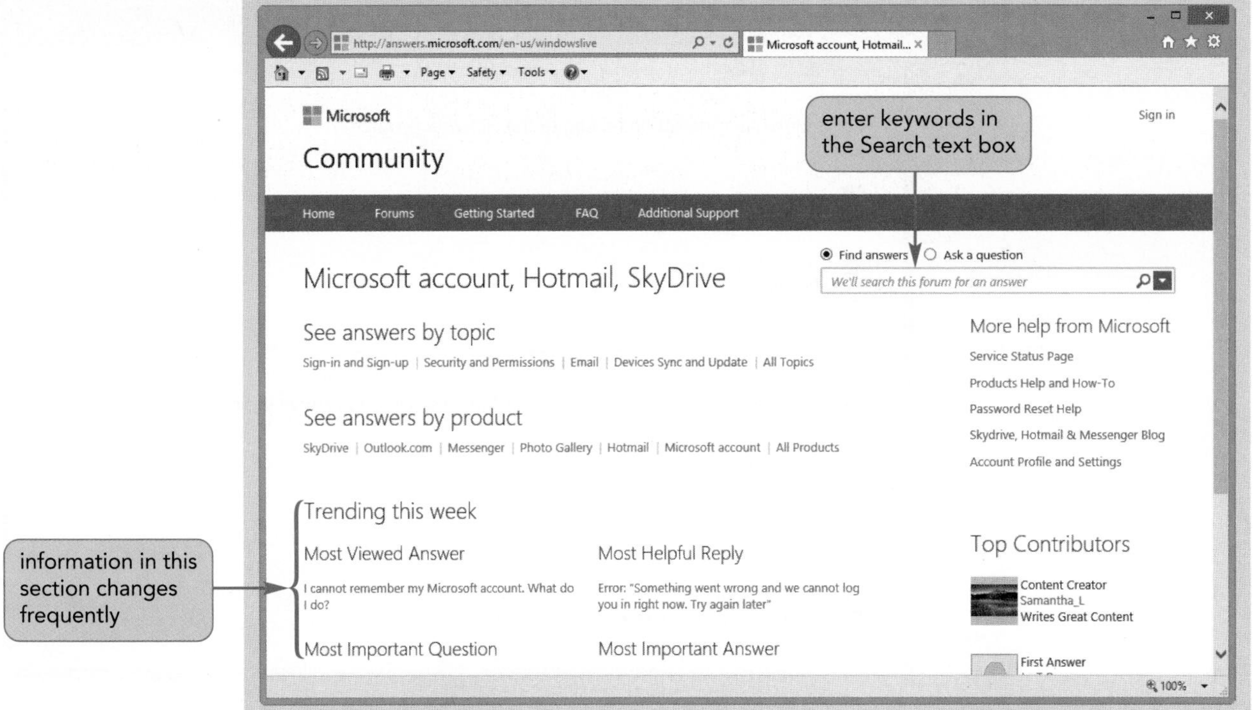

enter keywords in the Search text box

information in this section changes frequently

Microsoft

Community

Home   Forums   Getting Started   FAQ   Additional Support

Microsoft account, Hotmail, SkyDrive

● Find answers ○ Ask a question

We'll search this forum for an answer

See answers by topic

Sign-in and Sign-up | Security and Permissions | Email | Devices Sync and Update | All Topics

See answers by product

SkyDrive | Outlook.com | Messenger | Photo Gallery | Hotmail | Microsoft account | All Products

More help from Microsoft

Service Status Page

Products Help and How-To

Password Reset Help

Skydrive, Hotmail & Messenger Blog

Account Profile and Settings

Trending this week

Most Viewed Answer

I cannot remember my Microsoft account. What do I do?

Most Helpful Reply

Error: "Something went wrong and we cannot log you in right now. Try again later"

Top Contributors

Content Creator
Samantha_L
Writes Great Content

Most Important Question

Most Important Answer

First Answer

3. In the Trending this week section, click the link displayed below the Most Viewed Answer heading. A Web page opens displaying the question and answer. Scroll down to read the complete question and answer.

4. Click a link in the Related Threads section on the right side of the window to display a question and answer related to the ones you just read. (A **thread** is a discussion, a series of questions and answers about a topic.)

5. Scroll down, and then click a link in the More Microsoft Resources section on the right side of the window to display information related to the topic you selected in Step 4. Figure 10-35 lists several Microsoft account topics.

Figure 10-35 Microsoft account support topics

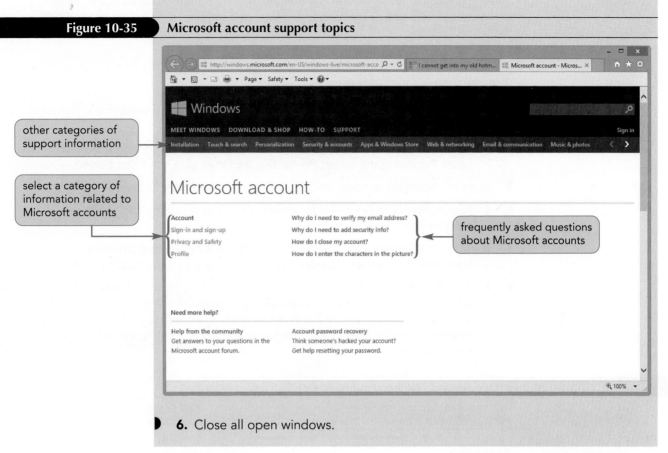

other categories of support information

select a category of information related to Microsoft accounts

frequently asked questions about Microsoft accounts

6. Close all open windows.

Now Kenny can help the employees at Fab Homes find answers to their Windows questions online.

Troubleshooting Printing Errors

You have already learned how to use the Devices and Printers window to install a printer and select the default printer to use with Windows applications. Besides using a troubleshooter to detect and repair problems for you, you can also use the Devices and Printers window to troubleshoot some typical printing errors, such as problems with print quality. You need to address certain printing problems, such as running out of paper or clearing a print jam, directly at the printer. For example, when the printer runs out of paper, you need to restock the paper tray with printer paper. To clear a jam, you need to follow the printer manufacturer's recommendations, which might involve pressing a button to clear the jam or opening the printer to remove paper.

However, these printing errors can also cause problems with the **print queue**, which is the list of documents waiting to be printed. While you clear a printer jam, for example, you might need to pause and then restart the print jobs in the print queue. The print queue also displays information about documents that are waiting to print, such as the printing status, document owner, and number of pages to print. You can use the print queue to view, pause, resume, restart, and cancel print jobs.

Kenny has not been able to print with a laser printer installed on his system. You'll try printing to the laser printer, and then show Kenny how to troubleshoot the problem using the Devices and Printers window and the print queue. To simulate a printing problem and perform the following steps, turn off the printer to which your computer is connected, if possible. The following steps use "Laser Printer" as the name of the printer causing problems. Substitute the name of the printer you turned off for "Laser Printer." If you cannot turn off a printer connected to your computer, read but do not perform the following steps.

To troubleshoot printing errors:

▶ **1.** Turn off your printer, start Notepad, and then type your name in the Notepad document.

▶ **2.** Click **File** on the menu bar, click **Print** to open the Print dialog box, click **Laser Printer** in the Select Printer list, and then click the **Print** button.

▶ **3.** In the Notepad window, press the **Enter** key and type today's date.

▶ **4.** Repeat Step 2 to print the document, and then minimize the Notepad window.

▶ **5.** Open the Control Panel, and then click **View devices and printers** in the Hardware and Sound category to open the Devices and Printers window.

▶ **6.** If necessary, right-click a blank spot in the window, point to **View** on the shortcut menu, and then click **Details** to display the window in Details view. Scroll down to display the Printers category, if necessary, and then click **Laser Printer** to display printer information at the bottom of the window. See Figure 10-36.

Figure 10-36	Devices and Printers window in Details view

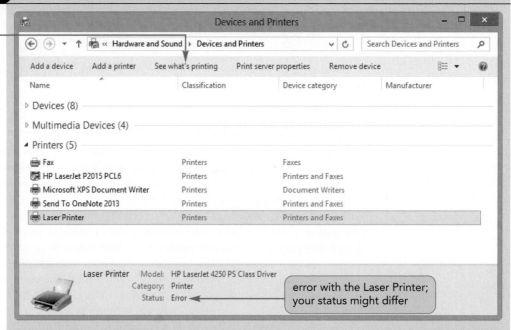

click to open the print queue for the selected printer

error with the Laser Printer; your status might differ

▶ **7.** Double-click **Laser Printer** to open the print queue. See Figure 10-37.

Trouble? If a Laser Printer window opens instead of a window showing the print queue, look for a link such as "See what's printing" or "Display Print Queue," and then click the link to open the print queue.

Figure 10-37   Laser Printer print queue

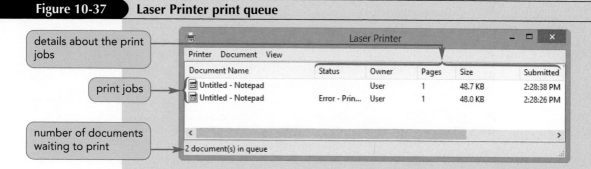

details about the print jobs

print jobs

number of documents waiting to print

▶ **8.** Right-click the second **Untitled – Notepad** print job in the queue, and then click **Pause** on the shortcut menu. This pauses the print job so you can solve the printer problem.

▶ **9.** Right-click the first **Untitled – Notepad** print job in the queue, and then click **Cancel** to prevent this print job from printing and delete it from the print queue. Click the **Yes** button when asked if you are sure you want to cancel the document.

▶ **10.** Reconnect the printer to your computer and turn it on, if necessary.

▶ **11.** In the Laser Printer print queue, right-click the paused **Untitled – Notepad** print job, and then click **Resume** on the shortcut menu. The Notepad document prints on the Laser Printer.

▶ **12.** Close all open windows without saving any changes.

Software errors also cause occasional problems for Fab Homes employees. You'll now show Kenny how to report software problems to Microsoft and find and apply solutions.

Recovering from Software Errors

To keep your computer running at peak performance, you need to know how to recover from two types of software errors: those produced by programs, such as an application closing unexpectedly, and those produced by Windows 8 itself, including Internet Explorer. You have already learned to use Task Manager to respond to an application that stops working or responding to your actions. Recall that you can open the Processes tab in Task Manager to identify unresponsive applications and then click the End task button to close the app. Another way to recover from software errors is to use the Programs and Features window to change the installed features of a program or to try to repair the installation. (To do so, you open Control Panel, click Programs, click Programs and Features, click the troublesome program, and then click the Repair button.) A third way to respond to software problems is to report the problem to Microsoft and have Windows check for a solution. Windows notifies you if you should take steps to prevent or solve the problem, or if it needs more information to find or create a solution.

Checking for Solutions to Software Problems

- Click the Action Center icon in the notification area of the taskbar, and then click Open Action Center.
- Expand the Maintenance section, if necessary, and then click Check for solutions.
- Follow any steps Windows provides.

In addition to reporting problems and checking for solutions, you can use the Action Center window to check for new solutions to past problems, review your problem history, change maintenance settings, and produce a reliability report, which gives you a history of the stability of your computer so you can be proactive in maintaining your computer.

Reporting and Solving Software Errors

If your computer is connected to the Internet, Windows can report software problems to a secure part of the Microsoft Web site. When an application closes unexpectedly, for example, a Windows dialog box appears asking if you want to send a problem report to Microsoft. If you agree, Windows sends a report to Microsoft that includes the name and version of the application, the date and time the problem occurred, and other technical information that can help diagnose the problem. Microsoft collects and reviews problem reports even for Windows software produced by companies other than Microsoft. You can review the information in any problem report before you send it.

When Microsoft receives a problem report, it checks for a solution, which might be a link to a Help article, a file to download, or steps to perform. When a solution is available, Microsoft sends the solution to your computer according to your problem reporting settings. Windows then displays a message regarding the solution in the Action Center and displays a Solve PC issues ScreenTip when you point to the Action Center icon in the notification area of the taskbar. To specify how you want Microsoft to check for solutions, you can select one of four problem reporting settings:

- Automatically check for solutions (recommended)—Microsoft checks for solutions as soon as it receives a problem report. If a solution is not available, Windows might display another dialog box asking for additional information about the problem. If you agree to send this additional information, Windows sends another problem report containing information from files such as event logs that can help solve the problem.
- Automatically check for solutions and send additional report data, if needed— Microsoft checks for solutions as soon as it receives a problem report. If a solution is not available and Microsoft needs additional information, Windows automatically sends another problem report with the requested information.
- Each time a problem occurs, ask me before checking for solutions—When you agree to send a problem report, Windows asks if you also want Microsoft to check for solutions.
- Never check for solutions (not recommended)—Microsoft does not check for solutions when you send a problem report.

In addition, you can use the Action Center at any time to check for solutions to software problems you've reported.

You'll start by showing Kenny how to use the Action Center to solve software problems.

To use the Action Center to solve software problems:

1. Point to the **Action Center** icon in the notification area of the taskbar. On Kenny's computer, a ScreenTip appears that indicates the Action Center detected one PC issue to resolve.

   Trouble? If the ScreenTip for your Action Center icon indicates that no current issues are detected, continue with the steps.

2. Click the **Action Center** icon in the notification area of the taskbar, and then click **Open Action Center**. The Action Center window opens. See Figure 10-38. In this case, the Action Center displays a message regarding a problem with the power management system driver on Kenny's computer.

Figure 10-38	Problem message in the Action Center window

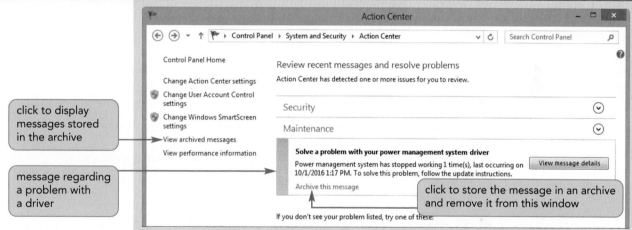

click to display
messages stored
in the archive

message regarding
a problem with
a driver

3. Click the **View message details** button to learn more about the problem and solve it, if possible. The Message Details window opens. See Figure 10-39.

   Trouble? If your Action Center window does not include a View message details button, skip Step 3 and read but do not perform the remaining steps.

Figure 10-39   Message Details window

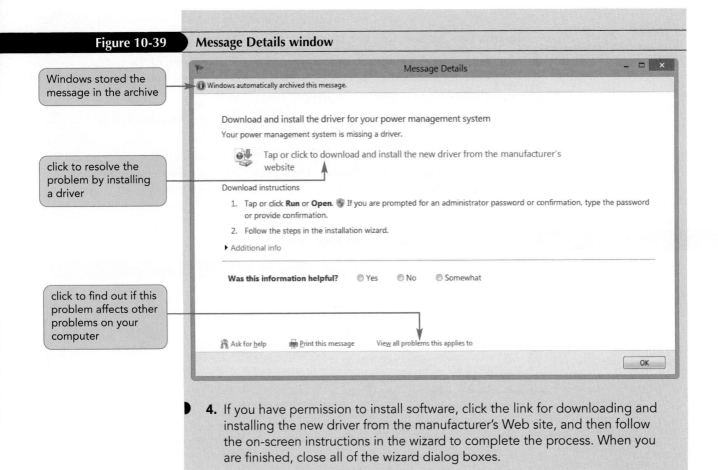

Windows stored the message in the archive

click to resolve the problem by installing a driver

click to find out if this problem affects other problems on your computer

4. If you have permission to install software, click the link for downloading and installing the new driver from the manufacturer's Web site, and then follow the on-screen instructions in the wizard to complete the process. When you are finished, close all of the wizard dialog boxes.

5. Click the **Back** button ⊙ to return to the Action Center window, which no longer displays the power management driver message.

When you view the details about an Action Center message, Windows usually archives the message, which means it adds the message to a list of solved or pending issues and removes it from the Action Center window. You can display this list by clicking the View archived messages link in the left pane of the Action Center window.

Kenny has sent reports to Microsoft about software problems, but he is not sure how his computer is set up to receive solutions. You'll make sure Windows is set to check for solutions to problem reports automatically, but to ask Kenny for additional information when necessary, which is the default problem reporting setting.

To set Windows to check for software solutions automatically:

1. In the Action Center window, click **Maintenance** to expand the Maintenance section and display the Maintenance options. See Figure 10-40.

Figure 10-40   **Maintenance options in the Action Center window**

click to make sure Windows is set to report software problems and check for solutions automatically

check for solutions to reported problems

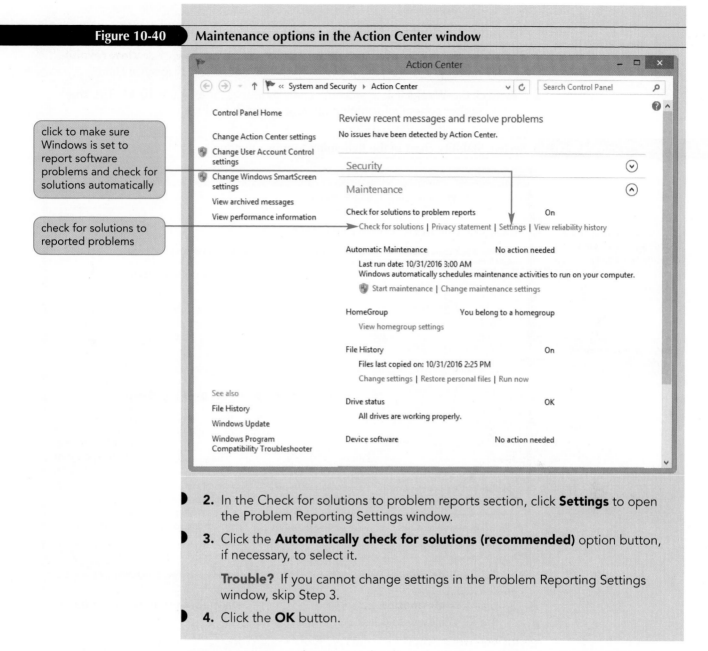

> **2.** In the Check for solutions to problem reports section, click **Settings** to open the Problem Reporting Settings window.

> **3.** Click the **Automatically check for solutions (recommended)** option button, if necessary, to select it.
>
> **Trouble?** If you cannot change settings in the Problem Reporting Settings window, skip Step 3.

> **4.** Click the **OK** button.

Now you are sure that Microsoft will send solutions to the Action Center on Kenny's computer as soon as they are available. If you wanted to check for solutions on your own, you could click the Check for solutions link in the Maintenance section of the Action Center window.

Viewing the Reliability History

The Reliability Monitor window includes information about the performance of your computer. It includes a chart tracking the stability of your computer, and it maintains up to a year of history on your system's stability and reliability events. For example, this tool tracks program failures, such as a program shutting down unexpectedly, and problems with the hard disk and memory, and records whether your computer successfully installed updates to keep the system running reliably. It displays these events on a chart, assigning each event a number from 1 (least stable) to 10 (most stable). You'll show Kenny how to use this tool to identify events that have affected the stability and reliability of his computer.

To view the System Stability chart:

1. In the Maintenance section of the Action Center window, click **View reliability history**. The Reliability Monitor window opens and displays a chart.

2. Click the **Weeks** link to view the chart by weeks. See Figure 10-41. The chart and other system information on your computer will differ.

Figure 10-41   System Stability chart in the Reliability Monitor window

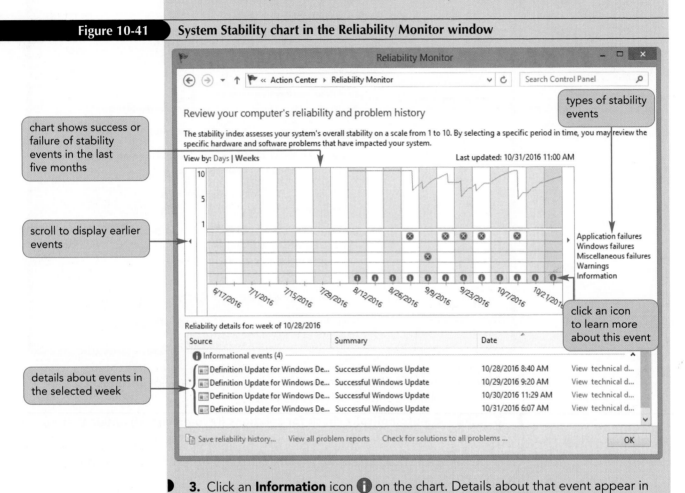

chart shows success or failure of stability events in the last five months

scroll to display earlier events

details about events in the selected week

types of stability events

click an icon to learn more about this event

3. Click an **Information** icon 🛈 on the chart. Details about that event appear in the Reliability details list. See Figure 10-42.

Figure 10-42   **Viewing information about a system stability event**

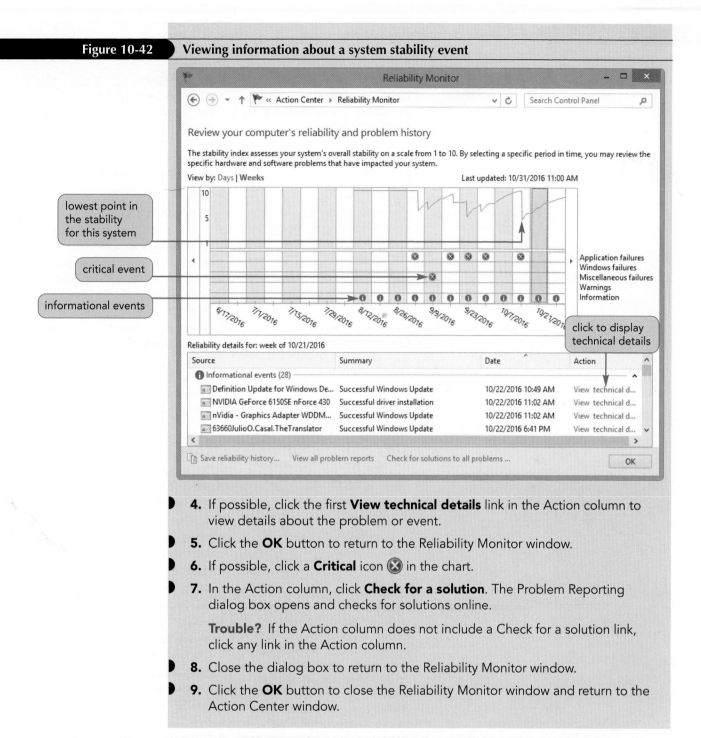

4. If possible, click the first **View technical details** link in the Action column to view details about the problem or event.

5. Click the **OK** button to return to the Reliability Monitor window.

6. If possible, click a **Critical** icon ⊗ in the chart.

7. In the Action column, click **Check for a solution**. The Problem Reporting dialog box opens and checks for solutions online.

   Trouble? If the Action column does not include a Check for a solution link, click any link in the Action column.

8. Close the dialog box to return to the Reliability Monitor window.

9. Click the **OK** button to close the Reliability Monitor window and return to the Action Center window.

The chart showed that the stability of Kenny's computer is usually between 7 and 10, though it has dipped as low as 5. Overall, this means his system has been fairly stable and reliable over the past year.

Recovering the Operating System

If Windows 8 doesn't start correctly or runs erratically, you can try the troubleshooting steps provided in Figure 10-43 to solve the problem. These solutions are listed in order of complexity, with the simplest solution listed first.

The correct key to display the Advanced Boot Options menu on your computer appears onscreen when the computer starts. If necessary, substitute the correct key name for the F8 key in the following steps.

Figure 10-43 **Recovering the operating system**

Tool	Description	How to Access
System Restore	Use System Restore to restore your computer's system files to an earlier point in time.	1. Open the Control Panel, click System and Security, click System, click System protection, and then click System Restore. 2. Click the Next button twice to accept the most recent restore point. 3. Click the Finish button.
Last Known Good Configuration	This advanced startup option starts Windows using the registry settings and drives that were in use the last time the computer started successfully.	1. Restart your computer. 2. Press and hold the F8 key before the Windows logo appears. 3. On the Advanced Boot Options screen, select Last Known Good Configuration, and then press the Enter key.
Safe mode	If the Last Known Good Configuration option doesn't work, use safe mode to try to identify and fix the problem. If your computer starts only in safe mode, try disabling recently installed hardware or programs.	1. Restart your computer. 2. Press and hold the F8 key before the Windows logo appears. 3. On the Advanced Boot Options screen, select Safe Mode, and then press the Enter key.
Startup Repair	In extreme cases, you can use Startup Repair to fix missing or damaged system files that might prevent Windows from starting.	1. Insert the Windows installation media. 2. Restart your computer. 3. Select your language settings, and then click the Next button. 4. Click Repair your computer. 5. Select the operating system to repair, and then click the Next button. 6. On the System Recovery Options menu, click Startup Repair.
Reinstall Windows	If your system has been severely damaged, you might need to reinstall Windows. A custom, or clean, installation of Windows permanently deletes all of the files on your computer and reinstalls Windows, so only use this option if all other recovery options have been unsuccessful. After the installation, you must reinstall your programs and restore your files from backup copies.	1. Insert the Windows installation media. 2. Display the Charms bar, and then click Change PC settings. 3. Click General, and then scroll down and click Get started in the "Remove everything and reinstall Windows" section. 4. Follow the instructions that appear on your screen.

© 2014 Cengage Learning

Last Known Good Configuration, Safe mode, and Startup Repair are advanced startup options that let you select settings before Windows 8 starts. **Last Known Good Configuration** uses the most recent system settings that worked correctly. Every time you turn your computer off and Windows shuts down successfully, it saves important system settings in the registry. If those new settings cause system problems, you can bypass the settings when you restart the computer by selecting the Last Known Good Configuration option on the advanced startup menu. When you do, Windows loads the settings it saved the second-to-last time you shut down the computer (the time before you shut down the computer after selecting the faulty new system settings). You can then disable a device or uninstall a program that is causing problems. Be sure you select the Last Known Good Configuration option *before* you sign in to Windows—you must press the F8 key right after the computer starts and before Windows does. If you sign in to Windows or start and wait for the desktop to appear, the Last Known Good Configuration will include the faulty new settings.

Safe mode is a troubleshooting option for Windows that starts your computer with only basic services and functionality. If a problem you experienced earlier does not reappear when you start Windows in safe mode, you can eliminate the default settings and basic device drivers as possible causes. While in safe mode, you can use Device Manager to disable a problematic device or restore a driver to its previous version. You can also restore your computer to an earlier point using System Restore.

Startup Repair is a Windows recovery tool that can fix problems such as missing or damaged system files, which might prevent Windows from starting. This tool is provided on the Windows installation media and, depending on how Windows was installed, might also be stored on your hard disk.

INSIGHT

Selecting a Restore Point or the Last Known Good Configuration

If your operating system is running erratically, the two least disruptive solutions to try are reverting to a restore point and using the Last Known Good Configuration. These two options are often confused. Choose System Restore when you notice your system behaving strangely and Windows is still running. Then you can select a restore point to return the system to an earlier point in time when things worked correctly. Unlike Last Known Good Configuration, you can undo the changes made with System Restore, so you can troubleshoot operating system problems by selecting a restore point first. Choose the Last Known Good Configuration option if you can't start Windows, but it started correctly the last time you turned on the computer.

Using the Problem Steps Recorder

If you are having trouble performing a task in Windows, you can use the Problem Steps Recorder to record the steps you take on a computer. The Problem Steps Recorder captures the screen each time you click, saves the screen image, and then includes a text description of where you clicked. Then, as part of the process, you can save the captured images and text in a zipped file and send it to a support professional or someone else helping you with a computer problem.

When you record steps on your computer, anything you type is not recorded. If what you type is an important part of re-creating the problem you're trying to solve, use the Add Comment feature in the Problem Steps Recorder to highlight where the problem is occurring and to provide other types of explanations or descriptions.

Kenny is having trouble installing a driver for a hardware device. He has been using Windows Update to download and install the driver. Each time he tries, Windows reports that the update failed. You'll show him how to use the Problem Steps Recorder to record the steps he takes to update the driver. He can then send the report to other system experts at Fab Homes to see if they can help him troubleshoot the problem.

To use the Problem Steps Recorder:

1. In the Action Center window, click the **Search** text box, type **problem steps**, and then click **Record steps to reproduce a problem** in the search results. The Steps Recorder window opens. See Figure 10-44.

Figure 10-44	Steps Recorder window

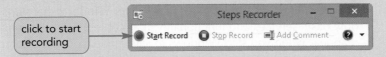

click to start recording

2. Click the **Start Record** button. The Steps Recorder starts recording your steps.

   Trouble? If a Steps Recorder warning dialog box opens indicating you might need to run the Steps Recorder as an administrator, click the OK button.

TIP

As you are recording steps, you can click the Add Comment button in the Steps Recorder window to write a note about a step.

3. Click the **Back** button in the Control Panel window, click **System and Security** in the Address bar, and then click **Windows Update**. While the Steps Recorder is recording, a red dot appears every time you click a button or press a key. The red dot indicates that the Steps Recorder has captured your every action.

4. Click the link for optional updates, and then click the **check box** for an optional update. See Figure 10-45.

   Trouble? If no optional updates are listed, skip Steps 4 and 5.

Figure 10-45	Recording the steps to install an optional Windows update

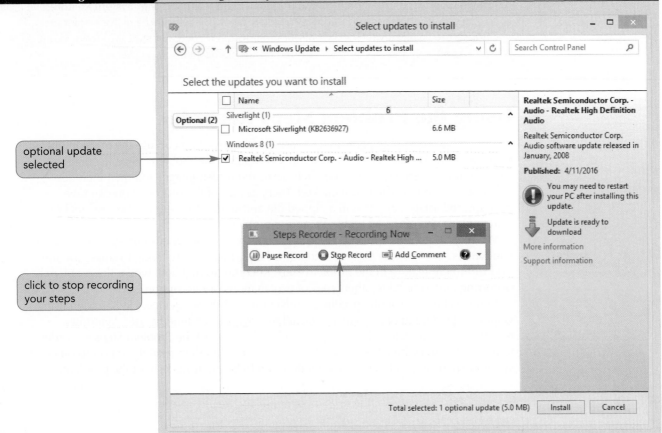

optional update selected

click to stop recording your steps

5. Click the **Install** button, and then wait while Windows prepares and then installs the update or fails to do so.

6. In the Steps Recorder window, click the **Stop Record** button. The Steps Recorder window opens. See Figure 10-46.

Figure 10-46 Captured steps

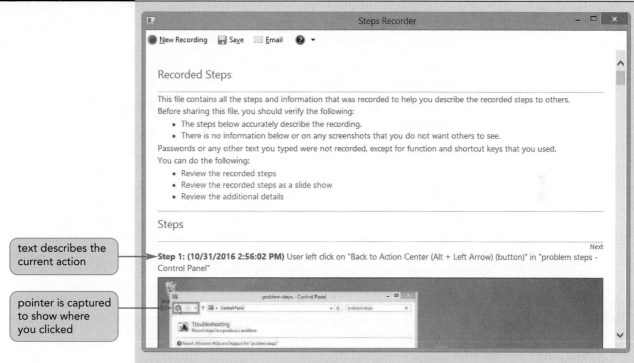

text describes the current action

pointer is captured to show where you clicked

7. Scroll to review the recorded steps, click the **Save** button at the top of the window, and then save the recorded steps as a ZIP file named **Optional Update** in the Windows10\Tutorial folder provided with your Data Files.

8. Close the Steps Recorder window.

Kenny will email this file containing the recorded steps to a technical support specialist later.

Requesting and Managing Remote Assistance

If you are experiencing a computer problem and can't find a solution yourself, you can use Windows Remote Assistance to have someone show you how to fix a problem. Remote Assistance is a convenient way for someone you trust, such as a friend, coworker, or technical support person, to connect to your computer and step you through a solution—even if that person isn't nearby. To help ensure that only people you invite can connect to your computer using Remote Assistance, all sessions are encrypted and password protected.

To request Remote Assistance, you can send an email message to invite someone to connect to your computer. After connecting, that person can view your computer screen and chat with you about what you both see on your computer screen. With your permission, your helper can even use a mouse and keyboard to control your computer and show you how to fix a problem. You can also help someone else in the same way.

Before you can use Windows Remote Assistance to connect two computers, you must enable the feature. You'll show Kenny how to enable Remote Assistance connections so that he can request help from you and vice versa.

To enable Remote Assistance connections:

▶ **1.** In the Address bar in the Control Panel window, click the **arrow** button ▶ after System and Security, and then click **System**. The System window opens.

▶ **2.** Click **Remote settings** in the left pane. The System Properties dialog box opens to the Remote tab.

Trouble? If a User Account Control dialog box opens requesting a password or your permission to continue, enter the password or click the Yes button.

▶ **3.** If necessary, click the **Allow Remote Assistance connections to this computer** box to insert a check mark.

To disable Remote Assistance invitations, you remove the check mark from the Allow Remote Assistance connections to this computer box on the Remote tab in the System Properties dialog box. You can also use the Remote tab in the System Properties dialog box to access advanced Remote Assistance settings, such as how much time you want enabled for Remote Assistance and how long invitations will be available.

When you allow Remote Assistance connections to your computer, you can send and receive Remote Assistance invitations using email or an option called Easy Connect. **Easy Connect** is a technology that connects two computers on a network so one computer can access the Start screen, desktop, and other resources of another computer.

You want to show Kenny how to limit the amount of time that a Remote Assistance invitation is available, so that an unauthorized person cannot control your computer without your knowledge.

> **TIP**
>
> Windows automatically allows the Remote Assistance program through Windows Firewall so you can receive assistance.

To select advanced Remote Assistance settings:

▶ **1.** On the Remote tab in the System Properties dialog box, click the **Advanced** button. The Remote Assistance Settings dialog box opens. See Figure 10-47.

Figure 10-47   **Remote Assistance Settings dialog box**

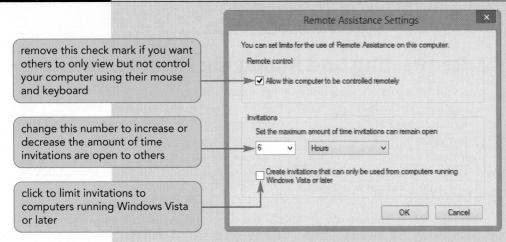

remove this check mark if you want others to only view but not control your computer using their mouse and keyboard

change this number to increase or decrease the amount of time invitations are open to others

click to limit invitations to computers running Windows Vista or later

▶ **2.** Under Invitations, click the box on the left to select the time that invitations can remain available, and then type **4** to reduce the amount of time a Remote Assistance invitation is available. Leave the Hours option set.

> **3.** Click the **OK** button to close the Remote Assistance Settings dialog box.

> **4.** Click the **OK** button to close the System Properties dialog box.

You can also use the Remote Assistance Settings dialog box to create invitations only for computers running Windows Vista or later, which protects the security of your computer. Although Kenny doesn't need to establish a Remote Assistance session now, you'll show him how to request assistance using the Windows Remote Assistance Wizard.

Requesting Remote Assistance

When you need help from someone else, you can request Remote Assistance using the Windows Remote Assistance Wizard, which you can start from the Control Panel.

You'll show Kenny how to use the Windows Remote Assistance Wizard to send an email message inviting you to help him troubleshoot a problem on his computer. When you perform the following steps, substitute the email address of a friend or classmate for the email address used in the steps.

To request Remote Assistance:

> **1.** In the Control Panel window, click the **Search** text box, type **remote**, and then click **Invite someone to connect to your PC and help you, or offer to help someone else** in the search results. The Windows Remote Assistance Wizard starts. See Figure 10-48.

Figure 10-48 **Starting the Windows Remote Assistance Wizard**

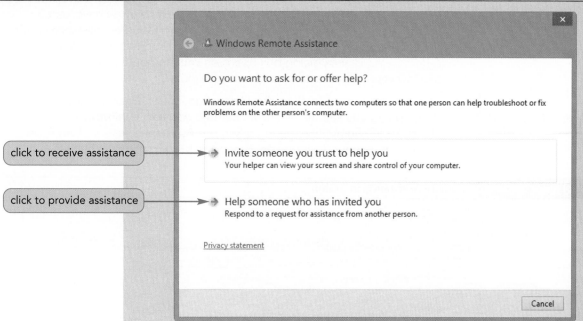

> **2.** Click **Invite someone you trust to help you**. The next wizard dialog box opens, asking how you want to invite someone to help you.

> **3.** Click **Use email to send an invitation**. Remote Assistance opens an invitation email in your default email program and fills in the subject and content of the message for you. See Figure 10-49.

Trouble? If you do not have a default email program set up on your computer, Windows asks you to select an email program to use. Select the program and wait for the invitation email to open, and then continue with Step 4.

Trouble? If a message appears regarding creating an email profile, close the message and then read but do not perform the remaining steps.

Trouble? If the Use email to send invitation option is grayed out, click Save this invitation as a file, use your email software to open a new email message, attach the file you just saved, and continue with the remaining steps.

Figure 10-49   **Email with Remote Assistance invitation**

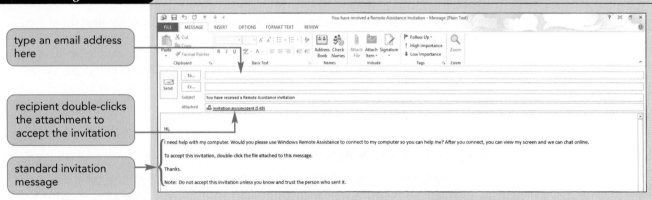

type an email address here

recipient double-clicks the attachment to accept the invitation

standard invitation message

---

4. Enter the email address of a friend or classmate, such as **Helper@FabHomes.com**, in the To box, and then click the **Send** button. A window opens displaying a connection password. Wait for your helper to receive and open the invitation, which might be an email attachment. If necessary, tell your helper the password in whatever way is convenient for you, such as a phone call. Your helper should start Remote Assistance on his or her computer, and then enter the password to connect to your computer. A Remote Assistance dialog box opens on your computer, asking if you want to allow your helper to connect to your computer.

5. Click the **Yes** button to allow the connection. Your helper can now see your desktop and you see the Windows Remote Assistance window shown in Figure 10-50. Sometimes during a Remote Assistance session, Windows might change your desktop background to black.

Figure 10-50   **Remote Assistance in action**

click when you are ready to stop sharing

you are sharing your computer with a helper

You can now perform the steps with which Kenny is having trouble. You can see Kenny's computer screen because you are playing the role of helper, and you and he can chat using the online Chat tool. With permission granted, you can control Kenny's computer to show him how to fix the problem. Right now you will just show him how to end the Remote Assistance session.

To end the Remote Assistance session:

▶ **1.** If your helper clicked the Request control button in the Remote Assistance window on his or her computer, click the **Stop sharing** button. Your helper no longer has access to your computer.

▶ **2.** Close the Remote Assistance window to end the Remote Assistance session.

▶ **3.** Close all other open windows.

Now that you're finished helping Kenny improve his computer's performance and troubleshoot system problems, you should restore your system settings.

Restoring Your Settings

If you are working in a computer lab or on a computer other than your own, complete the steps in this section to restore the original settings on your computer. If a User Account Control dialog box opens requesting an Administrator password or confirmation after you perform any of the following steps, enter the password or click the Yes button.

To restore your settings:

▶ **1.** Open the Control Panel, click **System and Security**, click **System**, and then click **Performance Information and Tools** in the See also section of the left pane.

▶ **2.** Click **Adjust visual effects** in the left pane.

▶ **3.** Restore your original settings, and then click the **OK** button to close the Performance Options dialog box.

▶ **4.** Open File Explorer, right-click the **USB flash drive**, and then click **Properties** on the shortcut menu.

▶ **5.** Click the **ReadyBoost** tab, and then click the **Do not use this device** option button. Click the **OK** button to close the Properties dialog box.

▶ **6.** In the Control Panel window, navigate to the System window, and then click **Remote settings** in the left pane.

▶ **7.** On the Remote tab of the System Properties dialog box, restore your original settings in the Remote Assistance section.

▶ **8.** Click the **Advanced** button, and then restore your original setting for the maximum amount of time Remote Assistance invitations can stay open, which is 6 hours by default. Click the **OK** button to close the Remote Assistance Settings dialog box.

▶ **9.** Click the **OK** button to close the System Properties dialog box.

▶ **10.** Close all open windows.

Session 10.2 Quick Check

1. The _____ Web site hosts a forum of users and Microsoft experts where you can search, browse, and post questions and answers.

2. What is a print queue?

3. How does Windows provide solutions when you use the Action Center to report a software problem?

4. How can you display details about an event that appears in the System Stability chart?

5. _____ is a troubleshooting option for Windows that starts your computer with only basic services and functionality.

6. Under what circumstances would you use the Problem Steps Recorder?

7. _____ is a convenient way for someone you trust to connect to your computer and step you through a solution, even if that person isn't nearby.

Review Assignments

There are no Data Files needed for the Review Assignments.

Now that you've helped Kenny Shen improve system performance and troubleshoot hardware and software problems on his computer, he asks you to show another Fab Homes manager, Helen Davison, how to optimize her computer. Complete the following steps, noting your original settings so you can restore them later:

1. Open the Control Panel, open the Performance Information and Tools window, and then rerun the assessment tool to calculate your computer's Windows Experience Index base score. Press the Print Screen key to capture an image of the screen. Paste the image in a new Paint file, and then save the file as **WEI Score** in the Windows10\Review folder provided with your Data Files.

2. To improve performance, adjust the visual effects on your computer. Do not animate controls and elements inside windows. In addition, do not animate windows when minimizing and maximizing. With the Performance Options dialog box open to the appropriate tab, press the Print Screen key to capture an image of the screen. Paste the image in a new Paint file, and then save the file as **Visual Effects** in the Windows10\Review folder provided with your Data Files.

3. Open the Advanced Tools window to display any issues that Windows identifies as detracting from the performance of your computer. Press the Print Screen key to capture an image of the screen. Paste the image in a new Paint file, and then save the file as **Issues** in the Windows10\Review folder provided with your Data Files.

4. Open the Event Viewer window and display details about a critical event. If your Event Viewer window does not list any critical events, display details about an error. Press the Print Screen key to capture an image of the screen. Paste the image in a new Paint file, and then save the file as **Events** in the Windows10\Review folder provided with your Data Files.

5. Open the Task Manager window and display the current apps and processes running on your computer. (*Hint:* To make sure that Task Manager groups processes by type, click View on the menu bar. If the Group by type option is not selected with a check mark, click Group by type.) Expand an app in the Apps section, and then press the Print Screen key to capture an image of the screen. Paste the image in a new Paint file, and then save the file as **Apps** in the Windows10\Review folder provided with your Data Files.

6. Open File Explorer, and then display a graph of CPU usage in the Task Manager window. Press the Print Screen key to capture an image of the dialog box. Paste the image in a new Paint file, and then save the file as **CPU Graph** in the Windows10\Review folder provided with your Data Files. Close the File Explorer and Task Manager windows.

7. Use the System Information window to display a system summary that shows details about the sound device component on your computer. Press the Print Screen key to capture an image of the screen. Paste the image in a new Paint file, and then save the file as **Sound Device** in the Windows10\Review folder provided with your Data Files.

8. Display the size of the paging file on your computer. Press the Print Screen key to capture an image of the dialog box. Paste the image in a new Paint file, and then save the file as **Paging File** in the Windows10\Review folder provided with your Data Files.

9. Generate a system health report for your computer. Save the report as **Health** in the Windows10\Review folder provided with your Data Files.

10. Attach a USB flash drive to your computer, and then increase the memory capacity of your system by turning on ReadyBoost. Select the maximum amount of available space on your USB flash drive to reserve for boosting your system speed. Press the Print Screen key to capture an image of the screen. Paste the image in a new Paint file, and then save the file as **USB ReadyBoost** in the Windows10\Review folder provided with your Data Files.

11. Display the Windows forum at the Microsoft Community Web site. Select the most viewed answer, and then press the Print Screen key to capture an image of the screen. Paste the image in a new Paint file, and then save the file as **Most Viewed** in the Windows10\Review folder provided with your Data Files.

12. Use the Action Center window to view the archived problem messages on your computer. Press the Print Screen key to capture an image of the screen. Paste the image in a new Paint file, and then save the file as **Archive** in the Windows10\Review folder provided with your Data Files.

13. Display your computer's reliability and problem history. View this information by Weeks. Select the current week, and then press the Print Screen key to capture an image of the screen. Paste the image in a new Paint file, and then save the file as **History Chart** in the Windows10\Review folder provided with your Data Files.

14. Use the Problem Steps Recorder to record the steps for opening an accessory on your computer, such as the Calculator. Save the steps in a Zip file named **Accessory Steps** in the Windows10\ Review folder.

15. Set the maximum amount of time Remote Assistance invitations can stay open to **5** hours. Press the Print Screen key to capture an image of the screen. Paste the image in a new Paint file, and then save the file as **Remote** in the Windows10\Review folder provided with your Data Files.

16. Restore your settings by completing the following tasks:
    - Adjust the visual effects on your computer by letting Windows choose what's best for your computer.
    - Turn off ReadyBoost.
    - Return the maximum amount of time Remote Assistance invitations can stay open to its original setting, which is **6** hours by default.

17. Close all open windows.

18. Submit the results of the preceding steps to your instructor, either in printed or electronic form, as requested.

Case Problem 1

APPLY

There are no Data Files needed for this Case Problem.

Hinsley Design   Roberta Hinsley owns a Web design company named Hinsley Design in Corvallis, Oregon. Roberta hired you as a computer specialist and is particularly interested in getting your help to improve the performance of her company's computers. She also wants to know how to find troubleshooting information for problems with Windows Media Player. Complete the following steps, noting your original settings so you can restore them later:

1. Display your computer's Windows Experience Index base score and subscores. Press the Print Screen key to capture an image of the screen. Paste the image in a new Paint file, and then save the file as **Scores** in the Windows10\Case1 folder provided with your Data Files.

2. To improve performance, adjust the visual effects on your computer to deselect settings that involve fading or sliding menus into view, and fading or sliding ToolTips into view. (*Hint:* ToolTips are similar to ScreenTips.) With the Performance Options dialog box open to the appropriate tab, press the Print Screen key to capture an image of the screen. Paste the image in a new Paint file, and then save the file as **Fading** in the Windows10\Case1 folder provided with your Data Files.

3. Open the Event Viewer window and display details about a warning. Press the Print Screen key to capture an image of the screen. Paste the image in a new Paint file, and then save the file as **Warning** in the Windows10\Case1 folder provided with your Data Files.

4. Display a resource overview, including graphs of CPU, Disk, Network, and Memory usage. Press the Print Screen key to capture an image of the screen. Paste the image in a new Paint file, and then save the file as **Resources** in the Windows10\Case1 folder provided with your Data Files.

5. Open the Task Manager window and display the apps and processes running on your computer. Display details about one of the apps in the Details tab. Press the Print Screen key to capture an image of the screen. Paste the image in a new Paint file, and then save the file as **Details** in the Windows10\Case1 folder provided with your Data Files.

6. In the System Information window, display a list of running tasks in the software environment. Press the Print Screen key to capture an image of the screen. Paste the image in a new Paint file, and then save the file as **Tasks** in the Windows10\Case1 folder provided with your Data Files.

7. Attach a USB flash drive to your computer, and then increase the memory capacity of your system by turning on ReadyBoost. Select the minimum amount of available space on your USB flash drive to reserve for boosting your system speed. Press the Print Screen key to capture an image of the dialog box. Paste the image in a new Paint file, and then save the file as **Minimum** in the Windows10\Case1 folder provided with your Data Files.

8. Use a Windows troubleshooter to find troubleshooting information about common problems with settings in the Windows Media Player program. In the wizard, do not have Windows apply repairs automatically. Press the Print Screen key to capture an image of the wizard listing a suggested fix for Windows Media Player settings. Paste the image in a new Paint file, and then save the file as **WMP Settings** in the Windows10\Case1 folder provided with your Data Files.

9. Use the Microsoft Community Web site to find solutions to problems with Windows Media Player settings. Use the Search box as necessary. Display the question and answer with the most helpful votes, and then press the Print Screen key to capture an image of the screen. Paste the image in a new Paint file, and then save the file as **Media Player Solution** in the Windows10\Case1 folder provided with your Data Files.

10. Click a link in the Related Threads section for the solution you found in Step 9. Press the Print Screen key to capture an image of the screen. Paste the image in a new Paint file, and then save the file as **Related Thread** in the Windows10\Case1 folder provided with your Data Files.

11. Start the Windows Remote Assistance Wizard and prepare to send an invitation to your instructor. Press the Print Screen key to capture an image of the open email invitation. Paste the image in a new Paint file, and then save the file as **Remote Invitation** in the Windows10\Case1 folder provided with your Data Files.

12. Restore your settings by adjusting the visual effects so that Windows chooses what's best for your computer. Turn off ReadyBoost.

13. Close all open windows.

14. Submit the results of the preceding steps to your instructor, either in printed or electronic form, as requested.

Case Problem 2

CHALLENGE

There are no Data Files needed for this Case Problem.

Green Clean   Larry Tollinos and George Lybrand are partners in Green Clean, a janitorial service company in Cleveland, Ohio. Larry and George upgraded their computers to Windows 8 a few months ago, and they have noticed that the computers are not running as efficiently as they were when Windows 8 was first installed. As the office manager of Green Clean, you share responsibility for optimizing the computers. Larry asks you to help him improve the performance of his computer and to troubleshoot problems he's having playing video files. Complete the following steps, noting your original settings so you can restore them later:

1. Find the hardware component with the lowest Windows Experience Index subscore on your computer, and then display details about it. Press the Print Screen key to capture an image of the screen. Paste the image in a new Paint file, and then save the file as **Low Subscore** in the Windows10\Case2 folder provided with your Data Files.

✚ **Explore** 2. Find more information about the Windows Experience Index in Windows Help and Support or at the Microsoft Web site. Press the Print Screen key to capture an image of the Web page displaying this information. Paste the image in a new Paint file, and then save the file as **Index Help** in the Windows10\Case2 folder provided with your Data Files.

⊕ **Explore** 3. Open Task Manager to display a list of running apps and processes. Sort the list by memory, with the app or process requiring the most amount of memory at the top of the list. Press the Print Screen key to capture an image of the dialog box. Paste the image in a new Paint file, and then save the file as **High Memory** in the Windows10\Case2 folder provided with your Data Files.

4. Open the Event Viewer window and display details about an error. Press the Print Screen key to capture an image of the screen. Paste the image in a new Paint file, and then save the file as **Error** in the Windows10\Case2 folder provided with your Data Files.

5. Open the Performance Monitor window and graph the percentage of time your processor is working. Add a counter to graph the percentage of paging file usage. Change the color of the % Usage counter to blue. After the Performance Monitor graphs the two counters for a few seconds, press the Print Screen key to capture an image of the screen. Paste the image in a new Paint file, and then save the file as **Performance Counters** in the Windows10\Case2 folder provided with your Data Files.

6. In the System Information window, show details about the display device on your computer. Press the Print Screen key to capture an image of the screen. Paste the image in a new Paint file, and then save the file as **Display Device** in the Windows10\Case2 folder provided with your Data Files.

⊕ **Explore** 7. Open the Action Center window and display the archived problem messages. Double-click a message to display its details, and then press the Print Screen key to capture an image of the screen. Paste the image in a new Paint file, and then save the file as **Problem Details** in the Windows10\Case2 folder provided with your Data Files.

8. Use a Windows troubleshooter to troubleshoot problems with playing DVDs in Windows Media Player. In the wizard, do not have Windows apply repairs automatically. Press the Print Screen key to capture an image of the screen listing the results. Paste the image in a new Paint file, and then save the file as **DVD** in the Windows10\Case2 folder provided with your Data Files.

9. Search the Windows forum at the Microsoft Community Web site for questions and answers about video cards. Select an answer that has at least one helpful vote, and then press the Print Screen key to capture an image of the screen. Paste the image in a new Paint file, and then save the file as **Video Card** in the Windows10\Case2 folder provided with your Data Files.

10. Use the Problem Steps Recorder to record the steps for starting the Windows 8 Video app, selecting a video, and exploring the movie. Save the recorded steps as a file named **Video Steps** in the Windows10\Case2 folder provided with your Data Files.

11. Close all open windows.

12. Submit the results of the preceding steps to your instructor, either in printed or electronic form, as requested.

CHALLENGE

Case Problem 3

There are no Data Files needed for this Case Problem.

Prism Investments   Gail Essex manages Prism Investments in Athens, Georgia, and works primarily on her Windows 8 computer. Recently, she has noticed that new software is running erratically, and that after she shuts down her computer, Windows is slow to start. As her office assistant, you offer to help her solve these problems. Complete the following steps, noting your original settings so you can restore them later:

✦ **Explore** 1. Display basic information about your computer, including its Windows Experience Index base score, subscores, processor, memory, and storage details. Press the Print Screen key to capture an image of the screen. Paste the image in a new Paint file, and then save the file as **System** in the Windows10\Case3 folder provided with your Data Files.

2. In the System Information window, display a list of running tasks. Note the filename of one task listed in the right pane.

✦ **Explore** 3. Open Task Manager to display details about the currently running processes. Sort the processes alphabetically by Name. Click a filename you displayed in the previous step. Arrange the windows on the desktop so you can see the System Information and Task Manager windows clearly. Press the Print Screen key to capture an image of the desktop. Paste the image in a new Paint file, and then save the file as **Running Tasks** in the Windows10\Case3 folder provided with your Data Files.

4. Display system information about print jobs on your computer. Use the Devices and Printers window to display the same information about print jobs on the default printer. Arrange the windows on the desktop so you can see the System Information window and the dialog box showing the print queue. Press the Print Screen key to capture an image of the desktop. Paste the image in a new Paint file, and then save the file as **Print Jobs** in the Windows10\Case3 folder provided with your Data Files.

5. Open the Reliability Monitor and select a day when the reliability index is less than 10. Press the Print Screen key to capture an image of the screen. Paste the image in a new Paint file, and then save the file as **Reliability** in the Windows10\Case3 folder provided with your Data Files.

✦ **Explore** 6. Open the Performance Monitor window and graph the percentage of time your processor is working. Add a Memory counter to graph the percentage of committed bytes in use. Change the color of the Memory counter to green. After the Performance Monitor graphs the two counters for a few seconds, press the Print Screen key to capture an image of the screen. Paste the image in a new Paint file, and then save the file as **Memory Counter** in the Windows10\Case3 folder provided with your Data Files.

7. In the Task Manager window, display the startup programs on your computer. Press the Print Screen key to capture an image of the screen. Paste the image in a new Paint file, and then save the file as **Startup** in the Windows10\Case3 folder provided with your Data Files.

8. Display the Office forum on the Microsoft Community Web site. Display the answer to the Most Important Question currently listed, and then click a link in the More Microsoft Resources section. Press the Print Screen key to capture an image of the screen. Paste the image in a new Paint file, and then save the file as **Office** in the Windows10\Case3 folder provided with your Data Files.

✦ **Explore** 9. Search the Windows forum at the Microsoft Community Web site for information about safe mode. Display one answer to a question about safe mode, and then press the Print Screen key to capture an image of the screen. Paste the image in a new Paint file, and then save the file as **Safe Mode** in the Windows10\Case3 folder provided with your Data Files.

10. Close all open windows.

11. Submit the results of the preceding steps to your instructor, either in printed or electronic form, as requested.

TROUBLESHOOT

Case Problem 4

There are no Data Files needed for this Case Problem.

Enjon Corporation   Jonathon Portman owns Enjon Corporation, an environmental engineering company in Towson, Maryland. He recently set up a small network in his office so he and his staff can share computer resources. Everyone at Enjon Corporation has Windows 8 installed on their computers. Jonathon uses a broadband digital subscriber line (DSL) to connect to the Internet, but the connection is frequently interrupted. His Internet service provider suspects he is having Winsock2 problems. As the Enjon Corporation office manager, you offer to research how to solve Jonathon's Internet connection problems. Complete the following steps:

⚙ **Troubleshoot** 1. Use Windows Help and Support to find information about and suggested solutions for Jonathon's Internet connection problems.

⚙ **Troubleshoot** 2. Search the Microsoft Web resources for similar troubleshooting information, including articles about Winsock2 problems.

3. Use your favorite search engine to find a description of Winsock2.

4. Based on your research, write one to two pages recommending how Jonathon can solve his problem. List the possible causes along with suggested steps to solve his problem. Save the document as **Connection Problem** in the Windows10\Case4 folder provided with your Data Files.

5. Submit the results of the preceding steps to your instructor, either in printed or electronic form, as requested.

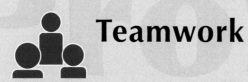

Teamwork

Preparing a Team Presentation

Most of your professional work will likely involve participating in a variety of groups and teams. According to *The American Heritage Dictionary of the English Language*, a team is a "group organized to work together." When you are part of a team, you collaborate with other team members to reach a common goal or outcome. You take advantage of the complementary skills, talents, and abilities that each team member contributes to produce results that are greater than those a single person could achieve. Because so many businesses and other organizations use teams to perform many day-to-day and special tasks, learning to be a contributing member of a successful team is a professional skill everyone needs to develop. Employers look for strong teamwork skills when hiring new employees and promoting current employees to leadership positions.

In this ProSkills exercise, you work with other students as a team to create a presentation that trains other people to use Windows 8. To be effective, your team must be more than a collection of people performing similar tasks. Because a team's efforts center on reaching a goal, your team should start by discussing your goal and brainstorming about how to reach it. Because team members ideally complement each other, your team should also strengthen the bonds between each member. To keep your team running smoothly, keep the following guidelines in mind as you work together to complete tasks:

- Remember that everyone brings something of value to the team.
- Respect and support each other as you work toward the common goal.
- When criticisms or questions arise, try to see them from the other person's perspective before taking offense or jumping to conclusions.
- When a team member needs assistance, seek ways to encourage or support him or her so the team's work is not affected.
- Decide early how the team will keep in touch and communicate with each other.
- Deal with negative or unproductive attitudes immediately so they don't have a negative effect on the team's energy and attitude.
- Get outside assistance if team members can't move beyond the obstacles facing them.
- Provide periodic positive encouragement or rewards for contributions.

PROSKILLS

Training Others to Use Windows 8

Explaining a concept to someone else or teaching a person how to perform a task is often the most effective way to retain information yourself. To make sure you thoroughly understand Windows 8, you can train other people to use it productively. Because you can do so much with Windows 8, a training effort is more practical if you collaborate with other people and form a team. Working as a team, assign tasks for completing the following project:

1. Select the features your team will cover. Each team member should be responsible for at least two Windows 8 features: one general feature (such as the Start screen or the desktop), and one feature covered in Tutorials 7–10 of this book.

2. Select a format for the presentation. For example, you could create a slide show, a series of informative graphics, or an illustrated document.

3. Select the software you will use to create the presentation. For example, you could create a slide show using Microsoft PowerPoint.

4. Based on your selections, prepare a presentation designed to train people how to use Windows 8. Assume your audience has worked with computers before, but not with Windows 8. The purpose of the presentation is to introduce people to Windows 8 features that can increase their efficiency and productivity.

5. Include the following types of information in the presentation:
    *   Title and introduction, including the names of everyone on the team
    *   Graphics, such as diagrams and screen shots, of each Windows tool your team describes
    *   Description of the applications, tools, and other features of Windows 8 you are covering, including their features and benefits
    *   Step-by-step explanations of how to perform a typical task using the application or tool
    *   Conclusion or summary

6. Prepare the presentation as a file your instructor can view.

7. Submit the presentation to your instructor, either in printed or electronic form, as requested.

OBJECTIVES

- Use touch gestures
- Navigate the Start screen
- Use Windows 8 and desktop applications
- Enter text on a touch keyboard
- Adjust touchscreen settings

Using Windows 8 with a Touchscreen Device

Mastering Touch Features in Microsoft Windows 8

If you use a computing device with a touchscreen, you can take advantage of the touch features in Windows 8 to perform all of your computing tasks. For example, you can start apps, switch from one app to another, and organize the Start screen using your finger as a pointing device. With the built-in touch keyboard, you can enter text anywhere you need to, such as in search boxes, email messages, and documents.

Windows 8 is designed to let you use any type of computer to interact with the operating system and applications. For example, you can use a mouse and keyboard connected to a desktop PC, a touchpad on a laptop, a pen or stylus on a slate, or a touchscreen on a tablet. This appendix is designed for people with touchscreen devices. It explains how to use touch gestures to select objects, navigate the computer, and start apps. It also provides step-by-step instructions for using a touch keyboard, interacting with the Start screen and desktop, and using Windows 8 apps and desktop programs. Finally, the appendix describes how to adjust touchscreen settings.

STARTING DATA FILES

There are no starting Data Files needed for this appendix.

Appendix A Visual Overview:

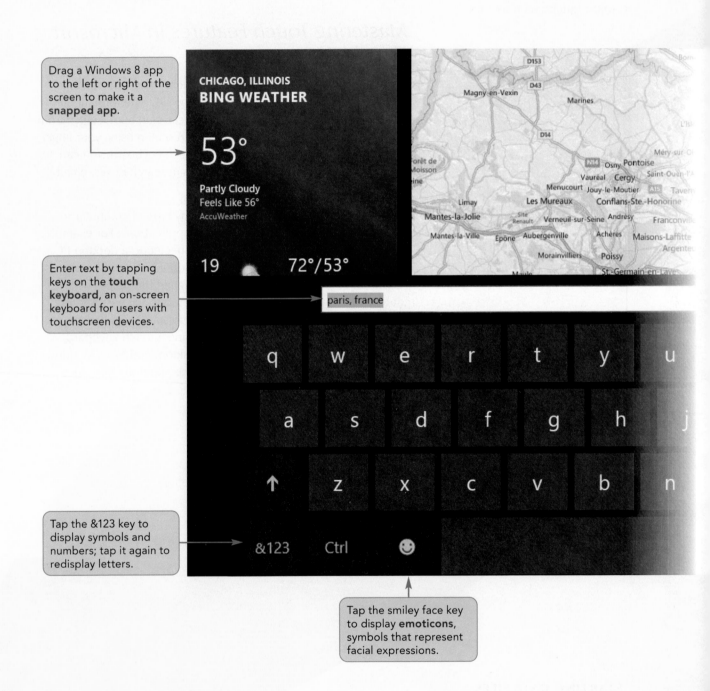

Drag a Windows 8 app to the left or right of the screen to make it a **snapped app**.

Enter text by tapping keys on the **touch keyboard**, an on-screen keyboard for users with touchscreen devices.

Tap the &123 key to display symbols and numbers; tap it again to redisplay letters.

Tap the smiley face key to display **emoticons**, symbols that represent facial expressions.

Using Touch Features

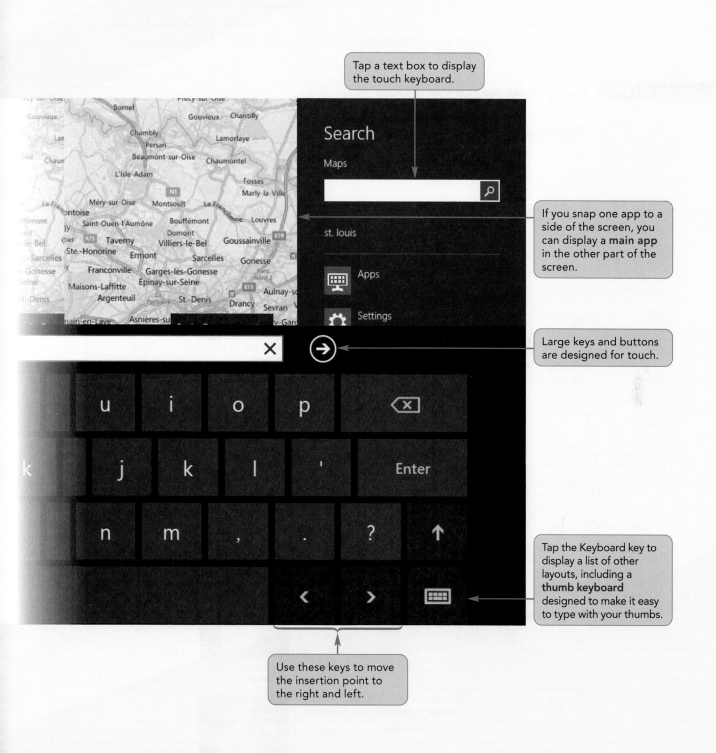

Tap a text box to display the touch keyboard.

If you snap one app to a side of the screen, you can display a **main app** in the other part of the screen.

Large keys and buttons are designed for touch.

Tap the Keyboard key to display a list of other layouts, including a **thumb keyboard** designed to make it easy to type with your thumbs.

Use these keys to move the insertion point to the right and left.

Using Touch Gestures

If you have a computer with a touchscreen, such as a tablet or laptop with a multitouch monitor, you can touch the screen directly to interact with Windows 8. The movements you make as you touch the screen with your fingertips are called **touch gestures**. You use the same touch gesture to perform a particular task in Windows 8 as you do in its applications. For example, to select an item on the Start screen or in a Windows 8 app, you tap the item, which means you use your fingertip to touch the item briefly. The six basic touch gestures are tap, press, swipe, slide or drag, pinch, and rotate. Figure A-1 illustrates these six touch gestures.

Figure A-1	Touch gestures and mouse equivalents

Touch Gesture	Description	Illustration
Tap	Touch an item with a fingertip	Tap **for primary Action**
Press	Touch and hold an item	Press and hold **to learn**
Swipe	Drag a fingertip across the screen and then release	Swipe **to select**
Slide or drag	Drag a fingertip across the screen without releasing	Slide **to pan**
Pinch	Touch the screen with two fingers and then drag your fingertips toward each other	Pinch and stretch **to zoom**
Rotate	Touch the screen with two fingers and then drag either clockwise or counterclockwise	Turn **to rotate**

© 2014 Cengage Learning

In the following steps, you use touch gestures to start the Calendar app, select a date and use other features, and then close the app. To perform these steps, make sure your Windows 8 touchscreen device is turned on and displays the Start screen.

To start and close an app:

1. Tap the **Calendar** tile on the Start screen to open the Calendar app.

2. Tap a date on the calendar to select the date and display its details. See Figure A-2. Your details might differ.

Figure A-2	Details of the selected date

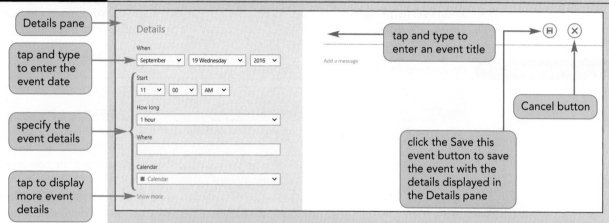

Details pane

tap and type to enter the event date

specify the event details

tap to display more event details

tap and type to enter an event title

Cancel button

click the Save this event button to save the event with the details displayed in the Details pane

3. Press the **Cancel** button ⊗ to display its name in a ScreenTip.

   Trouble? If the Details screen closes, you tapped the Cancel button instead of pressing it. To press the Cancel button, continue touching the button until the ScreenTip appears, and then repeat Steps 2 and 3.

4. Tap the **Cancel** button ⊗ to close the Details screen.

5. Swipe from the bottom edge of the screen toward the center to display the Calendar Apps bar. See Figure A-3.

Figure A-3	Calendar Apps bar

September 2016

Sunday	Monday	Tuesday	Wednesday	Thursday	Friday	Saturday
26	27	28	29	30	31	1
2	3 Labor Day	4	5	6	7	8
9	10	11	12	13	14	15
16	17	18	19	20	21	22
23	24	25	26	27	28	29

tap a button to change the display of the calendar to show the day, week, or month

Apps bar

Day   Week   Month   Today   New

▶ **6.** Tap the **Week** button on the Apps bar to display the Calendar in Week view.

▶ **7.** Drag the top of the Calendar app to the bottom of the screen to close the app.

> **Trouble?** If the Calendar app shrinks instead of closes, press the top edge of the app, drag it down until the app shrinks, continue dragging it to the very bottom of the screen, and then release your finger.

Touch gestures are often more comfortable than mouse actions, but mouse actions are more familiar for most computer users. In general, if you are using a mouse, you locate on-screen items by pointing to the screen corners. If you are using a touch-screen, you swipe from the screen edges. You can use your forefinger and thumb when you need two fingers to gesture. To help you make the transition from mouse to touch, Figure A-4 lists common Windows 8 tasks and their touch and mouse equivalents.

| Figure A-4 | Performing tasks with touch or mouse |

Task	Touch Gesture	Mouse Action
Display a ScreenTip	Press an object such as a button	Point to an object such as a button
Display an Apps bar	Swipe from the top or bottom of the screen toward the center	Right-click the bottom edge of the screen
Display the Charms bar	Swipe from the right edge of the screen toward the center	Point to the upper-right or lower-right corner of the screen
Display thumbnails of open apps (the Switch List)	Swipe from the left edge of the screen toward the center	Point to the upper-left corner of the screen
Drag an object	Touch, hold, and then drag	Click, hold, and then drag
Scroll the Start screen	Swipe from the right edge of the screen to the left	Click the scroll arrows, or drag the scroll bar
Select an object or perform an action such as starting an app	Tap the object	Click the object
Zoom	Pinch two fingers to zoom in or move the fingers apart to zoom out	Click the Zoom button

© 2014 Cengage Learning

Navigating the Start Screen

The Start screen is where you begin your work in Windows 8. The Start screen is designed to be especially easy to use on touchscreen devices. To start apps, use Windows 8 tools, and navigate from one app to another, you use the touch gestures described in the previous section of this appendix. In the following sets of steps, you perform some of the same tasks using touch gestures that you have already performed with a mouse: scroll and zoom the Start screen, switch between two apps, and snap an app to a side of the screen. When you use two or more fingers to manipulate objects, you are using the **multitouch** feature of Windows 8.

To navigate the Start screen:

▶ **1.** Touch the right side of the screen and then swipe your finger to the left side of the screen. The Start screen scrolls to show additional tiles not displayed on the main Start screen.

Trouble? If the screen does not scroll, your Start screen does not contain additional tiles.

▶ **2.** Touch the left side of the screen and then swipe to the right to scroll back to the main Start screen.

▶ **3.** Touch a blank part of the Start screen with your forefinger and thumb, and then pinch them together to zoom out and reduce the size of the tiles. See Figure A-5.

Figure A-5 **Zoomed Start screen**

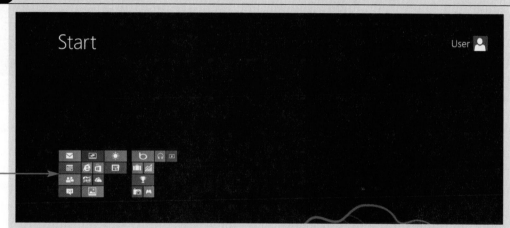

tiles are reduced in size

▶ **4.** Touch a blank part of the Start screen with your forefinger and thumb again, and then move them apart to zoom in and increase the size of the tiles.

Next, you start two apps, use the Charms bar to return to the Start screen, and then switch from one app to another.

To switch between apps:

▶ **1.** On the Start screen, tap the **Weather** tile to start the Weather app, which displays the current weather conditions in a specified location and provides a five-day forecast.

Trouble? If a message appears asking whether you want to turn on location services and allow Weather to use your location, tap the Block button.

▶ **2.** Swipe from the right side of the screen toward the center to display the Charms bar. See Figure A-6. The information displayed in your Weather app will differ from Figure A-6.

Trouble? If your Charms bar is active, status information such as the current date and time appear on the left side of the screen.

Figure A-6	Charms bar and Weather app

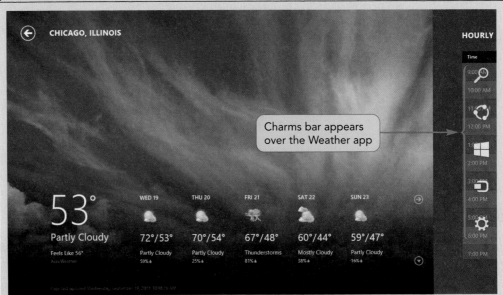

3. Tap the **Start** button on the Charms bar to return to the Start screen.

4. Tap the **Maps** tile to start the Maps app, which displays a map of a specified location.

   Trouble? If a message appears asking whether you want to turn on location services and allow Maps to use your location, tap the Block button.

5. Swipe from the left side of the screen toward the center to switch to the Weather app.

6. Slide a finger from the left side of the screen and then swipe back to the left (quickly tracing a ">" with your finger) to display the Switch List, which includes thumbnails of the other open application and the Start screen. See Figure A-7.

Figure A-7	Switch List

7. Tap the **Maps** thumbnail to switch to the Maps app.

Finally, you can snap an app to the screen. When you snap an app, you reduce it to a pane on the left or right side of the screen. If another app is open, it appears in the rest of the screen and is called the main app. You can drag the separator bar between the snapped app and the main app to change the amount of screen each app occupies. Your touchscreen device must be using a screen resolution of at least 1366 × 768 to snap apps.

The easiest way to snap an app is to display it on the screen and then drag it to the right or left, which is the technique you use in the following steps.

To snap an app:

1. Swipe from the left side of the screen toward the center to switch to the Weather app.

2. Drag the **Weather** app from the top of the screen down until the app appears as a large thumbnail, and then drag the thumbnail to the left until it expands and snaps to the left side of the screen.

   Trouble? If the Weather app did not snap to the left side of the screen, your screen resolution is probably not high enough to snap apps.

3. Swipe from the left and then back to display the Switch List, and then tap the Maps app to display it as the main app. See Figure A-8.

Figure A-8	Weather app snapped to the left side of the screen

Maps is the main app

Weather is the snapped app

According to Microsoft, Windows 8 apps running in the background don't slow down your computer the way desktop applications do. You can open Windows 8 apps and leave them running without affecting the performance of your computer. If you don't use an open Windows 8 app for a period of time, Windows eventually closes it. However, if the Switch List becomes crowded or you have to swipe many times to find the open app you want to work with, it's a good idea to close apps. In the following steps, you close the snapped Weather app and the main Maps app.

To close Windows 8 apps:

▶ **1.** Drag the top of the **Maps** app down to the bottom of the screen to close it.

▶ **2.** Drag the top of the **Weather** app down to the bottom of the screen to close it and display the Start screen.

Using Windows 8 Apps

Windows 8 provides a number of apps when you install the operating system. These apps use the streamlined Modern design, which features large, clear text and an uncluttered workspace. Windows 8 apps do not run in windows the way desktop applications do; instead, they expand to cover the entire screen unless you snap them. For example, Figure A-9 shows the Windows 8 version of Internet Explorer with its clean interface and touch-friendly controls.

Figure A-9	Windows 8 Internet Explorer

In addition to the built-in Windows 8 apps, you can purchase and download Windows 8 apps from the **Windows Store**, a Web site where Microsoft developers and independent programmers showcase Windows 8 apps they designed and posted. If you are connected to the Internet, you can visit the Windows Store by selecting the Store tile on the Start screen. Because Microsoft wants to protect Windows 8 apps from security threats by restricting them to a central distribution site, the Windows Store is the only place to purchase Windows 8 apps.

Using a Touch Keyboard

If you do not have a physical keyboard attached to your touchscreen device, you can use the touch keyboard, which is a keyboard that appears on the screen when you need to enter text. For example, you can use the touch keyboard to enter a search term on the Search menu and type text in any Windows 8 or desktop application. As you type, Windows suggests complete words that begin with the letters you typed, a feature called **AutoComplete**.

In addition to typing letters and common punctuation symbols such as the question mark (?) and period (.), you can tap the Symbols and numbers key (marked as &123) to display symbols such as an ampersand (&) and numbers from 0 to 9. If you are writing an email or a chat message, for example, you can tap the Smiley key to display smiley face symbols and emoticons, combinations of keyboard symbols that represent facial expressions. In informal messages, you can insert smiley face symbols and emoticons to express your mood or to help readers interpret the text.

To display the touch keyboard, tap a text box or another location where you want to enter text. In the following steps, you use the touch keyboard to search for a location in the Maps app.

To use the touch keyboard with the Search menu:

1. On the Start screen, swipe from the right to the center of the screen to display the Charms bar.

2. Tap the **Search** button to display the Search menu.

3. Tap the **Search** box to display a full-size touch keyboard. See Figure A-10.

| Figure A-10 | Full-size touch keyboard |

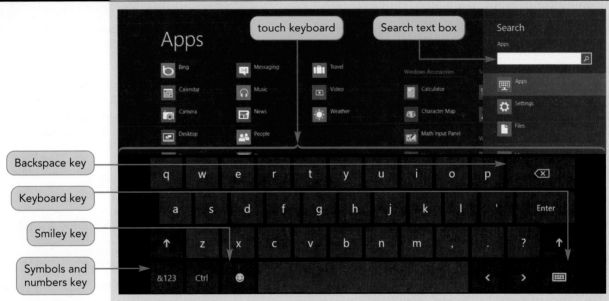

4. Tap the keys on the touch keyboard to enter **paris, france** in the Search box.

   Trouble? If you make a typing error, tap the Backspace key in the upper-right corner of the keyboard to delete the error and then retype.

5. Tap **Maps** on the Search menu to display Paris, France, in the Maps app. See Figure A-11.

TIP

Use the left and right arrow keys (< and >) to move the insertion point through the text you typed.

Figure A-11	Searching for Paris, France, in the Maps app

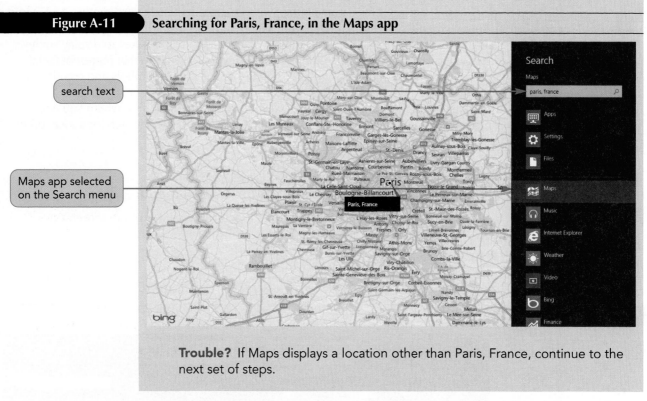

search text

Maps app selected
on the Search menu

Trouble? If Maps displays a location other than Paris, France, continue to the next set of steps.

The touch keyboard has two layouts: the full-size keyboard with large buttons and a split thumb keyboard. The full-size keyboard is designed for typing when your touchscreen device is on a surface such as a table or desk. The thumb keyboard, which splits the keyboard into three sections, is ideal when you are holding your touchscreen device with both hands and want to type with your thumbs.

TIP

When you're working on the desktop, tap where you want to enter text, and then tap the keyboard icon on the taskbar to display the touch keyboard.

To use the thumb keyboard:

1. Swipe from the right to display the Charms bar, and then tap the **Search** button to display the Search menu.

2. Tap the **Search** box to display the full-size touch keyboard.

3. Tap the **Keyboard** key ⌨ in the lower-right corner of the touch keyboard to display a list of layouts.

4. Tap the **Split keyboard** button ⌨ to display the thumb keyboard. See Figure A-12.

Figure A-12 **Thumb keyboard**

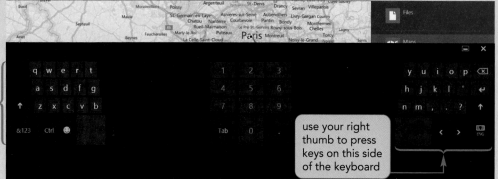

use your left thumb to press keys on this side of the keyboard

use your right thumb to press keys on this side of the keyboard

▶ **5.** Tap the keys on the thumb keyboard to type **helsi** in the Search box. As you type, Windows suggests complete words that begin with those letters.

▶ **6.** Tap **helsinki** in the list of suggestions to display a map of Finland with Helsinki identified.

Trouble? If a list of suggestions does not appear, type *helsinki* and then tap the Search button .

▶ **7.** Swipe from the right to display the Charms bar, and then tap the **Start** button to return to the Start screen.

Adjusting Touch Keyboard Settings

When you use a touch keyboard, Windows 8 applies the following settings by default:

- Shows text suggestions as you type
- Adds a space after you choose a text suggestion
- Adds a period after you double-tap the Spacebar
- Capitalizes the first letter of each sentence
- Uses all uppercase letters when you double-tap the Shift key
- Plays key sounds as you type
- Makes the standard keyboard layout available

To change a touch keyboard setting, you use the PC settings screen, which you can access on the Settings menu.

To display the touch keyboard settings:

▶ **1.** Swipe from the right to the center of the screen to display the Charms bar.

▶ **2.** Tap the **Settings** button to display the Settings menu.

▶ **3.** Tap **Change PC settings** to display the PC settings screen.

▶ **4.** In the left pane, tap **General** to display General settings on the right.

▶ **5.** Slide down to scroll the General settings and display the Touch keyboard section. See Figure A-13.

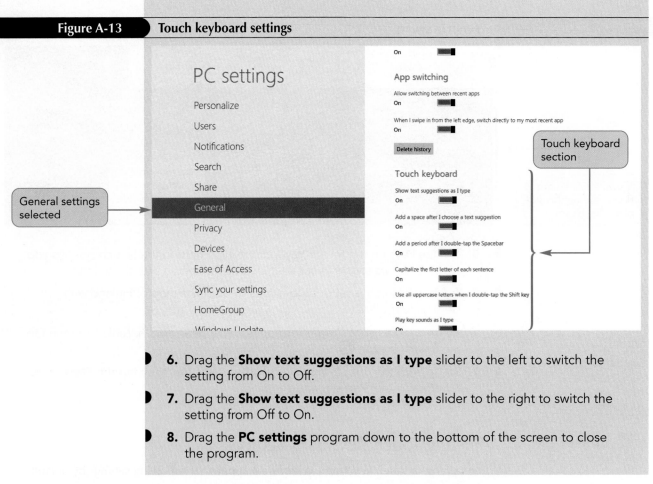

Figure A-13   Touch keyboard settings

General settings selected

Touch keyboard section

> **6.** Drag the **Show text suggestions as I type** slider to the left to switch the setting from On to Off.

> **7.** Drag the **Show text suggestions as I type** slider to the right to switch the setting from Off to On.

> **8.** Drag the **PC settings** program down to the bottom of the screen to close the program.

You change other PC settings the same way: by dragging the slider from right to left to enable a setting, and from left to right to disable a setting.

Interacting with the Desktop

Touch gestures work on the desktop just as they do on the Start screen. You tap the File Explorer button on the taskbar to display a folder window, tap an icon in the Navigation pane, and then double-tap (tap twice quickly) to open a file or folder in the right pane. You also tap a button on the ribbon to change the view, select a setting, and perform other File Explorer tasks.

One feature unique to touchscreen devices is the technique you use to select files. By default on a touchscreen device, files and folders are displayed in File Explorer with a check box to their left. You tap a check box to select the corresponding file or folder. This feature is especially useful if you are selecting more than one file or folder. For example, if you want to copy a few files, tap the check box next to each file, tap the Home tab (if necessary), and then tap the Copy button in the Clipboard group.

In the following sets of steps, you use touch gestures to explore the desktop. You display the desktop, open a shortcut menu, start File Explorer, navigate to a folder, and change the view of the icons in a folder window.

To display the desktop and open a shortcut menu:

▶ **1.** On the Start screen, tap the **Desktop** tile to display the desktop.

▶ **2.** Press the **Recycle Bin** icon on the desktop (that is, touch the icon and keep your finger pressed down).

▶ **3.** When a box appears around the icon, lift your finger to display the shortcut menu, which lists all the actions you can take with the Recycle Bin icon. See Figure A-14. For example, you can open the Recycle Bin, empty it, or display its properties.

| Figure A-14 | Recycle Bin shortcut menu |

Recycle Bin icon is selected

box appears around the icon

shortcut menu

▶ **4.** Tap a blank spot on the desktop to close the shortcut menu.

Next, you can start File Explorer, navigate to the Computer folder, and then change the view of the icons in that folder window.

To use File Explorer:

▶ **1.** Tap the **File Explorer** button on the taskbar to start File Explorer and display the standard libraries.

▶ **2.** In the Navigation pane, tap the **Desktop** icon to display the resources available from the desktop.

▶ **3.** In the right pane, double-tap the **Computer** icon to display the drives and devices on the computer.

▶ **4.** Tap the **Expand the Ribbon** button to expand the ribbon.

▶ **5.** Tap the **View** tab on the ribbon, and then tap **Medium icons** in the Layout group to display the drive icons in Medium icons view. See Figure A-15. The icons on your screen might differ.

Trouble? If the Details pane or Preview pane is open in the Computer window, your screen will look different from the figure, though the size of the icons should be the same.

Figure A-15   **Drive icons in Medium icons view**

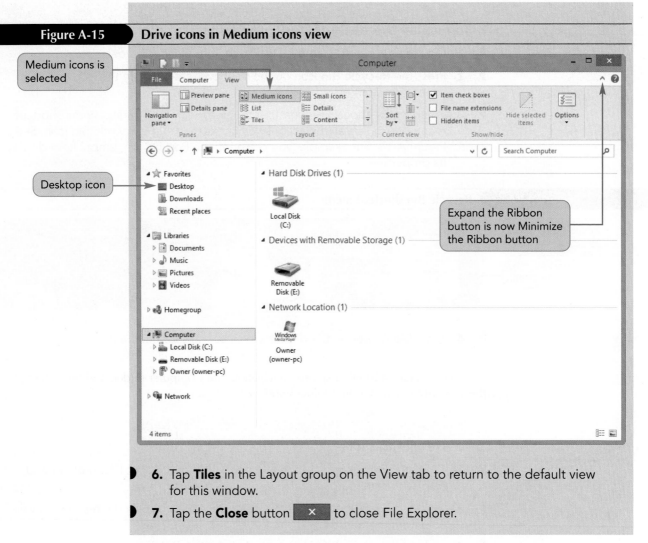

6. Tap **Tiles** in the Layout group on the View tab to return to the default view for this window.

7. Tap the **Close** button [×] to close File Explorer.

In this appendix, you learned how to use touch gestures to interact with Windows 8 on a touchscreen device, such as a tablet computer. You navigated the Start screen, started Windows 8 apps, switched from one app to another, and used two types of touch keyboards. You also used touch gestures while working with the classic desktop and File Explorer.

APPENDIX B

Exploring Additional Windows 8 Tools

OBJECTIVES

- Explore the Bing and Messaging apps
- Examine PC settings that sync data, protect data, and manage storage
- Set AutoPlay defaults and change the sound scheme
- Specify file and application defaults, Family Safety options, and credentials
- Use Ease of Access options
- Compare Windows 8 and Windows RT

Using Windows 8 Apps and Tools

Windows 8 provides a wealth of apps and tools for maintaining and enjoying your computer and for working productively. You have already used most of the built-in Windows 8 apps, such as Mail, People, and Calendar. You have also used tools provided on the PC settings screen, such as those that set the color and design of the Start screen, and in the Control Panel System and Security, Network and Internet, Hardware and Sound, Programs, User Accounts and Family Safety, and Appearance and Personalization categories.

In this appendix, you will learn about Windows 8 Bing and Messaging apps as well as additional PC settings that give you even greater control over your Windows 8 environment. You will use a System and Security tool called BitLocker Drive Encryption and then work with other tools in the Hardware and Sound category to set AutoPlay options and customize sound schemes. You will also examine how to select default applications and protect your computer by setting family safety options and managing credentials, which are the passwords you use frequently. To optimize your Windows experience, you will use Ease of Access tools, including those that make the computer easier to use. Finally, you will learn about Windows RT, short for Windows Runtime, which is specially designed for tablet computers and other small mobile devices, and then compare it to the Windows 8 edition, which you have used throughout this book.

STARTING DATA FILES

There are no starting Data Files needed for this appendix.

Appendix B Visual Overview:

One useful System and Security tool is **BitLocker Drive Encryption** (or **BitLocker**), which protects the data on hard drives and removable drives.

Use the Control Panel to change settings that control nearly everything about how Windows looks and works.

Select **Family Safety** settings to help manage how children use the computer.

AutoPlay is a Hardware and Sound feature that lets you choose which program to use to play media.

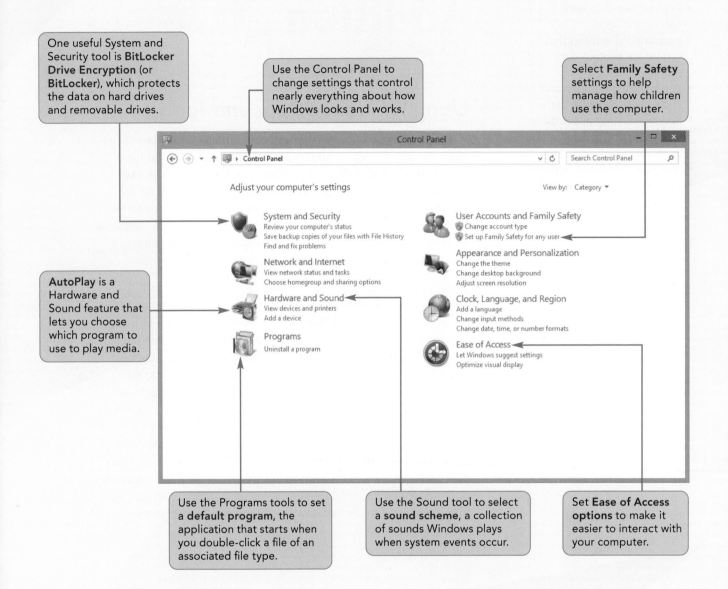

Use the Programs tools to set a **default program**, the application that starts when you double-click a file of an associated file type.

Use the Sound tool to select a **sound scheme**, a collection of sounds Windows plays when system events occur.

Set **Ease of Access options** to make it easier to interact with your computer.

Windows 8 and Control Panel Tools

Set preferences for working with **notifications**, messages that appear on the screen when apps and system tools need your attention.

By default, Windows 8 syncs settings with other Windows 8 computers.

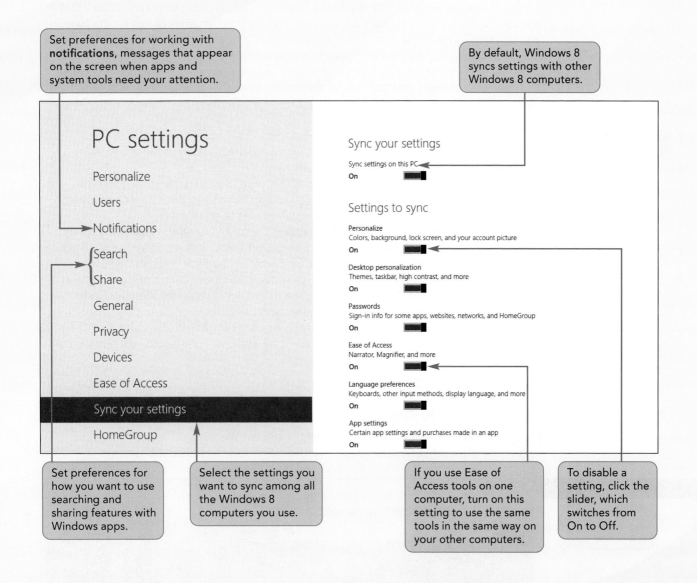

Set preferences for how you want to use searching and sharing features with Windows apps.

Select the settings you want to sync among all the Windows 8 computers you use.

If you use Ease of Access tools on one computer, turn on this setting to use the same tools in the same way on your other computers.

To disable a setting, click the slider, which switches from On to Off.

Exploring the Bing App

Bing is the Microsoft search engine you can use to search for information on the Web. Instead of starting Internet Explorer on the Start screen or the desktop, you can start the Windows 8 Bing app from the Start screen. As you enter search text, the Bing app presents suggested search expressions as tiles, which are easier to select than lines of text if you are using a touchscreen device. Search results are also displayed as tiles that include the Web page title, the Web address, and the first two lines of text on the page. You can scroll from left to right to browse the results and then click a tile to display the full Web page in IE Windows 8. If your screen resolution is 1366 x 768 or higher, you can snap the Bing app to one side of the screen, where it appears as a panel, and leave IE Windows 8 open in the main part of the screen. With this arrangement, you can click a tile in the Bing app and display the page in IE Windows 8 without leaving the search results.

If you search for images rather than Web pages, Bing displays the results as a collage. Click an image in the results to display a full-size version of the image with a thumbnail of the Web page displaying the image.

If you want to find out what topics are popular right now, you can click a **trending** topic or the More button at the bottom of the screen. When you click the More button, Bing displays tiles that preview topics of recent interest to other users.

Unlike the Bing search engine, the Bing app is connected to other Windows 8 apps, including Maps, Weather, News, Finance, Sports, and Travel. Use the Bing app to search for the weather forecast in a particular city, for example. The search results include a tile you can click to start the Weather app, which shows the current conditions and forecast for the city you specified. In addition, Bing and its connected apps are designed to be faster and more responsive than search engines you use in Internet Explorer.

In the following steps, you use the Bing app to search for information about Windows 8. Information on the Web changes frequently, so your results will differ from those shown in the steps.

To use the Bing app:

1. On the Start screen, click the **Bing** tile to start the Bing app. See Figure B-1. The photo that Bing displays changes daily, so your photo will differ.

| Figure B-1 | Bing app |

text box for search text

More button

click to display information about this photo

trending topics

▶ **2.** Click the text box to display tiles containing search terms that are popular now, and then type **win**. Bing suggests a few search terms that start with "win," such as "windows 8" and "windows update."

Trouble? If "windows 8" does not appear as a suggested term, continue typing "windows 8" until it does appear as a suggested term.

▶ **3.** Click the **windows 8** search suggestion to display tiles containing the search results. See Figure B-2.

Figure B-2	Search results in the Bing app

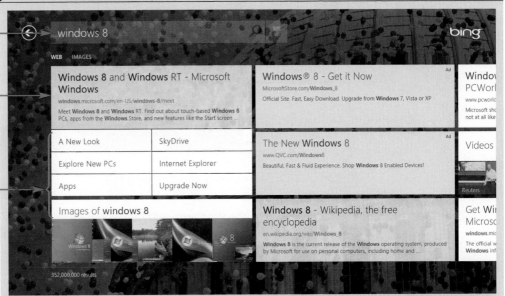

"windows 8" selected as the search term

Web page containing the search term

categories of Windows 8 Web pages

▶ **4.** Click the first tile in the search results to open the Web page in IE Windows 8.

▶ **5.** Point to the upper-left corner of the screen, and then click the **Bing** thumbnail to return to the Bing app while leaving IE Windows 8 open and running.

▶ **6.** Below the text box, click **IMAGES** to display images related to Windows 8.

▶ **7.** Point to the top of the screen until a hand pointer 🖑 appears, and then drag the Bing app to the left to snap it to the left side of the screen.

Trouble? If you are not using a screen resolution of 1366 × 768 or higher, you cannot snap apps to the side of the screen. Skip Step 7, and keep in mind that your results will not match the figure at the end of the steps.

▶ **8.** Point to the upper-left corner of the screen, and then click the **Internet Explorer** thumbnail to display the Web page in IE Windows 8 in the main part of the screen.

▶ **9.** In the Bing app, click **WEB** to display Web pages in the search results.

▶ **10.** Point to the lower-right corner of the Bing app until a minus sign button appears, and then click the **minus sign** button 🔳 to display tiles of search terms related to your original search term, "windows 8." Click a tile in the search results to display a list of Web pages related to the term.

▶ **11.** Click a tile in the search results to display the Web page in IE Windows 8. See Figure B-3.

Figure B-3	Viewing results and a Web page at the same time

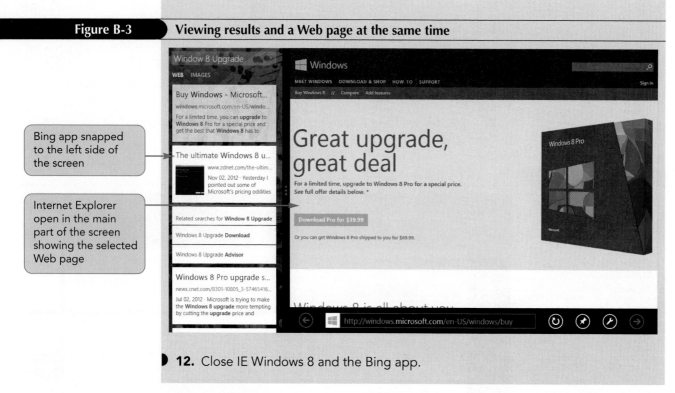

Bing app snapped to the left side of the screen

Internet Explorer open in the main part of the screen showing the selected Web page

▶ **12.** Close IE Windows 8 and the Bing app.

You can also use the Bing app with the Search menu. Display the Charms bar, click the Search charm, enter your search text, and then click Bing on the Search menu.

Exploring the Messaging App

The Windows 8 Messaging app lets you send and receive instant messages, or chat. An **instant message (IM)** is an online text-based conversation between two or more people using computers. Unlike email messages, which collect in your electronic mailbox until you view them, you exchange IMs in **real time**, which means the actual time you are sending and receiving messages. You can exchange IMs only if you and your contact are online at the same time. As you and your contact exchange IMs, you have an online conversation, also called a **thread**.

The Messaging app works with the People app so you can exchange IMs using the email addresses and other contact information stored on your computer. When you click the New message button in the Messaging app, the People app opens and displays available contacts. These are contacts currently online and connected to a service compatible with the one that Messaging uses. By default, the Messaging app uses the Windows Messenger service in your Microsoft account for instant messaging. You can also connect your Microsoft account to your Facebook account so you can chat with your Facebook friends using the Messaging app.

The Messaging app screen is divided into two panes: the Threads pane and the Messages pane. See Figure B-4.

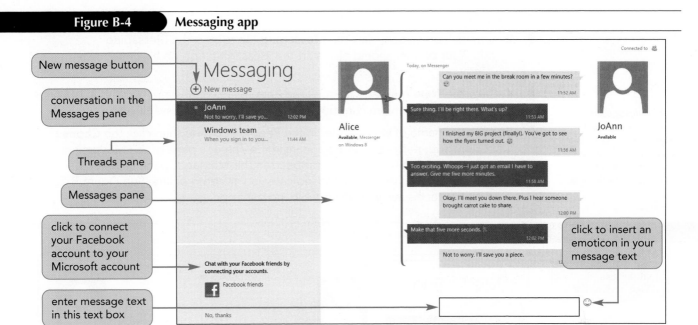

Figure B-4 Messaging app

- New message button
- conversation in the Messages pane
- Threads pane
- Messages pane
- click to connect your Facebook account to your Microsoft account
- enter message text in this text box
- click to insert an emoticon in your message text

The Threads pane lists the conversation threads you have with your contacts. The IMs in the selected thread appear in the Messages pane along with your contact's user picture and your user picture. You enter an IM in the text box that appears at the bottom of the Messages pane. The IM can include text and emoticons, which are small graphics that illustrate a concept, provide an example, or reflect your mood, such as a smiley face. You press the Enter key to send the IM, and your contact receives it instantly. If the Messaging app is running in the background when you receive an IM, a notification appears in the upper-right corner of the screen displaying the contact's name and message text. You can also snap the Messaging app to the screen if your screen resolution is 1366 × 768 or higher, so you can keep track of your IMs as you do other tasks.

To perform the following steps, you must be signed in to Windows using a Microsoft account. You should be working with a partner who is also signed in to his or her Microsoft account so you can exchange messages. In the following steps, you start by adding your partner's email address to the People app.

TIP

Another way to chat is to invite someone by right-clicking the Messaging screen to display the Apps bar and then clicking the Invite button.

To exchange IMs using the Messaging app:

1. On the Start screen, click the **People** tile to start the People app.

   Trouble? If you haven't signed in using your Microsoft account, a screen appears where you can enter your email address and the password for your Microsoft account.

2. Right-click the screen to display the Apps bar, click the **New** button to add contact information, and then enter your partner's name and email address. Click the **Save** button, and then close the People app.

   Trouble? If your People app already includes your partner's name and email address, skip Step 2.

3. On the Start screen, click the **Messaging** tile to start the Messaging app. Your partner should also start the Messaging app on his or her own computer.

4. Click the **New message** button. The People app opens and displays a list of your contacts who are currently online and using the Messaging app.

5. Click the name of your partner in the People app, and then click the **Choose** button. Your partner's name appears in the Threads pane of the Messaging app and his or her user picture appears in the Messages pane. A green bar appears in each user picture to indicate you are both online. See Figure B-5. If the contact is away or unavailable, no bar appears.

Figure B-5	Selecting a contact for chatting

green bar indicates that this user is online and available

contact using the Messaging app

current user on this computer

click to display a gallery of emoticons

type a message or response here

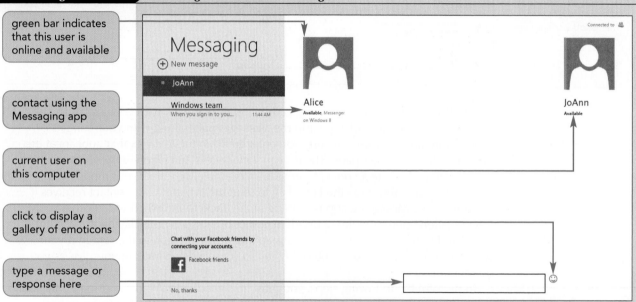

6. If necessary, click the text box at the bottom of the Messages pane, and then type a message, such as **Can you meet me in the break room in a few minutes?**.

7. Click the **Emoticon** icon 😊, click an emoticon to insert it in the text box, and then press the **Enter** key to send the IM.

8. If necessary, ask your partner to respond to the IM. The IM you receive appears in the Messages pane.

9. Close the Messaging app.

Keep in mind that you can add your friends and contacts from Facebook, Twitter, Outlook, and LinkedIn to your People app, so all of these contacts can be available for chatting in the Messaging app.

Changing PC Settings

The PC settings screen lists 13 categories of system settings you can select to customize Windows 8 according to your preferences. You have already selected preferences in many of these categories. This section discusses settings in the Notifications, Search, Share, Privacy, and Sync your settings categories. To display the PC settings screen, you select the Settings charm on the Charms bar and then click the Change PC settings link on the Settings menu.

Notifications are messages that appear onscreen when apps and system tools need your attention. By default, Windows displays app notifications on the Start screen, desktop, and lock screen and plays a sound to alert you when a notification appears. The apps that display notifications include Calendar, Mail, Music, and Store. In the following steps, you turn off notifications from the Music app to reduce the number of distractions that appear as you work.

To turn off a Notification setting:

▶ **1.** Display the Charms bar, click the **Settings** charm, and then click **Change PC settings** to display the PC settings screen.

▶ **2.** In the left pane, click **Notifications** to display the Notifications category of settings. See Figure B-6.

| Figure B-6 | Notifications category of settings |

general notification settings

settings for notifications from specific Windows 8 apps

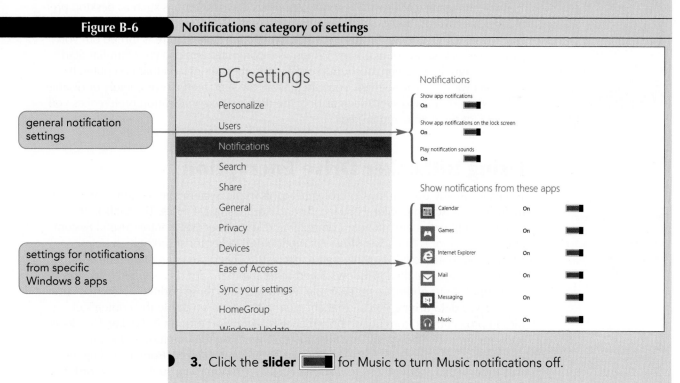

▶ **3.** Click the **slider** for Music to turn Music notifications off.

You work with the Search and Share settings in a similar way. In the Search category, you can set preferences for your search history and choose which Windows 8 apps you want to search, including Bing, Internet Explorer, Mail, Maps, and People. Recall that the Search menu includes a search text box; the Apps, Settings, and Files categories; and a list of apps you can search. By default, Windows displays the apps you search most at the top of the apps list on the Search menu. Windows also saves your search text as a suggestion for later searches. These settings are turned on by default; you click a slider to turn the setting off. You can also click the Delete history button to delete your search history, which is all of the search text you've used with the Search feature.

In the Share category, you set preferences for sharing files and information among apps and specify which apps can share, such as Mail, People, and SkyDrive. When you install other Windows 8 apps that can share, they also appear in the apps list in the Share category of the PC settings screen. When you are working in an app that can share information, such as SkyDrive, you can select a photo, for example, and then use the Share charm to display a list of Windows apps with which you can share the photo, including Mail and People. By default, Windows displays the apps you use most often and share most often at the top of this list, which includes up to five apps. You can change the number of apps the list displays or clear the list altogether.

The Privacy category lists settings you can turn on and off to protect your privacy or to share private information. For example, when you start the Maps apps, it shows your location by default. If you don't want the Maps app to show your location, you can turn off the Let apps use my location setting in the Privacy category.

If you are using a Microsoft account, Windows 8 syncs settings such as desktop preferences, passwords, and browser favorites with other Windows 8 computers by default. (See the Visual Overview for this appendix.) When the sync feature is turned on, you can sign in to your account on any Windows 8 computer and use your familiar Start screen design, lock screen, account picture, and other settings on that computer. If you don't want to sync settings, you can turn off the sync feature completely or disable only certain settings to sync, such as only the desktop personalization preferences you selected for the theme and taskbar.

Using BitLocker Drive Encryption

TIP

BitLocker is available for Windows 8 Pro and Enterprise editions, but not Windows Core or Windows RT editions.

You have already used many Control Panel tools in the System and Security category, including the Action Center, File History, and Administrative Tools. The tools in this category help you maintain your computer and keep it secure. Another useful System and Security tool is BitLocker Drive Encryption (BitLocker for short), which helps protect your data from loss, theft, and hackers. BitLocker can encrypt the entire hard drive where you installed Windows 8 and other internal hard drives where you store only applications and data, for example. Windows calls these additional internal hard drives **fixed data drives**. (Recall that encrypting means to scramble the contents of files to protect them from unauthorized access.) After you turn on BitLocker, Windows locks the drive by encrypting any files you save on that drive, including documents, passwords, and temporary files. The encryption prevents hackers from accessing the files they might otherwise use to discover sensitive information, such as passwords to financial accounts. When BitLocker is turned on, you can still sign in to Windows and use your files as you normally do.

To protect data on removable media such as USB flash drives and external hard drives, you can use BitLocker To Go. When you turn on BitLocker To Go, Windows locks the removable drive by encrypting all of its personal and system files.

Creating BitLocker Credentials

When you turn on BitLocker or BitLocker To Go for the first time, Windows asks you to create credentials to use for unlocking the drive. The credentials can be a password you create that includes uppercase and lowercase letters, numbers, spaces, and symbols. As an alternative, you can use a personal identification number (PIN) and a **smart card** (also called a **security card**), which is a plastic card containing a computer chip encoded with identifying information. To use a smart card, you need a **card reader**, which is a hardware device installed in or connected to your computer. In case you lose the smart card or forget your password, Windows also generates a **recovery key**, a string of 48 random characters that allows access to a locked drive. If you cannot provide the password, smart card, or recovery key, you lose access to the files on the drive, so be sure to store your credentials in a safe place and keep track of where you stored them.

A typical scenario involves a computer where Windows is installed on an internal hard drive, such as drive C, and a fixed data drive, such as drive D. In that case, if you turn on BitLocker for both drives, you can unlock drive D automatically when you sign in to Windows by providing the name and password for your user account. BitLocker still generates a recovery key for you in case you can't sign in for some reason.

Turning BitLocker On and Off

To use BitLocker to encrypt the internal hard drive where Windows is installed, your computer must have two partitions: a system, or boot, partition (which contains the files needed to start your computer) and an operating system partition (which contains Windows). BitLocker encrypts the operating system partition and then leaves the system partition unencrypted so your computer can start. The first time you turn on BitLocker, Windows creates these partitions for you, if necessary, using 200 MB of available disk space for the system partition.

When you start the computer, BitLocker checks for any conditions that might present a security risk, such as changes to a startup file. If it detects a potential security risk, BitLocker locks the internal hard drive where Windows is installed. To unlock the drive and access its files, you can enter the password, insert the smart card into the card reader and enter the PIN, or enter the recovery key.

To detect changes to the startup process on the operating system drive, BitLocker uses a **Trusted Platform Module (TPM)** component. The TPM is a microchip your computer needs to take advantage of advanced security features, such as BitLocker. If you want to use BitLocker to protect your Windows drive, check the information that came with your computer to make sure the TPM is installed.

When you turn on BitLocker To Go for a removable drive, BitLocker encrypts the entire drive. If you take the removable drive out of one computer and plug it into another, BitLocker requests your credentials. After entering the correct password, smart card and PIN, or recovery key, you can open and save files on the drive the way you normally do.

You can turn off BitLocker at any time, either temporarily by suspending it or permanently by decrypting the drive.

In the following steps, you turn on BitLocker To Go for a USB flash drive.

To turn on BitLocker To Go for a USB flash drive:

1. If necessary, insert a USB flash drive into a USB port on your computer, and then close the PC settings screen.

2. Open the Control Panel in Category view, click **System and Security**, and then click **BitLocker Drive Encryption** to open the BitLocker Drive Encryption window. See Figure B-7.

Figure B-7	BitLocker Drive Encryption window

click to turn on BitLocker for the system drive

click an expand button to display a link for turning on BitLocker for a removable drive

3. If necessary, click the **expand** button ✔ for your USB flash drive, and then click the **Turn on BitLocker** link next to your USB flash drive. Windows initializes BitLocker and then starts the BitLocker Setup Wizard. In the first dialog box of the wizard, you select how you want to unlock the drive. See Figure B-8.

   Trouble? If a User Account Control dialog box opens requesting a password or your permission to continue, enter the password or click the Yes button.

Figure B-8 Selecting how to unlock a drive

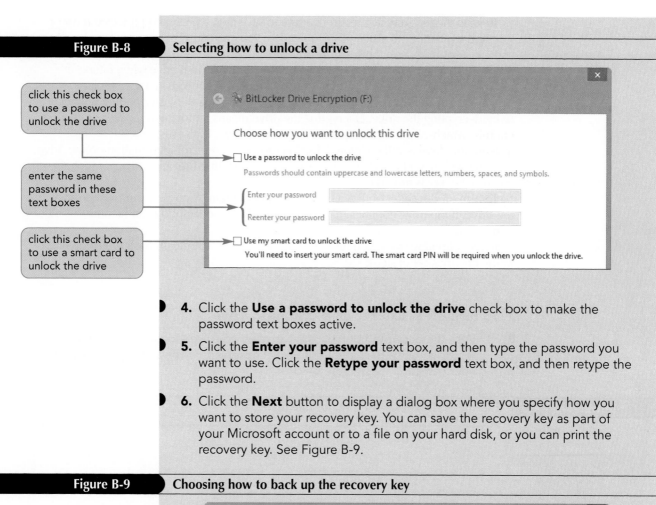

click this check box to use a password to unlock the drive

enter the same password in these text boxes

click this check box to use a smart card to unlock the drive

▶ **4.** Click the **Use a password to unlock the drive** check box to make the password text boxes active.

▶ **5.** Click the **Enter your password** text box, and then type the password you want to use. Click the **Retype your password** text box, and then retype the password.

▶ **6.** Click the **Next** button to display a dialog box where you specify how you want to store your recovery key. You can save the recovery key as part of your Microsoft account or to a file on your hard disk, or you can print the recovery key. See Figure B-9.

Figure B-9 Choosing how to back up the recovery key

choose an option for backing up your recovery key

▶ **7.** Click **Save to a file**. The Save BitLocker recovery key as dialog box opens. Navigate to the folder where you want to save the recovery key, and then click the **Save** button.

▶ **8.** Click the **Next** button to display a dialog box where you choose how much of the selected drive to encrypt. Make sure the first option button is selected, which encrypts used disk space only, and then click the **Next** button to display a dialog box asking you to confirm you are ready to encrypt this drive.

▶ **9.** Click the **Start encrypting** button. BitLocker encrypts the drive you selected, which takes a few minutes.

▶ **10.** When the encryption is complete, click the **Close** button.

To keep the recovery key secure, be sure to save it on a password-protected drive or store the printed key in a safe place. If needed, you can enter the recovery key directly or you can copy and paste the key from a file. If you store the recovery key on removable media, such as a USB flash drive, you can insert the USB flash drive when BitLocker requests the recovery key. Be sure to store that removable media in a secure place.

You can turn off BitLocker on a system drive in two ways: by suspending BitLocker or by decrypting the drive. Decrypting the drive means removing BitLocker protection entirely, which can take a long time on a system drive. If you suspend BitLocker instead, the drive is still encrypted, but Windows can read the information on the drive. You might suspend BitLocker so you can update a startup file, which you cannot access when BitLocker is turned on.

To turn off BitLocker on a drive that does not contain Windows, you must decrypt the drive. If the drive contains many gigabytes of data, decrypting can be time consuming.

In the following steps, you turn off BitLocker for the same USB flash drive you used in the previous set of steps.

To turn off BitLocker on a USB flash drive:

▶ **1.** With the encrypted USB flash drive attached to your computer, open the BitLocker Drive Encryption window, if necessary, which shows the drives on your computer. See Figure B-10.

| Figure B-10 | Turning off BitLocker for a removable drive |

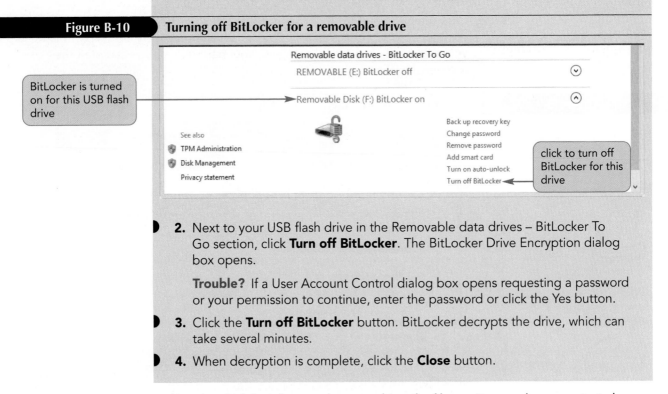

▶ **2.** Next to your USB flash drive in the Removable data drives – BitLocker To Go section, click **Turn off BitLocker**. The BitLocker Drive Encryption dialog box opens.

Trouble? If a User Account Control dialog box opens requesting a password or your permission to continue, enter the password or click the Yes button.

▶ **3.** Click the **Turn off BitLocker** button. BitLocker decrypts the drive, which can take several minutes.

▶ **4.** When decryption is complete, click the **Close** button.

Keep in mind that after you decrypt a drive, the files on it are no longer protected.

Managing Storage Spaces

Windows 8 introduces a feature called **Storage Spaces**, which lets you manage storage space on internal and external drives, including external hard drives and USB flash drives. To protect your data and increase the amount of storage space you can use, Storage Spaces lets you connect two or more drives to your computer and treat them as a single storage drive, or **pool**. The drives can use different interfaces; for example, one can be an internal hard drive, and another can be an external USB flash drive. Storage Spaces combines the storage capacities of these drives so you can store more files than you could on the separate drives. In addition, the pool **mirrors** the arrangement of the original drives: for each drive, the pool stores files in the same folders as in the original drives. If the USB flash drive in the pool fails, for example, your copy of the data is still available on another drive in the pool.

To perform the following steps, you need two USB flash drives that can be formatted, so they should not contain any data you want to save.

To create a storage pool:

▶ **1.** Attach two USB flash drives to your computer that do not contain data you want to save.

▶ **2.** In the BitLocker Drive Encryption window, click **System and Security** in the Address bar to return to the System and Security window, and then click **Storage Spaces** to open the Storage Spaces window. See Figure B-11.

| Figure B-11 | Storage Spaces window |

▶ **3.** Click the **Create a new pool and storage space** link to display a list of drives attached to your computer.

Trouble? If necessary, select a drive, and then click the **Create pool** button.

Trouble? If a drive attached to your computer does not appear in the Storage Spaces window, it is not compatible with Storage Spaces. Click the Cancel button. Read but do not perform the remaining steps.

Trouble? If a User Account Control dialog box opens requesting a password or your permission to continue, enter the password or click the Yes button.

▶ **4.** In the Name text box, enter a name for the pool, such as **John's movies** if you are storing copies of videos, for example. You can accept the defaults for the other settings in this window.

▶ **5.** Click the **Create storage space** button to format the USB flash drives and create the storage space.

When Windows is finished creating the storage space, the Storage Spaces window displays the drives contained in the storage space. Each storage space appears as a hard drive in File Explorer so you can store files in the storage space as you would any other drive. After you create a storage space, you can use it with File History to create continuous backups of your files in a very large drive.

Selecting AutoPlay Defaults

AutoPlay is a Windows feature that lets you choose which application to use for playing media content, such as music stored on a portable device or photos stored on a DVD. For example, if you have more than one media player installed on your computer, AutoPlay asks which one you want to use when you play a music file for the first time. You can change AutoPlay settings for each type of media file on your computer. AutoPlay also lets you select an action to take when you attach removable media to your computer.

When you turn AutoPlay on in the Control Panel, you can choose what should happen when you insert removable drives or different types of digital media into your computer. When AutoPlay is turned off, Windows displays a notification and asks you to choose what to do. A notification also appears if the Ask me every time setting is selected for the removable drive or media you insert or if no default has been selected. You can prevent the notification from appearing by selecting a default for the drive or type of media you plan to use.

In the following steps, you turn on AutoPlay, and then select a default action to play music using Windows Media Player.

To turn on AutoPlay and select a default action:

▶ **1.** In the Address bar of the Storage Spaces window, click **Control Panel** to return to the Control Panel Home window. Click **Hardware and Sound**, and then click **AutoPlay** to open the AutoPlay window. See Figure B-12.

Figure B-12 **AutoPlay window**

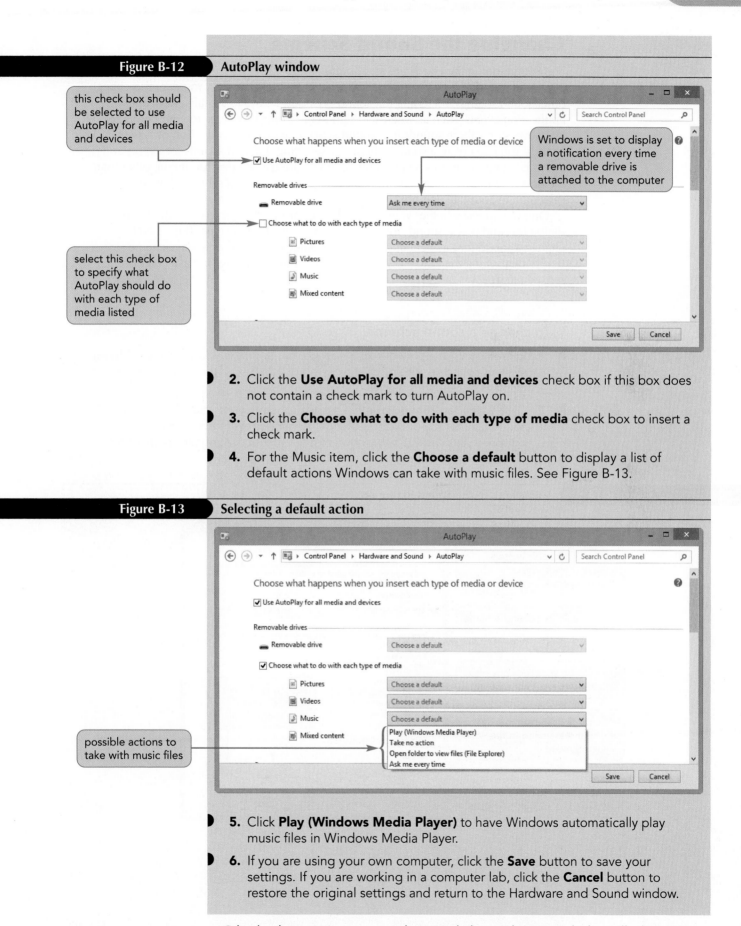

this check box should be selected to use AutoPlay for all media and devices

Windows is set to display a notification every time a removable drive is attached to the computer

select this check box to specify what AutoPlay should do with each type of media listed

possible actions to take with music files

2. Click the **Use AutoPlay for all media and devices** check box if this box does not contain a check mark to turn AutoPlay on.

3. Click the **Choose what to do with each type of media** check box to insert a check mark.

4. For the Music item, click the **Choose a default** button to display a list of default actions Windows can take with music files. See Figure B-13.

Figure B-13 **Selecting a default action**

5. Click **Play (Windows Media Player)** to have Windows automatically play music files in Windows Media Player.

6. If you are using your own computer, click the **Save** button to save your settings. If you are working in a computer lab, click the **Cancel** button to restore the original settings and return to the Hardware and Sound window.

Other hardware settings you can change include sound options, which you'll adjust next.

Changing the Sound Scheme

The Sound tool in the Hardware and Sound category lets you set the volume of the computer sound (which you learned to do in a previous tutorial). You can also change other sound settings, including the sounds Windows plays to signal system and application events, such as when you sign in or connect a device to your computer. Windows stores these sounds in a **sound scheme**, which is a collection of system sounds. You can create a sound scheme by selecting different sounds for events and then saving the sounds as a new scheme. If you are using a desktop theme other than the default Windows theme, it might also have its own sound scheme that you can select in the Sound dialog box.

One way to test whether your sound devices are working is to open the Sound dialog box and play a sound. You'll do that in the next set of steps. Then, you'll change a sound for an event and save all the selected sounds as a new scheme. Before performing the following steps, note the original settings in case you need to restore them.

To change a sound scheme:

▶ 1. In the Sound category of the Hardware and Sound window, click the **Change system sounds** link to open the Sound dialog box to the Sounds tab, which displays the sound schemes on your computer.

▶ 2. Click **Calendar Reminder** in the list of program events. See Figure B-14. The sound file that plays for the Calendar Reminder event appears on the Sounds button. In this case, the Windows Notify Calendar sound file plays for the Calendar Reminder event.

| Figure B-14 | Sounds tab in the Sound dialog box |

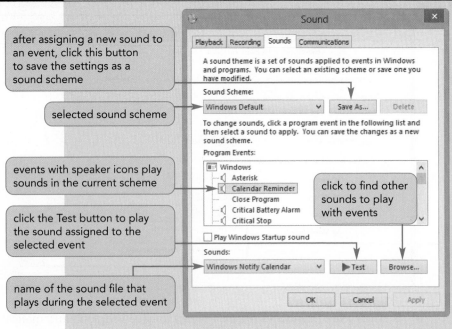

after assigning a new sound to an event, click this button to save the settings as a sound scheme

selected sound scheme

events with speaker icons play sounds in the current scheme

click the Test button to play the sound assigned to the selected event

name of the sound file that plays during the selected event

click to find other sounds to play with events

3. Click the **Test** button. The sound stored in the Windows Notify Calendar file plays.

   Trouble? If a sound does not play on your computer speakers, click the Volume or Speakers icon in the notification area, and then click the Mute button, if necessary, to turn on the speakers. Repeat Steps 2 and 3. If a sound still does not play and you are using external speakers, make sure the speakers are properly connected to your computer and are plugged into a power source, if necessary.

4. Scroll the Program Events list, and then click **Open Program** to assign a sound that plays when you start a Windows 8 or desktop application.

5. Click the **Sounds** button, and then click **chimes**.

6. Click the **Test** button to play the chimes sound.

7. Click the **Save As** button to open the Save Scheme As dialog box.

8. Type **App Open** as the name of the new sound scheme, and then click the **OK** button. App Open is now the current sound scheme on your computer.

9. Click the **OK** button to close the Sound dialog box.

The next time you start a Windows 8 app or desktop application, the chimes sound will play.

Setting Default Programs

When you double-click a data file such as a graphic or text document, an application starts and opens the file. Most computers have more than one application that can open certain types of files. For example, to open a photo file with a .jpg extension, you can use applications such as Photos, Paint, and Windows Photo Viewer. How does Windows choose the application to start when you double-click the .jpg file? It chooses the one set as the default application for that file type.

You can set default applications by using the Default Programs tool in the Control Panel to associate file types with an installed application. For example, if you associate .jpg files with Photos and .png files with Paint, you can use two default programs to work with graphics files. You can also set the default program you want to use for certain activities, such as browsing the Web. For example, if you have more than one browser installed on your computer, you can select the one you want to use by default. That browser will open when you click a Web page link in a document, for example.

By default, .png files are set to open in the Photos app. In the following steps, you set Paint as the default application to open .png files.

To set a default program:

▶ **1.** In the Hardware and Sound window, click **Programs** in the left pane to display the Programs window.

▶ **2.** In the Default Programs category, click **Set your default programs**. The Set Default Programs window opens and scans the programs installed on your computer.

▶ **3.** In the Programs list, click **Paint**. See Figure B-15.

Figure B-15 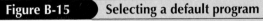 **Selecting a default program**

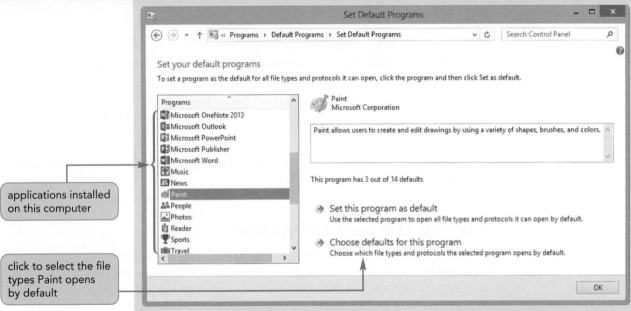

▶ **4.** Click **Choose defaults for this program** to open the Set Program Associations window, which lists file types that Paint can open.

▶ **5.** Click the **.png** check box, and then click the **Save** button to save the selected setting and return to the Set Default Programs window.

Now when you double-click a .png file, Paint will start so you can edit the graphic if necessary.

Selecting Family Safety Settings

To preserve the privacy of user accounts, you can use the Family Safety feature. If children use your computer, set up an account for each child. Then use Family Safety to set limits on how children can use the computer, such as the Web sites they can access, the hours they can use the computer, and the types of Windows Store apps and installed apps they can run (including games). Using Family Safety prevents children from accessing inappropriate content with your computer.

Before you set up Family Safety, make sure that each child using the computer has a Standard account—you can apply Family Safety settings only to Standard accounts. Figure B-16 describes the settings you can apply to limit a child's access to the computer:

| Figure B-16 | Family Safety settings |

Setting	Use to
Web filtering	Let children access all Web sites or only those you allow. You can also allow or block Web sites by rating and content types or only certain Web sites.
Time limits	Set time limits to prevent children from signing in during specified hours. If they are already signed in during a restricted time, Windows signs them out. You can set different sign-in hours for every day of the week.
Windows Store and game restrictions	Control access to Windows Store apps and games installed on your computer, choose an age rating level, and allow or block specific games.
App restrictions	Prevent children from running apps that you don't want them to run.

© 2014 Cengage Learning

Before applying the Family Safety settings, you need to be signed in to Windows using a password-protected Administrator account, and your computer must also have a Standard account. If one is not available on your computer, create a new Standard account and turn on Family Safety for that account as you create it. If you cannot sign in as an Administrator or change the settings for a Standard account, read but do not perform the following steps.

The following steps use a Standard account named Child User. If the Standard account you are using has a different name, substitute that name as you perform the steps. You'll set Family Safety settings on the Child User account so that this user can use the computer for a maximum of one hour on weekdays and a maximum of three hours on weekends.

To select Family Safety settings for a Standard user account:

▶ **1.** Return to the Control Panel Home page, and then click **Set up Family Safety for any user** in the User Accounts and Family Safety category to open the Family Safety window. See Figure B-17.

Trouble? If a User Account Control dialog box opens requesting a password or your permission to continue, enter the password or click the Yes button.

Figure B-17   **Family Safety window**

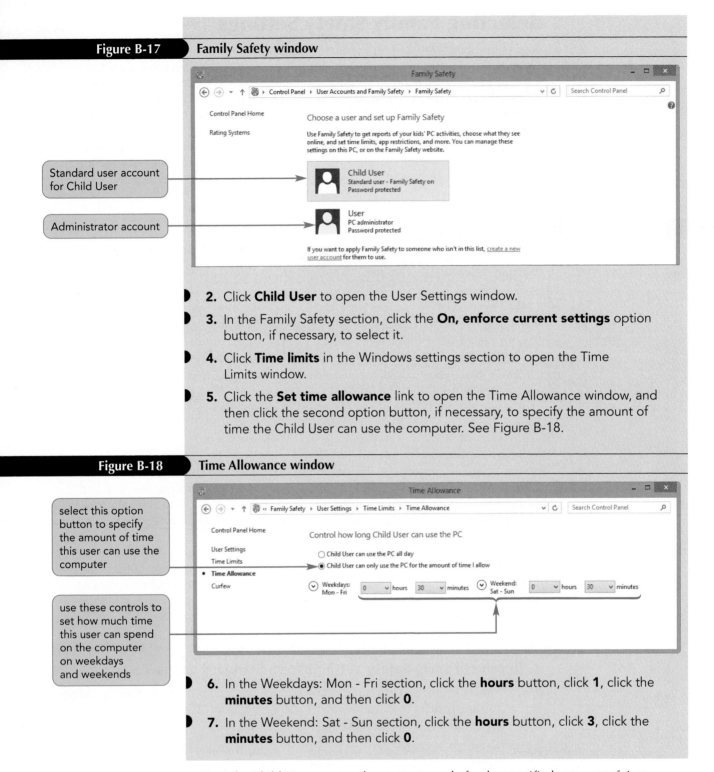

Standard user account
for Child User

Administrator account

2. Click **Child User** to open the User Settings window.

3. In the Family Safety section, click the **On, enforce current settings** option button, if necessary, to select it.

4. Click **Time limits** in the Windows settings section to open the Time Limits window.

5. Click the **Set time allowance** link to open the Time Allowance window, and then click the second option button, if necessary, to specify the amount of time the Child User can use the computer. See Figure B-18.

Figure B-18   **Time Allowance window**

select this option button to specify the amount of time this user can use the computer

use these controls to set how much time this user can spend on the computer on weekdays and weekends

6. In the Weekdays: Mon - Fri section, click the **hours** button, click **1**, click the **minutes** button, and then click **0**.

7. In the Weekend: Sat - Sun section, click the **hours** button, click **3**, click the **minutes** button, and then click **0**.

Now the Child User can use the computer only for the specified amounts of time.

Managing Credentials

Credential Manager helps to protect your privacy by storing passwords you frequently use to access Web sites or networks. If you save these passwords using Credential Manager, you don't have to retype them each time you return to the Web site or network. Windows saves your credentials in special folders on your computer called **vaults**. When you sign in to Web sites or other computers on a network, Windows and applications, such as a Web browser, can securely provide the credentials in the vaults so you can sign in automatically.

In the following steps, you store the user name and password for signing in to a Web site or network location for which you want to store a password.

To manage network passwords:

▶ 1. In the Time Allowance window, click **User Accounts and Family Safety** in the Address bar to display the User Accounts and Family Safety window, and then click **Credential Manager** to open the Credential Manager window. This window shows the credentials already set up on the computer, if any.

▶ 2. Click **Windows Credentials** to display options for working with credentials. See Figure B-19.

| Figure B-19 | Credential Manager window |

click to add a credential for a Web site or network location

use these links to back up your credentials and then restore them in case the originals are damaged

Generic Credentials are for applications that manage authorization separate from the credentials of the current user

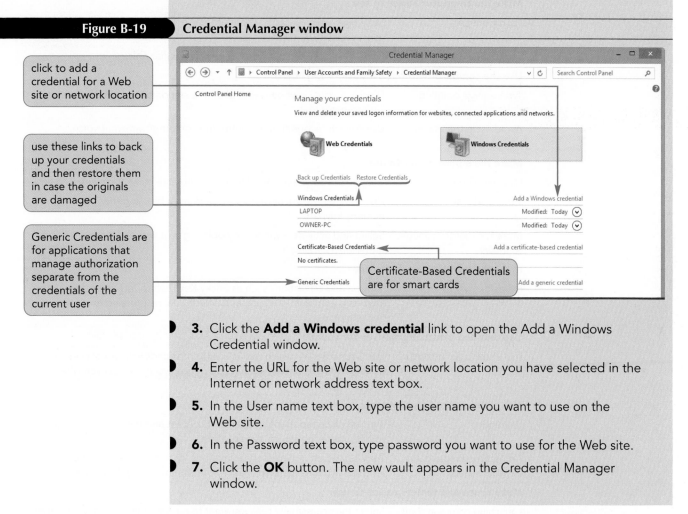

▶ 3. Click the **Add a Windows credential** link to open the Add a Windows Credential window.

▶ 4. Enter the URL for the Web site or network location you have selected in the Internet or network address text box.

▶ 5. In the User name text box, type the user name you want to use on the Web site.

▶ 6. In the Password text box, type password you want to use for the Web site.

▶ 7. Click the **OK** button. The new vault appears in the Credential Manager window.

If you could use your browser to visit *www.bank.com*, Windows would provide your user name and password so you could sign in automatically, if the site allows you to do so.

Setting Ease of Access Options

Ease of Access options are Windows 8 settings that you can change to make it easier to interact with your computer. Although designed primarily for users with special vision, hearing, and mobility needs, any user might find it helpful to adjust Ease of Access settings when working with software such as graphics programs that require more control over mouse and keyboard settings or when working in a poorly lit or noisy room.

To use Ease of Access options, you open the Ease of Access Center from the Control Panel. In this window, you can adjust settings that make it easier to see your computer or use the mouse and keyboard. Figure B-20 summarizes some of the accessibility settings you can change using the Ease of Access Center.

| Figure B-20 | Common Ease of Access options |

Option	Description
Use the computer without a display	
Turn on Narrator	Have Narrator read on-screen text aloud and describe some computer events, such as error messages.
Turn on Audio Description	Have Audio Description describe the action displayed in videos.
Make the computer easier to see	
High Contrast	Set a high-contrast color scheme to make some text and images on your screen more distinct.
Turn on Magnifier	Point to an area of the screen to have Magnifier enlarge it.
Use the computer without a mouse or keyboard	
Type using a pointing device	Display a visual keyboard with all of the standard keys, which you can click to enter text.
Avoid using the mouse and keyboard	Use speech recognition to control the computer with your voice.
Make the mouse easier to use	
Mouse pointers	Change the color and size of mouse pointers to make them easier to find.
Turn on Mouse Keys	Control the movement of the mouse pointer by using the numeric keypad.
Make it easier to manage windows	Select and activate a window by pointing to it with the mouse rather than clicking it.
Make the keyboard easier to use	
Make it easier to type	Turn on and off options such as Sticky Keys, which lets you select keyboard combinations such as Ctrl+Alt+Del by pressing only one key at a time.
Use text and visual alternatives for sounds	
Use visual cues instead of sounds	Use Sound Sentry, which replaces system sounds with visual cues, such as a flash on the screen, so that you notice system alerts even when you don't hear them.
Make it easier to focus on tasks	
Reading	Turn off all unimportant, overlapped content and background images to help make the screen easier to see.
Adjust time limits and flashing visuals	Turn on and off unnecessary animations when possible, and choose how long notifications are displayed on the screen before they close.
Make touch and tablets easier to use	
Launching common tools	Select the accessibility tool you want to run when you press two buttons at the same time on your tablet.

You can open the Ease of Access Center to explore its options.

To open the Ease of Access Center:

1. Click **Control Panel** in the Address bar of the Credential Manager window, and then click **Ease of Access** to open the Ease of Access window.

2. Click **Ease of Access Center**. The Ease of Access Center window opens. A narrator might explain what you can do with this window as Windows scans the text. As Windows scans, it moves a selection box in the Ease of Access Center window so you can make a selection. See Figure B-21.

Figure B-21	Ease of Access Center window

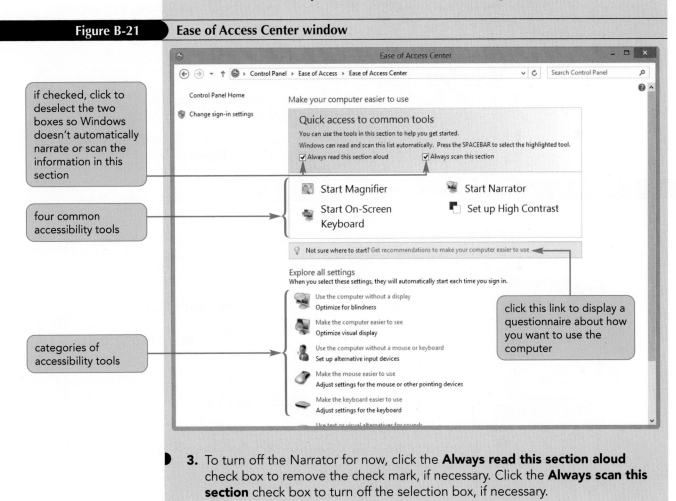

if checked, click to deselect the two boxes so Windows doesn't automatically narrate or scan the information in this section

four common accessibility tools

categories of accessibility tools

click this link to display a questionnaire about how you want to use the computer

3. To turn off the Narrator for now, click the **Always read this section aloud** check box to remove the check mark, if necessary. Click the **Always scan this section** check box to turn off the selection box, if necessary.

The Ease of Access Center window includes three sections. In the Quick access to common tools box, you can quickly turn on tools that make your computer easier to use: Magnifier, Narrator, On-Screen Keyboard, and High Contrast. When you turn on a tool, it stays on until you sign out of Windows or shut down.

The second section includes a Get recommendations to make your computer easier to use link. Click the link to display a questionnaire about how you want to use your computer. When you submit the questionnaire, Windows provides a list of settings that can make your computer easier to use. You can then select the settings you want.

The third section, Explore all settings, contains the seven categories of accessibility tools listed earlier. When you select these tools and set their options, they start immediately and each time you sign in to Windows.

You can start a couple of Ease of Access tools to determine whether they improve your computing experience.

To use Ease of Access tools:

1. In the Ease of Access Center window, click **Start Magnifier**. The Magnifier dialog box opens and the magnification is increased to 200%.

2. Click the **Minimize** button ▬ to minimize the dialog box. The screen is now magnified to make it easier to see. See Figure B-22.

Figure B-22   **Using Magnifier to make the screen easier to see**

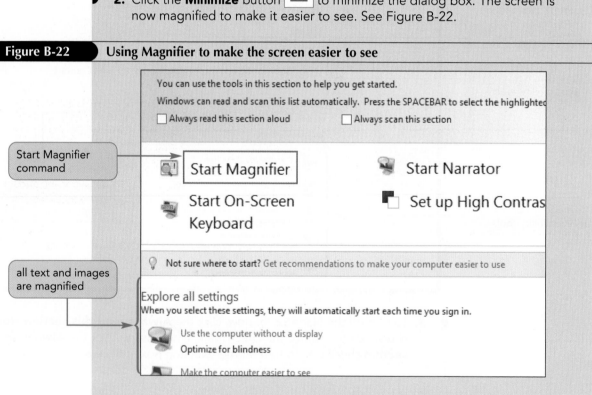

You can use the tools in this section to help you get started.

Windows can read and scan this list automatically. Press the SPACEBAR to select the highlighted

☐ Always read this section aloud   ☐ Always scan this section

Start Magnifier command →   Start Magnifier   Start Narrator

Start On-Screen Keyboard   Set up High Contras

💡 Not sure where to start? Get recommendations to make your computer easier to use

all text and images are magnified →

Explore all settings
When you select these settings, they will automatically start each time you sign in.

Use the computer without a display
Optimize for blindness

Make the computer easier to see

3. Move the pointer around the desktop.

4. Move the pointer to the bottom of the screen to display the taskbar, click the **Magnifier** button 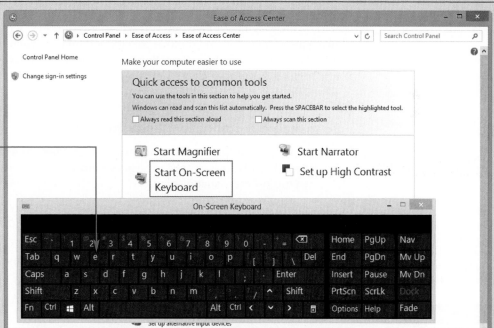 on the taskbar to open the Magnifier dialog box, and then click the **Close** button ⬛×⬛ to close the dialog box and turn off Magnifier.

TIP
You can also hold down the Windows key and then press the Esc key to turn off Magnifier.

5. Click **Start On-Screen Keyboard** to open the On-Screen Keyboard window. See Figure B-23. Your On-Screen Keyboard window might appear in a different position.

Figure B-23   **Using the On-Screen Keyboard to enter data**

click a key instead of pressing it on the physical keyboard

6. If necessary, drag the On-Screen Keyboard window to the bottom of the screen. Open Notepad, and then click keys on the On-Screen Keyboard to enter your name in a new Notepad document. As you begin to type, the On-Screen Keyboard might display a key containing your name. If so, click the key to insert your name in the Notepad window.

7. Close Notepad without saving any changes, and then close the On-Screen Keyboard window.

You can also use the Ease of Access Center window to change accessibility settings, such as those that optimize the visual display, adjust settings for the mouse or other pointing device, and set up alternatives to sound. You'll explore one of these tools to change accessibility settings next.

Making the Computer Easier to See

If you want to optimize the visual display on your computer, you can open a window where you can select settings to turn on a High Contrast theme, read screen text or video descriptions aloud, or turn on the Magnifier tool when you sign in to Windows. By default, High Contrast themes use one or two colors for text on a black background on the Start screen and desktop. If you have limited vision or if you're in a dark office, using a High Contrast theme can make it easier to see what's on your screen. You can also select a different High Contrast theme to use instead of the default one. After selecting a High Contrast theme, you can turn it on by pressing the left Alt+left Shift+Print Screen keys.

If you are having problems seeing text on a screen or viewing a video, you can turn on the Narrator or Audio Description, which narrates the action in a video. (This feature is available only for videos that provide audio descriptions.) You can also select settings to turn on the Magnifier tool when you sign in to Windows, set the thickness of the blinking insertion point, and remove background images when they appear in windows.

You'll turn on the High Contrast theme, and then explore other settings that make your computer easier to see.

To make your computer easier to see:

1. In the Ease of Access Center window, click **Make the computer easier to see** in the Explore all settings list. A window opens providing options for optimizing the visual display.

TIP

When you use a High Contrast theme, it affects all apps and windows you open, including the Start screen.

2. To test the current High Contrast theme, turn it on by pressing the **left Alt+left Shift+Print Screen** keys. A dialog box opens asking if you want to turn on High Contrast.

3. Click the **Yes** button. The desktop color scheme changes to the one in the default High Contrast theme. See Figure B-24.

Figure B-24   **Default High Contrast theme**

change this setting if you do not want to use a keyboard shortcut to turn High Contrast on or off

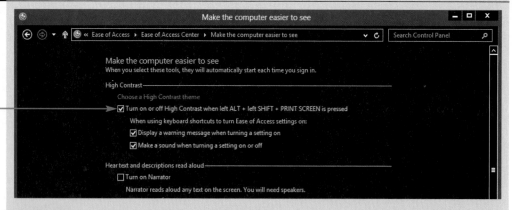

4. Press the **left Alt+left Shift+Print Screen** keys to turn off High Contrast.

5. Scroll the window, if necessary, to display all of the options in the Make things on the screen easier to see section.

6. Click the **Set the thickness of the blinking cursor** button (which displays a 1 by default), and then click **3**. The sample insertion point in the Preview box is thicker.

> **7.** Click the **Set the thickness of the blinking cursor** button, and then click **1** to restore this setting.

> **8.** Close all open windows.

Many Ease of Access Center windows include a link you can click to learn more about assistive technologies online.

Using Windows 8 and Windows RT

Besides Windows 8, which you have used throughout this book, Microsoft provides a second, related operating system called **Windows RT**, short for Windows Runtime, which is specially designed for tablet computers and other small mobile devices. While Windows 8 can run software created for earlier versions of Windows, Windows RT runs only apps that come with the operating system and those you install from the Windows Store, not those created for earlier versions of Windows. You start Windows RT apps from the Start screen and work with them as full-screen, tile-based apps with two exceptions: Windows RT versions of Microsoft Office and Internet Explorer run on the desktop. Both are already installed when you buy a Windows RT device.

One thing to keep in mind is that Windows RT is significantly different from Windows 8. If you buy a Windows RT tablet, remember that it cannot run legacy applications. That means you will have to purchase, download, and install apps from the Windows Store (though many of the current apps are offered free of charge). It may take a while for developers to create Windows RT versions of popular desktop applications and make them available at the Windows Store.

Another important difference is that Windows 8 runs on computers that use an Intel or AMD processor. These are called x86 computers because they use a processor based on the original Intel 8086 product line, which powered early PCs. In contrast, most tablet computers use ARM processors developed by a company named ARM Holdings. ARM processors allow computer manufacturers to create thin, lightweight, inexpensive tablets with long battery lives. To take advantage of these benefits, Windows RT runs only on computers with ARM processors. In short, you cannot run Windows 8 on an ARM computer, nor can you run Windows RT on an x86 computer. (However, some tablets do use processors in the x86 product line, so you can run Windows 8 on those tablets.)

Because Windows RT is a streamlined operating system, it does not include all of the features and tools provided with Windows 8. Figure B-25 lists popular features provided with both operating systems and those included only in Windows 8 Pro.

Popular Windows 8 and Windows RT features

Feature	Windows 8 Pro	Windows RT
BitLocker	•	
Browsers other than Internet Explorer	•	
Homegroup creation	•	
Homegroup joining	•	•
Internet Explorer 10	•	•
Multiple languages	•	•
Power plans	•	•
Remote Desktop Connection	•	
Storage Spaces	•	
Touch, mouse, and keyboard support	•	•
Upgrade from a previous Windows version, such as Windows 7	•	
Windows 8 apps such as Calendar, Mail, and Weather	•	•
Windows Defender	•	•
Windows Media Player	•	
Windows Update	•	•

© 2014 Cengage Learning

Restoring Your Settings

If you are working in a computer lab or on a computer other than your own, complete the steps in this section to restore the original settings on your computer.

To restore your settings:

1. Display the PC settings screen, click **Notifications**, and then click the **slider** for Music to turn Music notifications on.

2. Navigate to the folder where you saved the BitLocker recovery key, and then delete the recovery key file.

3. Open the Hardware and Sound window in the Control Panel, click **Change system sounds** in the Sound category, click the **Delete** button to delete the App Open sound scheme, and then click the **Yes** button to confirm the deletion.

4. If necessary, click the **Sound Scheme** button, click your original sound scheme, and then click the **OK** button to restore the default sound scheme.

5. Return to the Hardware and Sound window, click **AutoPlay**, and then restore your original settings for playing media.

6. Navigate to the User Accounts and Family Safety window, click **Set up Family Safety for any users**, type the administrator password in the UAC box and click the **Yes** button if necessary, click **Child User** (or the name of the user whose account you modified in this appendix), and then click the **Off** option button under Family Safety.

7. Return to the User Accounts window, and then click **Manage your credentials** in the left pane. Click **Windows Credentials**, click the **expand** button ☑ for the Web site or network location you used earlier, if necessary, click **Remove**, and then click the **Yes** button to confirm you want to remove the credential.

8. Navigate to the Ease of Access Center, and then restore your original settings for the **Always read this section aloud** check box and the **Always scan this section** check box, if necessary.

9. Return to the Control Panel Home page, click **Programs**, click **Set your default programs**, and then restore your original settings for the file types that Paint opens by default.

10. Display the Start screen, click the **People** tile, click the name of the contact you added in this appendix, right-click the contact, and then click the Delete button.

11. Close all open windows.

GLOSSARY/INDEX

TASK REFERENCE

TASK	PAGE #	RECOMMENDED METHOD
Accelerator, use	WIN 190–191	Display Web page with accelerator, click ⬀, click the Accelerator you want to use
Action Center window, open	WIN 225	Click ▥ in the notification area of the taskbar, click Open Action Center
App, install from Windows Store	WIN 474–475	Click the Store tile on the Start screen, scroll to display the desired category of apps, click the app you want to install, click Install
App, search for	WIN 285	Display Start screen, type the name of the app
App, uninstall Windows 8 app	WIN 476	Right-click the Windows app tile on the Start screen, click Uninstall on the Apps bar, click Uninstall
Application, start	WIN 14	*See* Reference box: Starting an Application
AutoPlay, turn on	WIN B14	Open the Hardware and Sound window in the Control Panel, click, click AutoPlay, select Use AutoPlay for all media and devices
Base score, view and calculate	WIN 521	*See* Reference box: Viewing and Calculating Your Base Score
Bing, start	WIN B4	Click the Bing tile on the Start screen
BitLocker To Go, turn off for a USB flash drive	WIN B11–B12	Insert the encrypted USB flash drive into a USB port, open the System and Security window in the Control Panel, click BitLocker Drive Encryption, click Turn off BitLocker, click Turn off BitLocker, click Close
BitLocker To Go, turn on for a USB flash drive	WIN B11–B12	Insert a USB flash drive into a USB port, open the System and Security window in the Control Panel, click BitLocker Drive Encryption, click Turn on BitLocker, follow the instructions in the wizard
Calculator, use	WIN 285–286	Display Start screen, type *cal*, click Calculator
Calendar, set appointment in	WIN 208	*See* Reference box: Scheduling an Appointment in Calendar
Calendar, start	WIN 208	Click the Calendar tile on the Start screen
Charms bar, display	WIN 8	Point to upper-right corner of Start screen (or press ⊞+C)
Compressed folder, create	WIN 86–87	In a folder window, select files and folders to be compressed, click Share tab, click Zip button in the Send group, type a folder name, press Enter
Compressed folder, extract all files and folders from	WIN 87–88	In a folder window, click Extract tab, click Extract all to start wizard, navigation to a location, click Extract
Computer, restore using a system restore point	WIN 471	Open the System and Security window in the Control Panel, click System, click System protection, click System Restore, click Next, choose a system restore point, click Next, click Finish (or Cancel)
Contact, add to People app	WIN 206	*See* Reference box: Adding a Contact to People
Control Panel, open	WIN 132	Display Charms bar from the desktop, click Settings charm, click Control Panel
Credential Manager, open	WIN B22	Open the User Accounts and Family Safety window in the Control Panel, click Credential Manager
Desktop, display	WIN 10	Click the Desktop tile on the Start screen
Desktop application, close	WIN 26	*See* Reference box: Closing an Application

TASK	PAGE #	RECOMMENDED METHOD
Desktop application, switch to another open	WIN 19	Click the program button on the taskbar
Desktop application, switch to Windows 8 app	WIN 19	Point to upper-left corner of the desktop, click the thumbnail of the app in Switch List
Desktop apps, pin to Start screen	WIN 101	*See* Reference box: Pinning an App to the Start Screen
Desktop apps, pin to taskbar	WIN 149	*See* Reference box: Pinning Desktop Apps to the Taskbar
Desktop background, change	WIN 136–138	Open the Personalization window in the Control Panel, click the Desktop Background link, click the image in the category you want to use, click Save changes
Desktop colors, change	WIN 138–139	Open the Personalization window in the Control Panel, click the Color link, click color you want to use, Click Save changes
Desktop icon, change image of	WIN 129	Right-click the desktop, click Personalize, click Change desktop icons, click the desktop icon you want to change, click Change Icon, click the icon you want to use, click OK, click OK
Desktop icon, display standard	WIN 127	*See* Reference box: Displaying Standard Desktop Icons
Desktop shortcut, create to drive	WIN 131	Insert the USB flash drive, click 🖿 on the taskbar, click the Computer icon in the Navigation pane, point to the Removable Disk icon, press and hold the left mouse button and drag the Removable Disk icon from the Computer window into an empty area of the desk-top, release the mouse button
Desktop shortcut, create to file or folder	WIN 130	Navigate to the folder window to locate the file or folder icon, right-click the icon, point to Send to, click Desktop
Desktop shortcut, delete	WIN 112	Right-click the shortcut icon on the desktop, click Delete
Desktop theme, save	WIN 142	Open Personalization window in the Control Panel, click Save theme, type a name for the theme you want to save, click Save
Desktop theme, select	WIN 135	*See* Reference box: Selecting a Theme
Device, enable and disable	WIN 498	*See* Reference box: Enabling and Disabling Devices
Device driver, roll back	WIN 502	Open Device Manager, double-click the device, click Driver tab, click Roll Back Driver
Device driver, update and install	WIN 499	Open Device Manager, double-click the device, click Driver tab, click Update Driver, click Search automatically for updated driver software, click Yes
Device Manager, open	WIN 498	Open the System and Security window in the Control Panel, click System, click Device Manager
Disk Cleanup, start	WIN 486	Right-click the disk in a folder window, click Properties, click General tab, click Disk Cleanup
Disk Optimizer, configure	WIN 493–494	Right-click the disk in a folder window, click Properties, click Tools tab, click Optimize, click Change settings, specify frequency, click Choose, select drives, click OK, click OK
Disk Optimizer, start	WIN 493–494	Right-click the disk in a folder window, click Properties, click Tools tab, click Optimize, click Optimize
Ease of Access Center, open	WIN B24	Open Control Panel, click Ease of Access, click Ease of Access Center
Email message, attach file to	WIN 204	Right-click a blank spot on the Mail screen, click Attachments on the Apps bar, navigate to and click the file you want to attach, click Attach
Email message, create	WIN 200	*See* Reference box: Creating and Sending an Email Message

TASK	PAGE #	RECOMMENDED METHOD
Email message, delete	WIN 203	Click the email message in the Message list, click (🗑)
Email message, reply	WIN 203	Select email message in the Message list, click (↩), click Reply, type message, click Send
Email message, send	WIN 200	*See Reference box: Creating and Sending an Email Message*
Event Viewer, open	WIN 532	Open the Performance Information and Tools window, click Advanced tools, click View performance details in Event log
External display device, connect a mobile PC to	WIN 414	*See Reference box: Connecting to an External Display Device*
Family Safety settings, select	WIN B20–B21	Open the User Accounts and Family Safety window in the Control Panel, click Set up Family Safety for any user, click a user, click the On, enforce current settings link, select options link
Favorites bar, display	WIN 187	Click Tools on the Command bar, point to Toolbars, click Favorites bar
Favorites Center, open in Internet Explorer Desktop	WIN 184	Start Internet Explorer Desktop, click ⭐
Favorites list, add Web page to	WIN 185	*See Reference box: Adding a Web Page to the Favorites List*
Favorites list, open	WIN 185	Open Favorites Center, click Favorites tab
Favorites list, organize	WIN 186	*See Reference box: Organizing the Favorites List*
Feed, subscribe to	WIN 188	Click 📶, click Subscribe to this feed, click Subscribe
File, copy	WIN 66	*See Reference box: Copying a File or Folder in a Folder Window*
File, create	WIN 72	Start application and enter data
File, delete	WIN 71	*See Reference box: Deleting a File or Folder*
File, move	WIN 63	*See Reference box: Moving a File or Folder in a Folder Window*
File, open from folder window	WIN 76	Navigate to the file, double-click the file
File, rename	WIN 71	Right-click the file, click Rename on shortcut menu, type new filename, press Enter
File, restore previous version from backup using File History	WIN 465	Display a folder window, click History in the Open group on the HOME tab, click the Previous version button until the original version of the file you want to restore is displayed, click (↺), click Replace the file in the destination
File, save	WIN 74	Click File menu, click Save As, navigate to a location, type the filename, click Save
File, search for by name, content, or file type from Start screen	WIN 290–292	Type search text on the Start screen, click Files, click the file you want to open
File, search for by name, content, or file type on the desktop	WIN 290–292	Open a folder window, type search criteria in the Search text box, press Enter
File, search for within a folder window	WIN 60	In a folder window, click the Search text box, enter text associated with the file (including filename, tags, or other file properties), press Enter
File, search for using AND or OR	WIN 307	Open a folder window, click the Search text box, type search text AND (or OR) search text
File, search for using Boolean filter and file properties	WIN 308	Open a folder window, click the Search text box, type property: search text
File, search for using property	WIN 305	Open a folder window, click the Search text box, type a property

TASK	PAGE #	RECOMMENDED METHOD
File, test for viruses with Download Manager	WIN 248–249	Click ⚙, click View downloads, right-click a file, click Rerun security checks on this file, click Close
File Explorer, open	WIN 30	Click 📁 on the taskbar
File History, exclude folders from backup	WIN 459–460	Click Exclude folders in the File History window, click Add, navigate to the folder you want to exclude from the backup, click Select Folder, repeat for each folder to be excluded
File History, set backup schedule	WIN 460–461	Click Advanced settings in the File History window, click Every hour (default), click a time interval option, click Save changes
File History, set up to back up files	WIN 455	See Reference box: Setting Up File History to Back Up Files
File History window, open	WIN 458	Open Control Panel, click System and Security, click File History
Filename extension, show or hide	WIN 83	Click View tab, click the File name extensions check box in the Show/hide group
Files, back up using File History	WIN 462	Click Turn on in the File History window
Files, select multiple	WIN 66	Hold down Ctrl key and click the files
Files, sort files in	WIN 78	In a folder window, click a column heading
Files, sync	WIN 435–436	Open Sync Center, click Sync All
Flip ahead, turn on in Internet Explorer Windows 8	WIN 177	See Reference box: Turning on Flip Ahead
Folder, copy	WIN 66	See Reference box: Copying a File or Folder in a Folder Window
Folder, create	WIN 62	See Reference box: Creating a Folder in a Folder Window
Folder, delete	WIN 71	See Reference box: Deleting a File or Folder
Folder, expand	WIN 33	In a folder window, click ▷ in the Navigation pane
Folder, filter files In	WIN 78	In a folder window, point to a column heading, click ▾, click filtering option
Folder, group files in	WIN 80	Click View tab, click 🔲 in Current view group, click group by option
Folder, move	WIN 63	See Reference box: Moving a File or Folder in a Folder Window
Folder, pin to Start screen	WIN 106–107	Open a folder window, navigate to and right-click the folder you want to pin, click Pin to Start on the shortcut menu
Folder window, return to previously visited location	WIN 34	Click ⊕
Hard disk, check for errors	WIN 489–490	Open the File History window, right-click the disk in a folder window, click Tools tab, click Check, click Scan drive, click Close
Hard disk, clean up using Disk Cleanup	WIN 486	Right-click the disk in a folder window, click Properties, click General tab, click Disk Cleanup
Hard disk, view partitions	WIN 485	Open the System and Security window in the Control Panel, click Create and format hard disk partitions in the Administrative Tools category
Hard disk, view properties	WIN 482	See Reference box: Viewing Hard Disk Properties
Help and Support, find topic	WIN 36	Click Browse help link
Help and Support, search	WIN 37	Click Help home link, type search text in the Search box
Help and Support, start	WIN 34–35	On the Start screen, type help, click Help and Support

TASK	PAGE #	RECOMMENDED METHOD
High contrast color scheme, turn off	WIN B26	Press the left Alt+left Shift+Print Screen keys
High contrast color scheme, use on the desktop	WIN B26–B27	Press the left Alt+left Shift+Print Screen keys, click Yes
Homegroup window, open	WIN 426	Open the Control Panel, type *homegroup* in the Search text box, click HomeGroup
Homegroup, access shared files	WIN 429	Open File Explorer, click the Homegroup computer in the Navigation pane, open folder containing the files
Homegroup, create	WIN 426–427	Open the HomeGroup window, click Create a homegroup, click Next, set libraries and resources to share, click Next, click Print password and instructions, click Print this page, click Finish
Homegroup, join	WIN 427–428	Open the HomeGroup window, click Join now, click Next, select libraries and resources to share, click Next, type the homegroup password, click Next, click Finish
Homegroup, leave	WIN 425	Open the Homegroup window, click Leave the homegroup, click Leave the homegroup
Homegroup, share files with	WIN 428	Open File Explorer, navigate to the folder, select the document, click Share tab, click Homegroup (view) in the Share with group
Homegroup, use to connect to a shared printer	WIN 431	Open the Hardware and Sound window in the Control Panel, click View devices and printers, click the Windows found a homegroup printer message
Homegroup, stop sharing a file or folder	WIN 430	Select the file or folder, click Stop sharing button in the Share with group on the Share tab
Internet, search using search expression	WIN 313	Type search expression in the Address bar, press Enter
Internet Explorer, block ActiveX controls	WIN 261	Click ⚙, point to Safety, click ActiveX Filtering to turn on
Internet Explorer, block content using Tracking Protection	WIN 260	Click ⚙, point to Safety, click Tracking Protection, click Your Personalized List, click Settings, click content provider, click Block, click OK, click Close
Internet Explorer, change settings using Pop-up Blocker	WIN 252	Display Web page, click ⚙, click Internet options, click Privacy tab, click Turn on Pop-up Blocker check box, click Settings, select Blocking level, click Close, click OK
Internet Explorer, delete browsing history in	WIN 257	Click ⚙, click Internet options, click General tab, click Delete in the Browsing history section, select options, click Delete, click OK
Internet Explorer, manage add-ons in	WIN 253	Click ⚙, click Manage add-ons
Internet Explorer, select privacy settings in	WIN 255	*See* Reference box: Selecting Privacy Settings
Internet Explorer, start from desktop	WIN 180	Display desktop, click 𝑒
Internet Explorer, start from Start screen	WIN 166	Click the Internet Explorer tile on the Start screen
Internet Explorer, turn on SmartScreen Filter	WIN 245–246	Click ⚙, point to Safety, click Turn on SmartScreen Filter, click Turn on SmartScreen Filter, click OK

TASK	PAGE #	RECOMMENDED METHOD
Internet Explorer Desktop, turn on InPrivate Browsing	WIN 258	Click ⚙, point to Safety, click InPrivate Browsing, type URL in the Address bar, press Enter
Internet Explorer Windows 8, turn on InPrivate Browsing	WIN 258	Right-click a blank spot on a Web page, click Tab tools, click New InPrivate tab
Internet search provider, add	WIN 317	*See* Reference box: Adding a Search Provider
Jump list, pin file to	WIN 150	Right-click the taskbar button, point to file, click 📌
Library, expand	WIN 33	In File Explorer, click ▷
Library, open	WIN 31	In File Explorer, click a library In the Navigation pane
Lock screen, clear	WIN 4	Press any key, or click anywhere on the screen
Magnifier, start	WIN B25	Open the Ease of Access Center window, click Start Magnifier, click Minimize
Mail, start	WIN 198	Click the Mail tile on the Start screen
Messaging, use for instant messaging	WIN B7–B8	Click the Messaging tile on the Start screen, click New message, choose partner, type message, press Enter
Microsoft account, set up	WIN 265	Start Internet Explorer Desktop, type https://signup.live.com in the Address bar, press Enter, enter your email address and other required information, click I accept
Microsoft Community website, open	WIN 557	Click Microsoft Community website on the Help and Support home page
Microsoft Community website, search for answer on	WIN 557–558	Open Microsoft Community website on the Help and Support home page, click the appropriate forum, search questions and answers for topics
Navigation bar, display in Internet Explorer Windows 8	WIN 172	Right-click the background of the Web page
Network and Sharing Center, open	WIN 432	Open Control Panel, type *network* in the Search text box, click Network and Sharing Center
Network files, make available offline	WIN 432	Open Control Panel, type *offline* in the Search text box, click Manage offline files in the Sync Center category, click Enable offline files, click OK
Network passwords, manage	WIN B22	Open Credential Manager, click Windows Credentials, click Add a Windows credential, type a URL, user name, and password, click OK
Offline files, enable	WIN 432	Open the Control Panel, type *offline* in the Search text box, click Manage offline files, click Enable offline Files, click OK
Offline files, make available	WIN 434	Right-click the folder you want to make available offline, click Always available offline
Offline files, work with	WIN 434	Click the offline file, click Easy access in the New group on the Home tab, click Work offline
On-screen keyboard, start	WIN B25	Open the Ease of Access Center window, click Start On-Screen Keyboard
Paging file, change size	WIN 546–548	Open the Performance Information and Tools window, click Advanced tools, click Adjust the appearance and performance of Windows, click Advanced tab, click Change, change settings, click OK
Paint, add text to a graphic in	WIN 344	*See* Reference box: Adding Text to a Graphic

TASK	PAGE #	RECOMMENDED METHOD
Paint, copy and paste graphic in	WIN 357	Select a portion of the graphic, click Copy button in the Clipboard group, click Paste button in the Clipboard group, drag selection to new location, click outside the image
Paint, crop a graphic	WIN 359	Select the portion of the graphic you want to retain, click Crop button in the Image group
Paint, delete a part of a graphic	WIN 354	Click Select button in the Image group, click a selection tool, drag to select the area of the shape with selection pointer, press Delete
Paint, display gridlines in	WIN 357	Click View tab, click the Gridlines check box
Paint, draw a shape	WIN 349–350	Click the desired shape tool in the Shapes gallery, drag the drawing pointer to draw the shape
Paint, fill an area with color in	WIN 355	*See* Reference box: Filling an Area with Color
Paint, magnify a graphic in	WIN 344	*See* Reference box: Magnifying a Graphic
Paint, move an image	WIN 340	Point to the image, drag to a new location
Paint, open a graphic file in	WIN 337	Click File tab, click Open, navigate to the file, click the file, click Open
Paint, paste graphics file from	WIN 340	Click Paste button arrow in the Clipboard group, click Paste from, navigate to the graphics file, click the file, click Open
Paint, resize the canvas in	WIN 342	Drag a sizing handle on the canvas
Paint, select a fill color for a shape in	WIN 350	Click Fill button in the Shapes group, click fill option
Paint, select a outline for a shape in	WIN 350	Click Outline button in the Shapes group, click outline option
Paint, select an entire graphic in	WIN 342	Click Select button arrow in the Image group, click Select all (or press Ctrl+A)
Paint, select background color for a shape in	WIN 353	Click Color 2 button, click a color square in the Colors gallery
Paint, select foreground color for a shape in	WIN 345	Click Color 1 button, click a color square in the Colors gallery
Paint, select size for a shape in	WIN 350	Click Size button arrow in the Shapes group, click size option
Paint, start	WIN 334	Type *paint* on the Start screen, click Paint in the Apps screen
Partitions, view for hard disk	WIN 485	Open Control Panel in Category view, click System and Security, click Create and format hard disk partitions in the Administrative Tools category
Password, change	WIN 266–267	Display Charms bar, click Settings charm, click Change PC settings, click Users, click Change your password, enter old password, enter new password, reenter new password, click Next, click Finish
Password, create picture password	WIN 268–269	Display Charms bar, click Settings charm, click Change PC settings, click Users, click Create a picture password, enter your password, click OK, click Choose picture, navigate to and click a picture file, click Open, click Use this Picture, draw three gestures, repeat the gestures, click Finish
Password, create PIN	WIN 267–268	Display Charms bar, click Settings charm, click Change PC settings, click Users, click Create a PIN, enter password, click OK, enter PIN, reenter to confirm, click Finish
PC settings, set	WIN B9	Click Settings charm on Charms bar, click Change PC settings, change settings as needed

TASK	PAGE #	RECOMMENDED METHOD
Peek, use	WIN 144	Click the far right side of the taskbar to minimize all of the open windows, point to the taskbar button to display thumbnails of opened files
Performance details, view and print	WIN 522	Open the Performance Information and Tools window, click View and print detailed performance and system information
Performance Information and Tools window, open	WIN 522	Open the System and Security window in the Control Panel, click System, click Windows Experience Index
Performance issues, view	WIN 529–531	Open the Performance Information and Tools window, click Advanced tools, click the Performance can be improved by changing visual settings. View details. link
Performance Monitor, open	WIN 533	See Reference box: Monitoring System Performance
Photos, share via SkyDrive	WIN 373	Click the SkyDrive tile on the Start screen, sign in, expand the Public folder, select a folder or create a new folder where you want to place the photos, display Apps bar, click Upload button, click Files, navigate to the folder with photos, select the photos, click Add to SkyDrive button
Photos, share via the Mail app	WIN 374–375	Start Photos app, expand Pictures library, navigate to the folder containing the photo, right-click the photo, display Charms bar, click Share charm, click Mail on the Share menu, enter email address(es), enter subject and message, click ⊞
Pictures library, arrange pictures in	WIN 367	Click Group by button in the Current view group, click grouping option
Power options, change	WIN 403–405	Open the Hardware and Sound window in the Control Panel, click Power Options, click Choose what the power buttons do, change settings, click Save changes
Power plan, modify	WIN 406	See Reference box: Modifying a Power Plan
Power plan, select	WIN 401	See Reference box: Selecting a Power Plan
Presentation, turn on or off	WIN 412	Open Windows Mobility Center, click Turn on or Turn off button in the Presentation Settings tile
Presentation settings, customize for a mobile PC	WIN 411–412	Open Windows Mobility Center, click 🖳, change settings, click OK
Printer, install local	WIN 506	See Reference box: Installing a Local Printer
Printer, set default	WIN 509	Open the Hardware and Sound window in the Control Panel, click Devices and Printers, right-click a printer, click Set as default printer
Problem Steps Recorder, start	WIN 570	Open Control Panel, type problem steps in the Search text box, click Record steps to reproduce a problem, click Start Record, follow instructions
Program, resolve compatibility issues using Program Compatibility Troubleshooter	WIN 477–478	Open the Programs window in the Control Panel, click Run programs made for previous versions of Windows, click Next, select the program that is causing problems, select Try recommended settings, click Test the program button, close the program, click Next, click Yes, save these settings for this program
Program, set as default	WIN B19	Open the Hardware and Sound window in the Control Panel, click Programs, click Set your default programs, select program, click Choose defaults for this program, select file types the program can open, click Save

TASK	PAGE #	RECOMMENDED METHOD
Public folder sharing, turn on	WIN 432–433	Open Network and Sharing Center, click Change advanced sharing settings, expand All Networks, click Turn on sharing so anyone with network access can read and write files in the Public folders, click Save changes
Recycle Bin, view	WIN 11	Double-click Recycle Bin icon
Remote Assistance, enable	WIN 572	Open the System and Security window in the Control Panel, click System, click Remote settings, select the Allow Remote Assistance connections to this computer check box
Remote Assistance, request	WIN 573–574	Open Control Panel, type *remote* in the Search text box, click the Invite someone to connect to your PC and help you, or offer to help someone else link, click the Invite someone you trust to help you link, click Use email to send an invitation, enter the email address of the person from whom you are requesting assistance, click Send
Remote Desktop Connection, set up	WIN 440	Open the System and Security window in the Control Panel, click System, click Remote settings, click Allow remote connections to this computer, click Select Users, click OK, click OK
Remote Desktop Connection, start and connect to remote computer	WIN 441	Type *Remote Desktop Connection* on the Start screen, click Remote Desktop Connection, select the name of the remote computer, click Connect, enter your user name and password, click OK
Resource Monitor, open	WIN 539	Open the Performance Information and Tools window, click Advanced tools, click Open Resource Monitor
Screen refresh rate, adjust	WIN 503	*See* Reference box: Adjusting the Screen Refresh Rate
Screen resolution, change	WIN 146–147	Right-click the desktop, click Screen resolution, click Resolution, drag the slider to the settings you want to use, click OK
Screen saver, activate	WIN 140–141	Open the Personalization window in the Control Panel, click the Screen Saver link, click Screen saver, click the screen saver you want to activate, click OK
Screen, capture	WIN 122	Display the screen you want to capture, press Print Screen
ScreenTip, display	WIN 24	Point to the object
Search, save	WIN 297	Click Save search, enter a name for the search, click Save
Search menu, display	WIN 9	Display Charms bar, click Search charm
Search results, filter	WIN 293	*See* Reference box: Filtering Search Results
Settings, search for	WIN 287	Display Start screen, type the name of the setting, click Settings
Shake, use	WIN 145	Open several windows on the desktop, point to the title bar of the window you want to keep open, hold down the mouse button and quickly drag the window about an inch to the right and left to shake it, minimizing all other open windows
Shortcut, change icon	WIN 109–110	Right-click the shortcut icon on the desktop, click Properties, click the Shortcut tab, click Change Icon, click the image you want for the shortcut icon, click OK, click OK
Shortcut, create custom	WIN 108–109	Right-click a blank area of the desktop, point to New, click Shortcut, type a command, click Next, type a name for the shortcut, click Finish
Shortcut, pin to Start screen	WIN 111	Right-click the shortcut icon on the desktop, click Pin to Start